Profession
DotNetNuke 4:
Open Source Web Application
Framework for ASP.NET 2.0

Professional
DotNetNuke™ 4:
Open Source Web Application
Framework for ASP.NET 2.0

Shaun Walker

Joe Brinkman

Bruce Hopkins

Scott McCulloch

Scott Willhite

Chris Paterra

Patrick Santry

Dan Caron

Wiley Publishing, Inc.

Professional DotNetNuke™ 4:
Open Source Web Application Framework for ASP.NET 2.0

Published by
Wiley Publishing, Inc.
10475 Crosspoint Boulevard
Indianapolis, IN 46256
www.wiley.com

Published simultaneously in Canada

ISBN-13: 978-0-471-78816-4
ISBN-10: 0-471-78816-3

Manufactured in the United States of America

10 9 8 7 6 5 4 3

1B/SZ/QW/QW/IN

Library of Congress Cataloging-in-Publication Data:

Professional DotNetNuke 4 : open source Web application framework for ASP.NET 2.0 / Shaun Walker ... [et al.].
   p. cm.
 ISBN-13: 978-0-471-78816-4 (paper/website)
 ISBN-10: 0-471-78816-3 (paper/website)
 1. Active server pages. 2. Web sites—Design. 3. Microsoft .NET. I. Walker, Shaun, 1971-
 TK5105.8885.A26P78952 2006
 005.2'76—dc22

                    2006017016

For general information on our other products and services please contact our Customer Care Department within the United States at (800) 762-2974, outside the United States at (317) 572-3993 or fax (317) 572-4002.

About the Authors

Shaun Walker

Shaun Walker, founder and president of Perpetual Motion Interactive Systems Inc., a solutions company specializing in Microsoft enterprise technologies. Shaun has 15 years professional experience in architecting and implementing large scale IT solutions for private and public organizations. Shaun is responsible for the creation and management of DotNetNuke, an open source content management system written for the Microsoft ASP.NET platform. Based on his significant community contributions he was recently recognized as a Microsoft Most Valuable Professional (MVP) in 2004. In addition, he was recently added as a featured speaker to the MSDN Canada Speakers Bureau which allows him to evangelize DotNetNuke to User Groups across Canada. Shaun resides in British Columbia, Canada, with his wife and two children.

Joe Brinkman

Joe Brinkman, formerly the founder and President of TAG Software Inc, is the Chief Technology Officer for DataSource Inc. (www.datasourceinc.com) a J2EE development company focused on simplifying and automating development of N-Tier applications with Java. With more than 22 years of IT experience and a Computer Science degree from the United States Naval Academy, he brings a broad range of experience and expertise in a variety of software and hardware architectures. Having worked with DotNetNuke since February 2003, and being a founding Core Team member, Joe currently serves as a member of the DotNetNuke Board of Directors, a Lead Architect, and Security Specialist.

Bruce Hopkins

Bruce Hopkins, Microsoft MVP (ASP.NET) holds a BSCIS from DeVry University and holds certifications as an MCSE and several flavors of Linux. Bruce is currently the IT Director for Chattahoochee Technical College in Marietta GA and has held a wide variety of positions in technology throughout his career ranging from programming and web design to network administration and management. Bruce remarks that this varied experience is crucial to determining the correct tool for the task at hand. This is shown by the many technologies he uses everyday, including Windows, Unix, SQL Server, Oracle, MySQL and many different Linux-based applications that are an integral part of maintaining the college's infrastructure. Bruce makes his home in Marietta, Georgia, with his wife and son.

Scott McCulloch

Scott McCulloch is an Application Developer for the Computer Science Corporation, Australia. At 26 years of age, Scott holds Bachelor and Masters degrees in Computer Science, as well as the three major Microsoft Certifications (MCSD, MCDBA, MCSE). Scott has been part of the DotNetNuke community since the project began (late December, 2002). Today, his role within the DotNetNuke team is contributing as an Architect and Core Developer. He currently resides in Wollongong, Australia, with his fiancé, Lenise.

Scott Willhite

Scott Willhite is an accomplished business and technology professional turned family man. Semi-retired from technology as a profession, his days are spent teaming with his wife Allison as professional Realtors. (www.alkihomes.com) and supporting a variety of community endeavors. A distinguished technology pedigree includes a BS in Computer Science and MBA in Information Systems Management degrees from Baylor University. And a proven track record of achievement includes service as an architect for Andersen Consulting (now Accenture), vice-president of Technology for 10x Labs, and Program Director for Safeco's Office of the CIO. An ASP.NET moderator and member of DotNetNuke's Board of Directors, Scott was recognized as a Microsoft Most Valuable Professional (MVP) in 2005 for significant contributions to the community. Ever the "Don Quixote" type, Scott's currently tilting at the windmills of open source, brandishing a Microsoft lance. Among other things, he oversees the Projects initiatives at DotNetNuke cultivating BSD licensed (unencumbered) practical applications of Microsoft technology and programming to share with the world. His favorite mantra is the core values developed with his partners for their former startup company, 10x Labs: "Speak the truth. Share the wealth. Change the world!" Scott currently lives in West Seattle, WA with his lovely wife Allison, "crazy smart" son Kyle, a whiny German Shepherd dog, three neurotic housecats, and a cast of wonderful friends and neighbors that he wouldn't trade for gold!

Chris Paterra

Chris Paterra is Lead Architect/Project Manager for Trend Core Group of Atlanta, which produces .NET marketing and communication tools. He also is a contributing author for *DotNetNuke For Dummies*. He enjoys writing magazine articles on project management and speaking at local Atlanta User Groups. A founding Core Team Member, Chris is currently serving as an Inner Core Team member in addition to being Project Lead for both the Gallery and the Forum DotNetNuke projects.

Patrick Santry

Patrick Santry, Microsoft MVP (ASP/ASP.NET) holds a MCSE, MCSA, MCP+SB, i-Net+, A+, and Certified Internet Webmaster certifications. He has authored and co-authored several books and magazine articles on Microsoft and Internet technologies. Patrick is frequent presenter on Web technologies, having presented at several events including the Exchange 2000 launch, DevDays 2004 in Pittsburgh, PA, and to area .NET SIGs on DotNetNuke module development. In addition, Patrick owns and maintains www.WWWCoder.com, a popular site for news, tutorials, and information for the Web development community. Patrick resides in Girard, PA, with his wife Karyn, and their four children, Katie, Karleigh, P.J, and Danny.

Dan Caron

Dan Caron is a Lead Application Designer & Developer with MassMutual Financial Group, a Fortune 500 global, diversified financial services organization. With MassMutual, Dan designs technical solutions for financial web applications using Microsoft and Java technologies. For more than 10 years, Dan has been designing and developing applications with various programming technologies including Microsoft ASP.NET, XML/XSL, SQL, Java and JSP. He has been a major contributor to the DotNetNuke open-source portal project since the core team was founded in 2003. Some of Dan's noteworthy contributions include the exception-handling framework, event-logging provider, and the scheduler. Dan continues to contribute his talent to the project as a Lead Architect, Core Developer, and member of the Board of Directors. Dan lives in Connecticut with his wife and two children.

Credits

Senior Acquisitions Editor
Jim Minatel

Development Editor
Maryann Steinhart

Technical Editor
Scott Willhite
Steve Fabian
Jon Henning
Philip Beadle
Michael Washington

Production Editor
Angela Smith

Copy Editor
Kim Cofer

Editorial Manager
Mary Beth Wakefield

Production Manager
Tim Tate

Vice President and Executive Group Publisher
Richard Swadley

Vice President and Executive Publisher
Joseph B. Wikert

Graphics and Production Specialists
Jennifer Click
Lynsey Osborn
Heather Ryan
Alicia South

Quality Control Technician
Brian H. Walls

Project Coordinator
Bill Ramsey

Proofreading and Indexing
Techbooks

Contents

Contents

Contents

Contents

Contents

Contents

Preface

DotNetNuke is a web application framework built utilizing ASP.NET and allowing for the easy creation of web sites. The system can be used as is or you can leverage the many capabilities of the platform to develop your own custom ASP.NET Web Applications. This book is aimed at people with development knowledge and those who are just interested in learning more about how DotNetNuke works.

Experienced developers of ASP.NET and those who are knowledgeable about DotNetNuke may want to skip Chapters 1–6. These chapters provide an overview of DotNetNuke and its operations. Chapters 7–17 tackle DotNetNuke architecture and development. However, you'll gain valuable insight into how DotNetNuke works by reading the entire book from front to back.

What This Book Covers

This book is split into two primary sections. The first half explores the history of the project, shows how to install DotNetNuke on the server, and explains how to manage and administer a DotNetNuke portal.

The second half of the book examines the DotNetNuke application architecture, how the application works, and how you can extend the portal framework by developing modules that plug into a DotNetNuke portal. Finally, you'll discover the flexible skinning capabilities of DotNetNuke and how you can create your own unique look for your portal.

What You Need to Use This Book

To install DotNetNuke and a supporting database you need either Windows 2003 Server or Windows XP (development only). This book covers a basic install of DotNetNuke using a SQL Server database as the data provider. You must have access to either SQL Server 2000/2005 or MSDE/SQL Express (development only) on the same machine or a remote machine.

To participate in the development chapters, you need Visual Studio.NET 2003 and Visual Web Developer of Visual Studio 2005.

Contributors

In addition to the authors, the DotNetNuke development team is comprised of many individuals working together from around the world. We want to acknowledge these people and their contributions to the project. Following are the DotNetNuke contributors and their roles within the community.

Board of Directors

The Board of Directors is responsible for managing the long-term strategic vision of the project. Its members are:

Dan Caron, see *About the Authors*.

Joe Brinkman, see *About the Authors*.

Nik Kalyani is the founder and CEO of Speerio, Inc., a Washington, D.C.-based software company. Kalyani, a serial entrepreneur, is proficient in many areas of software development but has a special focus on web application usability. He has contributed several DotNetNuke modules to the community and continues to focus Speerio's growth as a leading developer of enterprise-class DotNetNuke modules. On the Core Team, in addition to working on DotNetNuke strategy with other Board members, Kalyani coordinates the marketing efforts. In 2005, Kalyani worked closely with DotNetNuke leadership to develop the current DotNetNuke logo and brand elements. More recently, he founded Capital DUG, the DotNetNuke users group for the metro-D.C. area. A Western Michigan University computer science alumnus, Kalyani blogs regularly about his experiences developing .NET applications using C# and about the nascent web. Kalyani, his wife, and year-old daughter live in Washington, where he continues to learn more about the political process in preparation for a future run for Congress.

Scott Willhite, see *About the Authors*.

Shaun Walker, see *About the Authors*.

Core Team

The DotNetNuke Core Team is divided into two levels of participation—a Trustee Role and the Core Team. They represent different levels of trust and responsibility within the DotNetNuke organization.

Trustee Role

A Trustee Role is granted to individuals who have demonstrated their long-term commitment to the project. They have acted professionally, accepted responsibility, delivered assigned tasks successfully, and are actively engaged with the community. They act as Managers in key functional areas and manage communication with sub-teams of Core Team members.

Bruce Hopkins, see *About the Authors*.

Charles Nurse has been developing software for more than 25 years. He is the owner of his own consulting business, Keydance Computer Services, and has been a DotNetNuke developer for two years (the last 18 months as an Inner Core Team member, now Trustee). He was lead developer on the .NET 2 version of DotNetNuke (DNN 4.0). He is in the process of developing his own DotNetNuke Developer Resource site (www.dnndevzone.com), where he will be providing articles on developing for and with DotNetNuke. He was born in Bristol, England, but has been living in beautiful British Columbia on the west coast of Canada for the last 27 years. He and his wife Eileen have two teenage children.

Cathal Connolly works as a Senior Developer and Consultant with EG Information Consulting (www.eg-consulting.com), based in Belfast, Northern Ireland. Cathal has previously worked for IT companies in the UK, U.S., and Austria, developing both web and client/server applications using Microsoft technologies. His current focus is the development of secure banking applications and bespoke Smart Client .NET products. He is an MCSD, holds a BSc in Computer Science, and is an MVP in Visual Studio/VB.NET.

Christopher Paterra, see *About the Authors*.

Dan Caron, see *About the Authors*.

Joe Brinkman, see *About the Authors*.

Jon Henning is a senior consultant with Solution Partners Inc. (www.solpart.com), a Chicago-based consulting company specializing in Microsoft technologies. He is an MCSD who has been working with Visual Studio .NET since the PDC release. While he has written several articles dealing with all aspects of programming, his current love is the development of rich client-side functionality. Recently for version 3, Jon initiated the development of the DotNetNuke ClientAPI, which enabled developers to write rich client-side cross-browser logic against a simple API. The use of this API can be found throughout DotNetNuke, including the DotNetNuke TreeView, DotNetNuke LabelEdit, and DotNetNuke TextSuggest controls. Jon resides in Aurora, Illinois, with his wife Holly, and two children, Kyle and Carter.

John Mitchell is the founder and president of Snapsis Software, Inc. (www.snapsis.com). John has more than 20 years of development experience and has been working on the leading edge of Internet technologies for the past seven years. He specializes in the architecture, design, development, and implementation of portal/e-commerce applications. John has led teams in the development of several web sites including www.SamsClub.com and www.Maytag.com. He has been using and enhancing DotNetNuke since May 2003 and is a founding member of the Tulsa .NET Users Group (www.TulsaDnug.org).

Philip Beadle (MCAD, MVP) of Byte Information Technology in 2004 (www.byte.com.au) is a foundation member of the DotNetNuke Core Team and a Microsoft Certified Application Developer. He is experienced in the development and commercial application of the DotNetNuke Framework based on Microsoft's .NET technology. He has successfully developed and implemented sites for clients in Australia and overseas and was recently awarded the Microsoft Most Valuable Professional (MVP) award in ASP/ASP.NET.

Scott McCulloch, see *About the Authors*.

Scott Willhite, see *About the Authors*.

Shaun Walker, see *About the Authors*.

Vicenç Masanas is a developer and analyst at the Universitat de Girona, Spain. He has been developing web sites with Microsoft technologies, including ASP, VB, ASP.NET, Access, and SQL Server, since 1998. Vicenç joined the DotNetNuke community in summer 2003 coming from IBS portal. Today, his role within the DotNetNuke team is contributing as a Core Developer, Bugs & Enhancement Specialist, and DotNetNuke Evangelist for the Spanish area. Currently, Vicenç is working on a number of projects based on the DotNetNuke platform. Specializing on this platform as a framework for future works, he has also written VS.NET tools and tutorials for DNN developers that have been highly acclaimed (available at http://dnnjungle.vmasanas.net). He provides online support and training for DotNetNuke and custom module development and consultancy for DotNetNuke projects.

Geert Veenstra, a member of the DotNetNuke Inner Core Team, is currently working for Schmit (www.schmit.nl), a company that specializes in Parking solutions as a technical support specialist. In his daily job, he works with a multitude of operating systems (both Windows and Unix variants) and databases (such as Oracle, SQL and MySql Server). He has created the company's intranet and a customer bug-reporting web site (now both using DotNetNuke, of course). He joined the DotNetNuke team in mid 2003 and has been working mainly on Localization and Bug Fixing. He created the first third-party DotNetNuke dataprovider (for MySql) as well as a DNN installer.

Core Team

The Core Team is comprised of individuals who have achieved recognition within the DotNetNuke community—sometimes based on technical prowess but most often based upon their unselfish actions assisting other community members. Team members work closely with Trustee members to help manage various aspects of the project. Once a Core Team member gains a unanimous vote of respect and trust in the DotNetNuke Core, they are offered a promotion to the Trustee Role.

Bo Nørgaard holds a bachelor's degree in Electronic Engineering, is a certified Psion developer and engineer, and is a certified Internet Security Systems security engineer. He has been programming since 1979 and has been through Comal 80, Pascal, ANSI C, ADA, PLM, ASM (Intel), OO Pascal, Delphi, C++, Perl, PHP, Visual Basic, Java, and now C#. He started teaching in 1991 at the Copenhagen University College of Engineering, and later at the National Theatre School of Denmark. Bo has presented at several events including detailed security practices at CA-World in New Orleans. He is CEO of Bonosoft and operates the DotNetNuke developer community site (www.dotnetnuke.dk), which has numerous resources for both Visual Basic and Visual C# programmers writing plug-in modules for DotNetNuke.

Bryan Andrews has been developing web applications since Netscape 1.0 and has worked in many different capacities in the past 12 years from infrastructure architecture and management, to the development of collaborative and knowledge management tools. He is president and one of the founders of an Atlanta-headquartered marketing agency (TrendCRM) and associated development company (AppTheory), which produces marketing and communication tools. DotNetNuke has become the platform of choice for many of their clients and as such they have developed a complete suite of tools and agency-specific modules to support these clients.

Chris Hammond is the Product Manager for Internet Solutions with Engage Software in St. Louis, Missouri (www.engagesoftware.net). Engage Software's DotNetNuke work includes custom module and skinning implementation for some of the larger DNN implementations on the Internet including www.stlouischildrens.org and www.tamko.com. Chris has started a DotNetNuke user group in St. Louis (www.dnnug.com) and taken time to speak at user groups around the Midwest to evangelize and teach DNN. In his free time Chris participates in various activities with the Sports Car Club of America, including autocross and club racing, and manages multiple community portals dedicated to his hobbies. (www.solo2.org, www.sccaforums.com).

Jeremy White, founder and president of Webstone Technologies, LLC, is a founding member of the DNN Core Team. He holds MCSE, MCP+I, and MCT certifications and has many years of experience in programming, networking, WiFi, VoIP, and CMS technology implementations for a multi-national company. Jeremy has been actively involved in designing and developing web solutions with various Microsoft Internet technologies including ASP and ASP.NET. He is the author of the popular Shadow module for DNN 1.x and 2.x and has been a frequent DNN forums contributor since February 2003. Jeremy resides in Long Island, NY, with his wife and two dogs.

Leigh Pointer is an accomplished Microsoft Most Valuable Professional (MVP) with years of experience in the IT sector since 1988. He is highly experienced in user interaction design, web design, software engineering, software analysis and design, problem solving, and user relations. He demonstrates leadership in resource and project management, and has an in-depth understanding of Microsoft development tools. Leigh is results-oriented and thrives in an innovative, creative, challenging, fast-paced workplace. He consults on DotNetNuke, and can manage the process from installation to going live, whether the solution is Internet or intranet. Leigh is constantly designing and developing new modules for DotNetNuke, giving even more added functionality to what is already in the box. He is also the founder of the Netherlands and European DNN user groups.

Lorraine Young is a business analyst for Byte Information Technology based in Melbourne, Australia (www.byte.com.au). She is a founding member of the DotNetNuke Core Team who provides assistance in the user experience and documentation areas of the DotNetNuke Project. Lorraine holds a Bachelor of Arts degree in Professional Writing and Literature and a post-graduate degree in Orientation and Mobility for vision-impaired adults and children.

Patrick Santry, see *About the Authors*.

Mark Hoskins is the founder of KodHedZ Software Development (www.KodHedZ.net) based out of Victoria, BC, Canada, where he has been developing ASP.NET Business Management, eCommerce, and Dynamic Internet applications for more than three years, primarily using DotNetNuke as the development platform since its conception in December 2002. In addition to web applications, he has authored many articles and tutorials for developers on implementing and developing solutions using DotNetNuke and provides a wealth of resources at his flagship domain, www.KodHedZ.net.

Michael Washington is a web site developer and an ASP.NET C# and Visual Basic programmer. He has extensive knowledge in process improvement, billing systems, and credit card transaction processing. He has been involved with DotNetNuke for nearly three years and has worked on DotNetNuke Data Access Layer enhancements. He is the author of numerous DotNetNuke modules and tutorials including "Creating a DotNetNuke Module for Absolute Beginners!" He has a son, Zachary, and resides in Los Angeles with his wife Valerie.

Nina Meiers is a self-employed DotNetNuke web site skinner whose Core Team roles include User Experience Specialist, DotNetNuke Evangelist, and Technical Writing & Marketing Specialist. Nina's experience in graphics, her eye for technical perfection, and her ability to work well with developer and clients alike have helped secure her niche in the DotNetNuke community with more than 12,500 downloads of many quality free skins available from www.xd.com.au. Nina also has an extensive portfolio of projects from small business to Fortune 500 companies on her web site. Nina is married with children and enjoys renovations, reading, writing, and driving her muscle sports car.

Robert J. Collins is the founder and president of WillowTree Software, Inc., a custom software and DotNetNuke consulting company (www.willowtreesoftware.com). Robert is a veteran developer with more than a decade of web development experience, specializing in the design, development, and implementation of e-commerce applications, corporate intranet tools, and high availability data-driven web applications. He has established himself as a worldwide leader in the web development community. Robert founded the very successful Boise .NET Developers User Group (www.netdug.com), which is dedicated to the promotion of the Microsoft .NET Framework and Services. Rob formerly worked for Microsoft Corporation, where he was responsible for providing high availability web and database application solutions for Microsoft internal services and Microsoft partners. He also is an established desktop/client server applications developer, network systems engineer, and cluster services specialist with more than five years of experience working as a systems integrator (MCP, MCP+I, MCSE, MCSE+I).

Salar Golestanian specializes in skinning and UI, working solely in the DotNetNuke environment. He has years of creative design experience and is currently targeting clients wanting content management solutions. Salar is working on a number of projects based on the DotNetNuke platform; the links to various projects and showcases are available on www.salaro.com. Salar's background is in Internet technology using Microsoft tools. He has Bachelor of Science and MPhil degrees in Physics. He lives with his fiancé and daughter near London, U.K.

Shawn Mehaffie holds a MCP (ASP.NET) certification and is working on his MCSD certification. Shawn has 14 years' programming experience in VB.NET, ASP.NET, and C# and has worked with .NET since its release. He was on a team that wrote a payment engine web service as part of the Microsoft .NET Blaze program. Shawn also owns his own company, PC Resources, LLC (www.pcrresourcesllc.com). He has been a part of the DotNetNuke community since v1.0 and currently uses DotNetNuke to create web sites for his customers. Shawn is the QA Team Leader and a member of the Bug & Enhancement Team. Shawn is excited about being on the DotNetNuke Core Team and the positive contributions his team can have on future releases of DotNetNuke. Shawn lives in Blue Springs, Mo., with his wife and sons Austin and Tyler.

Steve Fabian has been designing and developing software solutions for 19 years. In addition to programming in more than a dozen different languages, Steve is proficient in graphics and web design and for the past few years has focused on user interface design, .NET development, both client and browser based, and most recently, DotNetNuke. Steve lives in New Jersey with his wife and their five dogs, Kahlua, Amaretto, Sambucca, Daiquiri, and Whiskey. In his extremely limited free time, Steve and his wife do volunteer work for BARKS, an animal rescue shelter in Byram, New Jersey (see www.gooddogs.com).

Tam Tran Minh holds a degree in architecture from HCMC-Vietnam University of Architecture. He is currently chairman and CIO of TTT Corporation in Vietnam (www.tttcompany.com). Since 2003, DotNetNuke has been the main content management portal for his company. Tam has developed and contributed several DotNetNuke modules to the community. Tam is currently developing a management and collaboration system for TTT with Visual Basic, Exchange/Outlook and now VB.NET. He is author of several articles in PC-World Vietnam and has published a book titled *Architectural Space— Virtual and Reality* (winner of the National Architectural Awards 2002 in Vietnam) based on projects of TTT using computer graphic technologies. Tam speaks both Vietnamese and English.

Michael Washington is a web site developer and an ASP.NET C# and Visual Basic programmer. He has extensive knowledge in process improvement, billing systems, and credit card transaction processing. He has been involved with DotNetNuke for nearly 3 years and has worked on the DotNetNuke Data Access Layer enhancements. He is the author of numerous DotNetNuke modules and tutorials including "Creating a DotNetNuke Module for Absolute Beginners!" He, his wife Valerie, and their son Zachary and reside in Los Angeles.

Conventions

To help you get the most from the text and keep track of what's happening, we've used a number of conventions throughout the book.

> Boxes like this one hold important, not-to-be forgotten information that is directly relevant to the surrounding text.

Tips, hints, tricks, and asides to the current discussion are offset and placed in italics like this.

As for styles in the text:

❑   New terms and important words are *highlighted* when they're introduced.

❑   Keyboard combination strokes appear like this: Ctrl+A.

❑   Filenames, URLs, and code within the text appear in a monospaced font, like this: `persistence.properties`.

❑   Code is presented in two ways:

```
A gray background highlights examples of new and important code.
```

```
The gray highlighting is not used for code that's less important in the present
context, or that has been shown before.
```

Source Code

As you work through the examples in this book, you may choose either to type in all the code manually or to use the source code files that accompany the book. All of the source code used in this book is available for download at `http://www.wrox.com`. At the site, simply locate the book's title (either by using the Search box or by using one of the title lists) and click the Download Code link on the book's detail page to obtain all the source code for the book.

Because many books have similar titles, you may find it easiest to search by ISBN; this book's ISBN is 0-471-78816-3 (changing to 978-0-471-78816-4 as the new industry-wide 13-digit ISBN numbering system is phased in by January 2007).

Decompress the downloaded code with your favorite compression tool. Alternatively, you can go to the main Wrox code download page at `http://www.wrox.com/dynamic/books/download.aspx` to see the code available for this book and all other Wrox books.

Errata

We make every effort to ensure that there are no errors in the text or in the code. However, no one is perfect, and mistakes do occur. If you find an error in one of our books, like a spelling mistake or faulty piece of code, we would be very grateful for your feedback. By sending in errata you may save another reader hours of frustration and at the same time you will be helping us provide even higher quality information.

To find the errata page for this book, go to http://www.wrox.com and locate the title using the Search box or one of the title lists. Then, on the book details page, click the Book Errata link. On this page you can view all errata that has been submitted for this book and posted by Wrox editors. A complete book list including links to each's book's errata is also available at www.wrox.com/misc-pages/booklist.shtml.

If you don't spot "your" error on the Book Errata page, go to www.wrox.com/contact/techsupport.shtml and complete the form there to send us the error you have found. We'll check the information and, if appropriate, post a message to the book's errata page and fix the problem in subsequent editions of the book.

p2p.wrox.com

For author and peer discussion, join the P2P forums at p2p.wrox.com. The forums are a Web-based system for you to post messages relating to Wrox books and related technologies and interact with other readers and technology users. The forums offer a subscription feature to e-mail you topics of interest of your choosing when new posts are made to the forums. Wrox authors, editors, other industry experts, and your fellow readers are present on these forums.

At http://p2p.wrox.com you will find a number of different forums that will help you not only as you read this book, but also as you develop your own applications. To join the forums, just follow these steps:

1. Go to p2p.wrox.com and click the Register link.
2. Read the terms of use and click Agree.
3. Complete the required information to join as well as any optional information you want to provide and click Submit.
4. You will receive an e-mail with information describing how to verify your account and complete the joining process.

   You can read messages in the forums without joining P2P but in order to post your own messages, you must join.

Once you join, you can post new messages and respond to messages other users post. You can read messages at any time on the Web. If you would like to have new messages from a particular forum e-mailed to you, click the Subscribe to this Forum icon by the forum name in the forum listing.

For more information about how to use the Wrox P2P, be sure to read the P2P FAQs for answers to questions about how the forum software works as well as many common questions specific to P2P and Wrox books. To read the FAQs, click the FAQ link on any P2P page.

Professional
DotNetNuke™ 4:
Open Source Web Application
Framework for ASP.NET 2.0

An Inside Look at the Evolution of DotNetNuke

By Shaun Walker
Project Founder

As much as DotNetNuke is an open source software application written for the Microsoft ASP.NET platform, it is also a vibrant community with developers, end users, vendors, and volunteers — all working together collaboratively in a rich and diverse ecosystem. This chapter attempts to capture the essence of the project, expose its humble beginnings, provide insight into its evolution, and document its many achievements, but not shy away from some of the hard lessons learned in the process. The lifeblood of any community is its people; therefore, it is a distinct honor and privilege to be able to share some of the emotion and passion that has gone into the DotNetNuke project so that you may be able to establish a personal connection with the various stakeholders and perhaps precipitate your own decision to join this burgeoning ecosystem.

In 2001–2002, I was working for a medium-sized software consulting company that was providing outsourced software development services to a variety of large U.S. clients specializing primarily in e-Learning initiatives. The internal push was to achieve CMM 3.0 on a fairly aggressive schedule so that we could compete with the emerging outsourcing powerhouses from India and China. As a result there was an incredible amount of focus on process and procedure and somewhat less focus on the technical aspects of software engineering. Because the majority of the client base was interested in the J2EE platform, the company primarily hired resources with Java skills — leaving me with my legacy Microsoft background to assume more of an internal-development and project-management role. The process improvement exercise consumed a lot of time and energy for the company, attempting to better define roles and responsibilities and ensuring proper documentation throughout the project life cycle. Delving into CMM and the PMBOK were great educational benefits for me — skills that would prove to be invaluable in future endeavors. Ultimately the large U.S. clients decided to test the overseas outsourcing options anyway, which resulted in severe downsizing for the company. It was during these tumultuous times that I recognized the potential of the newly released .NET Framework (beta) and decided that I would need to take my own initiative to learn this exciting new platform to preserve my long-term employment outlook.

For a number of years, I had been maintaining an amateur hockey statistics application as a sideline hobby business. The client application was written in Visual Basic 6.0 with a Microsoft Access backend and I augmented it with a simplistic web publishing service using Active Server Pages 3.0 and SQL Server 7.0. However, better integration with the World Wide Web was quickly becoming the most highly requested enhancement, and I concluded that an exploration into ASP.NET was the best way to enhance the application, and at the same time acquire the skills necessary to adapt to the changing landscape. My preferred approach to learning new technologies is to experience them firsthand rather than through theory or traditional education. It was during a Microsoft Developer Days conference in Vancouver, British Columbia in 2001 that I became aware of a reference application known as the IBuySpy Portal.

IBuySpy Portal

Realizing the educational value of sample applications, Microsoft built a number of source projects that were released with the .NET Framework 1.0 Beta to encourage developers to cut their teeth on the new platform. These projects included full source code and a liberal End User License Agreement (EULA), which provided nearly unrestricted usage. Microsoft co-developed the IBuySpy Portal with Vertigo Software and promoted it as a "best practice" example for building applications in the new ASP.NET environment. Despite its obvious shortcomings, the IBuySpy Portal had some strong similarities to both Microsoft Sharepoint as well as other open source portal applications on the Linux/Apache/mySQL/PHP (LAMP) platform. The portal allowed you to create a completely dynamic web site consisting of an unlimited number of virtual "tabs" (pages). Each page had a standard header and three content panes — a left pane, middle pane, and right pane (a standard layout for most portal sites). Within these panes, the administrator could dynamically inject "modules" — essentially mini-applications for managing specific types of web content. The IBuySpy Portal application shipped with six modules designed to cover the most common content types (announcements, links, images, discussions, html/text, and XML) as well as a number of modules for administrating the portal site. As an application framework, the IBuySpy Portal (see Figure 1-1) provided a mechanism for managing users, roles, permissions, tabs, and modules. With these basic services, the portal offered just enough to whet the appetite of many aspiring ASP.NET developers.

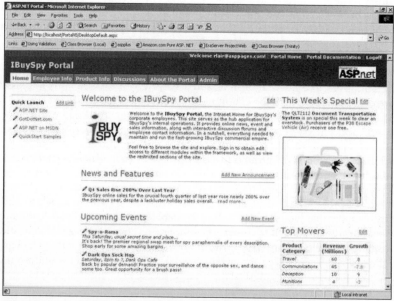

Figure 1-1

ASP.NET

The second critical item that Microsoft delivered at this point in time was a community forums page on the www.asp.net web site (see Figure 1-2). This forum provided a focal point for Microsoft developers to meet and collaborate on common issues in an open, moderated environment. Prior to the release of the forums on www.asp.net, there was a real void in terms of Microsoft community participation in the online or global sphere, especially when compared to the excellent community environments on other platforms.

One discussion forum on the www.asp.net site was dedicated to the discussion of the IBuySpy Portal application, and it soon became a hotbed for developers to discuss their enhancements, share source code enhancements, and debate IT politics. I became involved in this forum early on and gradually increased my community participation as my confidence in ASP.NET and the IBuySpy Portal application grew.

To appeal to the maximum number of community stakeholders, the IBuySpy Portal was available in a number of different source-code release packages. There were VB.NET and C#.NET language versions, each containing their own VS.NET and SDK variants. Although Microsoft was aggressively pushing the newly released C# language, I did not feel a compelling urge to abandon my familiar Visual Basic roots. In addition, my experience with classic ASP 3.0 allowed me to conclude that the new code-behind model in VS.NET was far superior to the inline model of the SDK. As luck would have it, I was able to get access to Visual Studio.NET through my employer. So as a result, I moved forward with the VB.NET/VS.NET version as my baseline framework. This decision would ultimately prove to be extremely important in terms of community acceptance, as I'll explain later.

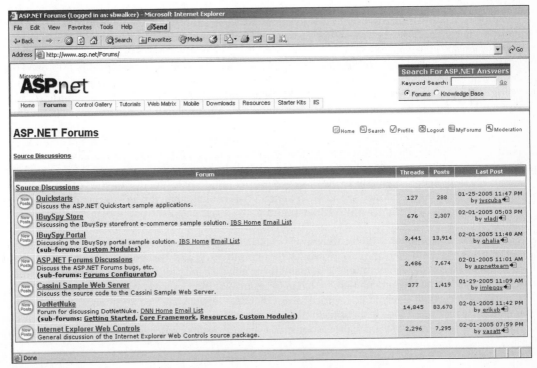

Figure 1-2

When I first started experimenting with the IBuySpy Portal application, I had some specific objectives in mind. To support amateur sports organizations, I had collected a comprehensive set of end-user requirements based on actual client feedback. However, after evaluating the IBuySpy Portal functionality, it quickly became apparent that some significant enhancements were necessary if I hoped to achieve my goals. My early development efforts, although certainly not elegant or perfectly architected, proved that the IBuySpy Portal framework was highly adaptable for building custom applications and could be successfully used as the foundation for my amateur sports hosting application.

The most significant enhancement I made to the IBuySpy Portal application during these early stages was a feature that is now referred to as "multi-portal" or "site virtualization." Effectively this was a fundamental requirement for my amateur sports hosting model. Organizations wanted to have a self-maintained web site, but they also wanted to retain their individual identity. A number of vendors emerged with semi-self-maintained web applications, but nearly all of them forced the organization to adopt the vendor's identity (that is, www.vendor.com/clientname rather than www.clientname.com). Although this may seem like a trivial distinction for some, it has some major effects in terms of brand recognition, site discovery, search engine ranking, and so on. The IBuySpy Portal application already partitioned its data by portal (site), and it had a field in the Portals database table named PortalAlias that was a perfect candidate for mapping a specific domain name to a portal. It was as if the original creators (Microsoft and Vertigo) considered this use case during development but did not have enough time to complete the implementation, so they simply left the "hook" exposed for future development. I immediately saw the potential of this concept and implemented some logic that allowed the application to serve up custom content based on domain name. Essentially, when a web request was received by the application, it would parse the domain name from the URL and perform a lookup on the PortalAlias field to determine the content that should be displayed. This site virtualization capability would ultimately become the "killer" feature that would allow the application to achieve immediate popularity as an open source project.

Over the next 8 to 10 months, I continued to enhance and refactor the IBuySpy Portal application as I created my own custom implementation (now code-named SportsManager.Net). I added numerous features to improve the somewhat limited portal administration and content management aspects. At one point, I enlisted the help of another developer, John Lucarino, and together we steadily improved the framework using whatever spare time we were able to invest. Unfortunately, because all of this was going on outside of regular work hours, there was little time that could be focused on building a viable commercial venture. So at the end of 2002, it soon became apparent that we did not have enough financial backing or a business model to take the amateur sports venture to the next level. This brought the commercial nature of the endeavor under scrutiny. If the commercial intentions were not going to succeed, I at least wanted to feel that my efforts were not in vain. This forced me to evaluate alternative non-commercial uses of the application. Coincidentally, I had released the source code for a number of minor application enhancements to the www.asp.net community forum during the year and I began to hypothesize that if I abandoned the amateur sports venture altogether, it was still possible that my efforts could benefit the larger ASP.NET community.

The fundamental problem with the IBuySpy Portal community was the fact that there was no central authority in charge of managing its growth. Although Microsoft and Vertigo developed the initial code base, there was no public commitment to maintain or enhance the product in any way. Basically the product was a static implementation, frozen in time, an evolutionary dead-end. However, the IBuySpy Portal EULA was extremely liberal, which meant that developers were free to enhance, license, and redistribute the source code in an unrestricted manner. This led to many developers creating their own customized versions of the application, sometimes sharing discrete patches with the general community, but more often keeping their enhancements private, revealing only their public-facing web sites for community recognition (one of the most popular threads at this time was titled "Show me your Portal"). In hindsight, I really don't understand what each developer was hoping to achieve by keeping his enhancements private. Most probably thought there was a commercial opportunity in building a portal application with a richer feature set than their competitor. Or perhaps individuals were hoping to estab-lish an expert reputation based on their public-facing efforts. Either way, the problem was that this mindset was really not conducive to building a community but rather to fragmenting it—a standard trap that tends to consume many things on the Microsoft platform. The concept of sharing source code in an unrestricted manner was really a foreign concept, which is obviously why nobody thought to step forward with an organized open source plan.

I have to admit I had a limited knowledge of the open-source philosophy at this point because all of my previous experience was in the Microsoft community—an area where "open source" was simply equated to the Linux operating system movement. However, there was chatter in the forums at various times regarding the organized sharing of source code, and there was obviously some interest in this area. The concept of incorporating the best enhancements into a rapidly evolving open-source application made a lot of sense because it benefited the entire community and created a wealth of opportunities for everyone. Coincidentally, a few open-source projects had recently emerged on the Microsoft platform to imitate some of the more successful open-source projects in the LAMP community. In evaluating my amateur sports application, I soon realized that nearly all of my enhancements were generic enough that they could be applied to nearly any web site—they were not sports-related whatsoever. I concluded that I should release my full application source code to the ASP.NET community as a new open source pro-ject. So, as a matter of fact, the initial decision to open source that would eventually become DotNetNuke happened more out of frustration of not achieving my commercial goals rather than predicated philan-thropic intentions.

IBuySpy Portal Forum

On December 24, 2002, I released the full open source application by creating a simple web site with a ZIP file for download. The lack of foresight of what this would become was extremely evident when you consider the casual nature of this original release. However, as luck would have it, I did do three things right. First, I thought I should leverage the "IBuySpy" brand in my own open source implementation so that it would be immediately obvious that the code base was a hybrid of the original IBuySpy Portal application, an application with widespread recognition in the Microsoft community. The name I chose was IBuySpy Workshop because it seemed to summarize the evolution of the original application—not to mention the fact that the IBSW abbreviation preferred by the community contained an abstract per-sonal reference (SW are my initials). Ironically I did not even have the domain name resolution properly configured for www.ibuyspyworkshop.com when I released (the initial download links were based on an IP address, http://65.174.86.217/ibuyspyworkshop). The second thing I did right was to require people to register on my web site before they were able to download the source code. This allowed me to track the actual interest in the application at a more granular level than simply by the total number of downloads. Third, I publicized the availability of the application in the IBuySpy Portal Forum on www.asp.net (see Figure 1-3). This particular forum was extremely popular at this time; and as far as I know, nobody had ever released anything other than small code snippet enhancements for general consumption. The original post was made on Christmas Eve, December 24, 2002, which had excellent symbolism in terms of the application being a gift to the community.

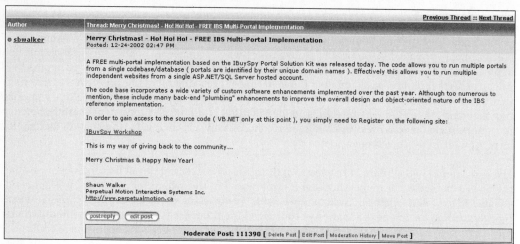

Figure 1-3

IBuySpy Workshop

The public release of the IBuySpy Workshop (see Figure 1-4) created such a surge in forum activity that it was all I could do to keep up with the feedback; especially because this all occurred during the Christmas holidays. I had a family vacation booked for the first two weeks of January, and I left for Mexico on January 2, 2003 (one week after the initial IBuySpy Workshop release). At the time, the timing of this family vacation seemed poor as the groundswell of interest in the IBuySpy Workshop seemed like it could really use my dedicated focus. However, in hindsight the timing could not have been better, because it proved that the community could support itself—a critical element in any open source project. When I returned home from vacation, I was amazed at the massive response the release achieved. The IBuySpy Portal Forum became dominated with posts about the IBuySpy Workshop and my Inbox was full of messages thanking me for my efforts and requesting me to provide support and enhancements. This certainly validated my decision to release the application as an open source project but also emphasized the fact that I had started a locomotive down the tracks and it was going to take some significant engineering to keep it on the rails.

Over the next few months, I frantically attempted to incorporate all community suggestions into the application while at the same time keep up with the plethora of community support questions. Because I was working a day job that prevented effort on the open source project, most of my evenings were consumed with work on the IBuySpy Workshop, which definitely caused some strain on my marriage and family life. Four hours of sleep per night is not conducive to a healthy lifestyle but, like I said, the train was rolling and I had a feeling the project was destined for bigger things.

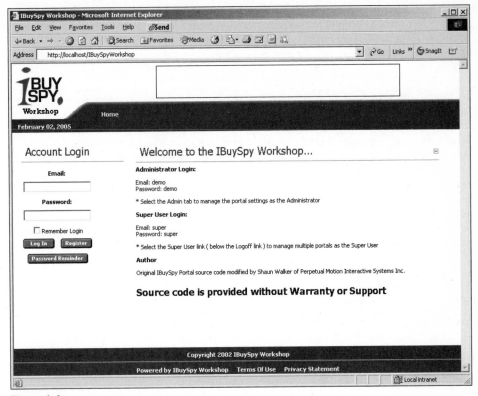

Figure 1-4

Supporting a user base through upgrades is fundamental in any software product. This is especially true in open source projects where the application can evolve quickly based on community feedback and technical advancements. The popular open source expression is that "no user should be left on an evolutionary dead-end." As luck would have it, I had designed a reliable upgrade mechanism in the original sports management application that I included in the IBuySpy Workshop code base. This feature enabled users of the application to easily migrate from one release version to the next—a critical factor in keeping the community engaged and committed to the evolution of the product.

In February 2003, the IBuySpy Portal Forum had become so congested with IBuySpy Workshop threads that it started to become difficult for the two communities to co-exist peacefully. At this point, I sent an e-mail to the anonymous alias posted at the bottom of the forums page on the www.asp.net site with a request to create a dedicated forum for the IBuySpy Workshop. Because the product functionality and source code of the two applications diverged so significantly, my intent was to try and keep the forum posts for the two applications separated, providing both communities the means to support their membership. I certainly did not have high hopes that my e-mail request was even going to be read—let alone granted. But to my surprise, I received a positive response from none other than Rob Howard (an ASP.NET icon), which proved to be a great introduction to a long-term partnership with Microsoft. Rob created the forum and even went a step further and added a link to the Source Download page of the www.asp.net site, an event that would ultimately drive a huge amount of traffic to the emerging IBuySpy Workshop community.

There are a number of reasons why the IBuySpy Workshop became so immediately popular when it was released in early 2003. The obvious reason is because the base application contained a huge number of enhancements over the IBuySpy Portal application, and people could immediately leverage them to build more powerful web sites. From a community perspective, the open source project provided a central management authority that was dedicated to the ongoing growth and support of the application framework, a factor that was definitely lacking in the original IBuySpy Portal community. This concept of open source on the Microsoft platform attracted many developers; some with pure philosophical intentions, and others who viewed the application as a vehicle to further their own revenue-generating interests. Yet another factor, which I think is often overlooked, relates to the programming language on which the project was based. With the release of the .NET Framework 1.0, Microsoft spent a lot of energy promoting the benefits of the new C# programming language. The C# language was intended to provide a migration path for C++ developers as well as a means to entice Java developers working on other platforms to switch. This left the Visual Basic and ASP 3.0 developer communities feeling neglected and somewhat unappreciated. The IBuySpy Workshop, with its core framework in VB.NET, provided an essential community ecosystem where legacy VB developers could interact, learn, and share.

Subscription Fiasco

In late February 2003, the lack of sleep, family priorities, and community demands finally came to a head and I decided that I should reach out for help. I contacted a former employer and mentor, Kent Alstad, with my dilemma and we spent a few lengthy telephone calls brainstorming possible outcomes. However, my personal stress level at the time and my urgency to change direction on the project ultimately caused me to move too fast and with more aggression than I should have. I announced that the IBuySpy Workshop would immediately become a subscription service where developers would need to pay a monthly fee to get access to the latest source code. From a personal perspective, the intent was to generate enough revenue that I could leave my day job and focus my full energy on the management of the open source project. And with 2000 registered users, a subscription service seemed like a viable model (see Figure 1-5).

However, the true philosophy of the open source model immediately came to light, and I had to face the wrath of a scorned community. Among other things, I was accused of misleading the community, lying about the open source nature of the project, and letting my personal greed cloud my vision. For every one supporter of my decision, there were 10 more who publicly crucified me as the evil incarnate. Luckily for me, Kent had a trusted work associate named Andy Baron, a senior consultant at MCW

Technologies and a Microsoft Most Valuable Professional since 1995, who has incredible wisdom when it comes to the Microsoft development community. Andy helped me craft a public apology message (see Figure 1-6) that managed to appease the community and restore the IBuySpy Workshop to full open source status.

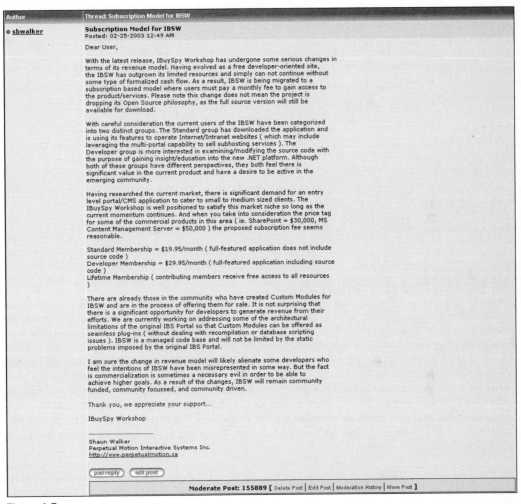

Author	Thread: Subscription Model for IBSW
● sbwalker	**Subscription Model for IBSW**

Posted: 02-25-2003 12:49 AM

Dear User,

With the latest release, IBuySpy Workshop has undergone some serious changes in terms of its revenue model. Having evolved as a free developer-oriented site, the IBSW has outgrown its limited resources and simply can not continue without some type of formalized cash flow. As a result, IBSW is being migrated to a subscription based model where users must pay a monthly fee to gain access to the product/services. Please note this change does not mean the project is dropping its Open Source philosophy, as the full source version will still be available for download.

With careful consideration the current users of the IBSW have been categorized into two distinct groups. The Standard group has downloaded the application and is using its features to operate Internet/Intranet websites (which may include leveraging the multi-portal capability to sell subhosting services). The Developer group is more interested in examining/modifying the source code with the purpose of gaining insight/education into the new .NET platform. Although both of these groups have different perspectives, they both feel there is significant value in the current product and have a desire to be active in the emerging community.

Having researched the current market, there is significant demand for an entry level portal/CMS application to cater to small to medium sized clients. The IBuySpy Workshop is well positioned to satisfy this market niche so long as the current momentum continues. And when you take into consideration the price tag for some of the commercial products in this area (ie. SharePoint = $30,000, MS Content Management Server = $50,000) the proposed subscription fee seems reasonable.

Standard Membership = $19.95/month (full-featured application does not include source code)
Developer Membership = $29.95/month (full-featured application including source code)
Lifetime Membership (contributing members receive free access to all resources)

There are already those in the community who have created Custom Modules for IBSW and are in the process of offering them for sale. It is not surprising that there is a significant opportunity for developers to generate revenue from their efforts. We are currently working on addressing some of the architectural limitations of the original IBS Portal so that Custom Modules can be offered as seamless plug-ins (without dealing with recompilation or database scripting issues). IBSW is a managed code base and will not be limited by the static problems imposed by the original IBS Portal.

I am sure the change in revenue model will likely alienate some developers who feel the intentions of IBSW have been misrepresented in some way. But the fact is commercialization is sometimes a necessary evil in order to be able to achieve higher goals. As a result of the changes, IBSW will remain community funded, community focussed, and community driven.

Thank you, we appreciate your support...

IBuySpy Workshop

Shaun Walker
Perpetual Motion Interactive Systems Inc.
http://www.perpetualmotion.ca

(post reply) (edit post)

Moderate Post: 155889 [Delete Post | Edit Post | Moderation History | Move Post]

Figure 1-5

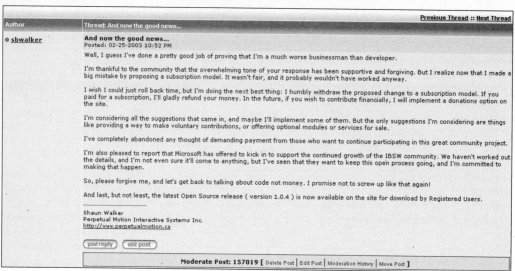

Figure 1-6

Microsoft

Coincidentally, the political nightmare I created in the IBuySpy Workshop Forum with my subscription announcement resulted in some direct attention from the Microsoft ASP.NET product team (the maintainers of the www.asp.net site). Still trying to recover from the damage I incurred, I received an e-mail from none other than Scott Guthrie (co-founder of the Microsoft ASP.NET Team), asking me to reexamine my decision on the subscription model and making suggestions on how the project could continue as a free, open source venture. It seemed that Microsoft was protective of its evolving community and did not want to see the progress in this area splinter and dissolve just as it seemed to be gaining momentum. Scott Guthrie made no promises at this point but he did open a direct dialogue that ultimately led to some fundamental discussions on sponsorship and collaboration. In fact, this initial e-mail led to a number of telephone conversations and ultimately an invitation to Redmond to discuss the future of the IBuySpy Workshop.

I still remember the combination of nerves and excitement as I drove from my home in Abbotsford, British Columbia to Microsoft's head office in Redmond, Washington (about a three-hour trek). I really did not know what to expect, and I tried to strategize all possible angles. Essentially all of my planning turned out to be moot, because my meeting with Scott Guthrie turned out to be far more laid back and transparent than I could have ever imagined. Scott took me to his unassuming office and we spent the next three hours brainstorming ideas about how the IBuySpy Workshop fit into the current ASP.NET landscape. Much of this centered on the evolving vision of ASP.NET 2.0 — an area where I had little or no knowledge prior to the meeting (the Whidbey Alpha had not even been released at this point).

At the beginning of the meeting, Scott had me demonstrate the current version of the IBuySpy Workshop, explaining its key features and benefits. We also discussed the long-term goals of the project as well as my proposed roadmap for future enhancements. Scott's knowledge of both the technical and community aspects of the ASP.NET platform really amazed me — I guess that's why he is the undisputed "Father of

ASP.NET." In hindsight, I can hardly believe my good fortune to have received three dedicated hours of his time to discuss the project — it really changed my "ivory tower" perception of Microsoft and forged a strong relationship for future collaboration.

Upon leaving Redmond, I had to stifle my excitement as I realized that, regardless of the direct interaction with Microsoft, I personally was still in the same situation as before the subscription model announcement. Because the subscription model failed to generate the much-needed revenue that would have allowed me to devote 100% of my time to the project, I was forced to examine other possible alternatives. There were a number of suggestions from the community and the concept that seemed to have the most potential was related to web hosting.

In these early stages, there were few economical Microsoft Windows hosting options available that offered a SQL Server database — a fundamental requirement for running the IBuySpy Workshop application. Coincidentally, I had recently struck up a relationship with an individual from New Jersey who was active in the IBuySpy Workshop forums on www.asp.net. This individual had a solid background in web hosting and proposed a partnership whereby he would manage the web hosting infrastructure and I would continue to enhance the application and drive traffic to the business. Initially there were a lot of community members who signed up for this service — some because of the low-cost hosting option, others because they were looking for a way to support the open source project. It soon became obvious that the costs to build and support the infrastructure were consuming the majority of the revenue generated. And over time the amount of effort to support the growing client base became more intense. Eventually it came to a point where it was intimated that my contributions to the web hosting business were not substantial enough to justify the current partnership structure. I was informed that the partnership should be dissolved. This is where things got complicated because there was never any formal agreement signed by either party to initiate the partnership. Without documentation, it made the negotiation for a fair settlement difficult and resulted in some bad feelings on both sides. This was unfortunate because I think the relationship was formed with the best intentions but the demands of the business resulted in a poor outcome. Regardless, this ordeal was an important lesson I needed to learn: regardless of the open-source nature of the project, it was imperative to have all contractually binding items properly documented.

DotNetNuke

One of the topics that Scott Guthrie and I discussed in our early conversations was the issue of product branding. IBuySpy Workshop achieved its early goals of providing a public reference to the IBuySpy Portal community. This resulted in an influx of ASP.NET developers who were familiar with the IBuySpy Portal application and were interested in this new open source concept. But as the code bases diverged, there was a need for a new project identity — a unique brand that would differentiate the community and provide the mechanism for building an internationally recognized ecosystem. Research of competing portal applications on other platforms revealed a strong tendency toward the "nuke" slogan.

The "nuke" slogan was originally coined by Francisco Burzi of PHP-Nuke fame (the oft-disputed pioneer of open source portal applications). Over the years, a variety of other projects adopted the slogan as well — so many that the term had obtained industry recognition in the portal-application genre. To my surprise, a WHOIS search revealed that dotnetnuke.com, .net, and .org were not registered and, in my opinion, seemed to be the perfect identity for the project. Again emphasizing the bare-bones resources under which the project was initiated, my credit card transaction to register the three domain names was denied, and I was only able to register dotnetnuke.com (in the long run an embarrassing

and contentious issue as the .net and .org domain names were immediately registered by other individuals). Equally as spontaneous, I did an Internet search for images containing the word "nuke" and
located a three-dimensional graphic of a circular gear with a nuclear symbol embossed on it. I contacted
the owner of the site and was given permission to use the image (it was in fact, simply one of many public domain images they were using for a fictitious storefront demonstration). A new project identity was
born — Version 1.0.5 of the IBuySpy Workshop was re-branded as DotNetNuke, which the community
immediately abbreviated to DNN for simplicity (see Figure 1-7).

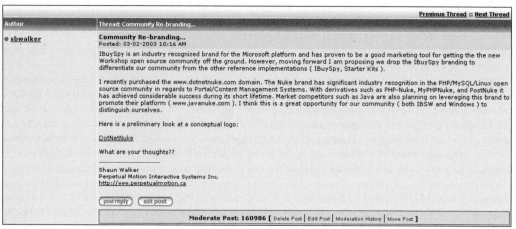

Figure 1-7

Licensing

A secondary issue that was not addressed during the early stages of the project was licensing. The original IBuySpy Portal was released under a liberal Microsoft EULA license that allowed for unrestricted
usage, modification, and distribution. However, the code base underwent such a major transformation
that it could hardly be compared with its predecessor. Therefore, when the IBuySpy Workshop application was released, I did not include the original Microsoft EULA, nor did I include any copyright or
license of my own. Essentially this meant that the application was in the public domain. This is certainly
not the most accepted approach to an open source project and eventually some of the more legal-savvy
community members brought the issue to a head. I was forced to take a hard look at open source licensing models to determine which license was most appropriate for the project.

In stark contrast to the spontaneous approach taken to finding a project identity, the licensing issue had
much deeper ramifications. Had I not performed extensive research on this subject, I would have likely
chosen a GPL license because it seemed to dominate the vast majority of open source projects in existence. However, digging beneath the surface, I quickly realized that the GPL did not seem to be a good
candidate for my objectives of allowing DotNetNuke to be used in both commercial and non-commercial
environments. Ultimately the selection of a license for an open source project is largely dependent upon
your business model, your product architecture, and understanding who owns the intellectual property
in your application. The combination of these factors prompted me to take a hard look at the open
source licensing options available.

For those of you who have not researched open source software, you would be surprised at the major differences between the most popular open source licensing models. It is true that these licenses all meet the standards of the Open Source Definition, a set of guidelines managed by the Open Source Initiative (OSI) at www.open-source.org. These principles include the right to use open source software for any purpose, the right to make and distribute copies, the right to create and distribute derivative works, the right to access and use source code, and the right to combine open source and other software. With such fundamental rights shared between all open source licenses, it probably makes you wonder why there is need for more than one license at all. Well the reason is because each license has the ability to impose additional rights or restrictions on top of these base principles. The additional rights and restrictions have the effect of altering the license so that it meets the specific objectives of each project. Because it is generally bad practice to create brand new licenses (based on the fact that the existing licenses have gained industry acceptance as well as a proven track record), people generally gravitate toward either a GPL or BSD license.

The GPL (or GNU Public License) was created in 1989 by Richard Stallman, founder of the Free Software Foundation. The GPL is what is now known as a "copyleft" license, a term coined based on its controversial reciprocity clause. Essentially this clause stipulates that you are allowed to use the software on the condition that any derivative works that you create from it and distribute must be licensed to all under the same license. This is intended to ensure that the software and any enhancements to it remain in the public domain for everyone to share. Although this is a great humanitarian goal, it seriously restricts the use of the software in a commercial environment.

The BSD (or Berkeley Software Distribution) was created by the University of California and was designed to permit the free use, modification, and distribution of software without any return obligation on the part of the community. The BSD is essentially a "copyright" license, meaning that you are free to use the software on the condition that you retain the copyright notice in all copies or derivative works. The BSD is also known as an "academic" license because it provides the highest degree of intellectual property sharing.

Ultimately I settled on a standard BSD license for DotNetNuke; a license that allows the maximum licensing freedom in both commercial and non-commercial environments — with only minimal restrictions to preserve the copyright of the project. The change in license went widely unnoticed by the community because it did not impose any additional restrictions on usage or distribution. However, it was a fundamental milestone in establishing DotNetNuke as a true open source project:

```
DotNetNuke(r) - http://www.dotnetnuke.com
Copyright (c) 2002-2006
by Perpetual Motion Interactive Systems Inc. (http://www.perpetualmotion.ca)

Permission is hereby granted, free of charge, to any person obtaining a copy of
this software and associated documentation files (the "Software"), to deal in the
Software without restriction, including without limitation the rights to use, copy,
modify, merge, publish, distribute, sublicense, and/or sell copies of the Software,
and to permit persons to whom the Software is furnished to do so, subject to the
following conditions:

The above copyright notice and this permission notice shall be included in all
copies or substantial portions of the Software.

THE SOFTWARE IS PROVIDED "AS IS", WITHOUT WARRANTY OF ANY KIND, EXPRESS OR IMPLIED,
INCLUDING BUT NOT LIMITED TO THE WARRANTIES OF MERCHANTABILITY, FITNESS FOR A
PARTICULAR PURPOSE AND NONINFRINGEMENT. IN NO EVENT SHALL THE AUTHORS OR COPYRIGHT
HOLDERS BE LIABLE FOR ANY CLAIM, DAMAGES OR OTHER LIABILITY, WHETHER IN AN ACTION
OF CONTRACT, TORT OR OTHERWISE, ARISING FROM, OUT OF OR IN CONNECTION WITH THE
SOFTWARE OR THE USE OR OTHER DEALINGS IN THE SOFTWARE.
```

Core Team

The next major milestone in the project's open source evolution occurred in the summer of 2003. Up until this point, I had been acting as the sole maintainer of the DotNetNuke code base, a task that was consuming 110% of my free time as I feverishly fixed bugs and enhanced the framework based on community feedback. Still I felt more like a bottleneck than a provider, in spite of the fact that I was churning out at least one significant release every month leading up to this point. The more active community members were becoming restless due to a lack of direct input into the progress of the project. In fact, a small faction of these members even went so far as to create their own hybrid or "fork" of the DotNetNuke code base that attempted to forge ahead and add features at a more aggressive pace than I was capable of on my own. These were challenging times from a political standpoint because I was eventually forced to confront all of these issues in a direct and public manner—flexing my "benevolent dictator" muscles for the first time—an act I was not the least bit comfortable performing. Luckily for me, I had a number of loyal and trustworthy community members who supported my position and ultimately provided the backing to form a strong and committed Core Team.

As a result of the single-threaded issues I mentioned earlier, most successful open source projects are comprised of a number of community volunteers who earn their positions of authority within the community based on their specific expertise or community support activities. This is known as a *meritocracy*, a term that means that an individual's influence is directly proportional to the ability that the individual demonstrates within the project. It's a well-observed fact that individuals with more experience and skills have less time to devote to volunteer activities; however, their minimal contributions prove to be incredibly valuable. Similarly, individuals with less experience may be able to invest more time but may only be capable of performing the more repetitive, menial tasks. Building a healthy balance of these two roles is exactly what is required in every successful open source project; and in fact, is one of the more challenging items to achieve from a management perspective.

The original DotNetNuke Core Team was selected based on their participation and dedication to the DotNetNuke project in the months leading up to the team's formation. In most cases this was solely based on an individual's public image and reputation established in the DotNetNuke Forum on the www.asp.net web site. And in fact, in these early stages, the online persona of each individual proved to be a good indicator of the specific skills they could bring to the project. Some members were highly skilled architects, others were seasoned developers, and others were better at discussing functionality from an end-user perspective and providing quality support to their community peers.

To establish some basic structure for the newly formed Core Team, I attempted to summarize some basic project guidelines. My initial efforts combined some of the best Extreme Programming (XP) rules with the principles of other successful open source projects. This became the basis of the DotNetNuke Manifest document:

❑ **Development is a team effort:** The whole is exponentially greater than the sum of its parts. Large-scale open source projects are only viable if a large enough community of highly skilled developers can be amassed to attack a problem. Treating your users as co-developers is your most effective option for rapid code improvement and effective debugging.

❑ **Build the right product before you build the product right:** Focus should be directed at understanding and implementing the high-level business requirements before attempting to construct the perfect technical architecture. Listen to your customers.

❑ **Incremental development:** Every software product has infinite growth potential if managed correctly. Functionality should be added in incremental units rather than attempting a monolithic implementation. Release often but with a level of quality that instills confidence.

❑ **Law of diminishing return:** The majority of the effort should be invested in implementing features that have the most benefit and widest general usage by the community.

DotNetNuke version 1.0.10 was the proving grounds for the original Core Team. The idea was to establish the infrastructure to support disconnected team development by working on a stabilization release of the current product. A lot of debate went into the selection of the appropriate source control system because, ironically enough, many of the Core Team had never worked with a formal source control process in the past (a fact that certainly emphasized the varied professional background of the Core Team members). The debate centered on whether to use a CVS or VSS model.

CVS is a source control system that is popular in the open source world that enables developers to work in an unrestricted manner on their local project files and handles any conflicts between versions when you attempt to commit your changes to the central repository. Visual SourceSafe (VSS) is a Microsoft source-control system that is supported by the Microsoft development tool suite, which requires developers to explicitly lock project files before making modifications to prevent version conflicts. Ultimately the familiarity with the Microsoft model won out and we decided to use the free WorkSpaces service on the GotDotNet web site (a new developer community site supported by Microsoft). GotDotNet also provided a simplistic Bug Tracker application that provided us with a means to manage the tracking of issues and enhancement requests. With these infrastructure components in place, we were able to focus on the stabilization of the application, correcting known defects and adding some minor usability enhancements. It was during this time that Scott Willhite stepped forward to assume a greater role of responsibility in the project; assisting in management activities, communication, prioritization, and scheduling.

A significant enhancement that was introduced in this stabilization release came from a third party who had contacted me with some specific enhancements they had implemented and wished to contribute. The University of Texas at El Paso had done extensive work making the DotNetNuke application compliant with the guidelines of the American Disabilities Association (ADA) and Section 508 of the United States Rehabilitation Act. The United States government made compliancy mandatory for most public organizations; therefore, this was a great enhancement for DotNetNuke because it allowed the application to be used in government, educational, and military scenarios. Bruce Hopkins became the Core Team owner of this item in these early stages, a role that required a great deal of patience as the rest of the team came to grips with the new concept.

Establishing and managing a team was no small challenge. On one hand, there were the technical challenges of allowing multiple team members, all in different geographic regions, to communicate and collaborate in a cost-effective, secure environment. Certainly this would have never been possible without the Internet and its vast array of online tools. On the other hand, there was the challenge of identifying different personality types and channeling them into areas where they would be most effective. Because there are limited financial motivators in the open source model, people must rely on more basic incentives to justify their volunteer efforts. Generally this leads to a paradigm where contributions to the project become the de facto channel for building a reputation within the community — a primary motivator in any meritocracy As a result of working with the team, it soon became obvious that there were two extremes in this area: those who would selflessly sacrifice all of their free time (often to their own detriment) to the open source project, and those who would invest the minimal effort and expect the maximum reward. As the creator and maintainer of the project it was my duty to remain objective and put the interests of the community first. This often caused me to become frustrated with the behavior of specific individuals, but in nearly all cases these issues could be resolved without introducing any hard feelings on either side. This is true in all cases except one.

XXL Fork

Early in the project history, I was approached by an individual from Germany with a request to maintain a localized DotNetNuke site for the German community. I was certainly not naïve to the dangers of forking at this point and I told him that it would be fine so long as the site stayed consistent with the official source code base, which was under my jurisdiction. This was agreed upon and in the coming months I had periodic communication with this individual regarding his localization efforts. However as time wore on, he became critical of the manner in which the project was being managed, in particular the sole maintainer aspect, and began to voice his disapproval in the public forum. There was a group who believed that there should be greater degree of transparency in the project — that developers should be able to get access to the latest development source code at anytime, and that the maintenance of the application should be conducted by a team rather than an individual. He was able to convince a number of community members to collaborate with him on a modified version of DotNetNuke, a version that integrated a number of the more popular community enhancements available, and called it DotNetNuke XXL.

Now I have to admit that much of this occurred due to my own inability to respond quickly and form a Core Team. In addition, I was not providing adequate feedback to the community regarding my goals and objectives for the future of the project. The reality is that the background management tasks of creating the DotNetNuke Core Team and managing the myriad other issues had undermined my ability to deliver source code enhancements and support to the community. The combination of these factors resulted in an unpleasant situation, one that I should have mitigated sooner but was afraid to act upon due to the fragility of the newly formed community. And you also need to remember that the creator of the XXL variant had broken no license agreement by creating a fork — it was completely legal based on the freedom of the BSD open source license.

Eventually the issue came to a head when members of the XXL group began promoting their full-source-code hybrid in the DotNetNuke Forum. Essentially piggy-backing on the primary promotion channel for the DotNetNuke project, they were able to convince many people to switch to the XXL code base. This had some bad consequences for the DotNetNuke community. Mainly it threatened to splinter the emerging community on territorial boundaries — an event I wanted to avoid at all costs. This situation was the closest attempt of project hijacking that I can realistically imagine. The DotNetNuke XXL fork seemed to be fixated on becoming the official version of DotNetNuke and assuming control of the future project roadmap. The only saving grace was that I personally managed the DotNetNuke infrastructure and therefore had some influence over key aspects of the open source environment.

In searching for an effective mechanism to protect the integrity of the community and prevent the XXL fork from gaining momentum, some basic business fundamentals came into play. Any product or service is only as successful as its promotion or marketing channel. The DotNetNuke Forum on the www.asp.net web site was the primary communication hub to the DotNetNuke community. Therefore it was not difficult to realize that restricting discussion on XXL in the forum was the simplest method to mitigate its growth. In probably the most aggressive political move I have ever been forced to make, I introduced some bold changes to the DotNetNuke project. I established some guidelines for Core Team conduct that included, among other things, restrictions on promoting competing open source hybrids of the DotNetNuke application. I also posted some policies on the DotNetNuke Forum that emphasized that the forum was dedicated solely to the discussion of the official DotNetNuke application and that discussion of third-party commercial or open source products was strictly forbidden. This was an especially difficult decision to make from a moral standpoint as I was well aware that the DotNetNuke application had been introduced to the community via the IBuySpy Portal Forum. Nonetheless, the combination of these two announcements resulted in both the resignation of the XXL project leader from the Core Team as well as the end of discussion of the XXL fork in the DotNetNuke Forum. It is important to note that such a defensive move would not have been possible without the loyalty and support of the rest of the Core Team in terms of enforcing the guidelines.

The unfortunate side effect, one about which I had been cautioning members of the community for weeks, was that users who had upgraded to the XXL fork were effectively left on an evolutionary dead-end — a product version with no support mechanism or promise of future upgrades. This is because many of the XXL enhancements were never going to be integrated into the official DotNetNuke code base (either due to design limitations or inapplicability to the general public). This situation, as unpleasant as it may have been for those caught on the dead-end side of the equation, was a real educational experience for the community in general as they began to understand the longer-term and deeper implications of open source project philosophy. In general the community feedback was positive to the project changes, with only occasional flare-ups in the weeks following. In addition, the Core Team seemed to gel more as a result of these decisions because it provided some much-needed policies on conduct, loyalty, and dedication as well a concrete example of how inappropriate behavior would be penalized.

Trademarks

Emerging from the XXL dilemma, I realized that I needed to establish some legal protection for the long-term preservation of the project. Because standard copyright and the BSD license offered no real insurance from third-party threats, I began to explore intellectual property law in greater detail. After much research and legal advice, I decided that the best option was to apply for a trademark for the DotNetNuke name. Registering a trademark protects a project's name or logo, which is often a project's most valuable asset. After the trademark was approved it would mean that although an individual or company could still create a fork of the application, they legally could not refer to it by the DotNetNuke name. This appeared to be an important distinction so I proceeded with trademark registration in Canada (because this is the country in which Perpetual Motion Interactive Systems Inc. is incorporated).

I must admit the entire trademark approval process was quite an educational experience. Before you can register your trademark, you need to define a category and description of your wares and/or services. This can be challenging, although most trademark agencies now provide public access to their database where you can browse for similar items that have been approved in the past. You pay your processing fee when you submit the initial application, but the trademark agency has the right to reject your application for any number of reasons — whereby, you need to modify your application and submit it again. Each iteration can take a couple of months, so patience is indeed a requirement. After the trademark is accepted, it must be published in a public trademark journal for a specified amount of time, providing third parties the opportunity to contest the trademark before it is approved. If it makes it through this final stage, you can pay your registration fee for the trademark to become official. To emphasize the lengthy process involved, the DotNetNuke trademark was initially submitted on October 9, 2003, and was finally approved on November 15, 2004 (TMA625,364).

Sponsorship

In August 2003, I finally came to an agreement with Microsoft regarding a sponsorship proposal for the DotNetNuke project. In a nutshell, Microsoft wanted DotNetNuke to be enhanced in a number of key areas; the intent being to use the open source project as a means of demonstrating the strengths of the ASP.NET platform. Because these enhancements were completely congruent with the future goals of the project, there was little negative consequence from a technical perspective. In return for implementing the enhancements, Microsoft would provide a number of sponsorship benefits to the project including web hosting for the www.dotnetnuke.com web site, weekly meetings with an ASP.NET Team representative (Rob Howard), continued promotion via the www.asp.net web site, and more direct access to Microsoft resources for mentoring and guidance. It took five months for this sponsorship proposal to come together, which demonstrates the patience and perseverance required to collaborate with such an influential partner as Microsoft. Nonetheless, this was potentially a one-time offer and at such a critical stage in the project evolution, it seemed too important to ignore.

An interesting perception that most people have in the IT industry is that Microsoft is morally against the entire open source phenomenon. In my opinion, this is far from the truth—and the reality is so much more simplistic. Like any other business that is trying to enhance its market position, Microsoft is merely concerned about competition. This is nothing new. In the past, Microsoft faced competitive challenges from many sources—companies, individuals, and governments. However, the current environment makes it much more emotional and newsworthy to suggest that Microsoft is pitted against a grassroots community movement rather than a business or legal concern. So in my opinion, it is merely a coincidence that the only real competition facing Microsoft at this point is coming from the open source development community. And there is no doubt it will take some time and effort for Microsoft to adapt to the changing landscape. But the chances are probably high that Microsoft will eventually embrace open source to some degree to remain competitive.

When it comes to DotNetNuke, many people probably question why Microsoft would be interested in assisting an open source project where it receives no direct benefit. And it may be perplexing why Microsoft would sponsor a product that competes to some degree with several of its own commercial applications. But you do not have to look much further than the obvious indirect benefits to see why this relationship has tremendous value. First and foremost, at this point the DotNetNuke application is only designed for use on the Microsoft platform. This means that to use DotNetNuke, you must have valid licenses for a number of Microsoft infrastructure components (Windows operating system, database server, and so on). So this provides the financial value. In addition, DotNetNuke promotes the benefits of the .NET Framework and encourages developers to migrate to this new development platform. This provides the educational value. Finally, it cultivates an active and passionate community—a network of loyal supporters who are motivated to leverage and promote Microsoft technology on an international scale. This provides the marketing value.

Enhancements

In September 2003, with the assistance of the newly formed Core Team, we embarked on an ambitious mission to implement the enhancements suggested by Microsoft. The problem at this point was that in addition to the Microsoft enhancements, there were some critical community enhancements, which I ultimately perceived as an even higher priority if the project should hope to grow to the next level. So the scope of the enhancement project began to snowball, and estimated release dates began to slip.

The quality of the release code was also considered to be so crucial a factor that early beta packages were not deemed worthy of distribution. Ultimately, the code base evolved so much that there was little question the next release would need to be labeled version 2.0. During this phase of internal development, some members of the Core Team did an outstanding job of supporting the 1.x community and generating excitement about the next major release. This was critical in keeping the DotNetNuke community engaged and committed to the evolving project.

A number of excellent community enhancements for the DotNetNuke 1.0 platform also emerged during this stage. This sparked an active third-party reseller and support community, establishing yet another essential factor in any largely successful open source project. Unfortunately, at this point the underlying architecture of the DotNetNuke application was not particularly extensible, which made the third-party enhancements susceptible to upgrade complications and somewhat challenging to integrate for end users. As a Core Team, we recognized this limitation and focused on full modularity as a guiding principle for all future enhancements.

Modularity is an architecture principle that basically involves the creation of well-defined interfaces for the purpose of extending an application. The goal of any framework should be to provide interfaces in all areas that are likely to require customization based on business requirements or personalization based on individuality. DotNetNuke provides extensibility in the area of modules, skins, templates, data providers, and localization. And DotNetNuke typically goes one step beyond defining the basic interface: it actually provides the full spectrum of related resource services including creation, packaging, distribution, and installation. With all of these services available, it makes it extremely easy for developers to build and share application extensions with other members of the community.

One of the benefits of working on an open source project is the fact that there is a high priority placed on creating the optimal solution or architecture. I think it was Bill Gates who promoted the concept of "magical software" and it is certainly a key aspiration in many open source projects. This goal often results in more preliminary analysis and design that tends to elongate the schedule but also results in a more extensible and adaptable architecture. This differs from traditional application development that often suffers from time and budget constraints, resulting in shortcuts, poor design decisions, and delivery of functionality before it is validated. Another related benefit is that the developers of open source software also represent a portion of its overall user community, meaning they actually "eat their own dog food" so to speak. This is really critical when it comes to understanding the business requirements under which the application needs to operate. Far too often you find commercial vendors who build their software in a virtual vacuum, never experiencing the fundamental application use cases in a real-world environment.

One of the challenges in allowing the Core Team to work together on the DotNetNuke application was the lack of high-quality infrastructure tools. Probably the most fundamental elements from a software development standpoint were the need for a reliable source-code-control system and issue-management system. Because the project had little to no financial resources to draw upon, we were forced to use whatever free services were available in the open source community. And although some of these services are leveraged successfully by other open source projects, the performance, management, and disaster recovery aspects are sorely lacking. This led to a decision to approach some of the more successful commercial vendors in these areas with requests for pro-bono software licenses. Surprisingly, these vendors were more than happy to assist the DotNetNuke open source project — in exchange for some minimal sponsorship recognition. This model has ultimately been carried on in other project areas to acquire the professional infrastructure, development tools, and services necessary to support our growing organization.

As we worked through the enhancements for the DotNetNuke 2.0 project, a number of Core Team members gained considerable respect within the project based on their high level of commitment, unselfish behavior, and expert development skills. Joe Brinkman, Dan Caron, Scott McCulloch, and Geert Veenstra sacrificed a lot of personal time and energy to improve the DotNetNuke open source project. And the important thing to realize is that they did so because they wanted to help others and make a difference, not because of self-serving agendas or premeditated expectations. The satisfaction of working with other highly talented individuals in an open, collaborative environment is reward enough for some developers. And it is this particular aspect of open source development that continues to confound and amaze people as time goes on.

In October 2003, there was a Microsoft Professional Developers Conference (PDC) in Los Angeles, California. The PDC is the premier software development spectacle for the Microsoft platform; an event that occurs only every two years. About a month prior to the event Cory Isakson, a developer on the Rainbow Portal open source project, contacted me, saying that "Open Source Portals" had been nominated as a category for a "Birds of Feather" session at the event. I posted the details in the DotNetNuke Forum and soon the item had collected enough community votes that it was approved as an official BOF session. This provided a great opportunity to meet with DotNetNuke enthusiasts and critics from all over the globe. It also provided a great networking opportunity to chat with the most influential commercial software vendors in the .NET development space (contacts made with SourceGear and MaximumASP at this event proved to be important to DotNetNuke, as time would tell).

Security Flaw

In January 2004, another interesting dilemma presented itself. I received an e-mail from an external party, a web application security specialist who claimed to have discovered a severe vulnerability in the DotNetNuke application (version 1.0). Upon further research, I confirmed that the security hole was indeed valid and immediately called an emergency meeting of the more trusted Core Team members to determine the most appropriate course of action. At this point, we were fully focused on the DotNetNuke 2.0 development project but also realized that it was our responsibility to serve and protect the growing DotNetNuke 1.0 community. From a technical perspective, the patch for the vulnerability proved to be a simple code modification.

The more challenging problem was related to communicating the details of the security issue to the community. On the one hand we needed the community to understand the severity of the issue so that they would be motivated to patch their applications. On the other hand, we did not want to cause widespread alarm, which could lead to a public perception that DotNetNuke was an insecure platform. Exposing too many details of the vulnerability would be an open invitation for hackers to try and exploit DotNetNuke web sites, but revealing too few details would downplay the severity. And the fact that the project is open source meant that the magnitude of the problem was amplified. Traditional software products have the benefit of tracking and identifying users through restrictive licensing policies. Open source projects have licenses that allow for free redistribution, which means the maintainer of the project has no way to track the actual usage of the application and no way to directly contact all community members who are affected.

The whole situation really put security issues into perspective for me. It's one thing to be an outsider, expressing your opinions on how a software vendor should or should not react to critical security issues in their products. It's quite another thing to be an insider, stuck in the vicious dilemma between divulging too much or too little information, knowing full well that both options have the potential to put your customers at even greater risk. Ultimately, we created a new release version and issued a general security alert that was sent directly to all registered users of the DotNetNuke application by e-mail and posted in the DotNetNuke Forum on www.asp.net:

```
Subject: DotNetNuke Security Alert

Yesterday we became aware of a security vulnerability in DotNetNuke.

It is the immediate recommendation of the DotNetNuke Core Team that all
users of DotNetNuke based systems download and install this security patch
as soon as possible. As part of our standard security policy, no further
detailed information regarding the nature of the exploit will be provided to
the general public.

This email provides the steps to immediately fix existing sites and mitigate
the potential for a malicious attack.

Who is vulnerable?

-- Any version of DotNetNuke from version 1.0.6 to 1.0.10d

What is the vulnerability?

A malicious user can anonymously download files from the server. This is not
the same download security issue that has been well documented in the past
whereby an anonymous user can gain access to files in the /Portals directory
if they know the exact URL. This particular exploit bypasses the file
security mechanism of the IIS server completely and allows a malicious user
to download files with protected mappings (ie. *.aspx).

The vulnerability specifically *does not* enable the following actions:

-- A hacker *cannot* take over the server (e.g. it does not allow hacker
code to be executed on the server)

How to fix the vulnerability?

For Users:

{ Instructions on where to download the latest release and how to install }

For Developers:

{ Instructions with actual source code snippets for developers who had diverged
from the official DotNetNuke code base and were therefore unable to apply a general
release patch }

Please note that this public service announcement demonstrates the
professional responsibility of the Core Team to treat all possible security
exploits as serious and respond in a timely and decisive manner.

We sincerely apologize for the inconvenience that this has caused.

Thank you, we appreciate your support...

DotNetNuke - The Web of the Future
```

The security dilemma brings to light another often misunderstood paradigm when it comes to open source projects. Most open source projects have a license that explicitly states that there is no support or warranty of any kind for users of the application. And while this may be true from a purely legal standpoint, it does not mean that the maintainer of the open source application can ignore the needs of the community when issues arise. The fact is, if the maintainer did not accept responsibility for the application, the users would quickly lose trust and the community would dissolve. This implicit trust relationship is what all successful open source communities are based upon. So in reality, the open source license acts as little more than a waiver of direct liability for the maintainer. The DotNetNuke project certainly conforms to this model because we take on the responsibility to ensure that all users of the application are never left on an evolutionary dead-end and security issues are always dealt with in a professional and expedient manner.

DotNetNuke 2.0

After six months of development, including a full month of public beta releases and community feedback, DotNetNuke 2.0 was released on March 23, 2004. This release was significant because it occurred at VS Live! in San Francisco, California — a large-scale software development event sponsored by Microsoft and Fawcette publications. Due to our strong working relationship with Microsoft, I was invited to attend official press briefings conducted by the ASP.NET Team. Essentially, this involved up to eight private sessions with the leading press agencies (Fawcette, PC Magazine, Computer Wire, Ziff Davis, and so on) where I was able to summarize the DotNetNuke project, show them a short demonstration, and answer their specific questions. The event proved to be spectacularly successful and resulted in a surge of new traffic to the community (now totaling more than 40,000 registered users).

DotNetNuke 2.0 was a hit. We had successfully delivered a high-quality release that encapsulated the majority of the most requested product enhancements from the community. And we had done so in a manner that allowed for clean customization and extensibility. In particular, the skinning solution in DotNetNuke 2.0 achieved widespread critical acclaim.

In DotNetNuke 1.X, the user interface of the application allowed for little personalization — essentially all DNN sites looked much the same, a negative restriction considering the highly creative environment of the World Wide Web. DotNetNuke 2.0 removed this restriction and opened up the application to a whole new group of stakeholders: web designers. As the popularity of portal applications had increased in recent years, the ability for web designers to create rich, graphical user interfaces had diminished significantly. This is because the majority of portal applications were based on platforms that did not allow for clear separation between form and function, or were architected by developers who had little understanding of the creative needs of web designers. DotNetNuke 2.0 focused on this problem and implemented a solution where the portal environment and creative design process could be developed independently and then combined to produce a stunningly harmonious end-user experience. The process was not complicated and did not require the use of custom tools or methodologies. It did not take long before we began to see DotNetNuke sites with richly creative and highly graphical layouts emerge — proving the effectiveness of the solution and creating a "Can you top this?" community mentality for innovative portal designs.

DotNetNuke (DNN) Web Site

To demonstrate the effectiveness of the skinning solution, I commissioned a local web design company, Circle Graphics, to create a compelling design for the www.dotnetnuke.com web site (see Figure 1-8). As an open source project, I felt that I could get away with an unorthodox, somewhat aggressive site design and I was impressed by some of Circle Graphic's futuristic, industrial concepts I had seen.

It turned out that the designer who had created these visuals had since moved on but was willing to take on a small contract as a personal favor to the owner. He created a skin that included some stunning 3-D imagery including the now infamous "nuke-gear" logo, circuit board, and plenty of twisted metallic pipes and containers. The integration with the application worked flawlessly and the community was wildly impressed with the stunning result. Coincidentally, the designer of the DotNetNuke skin, Anson Vogt, has since gone on to bigger and better things, working with rapper Eminem as the Art Director for 3-D animation on the critically acclaimed Mosh video.

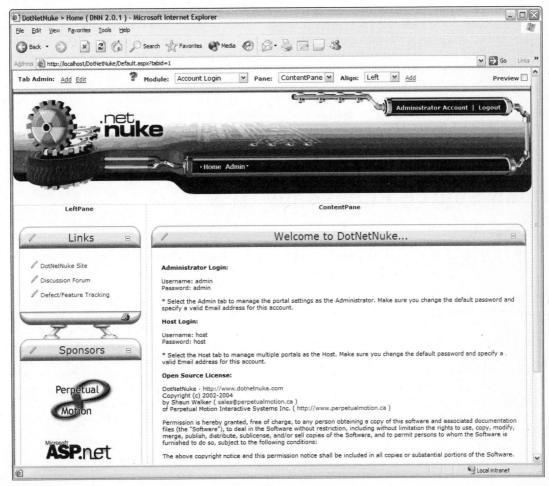

Figure 1-8

Provider Model

One of the large-scale enhancements that Microsoft insisted on for DotNetNuke 2.0 also proved to be popular. The Data Access Layer in DotNetNuke had been re-architected using an abstract factory model that effectively allowed it to interface with any number of relational databases. Microsoft coined the term "provider model" and emphasized it as a key component in the future ASP.NET 2.0 framework. Therefore, getting a reference implementation of this pattern in use in ASP.NET 1.x had plenty of positive educational benefits for Microsoft and DotNetNuke developers. DotNetNuke 2.0 included both a fully functional SQL Server and MS Access version, and the community soon stepped forward with mySQL and Oracle implementations as well. Again the extensibility benefits of good architecture were extremely obvious and demonstrated the direction we planned to pursue in all future product development.

Upon review of the DotNetNuke 2.0 code base, it was obvious that the application bore little resemblance to the original IBuySpy Portal application. This was a good thing because it raised the bar significantly in terms of n-tiered, object-oriented, enterprise-level software development. However, it was also bad in some ways because it alienated some of the early DotNetNuke enthusiasts who were in fact "hobby programmers," using the application more as a learning tool than a professional product. This is an interesting paradigm to observe in many open source projects. In the early stages, the developer community drives the feature set and extensibility requirements that, in turn, results in a much higher level of sophistication in terms of system architecture and design. However, as time goes on, this can sometimes result in the application surpassing the technical capabilities of some of its early adopters. DotNetNuke had ballooned from 15,000 lines of managed code to 46,000 lines of managed code in a little more than six months. The project was getting large enough that it required some serious effort to understand its organizational structure, dependencies, and development patterns.

Open Source Philosophy

When researching the open source phenomenon, there are a few fundamental details that are often ignored in favor of positive marketing rhetoric. I would like to take the opportunity to bring some of these to the surface because they provide some additional insight into some of the issues we face in the DotNetNuke project.

The first myth surrounds the belief that open source projects basically have an unlimited resource pool at their immediate disposal. Although this may be true from a purely theoretical perspective, the reality is that you still require a dedicated management structure to ensure that all of the resources are channeled in an efficient and productive manner. An army of developers without some type of central management authority will never consistently produce a cohesive application; and more likely, their efforts will result in total chaos. As much as the concept is often despised by hard-core programmers, dedicated management is absolutely necessary to set expectations and goals, ensure product quality, mitigate risk, recognize critical dependencies, manage scope, and assume ultimate responsibility. You will find no successful open source project that does not have an efficient and highly respected management team.

Also with regards to the unlimited resourcing myth, there are in fact few resources who become involved in an open source project that possess the level of competency and communication skills required to earn a highly trusted position in the meritocracy. More often, the resources who get involved are capable of handling more consumer-oriented tasks such as testing, support, and minor defect corrections. This is not to say that these resources do not play a critical role in the success of the project — every focused ounce of volunteer effort certainly helps sustain the health of the project. But my point is that there is usually a relatively small group on most open source projects who are responsible for the larger-scale architectural enhancements.

Yet another myth is related to the belief that anyone can make a direct and immediate impact on an open source project. Although this may be true to some degree, you generally need to build a trusted reputation within the community before you are granted any type of privilege. And there are few individuals who are ever awarded direct write access to the source code repository. Anyone has the ability to submit a patch or enhancement suggestion; however, there's no guarantee that it will be added to the open source project code base. In fact, all submissions are rigorously peer-reviewed by trusted resources, and only when they have passed all validation criteria are they introduced to the source code repository. In addition, although a specific submission may appear to be quite useful when judged in isolation, there may be higher-level issues to consider in terms of upgrade support (a situation that can lead to submitter frustration if the issues are not fully explained). From a control standpoint, this is not much different than source control management on a traditional software project. However, the open source model does significantly alter this paradigm in that everyone is able to review the source code. As a result, the sheer volume of patches submitted to this process can be massive.

There are also some interesting interpretations of open source philosophy that occasionally result in differences of opinion and, in the worst cases, all-out community revolts. This generally occurs because the guidelines for open source are quite non-explicit and subjective. One particularly hot topic that relates to DotNetNuke is source code access.

Some open source projects provide anonymous read-only access to the development source code base at all times. This full transparency is appreciated by developers who want to stay abreast of the latest development efforts — even if they are not trusted members of the inner project team. These developers accept the fact that the development code may be in various stages of stability on any given day, yet they appreciate the direct access to critical fixes or enhancements. Although this model does promote more active external peer review, it can often lead to a number of serious problems. If developers decide to use prerelease code in a production environment, they may find themselves maintaining an insecure or unstable application. This can lead to a situation in which the community is expected to support many hybrid variants rather than a consistent baseline application. Another possible issue is that a developer who succumbs to personal motivations may be inclined to incorporate some of the development enhancements into the current production version and release it as a new application version. Although the open source license may allow this, it seriously affects the ability for official project maintainer to support the community. It is the responsibility of the project maintainer to always ensure a managed migration path from one version to the next. This model can only be supported if people are forced to use the official baseline releases offered by the project maintainer. Without these constants to build from, upgrades become a manual effort and many users are left on evolutionary dead-ends. For these reasons, DotNetNuke chooses to restrict anonymous read access to the development source code repository. Instead, we choose to issue periodic point releases that allow us to provide a consistent upgrade mechanism as the project evolves.

Stabilization

Following the success of DotNetNuke 2.0, we focused on improving the stability and quality of the application. Many production issues were discovered after the release that we would have never anticipated during internal testing. As an application becomes more extensible, people find ingenious new ways to apply it, which often produces unexpected results. We also integrated some key Roadmap enhancements that were developed in isolation by Core Team members. These enhancements were actually quite advanced because they added a whole new level of professional features to the DotNetNuke code base, transforming it into a viable enterprise application framework.

It was during this time that Dan Caron single-handedly made a significant impact on the project. Based on his experience with other enterprise applications, he proceeded to add integrated exception handling and event logging to DotNetNuke. This provided stability and "auditability" — two major factors in most professional software products. He also added a complex, multi-threaded scheduler to the application. The scheduler was not just a simple hard-coded implementation like I had seen in other ASP.NET projects, but rather it was fully configurable via an administrative user interface. This powerful new feature could be used to run background housekeeping jobs as well as long-running tasks. With this in place, the extensibility of the application improved yet again.

Third-Party Components

An interesting concern that came to our attention at this time was related to our dependence on external components. To provide the most powerful application, we had leveraged a number of rich third-party controls for their expert functionality. Because each of these controls was available under its own open source license, they seemed to be a good fit for the DotNetNuke project. But the fact is there are some major risks to consider. Some open source licenses are viral in nature and have the potential to alter the license of the application they are combined with. In addition, there is nothing that prevents third parties from changing their licensing policy at any time. If this situation occurs, then it is possible that all users of the application who reference the control could be in violation of the new license terms. That's a fairly significant issue and certainly not something that can be taken lightly. Based on this knowledge, we quickly came up with a strategy that was aimed at minimizing our dependency on third-party components. We constructed a policy whereby we would always focus on building the functionality ourselves before considering an external control. And in the cases where a component was too elaborate to replicate, we would use a provider model, much like we had in the database layer, to abstract the application from the control in such a way that it would allow for a plug-in replacement. This strategy protects the community from external license changes and also provides some additional extensibility for the application.

With the great publicity on the www.asp.net web site following VS Live! and the consistent release of powerful new enhancements, the spring of 2004 brought a lot of traffic to the dotnetnuke.com community web site. At this point, the site was poorly organized and sparse on content due to a lack of dedicated effort. Patrick Santry had been on the Core Team since its inception and his experience with building web sites for the ASP.NET community became valuable at this time. We managed to make some fairly major changes to improve the site, but I soon realized that a dedicated resource would be required to accomplish all of our goals. Without the funding to secure such a resource, many of the plans had to unfortunately be shelved.

Core Team Reorganization

The summer of 2004 was a restructuring period for DotNetNuke. Thirty new community members were nominated for Core Team inclusion and the Core Team itself underwent a reorganization of sorts. The team was divided into an Inner Team and an Outer Team. The Inner Team designation was reserved for those original Core Team individuals who had demonstrated the most loyalty, commitment, and value to the project over the past year. The Outer Team represented individuals who had earned recognition for their community efforts and were given the opportunity to work toward Inner Team status. Among other privileges, write access to the source code repository is the pinnacle of achievement in any source code project, and members of both teams were awarded this distinction to varying degrees.

In addition to the restructuring, a set of Core Team guidelines was established that helped formalize the expectations for team members. Prior to the creation of these guidelines, it was difficult to isolate non–performers because there were no objective criteria by which they could be judged. In addition to the new recruits, a number of inactive members from the original team were retired, mostly to demonstrate that Core Team inclusion was a privilege, not a right. The restructuring process also brought to light several deficiencies in the management of intellectual property and confidentiality among team members. As a result, all team members were required to sign a retroactive non-disclosure agreement as well as an intellectual property contribution agreement. All of the items exemplified the fact that the project had graduated from its "hobby" roots to a professional open source project.

Microsoft Membership API

During these formative stages, I was once again approached by Microsoft with an opportunity to showcase some specific ASP.NET features. Specifically, a Membership API had been developed by Microsoft for Whidbey (ASP.NET 2.0), and they were planning on creating a backported version for ASP.NET 1.1 that we could leverage in DotNetNuke. This time the benefits were not so immediately obvious and required some thorough analysis. This is because DotNetNuke already had more functionality in these areas than the new Microsoft API could deliver. So to integrate the Microsoft components without losing any features, we would need to wrap the Microsoft API and augment it with our own business logic. Before embarking on such an invasive enhancement, we needed to understand the clear business benefit provided.

Well, you can never discount Microsoft's potential to impact the industry. Therefore being one of the first to integrate and support the new Whidbey APIs would certainly be a positive move. In recent months there had been numerous community questions regarding the applicability of DotNetNuke with the early Whidbey Beta releases now in active circulation. Early integration of such a core component from Whidbey would surely appease this group of critics. From a technology perspective, the Microsoft industry had long been awaiting an API to converge upon in this particular area, making application interoperability possible and providing best practice due diligence in the area of user and security information. Integrating the Microsoft API would allow DotNetNuke to "play nicely" with other ASP.NET applications — a key factor in some of the larger-scale extensibility we were hoping to achieve. Last, but not least, it would further our positive relationship with Microsoft — a factor that was not lost on most as the key contributor to the DotNetNuke project's growth and success.

The reorganization of the Core Team also resulted in the formation of a small group of highly trusted project resources that, for lack of a better term, we named the Board of Directors. The members included Scott Willhite, Dan Caron, Joe Brinkman, Patrick Santry, and me. The purpose of this group was to oversee the long-term strategic direction of the project. This included discussion on confidential issues pertaining to partners, competitors, and revenue. In August 2004, we scheduled our first general meeting for Philadelphia, Pennsylvania. With all members in attendance, we made some excellent progress on defining action items for the coming months. This was also a great opportunity to finally meet in person some of the individuals with whom we had only experienced Internet contact in the past. With the first day of meetings behind us, the second day was dedicated to sightseeing in the historic city of Philadelphia. The parallels between the freedom symbolized by the Liberty Bell and the software freedom of open source were not lost on any of us that day.

Returning from Philadelphia, I knew that I had some significant deliverables on my plate. We began the Microsoft Membership API integration project with high expectations of completion within three months. But as before, there were a number of high-priority community enhancements that had been promised prior to the Microsoft initiative, and as a result the scope snowballed. Scope management is an extremely difficult task when you have such an active and vocal community.

"Breaking" Changes

The snowball effect soon revealed that the next major release would need to be labeled version 3.0. This is mostly because of "breaking" changes: modifications to the DotNetNuke core application that changed the primary interfaces to the point that plug-ins from the previous version 2.0 release would not integrate without at least some minimal changes. The catalyst for this was due to changes in the Membership API from Microsoft, but this only led to a decision of "If you are forced to break compatibility, introduce all of your breaking changes in one breaking release." The fact is there was a lot of baggage preserved from the IBuySpy Portal that we were restricted from removing due to legacy support considerations. DotNetNuke 3.0 provided the opportunity to reexamine the entire project from a higher level and make some of the fundamental changes we had been delaying for years in some cases. This included the removal of a lot of dead code and deprecated methods as well as a full namespace reorganization that finally accurately broke the project API into logical components.

DotNetNuke 3.0 also demonstrated another technical concept that would both enrich the functionality of the application framework as well as improve the extensibility without the threat of breaking binary compatibility. Up until version 3.0, the service architecture for DotNetNuke was completely uni-directional. Custom modules could consume the resources and services offered by the core DotNetNuke framework but not vice versa. So although the application managed the secure presentation of custom modules within the portal environment, it could not get access to the custom module content information. Optional interfaces enable custom modules to provide plug-in implementations for defined core portal functions. They also provide a simple mechanism for the core framework to call into third-party modules, providing a bi-directional communication channel so that modules could finally offer resources and services to the core (see Figure 1-9).

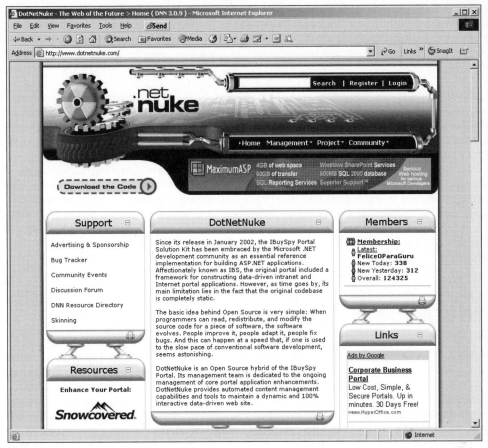

Figure 1-9

Web Hosters

Along with its many technological advances, DotNetNuke 3.0 was also being groomed for use by entirely new stakeholders: Web Hosters. For a number of years, the popularity of Linux hosting has been growing at a far greater pace than Windows hosting. The instability arguments of early Microsoft web servers were beginning to lose their weight as Microsoft released more resilient and higher-quality server operating systems. Windows Server 2003 had finally shed its clunky Windows NT 4.0 roots and was a true force to be reckoned with. Aside from the obvious economic licensing reasons, there was another clear reason why Hosters were still favoring Linux over Windows for their clients: the availability of end-user applications.

The Linux platform had long been blessed with a plethora of open source applications running on the Apache web server, built with languages such as PHP, Perl, and Python, and leveraging open source databases such as mySQL, (The combination of these technologies is commonly referred to as LAMP.) The Windows platform was really lacking in this area and was desperately in need of applications to fill this void.

For DotNetNuke to take advantage of this opportunity, it needed a usability overhaul to transform it from a niche developer–oriented framework to a polished end-user product. This included a usability enhancement from both the portal administration as well as the web host perspectives. Since Rob Howard left Microsoft in June 2004, my primary Microsoft contact was Shawn Nandi. Shawn did a great job of drawing upon his usability background at Microsoft to come up with suggestions to improve the DotNetNuke end-user experience. Portal administrators received a multi-lingual user interface with both field-level and module-level help. Enhanced management functions were added in key locations to improve the intuitive nature of the application. Web Hosters received a customizable installation mechanism. In addition, the application underwent a security review to enable it to run in a Medium Trust — Code Access Security (CAS) environment. The end result was a powerful open source, web-application framework that could compete with the open source products on other platforms and offer Web Hosters a viable Windows alternative for their clients.

DotNetNuke 3.0

Much of the integration work on the Membership API and usability improvements were fueled by a much larger hosting initiative that Microsoft was preparing to unleash in May 2005. This initiative included a comprehensive program aimed at increasing awareness for Windows-based hosting solutions on an international level. Based on its strength as a framework for building consumer web sites, Microsoft invited DotNetNuke to participate in the program as long as it could meet a defined set of technical criteria, including Membership API integration, Medium Trust CAS compliance, localization, and usability improvements. Nearly all of the enhancements were already identified on the product roadmap, so the opportunity to be included in the hosting program was really a win-win proposition for the project and the community. In addition, we believed that the benefit of participating in such a large-scale initiative would be enormous in terms of lending credibility to the DotNetNuke product, introducing the project to influential new stakeholders, and helping to build brand equity.

Core Team members made significant contributions during the development of DotNetNuke 3.0. Scott McCulloch, with the assistance of Jeremy White, implemented a full-featured URL rewriting component that allowed DotNetNuke to use standard URLs. Vicenc Masanas was instrumental in working on localization, templating, and stabilization tasks. Joe Brinkman implemented search-engine architecture, enabling content indexing across all modules in a portal instance. Jon Henning introduced a Client API library, enabling powerful client-side behavior in DotNetNuke modules. Perhaps the greatest code contributions were made by Charles Nurse. Realizing the massive amount of work that would be required to deliver the enhancements for the hosting program (and knowing that using only volunteer efforts would not hit the schedule deadlines), I hired the first full-time DotNetNuke contract resource. Charles was immediately put to work abstracting all of the core modules into independent private assemblies. At the same time, he reorganized entry fields in all application user interfaces and added full localization capabilities, including field-level online help.

The concept of localization was one the most commonly requested enhancements for the DotNetNuke application. Localization actually has multiple meanings when it comes to software applications because there is a distinct difference between static and dynamic content. Static content is information that is delivered as part of the core application typically implemented by developers. Dynamic content is information that is provided by users of the application and is typically entered by knowledge workers or webmasters. In DotNetNuke 3.0, we delivered full static localization for all administrative interfaces. This meant that all labels, messages, and help text could be translated and displayed in different languages based on the preference of the user. Developing a scalable architecture in this area turned out to be a challenging task because the solutions offered by Microsoft as part of the ASP.NET 1.x framework were better suited for desktop applications and had serious deficiencies and limitations for web applications. Instead, we decided to target the ASP.NET 2.0 localization architecture, which better addressed the web scenario. However, due to the specific business requirements of DotNetNuke, we soon realized that we were going to have to take some liberties with the proposed ASP.NET 2.0 localization architecture to enable us to achieve our goals for runtime updatability and scalability in a shared hosting environment. In the end, we were able to deliver a powerful solution that satisfied our business needs and provided forward compatibility to the upcoming ASP.NET 2.0 release.

The optional interface architectural model described earlier reaped rewards in DotNetNuke 3.0 in a number of key application areas. Registration of module actions in earlier versions of DotNetNuke was always less than optimal because they were dependent on page life-cycle events that were difficult to manage in a variety of scenarios. Optional interfaces finally provided a clean mechanism for the core framework to programmatically call into modules and retrieve their module actions. Other new features based on optional interfaces included content indexing, import, and export. In each of these cases, the core framework could rely on modules to provide content in a specific format that then allowed the core framework to provide advanced portal services.

After multiple beta releases (some of which were deemed not fit for public consumption), DotNetNuke 3.0 was officially released on March 12, 2005. Although there were breaking changes between DotNetNuke 2.0 and DotNetNuke 3.0, a number of modules were immediately available for DotNetNuke 3.0 due to the success of a pilot program named "30 for 3.0." This program was the shrewd strategy of Scott Willhite, and allowed a serious group of commercial module developers to have early access to beta releases of the DotNetNuke 3.0 product, enabling them to deal with any compatibility issues before the core framework became publicly available. Aside from the obvious benefits of having "applications" immediately available for the new platform, this program also provided some excellent business intelligence. It proved one of Scott's earlier assumptions that the vocal forums community represented only a small portion of the overall DotNetNuke user community. It also exposed the fact that DotNetNuke had found its way into Fortune 500 companies, military applications, government web sites, international software vendors, and a variety of other high-profile installations.

DotNetNuke 3.0 was released with two supported languages: English and German. Delivering two complete language packs adhered to one of our newer philosophies of always attempting to provide multiple functional examples to prove the effectiveness of a particular extensibility model. Before long, community members began submitting new language packs in their native dialects that were posted on the dotnetnuke.com site for download. The total number of supported language packs soon surpassed 30. This resulted in incredible growth and adoption for the DotNetNuke framework on an international basis.

Release Schedule

A common open source concept is referred to as "release early, release often." The justification is that the sooner you release, the sooner the open source community can validate the functionality, and the sooner you get feedback — good and bad — which helps improve the overall product. This concept is often combined with a "public daily build" paradigm, where continuous integration is used to automatically build, package, and publish a new application version every day. These concepts make a lot of sense for single-purpose applications; that is, applications that have closed APIs and have no external dependencies. But plug-in framework applications such as DotNetNuke possess a different set of requirements, many of which are not complementary with the "release early, release often" model.

Consider the case of any entity that has developed plug-in resources for the DotNetNuke framework. These could include modules, language packs, skins, or providers. Every time a new core version is released, each of these resources needs to be validated to ensure that it functions correctly. In many cases, this involves extensive testing, packaging a new version of the specific resource, publishing compatibility information, updating related documentation, communicating availability and/or issues to users, servicing compatibility support requests, updating commercial product listings, and so on. You must also consider the issues for the resource consumer. Consumers need to feel confident in the acquisition and installation of application resources. They are not keen on analyzing complicated compatibility matrices to manage their investment. And resellers such as Hosters represent an even larger superset of application consumers. The effort involved to perform application upgrades becomes more complicated and costly as the release frequency increases. This is clearly a case where "release early, release often" can lead to issues for framework consumers and suppliers.

For these reasons, DotNetNuke has always tried to follow a fairly well-structured release cycle. This has resulted in fewer major public releases but a much higher quality, more stable, core application. In general, it has enabled DotNetNuke resource suppliers and consumers to participate in a functional product ecosystem. However, as the number of serious platform adopters increased, so did the demands for better core-release communication.

DotNetNuke Projects

One of the goals of the DotNetNuke 3.0 product release that had tremendous value for the community at large was the abstraction of the modules that were traditionally bundled with the core framework. The core modules were neglected in favor of adding more functionality to the core framework services. This resulted in a set of modules that demonstrated limited functionality and were not evolving at the same pace as the rest of the project. The abstraction of the modules from the core framework led to the formation of the DotNetNuke Projects program: a new organizational concept modeled after the Apache Foundation that allowed many complementary open source projects to thrive within the DotNetNuke ecosystem. From a technical perspective, the modules were abstracted in a manner that conformed to our extensibility model for building "private assembly" modules and allowed each module to be managed as its own independent project. The benefit was that each module could form its own team of developers, with its own roadmap for enhancements, and its own release schedule. As a governing entity, DotNetNuke would provide infrastructure services such as a source code repository, issue tracker, project home page, and e-mail services for the project as well as a highly visible and respected distribution and marketing channel.

Obviously there are tradeoffs that need to be accepted when decomposing a monolithic system into its constituent components, but the overall benefits of this approach reaped substantial rewards for the project. For one thing, it provided a new opportunity for developer participation—basically providing a sandbox where developers could demonstrate their skills and passion for the DotNetNuke project. This helped promote the "meritocracy" model and aided in our Core Team recruitment efforts. The community benefited through the availability of powerful, free, open source components that were licensed under the standard DotNetNuke BSD license. It also allowed the modules to evolve much more rapidly and with more focus than they ever received as part of the monolithic DotNetNuke application. Abstracting the core set of modules was a good start; however, the platform was lacking some other essential modules—modules that were well integrated and provided the common functionality required by most consumer web sites. These items included a discussion forum, blog, and photo gallery.

Early in the DotNetNuke 3.0 life cycle, there were discussions with a high-profile third-party software development company that was actively developing an integrated suite of components with forum, blog, and gallery functionality. Although early indications seemed to be positive regarding collaboration, they unfortunately did not comprehend the opportunity of working with the DotNetNuke community and ultimately decided to instead focus their efforts on constructing their own proprietary solution. Because this decision was not communicated to us until late in the DotNetNuke 3.0 development cycle, it meant that we had to scramble to find a suitable alternative. Luckily, two of our own Core Team members—Tam Tram Minh of TTT Corporation and Bryan Andrews of AppTheory—had been collaborating on a comparable set of modules and had already been offering them for free download to the DotNetNuke community. Discussions with them led to the creation of three powerful new DotNetNuke Projects: the DotNetNuke Forums, Blog, and Gallery.

Integrating third-party modules is not without its share of challenges. An "incubation" period is required to make the module conform to the official DotNetNuke project standards. An official marketing name must be defined for the project and all references to the old module name need to be updated. This includes namespaces, folder names, filenames, code comments, database object names, release package metadata, and documentation. To allow legacy users of the contributed module to be able to migrate to the new DotNetNuke project, a robust upgrade mechanism must be created. The module also needs to be reviewed to ensure that it does not contain any security flaws or serious defects that could affect the general community. From an infrastructure perspective, the code needs to be uploaded to a dedicated source code repository, an issue tracker project must be created, and a project home page complete with discussion forum and blog needs to be created on dotnetnuke.com. These tasks represent the technical integration issues that need to be addressed; but an item of even greater importance for third-party modules is management of the associated intellectual property.

Intellectual Property

There are two main contributing factors when it comes to intellectual property: copyright and licensing. The copyright holder is the person who owns the rights to the intellectual property. Normally this is the creator; however, copyright can also be transferred to other individuals or companies. The copyright holder has the right to decide how his intellectual property can be used by others. When it comes to software, these usage details are generally published as a license agreement. License agreements can vary a great deal depending on the environment, but they generally resemble a standard legal contract, explicitly outlining the rights and responsibilities of each party. The copyright holder also has the right to change the license for the intellectual property at their discretion. It is this scenario that requires the most due diligence when dealing with third-party contributions.

Anybody who contributes source code to the DotNetNuke project must submit a signed Contributor License Agreement. This document ensures that the individual has the right to contribute intellectual property to the project without any type of encumbrance. It also transfers copyright for any contributed intellectual property to the project. This is important because DotNetNuke needs to be able to ensure all of its intellectual property is licensed consistently throughout the entire application. It protects the community from a situation where an individual copyright holder could change the license restrictions for a specific piece of intellectual property, forcing the entire community into a reactive situation (a situation we have already seen multiple times in the still nascent Microsoft open source community).

In the case of third-party modules that are fully functional applications with an existing and active user base, the intellectual property rights are owned by the external party. Under this scenario, we cannot adopt the intellectual property into the DotNetNuke project because it would mean that we would have no control over its licensing. Even if the contributor agreed to license the intellectual property under a complementary BSD open source license, the original copyright holder would still have the ability to change the license at any time in the future, which would put all users of the module in jeopardy. To mitigate this risk, we require that DotNetNuke must have sufficient rights to the intellectual property so that the community is adequately protected. However, we do not feel it would be fair to force a contributor to release all of the rights to their own intellectual property. Therefore, we have a Software Grant Agreement — a contract that provides both parties with full copyright to the specified intellectual property. Essentially this means that the intellectual property has been split into two independent versions. The contributor owns one version and is allowed to license it or modify it as they see fit. DotNetNuke owns the other version and licenses it under the standard DotNetNuke BSD License for distribution and enhancement. The end result is a win-win situation for both parties as well as the community.

Marketing

The success of any serious initiative must begin with the formulation of specific goals and the ability to measure progress as you work toward those goals. In terms of measuring the growth of the DotNetNuke project, we had traditionally monitored the total number of registered users on the dotnetnuke.com web site, the number of new users per month, and the number of downloads per month. These metrics revealed some definite trends but were rather myopic in terms of providing a relative comparison to other open source or commercial products. As a result, we looked for some other indicators that we could use to measure our overall market impact.

Alexa is a free service provided by Amazon that can be used to judge the popularity of an Internet web site. Popularity is an interesting metric because traffic distribution on the Internet conforms to a 90/10 rule: 10% of web sites account for 90% of the overall traffic, and 90% of web sites share the other 10%. This logarithmic scale means that it gets progressively more difficult to make substantial gains in your Alexa ranking as your web site popularity increases. Although the Alexa ranking is not a conventional progress indicator, we decided to use it as one of our key progress indicators (KPI) in determining the impact of our marketing efforts. The dotnetnuke.com web site had an Alexa ranking of 19,000 in April 2005.

SourceForge is the world's largest development and download repository of open source code and applications. Early in its project history, DotNetNuke had established a presence on SourceForge.Net (http://sourceforge.net/projects/dnn as shown in Figure 1-10) and continued to leverage its mirrored download infrastructure and bandwidth for hosting all project release packages. Because

SourceForge.Net contained listings for all of largest and most successful open source projects in existence, it also provided a variety of comparison and ranking statistics that could be used to judge activity and popularity. This seemed to be another good KPI to measure our impact in the open source realm. In April 2005, the DotNetNuke project had an overall project ranking of 1,271.

One of the items that had been neglected over the life of the project was the dotnetnuke.com web site. It had long been a goal to build this asset into a content-rich communication hub for the DotNetNuke community. Patrick Santry made some early progress in this area but recently found his volunteer time diminishing due to personal and family commitments. Because a web site is largely an extension of product marketing (another function that had long been ignored) the dotnetnuke.com web site suffered from sparse content, poor organization, and inconsistent focus. After the release of DotNetNuke 3.0, a significant effort was invested in improving all aspects of the web site. Much of the initial improvements came as a result of evaluating web sites of other open source projects. After extensive deliberation, we decided to organize the site information into three functional areas: user-oriented information, community collaboration, and developer information. New "sticky" content areas were added for project news and community events. The Home Page was completely revamped to provide summary marketing information and project metrics.

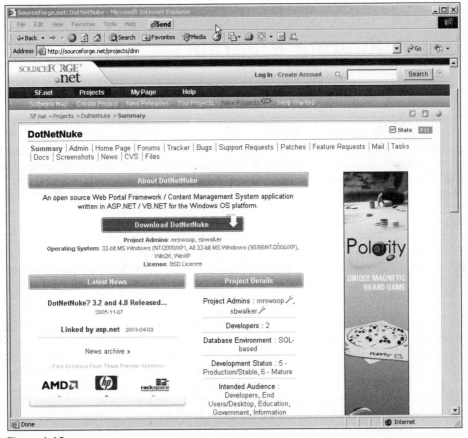

Figure 1-10

In March 2005, another significant milestone occurred in DotNetNuke history. Dan Egan, a passionate DotNetNuke community member, wrote a book for PackT Publishing entitled *Building Websites with VB.NET and DotNetNuke 3.0*. This was the first book published about DotNetNuke and was essential in proving the demand for the product, paving the way for future DotNetNuke books from a variety of other publishers. In addition, a handful of Core Team members, including me, were also collaborating on a book for WROX Press during this time frame, but the demands of getting the DotNetNuke 3.0 product ready for release forced us to slip the publication date. Regardless, any technical content that makes it to mass publication through traditional channels lends an incredible amount of credibility and equity to the project or technology for which it is written. In addition, books can have a positive marketing impact; especially if they reach wide circulation through online retailers and brick-and-mortar bookstores.

In May of 2005, Core Team member Jim Duffy was successful in securing a DotNetNuke session on DotNetRocks!, an Internet radio talk show hosted by Carl Franklin and Richard Campbell. This was our second appearance on the show (the first being in August of 2004), and it was a lot of fun to talk about DotNetNuke in such a relaxed and open atmosphere. The show focused on the recent DotNetNuke 3.0 release and proved to be great way to promote some of the incredible new application features. It is hard to estimate the impact of the appearance on the DotNetRocks! show, but it certainly made me a firm believer in the benefits of podcasting as a powerful broad distribution marketing medium.

Microsoft Hosting Program

Throughout the month of May 2005, Microsoft launched the aforementioned Hosting program. The purpose of the program was to encourage shared hosting providers to take advantage of Windows technology to grow their hosting businesses. The primary benefit of this program was the Service Provider License Agreement (SPLA), which allowed hosting companies to avoid large capital expenditures and pay their licensing fees based on actual usage. This lowered the barrier of entry in terms of cost and provided a risk-free model to test the demand for services. In addition to the SPLA, Microsoft recognized the value of end-user applications and included substantial promotion of DotNetNuke in the hosting seminars encompassing thirty cities around the globe. I was fortunate enough to attend the first seminar in Redmond, Washington, which provided an excellent opportunity to network with the Microsoft Hosting Evangelists, a group of hard-working individuals who were dedicated to the growth of Windows web hosting on an international basis. At the beginning of June, I was also privileged to attend a WSHA seminar in Amsterdam, Netherlands. The invitation was extended by Microsoft Europe, which was especially interested in the localization capabilities of the DotNetNuke application. This trip gave me a deeper understanding of the localization challenges of the international community and also provided me the opportunity to meet Geert Veenstra and Leigh Pointer — two Core Team members who actively participated in and evangelized DotNetNuke since its creation.

Although the Microsoft Hosting program did not reap any direct financial rewards for DotNetNuke, it provided a number of powerful benefits. It exposed the application to an influential group of organizations: large-scale web hosting companies that dominate the shared hosting market in terms of customer base and annual revenues. Companies such as GoDaddy, Pipex, and 1and1 began offering DotNetNuke as part of their Windows hosting plans. The hosting program also caught the attention of the largest hosting control panel vendors. Companies such as SW-Soft (Plesk), WebHostAutomation (Helm), and Ensim added integrated installation support for the DotNetNuke application within their control panel applications. All of these strategic partnerships exposed DotNetNuke to a much larger consumer audience and would not have been possible had it not been for the Microsoft Hosting program.

Collaboration with web hosts also resulted in new application features that were added to satisfy some of their specific business requirements. The ability for DotNetNuke to run in a web farm environment was one such feature that really addressed the application scalability questions beyond a single web server configuration. Dan Caron stepped up yet again to champion these enhancements, producing an architecture with two different caching providers to satisfy the widest array of use cases. Charles Nurse also completed the abstraction of all modules into isolated components that could be optionally installed and uninstalled from the core framework. This change provided additional flexibility for Web Hosters in terms of being able to customize their offering for clients.

Infrastructure

One of the benefits of the original sponsorship agreement with Microsoft was a free shared hosting account on the servers managed by the ASP.NET team at OrcsWeb. This arrangement served us well in the early stages but the fact that we had extremely limited access (that is, FTP) to the account and absolutely no control over the associated infrastructure services eventually created some challenges for the project. In addition, we had long been leveraging services from PortalWebHosting for back office items such as DNS, source control, issue tracking, and e-mail, but a recent change in ownership created some friction in regards to legacy promises and agreements. Approaching premium hosting provider MaximumASP in the fall of 2004, we were able to secure a generous formal sponsorship agreement that paved the way for a more centralized and professionally managed project infrastructure.

Initially, MaximumASP provided us with two dedicated servers and a Virtual Private Server (VPS) account on a shared server. One of the dedicated servers was configured as a SQL Server database server and the other as a back office server. The VPS account was provisioned as a web account for our public web site. This configuration served us well initially, but the rapid growth of membership and the lack of control over the web server soon forced us to look for other options. Further discussions with MaximumASP resulted in the allocation of a dedicated web server for our public web site. The combination of a dedicated web server and a dedicated database server proved flexible enough to handle our full web site requirements. It was not until we added discussion forums to our site and pushed our traffic past 4 million page views a month that we felt the need to consider a web farm configuration.

The physical abstraction of the core application into a more modular organization had a direct impact on our back office project infrastructure. Rather than simply managing a single source code repository and issue tracking database, we now had to deal with many Project sandboxes—each with their own membership and security considerations. In addition, establishing effective communication channels for different stakeholder groups was critical for managing the project. This is one of the reasons why the DotNetNuke Forums Project played such a significant role in the evolution of the DotNetNuke projects. It allowed for a variety of discussion forums to be created, some public and some private, providing focused communication channels for project members.

During 2005, Scott Willhite also made some huge contributions to the project in terms of infrastructure management. In a project of this size with so many active participants, there is an incredible amount of administrative work that goes on behind-the-scenes to keep the project moving forward. As most people know, administrative tasks are largely unappreciated and only seem to get attention when there is a problem. Scott does his best to keep the endless stream of infrastructure tasks flowing; receiving little or no recognition for his efforts, but playing an instrumental role in the success of the DotNetNuke project.

Branding

One of the things that became obvious during the writing of *Professional DotNetNuke ASP.NET Portals* (Wiley Publishing, Inc.) was that our branding message was not clear. Although our trademark and domain name reflected "DotNetNuke," our logo contained an abbreviated terminology of ".netnuke." This led to confusion for authors of the book as well as the publisher in terms of what was the correct product branding. As I mentioned earlier in this chapter, the initial branding was constructed with little or no foresight; therefore, it came as no surprise that a major overhaul was necessary.

Initial conversations within the Core Team offered some interesting and sometimes surprising opinions on the DotNetNuke brand. When discussion came to a stalemate, the topic was raised in the public forums that resulted in a similar scenario. Some folks considered the "nuke" term to be too offensive, unprofessional, or shocking to be used as a serious brand name. Others placed a significant metaphorical value in the current logo, which contained a gear embossed with a nuclear symbol. Some preferred a transition to the "DNN" acronym that was often used as a shorthand reference in various communication channels. Further debate ensued over the category we occupied (portal, content management system, framework, and so on) and the clear marketing message we wished to convey.

As the project founder, I had my own opinions on the brand positioning and ultimately decided to resort to an authoritarian model rather that a committee model so that we could make a decision and move forward. From my perspective, when it comes to technology companies, there is a lot of acceptance for non-traditional brand names (consider Google, Yahoo!, Go Daddy, and so on). In addition, due to the press coverage of the Microsoft Hosting program, the DotNetNuke name achieved a significant amount of exposure; therefore, a complete change in brand would impose a serious setback in terms of brand acceptance and market reach. Taking into consideration the valued perspectives of the Core Team and community, I felt there should be a way to provide a win-win solution for everyone.

I first tried working with a local design company (the same company that produced the DotNetNuke 2.0 site skin), and although they had a real talent for brand identity services, there were no concepts produced that really grabbed my attention or satisfied my goals for the project. Perhaps I was being overly critical in my judgment of various designs, but I knew that I absolutely did not want to settle for a concept unless I thought it met 100% of my criteria. Although Nik Kalyani had been on the Core Team for eight months and had even expressed a serious interest in the marketing activities of the project, it was not until the re-branding exercise where his talents were truly exemplified.

Nik and I started an offline dialog where we quickly established some complementary goals, at least at a conceptual level. The basic decision was that we wanted to retain the full "DotNetNuke" brand name and strengthen rather than dilute its brand emphasis. We also wanted to reduce or eliminate the negative imagery associated with the nuclear warning symbol in the current logo. Although the abbreviated form of the word "nuke" tended to evoke a negative response from the general population (relating it to bombs and radiation), the expanded form of "nuclear" and "nucleus" had a much more positive response (related to science, energy, and power). The word "nucleus" also had some complementary terms associated with it such as "core," "kernel," and so on that worked well with the open-source project philosophy. The trick was to find a way to emphasize one aspect over another.

Nik spent countless hours designing alternative logo concepts. From a typeface perspective, he suggested using the Neuropol font, and I really liked the fact that it had a strong technical overtone but not so much that it could not be used effectively in other mainstream media applications. To achieve a uniform appearance for the typeface, we decided to use all capital letters — even though the standard format for the brand name in regular print would continue to be mixed case. Nik included a unique customization for the "E" and the "T" letters that resulted in a distinctive, yet professional styling for the word-mark contained within the logo.

Creating the graphical element for the logo was a much bigger challenge because we were looking for a radically new design that exemplified so many diverse project attributes. To summarize some of the more important criteria, we were looking for something simple yet distinctive, with at least some elements that provided a visual reference to the old logo for continuity. It needed to be scalable and adaptable to a wide range of media (both digital and print) and cost-effective to reproduce. And perhaps the most subjective item I promoted was that the logo should be stylish — with my acceptance criteria being, "Would my wife permit me to wear clothing embossed with the logo when we went out in public together?" Nik created more than 40 unique logo concepts before arriving at a design that seemed to catch the full essence of what we were trying to accomplish (see Figure 1-11). After working at this for so long and dealing with the discouragement and frustration, it was a euphoric moment to discover the proverbial "love at first sight."

Figure 1-11

It is amazing how many diverse concepts can be represented in a single image. The saying "a picture is worth a thousand words" is cliché, but in this case, it certainly summarized the final product. The new logo had the basic shape of a nuclear atom. The nucleus of the atom was shaped like a gear to retain its heritage to the previous project logo. The logo was two basic colors — red and black (using shades of grey to achieve a 3-D effect) — making it much more adaptable and simple to reproduce in a wide variety of media formats than the previous logo (which used shadows and gradients for 3-D effects). The gear had twelve teeth (a number considered to be lucky in many cultures). The intersection of the three revolving electron trails (referred to as the "triad") could still be subtly viewed as a nuclear symbol reference. With some creative inference, they could also be viewed as the three-letter project acronym: DNN. Later, someone on the Core Team mentioned that the triad bore some resemblance to the Perpetual Motion Interactive Systems Inc. "infinity" logo—a reference I had never formally recognized but something that I am sure played a subliminal role in my selection.

In terms of brand acceptance, we realized there may be significant community backlash related to the new creative brand, especially from companies who were currently leveraging the existing DotNetNuke branding in their marketing materials. Therefore we were pleasantly surprised at the overwhelming positive feedback we received regarding the new brand identity. Our goal was to roll out the brand in progressive stages with the DotNetNuke 3.1 product release representing the official brand launch to the general community.

With the creative elements out of the way, it was time to finalize the rest of the branding process. Because DotNetNuke serves many different stakeholder groups, it was difficult to come up with a product category that was focused but not too limiting in scope. From a marketing perspective, the board agonized over the optimal brand message. "Content management" was a powerful industry buzzword, but if you compared the capabilities of DotNetNuke in this area with other enterprise software offerings, it became obvious that it would be some time before we could be considered a market leader. The term "portal" had been so overused in recent years that it became severely diluted and lost its clarity as an effective marketing message. Conversely, the emerging term "framework" began to surface more regularly and was starting to gain industry acceptance with both developers and management groups as a powerful software development category. Because DotNetNuke's architectural principles were predicated on simplicity and extensibility, the framework category seemed to be a natural fit. The next step involved clarifying the type of framework. DotNetNuke was primarily designed for use in a web environment and its breadth of features made it well-suited for building advanced data-driven Internet applications. The resulting "web application framework" was an emerging industry category in which DotNetNuke could take an immediate leadership role. Where applicable, we could also leverage our "open source" classification to emphasize our community philosophy and values.

One of the toughest parts of any re-branding exercise involves updating all existing brand references to reflect the new identity. In DotNetNuke's case, this affected the content and design of the dotnetnuke .com web site, the marketing references in the DotNetNuke release package, and all technical and user documentation. Compared to the time it took to construct the new logo, the time it took Nik Kalyani to create a new site design was minimal (which is truly amazing considering the amount of time and effort that typically goes into a custom site design). I had long been a fan of Nik's minimalist style, which emphasized clean presentation, lightweight graphics. and plenty of whitespace. Nik's expert grasp of the DotNetNuke skinning architecture enabled him to create a combination of skin and containers that were applied in a matter of minutes to completely transform the entire web site. The new site design was creative yet professional and eliminated the "cartoonish" criticisms of the previous site design (see Figure 1-12). Nik also created our first professional document templates that would provide consistency and emphasis of our branding elements within our technical and user documentation.

Figure 1-12

Tech Ed

At the beginning of June, there was a massive Microsoft technology conference, Tech Ed, in Orlando, Florida. Based on a generous invitation from the International .NET Association (INETA), Scott Willhite and I were provided with an opportunity to attend the event as their special guests. The timing was perfect because *Professional DotNetNuke ASP.NET Portals* was officially released at this event, as was the new project branding. Joe Brinkman and Dan Caron were able to attend some aspects of the book launch festivities, and we managed to jam a substantial amount of marketing activities into the five-day event. We had a dedicated Birds of Feather session, two community focus sessions at the INETA booth, a guest appearance at an INETA User Group workshop related to building effective web sites (where we learned 90% of .NET user groups were already using DotNetNuke), and a number of book signings scheduled by WROX Press at the Tech Ed bookstore. The DotNetNuke book was the top-selling developer book at the Tech Ed bookstore for the event—a fact that emphasized the growing popularity of the project. We also distributed official DotNetNuke T-shirts that showcased the new project branding, a popular item amid all the typical free swag provided at these events.

Seizing the opportunity of having the majority of the DotNetNuke Board of Directors together in one place, we had our second official board meeting — an all-day session in the conference room of our hotel in Orlando. On the agenda was a serious discussion related to Core Team reorganization and key project roles. For quite some time, we had realized that the current flat organizational structure was somewhat dysfunctional and that we ultimately needed more dedicated management resources to accomplish our goals. However, to support these resources, we needed a sufficient financial model. Discussion focused on the pros and cons of various revenue opportunities, their revenue potential, and their perceived effect on the community ecosystem. We also talked about what it would take for the current Board members to commit to full-time dedicated roles in the organization and the associated financial and security implications. A lot of really deep discussion ensued, which gave us a much better mental picture of the challenges that lay ahead if we truly wanted to take the project to the next level.

Following the publication of *Professional DotNetNuke ASP.NET Portals*, there was a bit of a media frenzy around the relationship between Microsoft and the open source phenomenon. Some of my personal opinions and quotes from the book found their way into an article published on CNET (one of the leading mainstream news sites), resulting in a lot of additional exposure for the project. It was interesting to see the power of the media at work, where a reference in a highly visible and trusted journalism channel can lead to broad distribution of a particular message (much like a stone in a pond leads to a concentric series of expanding ripples). For the most part, large companies are the most successful at leveraging these medial channels, but special-interest organizations also have the opportunity to make a significant impression.

Credibility

Although DotNetNuke had experienced a healthy growth rate through its open source philosophy, it had largely done so by appealing to the needs of grass-roots developers. Although these stakeholders represent an integral part of the high-tech marketplace, there is another group that is far more influential in terms of market impact. The so-called "decision-makers" represent the management interests in serious enterprise-level business organizations. For DotNetNuke to make the transition from a developer-oriented open source project to a serious enterprise software contender, it needed to appeal to the decision-maker mentality.

Where developers think in terms of short-term technical decisions (that is, "What tool can I use to get this job done as quickly as possible so that I can impress my boss?"), decision-makers think in terms of long-term business decisions. They are interested in the future support of a platform or product. They consider solutions in terms of "investments," "security," and how much "risk" is associated with adopting a particular technology as part of their company infrastructure. And regardless of the technical superiority of a software solution, the adoption criteria always come down to basic trust and consumer confidence. So the challenge for an open source project like DotNetNuke is establishing the necessary level of credibility to be taken seriously.

In the commercial world, customers get a sense of confidence based on the fact that they have paid licensing fees to a vendor that generally provides them with a certain level of future support. Obviously nothing is guaranteed, but this financial model provides both parties with a sense of security and responsibility. Another thing that the financial model affords is the ability to market the product through traditional channels — channels that "decision-makers" tend to monitor on a regular basis.

In the open source world, there are no licensing fees, which helps contribute to the lower cost of ownership but also leaves the investment/security aspect somewhat lacking. If you look at Linux, for example, you will notice that the broad industry buy-in for the operating system did not occur until after some serious market vendors (Sun and IBM) pledged their support. As soon as this happened, many medium-large companies began to take Linux more seriously. And this was not because Linux received any product improvements through these relationships, but rather because it reduced its risk perception in the general marketplace. And without traditional licensing fees, open source products generally do not have the budget to leverage traditional marketing channels and must instead rely on grassroots and viral marketing techniques.

So let's consider some of the ways in which an open source product can improve its credibility and reduce its risk perception for decision-makers. Clearly one way is that it can align itself with large, respected vendors who lend credibility (that is, "If vendor X thinks its good, then so do we."). Another way is to have mainstream books, magazines, and mass media distributors publish information about the product, contributing to the overall community knowledge base and providing recognition. Yet another option is to identify reference implementations that exemplify the best qualities of the product and impress people with their performance, elegance, or extensibility. Another way is to demonstrate a proven track record and history for supporting the community, especially through platform transitions where the likelihood of project failure is high. The overall size of the community ecosystem, including the open source participants, consumers, and third-party service providers, is another critical aspect in demonstrating credibility.

DotNetNuke definitely made some significant advancements in credibility in 2005. The strong working relationship with Microsoft reaped rewards with the Hosting program. The publication of *Professional DotNetNuke ASP.NET Portals* by Wiley Publishing, Inc. and *Building Websites with VB.NET and DotNetNuke 3.0* by PackT Press provided some excellent recognition through traditional publishing channels. Articles and references in mainstream magazines such as *Visual Studio Magazine*, *ASP.NET Pro*, *CoDe Magazine*, and *.NET Developers Journal* also provided some great benefits. The showcase on dotnetnuke.com contained many diverse reference implementations and we had proven through three years of product upgrades that we were committed to supporting the community. The membership and download metrics continued to grow exponentially, as did the number of independent software vendors (ISVs) providing products or services within the DotNetNuke ecosystem.

Trademark Policy

Unfortunately, an unexpected issue arose in the summer of 2005 that immediately put the project into crisis mode. Based on some invalid assumptions, a software consultant from Australia recommended that their client register a trademark for the DotNetNuke name in Australia. Aside from the obvious ethical implications, the immediate reaction was that this move was based on ulterior motives that could potentially hold the entire Australian DotNetNuke community hostage. Further communication revealed that the Australian company had concerns over the official trademark registered in Canada; specifically in regards to the fact it was embedded within the application source code and binaries, and that their business investment could be compromised if restrictions were ever put on trademark usage. Ultimately this whole situation revealed a number of critical issues when it comes to trademarks. First, the holder of the trademark must publish a policy that clearly defines the allowable usage of the mark under a wide range of use cases. Second, the trademark holder must make every attempt to enforce the policy so that the mark does not become a common term and lose its value as a protected asset. Third, a trademark must be registered in every jurisdiction where it intends to be used.

To satisfy the first requirement, I firmly believe in the philosophy of "standing on the shoulders of giants." Research revealed that Mozilla had recently gone through a similar project challenge, so we decided to use their recently published trademark policy as a template for our own. The political ramifications of introducing the policy at this point seemed controversial, but absolutely necessary if we intended to protect our brand. After extensive research, review, and legal advice, we finally announced the trademark policy in conjunction with the logo guidelines in July 2005. The overall community feedback was quite positive, because the policy made every effort to emphasize our open source roots and strong community ideals.

To satisfy the second requirement, all marketing materials were updated to reflect the trademark policy guidelines, and many community sites made changes to bring their use of the trademark into compliance. We also obtained legal advice on the creation of a Trademark License Agreement to be used in situations where third parties required the right to use the DotNetNuke trademarks for specific business purposes.

The third requirement was somewhat more challenging to deal with because it had substantial financial implications. The cost to register an individual trademark in a specific jurisdiction (country) can cost anywhere from $2000.00 to $5000.00. As an organization, we simply do not have the financial means to support such a large expenditure. So instead of considering all jurisdictions, we instead decided to focus on those jurisdictions that had a large project following. These included the United States, Canada, Australia, Japan, and the European Union. This whole experience gave me a much deeper understanding of the financial commitment required by large multinational companies who wish to protect their brand around the world.

ASP.NET 2.0

In July 2005, we recognized that we had approximately four months to prepare for the launch of Microsoft's next-generation software development platform. ASP.NET 2.0 had been under development for three years and had finally reached the point where it was ready for public release. Aside from reading the standard marketing propaganda in the various trade magazines catering to the Windows platform, I had not done significant research into the specific challenges DotNetNuke faced as a product related to this platform upgrade. And, as is usually the case, we quickly found out it was going to be some of the unpublicized platform changes that were going to cause us the most difficulty.

Based on early community feedback for the ASP.NET 1.0 release, Microsoft decided to completely overhaul the way web projects operated, including substantial changes to the underlying compilation model. Because DotNetNuke's advanced modular architecture strayed so far from the traditional monolithic ASP.NET application model, these platform changes had a significant impact on the project. Our solid working relationship with Microsoft reaped benefits in that we were able to engage in some focused dialog and onsite meetings in Redmond with the Microsoft Product Managers who understood the nuances of the new ASP.NET 2.0 platform better than anyone. Scott Guthrie, Simon Calvert, Omar Khan, and a number of other key Microsoft resources got personally involved in assisting us to find a suitable migration path.

I have to admit I was a vocal critic during these early discussions, because I could not understand the business cases that precipitated some of the major architectural changes. But after working closely with the Microsoft Product Managers, I began to warm up to the benefits of the new model and started to envision how we could leverage its capabilities to expose some powerful new options to the DotNetNuke community. But before we could focus on these new options, our most critical requirement was that we could not have breaking changes in the DotNetNuke framework in our ASP.NET 2.0 release. The main business criteria driving this requirement was the fact we had just had a major release with significant breaking changes in March 2005, and we could not risk an all-out community revolt (or product fork) based on compatibility issues.

Research and discussion proceeded throughout the months of July and August as we worked with Microsoft to find an optimal solution. Feedback from the community seemed to be mixed. People who were victims of the Microsoft propaganda machine seemed to think that the release of ASP.NET 2.0 would signal the end of DotNetNuke, because it promised to deliver so many overlapping application features. Other people who had adopted DotNetNuke as part of their business infrastructure expressed apprehension and fear regarding ASP.NET 2.0, based on their past experience that a significant platform upgrade usually resulted in a costly migration effort. Surprisingly, out of all the feedback collected, it appeared that nobody was making a serious attempt to perform the upgrade on their own, and that they were waiting for us to provide a migration path (as we had always done in the past). This element of trust was not lost on me, and I did my best to blog on a regular basis to provide public communication of our progress.

Reorganization

Throughout the summer and fall of 2005 there was ongoing discussion related to Core Team reorganization. Based on the guidelines that had been created when individuals were invited to join the team in the summer of 2004, there was clearly a group of members who had not lived up to their commitments. The list of responsibilities included staying involved in Core Team business through the private discussion forum; participating in weekly Core Team chats; contributing bug fixes, enhancements, or documentation to the core product; and being active in community support channels. There were many legitimate reasons, both personal and business-related, which led to inactivity for team members. However, the unfortunate side effect is that it led to a community perception that based on the total number of Core Team members, we were underachieving in terms of our capabilities as a whole. The Core Team reorganization meant that a number of team members needed to be retired to make way for some new members who had earned the right to participate based on their community accomplishments over the past year. The project had never had to deal with a situation like this in the past, and it's safe to say that as software developers, we are much more adept at solving technical problems than human-resources issues. So the dilemma was how to break the news to the inactive members in a professional and courteous manner that still respected their past accomplishments and left the door open for future DotNetNuke participation. It was Scott Willhite who demonstrated the most experience and wisdom in this area, as we worked on establishing effective human resources processes for the organization.

Since the original formation of the Core Team, all members had received equal rights in terms of project participation. This included not only communication channels but also permissions to the product source code repository. This model worked well when the team was small and all members were on equal footing in terms of their technical abilities. However, it proved to be a challenge when the team grew in size and members were added with varying technical backgrounds. DotNetNuke had grown into a mission-critical web application framework that many businesses now relied on for rock solid performance and reliability. We could no longer accept the risk of inexperienced team members checking in code that could compromise the stability of the application. As a result, we needed to re-factor our project roles to reflect the new project requirements.

A common theme that helped drive the re-factoring of the project roles was accountability. In the past, we had witnessed the fact that without accountability, an individual would not exhibit the same level of commitment, dedication, or passion for the project. As a result, it was important to provide Core Team members with areas of accountability where their contributions would be highly visible and easily recognized by the general public. This public aspect provided them with a much greater benefit in terms of visibility in the community, but it also made them a target for criticism if they were inactive because they were personally responsible for specific areas of the project.

Using the Apache Foundation as a meritocracy reference, we made some significant changes to the organizational model of the project. The old "Inner Team" designation was abolished in favor of a new "Core Team Trustee" role. Scott Willhite came up with this new name based on the desire for industry-accepted terminology and the fact that this innermost project role assumed the highest level of trust from a development perspective. Core Team Trustees had multiple years of experience on the project, had successfully demonstrated their technical aptitude, and as a result were granted write access to the core repository. The old "Outer Team" designation was simplified to "Core Team Member" — a role that was able to participate in all Core Team communication channels, but was only provided read access to the source code repository. In addition, we added a role for the DotNetNuke Projects of "Project Team Lead." This role was responsible for managing the project infrastructure and communicating project status to the Core Team.

Conferences

The month of September 2005 began with the Professional Developer Conference (PDC) in Los Angeles, California. Based on a kind gesture from Microsoft, a large number of Core Team members were provided with free registration for the event in exchange for analysis of key ASP.NET 2.0 features that could be used in the DotNetNuke framework. Scott Willhite, Dan Caron, Nik Kalyani, Jon Henning, John Mitchell, Charles Nurse, and I were all able to attend the event, bringing together in one place the largest group of Core Team members ever. It was an excellent opportunity to get to know one another and we spent a lot of time hanging out together, exploring the exhibitor area, hosting a Birds of Feather session, visiting Universal Studios, and attending a variety of conference sessions.

The DotNetNuke Board, with the recent inclusion of Nik Kalyani, also took the opportunity to have some serious meetings regarding the progress of the revenue opportunities discussed at Tech Ed. The summer had not been productive in getting any programs launched other than Advertising and Sponsorship, and Nik took a lead role in attempting to clarify both our marketing and financial initiatives for the next 12 months. Specific board members were assigned to each major opportunity, and projections were presented and discussed in terms of assumptions, benefits, and execution tasks. We had a lot of work ahead of us, including a major platform transition, now firmly scheduled for November 7, 2005.

Later in September, Microsoft hosted a three-day summit for its Most Valuable Professional (MVP) community members. Based on public achievements, a number of DotNetNuke Core Team members earned this award of distinction in 2005. Bruce Hopkins (Georgia, USA), Phil Beadle (Australia), Cathal Connelly (Ireland), Jim Duffy (USA), and I (Canada) were all able to attend the private summit in Redmond, Washington. The summit provided the opportunity to get to know these Core Team members on a more personal level, including their appetite for social festivities. I was also able to spend some time with a number of prominent ASP.NET personalities and DotNetNuke evangelists whom I greatly respected in terms of their contributions to the community. In addition, there was also a large representation of Microsoft employees at the MVP summit that resulted in some excellent networking opportunities and offline discussions. Steve Balmer's keynote address provided some valuable insight into the roadmap for Microsoft's products and revealed areas where DotNetNuke could focus its efforts to strengthen its market position in the coming year.

Directly following the MVP summit, I had the privilege of attending my first ASPInsiders summit as well. The ASPInsiders represent a group of well-respected industry leaders in the Microsoft ASP.NET community. I had recently been inducted as an official member and appreciated the opportunity to be included in such an elite group of professionals. Perhaps the most important benefit of being an ASPInsider was that it provided representation for the DotNetNuke development community and validation of our extensive contributions to the industry. Due to its small focused membership, the ASPInsiders summit had a personal and direct interaction with Microsoft employees, allowing its members to provide feedback on a number of exciting new technologies. The networking opportunity was incredible, and the intricate dynamics of the various personalities and companies represented was especially interesting.

DotNetNuke 4.0

Throughout the months of September and October, Charles Nurse was instrumental in working on the migration to the ASP.NET 2.0 platform. He invested a massive amount of time researching compatibility issues, creating various proof of concepts, and communicating regularly with Microsoft. He actually pursued two different agendas simultaneously: the upgrade of DotNetNuke 3.0 to ASP.NET 2.0 from a runtime perspective, and the creation of a new web project model for DotNetNuke 4.0 that provided a development strategy for the future.

To support the community, we concluded that we would need to support two parallel code bases for an undetermined period of time: DotNetNuke 3.x (ASP.NET 1.1) and DotNetNuke 4.0 (ASP.NET 2.0). Obviously, a more optimal solution would have been a single code base that worked on both platforms; however, this simply was not possible based on the platform compilation changes in ASP.NET 2.0. In addition, we did not know what to expect in terms of the adoption rate for the new Microsoft platform. Therefore, it seemed natural that we focus on developing for both ASP.NET 1.1 and 2.0 in the short term. An unfortunate side effect of this model involved a general recommendation to develop to the lowest common denominator (that is, not leverage ASP.NET 2.0-specific technology) and synchronizing all fixes and enhancements across the two code bases.

One of the greatest achievements in the platform migration was that we were able to fully satisfy our business requirement for no breaking changes. DotNetNuke modules and skins developed on ASP.NET 1.1 could be installed directly into the ASP.NET 2.0 environment without any changes whatsoever. This had massive benefits for the commercial DotNetNuke ecosystem because vendors could continue developing their modules as a single code base on the ASP.NET 1.1 platform but offer their packaged products for sale in both channels.

The only item that remained outstanding right up until the week before the November 7th launch was how to develop DotNetNuke 4.0 modules on the ASP.NET 2.0 platform. The new dynamic compilation model in ASP.NET 2.0 created some challenges for many of our runtime extensibility features, especially where they relied on object instantiation through reflection. As is often the case with technical problems, the answer is out there — it's just a matter of finding the right person to ask. As luck would have it, a Microsoft developer (Ting-Hao Yang) who was copied on some of the communication between our team and the Microsoft ASP.NET Product Manager group finally responded with details on a new ASP.NET 2.0 framework method that ultimately solved all of our remaining reflection issues. In the end, all that was required was a change to a single method in the DotNetNuke 4.0 core framework (to use BuildManager.GetType).

One of the benefits of the new ASP.NET 2.0 platform was that Microsoft had put a lot of focus on making the technology more accessible to the general developer community. A key deliverable in this strategy was the release of an entire suite of free "Express" tools. Included in the Express line was a tool named "Visual Web Developer" that provided a functional Integrated Development Environment (IDE) for ASP.NET 2.0. Leveraging the benefits of this powerful new tool, we created a DotNetNuke 4.0 Starter Kit that enabled a developer to configure a fully functional development environment within minutes. This had significant implications on the DotNetNuke development community because it lowered the barrier of entry and now made it possible for any aspiring software developer, from beginner to advanced, to be instantly productive with the DotNetNuke web application framework. Combine this with the free SQL Server 2005 Express database engine and you have a zero cost development environment. Visual Web Developer could not be used to develop server controls or class libraries; however, the fact that the DotNetNuke extensibility architecture was based on user controls made it a perfect fit.

Not wanting to neglect the existing DotNetNuke 3.0 community by focusing solely on ASP.NET 2.0 migration, we decided to integrate a few powerful new features that had long been requested by the general community. Core Team member Tam Tran Minh had been developing an Active Directory integration component for a number of years and agreed to contribute it as a fully supported core framework component. Additionally, Jon Henning had been busy working on a full-featured JavaScript API that would allow developers to leverage powerful client-side behavior in their modules. This included a new menu control, the DNN Menu, and an implementation of the popular Asynchronous JavaScript for XML (or AJAX) technology. AJAX technology had become one of the hottest new trends for web development, and it is important to note that DotNetNuke included a powerful AJAX library well before the announcement of ATLAS by Microsoft. The combination of these features offered benefits to both platform consumers and application developers, and further strengthened our core platform offering.

The official Microsoft launch date for ASP.NET 2.0 was set for November 7, 2005. We knew if we could release DotNetNuke 4.0 to coincide with this event, we would be able to ride the huge marketing wave created by Microsoft. Because we had always advocated "releasing software when it is ready," this hard deadline imposed some serious challenges on our meager project resources. Aside from the obvious technical deliverables, we had communication and marketing deliverables that also needed to roll out in unison. Nik Kalyani and Bill Walker showed their agility to pull things together on a tight schedule, and we launched our first monthly newsletter to the entire DotNetNuke registered user base (now 200,000 registered users) on November 7. The response was overwhelmingly positive as the significance of the achievement began to sink in. In the month of November, we recorded 165,000 downloads, far eclipsing any previous monthly download total in the history of the project.

An interesting aspect to consider in the ASP.NET 2.0 migration was that we delivered a fully managed upgrade to users of the DotNetNuke web application framework. Anyone who has ever attempted a major platform upgrade on their own should recognize the incredible value of this accomplishment. We had effectively eliminated a budget line item of considerable cost and effort from thousands of IT departments and business entities around the world. Compare this to scenarios where companies create their own custom ASP.NET 1.1 applications. In these cases, each company would need to invest significant resources and funding to work out their own web application migration strategy. Or compare this to another scenario where you adopt another web application framework, commercial or open source, which had not even considered the upgrade challenges posed by ASP.NET 2.0 and were going to force you to postpone your upgrade until it fit their own release schedule. In either case, the decision to adopt DotNetNuke as part of an organization's business infrastructure had certainly paid dividends worthy of the attention of any business decision maker.

Immediately following the DotNetNuke 4.0 release, we focused on stabilization issues that were exposed through testing by a larger community audience. Another area that received dedicated focus was the Module Item Template feature of the DotNetNuke 4.0 Starter Kit. Through research and persistence, we were able to construct a DotNetNuke Module Template that could automatically create all of the development resources required to build a fully functional module in DotNetNuke 4.0. It even had some parameterization capabilities so that the template could be customized at runtime to meet the needs of the developer. I wrote an article describing the Starter Kit and Module Template and posted it on the public forums on www.asp.net. The article proved to be popular, with nearly 30,000 views recorded in the six weeks following its publication. It turned out that the changes in ASP.NET 2.0 resulted in some decent productivity benefits for module developers, further improving the capabilities of the DotNetNuke framework.

An interesting event occurred in December 2005, well after the official launch of ASP.NET 2.0. Based largely on the feedback that we provided Microsoft during our product migration efforts, Microsoft announced some add-ons for Visual Studio 2005 that added back ASP.NET 1.1 development support through Web Application Projects as well as compilation and merge support through Web Deployment Projects. Based on its superior architecture and incredible popularity, DotNetNuke was able to unite a significant portion of the Microsoft developer community and create a much stronger voice and more compelling argument in favor of specific platform features than would have ever been possible for individual developers. Beside the fact that these add-ons provided some critical options for web application developers, it was really gratifying to see that our direct feedback could have such an immediate and influential effect on the industry.

Slashdotted

In October 2005, I wrote a blog titled "No Respect for Windows Open Source." The blog was a political rant based on the fact that because DotNetNuke did not run on a fully open source stack of software components (that is, Linux/Apache/MySQL/PHP or LAMP), it did not get any respect from the general open source community. Further, it argued that all open source projects regardless of platform should be judged solely on the validity of their open source license and ideals. The blog was picked up by Slashdot, the largest independent news site for information technology, and resulted in a lot of exposure for the project (see Figure 1-13). The posting on Slashdot generated more than 500 comments, each with their unique perspective on the Windows open source paradigm.

In October, we were approached by *.NET Developers Journal* (*.NETDJ*) to do a series of articles on the DotNetNuke project. This was an excellent opportunity to showcase various aspects of the project in a mainstream magazine. A number of Core Team members were identified as potential authors and the first article in a series of six was published in the November edition of *.NETDJ*. Forging relationships with publishers is a great way to raise the profile of the project and open doors for future opportunities. In this case, working with SYS-CON (the publisher of *.NETDJ*) reaped rewards in terms of being approved as a featured speaker in the upcoming SYS-CON Enterprise Open Source conference in June 2006.

By the end of 2005, the dotnetnuke.com web site had achieved an impressive Alexa ranking of 6,741 and our SourceForge.Net ranking had climbed to #75 (out of all the open source projects in the world). We were consistently getting 15,000 new registered users per month and our project downloads averaged 120,000 per month. The dotnetnuke.com site was now serving 4.5 million page views per month, and every indication was pointing to even more improvement in 2006.

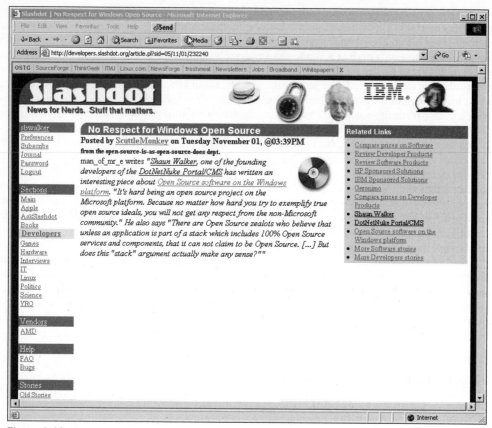

Figure 1-13

Benefactor Program

As much as there is a romantic notion regarding a distributed group of purely volunteer resources working together in their free time to produce an enterprise-level software product, it does not represent reality. To effectively manage all of the aspects of a professional software product, dedicated management is an absolute requirement. This does not just entail the standard project management principles for software development, but also the legal and marketing aspects of managing a high-profile technology asset. Since the project inception, I had been able to commit 100% of my time to the project only because there was a sufficient stream of project revenue to support my needs. And throughout the life of the project, a number of team members had been financially compensated for various deliverables so that we could meet obligations and scheduled deadlines. The financial resources came from a variety of sources, including third-party sponsorship, advertising, and custom consulting opportunities. Unfortunately, the revenue streams were not sizable or stable in terms of securing multiple resources for long-term engagements. Essentially, we were trying to operate a product company without any direct product revenue. And with the constant growth of the project, the demands were increasing rather than decreasing, putting even more pressure on the minimal set of project resources.

Back in July 2005, I concluded that without a dedicated sales effort, the dotnetnuke.com web site was never going to reach its full potential as a revenue-generating asset. (We had published ad rates on the site months earlier and had not received many serious inquiries.) I decided it was time to more actively cultivate our advertising and sponsorship revenue streams and that it was going to require spending some money to make money. Armed with a huge number of industry contacts collected at Tech Ed, I hired a full-time resource to actively manage the advertising and sponsorship program. Due to major content improvements made in the previous four months, the dotnetnuke.com web site became a targeted channel for the Microsoft development community. By simplifying the advertising rate sheet and employing traditional sales techniques, we were successfully able to grow this revenue stream in a relatively short time frame.

In the fall of 2005, while driving home from a business trip, I spent some dedicated time immersing myself in the revenue model dilemma. Over the years, I did a lot of research on business models for open source projects, and the big question was, "How do you sustain an open source organization while still adhering to its open source ideals?" There were obviously a number of companies that had demonstrated their ability to succeed in this area by employing a variety of financial options; however, I was keenly aware that each model had its own set of disadvantages.

One of the other recurring themes I kept thinking about is "who we serve." In a traditional business model, you serve your customers—but this generally assumes that some money is changing hands. For DotNetNuke, I would like to think that our open source community is who we serve—but because they are essentially using the product for free, it becomes challenging when other stakeholders step forward with financial support. Examining each of the more popular open source revenue models based on this theme proved to be a useful exercise.

The Pure Volunteer option has no revenue model. As a result, it has no resource cost—but at the same time it has no accountability, responsibility, or dedicated management. It could be argued that although it is supposed to serve the open source community, it really does not because there are no motivating factors driving the development and support.

The Dual License model has become popular in recent years because it allows for an open source version as well as a commercial version of the same product. The commercial version provides traditional licensing revenue that helps sustain dedicated management and developer resources, resulting in improved accountability. Unfortunately, it tends to lead to a number of conflict-of-interest scenarios within the ecosystem that can be quite damaging. For one thing, the open source version of the product is often stripped of its more valuable features in favor of promoting sales of the commercial version. The open source license is often tarnished to protect the intellectual property rights of the company in the commercial version. Extensibility options are throttled as the company attempts to control the financial ecosystem around the product. And the company typically shows favoritism through support and marketing channels to its paying commercial customers over the organic open source community. In the worst-case scenario, the company can be accused of taking the most valuable intellectual property from the community and using it for their own financial gain.

The Sponsorship model involves utilizing a revenue stream from one or more third-party funding sources. Although this revenue model results in funding for dedicated management, it often compromises the project ideals as the sponsor attempts to exert their influence over the project roadmap and marketing goals. It also results in a revenue stream that is variable, creating challenges in terms of cash-flow requirements. In addition, the project needs to be extremely diligent regarding the ownership of the intellectual property so as not to put itself in a situation where the third party could sue the project for copyright infringement or affect the open source project licensing.

The Professional Services model is based on a concept where the platform maintainer does a significant amount of custom consulting for a third-party client. The revenue from the custom consulting is used to fund the dedicated management for the open source product. Unfortunately, this model tends to consume a high level of resources to qualify leads, formulate contracts, manage accounts, obtain signoff, and keep the pipeline full of revenue opportunities. The revenue stream is variable, affecting cash flow, and key project resources are often required to focus on specific client requirements rather than supporting and improving the open source product.

The Charitable Donations model is popular in the traditional open source world because it involves voluntary community financial support of the project. The problem is that it does not generate a consistent, sustainable revenue stream, which means it is unable to secure dedicated management resources. In addition, there is a tendency for community members to assume that other members are making financial donations, when in reality the project is receiving no financial contributions from anyone.

The Vertical Application model leverages the open source product to create a highly specialized, commercial, vertical market application. The vertical market application typically generates revenue through as application service provider (ASP) revenue model, which contributes funding back to the open source project. The challenge is that it requires focused management and marketing in the vertical market, complete with domain challenges, competition, legal considerations, and political constraints. The open source application also tends to cater the product roadmap to the needs of the vertical market application, resulting in a less robust application framework.

Because each of the common revenue models seem to have their own set of issues, it made me brainstorm what I would consider to be an optimal open source revenue model. The main criterion is that the project should serve the open source community ("by the people, for the people"). It should be objective and open, avoiding conflict of interest and adhering to open source ideals. Finally, the revenue stream must be consistent and sustainable, capable of sustaining multiple dedicated resources.

An interesting economics philosophy that Scott Willhite turned me on to was the concept of the "abundance mentality." In terms of business value, an "abundance mentality" refers to an attitude of growth. Essentially, it means that the overall size of the ecosystem becomes larger as the number of opportunities within the ecosystem increases. By working together with various stakeholders in the ecosystem, all members of the collective group benefit through a greater abundance of revenue-generating opportunities. The opposite of the "abundance mentality" is the "scarcity mentality," where participants consider the size of the ecosystem to be constant and the goal is to capture as much of the market share as possible (choking out the smaller competitors in the process). DotNetNuke's extensible architecture and open source philosophy constantly pushes the envelope in terms of creating new business opportunities within the community. It was another principle that needed to be adhered to in our quest for a suitable revenue model.

With all of these ideas swirling in my head, I concluded that a Membership concept would be an effective revenue model for advancing our goals. It would mean that the open source project was funded by the community. It would also mean that the project was accountable and responsible to the community. Through the creation of new benefits, we would be able to provide more opportunities for community members to participate in the project ecosystem. From a public perspective, it would provide a defined method for any supporter, big or small, to contribute to the project. And we would not need to compromise any of our open source ideals. Membership would be available by subscription that would create on ongoing, consistent revenue stream.

The DotNetNuke Benefactor Program (see Figure 1-14) was officially launched in December 2005. Nik Kalyani came up with the marketing term "benefactor" because it clearly communicated the financial support goal of the program. The program had four levels of participation to cater to the needs of various stakeholders in the community, from individual developers to enterprise business organizations. The initial set of benefits was targeted to each program level and the administrative aspects of the program were automated as much as possible to provide a seamless user experience. The overall response to the program was positive and paved the way for future revenue opportunities.

Figure 1-14

DotNetNuke Marketplace

The extensibility model in DotNetNuke spawned an active commercial ecosystem. By January 2006, there were hundreds of commercial modules and skins available for the DotNetNuke application. In addition, there were many companies who were providing business services exclusively to the DotNetNuke market. This dynamic ecosystem was helping propel the growth of the project, but it was not without its share of issues.

Early in project's history, a third party created a reseller environment that allowed developers to sell their DotNetNuke products to consumers. This made it extremely easy for anyone, from a hobbyist developer to a serious independent software vendor, to get involved in the DotNetNuke commercial ecosystem. In the early stages, the existence of an established business environment for commercial components was critical to the growth of the project and promotion of the "abundance mentality." However, one of the most common types of negative feedback that we received related to this environment as time went on was about the quality of third-party products and services.

Based on the low barrier of entry of the reseller environment, the quality of commercial DotNetNuke components was extremely inconsistent. Some vendors were providing high-quality components, with professional support, and explicit licensing terms. Others were essentially providing untested code snippets with no support or licensing considerations. The combination of these polar opposites in terms of product quality posed some real issues in terms of our goals to promote DotNetNuke as an enterprise-level framework. Effectively, the existing reseller environment was supporting a "buyer beware" mentality that was not complementary with our goals for taking the project to the next level. Some of the more serious independent software vendors told us that for them to get involved in the ecosystem, a more professional reseller channel would need to be made available.

One of the issues that we struggled with for quite some time was the creation of some review criteria for DotNetNuke components. This became increasingly more critical as many of the DotNetNuke Projects entered the release pipeline. Leveraging the revenue from the Benefactor Program, I was finally able to fund this effort, and Joe Brinkman was selected as the best resource for the task. The review criteria played a fundamental role in our internal organizational process, but we also had another strategic goal in mind.

The current reseller environment was managed by a third party. We had approached them a number of times in the past with hopes that we could form a business partnership. The critical points were that we were not receiving any revenue from the DotNetNuke ecosystem we created, and we were not collecting any business intelligence related to the users of the product. For us to effectively manage the product roadmap, it was becoming increasingly more important that we get in touch with our true user community. The discussion forums represented a small-but-vocal group of community members who offered feedback, but there was a much larger group of users with whom we had absolutely no contact. Unfortunately, the reseller was not interested in working with us in this capacity, which left us with a single alternative: establishing our own reseller channel.

Combining the concepts of the review criteria with a reseller channel seemed to be a great way to satisfy a variety of project goals. Our reseller channel would only sell components that passed our objective review criteria. This improved the overall perception of quality and confidence in the community, provided us with the necessary business intelligence, and exposed a new revenue stream to help us secure more dedicated management resources.

Summary

DotNetNuke is an evolving open source platform, with new enhancements being added constantly based on user feedback. The organic community ecosystem that has grown up around DotNetNuke is vibrant and dynamic, establishing the essential support infrastructure for long-term growth and prosperity. You will always be able to get the latest high-quality release, including full source code, from www.dotnetnuke.com.

2

Installing DotNetNuke

Traditionally, web applications are deployed via *xcopy* (the process of copying multiple files from one place to another) and the execution of structured query language (SQL) scripts to initialize and upgrade the appropriate database schema. Advanced web applications such as DotNetNuke contain powerful installers that automate this process, improving the user experience and reducing the risk of missing an install step.

This chapter presents a step-by-step guide to using the automated installer packaged with DotNetNuke and provides guidance in selecting a version of the software that is suitable for your organization. The objective of the chapter is to provide you with a working installation of DotNetNuke.

Specifically, this chapter covers the following areas:

❑   What version of DotNetNuke should you use?

❑   Installing DotNetNuke v3.x.

❑   Upgrading an existing installation to v3.x.

❑   Installing DotNetNuke v4.x.

❑   Upgrading an existing installation to v4.x.

Selecting a Version

At the time of writing, there are two major versions of DotNetNuke, each targeting a different version of the .NET Framework:

❑   DotNetNuke v3.x, directed at ASP.NET 1.1

❑   DotNetNuke v4.x, aimed at ASP.NET 2.0

Each is functionally identical and your choice of version is dependent on your infrastructure (version of .NET Framework) and chosen development environment (Visual Studio 2003 versus Visual Studio 2005).

You can upgrade a v3.x to a v4.x installation at a later date.

After you select a version, proceed to the corresponding installation section in this chapter.

Installing DotNetNuke v3.x

Ensure that you have met all prerequisites before proceeding to the installation steps for DotNetNuke v3.x.

Prerequisites

Table 2-1 lists the software prerequisites for DotNetNuke v3.x

Table 2-1: DotNetNuke v3.x Software Prerequisites

Software	Description
Web Server	Microsoft Internet Information Server 5 or greater (contained in Windows 2000 Server, Windows XP Professional, and Windows 2003 Server)
Microsoft .NET Runtime	ASP.NET 1.1 or later
Database	Microsoft SQL Server 2000 or greater

DotNetNuke v3.x has an additional prerequisite not supported by all third-party web hosts: you must be able to at least specify Read, Write, and Modify permissions on the root installation folder. Before signing up for a third-party hosting plan, ensure that you will be able to do so.

Installation Steps

To install DotNetNuke v3.x, follow these steps, which are fully explained in the subsequent sections:

1. Download the software.
2. Unzip the package.
3. Create a database in SQL Server.
4. Create a database login.
5. Set file permissions.
6. Configure IIS (Internet Information Server).
7. Configure web.config for installation.
8. Install.

Step 1: Download the Software

You can download the latest version of the DotNetNuke software from the official DotNetNuke web site (www.dotnetnuke.com), shown in Figure 2-1.

You must be a registered user to reach the download page. Registering is easy — just select the Register link in the top-right portion of the screen and follow the directions.

Figure 2-1

Choose the DotNetNuke 3.x package that's right for you:

❑ **Install package (DotNetNuke_X.Y.Z_Install.zip):** Contains only the files necessary to run the application. Use this package if you don't expect to do any modifications to core files.

❑ **Source package (DotNetNuke_X.Y.Z_Source.zip):** Contains all the files related to the core DotNetNuke project, including all Visual Basic source files. Use this package if you expect to modify core files or want to view the associated source.

Step 2: Unzip the Package

Extract the entire contents of the zip file to your chosen installation directory. On a local intranet installation, you can place your web site anywhere (for example, c:\websites\dotnetnuke\). On a remote hosting server, you need to upload the files to your web site following the procedures provided by your hosting provider.

To extract a zip file, you can use either the built-in zip functionality of Windows XP or a third-party compression tool such as WinZip, which you can obtain from www.winzip.com.

Step 3: Create a Database in SQL Server

Create the database to contain your data for the DotNetNuke application.

In a remote hosting environment, your hosting provider probably has configured a SQL Server database for you, and can provide you with instructions for connecting to the database.

In a local intranet installation, you need to manually create a new database. To perform this for SQL Server 2000, you need to have Enterprise Manager and the Microsoft SQL Server Client Tools installed. If you do not have these, you can install them from your Microsoft SQL Server installation CD.

Open Enterprise Manager and expand the database server you want to create your database. If it's not listed, you will have to register your SQL Server instance with Enterprise Manager. To do this, refer to the Enterprise Manager help.

Now that you have found your database server — in this case, it is a local machine known as (local) — create your database by right-clicking the Databases node under your server and selecting New Database, as shown in Figure 2-2.

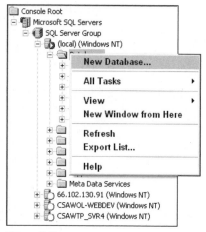

Figure 2-2

A dialog box appears asking for a database name. Put in any name and click OK. This example uses the name DotNetNuke, as shown in Figure 2-3.

> *Further configuration options are listed on the Data Files and Transaction Log dialog, but for this installation, just accept the defaults. For more information about these options, see the Help file that comes with Enterprise Manager.*

Figure 2-3

Step 4: Create a Database Login

Strictly speaking, you have two options in creating a user account to access your database:

❑ **Windows Security:** Uses the account that your application is running under to access the database. (This is the more secure option, but it is not supported in all environments, particularly in shared hosting).

❑ **SQL Server Security:** Uses a username-and-password combination to access the database.

For the purposes of this book, SQL Server Security is used, but we encourage you to explore Windows Security, especially in intranet environments.

Create a user account for the database in Enterprise Manager by first navigating to the Security node located at the top level of the server you are connecting to. Expand it and select the Logins node. A list of users who already have access to your database server appears in the right pane.

Right-click the Logins node and select New Login (as shown in Figure 2-4).

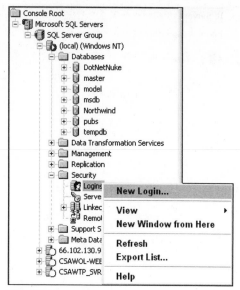

Figure 2-4

A dialog box appears that prompts you for details about the account. In this case, create a user called DotNetNukeUser, and use that name for the password as well. Make sure you select the SQL Server Authentication radio option (otherwise you'll be creating an account for Windows Authentication), and set the example database DotNetNuke as the default for this login. Figure 2-5 shows the dialog box with the details filled in.

> If you are unable to select the SQL Server authentication option, ensure that your database is running in Mixed Mode access, a setting that can be configured on the Properties dialog box of your database.

Before you click OK, there is one more step to perform. Although you selected DotNetNuke as the default database, you still need to grant the new user Read and Write access to it. To do this, select the Database Access tab and check the Permit check box next to the DotNetNuke database. In the Database Roles list at the bottom of the tab, check the Permit box for db_owner privileges, which the user must have to create and delete database objects.

Figure 2-6 shows the correct settings. After you have them set, click OK, confirm the password as prompted, and click OK again.

The new account should appear in the right task pane whenever you select the Logins node. You can come back here anytime to change details about this particular account.

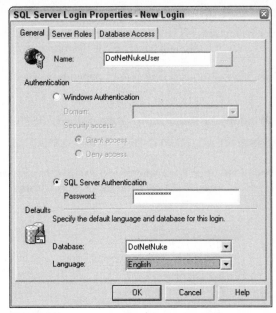

Figure 2-5

Figure 2-6

Step 5: Set File Permissions

The ASP.NET worker process requires NTFS (file) permissions to be set so that DotNetNuke can create directories and files for advanced functionality such as the file manager, multi-portal creation, and so on.

The user account that must have additional permissions depends on the version of Windows you are running:

❑ **Windows 2000/Windows XP Professional (IIS5):** {Server}\ASPNET User Account

❑ **Windows 2003 (IIS6):** NT AUTHORITY\NETWORK SERVICE User Account

To set the correct file permissions, open File Explorer and navigate to your installation folder (C:\ websites\DotNetNuke\, for instance). Right-click the folder, select Properties, and choose the Security tab (see Figure 2-7).

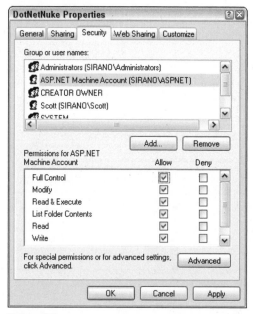

Figure 2-7

If you are cannot see the Security tab, you must disable Simple File Sharing. Here's how:

❑ *Select Start ⇨ My Computer ⇨ Tools ⇨ Folder Options ⇨ View.*

❑ *Scroll to the bottom of the list of advanced settings and un-check Use Simple File Sharing (Recommended).*

❑ *Click OK.*

The minimum permissions for the folders are as follows:

❑   **Root (and all child folders):** Read and Write access

❑   **/DesktopModules:** Write and Modify access

❑   **/Portals (and all child folders):** Write and Modify access

An additional permission is required if you plan to create child portals or install additional language packs:

❑   **Root (and all child folders):** Read, Write, and Modify access

Step 6: Configure IIS (Internet Information Server)

The next step in the process is to create a new web site pointing at the DotNetNuke installation files. To configure your web server, use the IIS management console.

To run the management console, select Start ⇨ Run, type **inetmgr**, and click OK.

Alternatively, you can access the console via the Windows Control Panel by selecting Administrative Tools ⇨ Internet Information Services.

The administration console for IIS appears, showing a node with the local computer's name. Expand this item to reveal the list of web sites on the local computer. Expand the Default Web Site node. Figure 2-8 shows the default web site that is automatically configured when IIS is installed.

If your IIS is not hosted on the local computer, you can remotely administer IIS by right-clicking the Internet Information Services node, selecting Connect, and following the on-screen prompts to connect to the remote computer.

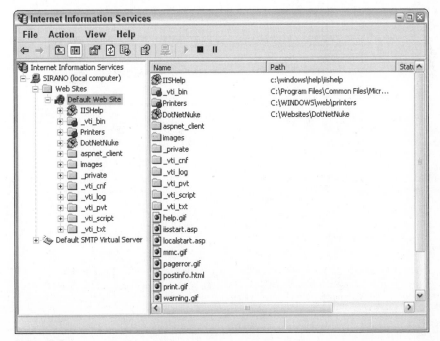

Figure 2-8

Right-click Default Web Site and select New ⇨ Virtual Directory. The Virtual Directory Creation Wizard appears as shown in Figure 2-9.

Figure 2-9

Click Next to proceed.

Enter the name of your virtual directory (DotNetNuke, for example) as shown in Figure 2-10, and then click Next.

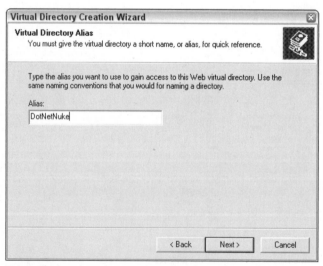

Figure 2-10

Select the installation directory chosen earlier (for example, C:\Websites\DotNetNuke), as shown in Figure 2-11.

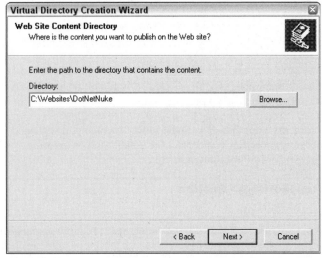

Figure 2-11

Click Next.

The last step is to specify the permissions applicable for the virtual directory. Keep the defaults of Read and Run Scripts, click Next, and then click Finish. Figure 2-12 shows the correct list of access permissions.

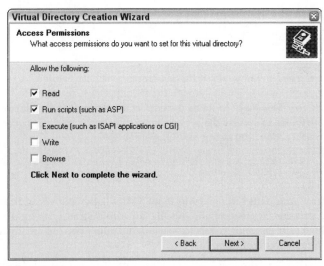

Figure 2-12

You have now completed configuration of IIS, so close the management console.

Step 7: Configure web.config for Installation

All ASP.NET applications require a central configuration file called web.config. This file is used to store application-specific settings such as database connection and encryption strings.

By default, DotNetNuke does not come with this configuration file. Instead, it contains release.config and development.config files, which are optimized for different environments, production or development, respectively.

For the purposes of this installation, use the release.config file by renaming it **web.config**. Once you have renamed the file, open it in your favorite text editor.

The web.config file contains a number of settings, some of which you will need to adjust. There are five settings in the <appSettings> section that control the installation or upgrade. Listing 2-1 shows the section with the settings that control installation in bold.

Listing 2-1: The <appSettings> Section

```
<appSettings>
    <add key="SiteSqlServer" value="Server=(local);Database=DotNetNuke;uid=;pwd=;" />
    <add key="MachineValidationKey"
value="F9D1A2D3E1D3E2F7B3D9F90FF3965ABDAC304902" />
    <add key="MachineDecryptionKey"
value="F9D1A2D3E1D3E2F7B3D9F90FF3965ABDAC304902F8D923AC" />
    <add key="MachineValidationMode" value="SHA1" />
    <add key="InstallTemplate" value="DotNetNuke.install.resources" />
    <add key="AutoUpgrade" value="true" />
    <add key="UseDnnConfig" value="true"/>
    <add key="InstallMemberRole" value="true" />
        <!-- Show missing translation keys (for development use) -->
    <add key="ShowMissingKeys" value="false" />
    <add key="EnableWebFarmSupport" value="false" />
    <add key="EnableCachePersistence" value="false" />
</appSettings>
```

Following is what you need to know about these settings:

❑   SiteSqlServer: This node contains the connection string to your database. Change the corresponding attributes to specify the server, name, username, and password of your database. Here's a sample connection string for SQL Server 2000:

```
<add key="SiteSqlServer" value="Server=(local);Database=DotNetNuke;uid=⊃
DotNetNukeUser;pwd=DotNetNukeUser;" />
```

❑   InstallTemplate: This setting points to an XML file that allows additional control over the installation process. By customizing this file, an administrator can modify the default security accounts, host settings, and portals to be created. Unless you are an advanced user, leave this file in the default configuration.

❑   AutoUpgrade: This setting determines whether the installation or upgrade process automatically runs when a difference in version is detected. If it is set to true, anytime DotNetNuke determines that the current running code is a higher version than the database, an install or an upgrade will automatically take place. If it is set to false, DotNetNuke will report the differences and then stop. The default setting is true. Set it to false only when you want to manually initiate the install process by navigating to (http://{siteURL}/Install/Install.aspx).

❏ `UseDnnConfig`: This setting is tied to the check that DotNetNuke performs when comparing the version of the assembly and the version of the database during the installation or upgrade process. To prevent multiple database hits, a file called dnn.config is cached in the install folder; it contains the current version number of the database's schema. This setting determines whether DotNetNuke examines this file or queries the database directly. The default is `true` and, for performance reasons, that works best in most cases.

❏ `InstallMemberRole`: This setting enables you to control the installation of the member role scripts that are packaged with DotNetNuke. These scripts initialize tables and stored procedures used to centrally store user and role information. They require a higher level of permission in your database (database owner) and may need to be initialized through another security account (pre-installation). The default setting is `true`. Use `false` only when you want to manually install those scripts.

A data provider section (see Listing 2-2) is defined further down the web.config file. There are two options in the default SQL Server provider that you may want to customize. Those options are bold in the listing.

Listing 2-2: The Data Provider Section

```
<data defaultProvider="SqlDataProvider">
  <providers>
    <clear />
    <add name="SqlDataProvider"
       type="DotNetNuke.Data.SqlDataProvider, DotNetNuke.SqlDataProvider"
       connectionStringName="SiteSqlServer"
       upgradeConnectionString=""
       providerPath="~\Providers\DataProviders\SqlDataProvider\"
       objectQualifier=""
       databaseOwner="dbo" />
  </providers>
</data>
```

Here's what you need to know about these settings:

❏ `objectQualifier`: This setting enables you to set a prefix to any of the objects created within your database. For example, if you specify an object qualifier of dnn_, the users table will be created as dnn_users. It is recommended that you specify this setting if multiple applications might need to use the same database.

❏ databaseOwner: This setting identifies the database user that owns the objects DotNetNuke will create in the database. By default, it is set to the database owner role (dbo) and in most cases should be left at this setting.

However, in some situations, the owner of the database might not grant you database owner (db_owner) privileges to the database (for example, third-party hosting). In these cases, set the databaseOwner attribute to the identity of your user. If the user is not a database owner, the user must have at least the following permissions:

  ❏ db_datareader (necessary for DotNetNuke)

  ❏ db_datawriter (necessary for DotNetNuke)

  ❏ db_ddladmin (necessary for MemberRoles)

  ❏ db_securityadmin (necessary during installation of MemberRoles)

Step 8: Perform the Installation

Verify that you have performed all seven of the preceding steps:

1. Obtained the latest source code from www.dotnetnuke.com.

2. Unzipped the latest source code to a local file directory.

3. Created a new database for the application.

4. Created a new database user to connect as.

5. Set file permissions on the local file directory.

6. Created a new virtual directory in IIS.

7. Configured web.config with your application-specific settings (for example, database connection, and so on).

If you have completed all of these steps, open your web browser and navigate to http://localhost/dotnetnuke/ for a local install or to http://www.mydomain.com/ for a remote install.

The AutoUpgrade function (discussed in step 7) detects if the database is empty. If the AutoUpgrade setting is false, a "Site Unavailable" page (see Figure 2-13) appears. The administrator can then trigger the install by navigating to one of the following URLs:

❑   **Local install:** http://localhost/dotnetnuke/Install/Install.aspx?mode=Install

❑   **Remote install:** http://www.mydomain.com/Install/Install.aspx?mode=Install

Figure 2-13

If the `AutoUpgrade` is set to `true`, the installation process begins automatically, as shown in Figure 2-14.

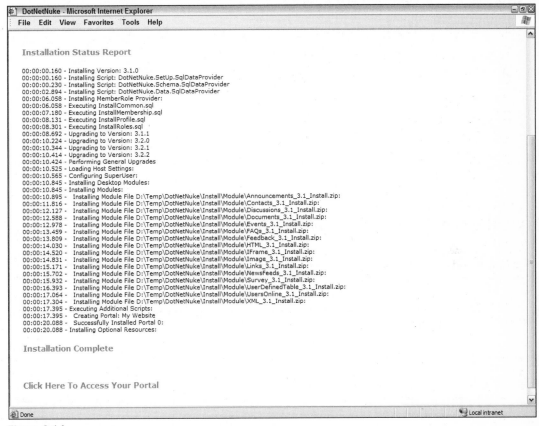

Figure 2-14

The installation process logs significant events on the page. Take a look at the steps performed:

1. The installer reports the version of the template being installed (`Installing Version: 3.1.0`).

2. The installer reports that the SQL installation scripts were executed:

❑ `DotNetNuke.Setup.SqlDataProvider`

❑ `DotNetNuke.Schema.SqlDataProvider`

❑ `DotNetNuke.Data.SqlDataProvider`

3. The install reports that the SQL common scripts were executed:

❑ `InstallCommon.sql`

❑ `InstallMembership.sql`

❑ `InstallProfile.sql`

❑ `InstallRoles.sql`

4. The install reports that the incremental upgrade SQL scripts were executed (`Upgrading to version: 3.1.1`, `Upgrading to version: 3.2.0`, and so on).

5. The sections of the Install template are parsed:

   ❏ `Host Settings`

   ❏ `SuperUser`

6. The modules are installed.

7. The portals are created.

8. Optional resources, such as additional skins, containers, and so on, are installed.

After the install is completed, follow the Click Here To Access Your Portal link to visit your new DotNetNuke site.

Upgrading to DotNetNuke 3.x

The upgrade process for DotNetNuke is very similar to the installation process. It contains an automated process but with fewer steps because the infrastructure is already in place. Here's what to do:

1. **Back up your site.** Before upgrading a site, it is recommended that you back up your entire site. This includes a backup of all site files and a full database backup. At a minimum, you must back up your web.config file.

2. **Download the software.** As described earlier in this chapter, obtain the latest release of the software from the official DotNetNuke site (`www.dotnetnuke.com`). Refer to the "Select a Version" section earlier in this chapter for information about which package to choose.

3. **Unzip the package.** After you have backed up your web.config file, you can extract the new version of DotNetNuke over your existing version.

4. **Configure web.config for upgrade.** As mentioned earlier, the installation package no longer includes a copy of web.config. The package does not contain this file because it contains password hash keys used for database encryption. If these keys had been changed in your existing install and were to be accidentally replaced, your users would no longer be able to log in to your site.

   The hash keys are found in the web.config file as shown in Listing 2-3.

Listing 2-3: Password Hash Keys

```
<add key="MachineValidationKey" value="B5EC9DAA0CFACE70BACD2462588555EEC85B6734" />
<add key="MachineDecryptionKey"
value="1FA6DB6E75EEC04AB58B7AC080AF471BF55EEC5D46BE95B9" />
<add key="MachineValidationMode" value="SHA1" />
```

The exact steps for configuring your upgraded site are as follows:

1. Make a backup copy of your existing web.config file (for example, **web.config.resources**).

2. Rename release.config to **web.config**.

3. Replace the values for the following in your new web.config, with the values in your backup:

```
SiteSqlServer
```

```
MachineValidationKey
```

```
MachineDecryptionKey
```

InstallationDate (This may not be present in web.config, so add the key that is in web.backup.resources to web.config.)

web.backup.resources is the recommended name for a backup of web.config.

4. Make any other changes to web.config that you made to support additional providers, and so on.

5. **Perform the upgrade.** First, verify that you have done the following:

   ❑ Backed up your entire site and database (or at least your web.config file).

   ❑ Obtained the most suitable package from `www.dotnetnuke.com`.

   ❑ Unzipped the package over the top of your existing installation.

   ❑ Renamed your web.config file (for example, to **web.config.resources**).

   ❑ Renamed release.config to **web.config**.

   ❑ Copied the password hash keys (and any other setting you customized) from your old web.config file to your new web.config file.

When you have completed all of those steps, open your web browser and navigate to `http://localhost/dotnetnuke/` for a local upgrade or `http://www.mydomain.com/` for a remote upgrade.

The `AutoUpgrade` function detects if the database requires an upgrade. If the `AutoUpgrade` setting (discussed earlier) is set to `false`, a "Site Unavailable" page like the one you saw in Figure 2-13 will appear. The administrator can then trigger the install by navigating to one of the following URLs:

   ❑ **Local install:** `http://localhost/dotnetnuke/Install/Install.aspx?mode=Install`

   ❑ **Remote install:** `http://www.mydomain.com/Install/Install.aspx?mode=Install`

If the `AutoUpgrade` is set to `true`, the installation process begins automatically as shown in Figure 2-15.

The upgrade process logs significant events on the page. Take a look at the steps performed:

1. The installer reports the new version of DotNetNuke to be installed (`Version: 3.2.2`).

2. The installer reports the current version of DotNetNuke installed (`Version 3.2.0`).

3. The installer reports that the incremental-version upgrade SQL scripts were executed (`Upgrading to version: 3.2.1`, `Upgrading to version: 3.2.2`, and so on).

4. The installer reports that general upgrades were performed.

5. The installer reports all modules that are installed as part of the package (these may be upgrades of existing modules).

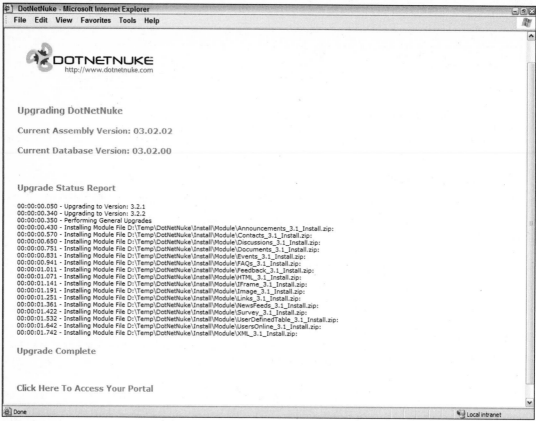

Figure 2-15

When the upgrade is complete, follow the Click Here To Access Your Portal link to visit your upgraded DotNetNuke site.

Installing DotNetNuke 4.x

DotNetNuke 4.0 is the first version of DotNetNuke to be targeted at ASP.NET 2.0. (Version 3.2 will run on ASP.NET 2, but it requires Visual Studio 2003 and .NET 1.1 for any development work.)

To further support ASP.NET 2.0, a new installation package — the DotNetNuke Starter Kit — has been added for DotNetNuke 4.0. A starter kit is a new project type for Visual Studio 2005 and Visual Web Developer Express. Essentially, it adds a new project type to your selected development environment and enables you to choose New DotNetNuke Site from the New Project menu.

Prerequisites

Table 2-2 lists the software prerequisites for DotNetNuke v4.x.

Table 2-2: DotNetNuke v4.x Software Prerequisites

Software	Description
Web Server	Microsoft Internet Information Server 5 or greater (contained in Windows 2000 Server, Windows XP Professional, and Windows 2003 Server)
Microsoft .NET Runtime	ASP.NET 2.0 or later
Database	Microsoft SQL Server 2000 or greater
Development Environment	Optional: If you plan to use the Starter Kit (not mandatory), you need either Visual Studio 2005 or Visual Web Developer.

DotNetNuke 4.x has an additional prerequisite that is not supported by all third-party web hosts: you must be able to specify at least Read, Write, and Modify permissions on the root installation folder. Before signing up for a third-party hosting plan, ensure that you will be able to assign these permissions.

Downloading the Software

The first step in the installation process is to obtain the DotNetNuke software. The latest version of the software can be downloaded at the official DotNetNuke web site, www.dotnetnuke.com. As noted earlier, you must be a registered user to reach the download page.

DotNetNuke 4.x is available in Source, Install, or Starter Kit packages:

❏ **Starter Kit package (DotNetNuke_X.Y.Z_StarterKit.vsi):** Contains a Project Template (based on the Install package), a Module Item Template (in both Visual Basic.NET and C#), and a Skin Item Template. The supporting class libraries, providers, and HttpModules are provided as precompiled assemblies (DLLs).

❏ **Install package (DotNetNuke_X.Y.Z_Install.zip):** Contains only the files necessary to run the application. Use this package if you don't expect to do any modifications to core files.

❏ **Source package (DotNetNuke_X.Y.Z_Source.zip):** Contains all the files related to the core DotNetNuke project, including all Visual Basic source files. Use this package if you expect to modify core files or want to view the associated source.

In deciding which package to use, determine what your development environment will be because Visual Web Developer Express (VWD) does not support any project type other than web sites. If you expect to do most of your development in VWD rather than Visual Studio 2005 (VS2005), you will not be able to use the Source package.

Visual Web Developer is an alternative, low-cost development environment available from http://msdn.microsoft.com/vstudio/express/vwd.

The following sections cover the installation of the new Starter Kit and the differences in the installation procedure for the Source/Install version. If you need more information on the Source/Install version, refer to the relevant section in the v3.x procedure.

Installing the Starter Kit

To install the Starter Kit, follow these steps:

1. Double-click the MSI file in Windows Explorer. The Visual Studio Content Installer, shown in Figure 2-16, launches.

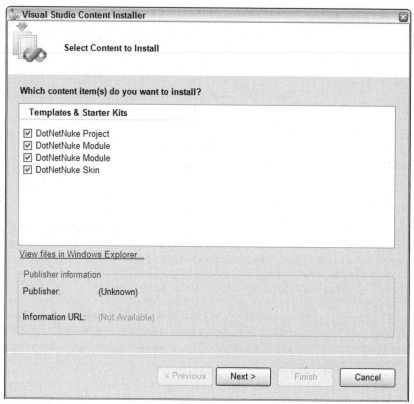

Figure 2-16

2. Select the templates you would like to install (by default, all are selected). Click Next.

3. The packages are not signed with a Digital Certificate, so you will get the warning shown in Figure 2-17. Select Yes.

4. The installer is ready to install the items you selected (see Figure 2-18). Click Finish.

Figure 2-17

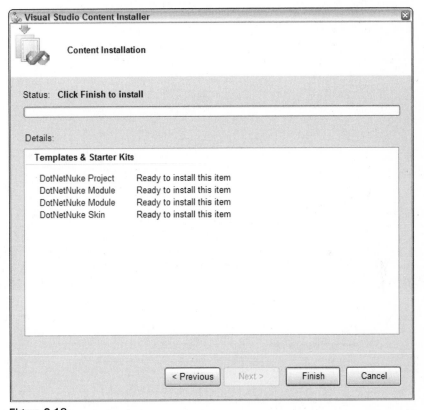

Figure 2-18

5. As Figure 2-19 shows, the installer lets you know when it has successfully completed its job. Click Close.

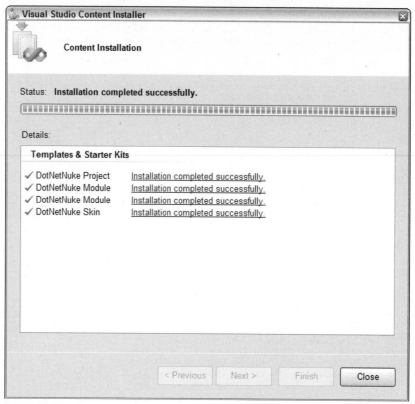

Figure 2-19

You can now create a new DotNetNuke project. In Visual Studio 2005 or Visual Web Developer Express, select File ➪ New Web Site. The New Web Site dialog box opens, as shown in Figure 2-20.

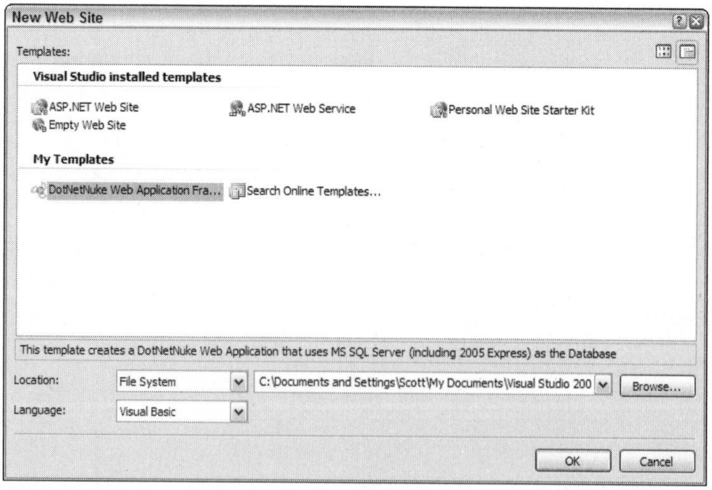

Figure 2-20

In the My Templates section, choose the DotNetNuke Web Application Framework template. At the bottom of the dialog box, specify a location and a language, and click OK. A web site is created in the folder you specified, and the Welcome.html file (see Figure 2-21) automatically opens in the internal browser.

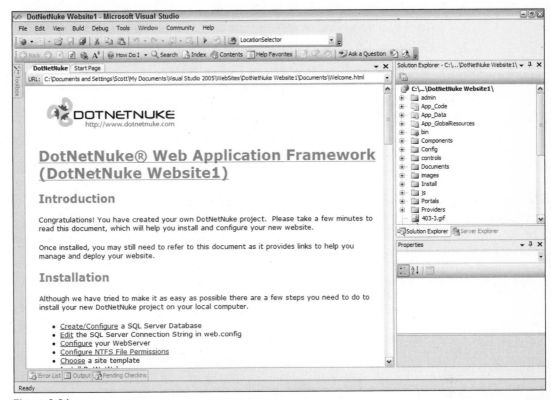

Figure 2-21

Welcome.html provides further instructions on how to complete the installation on your local machine.

Installing the Install/Source Package

This section focuses only on the differences between the v3.x and v4.x Install/Source installations. For more detailed instructions, see the appropriate section in the v3.x installation instructions. You've already downloaded the software, so we'll start with step 2.

Step 2: Unzip the Package

Like the v3.x installation, you have to extract your chosen installation package to a physical location on your computer.

Due to changes in the web project model for Visual Studio 2005, it is recommended that you extract the package as follows:

1. Create a directory where the application will reside (c:\websites\dotnetnuke, for example).

2. If you are using the Install package, do the following:

    ❑   Create a subdirectory called **website** (such as c:\websites\dotnetnuke\website).

    ❑   Extract the Install package into the website subdirectory you just created.

3. If you are using the Source package, extract the entire package to the original folder you created (c:\websites\dotnetnuke, for instance). The subfolders will be created automatically.

Steps 3–5: Set Up the Database, Login, and Permissions

Create the database to contain your data for the DotNetNuke application, create a user account to access your database, and set NTFS permissions. To do this, follow the relevant instructions in the "Install DotNetNuke v3.x" section at the beginning of the chapter.

Step 6: Configure IIS (Internet Information Server)

The next step in the process is to create a new web site pointing at the DotNetNuke installation files. Create a virtual directory in IIS called **DotNetNuke** (or whatever you choose) that points to the appropriate physical file directory.

The appropriate directory depends on how you extracted your chosen package. If you are using the Install package, point IIS to the folder you extracted the files to. If you are using the Source package, point IIS to the \website folder.

Ensure that your virtual directory is running ASP.NET 2.0 by right-clicking it and selecting Properties. The ASP.NET tab of the DotNetNuke Properties dialog box displays the version number (see Figure 2-22). You need version 2.0 or higher.

Step 7: Configure web.config for Installation

Although the web.config file for DotNetNuke v4.x differs quite a bit from that used in DotNetNuke v3.x, most of the disparity is due to .NET2.

As with v3.x, before doing anything else, rename release.config to **web.config**.

Three major differences exist between the v3.x web.config and the v4.x web.config:

❑   Version 4.x needs the SiteSqlServer setting in <appSettings> just as v3.x does, but v4.x also requires the same connection string to be set in the <connectionStrings> section (see Listing 2-4). In other words, v4.x requires the connectionStrings setting in two sections, not just one.

Listing 2-4: <connectionStrings> Section

```
<connectionStrings>
<add
  name="SiteSqlServer"
```

```
    connectionString="Server=(local);Database=DotNetNuke;uid=DotNetNukeUser;
pwd=DotNetNukeUser;"
    providerName="System.Data.SqlClient" />
</connectionStrings>
```

❑   The machine key settings in the v3.x `<appSettings>` section—`MachineValidationKey`,
     `MachineDecryptionKey`, and `MachineValidationMode`—are in v4.x's `<machineKey>`
     section (see Listing 2-5) located in the `<system.web>` section.

Listing 2-5: <machineKey> Section

```
<machineKey
    validationKey="F9D1A2D3E1D3E2F7B3D9F90FF3965ABDAC304902"
    decryptionKey="F9D1A2D3E1D3E2F7B3D9F90FF3965ABDAC304902F8D923AC"
    decryption="3DES"
    validation="SHA1"/>
```

Step 8: Perform the Installation

The v4.x installation process is identical to v3.x's. Open your web browser and navigate to `http://localhost/dotnetnuke/` for a local install or `http://www.mydomain.com/` for a remote install. When the installation completes, follow the Click Here To Access Your Portal hyperlink to access your new DotNetNuke 4.0 site.

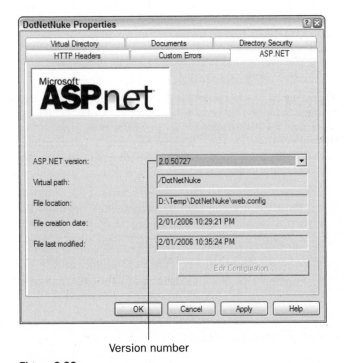

Version number

Figure 2-22

Upgrading to DotNetNuke 4.x

The upgrade process for DotNetNuke is very similar to the installation procedure. It contains an automated process with fewer steps because the infrastructure is already in place. This section focuses on the differences between the upgrades of v3.x sites and v4.x sites. Here are the steps:

1. **Back up your site.** As always, it is recommended that you back up your entire site before upgrading. This includes backing up all site files and your complete database. At a minimum, you must back up your web.config file.

2. **Download the software.** As described earlier in this chapter, obtain the latest release of the software from the official DotNetNuke site (`www.dotnetnuke.com`). Refer to the "Select a Version" section near the beginning of this chapter for information about which package to select.

3. **Unzip the package.** If you read the earlier section about installing a v4.x site, you know that the new web project model forced DotNetNuke to change its folder structure for the source version. This adds a level of complication for anyone upgrading from the v3.x source to the v4.x source.

   ❑ *Upgrading v3.x to v4.x install only:* If you are not worried about the source projects, you can upgrade your site in the following way by downloading the latest Starter Kit or install package:

   For the Starter Kit, create a new project in Visual Studio 2005 or Visual Web Developer Express (as described earlier in the chapter). Specify the location of your existing site. You are prompted with a warning that a site already exists at the location. Select the Create a New Web Site in the Existing Location option and press Enter.

   For the install package, extract the contents on to your existing site.

   When you are finished upgrading for install only, proceed to the "Configure web.config for Upgrade" section.

   ❑ *Upgrading v3.x to v4.x source only:* The situation is a little trickier if you want to upgrade to the Source version of DotNetNuke v4.0. Therefore, it's recommended that you follow the instructions earlier in this chapter on how to install a DotNetNuke v4.x site, rather than overwriting in some way your old site. Then move any custom content—such as Modules, Skins, and Portal content—you have on your old site, as well as your web.config file, to the new site. In IIS, re-point the virtual directory to the website folder of the DotNetNuke v4.x site.

   This is the safest and simplest way to move your development from v3.x to v4.x. After you have completed this process, you are ready to configure your web.config file.

4. **Configure web.config for upgrade**. As discussed earlier, the installation package no longer includes a copy of web.config. The exact steps for configuring your upgraded site are as follows:

   1. Make a backup copy of your existing web.config file (named **web.config.resources**, for instance).

   2. Rename release.config to **web.config**.

   3. Replace the following keys in your new web.config with the values in your backup:

      `SiteSqlServer`

      `MachineValidationKey`

MachineDecryptionKey

InstallationDate (This may not be present in the new web.config, so add the key that is in web.backup.resources to web.config.)

web.backup.resources is the recommended name for a backup of web.config.

4. Set `<connectionStrings>` to the same values as you just copied from your old web.config. This copies your database configuration to the new configuration file. Listing 2-6 shows the `<connectionStrings>` section.

Listing 2-6: <connectionStrings> Section

```
<connectionStrings>
<add
 name="SiteSqlServer"
    connectionString="??????"
    providerName="System.Data.SqlClient" />
</connectionStrings>
```

5. Set the values of the machineKey element to the values that used to be in the appSettings node, as shown in Listing 2-7.

Listing 2-7: Password Hash Keys

```
<machineKey
        validationKey="F9D1A2D3E1D3E2F7B3D9F90FF3965ABDAC304902"
        decryptionKey="F9D1A2D3E1D3E2F7B3D9F90FF3965ABDAC304902F8D923AC"
        decryption="3DES"
        validation="SHA1"/>
```

6. Make any other changes to web.config that you made to support additional providers, and so on.

5. **Perform the upgrade.** First, verify that you have done the following:

❑ Backed up your entire site and database (or at least your web.config file).

❑ Obtained the most suitable package from www.dotnetnuke.com.

❑ Installed the latest Starter Kit or unzipped the install package over the top of your existing installation.

❑ Renamed your web.config file (for example, to **web.config.resources**).

❑ Renamed release.config to **web.config**.

❑ Copied the password hash keys (and any other setting you customized) from your old web.config file to your new web.config file.

When you have completed all of those steps, open your web browser and navigate to http://localhost/dotnetnuke/ for a local upgrade or http://www.mydomain.com/ for a remote upgrade. Alternatively, if you are using the Starter Kit, you will need to run your site by pressing Shift + F5.

When you browse to your site, you get a report similar to the one shown in the v3.x upgrade section earlier in this chapter.

Installation Issues

The DotNetNuke Core Team has provided screens to assist in diagnosing problems associated with the installer. This section describes a couple of the more common error messages. If you cannot resolve your particular issue with this information, try the online support forums at www.dotnetnuke.com.

- ❑ **Invalid Connection String**. If you get the error message "Invalid Connection String," your connection string is invalid in the web.config file. Confirm that the connection string is correct, the database has been created, and the user has access to the database.

- ❑ **Insufficient File Permissions**. An "Insufficient File Permissions" error could mean that you have not granted the correct access to the root of the folder, or that you specified a different account than the account currently running the ASP.NET request. See the "Set File Permissions" section earlier in the installation section for more information. Figure 2-23 shows the error page DotNetNuke displays if it doesn't have the correct file permissions set.

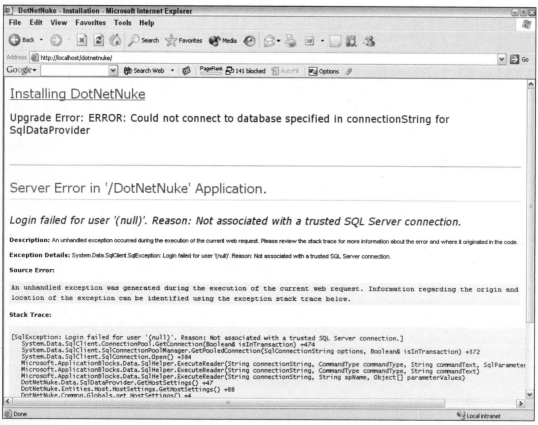

Figure 2-23

For the most current information about the installation process, refer to the "DotNetNuke Installation Guide" in the DotNetNuke documentation.

Summary

Installation for DotNetNuke comes in a variety of packages. Each package is targeted at a particular version of DotNetNuke (either v3.x or v4.x) and comes in a variety of flavors, as follows:

❑ **Install package:** Contains only the files necessary to run your portal. This package is recommended for non-developers.

❑ **Source package:** Contains all of the source code for DotNetNuke, allowing developers to modify and recompile their application.

❑ **Starter Kit:** Provides an additional project type for developers using Visual Web Developer Express or Visual Studio 2005. It enables them to easily create new DotNetNuke applications at the click of a button (v4.x only).

This chapter guided you through all of the necessary installation steps, including running an automated installer that provides guidance through the installation process.

3

Portal Overview

DotNetNuke is capable of serving many sites from a single installation. The term *portal* is often used to describe each site, although the term is somewhat narrow in its definition. So you might ask, what is a portal? The American Heritage Dictionary defines a web application portal as "a web site considered as an entry point to other web sites, often by being or providing access to a search engine." This can be true of DotNetNuke portals, but they really are more than just doorways to other applications or search engines — they also perform a host of other functions associated with displaying information to your users.

In DotNetNuke, a portal is one site, of *n* possible sites, in a single instance of DNN, with data and functionality completely discreet from other portals in the same instance. For the purposes of this discussion, a portal can be defined as the related data for one web site hosted within your DotNetNuke installation. The application natively provides the capability to host multiple web sites from the same code base, each containing different information and presented to the user at runtime based on the URL the user enters to access the code base. Exactly how the application accomplishes this task is covered later in the book.

As the portal administrator, you may set up hundreds of various web sites on the same portal. These can be a combination of parent and child portals (discussed later in this chapter), and at runtime the application will determine the proper content to display to the user based on the PortalID of the portal accessed. This is one of the most powerful features of DotNetNuke and has contributed to the rapid growth of the application since its inception.

Portal Organizational Elements

There are four main organizational elements for portals: parent/child portals, pages, panes, and containers. You'll examine all of them in the following sections.

Parent/Child Portals

A child portal has its own discreet membership, modules, and so on — essentially its own portal entirely — within the same domain as a parent. DotNetNuke creates a physical directory and file that enable IIS to recognize the portal's existence. Child portals make sense within a single domain, leveraged to intranets, SSO, and so forth.

A parent portal has no subdirectory, although it can remain within a domain by using cnames (sales.Domain.com, for example).

Let's look at the differences in the format of the URL between the two types of portals. A parent portal's URL takes the format of `http://www.YourDomain.com`, whereas a child portal takes the format of `http://www.YourDomain.com/YourChildPortal`. The application installation may contain any combination of parent or child portals. The only real difference between how you set up the various types of portals is how you define the portal. Figure 3-1 shows the options available in the Portal Setup module.

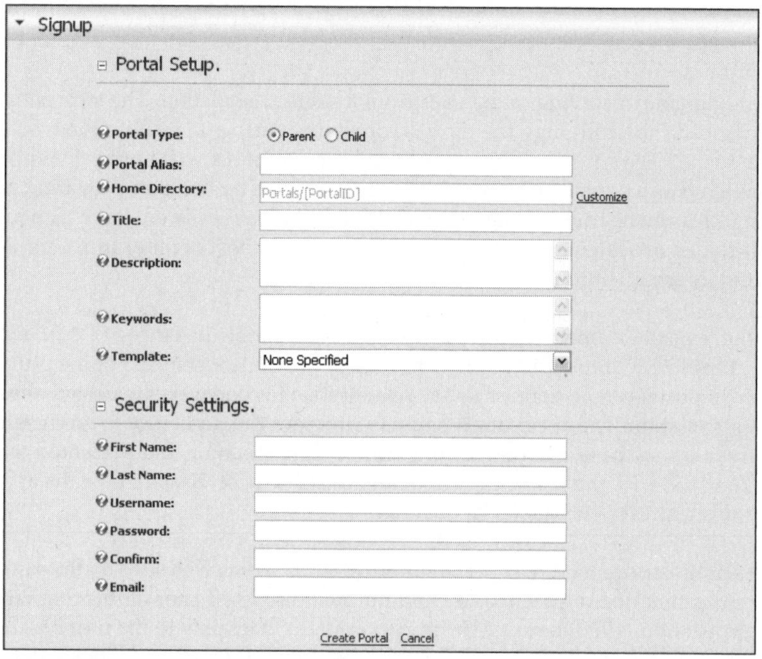

Figure 3-1

The module gives you several options when setting up a new portal. Notice the radio buttons for selecting a parent or child portal. Selecting the child portal requires no further configuration outside of the application. To set up a parent portal, you must perform some additional steps. You first need to set up an additional web site in your IIS Manager with host headers for your domain name, and then create a DNS record to point to the IP address of your web server. Information on how to perform these tasks is outside of the scope of this book, so please refer to your IIS and DNS help files for the steps. You can find specific details on how to use each of the functions for setting up a new portal in Chapter 5, which covers the host functions of DotNetNuke.

Pages

Pages are a relatively new term in DotNetNuke. Prior to version 3.x, these were called tabs. This change was made to allow for a more user-friendly experience for the novice who may not be a programmer by trade. You can think of a page in the same way you think of a static HTML page. The difference is that the application loads the content based on the parameters passed to it at runtime.

A page can also be only a navigational component. For example, when you specify the Link type in a Pages advanced setting, the Page element becomes either a link to an external element or simply a pointer to a real page within the site.

In reality, there is only one primary page in the application that displays all the content to your users. Exactly how this works is explained in detail in Chapters 7 and 8. Figure 3-2 shows the options for administering your portal pages.

Figure 3-2

On the left is a Page Functions menu. The buttons in this menu provide quick access to often-used page-management functions. They're described in Table 3-1.

Table 3-1: Page Functions

Function	Description
Add	Enables you to add a new page to the portal. After clicking this button, you are presented with the Page Management control, where you can define properties such as the page's name, title, keywords, permissions, and so on.
Settings	Enables you to modify an existing page.
Delete	Enables you to remove the current page from your portal.
Copy	By default, enables you to copy the modules located on the current page. You also have the option of duplicating the content in the modules of the current page, which can be a real time-saver when setting up your portal.
Preview	Enables you to view your page in the same manner your users will view it. This helps you ensure that your users see your content as you intended. This function also produces more questions than any other function for novices with DotNetNuke. If you are administering your portal and suddenly notice you can no longer edit the individual items of your modules, make sure that this Preview mode is turned off because it is likely your problem.

Clearly the name adequately describes each button's function. DotNetNuke attempts to follow this same structure throughout the application. Figure 3-3 illustrates the options available in the Page Management page, which you use to add new pages to your portal.

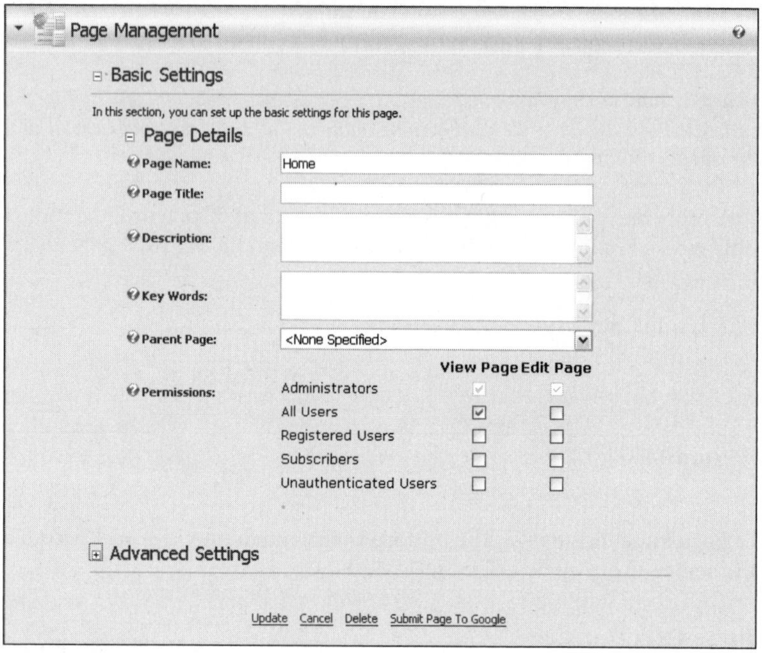

Figure 3-3

As you will see in later chapters, DotNetNuke uses an object-oriented approach in all functions, where feasible. You will see many of the same options available throughout the administration screens. The application uses the same user controls in numerous areas, which accomplishes two main functions: it allows a consistent look and feel to the application, and it simplifies the amount of code required to perform these functions.

Notice the question mark images in Figure 3-3. These images expand when you click them, offering some additional descriptions on the type of information the field expects. This reduces the learning curve associated with managing the portal content.

Panes

Panes are the areas of your skin that hold the various content modules you drop on each page. These enable you to organize your content in a manner that makes the best use of your site's real estate. The number and placement of panes is a function of your skin design. For a full discussion on creating skins, see Chapter 16. Panes are populated dynamically at runtime with the modules assigned to them. The types of modules you can use to display your content are discussed in the "Modules" section later in this chapter.

If DNN cannot find a pane—that is, a pane name that matches—it puts the modules in the ContentPane. If a skin is significantly different, the layout changes, but all the functionality is preserved (nothing breaks).

DotNetNuke ships with several prebuilt skins to help you get started launching your new site.

Containers

Containers enable you to enhance the look of your portal without any design changes to your skin. A container's purpose is to surround the content of a module with some design element, which allows you to bring more attention to the content of the module. You have two options for applying containers to your portal: You can apply a default container to your entire portal and, if desired, set a container for each module. Go ahead and add a module to a page and set up a container for a visual reference.

Now, modify the container of the Links module to change the look of the default page. First, select Settings from the module actions menu, as shown in Figure 3-4.

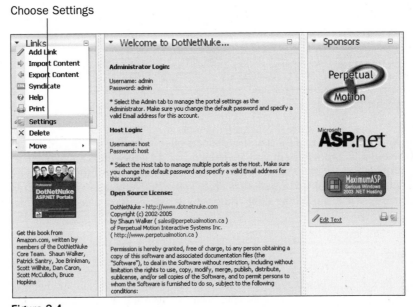

Figure 3-4

Selecting the Settings tab navigates you to the Module Settings page for the Links module. Notice that the Module Settings page contains many of the same options as the Portal Settings page. (This is an example of maintaining a consistent interface throughout the application through the use of the object-oriented programming used in DotNetNuke.) Scroll down to the Page Settings ⇨ Basic Settings Panel in the Module Settings control. (You may need to expand the panels by clicking the + sign for each panel and selecting a new container for this module.) Currently, this module is using one of the default containers that ship with the application. Select the DNN ⇨ Blue ⇨ Text Header ⇨ White Background container and update your module. You are then taken back to your original page and will immediately see the difference this one change makes. Update all the modules on this page so that you can really see the difference. Although it's much more exciting in color, the black-and-white illustration in Figure 3-5 shows how the entire look of this page changes with only a few mouse clicks.

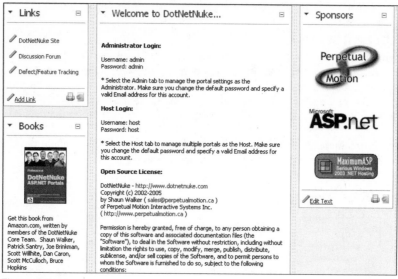

Figure 3-5

You can see by this example that the use of containers offers a lot of flexibility in "framing" the content of your site. Normally, you will want your containers to match the colors and design of your site, and most skins provide these complements as part of the package. Many commercial and free versions of skins are available for download or purchase. Refer to the DotNetNuke web site for links to a wide variety of skins and containers. Creating skins and containers is covered extensively in Chapter 16.

Modules

Modules are the meat and potatoes of a DotNetNuke site. They are the components that display relative, easy-to-update content to your visitors. Chapter 6 covers the applications of these modules and how to use them to add your content. Hundreds of free and commercial modules are available to extend the application functionality; simply perform a web search for "DotNetNuke modules" in your favorite search engine and you'll find a module to meet almost any need you may have for managing content.

This section provides an overview of many modules and prepares you for the detailed information in Chapter 6, which shows you how easy it is to use the modules to present content to site visitors. Beginning with version 3 of DotNetNuke, all the content modules were divided into separate projects, allowing you to pick and choose the modules you need for your specific installation. So, if your business requirement does not need an RSS module, for example, you can remove it from your installation without any adverse effects or any modifications of the core code. This is an important enhancement from a business perspective because it allows you to easily modify DotNetNuke to accommodate your unique business rules and needs, without programming or technical intervention.

It also should be mentioned that each of the modules is now been totally separated from the core framework and has its own release cycle. This allows for some interesting enhancements to the functionality of the modules over the coming year.

Table 3-2 describes a number of DotNetNuke modules that are installed by default.

Table 3-2: Default Modules

Module	Description
Account Login	Provides the login interface as a module. In can be useful in two scenarios: when you want the login dialog to appear on the home page (without the user clicking the login link), and when you want to use it on a login page, which could contain additional modules. You can specify any page within your portal as the login page via the administration screens at Admin ⇨ Site Settings ⇨ Advanced Setting ⇨ Page Management.
Announcements	Used to present a list of announcements. Each announcement includes a title, text, and a "read more" link. Optionally, the announcement can be set to expire after a specified date.
Banners	One of DotNetNuke's rich set of vendor management tools. It's used to display the advertising banners of vendors created within the portal (or as defined by the Host). Management of these vendors and creation of banners is performed in the administration area located at Admin ⇨ Vendors (or Host ⇨ Vendors). The module itself provides facilities to select the number of banners to display and the banner type, and tracks both their impressions and clicks.
Contacts	Renders contact information for a group of people, such as a project team, a sports team, or personnel within your department. It provides an edit page, which enables authorized users to edit and add contacts.
Discussions	A threaded discussion board. It provides groups of messages threaded on a single topic. Each message includes a Read/Reply Message page, enabling authorized users to reply to existing messages or add a new message thread. Although this is not a full-fledged forum module, it offers some functionality that you can use to enable light forum activities on your site. With the addition of the form module subproject, this module is likely to be discontinued in later releases because the Forum module offers the same functionality, but also adds many features not available with this module.
Documents	Renders a list of documents, including links to browse or download the document. It includes an edit page, which enables authorized users to edit or add the information about a document (for example, a friendly title).
Events	Renders a list of upcoming events, including time and location. Individual events can be set to automatically expire from the list after a particular date. The module includes an edit page, which enables authorized users to edit or add an event.

Table continued on following page

Module	Description
FAQs	Allows an authorized user to manage a list of frequently asked questions and their answers. This is a great module for reducing support calls to your customer service center because you can compile a list of the questions you receive about your business or services and present that data to your users.
Feedback	Enables visitors to send messages to the administrator of the portal. You have the ability to customize this module to send e-mails to various individuals within your organization, depending on the message content. This is one more example of how DotNetNuke enables you to assign different tasks to the correct individuals in your organization.
IFrame	A browser feature that enables you to display content from another web site within a frame on your site. Note that it is not supported consistently by all browsers. Internet Explorer displays this module very well, and it's also supported in Firefox, but other browsers have historically had problems displaying inline frames consistently.
Image	Renders an image using an HTML IMG tag. It includes an edit page that allows an authorized user to specify the location of the image that can reside internal or external to the portal. An authorized user can also specify height and width attributes, which permits the scaling of an image.
	The Image module is changing to the Media module (perhaps by the time this book is released), supporting a variety of still image formats as well as rich media including audio and video.
Links	Renders a list of hyperlinks. It includes an edit page, which allows authorized users to edit and add new links. Each link can be customized to launch new windows or capture information such as how many times that link has been clicked.
News Feeds (RSS)	Enables you to consume syndicated news feeds in Rich Site Summary (RSS) format. It includes an edit page that enables you to specify the location of the news feed and the style sheet (XSL) used to transform the news feed.
Search Input	Provides the capability to submit a search to a given Search Results module.
Search Results	Provides the capability to display search results.
Text/HTML	Renders a snippet of HTML or text. It includes an edit page, which enables authorized users to edit the HTML or text snippets directly (using the configured rich text editor).
User Account	Enables users to register and manage their accounts.
User Defined Table	Enables you to create a custom data table for managing tabular information.
XML/XSL	Renders the result of an XML/XSL transform. It includes an edit page that allows authorized users to specify a location for the XML document and the XSL style sheet used for transformation.

Remember, this is not a definitive list of the modules available within DotNetNuke. You have the option of installing modules provided by third parties or to even author your own. For complete instructions on how to use each of these modules, refer to Chapter 6. Chapters 9 through 12 cover the aspects associated with authoring your own modules to solve a unique business need for your organization.

DotNetNuke also provides some additional modules that are available in the download but not installed by default in the application. They include the following:

- ❑ **Users Online:** Enables you to display information about the current number of visitors accessing your portal at any given time.
- ❑ **Survey:** Enables you to conduct online surveys with your portal.
- ❑ **Forums:** Enables you to host a community forum for your visitors.
- ❑ **Blogs:** Enables you to host a web log on your site.

At the time of this writing, several other modules are under development that will enhance the usability of the application even further. In addition, many of the preceding modules are going through a major transition to enhance their current functionality.

User Roles

DotNetNuke offers a fairly robust method for dealing with permissions and controlling the tasks a particular user is allowed to perform. It does this with a roles-based security module, where every page and module in the application is assigned roles that determine what the user is allowed to do within the context of the application. You have the option of setting permissions at several levels within the portal. A user may be allowed access to edit certain modules or be given access to edit the entire page, as you deem necessary. These functions also apply to viewing a module's content or a specific page. Basically, all you need to do is create the necessary security roles and assign the permissions you want that role to perform to the module or page. After you have the roles and permissions defined, you can then place your users in the appropriate role, which will allow or restrict their access based on those permissions. This allows very granular control over the actions of users in your portal. At the time of this writing, versions 4.0 and 3.2 also included functionality that allows the use of an Active Directory user base within your portal. Chapter 4 has more information.

Summary

This chapter introduced basic DotNetNuke concepts and application functionality. The chapters that follow dive deeper into these items and describe how to implement each DotNetNuke function in your unique installation. As you can see from this chapter, the application offers a lot of functionality from a base installation and will allow you to quickly move your web site from conception to production. The next chapter looks at the host functions required to set up the application to host your various child and parent portals.

4

Portal Administration

Chapter 3 introduced basic concepts that define a portal in DotNetNuke. This chapter details the rich features and functions available to customize the look, feel, and function of your DotNetNuke portal and how to maintain it throughout its life.

To make this information more practical, examples in this chapter illustrate a real-world scenario of building a site for a pee-wee soccer team named the Gators. Where applicable, you'll not only learn how to accomplish tasks, but also when and why to do them. As the administrator of a DotNetNuke portal, you hold the keys to a powerful resource and you'll want to know how to manage it well.

In Chapter 3, you learned about the concept of hosting multiple portals on a single installation of DotNetNuke. This chapter assumes no knowledge of any portal in the installation other than the one you are currently administering. As far as the Portal Administrator is concerned, his portal exists alone in its own corner of cyberspace separate from any other.

Who Is the Portal Administrator?

When the Host creates your portal, a new user is created as well (see Chapter 5). This user is automatically associated with the portal in the Administrator security role and so becomes the default Portal Administrator. The features discussed in this chapter are available to users who belong to the Administrator security role (and SuperUsers such as the Host).

There is only one Portal Administrator — you! However, you have the authority to delegate privilege to other users to perform administrative tasks. Later in this chapter, you learn how to give Administrator access to another user. But regardless of how many users have administrative privileges, it is the user information of the one Portal Administrator that is used by DotNetNuke. For example, it is the Portal Administrator's e-mail address that appears as the "from" address for all e-mail sent by the portal and as the default to address for the Feedback module.

Ideally, a Host does not associate the Portal Administrator user with an individual, but rather with an account. In this way, the user information can be maintained separately and changed for the specific purpose of managing the portal (like specifying an appropriate e-mail address). The Portal Administrator account can be used to create additional users with administrative privileges that are associated with real people.

Where Do I Begin?

Begin at the beginning and go on until you come to the end; then stop. This little piece of advice is as wise today as it was when the King of Hearts delivered it to the White Rabbit. So with that cue from Lewis Carroll, let's start at the beginning — logging in. Follow these steps:

1. Navigate to your web site. This example is located at `http://soccer.dotnetnuke.com`, although your location will differ.

2. Click the Login link in the upper right corner of the page.

3. Log in to your portal using the Portal Administrator User Name and Password assigned by the Host account. Enter your User Name and Password and click Login (see Figure 4-1).

> If you are working with the default portal (the one created on first installation of DotNetNuke), the default Administrator User Name and Password are admin and admin, respectively. Likewise, the default Host values are host and host. It is highly recommended that you change these default values as soon as possible after installation to prevent unwanted access to your site.

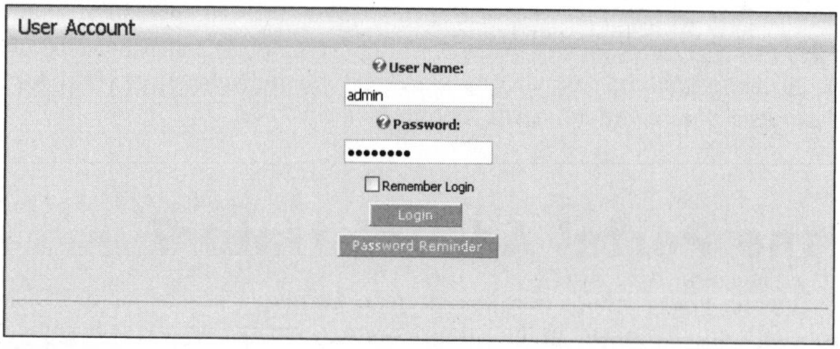

Figure 4-1

If you enter your User Name and Password correctly, the first thing you notice upon logging in is that the screen looks a little bit different than it did before (see Figure 4-2).

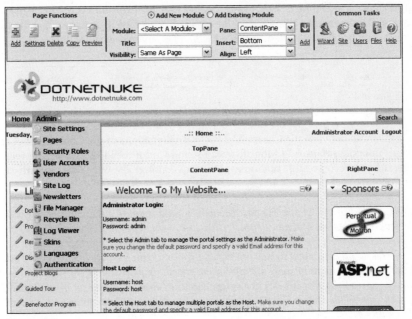

Figure 4-2

Three main differences are immediately obvious:

❑   The addition of the Control Panel, which spans the top of the browser window

❑   The layout of the skin panes

❑   The addition of the Admin menu

You learn more about panes and skinning in Chapter 16. For now you'll focus on the Control Panel.

The Control Panel

The Control Panel is primarily a palette of shortcuts for frequently used tasks, most of which are accessible from other pages through the Admin menu. In DotNetNuke version 3.0 and later, the Control Panel, an ICONBAR, is divided into three main sections: Page Functions, Add New Module and Add Existing Module, and Common Tasks (see Figure 4-3).

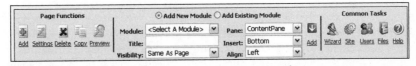

Figure 4-3

In DotNetNuke version 2.1, the Classic Control Panel had far fewer functions and a much thinner profile (see Figure 4-4). That version of the Control Panel is still an option in version 4.0 at the discretion of the Host. It's discussed briefly before the enhanced version is covered in more detail.

Figure 4-4

The main differences between the Classic and ICONBAR versions of the Control Panel are the addition of extra Page Functions, extra Add Module options, and Common Tasks. These differences are pretty straightforward and become more obvious as you move along. The only other difference is the deprecation of the Content check box.

> *In version 2.1, ill behavior of a poorly written module could result in a rather nasty error message that would keep a module from being displayed. In that case, it was virtually impossible for a Portal Administrator to remove the offending module. The Content check box provided a way to instruct modules not to display their content, which preempted the nasty error message and gave the Portal Administrator access to the modules settings where it could be deleted from the page. This condition rarely exists in versions after 2.1, so the Content check box does not appear on the ICONBAR version of the Control Panel. However, in the event that a seriously flawed module causes such behavior, the Classic Control Panel can be reinstated to leverage this functionality.*

The only functions on the Control Panel that can't be accessed through other navigation are the Site Wizard, Help, and Preview.

The Site Wizard

A slick addition to version 3.0 and later versions is the Site Wizard, which is the quickest way to make the most common customizations for those new to managing their own DotNetNuke web site. It walks you through a short conversational process, step by step, with extensive help and the ability to cancel at any time without saving the changes. Standard navigational controls appear on each page of the wizard for Back, Next, Finish, Cancel (without saving changes), and Help.

Clicking the Wizard button in the Control Panel takes you to step 1.

Step 1: Choose a Template for Your Site

The optional first step (see Figure 4-5) gives you the choice of applying a template to your portal. The purpose of a template is to add predefined functionality and content (pages, modules, and so on) to your site. For example, a Host might provide a variety of commonly used templates to jumpstart your club web site, family web site, small business web site, and so on.

> **For advanced users and developers, templates provide a powerful mechanism for sharing predefined portal functionality. Templates can carry rich information including portal settings, security roles, pages, modules, permissions, and so on. Template creation is a function available to Host Administrators (see Chapter 5).**

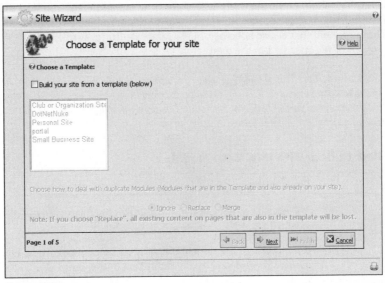

Figure 4-5

Clicking the check box for Build Your Site From A Template (Below) enables the list of available templates (see Figure 4-6). Select a template from the list by clicking it. If you do not want to apply a template to your site, simply leave the check box empty.

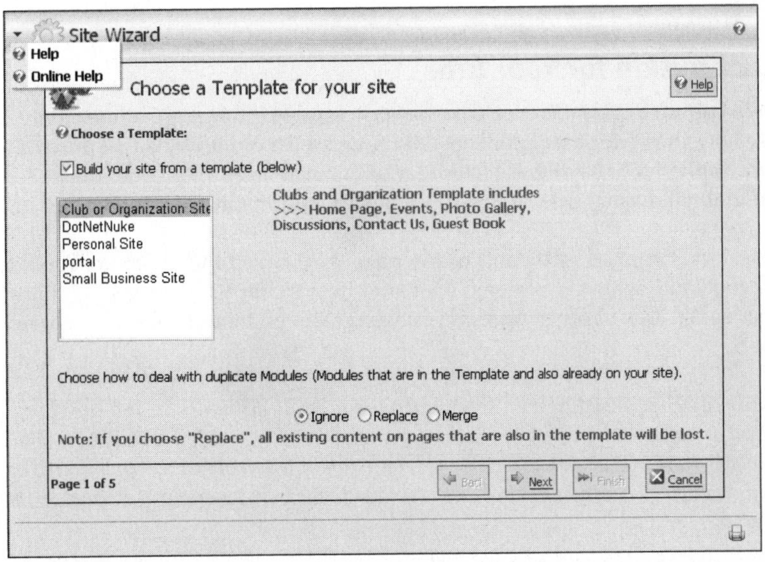

Figure 4-6

Radio buttons at the bottom of the page tell the wizard how to handle any conflicts that might be come up during the application of a template. A conflict is encountered when an existing component in your site matches a component that is also specified in the template (for example, when a module's title matches that of a module specified in the template). Table 4-1 summarizes the effects of each choice.

> *Site templates are additive. This means that when you apply a template, it incorporates those elements specified in the template into your existing web site. A template does not remove existing pages, modules, or content except as part of resolving a conflict. This is a mechanism developed to help prevent important content from being overwritten in your portal.*

Table 4-1: How to Deal with Duplicate Modules

Option	Description
Ignore	If a module of the same name and type as the one in the template already exists, the template definition is ignored.
Replace	If a module of the same name and type as the one in the template already exists, it is replaced by the definition in the template.
Merge	If a module of the same name and type as the one in the template already exists, the content is appended to the existing module content.

Select the option that best suits your needs. If you are beginning with a new (or empty) portal, the Replace option is most appropriate. Remember, you can click the Help button at any time for assistance.

Click Next to move on to step 2.

Step 2: Select a Skin for Your Site

Step 2 is where the fun begins. DotNetNuke has powerful skinning capabilities that enable administrators to choose how their site should look. Scroll though a list of the skins that are available and select the look you want applied to your site. If the author of the skin has provided an image for preview, it is displayed in a thumbnail format (see Figure 4-7). Click the thumbnail to view a larger image.

The skin you select is applied by default to any page that you add to your site. You'll be able to override that choice if you want, which is explored a bit later in this chapter. For now, just know that you'll be able to customize the look of other pages if you want to, even though you have chosen a default for all new pages here.

> *DotNetNuke comes preinstalled with several variations on its default skin. You can choose a version with vertical or horizontal menus, which display in fixed width or variable (browser) width and in any of five available colors (Blue, Gray, Green, Red, or Yellow). If your Host has enabled the option for your portal, you can upload additional skins that you can obtain from a variety of sources or that you can create yourself.*

When you have selected the default skin for your site, click Next.

> *Chapter 16 includes detailed information on how to create and package your own skins.*

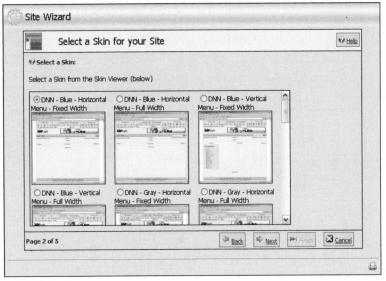

Figure 4-7

Step 3: Choose a Default Container for Your Site

In step 3, you choose a default container (see Figure 4-8). That container is automatically applied to every new module that you add to your pages. Just like with your default skin, you'll be able to override that choice if you need to display the module in another container. A good rule of thumb is to choose a container that you will use for the majority of the modules on your site and then set the individual exceptions as explained in Chapter 3. This also helps with the workload if you later decide to change the look of your site with a new skin because you won't have as many containers to update for your new design.

The container choices displayed in the wizard represent those that have been specifically packaged for the skin you chose in the previous step. Because a DNN - Blue skin was chosen for this example, the container choices are DNN - Blue also. However, clicking the Show All Containers check box at the top of the page displays all available containers for every skin that is available to you, so if you want to apply a yellow container as the default with the blue skin, you are free to do so.

DotNetNuke comes preinstalled with several variations on its default containers for each skin. You can choose a version with complementary background shading or white shading for the content area and image or text headers. Image headers provide a gradient fill image as the background for the module title, whereas text headers leave the background alone, matching the content area shading.

After you select the default container for your site, click Next. (At this point the wizard has enough information to display your site if you want to stop, so you could click Finish. However, for the purpose of this chapter, go on to the next step of the wizard.)

You can find detailed information on how to create and package your own containers in Chapter 16.

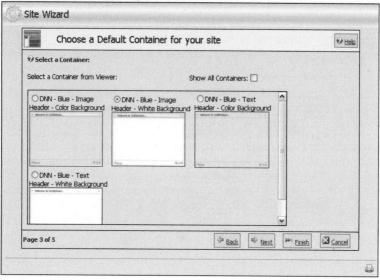

Figure 4-8

Step 4: Add Site Details

Every page in your site has a few simple attributes that help to identify it to web browsers and other services on the Internet, such as search engines. The Add Site Details page (see Figure 4-9) enables you to provide the necessary information.

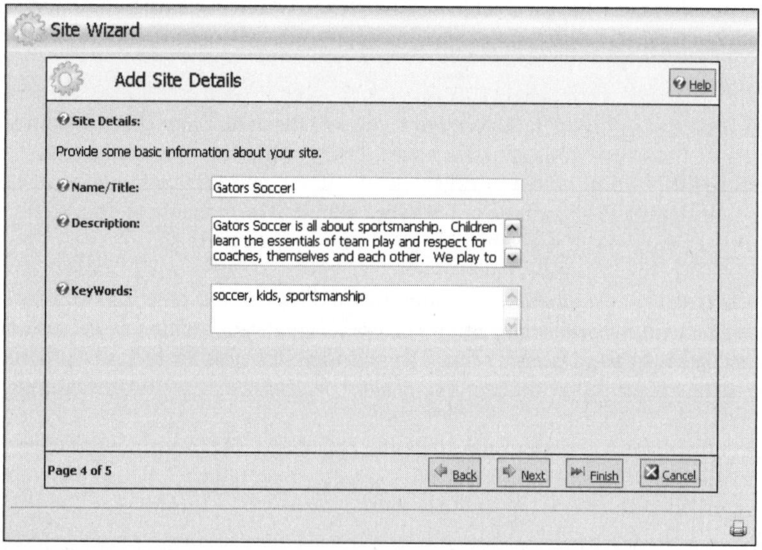

Figure 4-9

Table 4-2 lists each field and describes how its value affects your portal.

Table 4-2: Site Details

Field	Description
Name/Title	Used in several places in the portal operation. Most notably, it's displayed in the title bar of the user's browser window. It is also used to refer to your portal in outgoing mail for user registration, password reminders, and so on.
Description	The default value to populate the HTML META tag for DESCRIPTION in each page of your site. This tag is important because it provides search engines such as Google, Yahoo, and MSN with an informative description of your site (or page). The value can be set for each page individually; however, if it is omitted, this default description is used.
KeyWords	Keywords are also used as a default value to populate the HTML META tag for KEYWORDS in each page of your site. This tag can be useful to help improve search engine placement. Keywords and/or phrases are separated by commas. The value can be set for each page individually; however, if it is omitted these default keywords will be used.

When you have finished adding details for your site, click Next. (At this point, so you could click Finish. However, for the purpose of this chapter, go on to the next step of the wizard.)

Step 5: Choose a Logo

Step 5 is also optional. It invites you to select or upload an image for your logo (see Figure 4-10). For the default skins provided with DotNetNuke, the logo will appear in the upper left corner of the browser window. For this example, leave the logo unspecified.

Custom skins may place your logo in another location or ignore it altogether (that's a skin designer's choice). You'll want to make sure your logo design matches any new skin that you choose.

The File Location and File Name drop-down lists provide a simple way to locate the available files in your portal's root directory. Changing the File Location changes the list of files available (only web-friendly image files are listed). If your logo file is on your local computer and not your site, you can choose to upload it by clicking the Upload New File button. The page refreshes to reveal a standard upload control (see Figure 4-11). You still specify the File Location so the control will know in which sub-directory to store the image file. Click Save Uploaded File to get the file from your local computer to your portal, or click Select An Existing File to return to the previous selector.

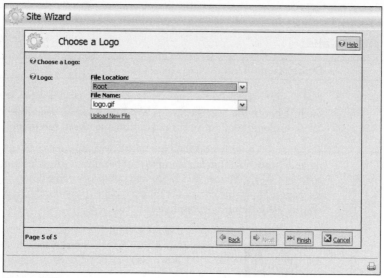

Figure 4-10

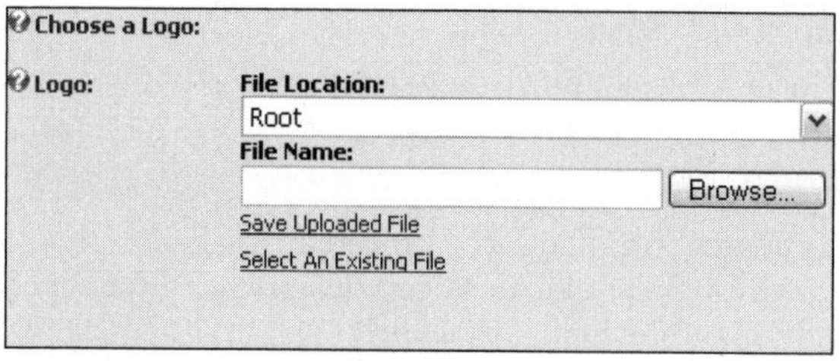

Figure 4-11

After you select the logo for your site, click Finish.

Now that you have completed the Site Wizard, take a look at your newly configured web site by navigating to any page (try clicking the Home menu item). Because you applied the Club or Organization Site template in step 1, the site now has some additional pages and example content instead of the empty web site that you began with. You can see the sample Gallery page in preview mode in Figure 4-12.

Figure 4-12

The Help Button

The Help button is a link that is configured by your Host (see Chapter 5). In the default installation, the link is configured to open the default help page at dotnetnuke.com. Your Host may opt to direct this link to another site that contains help that is more personalized or relevant to your specific hosting plan.

DotNetNuke has plenty of built-in help for its administrative functions. But the Help button gives Hosts some capability to create help completely customized for their (and your) purposes and put it right at your fingertips. For example, a Host-provided help site might have specific information related to customized templates available through the Site Wizard.

The Preview Button

The Administrator's view of the site differs from a regular user's view because of the need to see skin panes, edit icons, module actions, and so on. But sometimes you just need to know how things are going to look to a non-administrative user — that's what the Preview button on the Control Panel is for.

When you click the Preview button, you will notice two things. First, your view of the portal (below the Control Panel) changes: the pane definitions and the edit options vanish. Second, the Preview button icon changes (a plus becomes visible under the magnifying glass) to indicate that you are in Preview mode.

It can be easy to forget that you are in Preview mode, so make sure you toggle this setting back off when you no longer need it.

Configuring Your Portal

Now that your site has basic navigation, sample content, and a chosen look, you want to begin configuring other features to make your site special. The Portal Administrator has access to a wealth of configuration options to customize the look, content, and behavior of the site. This section discusses many of the set-it-and-forget-it types of configuration options. These are things that, for the most part, you want to include in your initial planning, set, and then leave alone until your next improvement project. This section also exposes you to a few tools that serve a purpose in both configuration and maintenance of your site (which is covered later in this chapter).

Site Settings

You can reach your site settings by clicking the Settings button in the Common Tasks area of the toolbar or by selecting Admin ➪ Site Settings. The Site Settings page contains expandable and collapsible categories of configuration options.

There are two important text buttons at the bottom of the page. Because a number of controls on the Site Settings page generate postbacks, you might occasionally be tempted to think that your changes have been saved—but no changes are saved until you click the Update button. The Submit Site To Google button formats and submits a request for Google to add your site to its search index.

> Search engine ranking is based on a number of factors. To improve your site's ranking, add appropriate Title, Description, and Keyword text to each page before submitting your site to Google or any other search engine.

In working with the Site Wizard, you already learned about all of the Details options available under Basic Settings, so those settings are skipped here and you can move on to the rest.

Basic Settings: Appearance

The Appearance settings control the configuration choices that affect the appearance of your site to visitors. Several of these settings involve the use of a selector similar to the one shown in Figure 4-13.

Figure 4-13

This selector uses a radio button to specify the source for populating the associated drop-down list box. The Host may provide skins or containers to all Portal Administrators and/or additional selections available only to your site (see Table 4-3). If the Host has enabled the Portal Administrator to upload skins, you'll be able to add your own and they will be available under the Sites option.

Table 4-3: Appearance Settings

Setting	Description
Logo	See the previous section on the Setup Wizard.
Body Background	This value is used in the HTML body tag of every page to render a tiled background image. If the selected skin hides background images, this setting may appear to have no effect. Leave this field clear if you don't intend to use a background image because it adds unnecessary weight to the rendered page.
Portal Skin	Specifies the skin for all non-administrator (and non-host) pages within the site. The skin is applied to all pages in the site where another skin has not been specifically chosen on those pages' individual settings. It also applies by default to all new pages.
Portal Container	Specifies the standard module container for all non-administrator (and non-host) pages within the site.
	The same rules of application and inheritance pertain to containers as well as skins. This choice applies to all modules in the site where another container has not been specifically chosen on those modules' individual settings. It also applies by default to all new modules.
Admin Skin	The look seen on Admin (and Host) menu pages within the site. Typically your choice of Admin Skin should be lightweight to reduce excessive image transfer and emphasize productivity over pizzazz.
	Some key pages are "system pages" implemented (under the covers) as Admin functions and retain the Admin skin, which complicates some aspects of site design. However, in the current version these pages (most notably the default Login, Registration, and Membership pages) are displayed using the same skin as the page that invoked them. You learn more about customizing the appearance of these pages later in this chapter.
Admin Container	Same as the Portal Container but affects only the Admin (and Host) pages.

If the Host has enabled Skin Upload Permissions for Portals, two additional text buttons appear at the bottom of the Basic Settings category: Upload Skin and Upload Container. These functions are covered in detail in Chapter 16.

The Preview link provides a convenient way to see what a skin or container will look like after you apply it to your portal. Clicking Preview launches another browser window, which opens to the front page of the site using the option selected. Close the window when you are finished previewing the skin.

Advanced Settings: Security Settings

Portal Registration drives fundamental behavior of your site that should be part of your initial design. Through registration, anonymous site visitors can join (or apply to join) the Registered Users role and be granted access to privileged content or site functionality. Because the Registered Users role requires registration and authorization (either explicit or automatic), these functions combine to provide for different options in the registration process (see Figure 4-14).

Figure 4-14

Choose your registration type based on the functional access requirements for visitors to your site. Table 4-4 summarizes the choices and how they impact site behavior.

Table 4-4: Security — Portal Registration Options

Option	Description
None	Registration is not an available option to site visitors. The Login button remains visible so that administrative access can be gained; however, the Registration button is hidden. Sites that select this option often change their skin to move the Login button to a less prominent location than where it normally appears on the default skin. This setting is appropriate for sites that do not publish privileged content or that process registration offline.
Private	Registrants apply for privileged access to the site. Until authorization is explicitly granted, access is limited to that of any anonymous user. This setting is appropriate for sites that require approval of registration requests (for example, a private family web site that invites friends and relatives to apply). An e-mail is sent to the registrant advising him or her of the private nature of the site. An additional e-mail is sent upon authorization (if and when it is performed).
	It is good practice to explain the process for approval of private registration prominently on your site.
Public	Registration is automatically (and immediately) authorized without validation of the e-mail address. A welcome e-mail is sent to the registrant. This setting is appropriate for sites that want to track usage but do not require validation of contact information.
Verified	Registration generates a verification code, which is included in the welcome e-mail sent to the address supplied by the registrant. Authorization is granted when the user supplies the verification code at the time of their first login. This process ensures that all registered users have supplied a valid e-mail address.

You can customize the content of the e-mails generated through the registration process by editing the appropriate language resources. You learn explicitly how to do this later in this chapter.

Remember that site registration is only the first step available for managing access to privileged content. After the site is registered, you can manage a user's access to pages and modules at a granular level through the application of security roles.

Advanced Settings: Page Management

Earlier you learned that the portal owns some standard pages. The Page Management settings give you the ability to customize those pages and a few other aspects of your site's general navigation (see Figure 4-15).

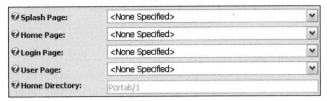

Figure 4-15

Each of the options consists of a drop-down list box for selecting a custom page within your portal. The <None Specified> selection for any of these configuration options results in default behavior. Table 4-5 explains the behavioral impact of each setting.

Table 4-5: Page Management Settings

Setting	Description
Splash Page	When a visitor reaches your site via its alias (for example, http://www .dotnetnuke.com), the default behavior is to display the Home page. If a Splash page is specified, it is what is displayed to the visitor instead. This affects only the initial landing page for site navigation or invalid links and does not change the location of Home for other purposes.
	It is left to you to determine the appropriate method and timing of redirection to the Home page. A typical implementation would be to specify a page that is defined as a link to a Flash introduction (which redirects when finished). Alternatively, a more traditional approach can be taken by utilizing a page setting (discussed later in this chapter) to add a META REFRESH directive to the HEAD area of a Splash page to redirect to Home after a specified interval.
Home Page	The default target for site navigation (in the absence of a Splash page). It is also used as the destination link for the site logo as well as any other default site behavior that results in redirection to the Home page (such as logging out). If no Home page is specified, the first page in the navigation order is used.
Login Page	The default Login page is provided for your convenience; however, as a system page it lacks the capability for skinning and may not be consistent with the look of your site (it retains the Admin skin). If specified, the Login page will be used as the target for login requests instead of the default Login page. This allows for full customization and skinning including additional modules and page elements. But don't forget to include the Account Login module on the page and be sure the page and module permissions specify visibility to Unauthenticated Users (or All Users). A simple example of a custom Login page would be to include the Account Login module on the Home page, visible only to the Unauthenticated Users role.

Table continued on following page

Setting	Description

	If a Login page is specified that does not actually contain an Account Login module, it is possible to get stuck. In the event this should occur, update the database directly to reset the Login page, as follows:
	
	`UPDATE PortalsSET LoginTabId = NULL`
	
	`WHERE PortalId = <the portal to fix>`

User Page	Displays a user's registration information and preferences, provides for password changes, and lists available membership services (see Figure 4-16). You can most readily see this by clicking the Registration button or by clicking your username if you are already logged in. The default User page is provided for your convenience. As another system page, it has the same skinning limitations and customization characteristics as the Login page. When you're creating a custom User page, be sure that the User Account module is visible to the All Users role. It serves the dual purpose of collecting registration information for Unauthenticated Users and displaying account information for Registered Users.
Home Directory	This display-only field identifies the path to the directory that holds all the portal's files. The directory is specified by the Host and represents a location relative to the web site root (for example, `http://www.dotnetnuke.com/ Portals/1`).

This is an opportune time to set defaults for what information is required for users to enter upon registration. On the User page, internal functions require that users enter a first and last name, username, password, and e-mail address. Other contact information fields are optional, but you can require them by clicking the check box next to the field.

Advanced Settings: Payment Settings

The Payment settings (see Figure 4-17) have been preserved from earlier versions of DotNetNuke for legacy support purposes. Only the PayPal option is supported using the POST method to emulate PayPal's Buy Now button functionality. Currently, these settings come into play only when public roles are defined with fees or when online portal signup is permitted. They are not used in any of the several eCommerce store and/or payment components available through third-party providers or in the free DotNetNuke Store module. These settings may be deprecated in a future version in favor of a more robust eCommerce API.

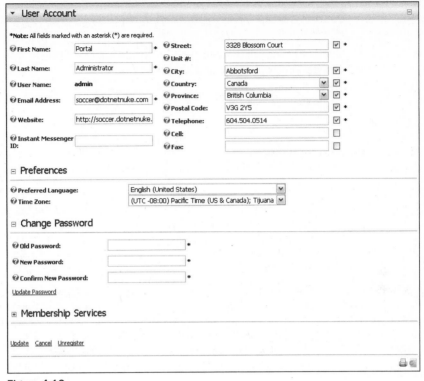

Figure 4-16

Figure 4-17

Because the Gators will offer at least one premium content area for subscription, you'll sign up for a PayPal account and use it to process payments for these services.

Other Settings

The group of miscellaneous settings (see Figure 4-18) has significant impact on several key display characteristics of your portal. Table 4-6 explains the impact of each setting.

Figure 4-18

Table 4-6: Miscellaneous Settings

Setting	Description
Copyright	Used to populate the text of the [COPYRIGHT] skin object token. In each of the default skins, the copyright notice appears at the bottom of the page. If your skin does not implement the COPYRIGHT skin object, this setting has no effect. For more information on skin object tokens, see Chapter 16.
Banner Advertising	Controls the behavior of the [BANNER] skin object token. The None option nullifies the token, resulting in no display of banners. The Site and Host options determine whether banners are displayed from your portal's Vendor List or from the Host's Vendor List. The Host option provides for leveraging a single Vendor List across all portals. If your skin does not implement the BANNER skin object, this setting has no effect. If you applied the DotNetNuke template in the Site Wizard, you will see a banner on the upper-right side of the default skin, which is a default banner that appears if none exist in the Vendors List.
Administrator	Recall that the Portal Administrator's contact information is used for the "from" address in outgoing e-mail, the default-to address in the Feedback module, and so on. You can designate another portal user (who is also in the Administrator role) as the primary Portal Administrator.
Default Language	DotNetNuke supports localization of text, dates, and currency within the portal framework. English language files are installed by default but many additional language packs are available at www.dotnetnuke.com (40 currently). The default language is displayed to anonymous site visitors and Registered Users who have not selected a default language in their own membership settings. If additional language packs are installed, they will be available in this drop-down list.
Portal TimeZone	DotNetNuke supports localization of time zone similarly to languages. The default time zone is used for anonymous site visitors and Registered Users who have not selected a default time zone in their own membership settings. This feature is primarily available for support of modules that may require it. Timestamps visible in the Log or for the creation and update events for individual records are based on server time, rather than localized time. There are no features in the default installation of DotNetNuke that display localized time.

The footer area of the default skins contains the [COPYRIGHT] skin object token, which displays the copyright notice specified in Other Site Settings (see Figure 4-19).

Copyright 2002-2005 DotNetNuke   Terms Of Use   Privacy Statement

Figure 4-19

Changing the default language setting causes DotNetNuke to reload all static portal content (labels, Admin and Host menus, and date and currency formats) from resource files that correspond to the language specified. You can even customize the static labels if desired. Compare Figure 4-18 and Figure 4-20 to see how the choice of default language affects your portal. Note that dynamic content (like the text of the Copyright notice) is not translated. Modules that are well behaved also implement this approach to static localization.

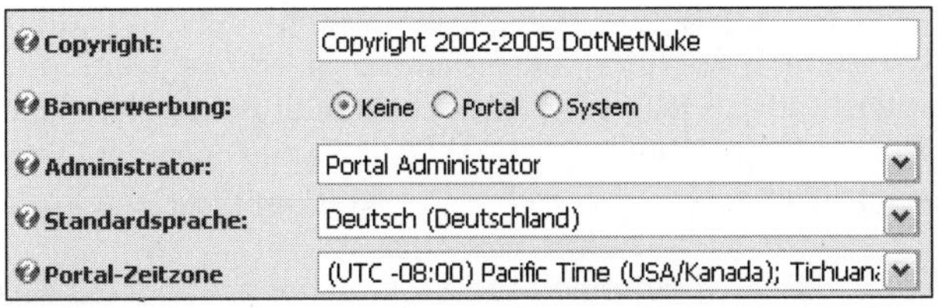

Copyright:	Copyright 2002-2005 DotNetNuke
Bannerwerbung:	⊙ Keine ○ Portal ○ System
Administrator:	Portal Administrator
Standardsprache:	Deutsch (Deutschland)
Portal-Zeitzone:	(UTC -08:00) Pacific Time (USA/Kanada); Tichuana

Figure 4-20

Core support for multi-language module content (and versioning) is on the development roadmap for a future version of DotNetNuke.

Stylesheet Editor

DotNetNuke supports cascading style sheets so that skin and container designers, as well as module developers, have a means to customize components they provide. The highest-level style sheet is located in the portal's home directory, appropriately named portal.css. The Stylesheet Editor gives you a convenient way to quickly update any style supported within the DotNetNuke framework (see Figure 4-21).

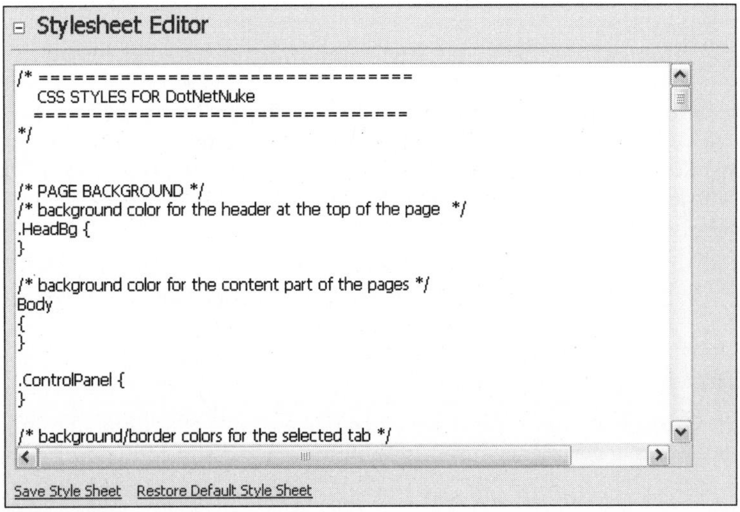

⊟ Stylesheet Editor

```
/* =================================
    CSS STYLES FOR DotNetNuke
   =================================
*/


/* PAGE BACKGROUND */
/* background color for the header at the top of the page  */
.HeadBg {
}

/* background color for the content part of the pages */
Body
{
}

.ControlPanel {
}

/* background/border colors for the selected tab */
```

Save Style Sheet   Restore Default Style Sheet

Figure 4-21

If you should ever need it, there is a Restore Default Style Sheet button, which returns the template to its original settings. Any customizations you made will be lost, so it's a good idea to make a backup copy of this file first.

> *DotNetNuke purposefully situates the portal.css file as the last in cascading order so that a Portal Administrator can quickly and easily update styles for a given site. However, if a skin designer adds a stylesheet reference or inline styles directly to a skin, the cascading order will be broken. A properly designed skin allows DotNetNuke to inject the skin's CSS file into the proper cascading order without an explicit reference.*

Security Roles

The DotNetNuke architecture enables you to control access to your content both at the page level and the module level through the application of user roles. A role can be thought of as a group with a purpose (for example, Newsletter Subscriber, Gallery Administrator, or Team Member). You learn to apply roles later in this chapter. Modules may extend the concept of permissions to include purposes relevant to their specific function, but for planning purposes you should consider that roles address two types of purposes (permissions) in the context of portal administration: View and Edit.

Some important security roles are predefined and you can define others as necessary. You are already acquainted with (and a member of) the Administrators role. You've also touched briefly on the Registered Users role, which includes all users that have registered on your site and have been authorized, whether by an Administrator, through public access, or through verification at login. Figure 4-22 shows the Security Roles page and predefined roles for a default portal.

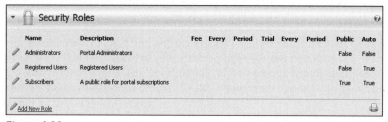

Figure 4-22

Two additional built-in roles you will find useful are the Unauthenticated Users and All Users roles. The Unauthenticated Users role has no explicit definition because it denotes anonymous users who belong to no real security role at all. Likewise, the All Users role includes both users who are currently logged in as well as those who are not. You will see how both of these roles are used later when you work with page and module permissions.

Your portal may have additional roles based on the template you specified using the Site Wizard earlier in this chapter.

Creating a New Role

In designing the Gators web site, it was determined that a couple of additional roles would be needed. You'll add an opt-out role that all new users are automatically assigned to. The preconfigured

Subscribers role is an example of this, but you'll create your own in this exercise. You'll also add a public role for subscription to premium services.

Basic Settings

Click the Add New Role link at the bottom of the Security Roles page to open the Edit Security Role page (see Figure 4-23). Table 4-7 describes the fields in the basic settings.

Role Name:	Newsletter Subscribers
Description:	Receive our monthly soccer newsletter!
Public Role?	☑
Auto Assignment?	☑

Figure 4-23

Table 4-7: Add New Role — Basic Settings

Field	Description
Role Name and Description	These are visible to Administrators on the list of Security Roles (previously shown in Figure 4-22) and also in the Membership Services area of the Account Profile page if the role is defined as Public (shown later in Figure 4-25).
Public Role	These show up as user-selectable options in the Membership Services area of the Account Profile page (shown later in Figure 4-25). This is useful to enable user selection of optional services.
Auto Assignment	If this is checked, the role is retroactively applied to all existing users and is automatically assigned to all new users.

You'll define a role that is used to determine who should receive your monthly newsletter. The role is automatically assigned to each new user but, as a public role, it can be canceled by the user at any time. Figure 4-23 illustrates the setup of the new role.

Alternatively, you might choose not to auto-assign the role in favor of allowing your users to opt-in specifically. This would be a more acceptable option for marketing-oriented communications because the default user registration does not currently include the capability to opt-out at the time of signup.

Advanced Settings

You'll also define an optional role with a fee, which you'll use to expose privileged content to paid subscribers. The Gators site will provide access to a gallery of photos and for a small fee users can download high-quality images for printing. For this, you need to apply some advanced settings (see Figure 4-24).

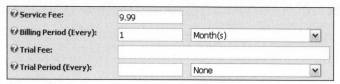

Figure 4-24

Table 4-8 describes the fields in the advanced settings area.

Table 4-8: Add New Role — Advanced Settings

Setting	Description
Service Fee	The fee associated with the service that is enabled via the role. The fee is applied in the currency specified in your portal settings. If you've specified PayPal as your payment processor, be sure that your account is set up to accept payments in the chosen currency.
Billing Period (Every)	These two fields define how often a user is billed for the service. It may be a one-time or recurring fee.
Trial Fee	You can choose to allow a trial period for services at a different rate than the full service amount. Free trial services are often offered for a limited time.
Trial Period	These two fields define the duration of the trial period. When a trial role is granted, it is given an expiration date that is based on this time period.

You'll apply a small monthly fee to this role. When users subscribe to it, they're taken to the PayPal web site where they can authorize a payment to your account. Upon completion of that process, they are transferred back to the home page of your web site. The update to the user's account is processed asynchronously.

Remove the preconfigured Subscriber role because you've just created your own.

Public Roles and Membership Services

Public roles, such as those you defined in the previous section, are made available to users via the Membership Services area of their Account Profile page (see Figure 4-25).

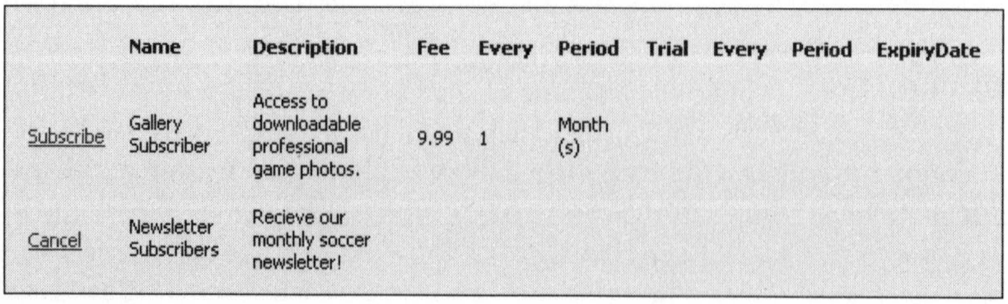

	Name	Description	Fee	Every	Period	Trial	Every	Period	ExpiryDate
Subscribe	Gallery Subscriber	Access to downloadable professional game photos.	9.99	1	Month (s)				
Cancel	Newsletter Subscribers	Recieve our monthly soccer newsletter!							

Figure 4-25

Delegating Authority and/or Assigning Privileges

Roles that are not public typically define privileged access for users or areas of responsibility for maintenance purposes. Assume you've already defined such a role for the individuals who will maintain the file download area called Gallery Maintenance. Navigate there by clicking the Manage Users In This Role button on the Edit Security Roles page.

To add a user to the role, simply select the user in the User Name drop-down list (see Figure 4-26) and click Add Role.

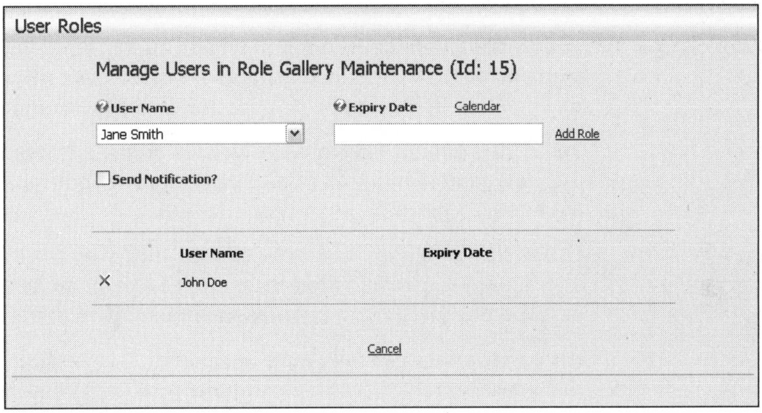

Figure 4-26

If appropriate, an expiry date can be specified, after which the role has no effect. The Send Notification check box (if checked) results in an e-mail being sent from the Portal Administrator to the user, advising her of her addition to the role.

All users currently assigned to the role appear in the list. Clicking the red X next to any user's name removes him or her from the role.

Now that you can create roles and assign users to them, you're ready to put those roles to use. In the next section, you create a page that your Gallery Subscriber role can access but a normal registered user cannot. Likewise, your Gallery Maintenance role should be able to edit the page while others (except Administrators) cannot.

Pages

Pages are the building blocks of your DotNetNuke portal. They are the real estate where you deposit content to create an interesting site. You can see them represented in menu items, bread crumbs, and site links. You've already dealt with a number of system pages, but in this section you learn all about creating and managing pages of your own.

Creating New Pages

The quickest way to create a new page is to click the Add button in the Page Functions area of the Control Panel. You can also create a page by selecting Admin ➪ Pages, navigating to the Page List, and clicking the Add New Page button. Table 4-9 explains the basic settings.

Table 4-9: Add New Page — Basic Settings

Setting	Description
Page Name	This value appears as the text in the menu item, Recycle Bin, and anywhere that pages are listed (for example, in drop-down selection lists).
Page Title	Displays in the title bar of the user's browser. Search engines typically use this as a key indicator of relevance, so be sure to make your page titles fully descriptive of the page content (for example, "Soccer Team Photos for Download").
Page Description	You added a default description when you imported your portal template (previously described in Table 4-2). However, it is recommended that you add a relevant description for each page within your site.
KeyWords	You added default keywords as well (as previously described in Table 4-2) but, again, unique keywords can improve your ranking for search engines.
Parent Page	Drives the navigation hierarchy of your site.* Any page that does not have a parent specified appears as a top-level menu item. Any page that has a parent specified appears as a submenu item to the parent page.
	Although a page can only have one parent, it is possible to create a page that is really just a reference to another (existing) page. So you can reference the same page from more than one place in the menu structure (see "Link URL" in Table 4-10).
Permissions	Each role in your portal can be explicitly assigned permissions to view or edit the page. Edit permissions are the same as those available to the Portal Administrator (for page-level actions only). View permissions determine whether the page is displayed to the role (as shown later in Figure 4-28).

* You can take this hierarchy as deep as you like, but conventional wisdom says that going more than about two levels deep becomes difficult to navigate. Not every page needs to be accessible from the main menu.

When you're creating a new page, you have the option to copy the structure and/or content of an existing page (see Figure 4-27).

Figure 4-27

If you have created a page that employs a layout of modules that will be common in your site, it may be useful to begin developing new pages using that same layout. You can specify which page to copy and whether the module content should be the same. If you select Copy Content, the modules on the new page will be shadows of existing modules on the Copy Modules From page. All of the shadow copies are linked so that changes to any one will update every instance on each copied page. This can be particularly helpful for things like links modules used for navigation, banner modules displayed on selected pages, and so on. If you do not select Copy Content, new empty modules are placed on the page in the same layout and with the same permissions as the page specified to copy from.

Table 4-10 explains the fields in the advanced settings area.

Table 4-10: Add New Page — Advanced Settings

Setting	Description
Icon	Identifies an image that will be displayed beside the page name in the menu. Menu text bottom aligns with the images, so 16x16 icons tend to look the best.
Page Skin	This optional setting associates a skin specifically to this page. It's useful if you have a skin with special formatting or a functional need to appear different than the rest of your site. If this option is <Not Specified>, the page inherits the default skin as specified in the Site Settings (previously shown in Figure 4-13).
Page Container	This setting associates a default container specifically to this page.
Hidden	This option has nothing to do with the visibility of your page. (Visibility is a function of roles that you were introduced to earlier.) You select this option to keep a page from being added to the (main) menu. You may have many pages that are not part of your top-level navigation but that are linked in other ways throughout your site. Any page that is a descendent of a hidden page is also suppressed from the main menu. However, if you are using third-party navigational components, this is often a convenient way to create sub- or "child" menus.
Disabled	If a page is disabled, it is not accessible to any user of the site who is not a member of the Administrator role. This feature is useful for suppressing content without manipulating roles (for example, universally hiding a page until it is updated).
Start Date	Specify a date that the page (and menu item) becomes visible. Before the start date, the page will function as if it were disabled.
End Date	Specify a date after which the page (and menu item) is no longer visible. The page will function as normal until that date.
Link Url	Change the target of your page. The default is a Link Type of None, which is interpreted as an internal page. The page will open in the same browser window. URL (A Link To An External Resource): The menu item acts as a direct link to the target URL specified by entering a new URL or selecting one previously used.

Table continued on following page

Setting	Description
	Page (A Page On Your Site): The menu item acts as a link to an existing page in your site. This option enables you to create multiple navigational items that point to the same place (for example, a descriptive page that applies to multiple products or an alternative navigational hierarchy for a child menu or site map). File (A File On Your Site): The menu item acts as a link to a file in your portal root (for example, a link to a PDF document or image).

Securing Privileged Content

Earlier in this chapter, you learned to create security roles to logically group users. Page (and module) permissions enable you to give privileges to those groups of users. The built-in Administrator role always has both View and Edit permissions on every page.

Figure 4-28 shows the permissions that you'll apply to the Gators Gallery page. By giving View Page permissions to All Users, even anonymous users browsing the site can access the menu item and the page. In addition, you will give edit access to the Gallery Maintenance role, which will have responsibility for keeping this page current (for example, adding new photos).

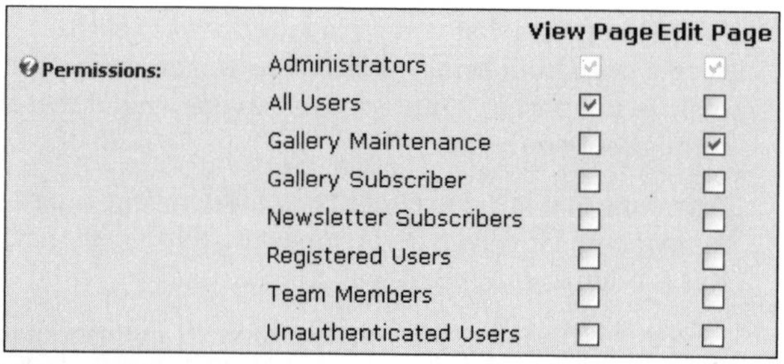

Figure 4-28

The permissions specified in Figure 4-28 only secure the edit privilege of the page. You'll recall that the Gators also have a paid role for Gallery Subscribers, which should give them access to premium content. When those pages are created, you'll uncheck All Users and give View Page permissions to the Gallery Maintenance and Gallery Subscriber roles only.

Now You See It, Now You Don't

The Unauthenticated Users role can be quite useful. It enables you to present a completely different view of your site to an anonymous user than to your registered users. If View Page permissions are assigned only to the Unauthenticated Users role, they will essentially disappear from view after a user is logged in.

One way of applying this concept is to define a Splash Page (shown previously in Figure 4-15) so that its View permissions are set only for Unauthenticated Users. This creates a landing page that is no longer visible when a user is logged in, but preserves the behavior of the Home page after login. Further, if the specified Home page is set only for Registered Users, its information remains private and the Splash page functions as a Home page for the anonymous user.

Take care when planning your site's navigation using the Unauthenticated User role. You don't want to hide a menu item if it has submenu items that you want to keep visible.

Changing Navigational Structure

You've used the Parent page setting to specify navigational structure. But if that were the only mechanism you had to reorganize your site, it would be a little challenging. So another method involves the Pages list (see Figure 4-29), which you access by selecting Admin ⇨ Pages.

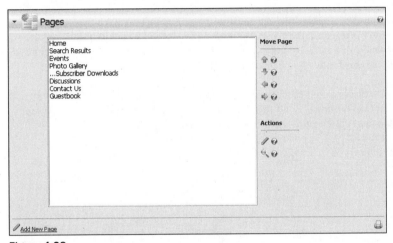

Figure 4-29

This list displays all the pages in your site in an organization that closely matches your menu structure. Items at the top of this list are leftmost in your menu, moving right along the menu as you move down the list. Items that are indented (for example, Subscriber Downloads) are submenu items. The buttons available on the right provide a means to change the defined parent of a selected page, moving it (and all its children) up or down within the menu hierarchy or changing its (and all its children's) position in the parent/child relationship. You can choose to Edit or View a page as well.

Regardless of the visibility settings of the page (whether by start/end dates, enable/disable, or hidden/unhidden), it will appear in this list, and so the menu hierarchy can become more difficult to see if you have a large number of pages on your site. For this reason, it may be advantageous to define a few phantom pages for organizational purposes. For example, you might define a hidden page called Orphans and assign it as the parent to pages that are suppressed from the menu.

Skins

The Skins page (see Figure 4-30), which is accessible from the Admin menu, gives you the ability to browse and apply skins and containers to customize the look of your site. You learned a bit about this functionality within the context of the Site Wizard, and you can access the functionality directly through this page.

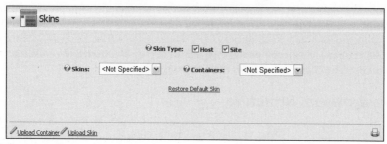

Figure 4-30

You can specify whether the drop-down containers list Host- and/or Site-supplied skins. If your Host has enabled the option, you may also see buttons to Upload Container and Upload Skin (otherwise, these buttons are not visible to you). Clicking the Restore Default Skin button changes your site's default settings to those originally specified by your Host.

Selecting a skin or container from their respective drop-down lists displays the available selections in a gallery format (see Figure 4-31). If provided by the designer, the galleries will include thumbnail previews and the skin gallery will include associated containers.

Chapter 16 covers the topic of developing custom skins and containers in detail.

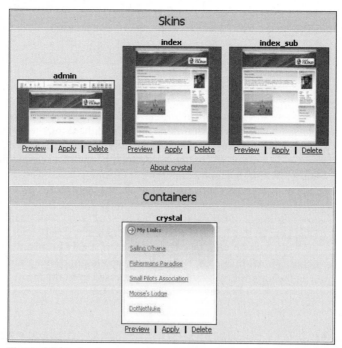

Figure 4-31

From the gallery you can click a thumbnail image to see a larger image (if provided by the designer). You can also see how a skin or container would look on your Home page by clicking Preview, or set it as the default for the portal by clicking Apply. You can specify whether it should be applied to Admin and/or Portal pages in a check box below the gallery. If you selected a Site skin from the drop-down list, you have the option to delete individual skins and containers as well.

If the skin designer included an about.htm file in the package, you'll also see an About <skin name> button below the gallery. Click it to open the designer-supplied file.

If you have pages with modules placed just the way you like them, be careful about changing your skin and moving things around. If you select a skin that has a different pane layout than the one you are currently using, DotNetNuke won't know where to put some of those modules and will temporarily display them in the ContentPane by default. Changing back to the old skin will restore the original position if you don't change anything. If you're experimenting with skins on a page with lots of content, make a copy of your existing page first and experiment on that. Or just stick with the Preview option in the gallery.

File Manager

File management is an area that was radically improved in version 3.0 and updated with version 4.0 and the introduction of the ClientAPI. Prior to introduction of the File Manager, all files were maintained in a flat structure in the portal root directory, which could easily become unwieldy. Now files can be managed in subdirectories, and those subdirectories can be protected through role-based permissions.

Figure 4-32 shows the basic features of the File Manager. Most operations are intuitive, and the interface is pretty forgiving, providing feedback if you do something incorrectly. Group file and folder operations require that you select either a group of files or a folder first. The ClientAPI is responsible for AJAX-style smooth scrolling in the tree view.

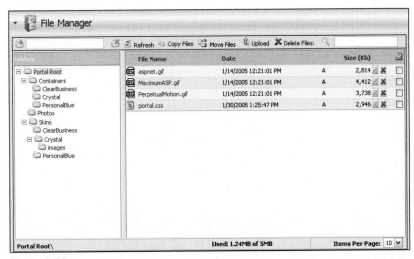

Figure 4-32

Folder Permissions

There are multiple folders within the portal root. By default, only the Administrators role has permission to view and write files in all of these folders (see Figure 4-33). If you want the users who administer your gallery to be able to upload photos, you need to grant appropriate permissions to the role that identifies them (Gallery Maintenance).

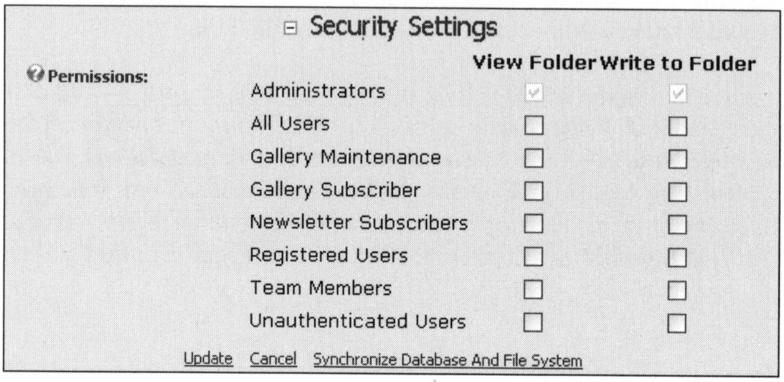

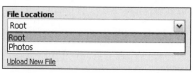

Figure 4-33

These security settings are applied everywhere that the DotNetNuke file-management controls are used. You've seen these controls in the Portal Administrators interface in a number of places, including the logo file selector in the Site Wizard (previously shown in Figure 4-11). These same controls are used in many modules (for example, the Documents module), which you'll learn more about in Chapter 6.

The Gallery Administrator needs permission to select files from the drop-down to add pictures to the gallery, and also needs to be able to write to the folder to upload new photos. So be sure to grant both View and Write permissions to the Gallery Maintenance role for the Photo folder.

Figure 4-34 shows both the Root and Photo folders available to the file upload control. Access to the portal root directory is provided by default to preserve functionality for users upgrading from version 2.x to version 3.0. It is recommended that upgraded sites review their file and folder management policies.

Figure 4-34

Uploading Files

Click the Upload button in the File Manager, and the original DotNetNuke File Upload page is displayed. The upload control provides a lot of rich functionality and is used in many places within DotNetNuke for uploading various component packages like modules, skins, language packs, and so on. This is the control in its plain vanilla state, waiting for you to specify generic files to upload.

The File Upload control includes a drop-down list that you can use to specify the target directory and an Add button that captures input from the basic file selector and includes it in a list of files to upload. This feature enables you to upload multiple files in one upload step.

The check box for Decompress ZIP Files allows you to upload a zipped file (preserving bandwidth) that is unzipped for you into the target directory. An invalid file type is stopped from unpacking in an upload. Both individual files and the content of zip files are matched against an allowable file types list, which is configurable by the Host.

> Properties of the .NET Framework HttpPostedFileClass dictate the size limits for uploading files. DotNetNuke sets these properties in the default web.config file as follows:
>
> ```
> <httpRuntime useFullyQualifiedRedirectUrl="true" ⤵
> maxRequestLength="8192" requestLengthDiskThreshold="8192" />
> ```

Using FTP with File Manager

The File Manager provides a convenient way to move files through the interface. For bulk operations, however, you may prefer to utilize FTP to transfer files (if permitted by your Host). If files are added to your site through any means other than the file upload interface, you need to click the Synchronize Database and File System button. That command instructs DotNetNuke to iterate through the portal root and resolve for any files and folders that may be added or missing. Your Host may have enabled a scheduled job to perform this synchronization for you on a periodic basis, but if you do it yourself, you'll see those files in your drop-down lists immediately.

Do not delete files outside of the File Manager. Using the File Manager ensures that database references are updated appropriately throughout the application where file references are made (in other modules, for example).

Languages

Languages and localization features are primarily controlled by the Host account; however, the Portal Administrator has limited control to override localization strings and to define the default language for your portal. These settings are specific to your portal and therefore no mechanism is provided to export or import these changes.

Changing Your Default Language

You set the default language for your site earlier in this chapter. The default language is used in cases where the user has not been authenticated, and therefore does not have a preferred language of their own (as specified in a registered user profile). Also, the default language will be used as the default choice for the preferred language when a new user registers on the portal. The default language is controlled from the Site Settings page, which you saw in Figure 4-18. After users (including the Portal Administrator and Host accounts) log on to the site, their preferred language is used instead of the default language.

The Language Editor

To create custom localization strings for the portal, select Admin ⇨ Languages. Then from the Module Actions menu on the Languages page, select Language Editor. The Language Editor screen (see Figure 4-35) provides the ability for Administrators to customize resource strings for any of the installed locales.

Figure 4-35

The tree on the left side of the screen enables you to easily navigate to any resource file. Each resource file corresponds to the various controls or shared resources in the portal. The first time you attempt to edit a resource file, you are asked to verify that you want to create a custom resource file (see Figure 4-36). The resource file will be saved in the directory alongside the other resources.

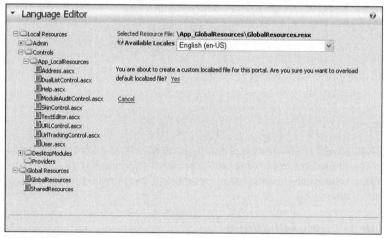

Figure 4-36

Resource files are named using a standard pattern based on the associated file: [FileName].resx for English resources, and [FileName].[Culture].resx for non-English resources. When portal-specific resource files are created, the system prepends the .resx extension with Portal-[PortalID]. In the example from Figure 4-37, the local portal copy of the English resource file would be named SkinControl.ascx .Portal-0.resx. The German (Deutsch) version would be named SkinControl.ascx.de-DE.Portal-0.resx.

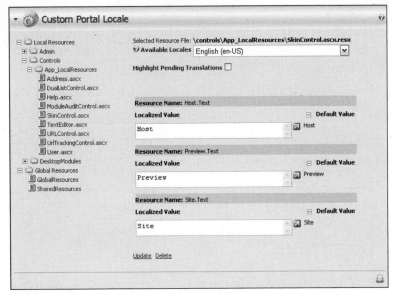

Figure 4-37

When the portal-specific localized file is created, all resource strings are included. After the portal resource file is created, any changes in the comparable host file are overridden by the portal file, even if the portal file strings were not changed. In Figure 4-37, the values for Host.Text, Preview.Text, and Site.Text are written to the resource file when the portal file is created.

Each resource displays the Resource Name, Default Value, and Localized Value. The Resource Name corresponds to the key used by the portal for looking up the localized value. The default System Locale for DotNetNuke is English (en-US). The English language resources are used for all default values.

Localized values correspond to the locale selected in the Available Locales drop-down list box. Localized values can be edited directly using the associated textarea boxes. After you have completed editing the localized values, click the Update link button to save your changes.

This works well for simple strings and enables you to edit multiple strings without requiring multiple postbacks to the server. Long strings, or resource strings that contain HTML are more difficult to edit using the text-area boxes. To edit these resources, click the arrow button to the right of the text area.

Because the button causes a postback to the server, and you are not yet ready to save changes for the associated localized value, you may lose any data that has been changed (but not updated) elsewhere on the page. To prevent data loss, DotNetNuke displays a dialog box that asks you to confirm that you want to proceed (see Figure 4-38).

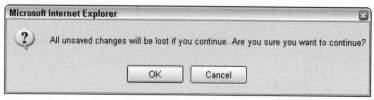

Figure 4-38

Click Cancel to return to the main editing screen to save any pending changes. Click OK to proceed to the Language Editor screen (see Figure 4-39).

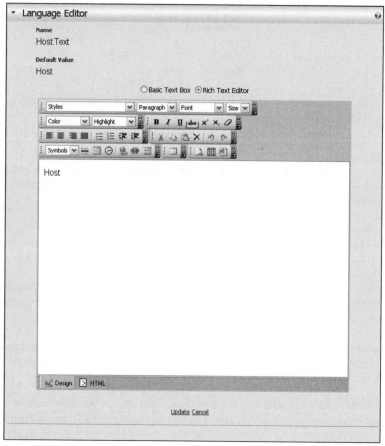

Figure 4-39

The Language Editor uses the HtmlEditorProvider defined in the web.config file. The editor provides advanced text and HTML editing functionality. After you make the changes to the resource string, select Update to save your changes and return to the Custom Portal Locale screen, or select Cancel to discard your changes and return.

Customizing Your E-mail Templates

Most Portal Administrators choose to keep almost all of the default resource strings for their web site. However, you should at least review the standard system messages used for generating e-mails to your web site users. Previous versions of DotNetNuke provided a central location for managing the e-mail templates used by the system. Starting with DotNetNuke version 3.0, the templates were incorporated into the resource files so that they could be localized like other static elements of the portal.

Because static e-mail templates would not be useful, DotNetNuke supports the use of special tokens, which are replaced at runtime with the specified property value. DotNetNuke currently recognizes six different tokens (see Table 4-11) that follow the pattern [TokenName:Property]. Valid properties for each of these tokens are defined in Appendix B.

Table 4-11: E-mail Template Tokens

Token Name	Description
Host	Provides access to a limited set of HostSettings properties.
Portal	Provides access to the PortalSettings properties. This token also supports the URL property that corresponds to the HTTP Alias for the current portal.
User	Provides access to UserInfo properties. This token also supports the VerificationCode property, which is dynamically generated based on the portal ID and user ID in the form [PortalID]-[UserID]. The user token is not valid for all templates (see Table 4-12).
Membership	Provides access to UserMembership properties. This information is specific to the currently selected user. The Membership token can only be used for templates that also support the User token.
Profile	Provides access to the UserProfile properties. This information is specific to the currently selected user. The Profile token can only be used for templates that also support the User token.
Custom	Used when arbitrary data needs to be included in the template. The data is passed as an ArrayList and is specific to each e-mail template. Not all templates support the use of custom values (see Table 4-12).

Table 4-12 describes each of the e-mail templates supported by the core portal. These templates can all be found in the global resources file: \App_GlobalResources\GlobalResources.resx.

Table 4-12: Site-Generated E-mail Templates

Resource	User Token	Custom Token
EMAIL_USER_REGISTRATION_PUBLIC_SUBJECT EMAIL_USER_REGISTRATION_PUBLIC_BODY Sent to users when they register on a site that is not set to Private Registration. This e-mail is also sent when a registration is manually authorized.	Yes	None
EMAIL_USER_UNREGISTER_SUBJECT EMAIL_USER_UNREGISTER_BODY Sent to the Portal Administrator when a user is unregistered whether by user self-service or through deletion.	Yes	None
EMAIL_SMTP_TEST_SUBJECT Sent to the Host when testing SMTP configuration.	No	None
EMAIL_PORTAL_SIGNUP_SUBJECT EMAIL_PORTAL_SIGNUP_BODY Sent to the new Portal Administrator whenever a portal is created, whether by the Host or by a user when he or she signs up for a portal as a free trial (Host option).	Yes	None
EMAIL_USER_REGISTRATION_PRIVATE_SUBJECT EMAIL_USER_REGISTRATION_PRIVATE_BODY Sent to the user at the time of registration, only on sites where Private Registration is set. This is the e-mail that should explain your approval policy.	Yes	None
EMAIL_USER_REGISTRATION_ADMINISTRATOR_SUBJECT EMAIL_USER_REGISTRATION_ADMINISTRATOR_BODY Sent to the Portal Administrator on every registration.	Yes	None
EMAIL_PASSWORD_REMINDER_SUBJECT EMAIL_PASSWORD_REMINDER_BODY Sent to the user when a reminder is requested.	Yes	None
EMAIL_ROLE_ASSIGNMENT_SUBJECT	Yes	None
EMAIL_ROLE_ASSIGNMENT_BODY Sent to the user when a role is assigned by the Administrator and the Send Notification option is checked.	Yes	0: RoleName 1: Description 2: Expiry Date
EMAIL_ROLE_UNASSIGNMENT_SUBJECT	Yes	None
EMAIL_ROLE_UNASSIGNMENT_BODY Sent to the user when a role is removed by the Administrator and the Send Notification option is checked. For the purposes of unassignment, the value of the Expiry Date is hidden.	Yes	0: RoleName 1: Description 2: <blank>
EMAIL_AFFILIATE_NOTIFICATION_SUBJECT	Yes	None

Resource	User Token	Custom Token
EMAIL_AFFILIATE_NOTIFICATION_BODY Sent to the affiliate when the Send Notification button is clicked on the Edit Vendor page.	Yes	0: VendorName 1: AffiliateURL
EMAIL_BANNER_NOTIFICATION_SUBJECT EMAIL_BANNER_NOTIFICATION_BODY Sent to a vendor when the Email Status To Vendor button is clicked from the Edit Banner page in Vendor Management. The custom fields are available to both the subject and body.	No	0: BannerName 1: Description 2: ImageName 3: CPM/Cost 4: Impressions 5: StartDate 6: EndDate 7: Views 8: ClickThrus

The Privacy Statement and Terms of Use

Like e-mail templates, you are likely to need to customize the Terms of Use and Privacy Statement resources (see Table 4-13). Because these two resources are generic to the entire web site, the User, Membership, Profile, and Custom tokens are not usable. Links to the terms and privacy statement are included in the default skins (as previously shown in Figure 4-19).

Table 4-13: Terms of Use and Privacy Statement Resources

Resource	User Token	Custom Token
MESSAGE_PORTAL_TERMS	No	None
MESSAGE_PORTAL_PRIVACY	No	None

Authentication

Windows Authentication was officially introduced in version 3.2 (for ASP.NET 1.1) and version 4.0 (for ASP.NET 2.0), increasing DotNetNuke's capability to provide a robust platform for intranets. If your portal is in an intranet environment, Authentication allows you to specify an external authentication source for your users (that is, Open LDAP, ADAM). The configuration screen for Authentication is illustrated in Figure 4-40.

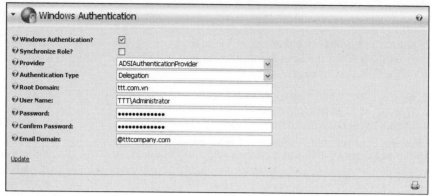

Figure 4-40

Table 4-14 explains the purpose of each of the fields and how they are configured.

Table 4-14: Windows Authentication

Field	Description
Windows Authentication	Indicates whether Windows Authentication is enabled for the site.
Synchronize Role	Indicates whether DotNetNuke should synchronize Security Role assignments to Users based on roles in the Active Directory. For this to work properly the Security Roles in the Portal must exactly match the ones in the Active Directory that you wish to replicate. This will not happen automatically, but the account will synchronize when users first log in to the portal with their Active Directory credentials.
Provider	Select the provider to use for the authentication of the user accounts. The ADSIAuthenticationProvider is provided with DotNetNuke and installed by default, although other providers may be available from third parties (or included with the default installation in the future).
Authentication Type	Specify the type of authentication you want to use (Delegation is the recommended setting and works for most instances). You may need to consult with your Network Administrator regarding Authentication Types for your network.
Root Domain	Specify the root domain that you want to authenticate against. If this value is left blank DotNetNuke will query the root forest of your network; however, in a strict network you may not have sufficient permissions for this default action. It is recommended that you supply a value in the yourdomain.com or DC-yourdomain,DC-com formats.
User Name	Specify the User Name that will access the LDAP information in Active Directory. This user must have read permissions to the AD structure and user accounts, specified in the DOMAIN\UserName format.

Field	Description
	If no User Name (and Password) is specified, DotNetNuke will attempt the operation using the credentials specified to the application in IIS.
Password	Specify the password associated with the User Name.
Confirm Password	Confirm the password.
Email Domain	Users in DotNetNuke are required to have an e-mail address associated with their account. If your authentication configuration does not supply an e-mail address, one will be assigned to the user in the following format: `Username + @ + email domain` For most configurations, leave this field blank and accept e-mail information from your Active Directory.

If your settings are properly configured, clicking Update generates an informational message that confirms successful access of the directory and a listing of network domains. Otherwise, an error message appears.

Table 4-15 explains four modes of Authentication that manifest different behavior. These modes are a function of whether Anonymous Access is configured in IIS for the site and for the page that invokes Windows sign-on (\Admin\Controls\WindowsSignin.aspx) and whether an HTTP module is activated for the installation.

To fully configure Authentication requires access to the server where your portal installation resides and the LDAP or Active Directory domain you will reference as well as IIS settings and the application root file system. This level of access is not typically afforded to a Portal Administrator, so assistance from your Host may be required.

Table 4-15: Configuration of Authentication Modes

Mode	Description	Site	Page	HTTP
DNN Forms Authentication	Standard DotNetNuke user authentication with no Active Directory. This is the default mode.	Yes	Yes	No
Windows Authentication	Typical for an intranet environment, where sign-on to the DotNetNuke portal is also sign-on to the local network. The portal bypasses the DotNetNuke login process, validating the user against Active Directory and creating the user in DotNetNuke if he or she did not previously exist.	No	No	Yes

Table continued on following page

133

Mode	Description	Site	Page	HTTP
Windows / Forms (Mixed Mode) Authentication	Best suited to a mixed environment where DotNetNuke is exposed both to intranet and Internet users. Authentication is provided inside your network via Active Directory, but users from outside the network can authenticate using the standard DotNetNuke form.	Yes	No	Yes
ADSI Forms Authentication against Active Directory	When Active Directory is used to authenticate users in an extranet environment, this mode uses the standard DotNetNuke authentication form but validates those credentials against the Active Directory.	Yes	Yes	No

Forms Authentication is the DotNetNuke default. No changes are required because the initial setup of your web site most likely defaults Anonymous Access to both the site and the individual pages. Likewise, ADSI Forms Authentication against Active Directory is a default behavior that requires only changes to the configuration page (basically turning Windows Authentication on with the check box).

Enabling Mixed or Windows-only modes is only slightly more complex. But the first step is to get your Authentication module working properly and authenticating against AD (in ADSI Forms Authentication). After this is completed, you need to update some IIS settings to enable Integrated Windows authentication for the web site that contains DotNetNuke and set the Anonymous Access attributes for the Site and sign-on page. For details on how to enable Integrated Windows Authentication in IIS or to enable Anonymous Access, refer to the documentation for your server and the appropriate version of IIS.

Finally, to complete your Mixed or Windows-only mode setup, you need to enable the Http Authentication module by un-commenting a line in the web.config file. Open web.config, find the following commented statement (located in the HTTP Modules section), and remove the following comments:

```
<!-- add name="Authentication" type="DotNetNuke.HttpModules.AuthenticationModule,
DotNetNuke.HttpModules.Authentication" / -->
```

If you're running DotNetNuke on a computer that is not a Windows server (for example, Windows XP), you might experience a "double-hop" issue (refer to http://support.microsoft.com/default.aspx?scid=kb;en-us;329986#3 for more information). To solve this problem, modify your web.config file by un-commenting identity impersonation as follows:

```
<identity impersonate="true"/>
<!--
<authentication mode="Windows">
</authentication>
-->
```

You also need to verify that the user account specified for Anonymous Access to your site has permission to access your Active Directory.

Maintaining Your Portal

After your portal is set up and working just the way you want, you'll start finding good reasons to enhance or change things. You'll delegate maintenance work to others; you'll pick up some site advertising or want to track affiliate referrals; you'll want to communicate with your registered users; you'll want to recover work that you've previously discarded; and you'll want to know what kind of traffic your site is getting.

You've already experienced a feature-rich environment for configuration of your portal's look, feel, and function. DotNetNuke provides an equally rich suite of tools for maintenance tasks as well.

User Accounts

The User Details page (previously shown in Figure 4-16) provides for user self-management. The Portal Administrator is able to manage users from the User Accounts page (see Figure 4-41). Access it by selecting Admin ➪ User Accounts.

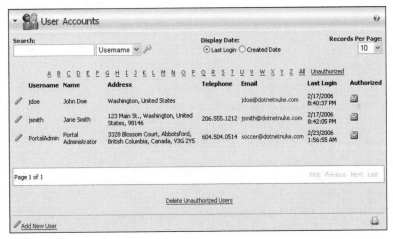

Figure 4-41

The page supports several methods of finding a user, which is helpful when your number of registered users becomes large. Clicking a letter filters the list by username, displaying a maximum of the number of records specified in the drop-down list box in the upper-right corner of the page. A standard paging control with buttons for First, Previous, Next, and Last appears if there are enough users in the list to require paging. If you need to find a specific user, the search box can accept either a username or an e-mail address.

Depending on the type of Portal Registration Options you selected (previously described in Table 4-4), you may have particular interest in finding unauthorized users. Private registration requires the Portal Administrator to manually approve users so the button to list them, the check box to indicate them, and the button to delete them are handy features. List the unauthorized users, approve the ones you'd like to permit access, and then click Delete Unauthorized Users to remove the remaining registrations you've deemed inappropriate for your site.

Clicking the pencil icon next to a user's name takes you to the Edit User Accounts page (see Figure 4-42). This page is similar to the User Account page previously shown in Figure 4-16, but it differs in a couple of key ways. There is an Authorized check box to flag the user, and the Membership Services control is missing in favor of a link button to Manage Roles For This User.

> *In early versions of DotNetNuke, it was possible to change the name of a user, but this feature is not present after version 3.0. The default Membership Provider used by DotNetNuke incorporates an ASP.NET 2.0 component (MemberRole) with lots of sophisticated security features. One of the security tenets of this component prohibits the changing of a user's identity after it is set.*

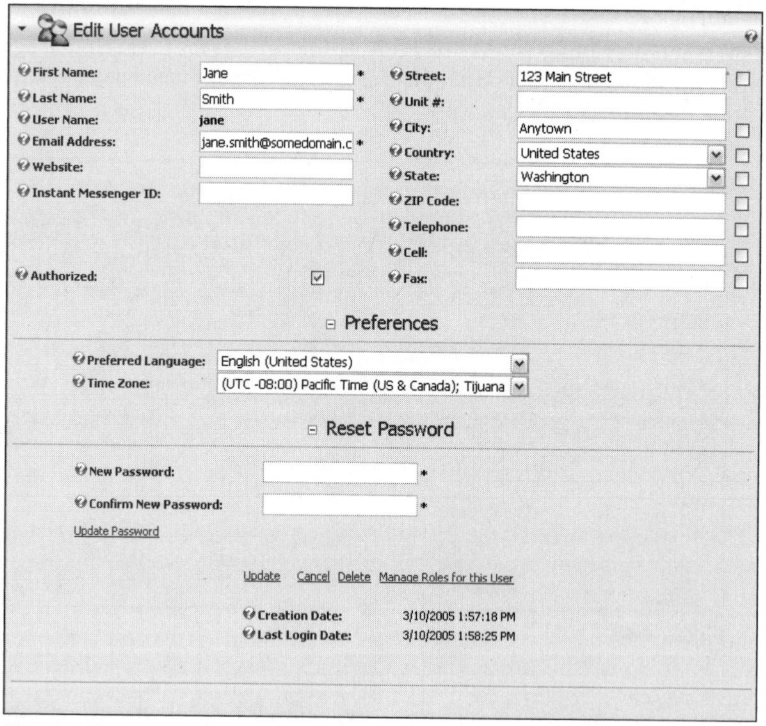

Figure 4-42

In support of the Private Registration option, checking Authorized causes an e-mail to be sent to users that provides them with their login credentials and a welcome message.

The Preferred Language and Time Zone settings work exactly as they do for the Site Settings (previously described in Table 4-6). These settings will override the default site settings when the user is logged in.

Managing Security Roles

Earlier in this chapter, you were introduced to managing security roles within the context of the list of roles (as previously shown in Figure 4-26). When you're approaching this task from the list of users, the Manage Roles For This User button takes you to a similar page (see Figure 4-43).

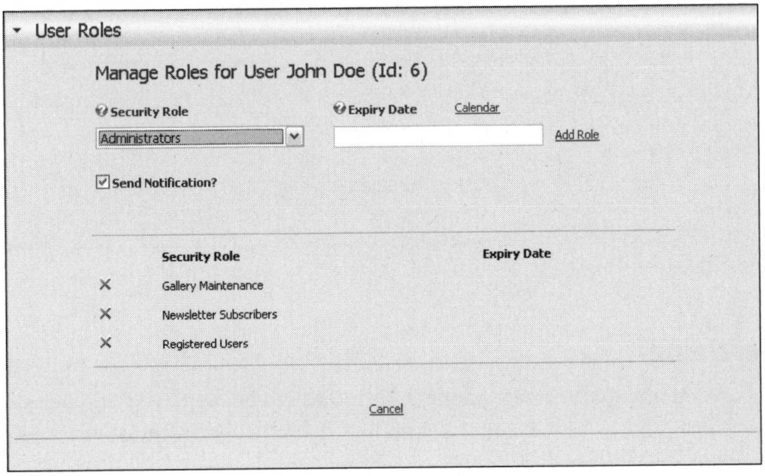

Figure 4-43

You can assign a role to your user along with an expiration date (if desired), or remove existing roles. You can also choose whether you'd like the user to receive e-mail notification of the change.

Vendors

At some point, you may want to develop partnerships with others in promoting your web site and/or complimentary products and services. DotNetNuke provides a number of built-in features to get you started in developing these relationships.

The vendor-management features provide a lot of basic functionality, but for enterprising developers there is also a lot of room to build on this foundation to provide additional services.

Creating a New Vendor

To create a new vendor, open the Vendors page (see Figure 4-44) by selecting Admin ⇨ Vendors. Then, select Add New Vendor from the bottom of the page or from the action menu.

On the Edit Vendors page (not pictured), you add basic contact information for the vendor as you would for any user. You also have the option to specify a vendor's web site, logo, key search words, and classification.

At the time of this writing, most of these optional fields are unused. However, they are reserved for future use as DotNetNuke architecture/services continue to develop in this area.

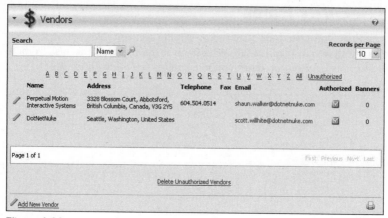

Figure 4-44

Banner Advertising

After you add a vendor, you can create banners for it that can be displayed on your site. Navigate to the Edit Vendor page for your vendor, expand the Banner Advertising section, and click Add New Banner. Table 4-16 explains the settings.

Table 4-16: Edit Banner Settings

Setting	Description
Banner Name	Identifies the banner in lists, and is used as the ALT text for graphic banners and as hyperlinked text on text banners.
Banner Type	Of the available banner types, only two really impact how the banner fields are used. When you place banners on your site with the Banner module, you select the type of banner it should display. Choosing Banner, MicroButton, Button, Block, and Skyscraper provides logical groupings of banners that fall into common width and height formats. There are no actual rules, but these groupings help to organize banners so that you don't wind up displaying wide banners in button-sized locations in your skin.
	Text and Script types are special cases. If you choose a Text banner, you can mimic the look of Google AdSense (see Figure 4-45). Choosing a Script banner allows free-form HTML in the text box, which is helpful for a number of generated links for things like Amazon products.
Banner Group	Further aids in the ad-hoc grouping of banners. For example, DotNetNuke.com displays rotating button banners for its sponsors. To keep sponsor buttons separate from other banners, each has Sponsor in its Banner Group field. Likewise, the Banner Options for the module specifies Sponsor in its Banner Group.
	Because this field is ad-hoc, there is no real way to track how or where it is used. You have to keep up with that on your own. But it does provide for all the logical separation you should ever need.

Setting	Description
Image	Specifies whether your image (if applicable) is to be rendered from a file on your site or from a remote URL.
Text/Script	The text in this field is handled differently depending on the Banner Type previously selected. For most banner types, just leave this field blank. For type Text, the value appears as simple text (unlinked) below the hyperlinked Banner Name field (see Figure 4-45). For the Script type, this field can contain raw HTML, supporting a variety of link types and formats. The field length is limited to 1000 characters.
URL	If this value is populated, it is used instead of the URL associated with the vendor. You can use this URL to point to specific pages in a vendor's site or to configure extra query string parameters. This field also displays as hyperlinked text on banners of the Text type (see Figure 4-45).
CPM/Cost	At the time of this writing, the CPM value is not used for any calculation. However, it does provide a convenient place to record this information in the context of the banner.
Impressions	If specified, this value is one of the criteria used to determine whether a banner should be shown. To limit a banner's display based on the number of impressions, this field removes it from rotation after the value has been reached.
Start Date	Use this field to set up banners in advance to begin displaying at a future date.
End Date	Together with Start Date, you can create banners to run for specific date durations for events, special deals, holidays, and so on.
Criteria	Specifies how the Impressions and Date constraints should be enforced. If they are enforced independently of one another (OR), a banner ceases to display outside of its date constraint or even within its date constraint if the number of impressions has been reached. If they are enforced jointly (AND), all criteria must be true for the banner to cease display. The AND option helps to address a lack of throttling control. On a busy site with few banners in rotation, a given number of impressions can be used up quickly and so displayed over only a brief time period. By jointly evaluating the criteria, a more equitable rotation is achieved by providing for additional banner impressions during the time period.

Figure 4-45

139

You can advise vendors of the status of a banner by clicking the Email Status To Vendor button at the bottom of the Edit Banner page. This sends an e-mail to the address specified in the Vendor details, which relays the banner field information (text, costs, and constraints) and performance (view and click-through counts).

Vendors as Affiliates

Just as your site links to vendors through the use of banners, your vendors may also link to you. If you would like to be able to track your vendors' click-through performance to your site, click Add New Affiliate. Define a tracking period and associated Cost Per Click (CPC) and Cost Per Acquisition (CPA), and e-mail the vendor the link information by clicking Send Notification (see Figure 4-46).

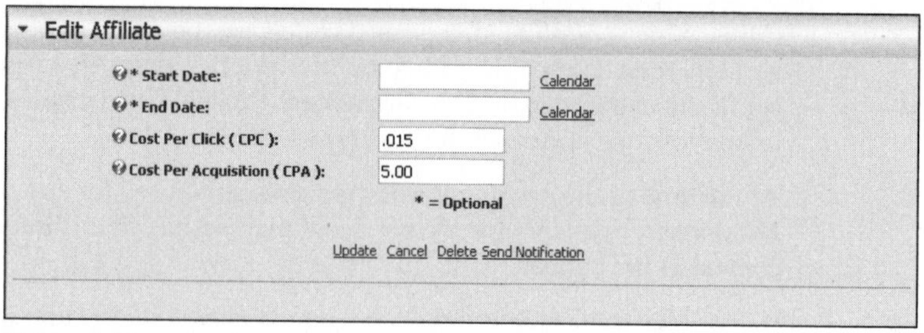

Figure 4-46

The CPC information for affiliate referrals is summarized in the Edit Vendor list, just as click-through is for banners. However, the CPA information is currently unused. You can specify multiple affiliate relationships under a single vendor to provide for tracking during discrete time periods.

At the time of this writing, it is possible to create affiliate referrals with overlapping date ranges. This produces double counts of vendor performance during the period of overlap, so be sure to end one affiliate period before starting another.

Newsletters

Periodically, you'll want to communicate with your users. The Newsletter page provides a convenient way for you to do this by enabling you to send e-mail to users in specified roles (see Figure 4-47). Remember when you set up the Newsletter Subscribers role? Here's where you put that to use.

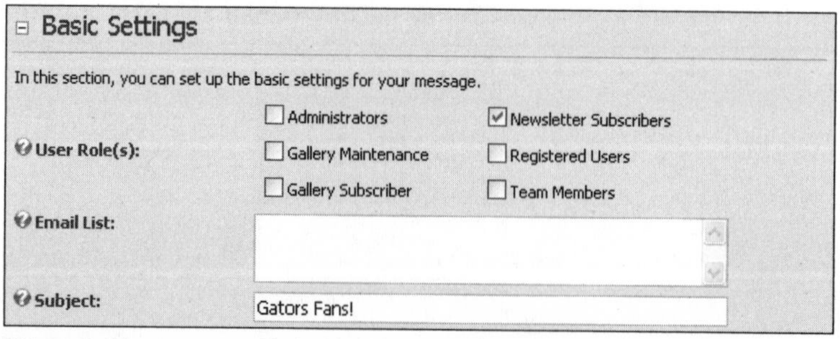

Figure 4-47

Just select the roles that you want to be included in the distribution. If users belong to more than one role, they'll still get only one e-mail. You can also specify additional recipients separated by semicolons in the Email List field. And you can format your e-mail as either text or HTML.

Figure 4-48 shows the advanced e-mail options, which include sending a file attachment and choosing the priority setting. The Send Method option enables you to specify whether your e-mail is personalized. Choosing the BCC method sends just one e-mail, which is delivered to all users. Choosing the TO method causes your e-mail to be personalized (for example, "Dear John Doe").

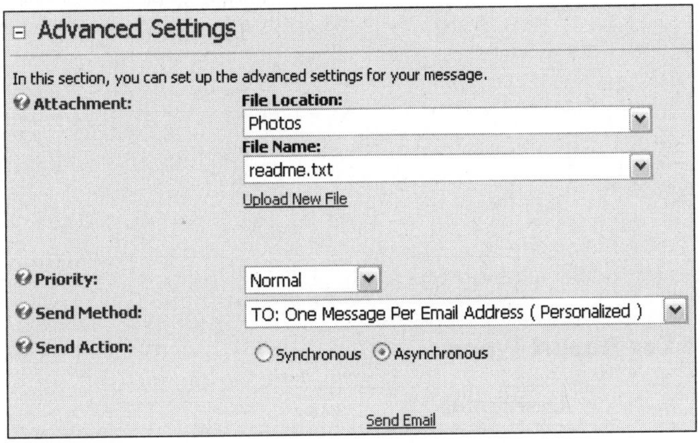

Figure 4-48

Using the TO method seems much more personal, but it comes at a cost. First, the processing required to create a separate e-mail for each user could be substantial (with large user volume). Second, it significantly increases your bandwidth utilization. The bandwidth associated with the BCC method is minimal — just one e-mail. However, the bandwidth associated with the TO version is the product of the size of the e-mail and the number of users.

You can also choose whether the sending of e-mail is processed synchronously or asynchronously. If you have a large list of users, asynchronously probably makes the most sense. In either case, a summary e-mail is sent to the Portal Administrator reporting on the number of recipients, number of pieces of e-mail actually sent (1 or n), and the start/stop times for processing the job. DotNetNuke batches e-mail addresses into groups in the background so you never actually try to send an e-mail with thousands of BCC recipients.

Site Log

The Site Log displays text-based reports only, as shown in Figure 4-49.

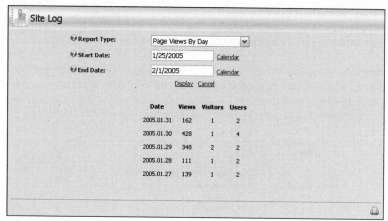

Figure 4-49

Table 4-17 identifies the available report types.

Table 4-17: Site Log Report Types

Type	Description
Affiliate Referrals	Tracks referrals from vendors who are defined as affiliates. By using their affiliate ID numbers in links to your site, you can capture how productive those affiliate links are.
Detailed Site Log	Includes all users and displays date and time, username, referrer, user agent, user host address, and page name.
Page Popularity	Displays the total number of visits to the pages on your site in the period specified. It includes the date and time of the last page visit.
Page Views By	This series of reports provides a summary of the number of visitors (anonymous) and users (logged in) that accessed your site in the intervals specified (Day, Day of Week, Hour, Month).
Site Referrals	Summary list of web pages (including search engines) that users have clicked to lead them to your site.
User Details	This series of reports provides a summary of the number of page visits recorded according to the characteristic specified (Agents, Frequency, Registrations by Country, and Registrations by Date). The Report by Frequency can be interesting — it identifies your most frequent visitors in any given period.

Logging occurs at the discretion of the Host, who has a number of options for how it is configured. If the Host chooses to generate text-based log files (like IIS logs), these reports become obsolete because they work only with database logging information (at this time). Chapter 5 provides more information on Host settings that control logging.

Recycle Bin

Have you ever deleted a file on your computer only to experience a panic moment? Portal Administrators might do that, too, once in a while, which is why DotNetNuke has a Recycle Bin feature (see Figure 4-50).

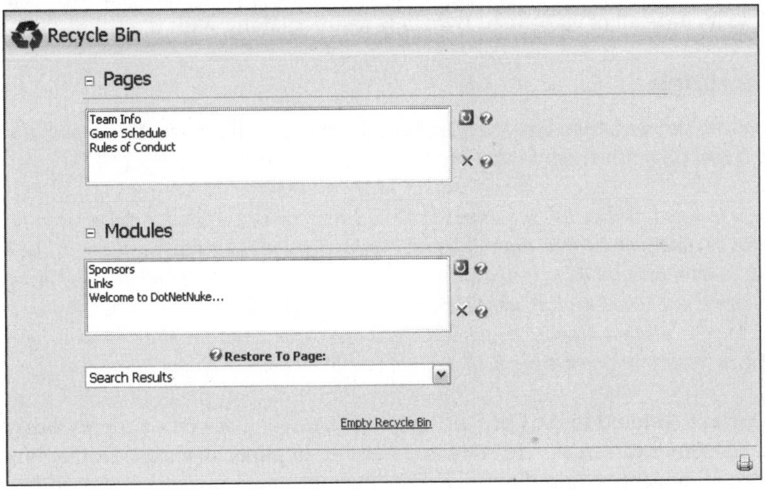

![Recycle Bin screenshot showing Pages section with Team Info, Game Schedule, Rules of Conduct and Modules section with Sponsors, Links, Welcome to DotNetNuke, Restore To Page: Search Results, Empty Recycle Bin]

Figure 4-50

The act of deleting a page or module doesn't really delete anything — it merely sets a flag that DotNetNuke understands internally as deleted and ignores it in the general interface. Items that have this flag set can be found in (and restored from) the Recycle Bin.

Developers can see this implementation by looking at the database fields Tab.IsDeleted and Modules.IsDeleted.

Recycling Pages

You can select single or multiple pages to restore or delete. However, when doing either you must follow the hierarchy of the pages for it to work. If you think about it, that makes perfect sense, but it is not obvious. In the example previously shown in Figure 4-50, the Team Info page was the parent to the others (in the menu structure). If you attempt to restore the Game Schedule page first it would have nowhere to go, so you would receive a warning like the one shown in Figure 4-51.

Figure 4-51

Likewise, if you try to permanently delete the top-level page (Team Info) before deleting the child pages, you would receive a warning like the one in Figure 4-52.

> ! **Team Info** Page Cannot Be Deleted Until Its Children Have Been Deleted First.

Figure 4-52

When a page is deleted, its modules are not listed individually in the Recycle Bin. That's because a page is considered to include all of its content (which is restored along with it).

Recycling Modules

When modules are deleted, they lose their association to a specific page. So when they are restored, you must select a target page for them to appear on.

Currently, a restored module has the same view and edit permissions that it did originally. However, this may not be what you have in mind if you are restoring a module that has been in the Recycle Bin for a while. In fact, because there is no convenient way to look at a module that is in the bin, you might be just restoring one to see what it was. The best way to do this is to restore modules to a page that is not visible to your users (a staging page). Then you can check it out for yourself and change whatever settings are necessary before moving it to its final (visible) home.

Modules are always restored to the ContentPane on the target page (shown previously in Figure 4-12). Because a skin designer can create virtually any number of panes in a skin, DotNetNuke can only rely on the existence of this one required pane. This is one more reason why it's a good practice to restore modules to a staging page before relocating them.

Cleaning Up

As you might have gathered, it's possible to accumulate quite a bit of junk in the Recycle Bin if you do a lot of creating and deleting of pages and/or modules. It's a good idea to do a little housecleaning here every once in a while so that when you really need it, the Recycle Bin is easier to navigate.

Log Viewer

The Log Viewer gives a Portal Administrator the ability to monitor a variety of events and associated details including (but not limited to) exceptions. Out of the box, DotNetNuke is configured to log exceptions only; however, any of the (approximately) 48 defined events can be logged at the discretion of the Host.

System logging is accomplished by means of either a database or an XML file-based provider (as configured by a Host). For all versions since 3.1.0, the database provider has been specified by default and can be verified by checking the following line in the web.config file:

```
<logging defaultProvider="DBLoggingProvider">
```

In the database provider, the EventLog table holds the records for all event types. However, in the XML file-based provider, a single set of logs is implemented as a group of XML files that are located in the default portal root directory. Records from these files are filtered to display only those generated by your portal. The Portal Administrator can filter the list by event type, limit the size of the list displayed, and even send an e-mail that lists the contents to a specified recipient if assistance is needed (as shown in Figure 4-53). There are no functional differences in use of either provider.

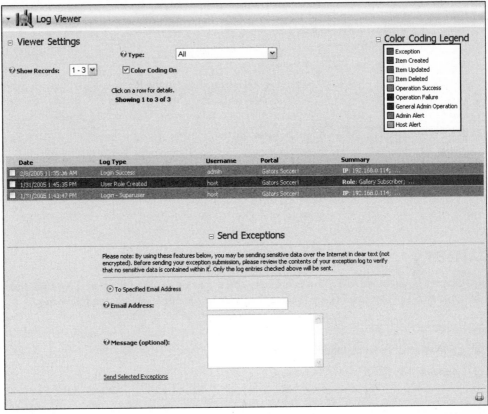

Figure 4-53

When you're sending log entries, the body of the e-mail message is populated with the XML text exactly as it appears in the log files.

Clicking an entry in the Log Viewer expands it to show the full details of the event. Some events contain as little as one or two items of detail, and others contain many more. The event detail for a module load exception is illustrated in Figure 4-54.

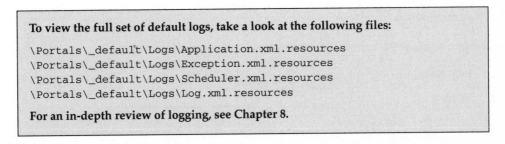

To view the full set of default logs, take a look at the following files:

```
\Portals\_default\Logs\Application.xml.resources
\Portals\_default\Logs\Exception.xml.resources
\Portals\_default\Logs\Scheduler.xml.resources
\Portals\_default\Logs\Log.xml.resources
```

For an in-depth review of logging, see Chapter 8.

```
ModuleId: 413
ModuleDefId: 102
FriendlyName: Sponsors
ModuleControlSource: DesktopModules/HTML/HtmlModule.ascx
AssemblyVersion: 03.00.10
Method: System.Data.SqlClient.SqlDataReader.Read
FileName:
FileLineNumber: 0
FileColumnNumber: 0
PortalID: 1
PortalName: Gators Soccer!
UserID: 2
UserName: admin
ActiveTabID: 55
ActiveTabName: Home
AbsoluteURL: /Default.aspx
AbsoluteURLReferrer:
ExceptionGUID: 00ea598e-e6be-4122-9722-8cd5a9e262bc
DefaultDataProvider: DotNetNuke.Data.SqlDataProvider, DotNetNuke.SqlDataProvider
InnerException: Syntax error converting the varchar value 'a' to a column of data type int.
Message: Syntax error converting the varchar value 'a' to a column of data type int.
StackTrace:
Source:
Server Name: MAIN
```

Figure 4-54

Summary

In this chapter, you learned just about everything there is to know about the Portal Administrator and the features and functions available to you in that role. Key features include the following:

- ❏ Control Panel
- ❏ Site Wizard, Preview Mode, and Help
- ❏ Preview Mode

You examined the tools available to configure your portal, such as the following:

- ❏ Site Settings
- ❏ Security Roles
- ❏ Pages
- ❏ Skins
- ❏ File Manager
- ❏ Languages
- ❏ Authentication

You also learned about the tools available to maintain your portal over time:

- ❏ User Accounts
- ❏ Vendors

- ❏ Newsletters
- ❏ Site Log
- ❏ Recycle Bin
- ❏ Log Viewer

You now have some understanding of how to do things, and when and why to do them.

5

Host Administration

In Chapter 4, you learned just about everything there is to know about administering a DotNetNuke portal. In this chapter, you'll learn everything there is to know about administering a collection of portals, their environment, and runtime features.

As the Host, you function essentially as the "creator" of the DotNetNuke universe in which the portals exist. This is a lofty sounding role, but it is an accurate description because the Host has absolute sway over what portals can and cannot do within their installation. Each Portal Administrator is subject to the "laws of nature" established by the Host, and the Host has complete authority to change those laws at will. Some of those laws apply universally to all portals in the installation, but others apply discretely to individual portals.

> *Understanding the Host role is essential. Each Portal Administrator considers his or her portal to be alone in its own corner of the cyber-universe, but the Host knows otherwise. Host options provide for differentiation between one installation of DotNetNuke and another. Configuration choices made by the Host can affect function and performance of all portals and must therefore be made wisely and with deliberate intent.*

When you complete this chapter, you'll know everything you need to know as a Host to effectively configure and manage a DotNetNuke installation.

Who Is the Host?

Continuing with the "Host as creator" analogy could get you in trouble in some circles (not to mention with your editor!). Because DotNetNuke is an "equal opportunity application," we'll find another way to describe the Host that is less prone to cause this particular brand of excitement. (DotNetNuke generates plenty of excitement in business and technology circles and we're quite content with that.)

To clearly identify the Host requires you to first review a defining characteristic of DotNetNuke. You'll recall from Chapter 3 that DotNetNuke supports "multiple web sites from the same codebase." With one installation of DotNetNuke, you can create as many unique portals as you like, each with its own URL(s), identity, features, users, data, and so on. You learned in Chapter 4 that each portal has its own administrator, but this begs the question, "Who administers the creation of portals?" So this is how the scope of the role first comes into focus. The Host is the user who creates portals. But the Host does a lot more — so much more that this entire chapter is devoted to the role.

Prior to version 3.0, the Host was alone in his sovereignty, carrying all the responsibility that went along with being the only user in that role — big title, big job. There was only one Host account. Version 3.0 introduced the role of SuperUser, so instead of being forced to play deity a Host could open ranks to allow for a more Justice League approach to configuration and maintenance. All SuperUsers have "superpowers" in the DotNetNuke universe, including all of the capabilities traditionally associated with the original Host account, such as access and full administrative permissions to every portal in the installation.

So the first thing you've learned is that "Host" is a legacy term, carried forward from previous generations of DotNetNuke. Understanding this, you can now feel free to interchange the terms Host and SuperUser — in all but one case. The default installation of DotNetNuke has one SuperUser account pre-installed whose username actually is "host."

Where Do You Begin?

If you're going to master a universe, you have to manifest your superpowers and take some cues from the most famous "in the beginning" of all! Breathe some life into a new user, or, in keeping with the Justice League theme, be a hero and get a sidekick.

The first thing you want to do is create another SuperUser account and then retire the default host account. It's a prudent security measure in any software installation to retire default administrative accounts to thwart dubious hacking efforts. At a minimum, you'll want to change the password for the default host account, although you can delete it entirely.

> *Starting with version 3.0, DotNetNuke utilizes a version of Microsoft's ASP.NET 2.0 MemberRole component in the default Membership Provider. One of the many distinct features of this component is the implementation of user lockout. After a specified number of invalid password attempts, a user account will be unable to log in. Although DotNetNuke resets the password lockout after 10 minutes (a default time period that you can modify), the nuisance can be avoided entirely by using a different account and username.*

Log in using your new SuperUser account username and password. Notice that you have a top-level Host menu (see Figure 5-1). You'll be getting into the details of each its menu items in this chapter, but right now just select the SuperUsers Accounts menu item.

When the SuperUsers Accounts page opens, you'll see a familiar view (see Figure 5-2). The page is literally the same control that is used for managing other users' accounts and works in the same way (if you need a refresher on how this works, consult Chapter 4). It's even titled User Accounts.

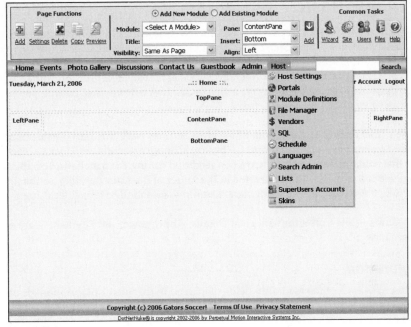

Figure 5-1

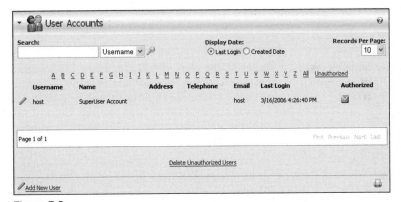

Figure 5-2

Configuring Your Installation

As you're about to see, the Host has a lot of options and tools for configuring the environment in which portals live. As you learned in Chapter 4, in the context of the Portal Administrator, some capability is specifically appropriate for initial configuration, some for routine operations, and some for ongoing maintenance, reporting, and issue resolution. As you move through each of the Host Settings, you'll see how they apply to those needs.

Host Settings: Basic

Host Settings (Host ⇨ Host Settings) is divided into two categories for the sake of organization: Basic Settings and Advanced Settings. Each category consists of a number of option groups.

As with Site Settings, there is an important text button at the bottom of the Host Settings page: Update. Despite the fact that a number of controls on the Host Settings page generate postbacks, no changes are saved until this button is clicked.

There is also a final control at the bottom of the Host Settings page that falls outside of any option group, the Upgrade Log For Version selector and Go button. Choose a version and click Go to view a log file (if one exists) that contains any errors or warnings recorded during the installation or upgrade process for the selected version. The log files are created in the folder of the Data Provider, so the default installation of DotNetNuke puts those files in \Providers\DataProviders\SqlDataProvider*.log.

The basic settings — Site Configuration, Host Details, Appearance, and Payment — are explored in the following sections.

Site Configuration

Table 5-1 describes each of the read-only fields displayed in the Site Configuration group under Basic Settings. This group is particularly helpful in identifying the context under which your installation of DotNetNuke is running. If you are communicating with an ISP or hosting company, these details may be useful in diagnosing any issue you might be investigating.

Table 5-1: Site Configuration Fields

Field	Description
DotNetNuke Version	Indicates the version of DotNetNuke that's currently running. Until version 3.0, the only way to verify the running version was to check a database value or to enable an option to display the version in the browser's title bar (see "Show Copyright Credits" in Table 5-3). The format of a DotNetNuke version number is `[Major Version].[Minor Version].[Package Version]`
	Major and minor versions combine to identify which functional version of DotNetNuke you are using (for example, 4.0). The Package Version indicates a particular package that may be an alpha or beta testing release, a public release, a security patch release, and so on.
Data Provider	Identifies the Data Provider that DotNetNuke is currently using.
.NET Framework	Indicates the version of the .NET CLR that DotNetNuke is running under. This can be helpful in ensuring proper setup when your server environment supports multiple versions of the ASP.NET framework. For developers, this is System.Environment.Version.
ASP.NET Identity	Identifies the Windows account name under which DotNetNuke is running (or the name of the account being impersonated). For developers this is System.Security.Principal.WindowsIdentity.GetCurrent.Name.

Field	Description
Host Name	Identifies the host name of the system DotNetNuke is running on. For developers this is Dns.GetHostName.

Host Details

The host details establish the identity of the installation for both internal processing and external identity (see Table 5-2). For the most part, the settings of individual portals define their own identity. However, skin object support is available to pass on host information into portal-level skins. This can be useful for portals whose support requirements are met by their host so that they can dynamically inject appropriate title and contact information where needed.

Table 5-2: Host Details Settings

Setting	Description
Host Portal	This drop-down selection identifies which portal in the installation is to be considered the default. The default portal attributes are used where no other portal context can be determined. For example, when an invalid URL is used to reach the installation, the request is answered on the first alias of the specified Host Portal.
Host Title	This value is used to populate the text for the [HOSTNAME] skin token.
	Prior to version 3.0, you could see the [HOSTNAME] skin token in action on the bottom of the default skin. It was often imposed by the host as a means of injecting a "powered by" link into each portal's skin.
Host URL	Specifies the link target for the [HOSTNAME] skin token. (This is not the same as an alias for the default portal.)
Host Email	Most e-mail in DotNetNuke is sent to or from the individual Portal Administrators. However, there are a few specific cases where the Host e-mail address is used (for example, an SMTP configuration test, a [HELP] skin token, and so on).

To avoid potential problems with outbound e-mail, ensure that the Host Email is a valid address on the SMTP Server (described later in Table 5-5).

Appearance

In Chapter 4, you learned about a number of optional settings for default portal appearance. If those choices are left unmade, the host default choices are applied. Additionally, the host has a couple of other configuration options that affect the appearance of portals in this installation. Table 5-3 summarizes the effects of each choice.

Table 5-3: Appearance Settings

Option	Description
Show Copyright Credits	Inserts the DotNetNuke version number into the browser's title bar and populates the [DOTNETNUKE] skin object. In the default skin, this is displayed as a small thin bar across the bottom of the page that shows the DotNetNuke copyright (see the bottom of Figure 5-3).
Use Custom Error Messages	Specifies whether DotNetNuke or ASP.NET will intercept module errors. If this option is selected, DotNetNuke displays only basic friendly messages to non-Admin users. If the user is an Admin (or Host) user, full error information is made available. Figures 5-4 and 5-5 illustrate the difference between the same error messages presented to Users and Administrators/SuperUsers, respectively. Detailed information is also retained in the error log.
Host Skin	If a skin is not specified in the portal Site Settings, this skin is used as the default for each page where a skin is not explicitly specified in Page Settings. The Host Skin, Host Container, Admin Skin, and Admin Container settings work exactly like their counterparts in the Portal Administrators Site Settings. For more detail, see Chapter 4.
Host Container	If a container is not specified in the portal Site Settings, this container is used as the default for each module where a container is not explicitly specified in Module Settings.
Admin Skin	If a skin is not specified in the portal Site Settings, this skin is used as the default for Admin pages.
Admin Container	If a container is not specified in the portal Site Settings, this container is used as the default for modules on every Admin page.
Upload Skin	Uploading a skin from the Host Settings loads it into the Host's default folder, which makes it available to all portals. This is in contrast to uploading from Site Settings, where it loads into the Portal Root folder. Skins uploaded from Host Settings are located in \Portals_default\Skins.
Upload Container	Uploading a container from the Host Settings loads it into the Host's default folder, which makes it available to all portals. This is in contrast to uploading from Site Settings, where it loads into the Portal Root folder. Containers uploaded from Host Settings are located in \Portals_default\Containers.

The Show Copyright setting can be helpful in a development environment for quick reference to the running version (see Figure 5-3). In a production environment, however, it can pose a risk of exposure to anyone trolling specifically to locate DotNetNuke web sites. A simple Google search of the copyright statement or DNN in the title bar yields results for sites that have not disabled this option.

Figure 5-3

ASP.NET error messages can be helpful and informative for developers, but the familiar "yellow screen of death" (the standard ASP.NET error page) doesn't do much for the confidence of users and clients. DotNetNuke's Custom Error Messages option intercepts errors and encapsulates them within either the offending module's container or, in the case of a non-module error, injects them into the top of the Content Pane (see Figure 5-4).

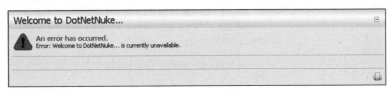

Figure 5-4

Because the error information is confusing for users but valuable for support personnel, DotNetNuke displays different error information based on the current user. If the current user is an Administrator or SuperUser, full detailed information is provided (see Figure 5-5). Other users are spared the gory details and presented with a friendlier message.

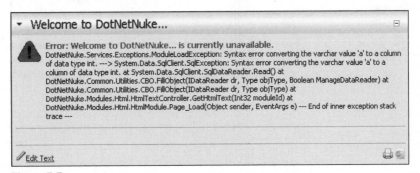

Figure 5-5

Payment Settings

You learned in Chapter 4 that many of these Payment Settings have been preserved from earlier versions of DotNetNuke for legacy support purposes. For the Host, these settings come into play only as defaults for new portal creation or for portal subscription renewal. These Payment Settings (see Table 5-4) will be deprecated in a future version in favor of more robust eCommerce APIs.

Table 5-4: Payment Settings

Setting	Description
Hosting Fee	Represents a default monthly charge associated with hosting a portal. This value is displayed on the Host's list of portals and is applied to new portals at the time of their creation. It can also be specified within a portal template, which would override this default value. If subscription renewal is activated, this fee is used for the monthly renewal rate.
Hosting Currency	Default host currency is used in conjunction with the specified Payment Processor (for example, as a required parameter for PayPal processing). This value is applied to new portals at the time of their creation but can also be overridden within a portal template.
Hosting Space (MB)	Specifies a default disk space limit for new portals. As with many other portal values, it can be overridden in a portal template. It is an enforced limit that's displayed at the base of the File Manager in the Portal Administrators view. As Host, you can change this value in the Site Settings for a specific portal.
Demo Period (Days)	If Anonymous Demo Signup is enabled, the Expiry Date for a new portal is set this many days into the future. As Host, you can change this value in the Site Settings for a specific portal.

Anonymous Demo Signup	This is a legacy feature and its use is highly discouraged.
	
	If this option is disabled, only the Host Administrator can create a new portal. If enabled, anonymous users can sign up and immediately log in as Portal Administrator to their own child portal. You have to create your own link somewhere to reach the signup page, but you can copy it from your browser's address bar after clicking Add New Portal on the Portals page. It should have a form like one of the following (depending upon your FriendlyUrls settings):
	
	`http://soccer.dotnetnuke.com/Default.aspx?tabid=17&ctl=Signup&mid=321`
	
	`http://soccer.dotnetnuke.com/tabid/17/ctl/Signup/mid/321/Default.aspx`
	
	This page is not illustrated specifically, but it uses the same control as standard portal signup, which is shown later in Figure 5-12.

Setting	Description
	A legacy feature of DotNetNuke, this setting was originally provided to showcase the capability of DotNetNuke to host private portals for potential clients. Although it's still supported in version 4.0, it is not without its share of legacy issues. Demo signup is enabled throughout the installation, not just on the Host Portal, so a clever anonymous user who locates a DotNetNuke site might try the demo portal signup. The Portal Root ensures file separation and the host File Upload Extensions setting protects from unsafe files, but a malicious user who finds your site could use you as an anonymous download location for the duration of the demo period (or until you catch him or her). Further, because the user chooses the child portal name, you could wind up with unpleasantly named folder paths indexed by search engines that you would rather not have. Because demo signup creates the user as Portal Administrator, a valid e-mail address is not even required.

The Hosting Space option is included with the Payment Settings because it is recognized as a factor that commands premium pricing from a web host, and therefore generally also from a VAR (value added reseller). If a file upload attempt causes the hosting space to be exceeded, an error message is displayed (see Figure 5-6).

Enforcing the file upload limit protects you from rampant file uploading by well-meaning clients who don't understand the value of limited disk space. It provides the ability to proactively allocate your available disk space among clients as well as an opportunity to assess charge-back for additional usage.

File upload capabilities through an HTML Provider can be disabled. Unless the control maker has made it possible to intercept and filter file upload requests, DotNetNuke cannot ensure integrity of the portal files based on hosting space, allowable file extensions, or directory security. By default, all file uploads should be performed through the File Manager.

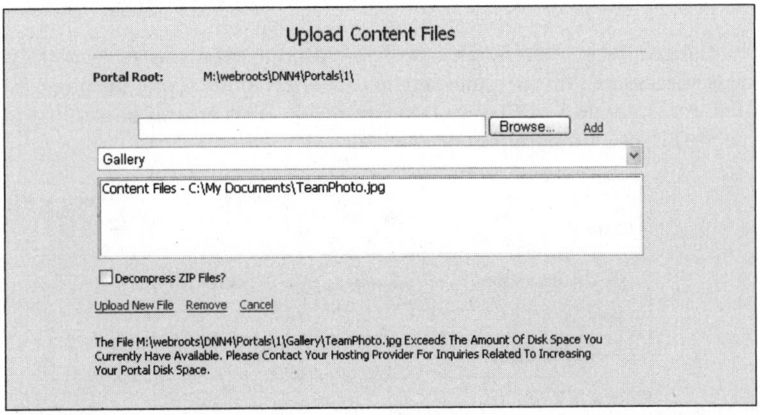

Figure 5-6

Host Settings: Advanced

The Advanced Settings category of Host Settings includes Proxy, SMTP Server, and other settings. These are explored in the following sections.

Proxy Settings

In general, DotNetNuke should not require specific Proxy Settings. However, some modules may address additional ports for which Proxy Settings are required in your environment (for example, RSS, FTP, NNTP, and so on). Standard settings are configurable for the Proxy Server Name, Port, UserID, Password, and Timeout duration.

Check with your network administrator about appropriate values for these settings in your location.

SMTP Server Settings

Outbound e-mail requires that a valid SMTP server be specified. Table 5-5 explains the SMTP Server Settings in more detail.

Table 5-5: SMTP Server Settings

Setting	Description
SMTP Server	This value must resolve to a valid SMTP server. You can specify the server by computer name (for example, MYSERVER or Localhost), IP address (for example, 127.0.0.1), or URL (for example, smtpauth.earthlink.net).
SMTP Authentication	Unless your SMTP server is an open relay or filtered by IP, you need to specify an authentication method. Most SMTP servers use Basic authentication, although MS Exchange servers prefer NTLM.
SMTP Username	Login name for the account on the SMTP Server (optional).
SMTP Password	Password for the account on the SMTP Server (optional).

After you've configured these settings, click the Test button to send a message to the Host Email. If the send operation is successful, you see a message to that effect at the top of the page. If the operation is unsuccessful, you may receive a CDO error (see Figure 5-7). This error is generally produced as a result of specifying an SMTP server that cannot be reached.

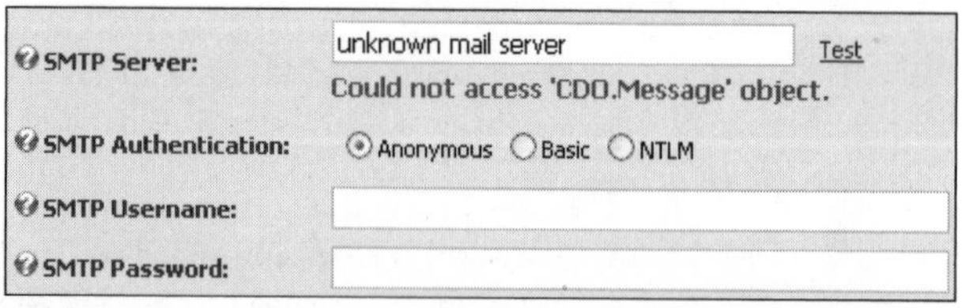

Figure 5-7

In hosting situations, the web server itself often runs a simple SMTP service for handling outbound e-mail generated by web sites. Although this setup initiates outbound e-mail, that mail is often flagged as SPAM by the target domains (especially domains like Hotmail.com, Yahoo.com, and so on). For best results, the SMTP server you specify should be the one in the MX record for your domain. Depending on your SMTP server's configuration, it may be necessary for Portal Administrators' e-mail addresses to be recognized on the server as well.

If you are testing from a home network via a broadband connection, be aware of your ISP's policies regarding SMTP servers. Generally speaking, most ISPs do not allow the trafficking of e-mail from other SMTP servers on their networks (as a SPAM control measure). You either need to configure DotNetNuke to use the credentials of your ISP account (just as you would in your local e-mail client) or configure a local SMTP server to relay through your ISP and specify that local server in DotNetNuke.

Other Settings

There are a number of other settings, including some that fall into the category of "super powers." Each setting is described in Table 5-6, but several of them are explained in greater detail later in the chapter when the functional aspects of the features that these settings control are discussed.

Table 5-6: Other Advanced Settings

Setting	Description
Control Panel	Select the Control Panel that Portal Administrators will use. Chapter 4 contains a full description of the choices.
	The capability to select the Control Panel exists largely to promote the concept of creating customized Control Panels for the host. If you created your own Control Panel, what would you make it look like?
Site Log Storage	Enables you to specify whether site log information is stored in the database or in files. File-based logs are written using the IIS 6 log conventions and are stored in the each portal folder with the following naming convention: /portals/<portalid>/logs/ex<yymmdd>.log. The database option is specified by default.
Site Log Buffer (Items)	This value defines the number of site log entries that are held in memory before storing them. Setting the buffer to 0 turns logging off entirely.
	Changing the buffer value does not affect the actual I/O cost of logging, but it does change where and when the cost is incurred. For example, if the log buffer is set to 1, every page request in every portal will incur the (slight) overhead of the log I/O, whereas if the log buffer is set to 20, only 1 in 20 requests will incur the overhead, but it will incur the overhead of all 20 I/O requests.

Table continued on following page

Setting	Description
	If the cache is cleared (whether by the restart of the application, in Host Settings, or by other means), any uncommitted items in the log buffer are lost.
	Individual buffers are cached for each portal, but this setting applies globally to all of them. Setting this value too high could result in data loss for low traffic sites whose cache might expire (and be lost) before reaching the buffer threshold.
Site Log History (Days)	DotNetNuke performs site logging on an individual portal level and retains that information for the number of days specified. This value represents the default duration that will be applied to each new portal created. Changing this value has no effect on the configuration of existing portals, although as Host, you can change this value in the Site Settings for a specific portal.
	Expiration of site log data is contingent upon execution of a scheduled job, which periodically truncates the buffer to the duration specified. The PurgeSiteLog job must be enabled in the Scheduler for this to occur; otherwise the SiteLog table can grow unchecked. Job scheduling is covered later in this chapter.
Disable Users Online	UsersOnline is a popular functionality in many online portal applications, tracking and displaying the number of users registered on the site, how many users are currently using the site, and so on. However, this functionality imposes unnecessary processing overhead on each page request for sites that don't need it. By checking this option, logic within DotNetNuke that populates UsersOnline tracking tables and cache objects is bypassed for the entire installation.
	Setting this option is only half the process required to enable or disable UsersOnline. An essential part of UsersOnline is a corresponding scheduled job that performs periodic cleanup on the associated AnonymousUsers and UsersOnline database tables. If this job is enabled without UsersOnline in use, it is an unnecessary drain on system resources. Conversely, if it is not enabled when UsersOnline is in use, these tables grow unchecked. Job scheduling is covered later in this chapter.
Users Online Time (Minutes)	UsersOnline tracks the presence of users who have been active on the system within this time period. When the scheduled job runs to clear the tracking tables, it uses this time period as a basis for determining which records to clear.

Setting	Description
	UsersOnline does not track or log personal information and is not a mechanism for "spying" on users. It makes temporary note of who is logged in, what page they are currently visiting (no history), and how many anonymous users are currently viewing the site. The data is deleted after this duration has passed.
Auto-Unlock Accounts After (Minutes)	As a security measure to thwart hacking attempts, DotNet-Nuke locks out a user account after a series of unsuccessful login attempts. Such an account can be automatically unlocked with a successful authentication after a certain period of time has elapsed. This value is the number of minutes to wait until the account is automatically unlocked. Enter **0** to disable the auto-unlock feature.
File Upload Extensions	This comma-separated list specifies the file extensions that are permissible through the File Manager. It comes prefilled with a variety of common "safe" file extensions and can be fully customized. The file management utilities within the portal are "intelligent" and reference this allowable file list. For example, a file that is renamed in the File Manager cannot be renamed with an invalid file extension. Likewise, files with invalid file extensions are ignored when an uploaded zip file is unpacked.
Skin Upload Permission	You can enable Portal Administrators to upload skin and container files by selecting Portal. To restrict them from uploading skin and container files, select Host.
Module Caching Method	Module instances have a Cache Time setting that can be modified to improve performance in relatively static modules. This setting controls whether module caching is performed on disk or in memory. Memory caching provides the most flexibility and is the highest performance method, but it also consumes the most system resources. When this option is enabled, HTML files are created and stored on the file system in the following format: `\Portals\<portalid>\Cache\TabModule_<tabmodule id>_<language>.htm`

Table continued on following page

161

Setting	Description
Performance Setting	A variety of cache objects in DotNetNuke provide for increased performance. They do not all have the same duration. They expire based on their specific functionality—for example, User objects expire more often than Portal objects. Changing this setting applies a common multiplier that affects their relative duration (or lifespan). The duration is enforced within DotNetNuke, but it's still subject to external settings that govern the site (such as recycling the ASP.NET worker process). Moderate caching is the default setting.
	The No Caching option is primarily developer- or support-oriented. Without the benefit of the caching features of ASP.NET, the amount of work performed on each page request renders DotNetNuke slow to run and is not recommended. However, this option can be useful in tracking down a caching-related issue.
Clear Cache	Enables the Host to manually clear the cache on demand. Generally this is not required; however, as Host, you typically have access to manipulate database tables directly. Table updates applied this way bypass the application and may not be reflected until the cache is updated. You can force an update of cache to reflect your manual changes by clearing it. (Clearing the cache this way also dumps buffered logs, so it should be performed only when necessary.)
Scheduler Mode	The Timer Method maintains a separate thread to execute scheduled tasks while the worker process is alive. Alternatively, the Request Method triggers periodic execution of tasks as HTTP Requests are made. You can disable the Scheduler by selecting Disabled. The Scheduler is examined in detail later in this chapter.
Enable Event Log Buffer?	Like the site log, the event log can also be buffered for performance to avoid the overhead associated with logging I/O on every request. If checked, this setting causes event log entries to be buffered into cache and periodically written to the data store. If unchecked, log entries are written immediately.
	Unlike site logging, event log buffering is governed by a scheduled task (PurgeLogBuffer). If this task is not enabled or if the Scheduler is stopped, this setting has no effect and logging occurs as if this setting were unchecked. Event Logging is covered in more detail later in this chapter.
Use Friendly Urls	If checked, DotNetNuke invokes the FriendlyUrl Provider. By default, DotNetNuke installs a provider that produces "machine friendly" URLs that enable better indexing by search engines.

Setting	Description
	For developers, the default provider behavior is controlled by a rule file (siteurls.config) located in the web root.
	The default modules provided with DotNetNuke work well with this provider. However, not every module may work well with any specific implementation of Friendly Urls. It is advisable to ensure that any module you employ works with your FriendlyUrl Provider. For more information on FriendlyUrls, see Chapter 8.
Help URL	The target URL for administrative help, including the Help button in the Control Panel and the Online Help menu item for administrative functions. If this field is blank, the Control Panel Help button is disabled and the Online Help menu item is not available on administrative functions.
	By default, DotNetNuke provides context-sensitive online help for all standard modules and administrative features at the following site:
	`http://www.dotnetnuke.com/default.aspx?` `tabid=787`
Enable Module Online Help	If enabled, an item for Online Help appears in every Module Actions Menu. This requires that a Help URL be configured in the Module Definitions for each module in use, although the developer may have provided this.

Managing Portals as Host

A number of settings defined at the portal level are limited to SuperUser access. Some of these were pointed out in the previous section but there are a few additional ones. Because these settings are applicable on a per-portal basis, you need to be in the context of the portal in question to change them. You can reach the site settings for any portal through the Portals page (Host ⇨ Portals). Just click the pencil icon next to one of the portal names (see Figure 5-8).

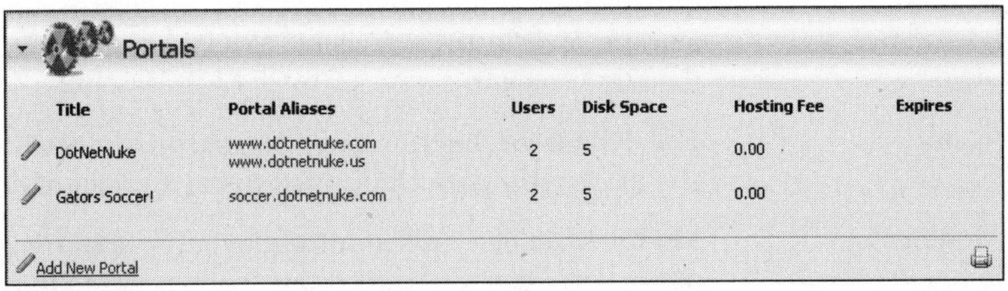

Title	Portal Aliases	Users	Disk Space	Hosting Fee	Expires
DotNetNuke	www.dotnetnuke.com www.dotnetnuke.us	2	5	0.00	
Gators Soccer!	soccer.dotnetnuke.com	2	5	0.00	

Add New Portal

Figure 5-8

Portals

From the Portals page you can create and maintain portals as well as generate a portal template for import into another DotNetNuke installation.

At a glance, the list enables you to see which portals are configured as well as their portal aliases, number of registered users, disk space threshold, hosting fee, and expiration date (if set). Click the pencil icon next to any entry to access its Site Settings page. When you are logged on as the Host, you have access to additional configuration items (see Figure 5-9) that the Portal Administrator cannot see.

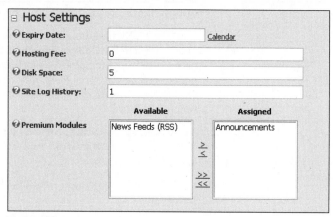

Figure 5-9

Table 5-7 explains how each of these advanced options affects the portal.

Table 5-7: Host-Only Site Settings

Setting	Description
Expiry Date	When the expiry date for a portal is exceeded, a friendly message is displayed in the place of regular content (see Figure 5-10).
Hosting Fee	The default for this value is established in the Host Settings. This is primarily a display field that indicates the value appropriate for monthly renewal.
Disk Space	The default for this value was set in the Host Settings. It limits the amount of disk space available to a Portal Administrator through the File Manager.
Site Log History	The default for this value was set in the Host Settings. It keeps the site log for this portal truncated to the number of days indicated.
Premium Modules	Modules can be installed for use by any portal or can be limited to use in specific portals by setting them as "premium." This set of controls identifies which premium modules have been applied to this portal. You learn more about host management of modules later in this chapter.

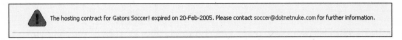

Figure 5-10

There's also a new control at the bottom of the Site Settings page for maintaining the list of aliases (domain names) for the portal (see Figure 5-11).

Figure 5-11

Prior to version 3.0, all portal aliases were maintained in a comma-delimited string, which restricted the number of aliases that could be assigned. Additionally, it made processing based on individual aliases more complex and inefficient. Starting with version 3.0, portal aliases are maintained as a list of separate items. To add an additional portal alias, simply click Add New HTTP Alias and enter it in the text box provided. A portal can answer to an unlimited number of portal aliases.

Adding a New Portal

To create a new portal, click Add New Portal on the bottom of the Portals page (or select it from the Action menu). The Signup page opens (see Figure 5-12).

The default root directory for the portal can be overridden. Aside from that, there should be only one field on this page that might be unfamiliar to you: Portal Type. You learn about Parent and Child portals in the next section.

Parent Portals and Child Portals

In Chapter 3, you were introduced to the concept of Parent and Child portals. Portal Setup is where you put those concepts into practice by specifying either a Parent or Child portal. The only real distinction between a Parent and a Child portal is that a Parent portal alias has a simple URL attributed to it, whereas a Child portal consists of a URL and subdirectory name. An example of a valid Parent portal name is www.dotnetnuke.com. Alternatively, you can specify an IP address instead of a domain name (for example, 209.162.190.188). An example of a valid Child portal name is www.dotnetnuke.com/soccer, and an IP address can be substituted here as well (for example, 209.162.190.188/soccer). A Child portal can be turned into a Parent portal simply by adding a URL to its list of portal aliases.

When a new Child portal is created, a physical directory is also created in the root of the web site with the Child portal's name. A page called subhost.aspx is copied into the directory as default.aspx. That's how DotNetNuke can implement addressing of the Child portal by the alias name (for example, www.dotnetnuke.com/soccer) without making modifications to IIS. Without existence of a physical path and filename (for example, www.dotnetnuke.com/soccer/default.aspx), IIS would normally process the request without ever handing it to ASP.NET, rendering an HTTP 404 Error or "page not found." You might wonder why a simple change to IIS would not be a better solution. It might be, but DotNetNuke is built to provide the functionality in environments where this level of access control may not be available (that is, in a shared hosting environment).

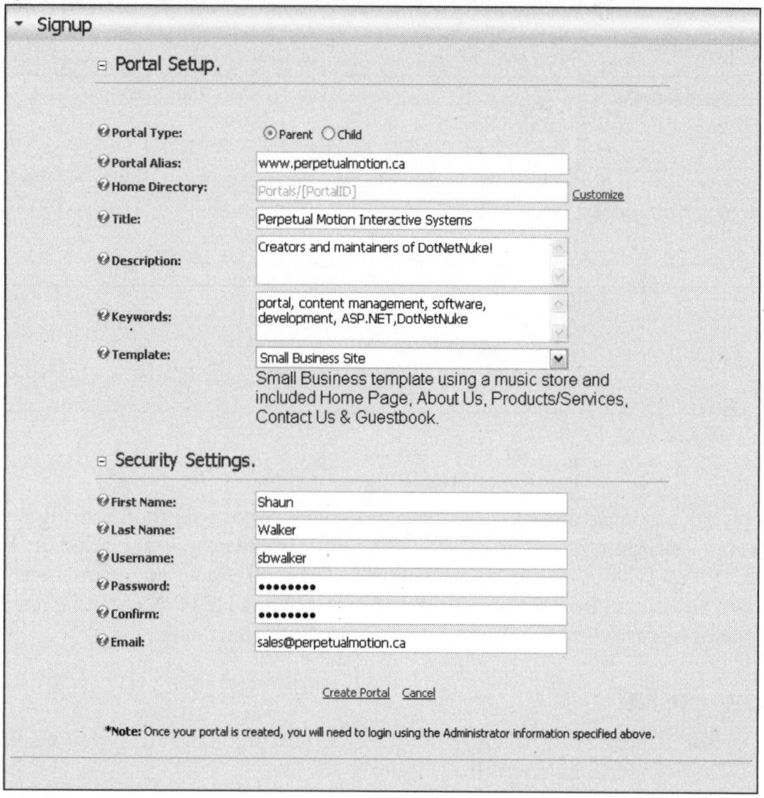

Figure 5-12

So why would you create a Child portal instead of a Parent? With a single registered domain name, you can create an infinite number of cname portals (for example, soccer.dotnetnuke.com) as long as your ISP supports a DNS wildcard for your domain. The most popular reason for creating a Child portal is the capability to emulate a single sign-on solution where credentials appear to be shared between portals. This is a common implementation in intranets where departmental portals are involved. Because Child portals exist in the same domain as the Parent portal, they can share access to a domain cookie, which preserves their logged-in status across subportals as long as the username and password are synchronized.

Portal Templates

In Chapter 4, you learned about portal templates in the context of importing one through the Site Wizard. As Host, you can create your own portal templates, which truly qualifies as a "superpower." Figure 5-13 illustrates the Export Template function, which is the second component of the Portals page on the Host menu.

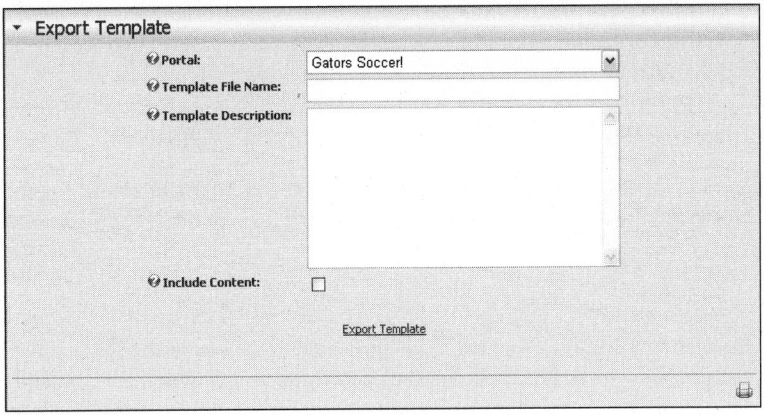

Figure 5-13

This feature enables you to select an existing portal, supply a name and description, and then generate a template that contains all the information necessary to re-create the portal on another installation (see Listing 5-1). Two files are generated in the `<name>.template` process, and `<name>.template .resources`. `.template` is a plain-text file that contains a complete XML representation of the portal, its pages, modules, settings, and file structure. `.resources` is just a zip file of the portal root that is exported as content (if that option is selected).

Listing 5-1: Portal Template (Settings Node)

```
<settings>
    <logofile>logo.gif</logofile>
    <footertext>Copyright 2002-2005 DotNetNuke</footertext>
    <expirydate>0001-01-01T00:00:00.0000000+11:00</expirydate>
    <userregistration>2</userregistration>
    <banneradvertising>1</banneradvertising>
    <currency>USD</currency>
    <hostfee>0</hostfee>
    <hostspace>5</hostspace>
    <backgroundfile />
    <paymentprocessor>PayPal</paymentprocessor>
    <siteloghistory>60</siteloghistory>
    <defaultlanguage>en-US</defaultlanguage>
    <timezoneoffset>-480</timezoneoffset>
</settings>
```

Portal templates are a powerful capability in DotNetNuke — but this capability is still "raw." This means that we've yet to provide user interface controls to direct how a template file is exported. At this point, template files contain everything including the kitchen sink! If you are creating templates, it would be wise to actually read through the generated file and make sure that there are no options specified that would be inappropriate for where you intend to apply them. As a standard XML file, this is a pretty simple thing to do and removing nodes that you don't want should work fine.

For example, a generated template contains nodes with all the settings for the current portal. As you can see in Listing 5-1, there are a few nodes here that you might not want to override in a portal that imports the template; nodes such as `<userregistration>`, `<hostspace>`, and `<paymentprocessor>`. These settings might be appropriate for a new portal, but templates located in the Host Root (\Portals_ default) are available to the Site Wizard and can be applied to existing portals as well.

Templates provide a lot of power and promise for automatic configuration and for sharing of portal information. However, they should be used with care until they're more fully "cooked."

Skins

The Portal Administrator and the Host each have their own version of the Skins page. As Host, both are visible and accessible to you, so it is essential that you understand which one you are working with.

When using the Admin ⇨ Skins page, you (as Host) always have access to the Upload Skin and Upload Container buttons. These are visible to the Portal Administrator only when the Skin Upload Permission is set to Portal (as previously described in Table 5-6). This enables you to upload skins and containers that are private to the specific portal — those files are uploaded to the Portal Root directory (\Portals\ <PortalId>). When using the Host ⇨ Skins page, the only difference is the target of the uploaded files. Skins and containers uploaded through the Host ⇨ Skins page are installed in the Default Portal directory (\Portals_default) and are available to every portal in the installation.

> To upload skins for a specific portal only, log in to that specific portal as a SuperUser and navigate to Admin ⇨ Skins. A quick way to navigate to any given portal is to go to the Portals list on the Host menu and click the portal alias name.

Log Viewer

Chapter 4 provided some basic information about the Log Viewer from the Portal Administrator's perspective. As the Host, there are two specific differences in your view of the logs as well as a few additional features. First, your view includes exceptions (and any other events that are hidden from the Portal Administrator). Second, your view can contain log entries from all portals (if selected as an option). You also have access to some additional functions, including the capability to select and delete specific log entries, clear the entire log, and edit the log configuration.

System logging is accomplished by means of either a database provider or an XML file-based provider. For all versions since 3.1.0, the database provider has been specified by default and can be verified by checking the following line in the web.config file:

```
<logging defaultProvider="DBLoggingProvider">
```

In the database provider, the EventLog table holds the records for all event types. In the XML file-based provider, a single set of logs is implemented as a group of XML files that are located in the default portal root directory. There are no functional differences in the use of either provider.

If you are using the XML file-based provider, the full set of logs is located in the following files:

\Portals_default\Logs\Application.xml.resources

\Portals_default\Logs\Exception.xml.resources

\Portals_default\Logs\Scheduler.xml.resources

\Portals_default\Logs\Log.xml.resources

From the Log Viewer, select Edit Log Configurations at the bottom of the page or from the Action menu to open the Edit Log Settings page illustrated in Figure 5-14.

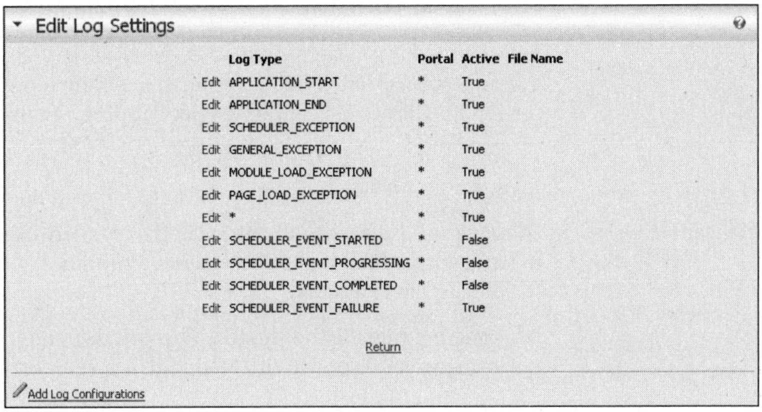

Figure 5-14

There are a number of preconfigured logging events — some enabled and some disabled. For example, because the Scheduler is disabled in the default installation of DotNetNuke, its logging events are also disabled. Click Add Log Configurations at the bottom of the page to add a new configuration, or click Edit next to an existing configuration to alter it. Figure 5-15 shows the Edit Log Settings page.

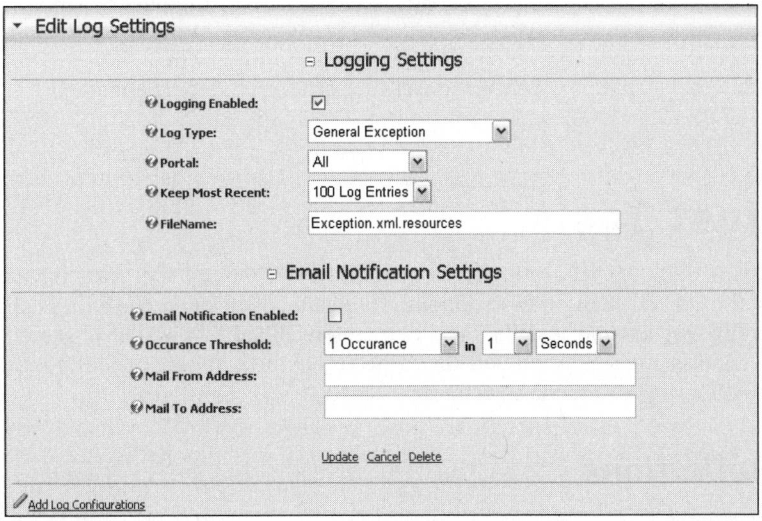

Figure 5-15

Table 5-8 explains each of the log configuration settings.

Table 5-8: Edit Log Settings

Setting	Description
Logging Enabled	Turns logging on for the item. Items can be defined in the log settings without being enabled (for example, the default Scheduler event logging settings).
Log Type	Select one of the system-defined event types to log or the All category (as appropriate). It is acceptable to define more than one log setting for the same event or for overlapping events.
Portal	Indicate a specific portal (or All portals) for which this event is to be logged.
Keep Most Recent	Selecting All preserves all entries in the log. Any other value results in truncation of the log to the maximum number of items specified for the log type selected.
FileName	Multiple log files can be created. This can be handy for monitoring performance and/or activity related to a given portal or event type.
Email Notification Enabled	When enabled, the SendLogNotifications scheduled job assembles and sends e-mail according to the Edit Log Settings when it runs.
Occurrence Threshold	Specifies how often an event must occur to trigger e-mail notification.
Mail From Address	Sent-from address specified on outgoing e-mail.
Mail To Address	Sent-to address specified on outgoing e-mail.

Other Host Tools

In addition to the portal-specific settings you've just learned about, SuperUsers have access to many other powerful tools and configuration options. These are not visible to the Portal Administrator and affect your entire DotNetNuke installation and, therefore, all portals. The level of sophistication of these configurable items is quite deep and will challenge you to think about how best to customize your installation to achieve your unique objectives.

Module Definitions

The Module Definitions page serves as the administration area for all of the modules installed in DotNetNuke. This page enables you to edit or delete existing module definitions and to add new modules.

DotNetNuke comes with a number of basic modules (identified in Chapter 3) preinstalled. Figure 5-16 shows the Module Definitions page for a default installation. Each module in the list is shown with a name, description, and a true/false option indicating whether it is marked as "premium."

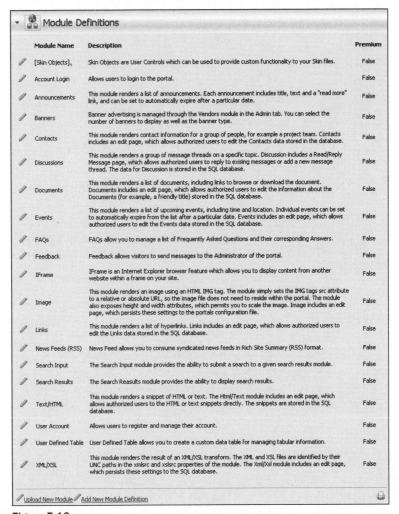

Figure 5-16

What Is a Premium Module?

A module that has been marked "premium" is not freely available to all Portal Administrators. Non-premium modules automatically show up in the selector on every Portal Administrator's Control Panel, but premium modules require Host configuration on a per-portal basis. The Premium module setting enables you to hide special-purpose modules installed or developed for one client from those installed or developed for another. It also enables you to segment your product offerings, providing extra functionality at a "premium" rate.

Editing Module Definitions

To edit a module definition (for example, if you want to mark an existing module as premium), click the pencil icon next to the module you want to edit (for example, Announcements).

Each module definition is comprised of three sections: the module description (see Figure 5-17), the module definitions, and the module controls (see Figure 5-18).

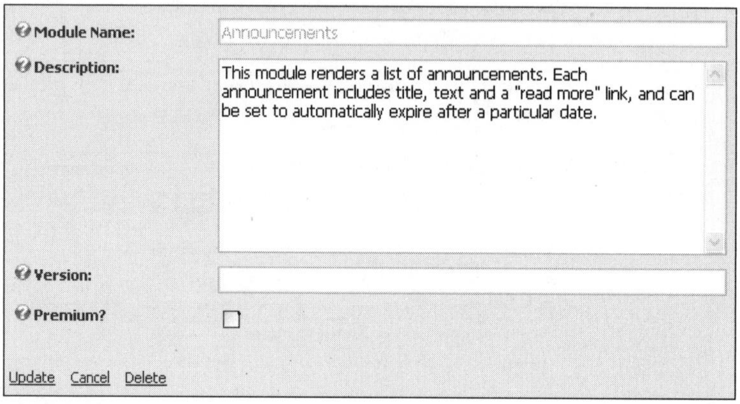

Figure 5-17

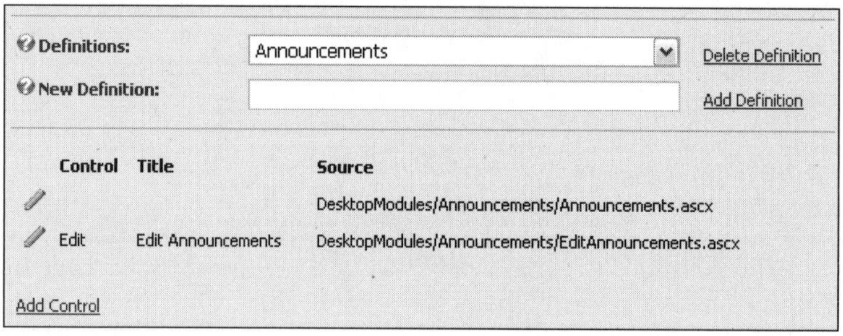

Figure 5-18

The module description settings (shown in Figure 5-17) hold the basic properties of the module. The Module Name is used in the drop-down list of modules available to Portal Administrators on the Control Panel. The Description is displayed on pages that describe the modules (for example, Module Definitions page). The Version is used by module developers when issuing updates of their modules. The Premium setting determines if a module is available to all portals or only those specifically given access.

A module can have any number of definitions. A definition directly matches to a single component of a module. For this reason, most modules usually have only one definition—they only add one component to the page. The Announcements module, for example, has only one component and it is called Announcements, as previously shown in Figure 5-18.

Some modules may add many components to a page, with each component providing differing functionality but part of a logical group. For example, a blogging module might contain a calendar, a list of blog entries, and a search module. These would be configured as three different definitions, but would still belong under the same Module Name (for example, myblog).

You can add definitions by typing in their name and clicking Add Definition (see Figure 5-18). Alternatively, you can select an existing definition from the drop-down list and click Delete Definition (see Figure 5-18).

Each definition may have a number of a controls associated with it. The controls directly map to ASP.NET user controls and each is marked with a name known as a key, which allows DotNetNuke to determine which control to load at runtime.

As previously shown in Figure 5-18, the Announcements module has only two controls: the user control that displays the announcements (announcements.ascx), and the edit announcement page (editannouncements.ascx). Complex modules may have a dozen or more configured controls.

The Control section enables you to add new controls by clicking the Add Control link; edit an existing control by clicking the pencil icon; or delete a control by editing it first and then clicking Delete on the Edit page.

Installing a New Module

There are two methods for installing new modules into your DotNetNuke environment. The first is an automated install. The second is manually adding the module definition. Chapter 17 contains a thorough examination of the packaging and installation of modules and other DotNetNuke add-ons, but the module installation processes are summarized here for the sake of continuity.

> *Developers generally use the manual method during the process of creating new modules. Hosts that are not involved in module development will probably never use it.*

Performing an automated install involves uploading a zip file containing the module (often referred to as a "module package" or "module install"). These zip files are generally available from independent developers and companies that create them.

DotNetNuke 3.0 was packaged with two sample modules that were not installed by default — Survey and Users Online — deferring their installation as a user exercise. As popular modules, they are now part of the default installation in DotNetNuke 4.0, so the following example reinstalls the Survey module. However, the process is the same for any module you may want to install.

> **Many free modules and other resources are available at** www.dotnetnuke.com. **These include robust forum, blog, and file repository modules; alternative editor providers, media players, and maps; and much more.**

Download a module zip file from www.dotnetnuke.com. The names of these files typically follow a format similar to modulename_xx.xx.xx_Install.zip or modulename_xx.xx.xx_Source.zip, indicating the name of the module, version, and content of the file. This format indicates whether the file also contains the source code for the module in addition to the files required for installation.

Click the Upload New Module button at the bottom of the Module Definitions page (previously shown in Figure 5-16) or on its action menu. The File Upload page opens (see Figure 5-19), with no options for selecting a target directory. This is because a module's install locations are not configurable. Modules are installed into a folder beneath the \DesktopModules directory as defined in the manifest file, supplied as part of the module package.

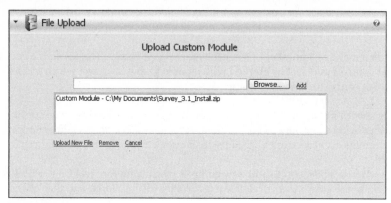

Figure 5-19

Click the Browse button and locate the module's zip file (for example, Survey_3.01.00_Install.zip). For the purposes of this example, any module zip file will do. After you make the selection, click the Add button. The filename is added to a list of files that enable you to upload multiple modules simultaneously. When you are satisfied with the list of files to upload, click the Upload New File button.

After the module is installed (or uploaded), a detailed log is displayed showing what happened during the install (see Figure 5-20). If any portion of the installation process fails, error messages appear in this log highlighted in red. If your module has a red error message, contact the module provider for technical support.

If there are no red error messages in the log, your module has been successfully installed and is now available to use within your installation.

Manually Installing a New Module

As previously mentioned, installing a new module manually is usually reserved for developers creating new modules. To install a new module manually, click the Add New Module Definition button at the bottom of the Module Definitions page (shown previously in Figure 5-16) or on its action menu.

The Add New Module Definition page opens and you can create your own module definitions using the same method as editing module definitions (described earlier in this chapter).

File Manager

The File Manager works for SuperUsers in the same way as it does for Portal Administrators, with a couple of minor exceptions. If you need a refresher on its basic operation, consult Chapter 4.

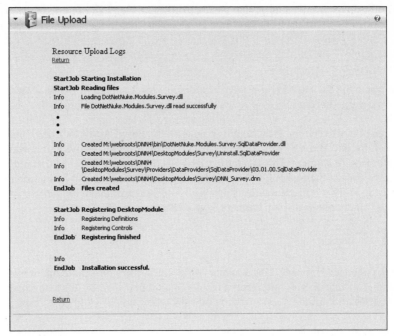

Figure 5-20

You learned previously that the Host can provide resources to all portals (for example, templates, skins, and so on) by making them available through the Host Root folder (that is, \Portals_default). Where Admin ⇨ File Manager provides access to each Portal Root, Host ⇨ File Manager provides access to the Host Root (see Figure 5-21).

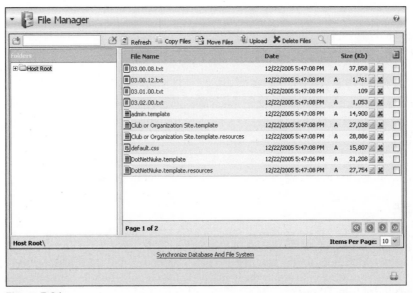

Figure 5-21

There is no additional control for applying permissions, because Host Root permissions are not configurable. Only SuperUsers can add, change, modify, or delete files in the Host Root.

Vendors

Like the File Manager, the Host Vendor page works for SuperUsers in the same way as it does for Portal Administrators. If you need a refresher on its basic operation, consult Chapter 4.

The only difference between the Host Vendor page and the Portal Administrator Vendor page is the underlying vendor list. You maintain a vendor list separate from the individual portals, which is visible by all of them through banners. This is a particularly useful feature for Hosts that maintain multiple portals of their own (rather than belonging to clients). One list of vendors can be maintained and used to serve advertising and/or affiliate relationships with multiple portals. In the Banner module, a Portal Administrator can choose to display banners from either source (Host or Site)

SQL

The Host SQL page (see Figure 5-22) is a handy utility for inquiry or remote maintenance. It provides for the processing of simple queries and returns results in a tabular format. It is also capable of executing compound queries and update queries when you select the Run As Script check box.

Figure 5-22 illustrates a couple of handy queries for managing user accounts locked out by the MemberRole Provider due to invalid password attempts. Although this can be accomplished on a user basis on each portal's User page (or by waiting 10 minutes), the query method can unlock all users in all portals with one query and is a convenient example.

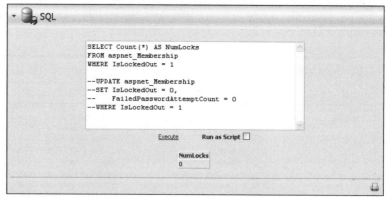

Figure 5-22

Schedule

Starting in DotNetNuke 2.0, two pieces of functionality were introduced that required recurring operations to be processed regularly — Users Online and Site Log — emulating batch processing. Ultimately, there are many applications for the services of a batch processor, and the Scheduler serves that function in DotNetNuke. Figure 5-23 illustrates the items available on the Schedule page and their default settings at the time of installation.

Carefully assess the items in the default schedule list, their settings, and enabled/
disabled status to ensure that they meet your specific operating requirements.

The Schedule page provides you with access to edit the settings of each item, or to add a new item by clicking the Add Item to Schedule button or selecting the Action menu item. It also provides appropriate at-a-glance information such as the enabled/disabled status, recurring frequency, and next scheduled execution time, as well as access to a detailed history report.

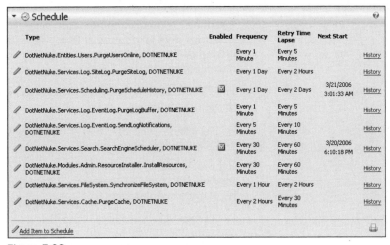

Figure 5-23

Schedule Item Details

Click the pencil icon next to an item to open the Edit Schedule page (see Figure 5-24). Table 5-9 explains each of the schedule item settings in detail. Setting changes made on the Edit Schedule page take effect immediately.

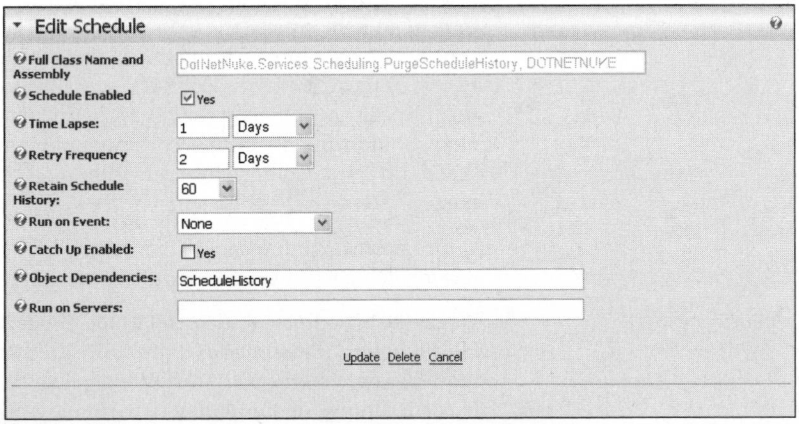

Figure 5-24

Table 5-9: Edit Schedule Settings

Setting	Description
Full Class Name and Assembly	This entry field should contain the full class name followed by the assembly name (such as "DotNetNuke.Entities.Users .PurgeUsersOnline, DOTNETNUKE"). Assemblies may belong to modules, skin objects, or other components you have installed that leverage the Scheduler's programming interface as long as they inherit from DotNetNuke.Scheduling .SchedulerCllient. Installing a component (or module) may actually create a Scheduler item for you rather than relying on you to create it yourself. Read the instructions carefully for any modules or components that you install.
Schedule Enabled	Enable or disable the schedule item. If disabled (unchecked), the Scheduler ignores the item when processing.
Time Lapse	Set the desired frequency for running this item (that is, every x minutes/hours/days).
Retry Frequency	If the task fails when it runs according to the specified frequency, it is retried according to this setting until the next regularly scheduled start.
Retain Schedule History	Each time a scheduled item is run, its success/fail status and a number of other useful information items are logged. This value determines the number of log records that are retained in this history. Older items are truncated from the log.
Run on Event	Enable a job to run on an event rather than on a schedule. The only event currently supported is APPLICATION_START because events triggered on APPLICATION_END are not guaranteed to run in ASP.NET.
Catch Up Enabled	If the Scheduler is unable to run when the scheduled start time of an item passes, the item is not run. This condition could be caused by any number of things, including a server reboot or recycling of the ASP.NET worker process. This setting indicates whether, at the next scheduled start time, an item should run only once according to the schedule or play "catch up" and run once for each scheduled start that was missed. Under normal circumstances this setting isn't necessary, but it is available for custom schedule items that require it.
Object Dependencies	When the Scheduler Mode is set to the Timer Method in the Host Settings, it executes as a multithreaded process. This requires some method of protection against possible deadlock conditions for simultaneously running threads.

Setting	Description
	This field provides for the specification of one or more comma-separated string values, which serve as semaphores to avoid deadlock. For example, if one scheduled item performs a `select` on the Users table and another item performs a massive update on the Users table, you might want to prevent these two items from running at the same time. So both items should have an object dependency on the same string value (for example, `"LockUsersTable"`). The dependency suppresses the start of any other items until the currently running item has finished.
Run on Servers	When you're running in a web farm environment, it may be necessary to limit the instances of any given scheduled process. If this comma-delimited field is empty, the scheduled process runs on any server that invokes it. However, if the field is not empty, a server only runs the process if it finds a match on its server name.
	Using this method a web farm can be configured to prevent multiple web servers from attempting the same database operation at the same time. Redundancy can be preserved by configuring the same processes to run on different web servers on complimentary schedules.

Schedule History

Click the History link next to an item to display the Schedule History page (see Figure 5-25). This page simply displays a log of results from previous runs of the scheduled item. The size of this log (number of items) is set in the Item Settings.

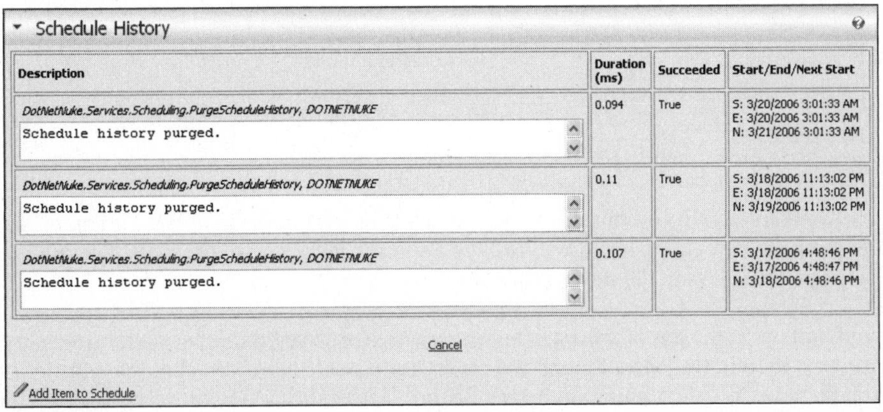

Figure 5-25

Schedule Status

You reach the Schedule Status page by selecting View Schedule Status from the action menu on any of the schedule-related pages (see Figure 5-26).

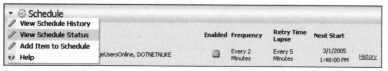

Figure 5-26

The Schedule Status page provides a detailed view of the current state of the Scheduler and running or pending items (see Figure 5-27). Refreshing the page quickly illustrates that DotNetNuke is busily working in the background to process your scheduled items.

Figure 5-27

There are two display areas on this page: Items Processing and Items In Queue. If you refresh while watching the Time Remaining run down to 0 for a specific item, you may catch it actually in execution, which is when it displays in the Items Processing area.

Command buttons at the top of this page enable you to stop/start the Scheduler if necessary. This suspends the execution of the jobs although the timers continue to run. Note that these buttons are not enabled if the Scheduler is running under the Request Method (previously described in Table 5-6).

Configuration

The Scheduler has a couple of useful settings that can be manipulated in the application's web.config file. To locate these settings, look for the section that resembles Listing 5-2. The effects of these settings are summarized in Table 5-10.

Listing 5-2: Schedule Provider Section of web.config

```
<add name="DNNScheduler"
        type="DotNetNuke.Services.Scheduling.DNNScheduling.DNNScheduler,
            DotNetNuke.DNNScheduler"
        providerPath="~\Providers\SchedulingProviders\DNNScheduler\"
        debug="false"
        maxThreads="-1"/>
```

Table 5-10: Schedule Provider Configuration Settings

Setting	Description
debug	When this is set to `"true"`, a lot of log file entries are generated that help in debugging Scheduler-related development (that is, developing your own Scheduler items). Debugging multithreaded applications is always a challenge. This is one setting that can help you figure out why a task is or isn't getting run.
maxThreads	Specifies the maximum number of threads to use for the Scheduler (when in Timer Method mode). `"-1"` is the default, which means "leave it up to the Scheduler to figure out." If you specify a value greater than 0, the Scheduler uses that number as the maximum number of thread pools to use.

Considerations

One limitation of the Timer Method mode of the Scheduler is that it cannot run 24/7 without help from an external program, the ASP.NET worker process. This is a constraint of ASP.NET, not of DotNetNuke. The web site's worker process periodically recycles according to settings in IIS or machine.config. Some hosts may have settings that recycle the worker process every 30 minutes (forced), whereas others may have more complicated settings, such as recycling the worker process after 3000 web site hits, or after 20 minutes of inactivity. It is this recycling of the worker process that shuts down the Scheduler until the worker process is started again (that is, by someone hitting the web site, which in turn starts up the worker process, starting up the Scheduler as well).

This functionality is actually a major benefit to web applications as a whole, in a hosted environment, because it keeps runaway applications from taking down the server. But it isn't without its drawbacks.

The bottom line is that the Scheduler will run 24/7 in the Timer Method mode as long as someone is visiting your web site frequently enough to keep the worker process active. It is during periods of inactivity that the worker process could possibly shut down. It is for this reason that you should carefully plan the types of tasks you schedule. Make sure that the tasks you schedule are not time critical — that is, don't have to run "every night at midnight" and so on. A more suitable task is one that runs "once per day" or "once every few minutes," and doesn't mind if it's not run during periods of inactivity.

The Request Method does not have the same dependency on the ASP.NET worker process. However, it is entirely dependent upon the timing of visitors to your web site. During periods of inactivity on your web site, scheduled jobs do not run.

Languages

In Chapter 4, you learned that Portal Administrators have some limited control over the supported languages and localized strings in their portal. The Host has access to a number of other features and configuration options. Selecting Host ⇨ Languages opens the Languages administration page as shown in Figure 5-28.

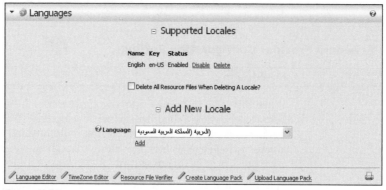

Figure 5-28

Background

Software applications are frequently used in many different countries, each with its own unique language and culture. This is certainly the case with DotNetNuke, which has users around the globe. In an effort to better support users from other countries and cultures, DotNetNuke implements a localization framework to allow the portal to better handle its users' needs. Not only do other cultures have different languages, but they also may be in different time zones, have different currencies, and express times and dates in a different format. Any localization framework has to take all these factors into account to be effective.

In developing the localization framework, the DotNetNuke developers examined many different implementations and ultimately chose a solution that closely followed the ASP.NET 2.0 framework. Although the underlying architecture may differ slightly, DotNetNuke uses the same resource file format and file locations, which thereby simplified the migration path to ASP.NET 2.0.

The Languages page is the primary stepping-off point when configuring language support. These settings determine the languages available to each portal and the default localized strings. Additionally, the Host controls the definitions of time zones within the associated portals.

To define localized strings, you must first create a locale. A locale identifies the culture associated with a group of localized strings. The culture is identified by a friendly name and a key value that corresponds to specific culture. The .NET Framework documentation defines the culture as follows:

The culture names follow the RFC 1766 standard in the format `"<languagecode2>-<country/regioncode2>"`, where <languagecode2> is a lowercase two-letter code derived from ISO 639-1 and <country/regioncode2> is an uppercase two-letter code derived from ISO 3166. For example, U.S. English is `"en-US"`.

To define a locale for your installation, select one from the drop-down list of .NET-recognized locales and click the Add link. This creates a new entry in the Locales.xml file and creates a localized copy of the TimeZones.xml file. After you have created a new locale definition, you are ready to create localized resource strings.

Select the Language Editor link on the Languages administration screen. This opens the Language Editor (see Figure 5-29). It's the same editor available to Portal Administrators and was covered in Chapter 4. The only difference is that any localized resources created by the Host become the default resource strings for all portals.

> If the Portal Administrator edits a resource file, it will override all resources loaded from the default resource file. Even if the Host subsequently makes changes to the same set of resource strings, these changes will not be reflected in the portal, which has its own copy of the original resources.

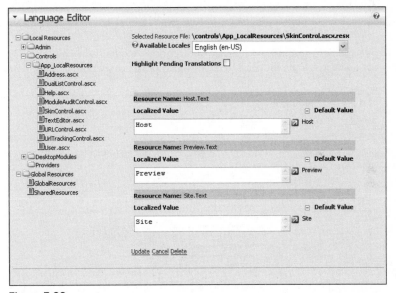

Figure 5-29

The standard portal installation includes more than 115 resource files for each locale. After a new locale is added by the host, DotNetNuke must create corresponding localized resource files for it. The portal only creates the new resource file when the Language Editor is used to edit the localized strings. If the resource for the new locale is never edited, the default locale (English en-US) is used when displaying localizing content.

Chapter 5

So, with 100-plus files to edit, you must be asking yourself, "How do I ensure I have created localized versions of each resource file?" That is where the Resource File Verifier (see Figure 5-30) comes in, which you reach by link from the Languages page.

Figure 5-30

Click the Verify Resource Files link to examine the portal for any old or missing resource files. After the portal has examined the available resource files, you get a list of missing resource files, resource files with missing entries, files with obsolete entries, and files that have entries created prior to any changes to the default resources (as shown previously in Figure 5-29).

> *The test for determining "Files Older than System Default" is based on file modification dates. Therefore, if you change multiple resources in the system default file and then change just one resource string in the localized file, this check will not be able to detect that other resource strings may still need to be updated.*

The Resource File Verifier examines each locale and reports the results as shown in Figure 5-31. Use this report to identify resources that still need to be localized or that may not be up-to-date.

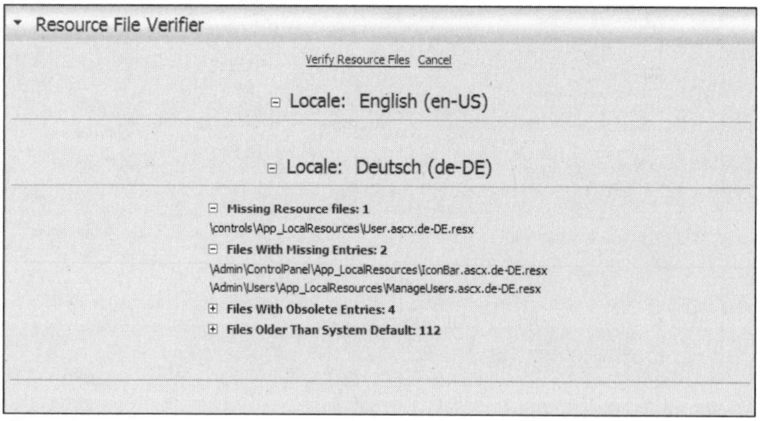

Resource File Verifier

Verify Resource Files Cancel

Locale: English (en-US)

Locale: Deutsch (de-DE)

Missing Resource files: 1
\controls\App_LocalResources\User.ascx.de-DE.resx
Files With Missing Entries: 2
\Admin\ControlPanel\App_LocalResources\IconBar.ascx.de-DE.resx
\Admin\Users\App_localResources\ManageUsers.ascx.de-DE.resx
Files With Obsolete Entries: 4
Files Older Than System Default: 112

Figure 5-31

Using the Verifier makes managing localized resources much easier, but ultimately it is still up to you to handle localization. If this still seems like too much work, DotNetNuke provides a shortcut. Instead of localizing resources yourself, you can load resource packs that were created by someone else. See Chapter 17 for more information about how to create and load resource packs.

Globalization

Globalizing an application requires more than just having content appear in a specific language. Another aspect of globalizing an application requires that the application understand the time zone of the current user. If the server logs show that a critical event happened at 1:00 AM, what does that really mean? If you are in Germany and the web server is in Texas, what time did the event happen? To solve this problem, DotNetNuke stores all time in Universal Time Coordinated (UTC) format. Each user can associate a TimeZone with his or her profile. This setting is used to localize the time for the current user.

The TimeZone Editor shown in Figure 5-32 is accessible from the Language Administration screen and allows the Host to edit the available TimeZone definitions. Like all other resources, the TimeZone definitions are localized, so when you're creating new locales, remember to edit their TimeZones, too.

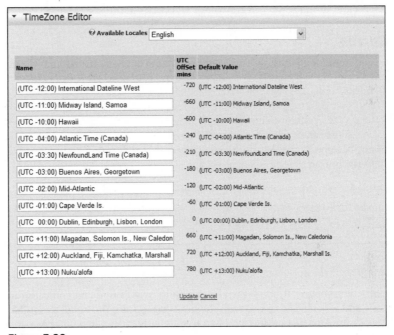

Figure 5-32

Search Admin

The Search Admin page enables you to configure certain aspects of the search engine features. It's important to remember that you are configuring the search for the entire installation, not just for any specific portal. There are just a few options, as shown in Figure 5-33.

Specifying the Maximum and Minimum Word Length settings helps prevent you from indexing unreasonable terms. The internal default values are currently 50 and 4, respectively. If you deselect Include Common Words, the search engine won't bother indexing words that exist in the SearchCommonWords database table. That table has the capability to create common word entries for each locale (for multilanguage customization), although only the English language common words are included by default. Likewise, you can choose to Include Numbers or to ignore them when content is indexed.

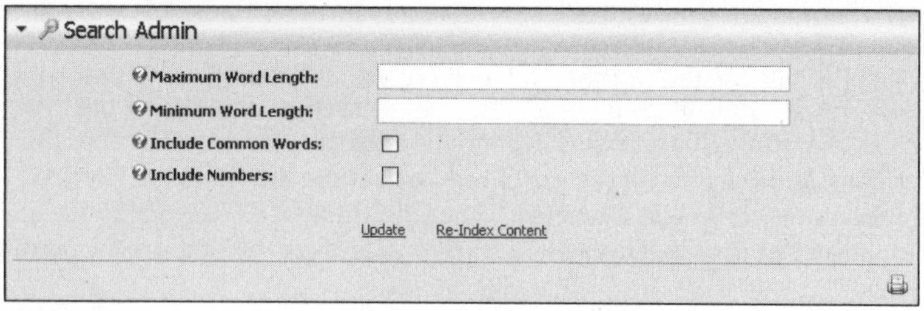

Figure 5-33

Clicking the Update button saves your preferences. Clicking Re-Index Content causes the search engine to empty its tables and re-index the full content of all portals in the installation.

Keeping It Current

When you learned about the Scheduler, you may have noticed a scheduled item for the search engine:

```
DotNetNuke.Services.Search.SearchEngineScheduler
```

If you want your portal's content to be current, it is essential that this job be configured to run periodically. As Portal Administrators add content to their web sites, it is not immediately available through site search. It does not become available until the new content is indexed the next time this job runs or until a SuperUser clicks the button to re-index content.

> The engine that drives search also drives RSS syndication. Updated content is not reflected in syndication until the next time the search index is run.

Background

Prior to DotNetNuke version 2.0, site search functionality was built using complex (and convoluted) database queries and was limited to use with the built-in modules provided by DotNetNuke. To make search work with a third-party module, you had to manually change the database queries or find an alternative search implementation. And its usage was fairly crude by today's standards, without any configuration options or advanced search features.

In version 2.0, the previous implementation became totally obsolete with the introduction of the Data Abstraction Layer and Data Providers. And so the design of a new search engine began in earnest. Before this effort progressed much beyond the design stage, the team development target shifted from version 2.2 to version 3.0, so DotNetNuke version 2 never did get a replacement for its lost search functionality.

Starting in DotNetNuke 3.0, the search engine is fully integrated into the core application and modules are able to hook into this powerful functionality easily. This means that any third-party module can participate in full site search and/or content syndication, simply by implementing the search API as documented in Chapter 8. Currently, the core framework provides a search input module that performs full site search and a default search results page.

Lists

DotNetNuke includes a common utility that enables you to manage the content of lists (where appropriate) and to augment the lists to customize your installation. Select Host ➪ Lists to open the Lists page (see Figure 5-34).

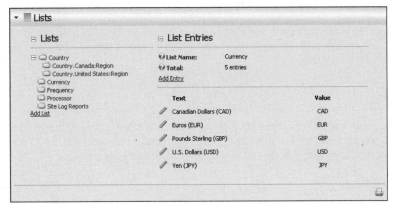

Figure 5-34

The list manager is fairly straightforward, providing an index of the lists it is currently tracking as well as a summary of the entries and the capability to add new entries or edit existing ones.

Not all lists are ones you should edit without an understanding of the potential impacts. For example, if you were to remove an entry from the Site Log reports list, it would prevent Portal Administrators from ever running that report on their portal. You might consider this a good thing if it was necessary to remove a report that was adversely affecting performance. However, adding a new item to that list would result in application errors because the Site Log report would not know how to process them.

One of the first customizations you might make to your installation's lists would be to add a new Country sublist, as illustrated in Figure 5-35.

Figure 5-35

This example adds region entries for the British Virgin Islands so that when users register from there, they are required to specify their island of residence. DotNetNuke is preconfigured for Canada and the United States, but you can customize your installation for any regional list that you require.

Skins

As mentioned earlier in this chapter, the only difference between working with skins from the Admin menu and working with skins from the Host menu is the target location of the upload, which determines availability to other Portal Administrators. For additional information on skins and skinning, see Chapters 4 and 16, respectively.

Summary

In this chapter, you learned just about everything there is to know about administering a collection of portals, their environment, and runtime features as the Host (or SuperUser) of a DotNetNuke installation. Key Host functions that you should understand include the following:

❑   Host Settings

❑   Portals

❑   Module Definitions

❑   File Managers

❑   Vendors

❑   SQL

❑   Schedule

❑   Languages

❑   Search Admin

❑   Lists

❑   SuperUsers Accounts

❑   Skins

You've learned which Portal Administrator–level functions contain Host configurable settings. These functions include the following:

❑   Site Settings

❑   Skins

❑   Log Viewer

You learned about the location and relevance of the Host Root directory (\Portals_default) versus the Portal Root directory (\Portals\<portalid>), and know that Host default settings are used to create new portals, but that (in most cases) changing them has no effect on existing portals.

Your SuperUser powers are now fully enabled and you are prepared to assume leadership of your own DotNetNuke "Justice League" (cape and superhero sidekick not included).

6

Modules

Now that you are familiar with the Host and Portal Administration capabilities available within DotNetNuke, this chapter looks at a concept familiar to most portals—modules.

A *module* is a pluggable user interface component that processes requests and generates dynamic content. This definition is similar to that of an ASP.NET page, with the exception that a module can appear only on an ASP.NET page, and a page may contain any number of module "instances."

DotNetNuke provides a number of modules out of the box. Each module provides its own unique functionality, such as discussion boards, picture galleries, and document management. Developers can also create their own modules that provide alternate functionality.

By the end of the chapter, you should have a good understanding of the architecture surrounding modules and how they relate to the DotNetNuke portal system. This chapter also discusses the practical aspects such as management and installation. An introduction is also given to each of the modules included within DotNetNuke.

Module Architecture

This section explains the concepts of a portal, page, module container, and the module itself. A walkthrough of how a page is constructed is also presented.

Portal

As discussed in earlier chapters, a *portal* can be defined as a web-based application that provides content aggregation from different sources and hosts the presentation layer (modules) of information systems.

Figure 6-1 depicts a portal's basic architecture. DotNetNuke needs to perform a number of steps to process a page request. The following steps execute during the initialization of the page and work to dynamically load modules at runtime. The dynamically created modules are then capable of handling their own life cycle including events such as initialization, load, and render.

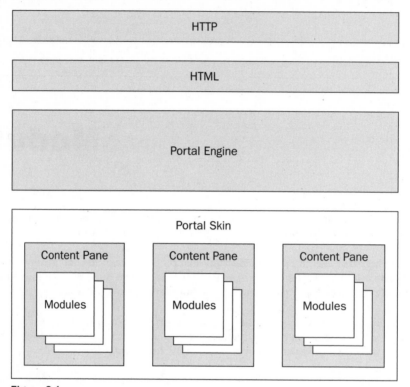

Figure 6-1

Step 1: Page Configuration Retrieval

The first step is to retrieve the modules for the requested page. The retrieval step comprises a number of important pieces of information, such as the modules that appear on the page, the section of the page on which they will appear (known as *content panes*), and, finally, the security roles associated with each module.

Step 2: Security Audit

The second step is to make some decisions about the security information retrieved in the previous step. By examining the current user roles (whether a registered user or anonymous) and the view roles associated with each module, you can form a list of "authorized" modules for the current page.

Step 3: Content Injection

The third (and final) step is to inject the "authorized" modules dynamically into the corresponding content panes of the page. After all of the modules have been loaded, each module is then able to execute its own series of events and render content.

Page

Figure 6-2 depicts the basic portal page components. The page itself represents a complete markup document consisting of a number of content panes, and in each content pane, a number of modules. In addition to the modules, a page consists of navigation areas and site banners. To learn more about how to customize the look of these other areas, see Chapter 16.

Each module consists of a title, decorations, and the content produced by the module. The decorations can include buttons, links, and a hover menu that can change the module's state or perform functionality specific to that module.

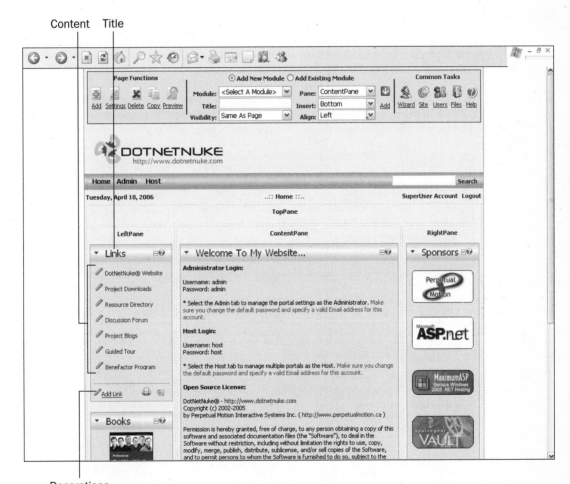

Figure 6-2

Module

As mentioned previously, a portal is a web-based application that processes requests and generates dynamic content. Each module produces its own piece of markup (known as a *fragment*) and together with the skin's markup shows a complete document.

Because each module produces its own markup, it can be viewed as a tiny application within a larger application. Usually, users interact with the content produced by each module by clicking links or submitting forms that are then processed by the portal system and the command passed to the corresponding module.

Module Container

The decorations surrounding a module are known as a *module container*. Through this container, a user is able to interact with the module and perform actions such as minimizing, maximizing, and more advanced features (if the user has edit privileges on that module).

Figure 6-3 shows the module container of a Links module when a user is logged in with edit access. It includes a number of items, such as the hover menu with a list of administration options (discussed later in this chapter), the title of the module, and the minimize/maximize option.

Figure 6-3

User Content Modules

Now that you are familiar with the concepts surrounding modules, this section examines the 16 user content modules that are bundled with DotNetNuke. Another five "internal" modules exist that are not really content modules, so this section does not discuss them.

Here's the complete list of modules:

- ❑ Account Login (internal)
- ❑ Announcements
- ❑ Banners (internal)
- ❑ Contacts
- ❑ Discussions
- ❑ Documents
- ❑ Events
- ❑ FAQs
- ❑ Feedback
- ❑ IFrame
- ❑ Image
- ❑ Links
- ❑ News Feeds (RSS)
- ❑ Search Input (internal)
- ❑ Search Results (internal)
- ❑ Survey
- ❑ Text/HTML
- ❑ User Account (internal)
- ❑ User Defined Table
- ❑ Users Online
- ❑ XML/XSL

The Core Team's policy on bundled modules is not to include every new module within the core, but to provide an extensible and rich platform that enables third parties to build on the functionality in the bundled modules. Still, the bundled modules are designed to meet the majority of needs.

To meet the growing needs of the community, a number of subprojects have been formed to further extend the initial modules bundled within DotNetNuke. These projects are managed separately from the core project and are typically released in shorter timeframes. Popular subprojects include the following:

- ❑ Blog
- ❑ Firebird Database Provider
- ❑ Forum
- ❑ Gallery
- ❑ Help
- ❑ Repository
- ❑ Store
- ❑ Wiki

You can download these modules or find out more information about them at
www.dotnetnuke.com/DotNetNukeProjects/tabid/824/Default.aspx.

Announcements Module

The Announcements module enables you to create short articles for your visitors and even to expire the older articles as the content becomes obsolete. This module provides an easy-to-use interface for keeping your content fresh and rotated. You can use the module to display news releases or a collection of related articles, or merely as a teaser to other content in your portal.

You'll now add an Announcements module to your base installation and see exactly how this module works. Start by opening your web browser to the application and logging in with the administrator account to add the module to your page. Then you will add some content to your module instance.

You do not have to be the administrator to accomplish this task. You could set up a role with edit permission to your page and offload this task to another individual in your organization. This is made possible by the roles-based security the application employs to control access to content and administration.

First, use the Add Module function, as shown in Figure 6-4, to add the module to your page.

Figure 6-4

This process is the same for every type of module you add. For clarity, these are the exact steps for adding the Announcements module, but as other modules are discussed, just the specifics related to the particular module will be discussed.

When you log in to your portal and navigate to a page where you have edit privileges, you see the Control Panel shown in Figure 6-4. In Chapter 4, you used this interface to add a new page to your portal using the Page Functions section. You are now going to use the module section of this interface to add an Announcements module. Remember that this is the interface you use to add any module to your portal pages. As in the Page Functions section, the titles of the available functions are self-documenting. The Module drop-down control lists all of the types of modules you have installed in your DotNetNuke instance, and you can select any available module type from the list. If you select the Add Existing Module radio button, the content of the Module drop-down list changes to reflect instances of other modules you have already added elsewhere in your portal instance. Assume you have a navigation module you need to show only on certain pages to enable navigation to deeper content areas of your site, but you do not want to show on all pages of the portal. This function enables you to easily duplicate your navigation for only the pages for which you need the functionality to be available. The Module control enables you to specify the pane where you want the module to appear and how you need the module aligned inside that pane, with the Pane and Align drop-down list controls, respectively. Notice that you can also specify the title for the module instance as you add the instance.

The preceding directions apply to any module you add to a page.

Now that you understand all available functions, take a look at Figure 6-5. Add the Announcements module, and define the settings of your module instance by choosing Settings from the Module menu.

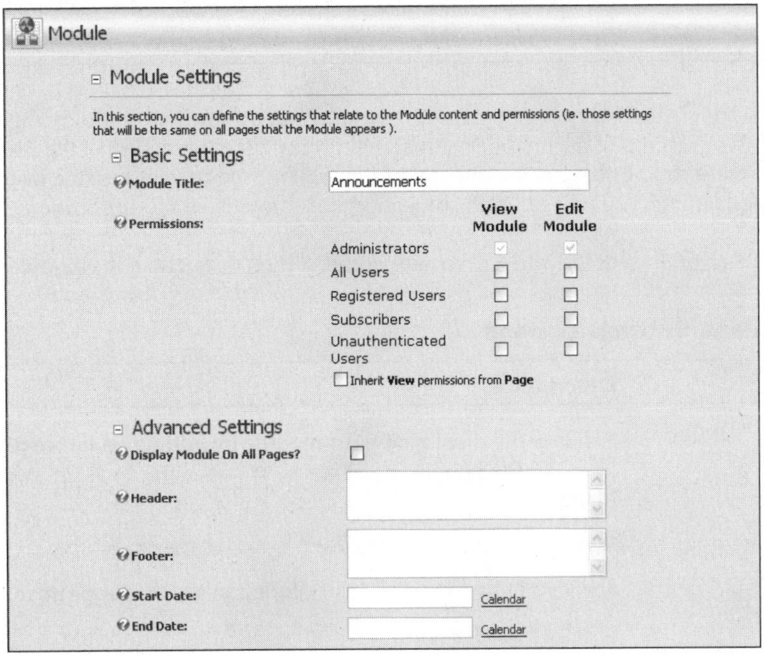

Figure 6-5

You've now added your announcements instance and navigated to the settings for your module. Notice that the Module Settings control looks similar to the Page Settings control used in Chapter 4. This is by design because it decreases the learning curve associated with managing the application. Notice that this control uses the same type of field-level help available in the Page Settings control, which enables you to get a description of the type of content the application expects for this module instance. Table 6-1 describes these associated settings.

Table 6-1: Module Settings Options

Option	Description
Module Title	The module's title.
Permissions	Set which roles will have access to edit the content in your module. Several options are available for controlling the security of the module's content. A special option is the Inherit View Permissions from Page check box, which allows the security settings specified at the page level to secure your module.
Display Module On All Pages	Define a module that will appear on all pages within your portal. This can be useful when you're defining advertising or navigation-type modules that you need to display to your users regardless of the page they are visiting.
Header	Define content to display above your module's content.
Footer	Define content to display under your module's content.
Start Date	The date you want the content to start displaying to your users. This can be useful for planning content that you want to appear only after a certain date.
End Date	Specify when outdated content should expire.

These options are virtually concurrent across all instances of the various modules. Figure 6-6 shows the panel for the Page Settings of the module. Although this may appear exactly like the Page Settings covered in Chapter 3, these settings have some unique options just for the current module instance. Figure 6-6 illustrates page settings you will see in the base modules throughout the application.

Table 6-2 lists each of the settings. You will encounter this section throughout the modules in the application.

Table 6-2: Page Settings Options

Option	Description
Icon	Enhance the display of your module by adding an image to the left of the title. The file you use must reside in one of the areas defined in your File Manager area.
Alignment	Specify the alignment of your module in the pane.
Color	Specify the background color of the content that appears in this module.
Border	Specify a border width for your content in the module.
Visibility	DotNetNuke exposes methods to allow your users to expand and collapse content to save real estate. The Visibility options enable you to define the default behavior of the module and whether you want users to be able to hide or display the module's content.
Display Title	Display or hide the module's title.
Allow Print	Enables you to expose the print module action, which displays a print icon users can select to print the module's content in a print-friendly format.

Option	Description
Allow Syndicate	Enables you to expose your module's content in an XML format, which allows other web authors to consume and display your content on another web site.
Module Container	Set the container to use for the module's display in the portal.
Cache Time	DotNetNuke uses caching to increase the performance of the application. This setting enables you to set the number of seconds the module should remain cached in memory.
Set As Default Settings	Use this module's settings as the default for all the modules you add to your portal.
Apply To All Modules	This is a time-saver if you decide you want the default behavior of all modules to be different from your original settings. You can apply the settings to one module and push those settings to all instances of modules in the portal.
Move To Page	Enables you to move this module instance to another page in the portal.

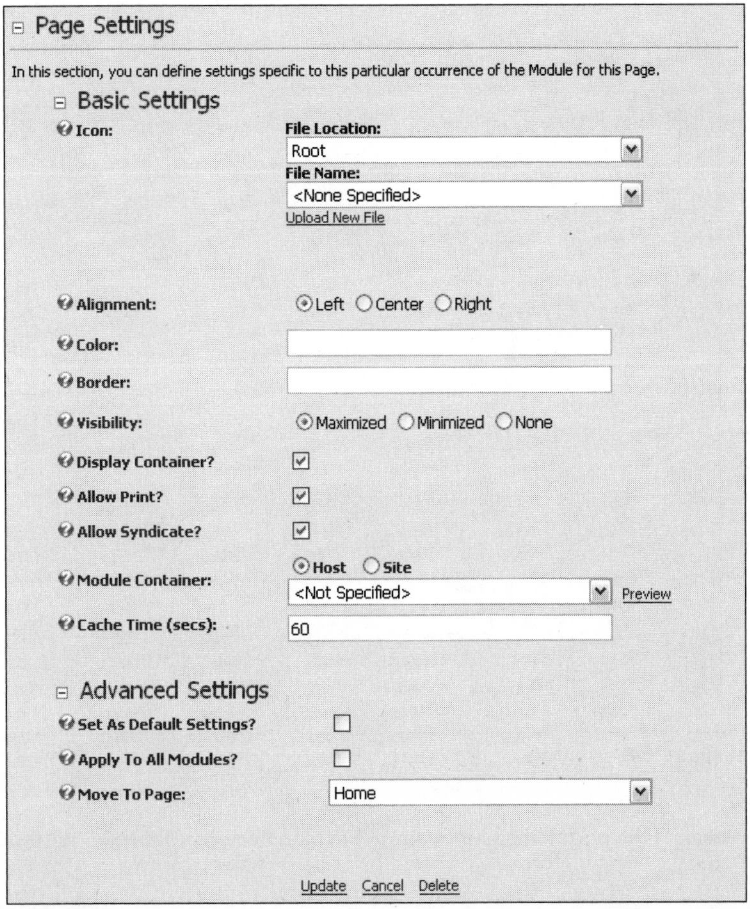

Figure 6-6

The settings listed in this section are implemented from the base module settings class, so this information is pertinent to all modules that inherit the classes, and it is a programming requirement that modules inherit the class. This means that you will have the preceding functionality no matter which module you are working with, whether it's a base module or another third-party module.

Now that you have updated your module settings, you can add a couple of announcements for your users. Figure 6-7 illustrates how the Announcements module shows the results of your changes to the settings.

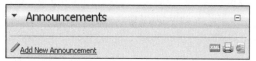

Figure 6-7

Assuming you set up your module to Allow Print and Allow Syndicate, the XML and Print icons appear in the module instance. If you have not enabled these options, those icons are not available. Click the Add New Announcement command link to navigate to the Edit control for your Announcements module. The Edit Announcements page (see Figure 6-8) opens, and you can define your announcement.

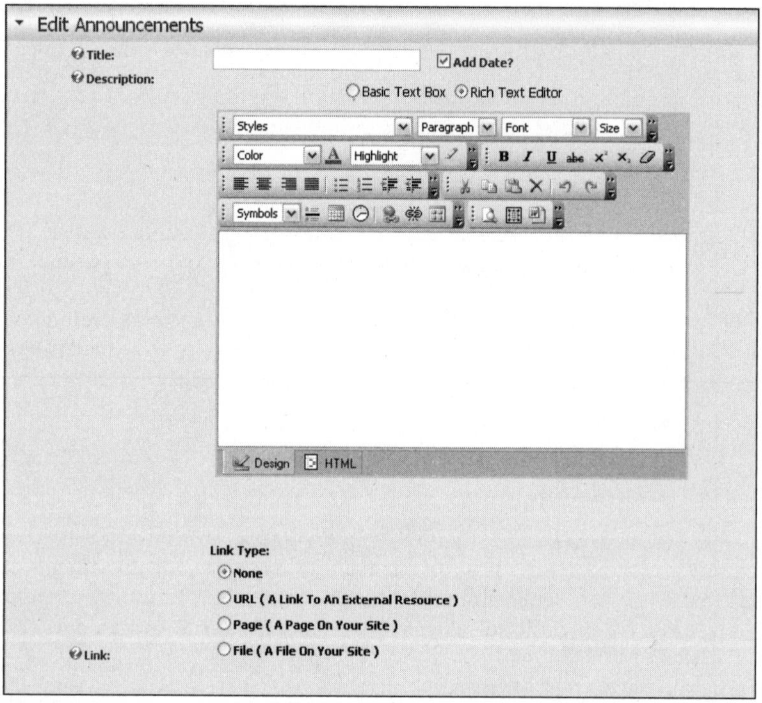

Figure 6-8

Like the other areas of the portal, the names are self-explanatory, but Table 6-3 describes each option.

Table 6-3: Edit Announcements Options

Option	Description
Title	The title that describes the individual announcement. By default, the date the announcement is created is appended to the title you define here. If you do not want this date to appear to your users, uncheck the Add Date check box.
Description	The content for your announcement. This module uses the FreeTextBox (FTB) control to make it easier for users to format the display of the text. If this particular announcement does not require rich text formatting functionality, you can use the text box option, which dynamically removes the instance of FTB and enables you to use only a text box for this function.
Link	Specify a location where users can obtain more information about the announcement. Enabling this option creates a link at the end of your announcement that, when clicked by the user, allows navigation to the link you define. The default option is to not provide a link (None). If you select the URL option, the location control changes to a text box, allowing you to specify an external URL. If you select the Page or File option, the Location control changes to a drop-down list, which enables you to select the page or file where the additional information resides. Additional options allow you to further customize the link to capture the number of times an article is clicked, who clicked it, and a choice to open it in a new window.
Expires	Set a date when the content should expire and no longer be viewable by your users.
View Order	By default, announcements are displayed in ascending order according to their creation date. The View Order option enables you to define the order in which you want announcements to appear.

You now have all the knowledge necessary to create and maintain announcements for your portal. The other base portal modules follow similar methods for creating content. Because many of these modules use the same methods for the common functions, these methods are not covered in detail in the later module descriptions, but the differences are emphasized. One thing to keep in mind if you have aspirations of creating your own modules to extend DotNetNuke is that the code contained in the Announcements module is a good head start for creating the layout of your own modules. For more on developing your own modules, refer to Chapters 12–15.

Banner Module

The Banner module provides a method of offering advertisements in the DotNetNuke application. Administering this module is a little different from any of the other base modules because this module works in conjunction with the Vendors module, which is an administrator-only module. Banners can be controlled from the Host level or Portal level, and the Host or SuperUser account controls this behavior.

Probably the first thing you will notice when you add this module to a page is that you see only a Banner Options action and not an Add New Action option, like the other modules display. This is because the banners will need to be added from either the Admin Vendors page or from the Host Vendors page. This is one of the functions that makes DotNetNuke a viable host platform, because you can offer free or inexpensive portals for your users and then recuperate your hosting costs by offering advertising on the individual portals in your DotNetNuke installation.

The previous two chapters discussed the Host and Admin functions and covered exactly how to add them. For now, assume you have already added a vendor and are ready to display a banner advertisement for that vendor. After you add the module to a page, click the Banner Options action. You are presented with the Edit Banner window, as shown in Figure 6-9.

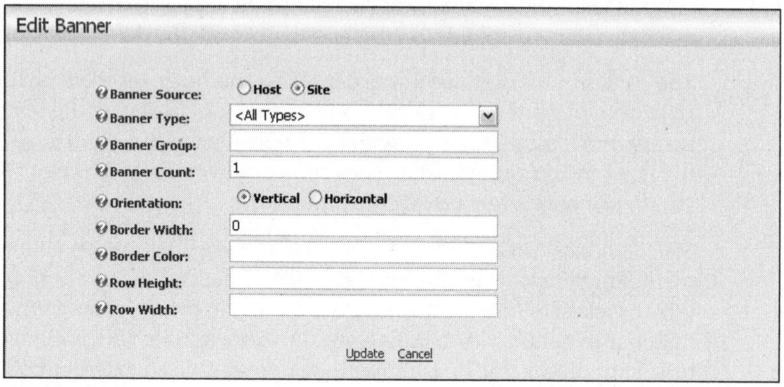

```
Edit Banner

        Banner Source:      ○ Host  ⊙ Site
        Banner Type:        <All Types>                    ▼
        Banner Group:
        Banner Count:       1
        Orientation:        ⊙ Vertical  ○ Horizontal
        Border Width:       0
        Border Color:
        Row Height:
        Row Width:

                            Update   Cancel
```

Figure 6-9

As you can see, there is no option to add a banner to this control. That action is handled in the respective Vendors module by the Host or Portal Administrator, and this module is the mechanism you use to display those settings to the user. For a full description of managing the Vendor functions in DotNetNuke, refer to Chapters 4 and 5. Table 6-4 describes the Edit Banner options.

Table 6-4: Edit Banner Options

Option	Description
Banner Source	Selecting one of these radio buttons enables you to specify whether the vendor banners shown in this module should originate from the host or from the portal.
Banner Type	The type of banner that should be shown in this module. Banner types include Banner, MicroButton, Button, Block, Skyscraper, Text, and Script. Selecting a specific type means the vendor must have that type assigned to its account or the module won't show that vendor's advertisements.
Banner Group	Enables you to associate a group of banners in the administrator vendor's module, such as the Site Banner group. Entering the banner group here enables you to group the same types of banners.
Banner Count	Defines the number of times a banner will display to the users.
Orientation	Enables you to display the banner either vertically or horizontally. The type of banner you chose usually dictates which option you should select.
Border Width	Defines the width of the border.
Border Color	Sets the border color.
Row Height	Sets a row height for your banner.
Row Width	Sets a row width for your banner.

After you have set up your vendor accounts on the vendor pages, you will be able to earn revenue from your DotNetNuke installation. As you saw, there is really no direct editing of content from this module. This is a design decision, so you can let other roles in your installation handle these remedial types of tasks while you control your revenue generation from the higher accounts. You will still need to set up the module settings for this module, but because this module contains the same functions as the Announcements module, those settings will not be covered again here.

Contacts Module

Almost every web site, regardless of content area, needs a method to provide information to contact the site's owners and employees. This is the purpose of the Contacts module. You can add your contact information and provide an easy-to-use interface for updating it to maintain current information. You can create an entire company directory from this module or display contact information for only a few individuals. The types of information you can display include the name, employee role, e-mail address, and telephone numbers for the individuals listed. Figure 6-10 shows the options for adding a Contacts module to your test portal.

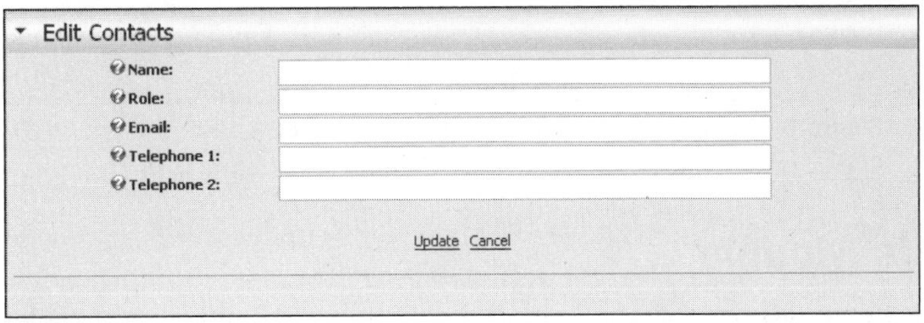

Figure 6-10

Here you can enter the information for each contact you want to display and the module will show the information to the roles you approve. When the module information is entered, the e-mail will be formatted as a mailto link that your users can use to send e-mail to the contact via their default mail client.

Discussions Module

The Discussions module is a lightweight forum module your users can use to share information. It isn't designed to be a full-fledged forum platform, but it will work for light forum activities you may need to offer on your web site. This module uses the same settings as the previous modules have used, so there's no need to cover those activities again. Figure 6-11 shows the interface for creating new threads in the module.

As you can see, this is the simplest interface you've encountered so far. This module is easy to use—just enter a title and write your message. To reply to your thread, users must click the thread and click Reply. Try out this module to see if it meets your need to provide the functionality to your users.

> *Several other full-fledged forum modules are available for DotNetNuke. Some of these are free and some require a small license fee. Refer to the DotNetNuke web site if you require a more robust forum system for your portal.*

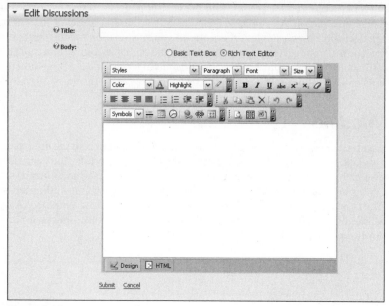

Figure 6-11

Documents Module

The Documents module enables you to upload files to your portal and offer those files to your users for download. This is a fairly useful module because you will likely need to offer examples or additional information in the form of Word documents or other types of files to your users. The types of files you can use with this module are controlled by the file type settings under the Host Settings page. By default, DotNetNuke allows the following extensions:

.jpg	.png	.txt
.jpeg	.doc	.xml
.jpe	.xls	.xsl
.gif	.ppt	.css
.bmp	.pdf	.zip

If you require additional file types not allowed by default, you will need to add the extension under the Host Settings page in the File Upload Extensions field. If you are going to allow your users to upload files, you should be careful as to the types of files allowed because users may introduce viruses or other undesirable files into your portal file system. The application offers no default protection in this area, so diligence is needed to protect the integrity of the system.

Figure 6-12 shows the interface you use to add new documents to this module. As in other areas of the application, the files you make available through this module will reside in your portal's default file directory.

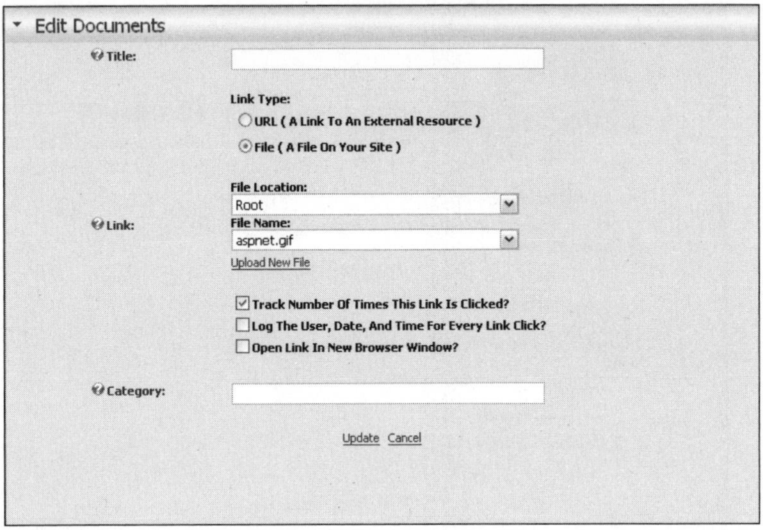

Figure 6-12

Enter the title, link, and category for your module. You may notice that the Link section appears similar to the Link control in the Announcements module. This is another example of the object-oriented nature of DotNetNuke, which reuses code wherever possible to enable a simpler user interface and to promote best programming practices. The only difference between the two is that the Announcements module enables you to select a page in your portal as one of the links. Because it should never be necessary to offer a page for download, this option is not included in the Documents module. Like the Announcements module, the Documents module enables you to track your users' actions to determine the content they are most interested in receiving. The Category field offers you the ability to group the files in the module logically. This category will be displayed as part of the Documents module so that users understand the type of file they are about to download or view.

Events Module

The Events module enables you to announce upcoming events to your users. Although this module has some additional settings that control the display of the module, the rest of the module settings are the same as the ones already discussed; so, this section looks only at the settings that are unique to this module.

As you can see from Figure 6-13, you can display the Events module in either a List or Calendar format. The options for setting the cell width and height are pertinent only if you select the Calendar option. Selecting the List option will format the information you enter into the module as a sequential list of upcoming events.

After you've decided on the view for the events, you can add the event, as shown in Figure 6-14. Table 6-5 explores the available options.

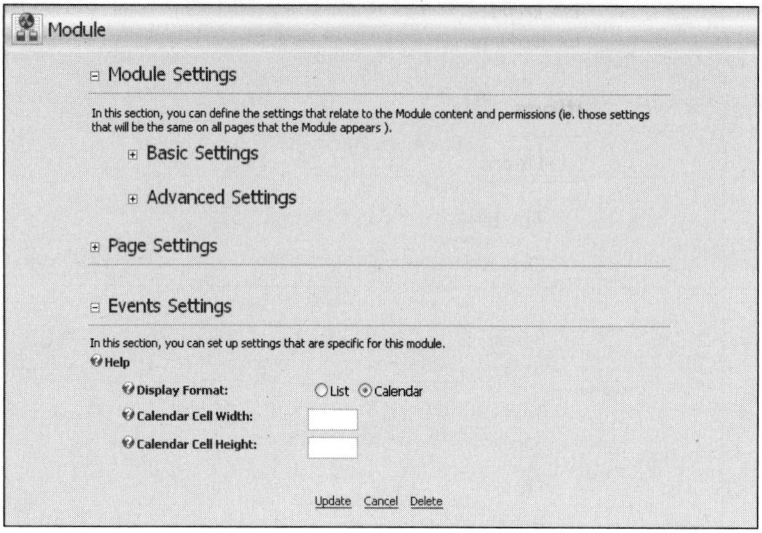

Figure 6-13

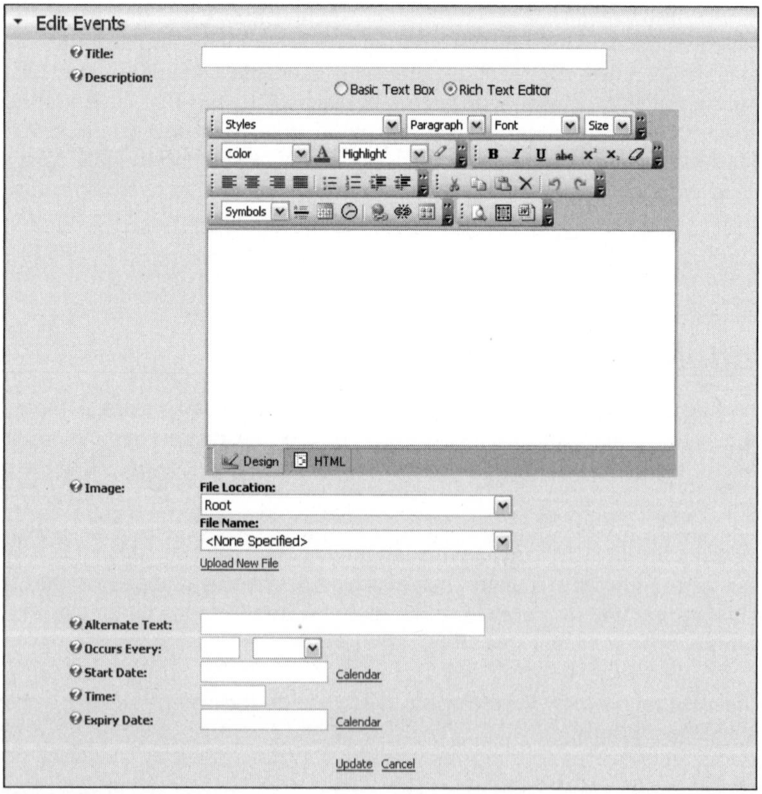

Figure 6-14

When using the Calendar view, keep the amount of text in the description minimal because the available space is limited. If your events need a longer description, use the List view instead.

Table 6-5: Edit Events Options

Option	Description
Title	The title of your individual event.
Description	Describe your event to provide users with detailed information that is not included elsewhere in the module.
Image	Select an image to be associated with your event. This is usually used to easily convey more information about your event to your users.
Alternate Text	Text describing your image. This is important for meeting web accessibility for users who may access your site using screen readers.
Occurs Every	How often this event will occur. Options are to set the event to occur periodically based on the day, week, month, or year. This is a time-saver because if you have recurring events to announce, you only need to set the event once and the module takes care of the rest.
Start Date	The first date your event will occur. Unlike the Announcements module, your content is visible before the date you enter here. This date signifies the start of your event.
Time	Time of day your event will occur.
Expiry Date	The last day of your event. This is useful when you are using the Occurs Every function and no longer need to show the event but would like to keep earlier events of this type for reference.

FAQs Module

You can use the FAQs (Frequently Asked Questions) module to answer questions users may have about your web site or products. It is one of the simpler modules in DotNetNuke, but it's also one of the more powerful ones because it can save you many hours of replying to e-mails. The interface for adding a new FAQ is quite simple and warrants little discussion. Basically, you enter a question you want to provide an answer for and then enter the answer. The module enables you to use the Rich Text editor to format your questions and answers in a way that is easy for your users to understand and to convey the intended message. Figure 6-15 shows the interface for the FAQ's module's Edit functions.

Feedback Module

The Feedback module offers you a mechanism for allowing users to contact you without exposing your e-mail address to the many spam bots that regularly scan the Internet. The module does not have an Add function like the other modules because the purpose of the module does not require that functionality. Basically, users are adding feedback when they send you e-mails. The module contains some settings to control its display to users and to specify the address to which the e-mails are sent. Prior to version 3 of the portal, the only option was to send these requests to the administrator account. Now you can change this behavior. One thing to be aware of is that this module relies on the mail server settings on the Host Settings page to function properly. Ensure that you have successfully added your mail server and tested the settings before attempting to utilize this module's functionality. You also have the option of setting the width and rows of the Feedback module to control its display (see Figure 6-16).

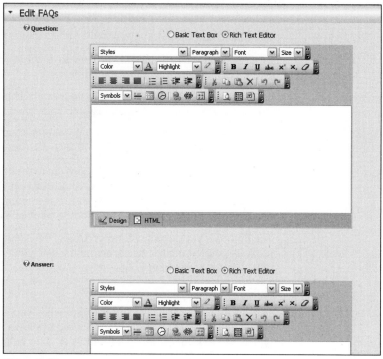

Figure 6-15

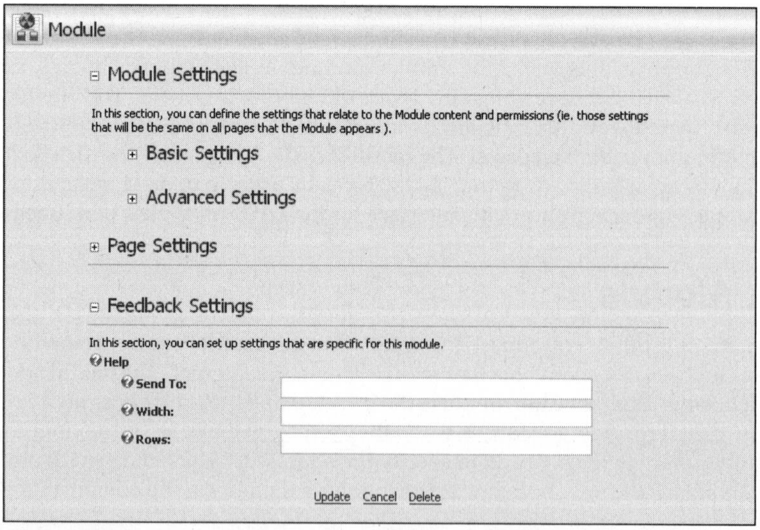

Figure 6-16

IFrame Module

The IFrame module enables you to display web pages from other web sites in your portal. When you set the page, the module should display and add an IFrame tag to your page and load the remote site into the frame. One of the main uses for this module mentioned in the DotNetNuke forums is to utilize legacy applications that were created with ASP or some other dynamic language that must still be used for some functionality. This enables companies to take advantage of the benefits of DotNetNuke while still using other functionality of previous applications. This usually is a short-term fix—as companies become more familiar with DotNetNuke module development, they can convert their legacy applications to fully compliant DotNetNuke modules to take advantage of full integration with DotNetNuke roles and user control functions. Figure 6-17 illustrates the Edit control for the IFrame module, and Table 6-6 describes the options available.

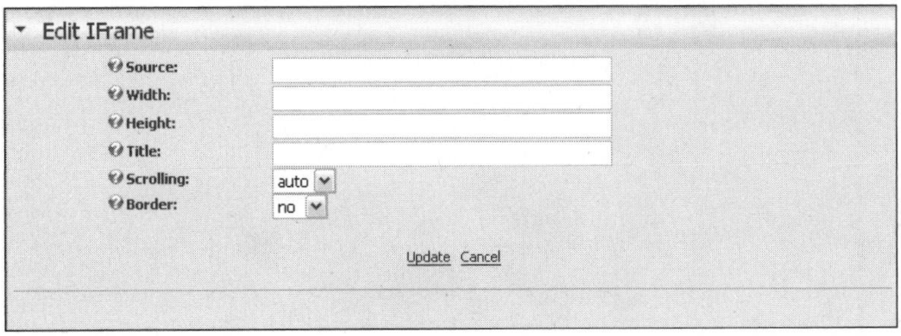

Figure 6-17

Table 6-6: Edit IFrame Options

Option	Description
Source	The location of the web page you want to display in your module.
Width and Height	Determines the size of the IFrame and should be adjusted to fit the page you need to display. The fields can be entered either as pixels or as a percentage, depending on your needs.
Title	This field is somewhat misleading because it neither refers to the module's title nor will it be shown in the web browser. The title, for which you should enter a descriptive value, is required to comply with Section 508 of the Rehabilitation Act.
Scrolling	Determines whether the IFrame adds scrollbars for the frame. This is important if the target web page is larger than you can show in your portal without impeding the display or omitting certain content of the target page. The auto setting usually is the best choice because the module will determine whether the bars are needed based on the dimensions of the target page.
Border	Defines whether a border will appear around the target page.

207

Image Module

As its name suggests, the Image module offers an easy way to add images to your portal. The module enables you to add an image to a page where it would not make sense to have a skin element and you do not require the capability to link to another site from the image. The image you display can reside either in your portal file system or on an external resource. Figure 6-18 shows the options available for adding a link.

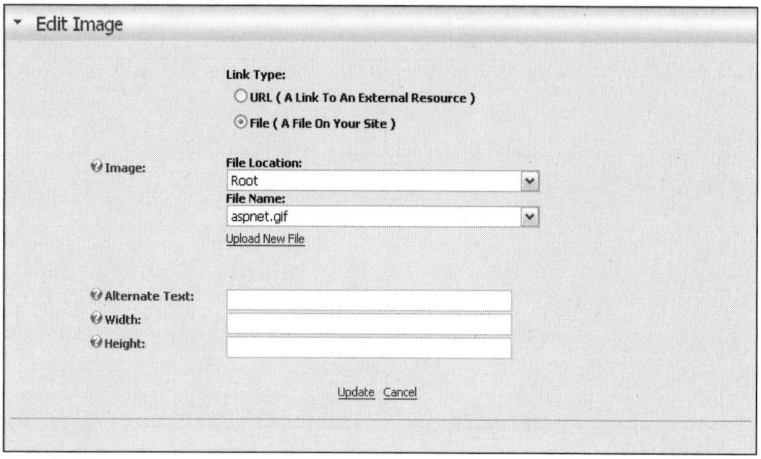

Figure 6-18

Notice the familiar file picker interface you have seen in other modules. Selecting the URL option for the Link Type produces a postback and presents you with a text box to enter in the path to the remote image. If you want to use an image that resides in your portal directories, simply select the image from the drop-down lists. This interface also enables you to enter alternate text for the image and to specify the image's width and height. Leaving the proportion text boxes blank causes the image to be displayed in its actual size.

Links Module

The Links module is likely one of the most used modules in DotNetNuke installations — it probably is only used less than the Text/HTML and Announcements modules. As its name suggests, this module enables you to add links to enable users to navigate to other areas of your site or to remote web sites. There are a few unique settings with which you need to be familiar. Figure 6-19 shows the Module Settings pane for the Links Settings.

You have several options for controlling the behavior and view of the Links module. The Control Type radio buttons enable you to define whether the link list displays as a drop-down list or a normal, data-bound list. You also have the option of controlling the orientation of the list with the List Display Format option. The last option, Display Info Link, enables you to show users a short description of the web page to which the link navigates, which is useful because it allows some additional keywords to be associated with the link. For this example, just accept the defaults in the Link Settings and move on to adding your link, as shown in Figure 6-20.

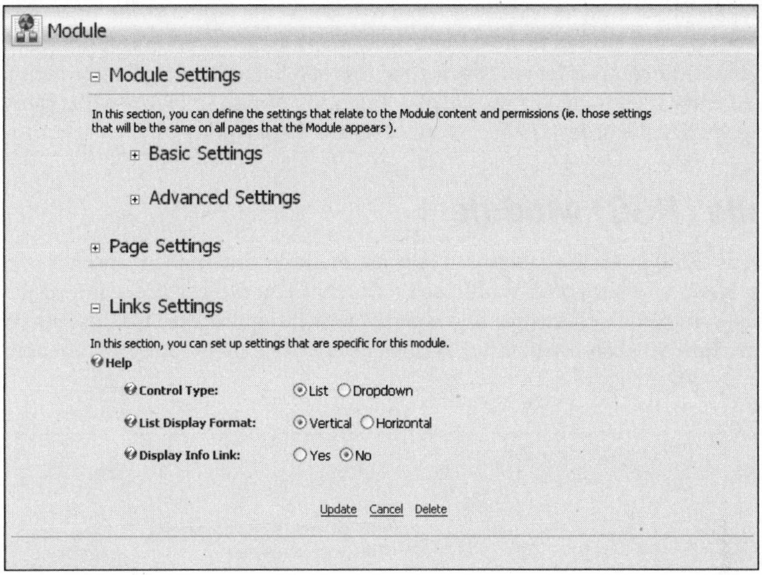

Figure 6-19

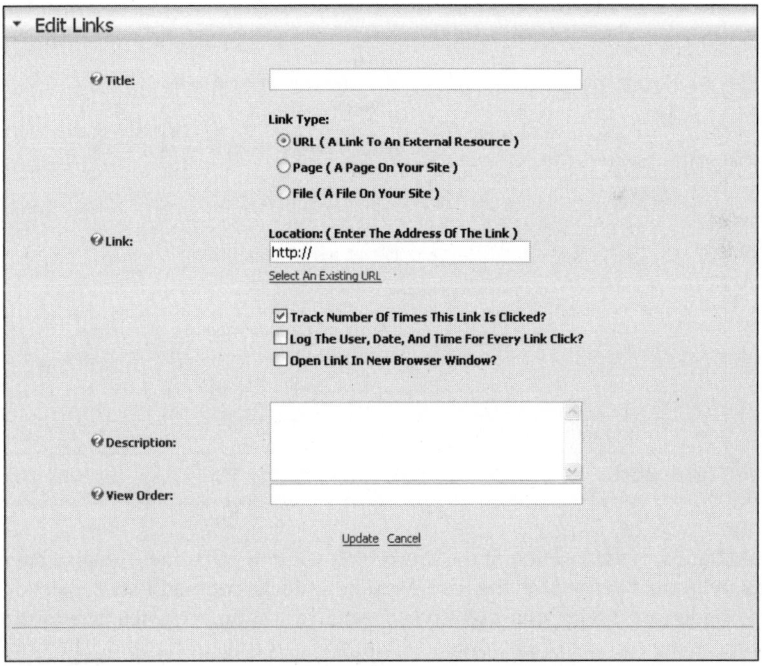

Figure 6-20

The text you enter in the Title field is what users will see as the link. As with other modules, the Link Settings offer options for linking to an external resource, a page on your site, or an internal file in your module, and the audit controls let you track your visitors' behavior. The Description field contains the text you would enter if you selected the Display Info Link option in Figure 6-19. The View Order option enables you to specify the order in which your links are displayed.

News Feeds (RSS) Module

The News Feeds (RSS) module enables you to consume RSS content from another resource and display it to your users. Many web sites offer syndicated feeds that you can consume and display relevant content for your portal, some of which are free and some of which require a fee to consume. With the News Feeds (RSS) module, you can use both types of feeds and display the information according to your feed style sheet, as shown in Figure 6-21.

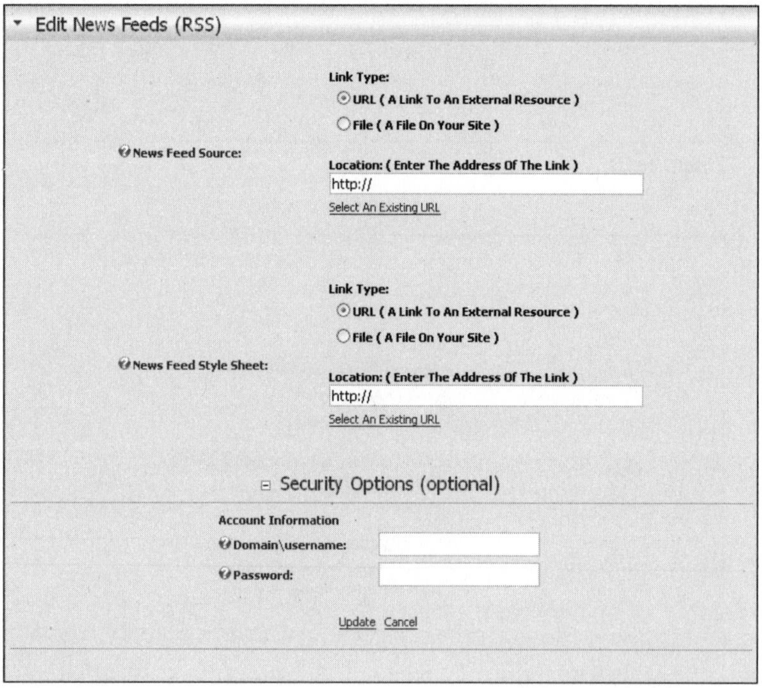

Figure 6-21

The News Feed Source is the location of the source you want to consume. You also have the option of specifying the style sheet to use with the feed. Most news feeds provide a style sheet designed specifically for their feed, or you can specify your own style sheet. In addition, some feeds require you to present credentials authorizing access to their content before you can consume a feed. The Domain\username and Password text boxes are where you enter this type of authentication information.

Text/HTML Module

The Text/HTML module—"HTML mod" for short—is probably one of the most-used DotNetNuke modules. It enables you to format your content with the easy-to-use FreeTextBox editor and also allows a large amount of content to be displayed. This module also fits with what most webmasters need for their content display. You have the option of using the editor or, if you're a hard-core HTML programmer, you can type in your HTML directly without relying on the controls rendering your markup. The Text/HTML module's interface is straightforward and includes only two controls, as shown in Figure 6-22.

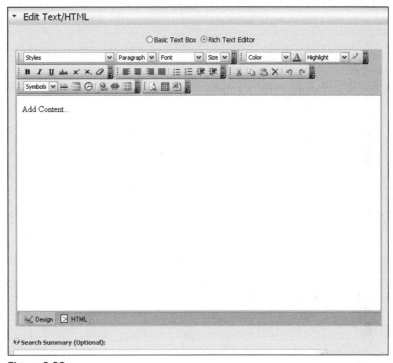

Figure 6-22

The first option is where you will enter your content to be displayed in the module, and the second is a search summary. The DotNetNuke search functions are capable of indexing all the content in this module. The type of content entered in this module may become quite large, so the Core Team felt it would be pertinent to allow a mechanism for the module administrator to add a summary of the content for the search engine to use. This accomplishes two functions. First, it enables you to provide the gist of the content that will be displayed to users when they search for similar content and, second, it helps with the performance of the search engine because there is no need to index all the content that may appear in this type of module.

Alternate editors with extended functionality can also be plugged into DotNetNuke via the Provider Model. A subproject for an alternate editor (FCKEditor) can be found at www.dotnetnuke.com/Default.aspx?tabid=934.

User Defined Table Module

The User Defined Table is a catch-all type of module that enables you to define your own data type and display that information to users in an organized manner. The easiest way to understand the use of this module is through an example. Suppose you need an additional field for your portal's contacts. You could open the Contacts project, modify the code to add your field, and then recompile, but you could also use the User Defined Table module to accomplish the same task. First, add the module to your page and open the Manage User Defined Table action item; then click the Add New Column link. The Manage User Defined Table dialog opens, as shown in Figure 6-23.

Figure 6-23

For simplicity, assume you need to display only the person's name, title, and birthday in your Contacts module. So, you add fields of these types and now have your fields defined, as shown in Figure 6-24.

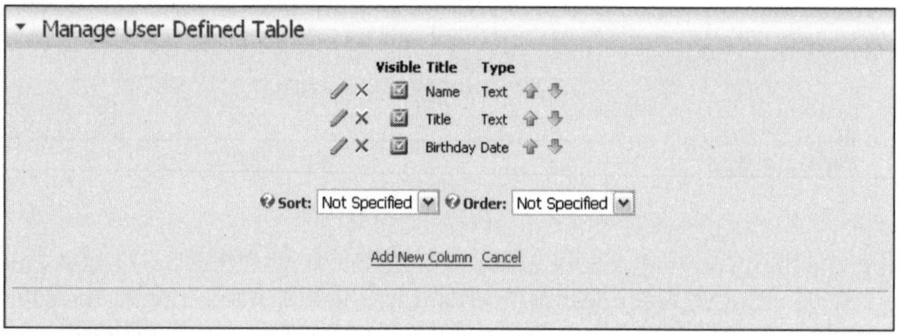

Figure 6-24

You not only can add your own unique fields, but you also have the ability to specify the data type. Data type options for this module include Text, Integer, Decimal, Date, and Boolean. Figure 6-25 shows the finished table. To add a new item to the module, select the Add New Row action from the module menu.

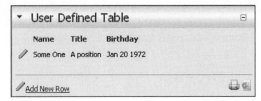

Figure 6-25

As you can see, you can display information in a manner that was previously not available with the portal, and you have accomplished your goal with just a few clicks and without ever opening an IDE to display your data. Spend some time exploring this module to see what other functions it may enable you to perform.

A subproject exists for the User Defined Module and includes an improved version. You can find out more at the official subproject page, www.dotnetnuke.com/Default.aspx?tabid=877.

XML/XSL Module

The XML/XSL module enables you to display XML data from an external data source in your portal according to the accompanying XSL transformation file. It further increases the type of data you can display in your portal and is limited only by the XML technology and your imagination. Figure 6-26 shows the module's Edit settings.

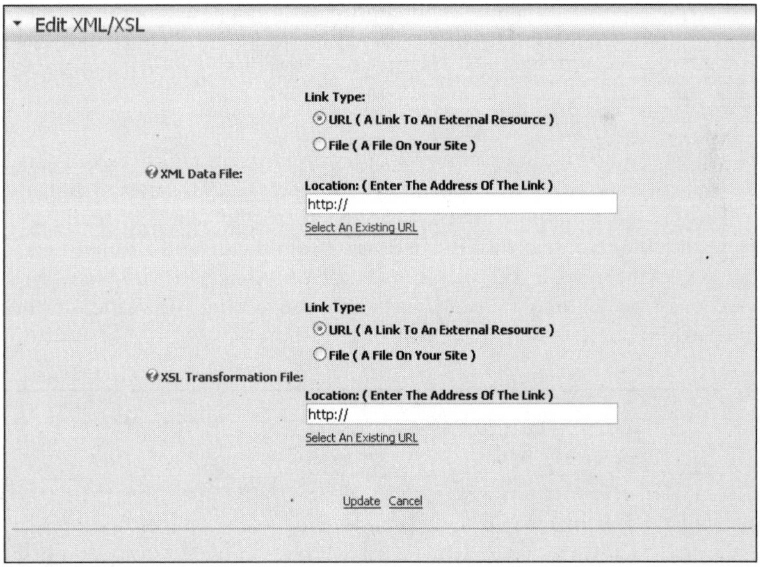

Figure 6-26

The module uses the file picker controls available in other modules to enable you to select the source of your XML data and the transformation file you will use to describe that data. It enables DotNetNuke to consume data from a wide variety of sources because most modern data sources enable a method for exporting data to the XML format.

Managing Modules

Now that you have seen the architecture and explored the modules bundled within DotNetNuke, it's time to examine their management functionality.

Page Management

Figure 6-27 shows the module section of the administration toolbar that appears for portal administrators or users with sufficient edit permissions.

Figure 6-27

This toolbar has two modes of operation, depending on the radio option you select. The default mode of operation is Add New Module, as shown in the figure. To add a new module, select the desired module from the Module drop-down list, specify the pane to inject the module into, specify a title for the desired module, and then choose the alignment for the text within the module. Click the Add button to inject the module into the current page.

The other mode of operation is Add Existing Module, as shown in Figure 6-28. This mode enables you to add the same instance of a module that appears on another page. This means that any updates done to the module will automatically appear in both locations no matter which page the update was performed on. To add an existing module, select the desired page from the drop-down list, specify the pane to inject the module into, select the module (populated from the page selected) you want to add to the current page, and then choose the alignment for the text within the module. Click the Add button to inject the module into the current page.

Figure 6-28

After you have added a module to a page, you may notice a red border around it with the keyword Administrators. The red border dictates that this module is not publicly viewable. The process has been designed so that only the administrators of the current page can see newly added modules. To make it viewable publicly, see the "The Hover Menu's Settings" section later in this chapter.

Module Management

When a module is on the page, there are several options available. Earlier this chapter discussed the concept of a module container. This section explains the various decorations (buttons, links, and hover menu) that are available in each module (provided that the user is authorized). The following features are described:

❑ **Drag-and-drop:** Enables you to reorganize modules on a single page.

❑ **Hover menu:** Provides a variety of options.

❑ **Minimize/Maximize:** Enables you to control the visibility of a module's content.

Drag-and-Drop

Drag-and-drop is a relatively new feature in DotNetNuke. It enables an authorized user to select a module, drag it to a new location (content pane), and then drop it there.

To relocate a module, select the title of a module with your left mouse button, hold down the button, and drag the module to the new location, as shown in Figure 6-29. The pane you are dragging the module to should be highlighted, indicating that it is okay to drop the module (by releasing the mouse button).

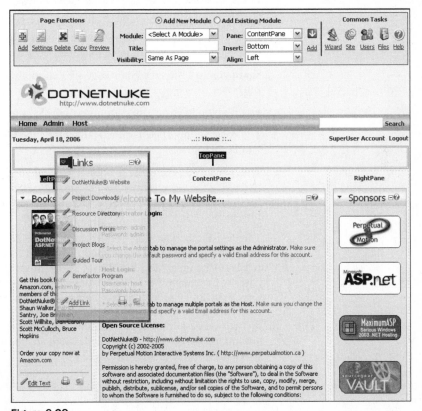

Figure 6-29

Using drag-and-drop provides a time-efficient method of reorganizing page content.

Hover Menu

The hover menu contains a variety of options and is ordered in a similar fashion for all modules. The first one or two options available in the menu are module-specific. For example, the first option on the Announcements module's hover menu is Add New Announcement, which is specific to that module.

Table 6-7 describes the general options available to all modules.

Table 6-7: General Hover Menu Options

Option	Description
Import Content	Enables you to import a module's content from another portal. Be aware that not all third-party modules support this option.
Export Content	Enables you export a module's content to a single file. Again, not all third-party modules support this option.
Syndicate	Links to a Rich Site Summary (RSS) feed for that module.
Help	Links to the configured help for that module. Module authors have a number of mechanisms for providing help, and this option links to the mechanism they have selected.
Print	Takes you to a screen containing only that module for printing purposes.
Settings	Enables you to edit various options of the selected module.
	The Basic Settings (see Figure 6-30) include the Module Title and Permissions.
	The Advanced Settings (also shown in Figure 6-30) enable you to display the module on all pages, provide a header or footer for the module, and provide a start and end date for display purposes.
	The Page Settings section (see Figure 6-31) includes options for controlling the look of the module, such as Icon, Color, Border, Alignment, and Visibility. Other options include Display Container, Allow Print, Allow Syndicate, Module Container, and Cache, which allows output caching of the module's content—something that's particularly useful on high-traffic sites. The last section of this area enables the authorized user to apply these settings to all modules, or to move the module to another page.

Option	Description
Delete	Prompts the user to confirm whether to the delete the selected module. Answering yes will remove the module from the page and place it in the recycle bin located in the administration section of the portal.
Move	The Move option—under which are additional menus, the number of which depends on the portal skin—enables you to specify a valid pane to which to move the selected module. This is an alternate method of moving a module to the drag-and-drop method discussed earlier.

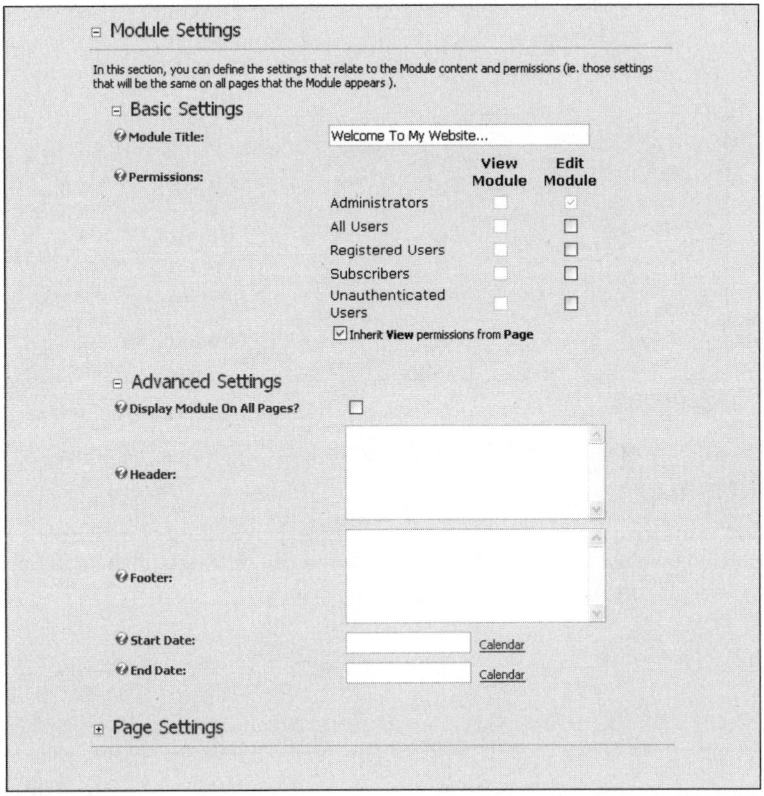

Figure 6-30

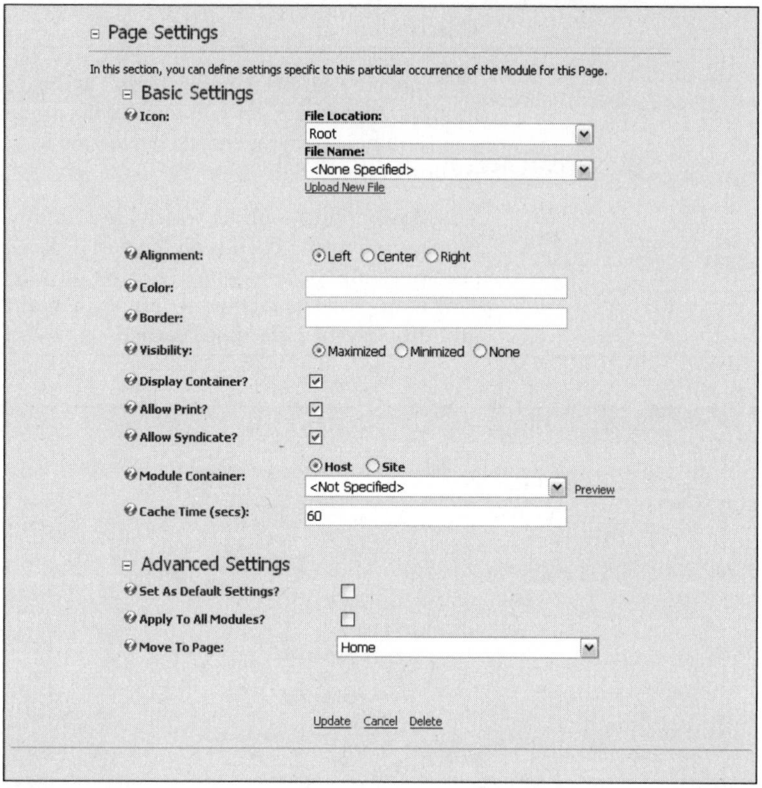

Page Settings

In this section, you can define settings specific to this particular occurrence of the Module for this Page.

Basic Settings

Icon:
File Location:
Root

File Name:
<None Specified>
Upload New File

Alignment: ⊙ Left ○ Center ○ Right

Color:

Border:

Visibility: ⊙ Maximized ○ Minimized ○ None

Display Container? ☑

Allow Print? ☑

Allow Syndicate? ☑

Module Container: ⊙ Host ○ Site
<Not Specified>   Preview

Cache Time (secs): 60

Advanced Settings

Set As Default Settings? ☐

Apply To All Modules? ☐

Move To Page: Home

Update   Cancel   Delete

Figure 6-31

Minimize/Maximize

The minimize/maximize feature enables a user to control the visibility of a module's content. This feature is personalized on a user-to-user basis, although you can set a default state in the Module Settings section of a module. Figure 6-32 shows a minimized module.

Figure 6-32

Installing Third-Party Modules

Now that you are familiar with the concept of modules and using the default modules within your portal, you can add third-party modules to your DotNetNuke installation. As discussed earlier, DotNetNuke is an extensible platform — that is, it enables you to install third-party modules into your portal environment. This section walks you through the steps of uploading a new module.

Chapter 5 introduced the Module Definitions page (see Figure 6-33), which enables you to install new DotNetNuke modules. To find this page, make sure you are logged in as a SuperUser and navigate to Host ⇨ Module Definitions.

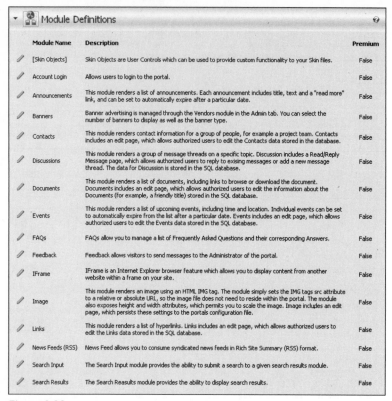

Figure 6-33

To add a third-party module from the Module Definitions page, follow these steps:

1. Move your mouse over the hover menu and select Upload New Module. The File Upload screenopens, as shown in Figure 6-34.

2. Before installing a module, of course, you need to find it. You can find many modules from either the DotNetNuke subprojects or the DotNetNuke module directory, both of which are located at www.dotnetnuke.com. After you find the module you want, upload it by clicking the Browse button and selecting the corresponding zip file. Click Add and then click Upload New File.

3. The resulting screen presents a series of log entries showing you what happened during the installation of the module. When you are satisfied with the installation (for example, there are no glaring red error messages), click the Return hyperlink or navigate to any page within your portal system. This page hit may take some time because installing a new module flushes the cache.

4. Confirm that the module has been installed successfully by checking the drop-down list in the top toolbar. Your new module should be in the list.

Figure 6-34

Summary

This chapter introduced the concept of modules and discussed their architecture in a portal context. You should now be familiar with a portal, page, module, and module container.

The chapter explored the types of modules included with DotNetNuke and the management of those modules from a site administrator's perspective. It also examined management from a page perspective and examined the various controls, such as the hover menu, that are included within a module.

In addition, the installation of modules was discussed, and instructions for installing a third-party module were provided.

7

DotNetNuke Architecture

The architecture of DotNetNuke has evolved from a simple rewrite of the IBuySpy Portal into a best-practice example of enterprise-level design patterns and coding standards that can be applied in the real world. This chapter explains the components of the architecture behind DotNetNuke and how they work together to form an enterprise-worthy web application framework.

Before tackling the architectural overview, however, you should understand some key technologies that DotNetNuke employs.

Technologies Used

As you know, DotNetNuke was originally derived from the IBuySpy Portal Starter Kit. IBuySpy was written in VB.NET and showcased some interesting development concepts of the "new" ASP.NET platform. If you look under the hood of DotNetNuke today, though, it doesn't even resemble IBuySpy. We've taken the basic principles of dynamic content from IBuySpy and applied many best-practice design patterns and coding standards that have evolved as the .NET Framework has grown.

DotNetNuke uses several key technologies in its supported architecture:

- ❏ An operating system that supports ASP.NET (that is, Windows 2000 with SP4, Windows 2003 Server, Windows XP with SP2, and so on).

- ❏ The ASP.NET framework (DotNetNuke 3.2 can be run on both ASP.NET 1.1 and 2.0, but the development project structure is specifically configured for ASP.NET 1.1. DotNetNuke 4 requires the ASP.NET 2.0 framework for both runtime and development.)

- ❏ Visual Basic .NET (C# can be used to write extensions to the platform).

❑   Web forms

❑   Microsoft Internet Information Services (or any web server capable of supporting ASP.NET such as the built-in web server in VWD Express and so on)

❑   ADO.NET

❑   Microsoft SQL Server 2000 or Microsoft SQL Server 2005 (Express, Standard, or Enterprise)

In addition, DotNetNuke showcases several key design patterns and concepts that differentiate it from many other web applications' frameworks and provide a foundation that demonstrates and encourages best-practice programming:

❑   Provider Model

❑   Custom Business Objects and Controllers

❑   Centralized Custom Business Object Hydration

❑   Membership, Roles, and Profile Providers using ASP.NET 2.0 API

❑   Localization framework that mirrors the ASP.NET 2.0 implementation

Provider Model

The Provider Model is a design pattern that is used in the DotNetNuke architecture to allow core functionality to be replaced without modifying core code. The introduction of the Provider Model started with Microsoft in its need to provide a simple, extensible API in .NET. The Provider Model was formalized in ASP.NET 2.0 as a best-practice design pattern. The purpose of the Provider Model is to provide a well-documented, easy-to-understand API that has the benefits of simplicity and the power of extensibility.

To provide both simplicity and extensibility, the API is separated from the *implementation* of the API. A provider is a contract between an API and the business logic that establishes the functionality that the implementation of the API must provide. When a method in the API is called, it is the implementation of the API that fulfills the request. Simply put, the API doesn't care how the job is done, as long as it is done. If there is one useful concept garnered from this section, let it be this oversimplification of the purpose of the Provider Model:

> *Build things so they do not depend on the details of other things.*

This fundamental design concept was recognized well before the Provider Model came to fruition, but it truly speaks to what the Provider Model brings to developers. The API in the Provider Model does not depend on the details of the implementation of the API. Therefore, the implementation of the API can be changed easily, and the API itself is unaffected due to the abstraction.

Provider Model Usage

There are several areas in DotNetNuke that use the Provider Model:

- Data Provider
- Scheduling Provider
- Logging Provider
- HTML Editor Provider
- Search Provider
- Friendly URL Provider

The first implementation of the Provider Model in DotNetNuke was the Data Provider. DotNetNuke originally supported only Microsoft SQL Server. The core of the portal was tightly coupled with the data tier. There were many requests from the community to extend DotNetNuke to support other data stores. We needed a way to support a diverse array of data stores while maintaining a simple Data Access Layer and allowing for extensibility. That's when the concept of the Provider Model was first introduced into DotNetNuke.

Figure 7-1 shows that the Data Provider API is not dependent on a tightly coupled implementation of the API. Instead, the Data Provider API doesn't even know what kind of data store is being used until you configure an XML setting in the web.config file. Other than the settings in web.config, the only other requirement of the Data Provider API is that the implementation of the API must fulfill its contract by providing the necessary functionality defined in the base class. For example, all methods marked with MustOverride in the Data Provider API must be overridden in the implementation of the API.

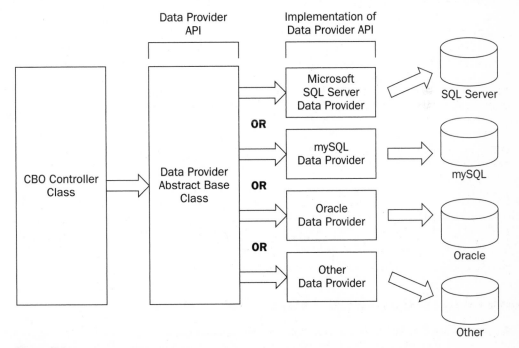

Figure 7-1

Provider Configuration

The Provider API has to be configured to work with the implementation of the API. The API needs to be configured to know which type and assembly to use for the implementation of the API. As mentioned in the previous section, this is handled in the web.config file.

The configuration settings are in XML in the web.config file. There is no standard for naming conventions or the structure of the configuration settings in the Provider Model in general. However, DotNetNuke has followed a consistent pattern in each Provider Model API and the associated configuration settings.

Each API may have different requirements for configuration settings. For example, the Data Provider API needs a connection string defined in its configuration settings. The XML Logging Provider needs its log configuration file location defined in its configuration settings. So each API has configuration settings that are specific to it.

The DotNetNuke core providers store the Provider Model API configuration settings in web.config under the /configuration/dotnetnuke node. When a Provider Model API is first instantiated, it collects these settings, which enable it to use the specified implementation of the API. The configuration settings are then cached so that in subsequent requests, the configuration settings are retrieved more quickly. Listing 7-1 shows a section of the web.config file that contains the Data Provider API's configuration settings.

Listing 7-1: Data Provider Configuration Settings

```
<data defaultProvider="SqlDataProvider">
    <providers>
        <clear />
        <add name="SqlDataProvider"
        type="DotNetNuke.Data.SqlDataProvider, DotNetNuke.SqlDataProvider"
        connectionStringName="SiteSqlServer"
        upgradeConnectionString=""
        providerPath="~\Providers\DataProviders\SqlDataProvider\"
        objectQualifier=""
        templateFile="DotNetNuke_template.mdf"
        databaseOwner="dbo" />
    </providers>
</data>
```

The Provider Model has brought great value to DotNetNuke in the way that it allows for functionality to be replaced without modifying the core code. In DotNetNuke, as in most open-source applications, the core code should not be modified by its consumers if at all possible. The Provider Model helps enforce this fundamental standard of open-source application development. It also provides a new level of abstraction between the Data Access Layer and the data store.

Custom Business Objects

A Custom Business Object (CBO) is essentially a blueprint, or representation, of an object that is important to the application. In DotNetNuke, an example of a CBO is an instance of the DotNetNuke.Services .FileSystem.FileInfo class in /components/FileSystem/FileInfo.vb. An instance of this class contains information about a single file as shown in Listing 7-2.

Listing 7-2: The FileInfo CBO Class

```
<XmlRoot("file", IsNullable:=False)> Public Class FileInfo
    Private _FileId As Integer
    Private _PortalId As Integer
    Private _FileName As String
    Private _Extension As String
    Private _Size As Integer
    Private _Width As Integer
    Private _Height As Integer
    Private _ContentType As String
    Private _Folder As String

    <XmlIgnore()> Public Property FileId() As Integer
        Get
            Return _FileId
        End Get
        Set(ByVal Value As Integer)
            _FileId = Value
        End Set
    End Property
    <XmlIgnore()> Public Property PortalId() As Integer
        Get
            Return _PortalId
        End Get
        Set(ByVal Value As Integer)
            _PortalId = Value
        End Set
    End Property
    <XmlElement("filename")> Public Property FileName() As String
        Get
            Return _FileName
        End Get
        Set(ByVal Value As String)
            _FileName = Value
        End Set
    End Property
    <XmlElement("extension")> Public Property Extension() As String
        Get
            Return _Extension
        End Get
        Set(ByVal Value As String)
            _Extension = Value
        End Set
    End Property
    <XmlElement("size")> Public Property Size() As Integer
        Get
            Return _Size
        End Get
        Set(ByVal Value As Integer)
            _Size = Value
        End Set
    End Property
    <XmlElement("width")> Public Property Width() As Integer
```

(continued)

Listing 7-2: *(continued)*

```
        Get
            Return _Width
        End Get
        Set(ByVal Value As Integer)
            _Width = Value
        End Set
    End Property
    <XmlElement("height")> Public Property Height() As Integer
        Get
            Return _Height
        End Get
        Set(ByVal Value As Integer)
            _Height = Value
        End Set
    End Property
    <XmlElement("contenttype")> Public Property ContentType() As String
        Get
            Return _ContentType
        End Get
        Set(ByVal Value As String)
            _ContentType = Value
        End Set
    End Property
    <XmlElement("folder")> Public Property Folder() As String
        Get
            Return _Folder
        End Get
        Set(ByVal Value As String)
            _Folder = Value
        End Set
    End Property
End Class
```

The FileInfo class has no methods, only properties. This is an important distinction to recognize—CBOs only have properties. The methods to manage the CBO are in a CBO Controller class specific to the CBO. A CBO Controller class contains the business logic necessary to work with its associated CBO class. For example, there is a FileController class in /components/FileSystem/FileController.vb that contains business logic for the FileInfo CBO. For the sake of the core File Manager module, the FileInfo data is stored in the database. Therefore, the FileController class contains the logic necessary to hydrate the FileInfo object (or a collection of FileInfo objects) with data retrieved from the database.

CBO Hydrator

One powerful core service is the CBO Hydrator, which is located in the CBO class in /components/ Shared/CBO.vb. It is a collection of methods that provide a centralized means of hydrating a CBO or a collection of CBOs.

Figure 7-2 shows how a CBO Controller class makes a call to the CBO Hydrator by sending in an open DataReader and the type of object to fill. Depending on the method called within the CBO Hydrator, it returns either a single hydrated object or a collection of hydrated objects. When the CBO Hydrator fills an object's properties, it discovers the properties of the CBO using reflection. Then it caches the properties that it has discovered so that the next time an object of the same type is hydrated, the properties won't need to be discovered. Instead, they can be pulled from the cache.

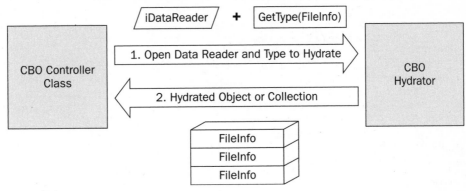

Figure 7-2

To hydrate a collection of CBOs, use the DotNetNuke.Common.Utilities.CBO.FillCollection method. The method accepts an IDataReader and a type as input parameters. It returns an ArrayList of objects of the type specified in the objType parameter. For example, the code-behind for the Portals module ($AppRoot/admin/Portal/Portals.ascx.vb) needs a collection of PortalInfo objects so it can display a list of Portals in the portal module's rendered output. The code-behind calls DotNetNuke.Entities.Portals .PortalController.GetPortals() to get an ArrayList of PortalInfo objects. That ArrayList is filled by the DotNetNuke.Common.Utilities.CBO.FillCollection method, which converts an iDataReader object (from a database query) into a collection of hydrated PortalInfo objects. Here's the DotNetNuke .Common.Utilities.CBO.FillCollection method signature:

```
Public Shared Function FillCollection(ByVal dr As IDataReader, ByVal objType As _
Type) As ArrayList
```

To hydrate a single CBO rather than a collection, use the CBO.FillObject method. It accepts the same input parameters, but returns a single object. For example, in the code-behind for the Site Settings module ($AppRoot/Admin/Portal/SiteSettings.ascx.vb), the control needs a PortalInfo object to display the portal settings in the module's rendered output. The code-behind gets the PortalInfo object from a call to DotNetNuke.Entities.Portals.PortalController.GetPortal. The GetPortal method uses the DotNetNuke.Common.Utilities.CBO.FillObject method to convert an iDataReader object (from a database query) into a hydrated PortalInfo object. Following is the method signature for DotNetNuke .Common.Utilities.CBO.FillObject:

```
Public Shared Function FillObject(ByVal dr As IDataReader, ByVal _
objType As Type) As Object
```

Using the CBO Hydrator

The FileController shown in Listing 7-3 is an example of a CBO Controller that utilizes the CBO Hydrator.

Listing 7-3: The FileController CBO Controller Class

```
Public Class FolderController
    Public Function GetFoldersByPortal(ByVal PortalID As Integer) As ArrayList
        Return _
        CBO.FillCollection(DataProvider.Instance().GetFoldersByPortal(PortalID), _
        GetType(Services.FileSystem.FolderInfo))
    End Function
    Public Function GetFolder(ByVal PortalID As Integer, ByVal FolderPath As _
    String) As FolderInfo
        Return CType(CBO.FillObject(DataProvider.Instance().GetFolder(PortalID, _
        FolderPath), GetType(Services.FileSystem.FolderInfo)), FolderInfo)
    End Function
    Public Function GetFolder(ByVal PortalID As Integer, ByVal FolderID As Integer)
    As ArrayList
        Return CBO.FillCollection(DataProvider.Instance().GetFolder(PortalID, _
        FolderID), GetType(Services.FileSystem.FolderInfo))
    End Function
    Public Function AddFolder(ByVal objFolderInfo As FolderInfo) As Integer
        Return DataProvider.Instance().AddFolder(objFolderInfo.PortalID, _
        objFolderInfo.FolderPath)
    End Function
    Public Sub UpdateFolder(ByVal objFolderInfo As FolderInfo)
        DataProvider.Instance().UpdateFolder(objFolderInfo.PortalID, _
        objFolderInfo.FolderID, objFolderInfo.FolderPath)
    End Sub
    Public Sub DeleteFolder(ByVal PortalID As Integer, ByVal FolderPath As String)
        DataProvider.Instance().DeleteFolder(PortalID, FolderPath)
    End Sub
End Class
```

Using the CBO Hydrator significantly reduces the amount of code needed to fill an object or collection of objects. Without using the CBO Hydrator, you would have to code at least one line per CBO property to fill that object with the contents of a DataReader. Listing 7-4 is an example of filling a single FileInfo object without using the CBO Hydrator.

Listing 7-4: Traditional Method of Filling an Object

```
Dim dr As IDataReader
Try
    dr = DataProvider.Instance().GetFolder(PortalID, FolderPath)
    Dim f As New FileInfo
    f.ContentType = Convert.ToString(dr("ContentType"))
    f.Extension = Convert.ToString(dr("Extension"))
    f.FileId = Convert.ToInt32(dr("FileId"))
    f.FileName = Convert.ToString(dr("FileName"))
    f.Folder = Convert.ToString(dr("Folder"))
    f.Height = Convert.ToInt32(dr("Height"))
    f.PortalId = Convert.ToInt32(dr("PortalId"))
    f.Size = Convert.ToInt32(dr("Size"))
    f.Width = Convert.ToInt32(dr("Width"))
```

```
        Return f
    Finally
        If Not dr Is Nothing Then
            dr.Close()
        End If
    End Try
```

Instead of writing all of that code, the CBO Hydrator can be used to greatly simplify things. The code in Listing 7-5 does the same thing as the code in Listing 7-4, except it uses the CBO Hydrator.

Listing 7-5: Filling an Object Using the CBO Hydrator

```
Return CType(CBO.FillObject(DataProvider.Instance().GetFolder(PortalID, _
        FolderPath), GetType(Services.FileSystem.FolderInfo)), FolderInfo)
```

Custom Business Objects are used throughout DotNetNuke to create a truly object-oriented design. The objects provide for type safety and enhance performance by allowing code to work with disconnected collections rather than with DataReaders, DataTables, or DataSets. Use the CBO Hydrator whenever possible to reduce the amount of coding and to enhance the maintainability of the application.

Architectural Overview

The DotNetNuke architecture permits the application tiers to be distributed across two servers: the web server and the database server, as shown in Figure 7-3. The web server contains the Presentation, Business Logic, and Data Access Layers. The database server contains the Data Layer.

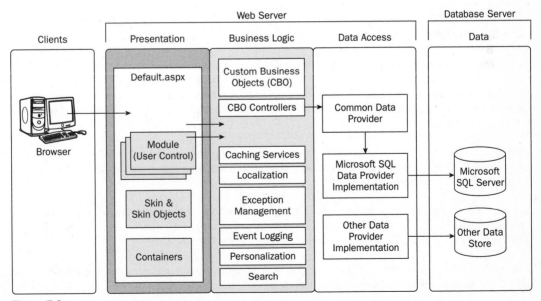

Figure 7-3

Presentation Layer

The Presentation Layer provides an interface for clients to access the portal application. This layer consists of the following elements:

- ❑ **Web forms:** The primary web form is Default.aspx. This page is the entry point to the application. It is responsible for dynamically loading the other elements of the Presentation Layer. Default.aspx is in the root installation directory.

- ❑ **Skins:** The Default.aspx web form loads the skin for the page based on the settings for each page or portal. The base Skin class is in /admin/Skins/Skin.vb.

- ❑ **Containers:** The Default.aspx web form also loads the containers for the modules based on the settings for each module, page, and portal. The base Container class is in /admin/Containers/Container.vb.

- ❑ **Module user controls:** Modules will have at least a single user control that is the user interface for the module. These user controls are loaded by Default.aspx and embedded within the containers and skin. The module user controls are in .ascx files in /DesktopModules/[module name].

- ❑ **Client-side scripts:** There are several client-side JavaScript files that are used by the core user-interface framework. For example, the /DotNetNuke/controls/SolpartMenu/spmenu.js script file is used by the SolPartMenu control. Custom modules can include and reference JavaScript files as well. Client-side JavaScript files that are used by the core are in the /js folder. Some skins may use client-side JavaScript, in which case the scripts are in the skin's installation directory. Any client-side scripts used by modules are located under the module's installation directory.

When visiting a DotNetNuke portal, the web form that loads the portal page is Default.aspx. The code-behind for this page ($AppRoot/Default.aspx.vb) loads the selected skin for the active page. The skin is a user control that must inherit from the DotNetNuke.UI.Skins.Skin base class. The Skin class is where most of the action happens for the Presentation Layer.

First, the Skin class iterates through all of the modules that are associated with the portal page. Each module has a container assigned to it. The container is a visual boundary that separates one module from another. The container can be assigned to affect all modules within the entire portal, all modules within a specific page, or a single module. The Skin class loads the module's container and injects the module control into the container.

Next, the Skin class determines whether the module implements the DotNetNuke.Entities.Modules .iActionable interface. If it does, the Skin class discovers the actions that the module has defined and adds them to the container accordingly.

Then, the Skin class adds references to the module's style sheets to the rendered page. It looks for a file named module.css in the specific module's installation directory. If it exists, the class adds an Html GenericControl to the page to reference the style sheet for the module.

All of this happens within the Skin class in the Init event as shown in Figure 7-4. The final rendering of the contents of a module is handled within each module's event lifecycle.

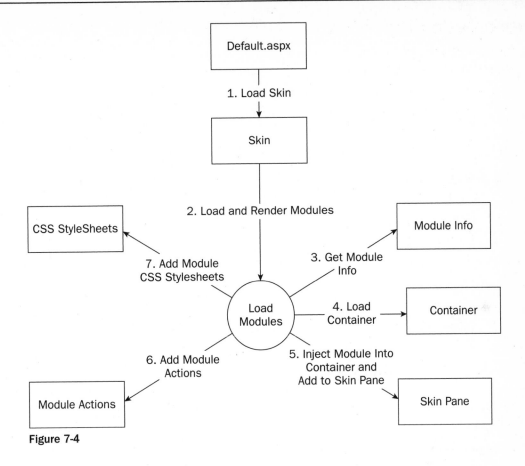

Figure 7-4

Finally, the code-behind ($AppRoot/Default.aspx.vb) renders the appropriate style-sheet links based on the configuration of the portal and its skin. See Chapter 16 for more details on style sheets and the order in which they are loaded.

Business Logic Layer

The Business Logic Layer provides the business logic for all core portal activity. This layer exposes many services to core and third-party modules. These services include:

- ❑ Localization
- ❑ Caching
- ❑ Exception management
- ❑ Event logging
- ❑ Personalization

❑ Search

❑ Installation and upgrades

❑ Membership, roles, and profile

❑ Security permissions

The Business Logic Layer is also home to Custom Business Objects (CBOs), whose fundamental purpose is to store information about an object.

Data Access Layer

The Data Access Layer provides data services to the Business Logic Layer. It allows for data to flow to and from a data store.

As described earlier in this chapter, the Data Access Layer uses the Provider Model to enable DotNetNuke to support a wide array of data stores. The Data Access Layer consists of two elements:

❑ **Data Provider API:** An abstract base class that establishes the contract that the implementation of the API must fulfill.

❑ **Implementation of Data Provider API:** A class that inherits from the Data Provider API class and fulfills the contract by overriding the necessary members and methods.

The core DotNetNuke release provides a Microsoft SQL Server implementation of the Data Provider API.

Beginning with the CBO Controller class, the following code snippets show how the Data Provider API works with the Implementation of the Data Provider API. Listing 7-6 shows how the IDataReader that is sent into CBO.FillObject is a call to DataProvider.Instance().GetFolder(PortalID, FolderPath).

Listing 7-6: The FolderController.GetFolder Method

```
Public Function GetFolder(ByVal PortalID As Integer, ByVal FolderPath As ↩
String) As FolderInfo
    Return CType(CBO.FillObject(DataProvider.Instance().GetFolder(PortalID, _
    FolderPath), GetType(Services.FileSystem.FolderInfo)), FolderInfo)
End Function
```

Figure 7-5 breaks down each of the elements in this method call.

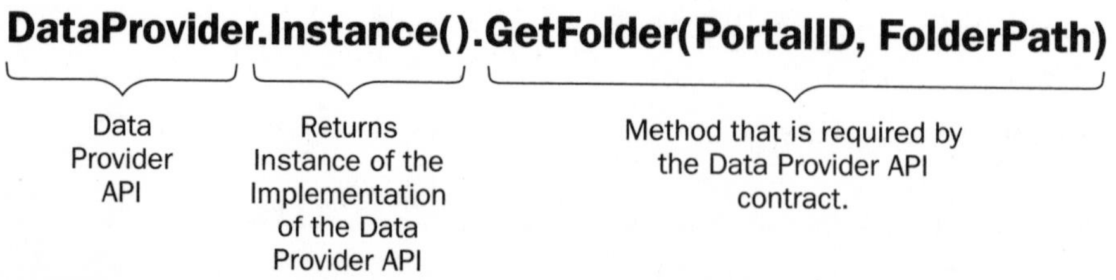

DataProvider.Instance().GetFolder(PortalID, FolderPath)

Data Provider API

Returns Instance of the Implementation of the Data Provider API

Method that is required by the Data Provider API contract.

Figure 7-5

The `Instance()` method returns an instance of the implementation of the Data Provider API, and therefore executes the method in the provider itself. The `GetFolder` method called in Listing 7-6 is an abstract method that is detailed in Listing 7-7.

Listing 7-7: The DataProvider.GetFolder Abstract Method

```
Public MustOverride Function GetFolder(ByVal PortalID As Integer, _
ByVal FolderPath As String) As IDataReader
```

This method is part of the contract between the API and the implementation of the API. It is overridden in the implementation of the API as shown in Listing 7-8.

Listing 7-8: The SQLDataProvider.GetFolder Method

```
Public Overloads Overrides Function GetFolder(ByVal PortalID As Integer, ByVal _
FolderPath As String) As IDataReader
    Return CType(SqlHelper.ExecuteReader(ConnectionString, DatabaseOwner & _
    ObjectQualifier & "GetFolders", GetNull(PortalID), -1, FolderPath), _
    IDataReader)
End Function
```

Listing 7-8 shows a reference to the SqlHelper class, which is part of the Microsoft Data Access Application Block. DotNetNuke uses the Data Access Application Block to improve performance and reduce the amount of custom code required for data access. The Data Access Application Block is a .NET component that works with ADO.NET to call stored procedures and execute SQL commands on Microsoft SQL Server.

Data Layer

The Data Layer provides data to the Data Access Layer. The data store used in the Data Layer must be supported by the implementation of the Data Provider API to fulfill the data requests.

Because the DotNetNuke Data Provider Model is so extensible, there are several Data Providers available, including core-released Data Providers and third-party providers such as Microsoft SQL Server, Firebird, MySQL, and Oracle providers. The core DotNetNuke release provides a Microsoft SQL Server implementation of the Data Provider API (which includes support for Microsoft SQL Server 2005 Express).

Installation Scripts

Included in the implementation of the API is a collection of scripts that create the database in the Data Layer during the installation process. These scripts collectively create the database tables, stored procedures, and data necessary to run DotNetNuke. The installation scripts are run only during a new installation and are run from the `DotNetNuke.Services.Upgrade.Upgrade.InstallDNN` method. The scripts are as follows:

- ❏ **DotNetNuke.SetUp.SqlDataProvider:** Prepares the database for the installation by dropping some key tables.

- ❏ **DotNetNuke.Schema.SqlDataProvider:** Installs the tables and stored procedures.

- ❏ **DotNetNuke.Data.SqlDataProvider:** Fills the tables with data.

Upgrade Scripts

For subsequent upgrades performed after the initial installation, a collection of scripts that modify the schema or data during the upgrade process is run from the `DotNetNuke.Services.Upgrade.Upgrade .UpgradeDNN` method. There is one script per baseline version of DotNetNuke. A baseline version is a working version of DotNetNuke that represents some internal milestone. For example, after the core team integrates a major new feature, such as the Member Role Provider, the code is tested, compiled, and zipped for distribution among the Core Team. This doesn't necessarily mean there is one script per released version of DotNetNuke—behind the scenes, we may have several baseline versions before a formal public release.

The file-naming convention includes the version of the script followed by the SqlDataProvider extension. The extension must be the same name as found in the DefaultProvider attribute of the Data Provider's configuration settings in the web.config file. For example, the filename for the upgrade script for upgrading from baseline version 4.0.2 to 4.0.3 is 04.00.03.SqlDataProvider.

When the DotNetNuke application is upgraded to another version, these scripts are executed in logical order according to the version number. Only the scripts with a version number that is less than or equal to the value of the constant DotNetNuke.Common.Globals.glbAppVersion are run. This constant is defined in the /components/Shared/Globals.vb file.

Script Syntax

The scripts are written in SQL, but there are two important non-SQL tags used in them: `{databaseOwner}` and `{objectQualifier}`. Both of these tags represent a programmatically replaceable element of the script. Earlier in this chapter, Listing 7-1 showed the configuration settings for the Microsoft SQL Server Data Provider implementation that included two XML attributes named `databaseOwner` and `object Qualifier`. The `databaseOwner` attribute defines the database owner to append to data objects in the scripts. The `objectQualifier` attribute defines a string to prefix the data objects with in the scripts.

For example, Listing 7-9 shows how the `GetSearchSettings` stored procedure is created in the 03.00.04.SqlDataProvider script.

Listing 7-9: A SqlDataProvider Upgrade Script

```
CREATE PROCEDURE {databaseOwner}{objectQualifier}GetSearchSettings
    @ModuleID int
AS
SELECT      tm.ModuleID,
            settings.SettingName,
            settings.SettingValue
FROM        {objectQualifier}Tabs searchTabs INNER JOIN
            {objectQualifier}TabModules searchTabModules
                    ON searchTabs.TabID = searchTabModules.TabID INNER JOIN
            {objectQualifier}Portals p
                    ON searchTabs.PortalID = p.PortalID INNER JOIN
            {objectQualifier}Tabs t
                    ON p.PortalID = t.PortalID INNER JOIN
            {objectQualifier}TabModules tm
                    ON t.TabID = tm.TabID INNER JOIN
            {objectQualifier}ModuleSettings settings
```

```
                        ON searchTabModules.ModuleID = settings.ModuleID
    WHERE       searchTabs.TabName = N'Search Admin'
    AND         tm.ModuleID = @ModuleID
    GO
```

This code looks like SQL with the addition of the two non-SQL tags. The first line creates a new stored procedure:

```
CREATE PROCEDURE {databaseOwner}{objectQualifier}GetSearchSettings
```

It is created in the context of the databaseOwner defined in web.config, and the name of the stored procedure is prefixed with the objectQualifier value from web.config.

If in web.config the databaseOwner is set to dbo and the objectQualifier is set to DNN, the preceding line would be programmatically converted to:

```
CREATE PROCEDURE dbo.DNN_GetSearchSettings
```

The `objectQualifier` attribute is useful when you want to maintain multiple instances of DotNetNuke in the same database. For example, you could have a single web server with 10 DotNetNuke installations on it, each using the same database. But you wouldn't want these 10 installations using the same data tables. The `objectQualifier` attribute adds the flexibility for you to store data from multiple DotNetNuke installations in the same database.

Security Model

In previous DotNetNuke releases, the framework offered only a single security solution; the forms-based security that was included with the core release. That security worked well, but it limited the capability to implement DotNetNuke in a way that tightly integrates with other security mechanisms. Third-party developers provided enhancements that allow Windows authentication to be used, and DotNetNuke 4.0 supports Windows authentication directly in the core release.

Examining how security works in ASP.NET 2.0 will help you understand the challenges that the Core Team faced in implementing the Membership API, as well as the finer details of how security works in DotNetNuke today.

Security in ASP.NET 2.0

In ASP.NET 1.x, the native authentication and authorization services relied on external data stores or configuration in the web.config file. For example, in ASP.NET 1.1, an application can provide forms-based authentication. This requires the developer to create a login form and associated controls to acquire, validate, and manage user credentials. After authenticatation, authorization is provided through XML configurations in the web.config file.

In ASP.NET 2.0, the introduction of several new security enhancements expands on these services in three distinct ways:

❑ **Login and user controls:** A new suite of login and user controls provides plenty of functionality out-of-the-box, reducing the need for each application to provide its own login and user controls. For example, it is easy to generate a set of pages for registering a new user, allowing an existing user to log in, and even handling forgotten passwords by simply placing the appropriate controls on a page and setting a few properties.

❑ **User management:** ASP.NET 2.0 provides a configuration interface for each application that allows for easy management of the application. One feature of the configuration interface is the capability to manage security for the application. For example, you can easily create a new user and a new role and then add the user to the role, all within the ASP.NET 2.0 native configuration interface. As an alternative, security can be managed by writing a custom management tool to access the same functionality programmatically.

❑ **Membership Provider:** This new provider is the conduit between the Presentation Layer (specifically the login/user controls and the configuration interface) and the persistence mechanism. It encapsulates all of the data access code required to manage users and roles.

Together these three components reduce the amount of code that is required to provide authentication and authorization services and persist the data to a data store.

DotNetNuke and ASP.NET 2.0

To build an application that fully supports authentication in ASP.NET 2.0, the Membership Provider has to be integrated into the application. There are several benefits to using this provider in an application. First, it can reduce the amount of code that is written to bring these services to the application. This is true as long as the business requirements fall within the functionality that the default Membership Provider supplies. Second, implementing the Membership Provider promotes developer and consumer confidence because Microsoft has taken on the responsibility of ensuring that its provider follows optimal security standards and has been subjected to rigorous threat modeling and penetration testing.

When the Membership/Roles Provider was first introduced in DotNetNuke 3.0, it leveraged a backported version of this component created by Microsoft because ASP.NET 2.0 had not yet been released. That version conformed to the same API found in ASP.NET 2.0, except that it ran in ASP.NET 1.1. This was a great addition to DotNetNuke for many reasons, but one key benefit is that it allowed DotNetNuke to conform to several ASP.NET 2.0 specifications even before ASP.NET 2.0 was released. DotNetNuke version 4.0 uses the ASP.NET 2.0 Membership/Role Provider.

Security in DotNetNuke 4.0

Security in DotNetNuke 4.0 was implemented with quite a bit of forward thinking. It combines the best features of prior versions of DotNetNuke with the features of the ASP.NET 2.0 Membership Provider. The result is an extensible security model that aligns DotNetNuke closely with best-practice security models in ASP.NET 2.0.

Portals and Applications

DotNetNuke supports running many portals from a single DotNetNuke installation. Each portal has its own users and roles that are not shared with other portals. A portal is identified by a unique key: the PortalID.

Because the default Membership Provider implementation is a generic solution, it does not natively support the concept of having multiple portals, each with its own users and roles. The default implementation was designed in a way that supports only a single portal site in a DotNetNuke installation. The Membership Provider refers to the DotNetNuke installation as an application, and without customization, that application can support only a single set of users and roles (a single portal instance).

To overcome this limitation, a wrapper was needed for the Membership Provider's SQL data providers. This customization allows application virtualization support. The end result is that the Membership Provider, as implemented in DotNetNuke, can support multiple applications (multiple portal instances in a single DotNetNuke installation).

Data Model for Membership

To achieve the full benefit from the Membership Provider, it is important to recognize that user information can be externalized from DotNetNuke and held in a data store that is independent of the main data store. For instance, DotNetNuke may use Microsoft SQL Server as its database to store content and system settings, but the Membership Provider may use Windows authentication, LDAP, or another mechanism to handle authentication and authorization. Because security can be externalized using the Provider Model, it was important to ensure that the implementation of the Membership Provider didn't customize any code or database tables used by the provider. Those data tables had to be independent from the other core DotNetNuke tables. We could not enforce referential integrity between DotNetNuke data and the Membership Provider data, nor could we use cascade deletes or other data level synchronization methods — all of the magic had to happen in the business layer.

One challenge in implementing the Membership Provider was dealing with the fields that DotNetNuke internally supports but that the Membership Provider does not support. Ideally, we would have completely replaced the DotNetNuke authentication and authorization tables with the tables used by the Membership Provider. However, we could not achieve this goal because the authentication and authorization tables in DotNetNuke were already tied to so many existing and necessary features of the application. For instance, the DotNetNuke Users table has a UserID column, which holds a unique identifier for each user. This UserID is used in nearly all core and third-party modules. The most significant problem with UserID was that it doesn't exist in the Membership Provider. Instead, the Membership Provider uses the Username as the unique key for a user within an application. We needed a way to maintain the UserID to preserve the DotNetNuke functionality that depended on it. This is just one example of an attribute that cannot be handled by Microsoft's default Membership Provider.

Ultimately, we decided that we would need to maintain satellite tables to support the DotNetNuke attributes that could not be managed by the Membership Provider. The goal was to maintain enough information in the DotNetNuke tables so that functionality was not lost, and offload whatever data we can to the Membership Provider tables. The end result is a data model that mirrors the Membership Provider data tables as shown in Figure 7-6.

Notice that none of the tables on top in Figure 7-6 have database relationships to the any of the tables on the bottom. The lines connecting them simply show their relationship in theory, not an actual relationship in the database.

Because the data for portals, profiles, users, and roles is stored in multiple unrelated tables, the business layer is responsible for aggregating the data. For example, you cannot get a complete representation of a user without collecting data from both the aspnet_Users table (from the Membership Provider) and the Users table (native DotNetNuke table).

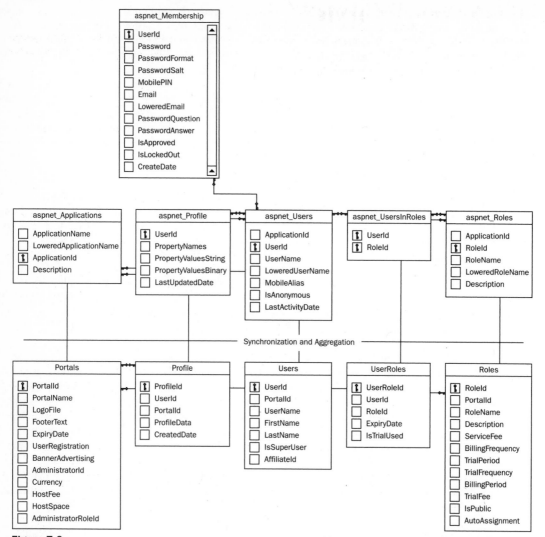

Figure 7-6

In addition to aggregation, data in the tables used by the Membership Provider and the native DotNetNuke tables must be automatically synchronized. Earlier in this chapter, you learned that the Membership Provider supports a wide array of data stores, and in ASP.NET 2.0, the data in those data stores can be managed through a common application configuration utility. If a user is added through that utility, the user is not added to the native DotNetNuke tables. Also, if your Membership Provider uses an LDAP implementation, for example, a user could be added to LDAP but would not be added to the native DotNetNuke tables. That's why synchronization services between the two data structures are provided.

DotNetNuke 4.0 fully leverages features of the ASP.NET 2.0 Membership API. Atypical of applications built on new platform releases, DotNetNuke 4.0 provides a tested and proven solution on the ASP.NET 2.0 framework based on the backported component utilized in DotNetNuke 3.0. These features bring demonstrated flexibility and extensibility to the security framework.

Namespace Overview

DotNetNuke 4.0 is a moderately large framework, but it is organized as a coherent set of namespaces and class locations to facilitate ease-of-use for the developer. Figure 7-7 shows the second-level namespaces that fall under the root DotNetNuke namespace.

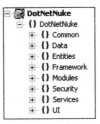

Figure 7-7

Here are brief descriptions of these namespaces:

- **DotNetNuke.Common:** Used for all classes used throughout the entire DotNetNuke application. For example, the global constants that are used throughout the application are found in the DotNetNuke.Common.Globals class.

- **DotNetNuke.Data:** Used for any classes relating to the Data Access Layer. For example, the DataProvider base class for the Data Provider API is in the DotNetNuke.Data namespace.

- **DotNetNuke.Entities:** Used for the classes that represent and manage the five entities that make a portal. They are Host, Portals, Tabs, Users, and Modules. The Modules namespace that falls under DotNetNuke.Entities is home to the functionality behind managing modules. The actual modules themselves have their own second-level namespace: DotNetNuke.Modules.

- **DotNetNuke.Framework:** Home to several base classes and other utilities used by the DotNetNuke application.

- **DotNetNuke.Modules:** Used for organizing portal modules. There is a child namespace in the core named DotNetNuke.Modules.Admin where the classes for all of the core admin modules reside. For example, the Host Settings module is found in the DotNetNuke.Modules.Admin.Host.HostSettingsModule class.

- **DotNetNuke.Security:** Used for authorization and authentication classes. This includes tab permissions, module permissions, folder permissions, roles, and other portal security classes.

- **DotNetNuke.Services:** Used for any services the core provides for modules. In this namespace, the child namespaces for exception management, localization, personalization, search, and several others reside.

- **DotNetNuke.UI:** Used for any user interface classes. For example, the Skin and Container classes are found in DotNetNuke.UI.Skins.Skin and DotNetNuke.UI.Containers.Container, respectively.

Summary

This chapter covered the architecture of the DotNetNuke application. Here are key points to understand about the architecture:

- ❑ The Provider Model design pattern enhanced DotNetNuke with greater extensibility without having to make core changes to realize that extensibility.

- ❑ The use of Custom Business Objects along with the CBO Hydrator created a foundation for developers to code using best-practice standards that enable them to build more maintainable modules and providers that perform well.

- ❑ The Membership Provider in DotNetNuke created an extensible security model that showcases an API that mirrors the API found in ASP.NET 2.0.

- ❑ The namespace model is organized in a logical hierarchy that makes it easy to find the classes used most often.

In the next chapter, you'll explore the core DotNetNuke APIs and discover many of the powerful services that the DotNetNuke core application provides developers.

Core DotNetNuke APIs

DotNetNuke provides significant capability straight out of the box. Just install and go. Sometimes, however, you may need to extend the base framework. DotNetNuke provides a variety of integration points: from HTTP modules to providers to custom modules. To fully take advantage of the framework, it is important to understand some of the base services and APIs provided by DotNetNuke.

This chapter examines some of the core services provided by DotNetNuke. You can use these services from within your own code. Because most of the core services are built using the Provider design pattern, it's also possible to swap out the base functionality. If you need your events logged to a custom database or the Windows Event Logs, then just create your own provider.

The second part of this chapter covers several HTTP modules that are installed with DotNetNuke. They provide features like Friendly URLs, Exception Management, and Users Online. Many of the providers installed with DotNetNuke use HTTP modules to hook into the request-processing pipeline. By examining the code used in the core HTTP modules, you can build your own custom extensions that can be used in DotNetNuke as well as other ASP.NET applications.

The final section examines some of the core interfaces that you can implement in your own modules. These interfaces simplify the process of adding common features to your module, whether it is the module menu, searches, importing and exporting, or even custom upgrade logic. By using these interfaces in your modules, you can provide some of the same features you see in the core DotNetNuke modules with very little coding effort.

Event Logging

The Logging Provider in DotNetNuke provides a very configurable and extensible set of logging services. It is designed to handle a wide array of logging needs including exception logging, event auditing, and security logging. As you may have gathered from its name, the Logging Provider uses the Provider Model design pattern. This allows the default DB Logging Provider to be replaced with another logging mechanism without having to make changes to the core code. This section covers the ways you can use the Logging Provider to log events in custom modules.

Before you dive into the details of how to use the Logging Provider API, it is important to understand some concepts and terminology that will be used in this section:

❑ **Log classification:** There are two different types of log classifications in the Logging Provider. The first is the *event log* classification. This encapsulates all log entries related to some type of event within DotNetNuke. For example, you can configure the Logging Provider to write a log entry when a login attempt fails. This would be considered an event log entry. The second log classification is the *exception* log classification. You can configure the Logging Provider to log exceptions and stack traces when exceptions are thrown within DotNetNuke. These two classifications are distinct only because they have different needs in terms of what type of information they log.

❑ **Log type:** A *log type* defines the type of event that creates the log entry. For example, an event log type is LOGIN_FAILURE. The Logging Provider can react differently for each log type. You can configure the Logging Provider to enable or disable logging for each of the log types. Depending on the Logging Provider, you can configure it to log each log type to a different file or to send e-mail notifications upon creating new log entries for that log type.

❑ **Log type configuration:** The Logging Provider is configured via a module that is accessible from the Log Viewer screen (the Edit Log Configuration Module Action). This enables you to configure each log type to be handled differently by the Logging Provider.

The API

The Logging Provider functionality lives in the DotNetNuke.Services.Log.EventLog namespace. In this namespace, you will find the classes that comprise the Logging Provider API. These are described in Table 8-1.

Table 8-1: Logging Provider Classes

Class	Description
EventLogController	Provides the methods necessary to write log entries with the event log classification. It inherits from LogController.
ExceptionLogController	Provides the methods necessary to write log entries with the exception log classification. It inherits from LogController.
LogController	Provides the methods that interact with the Logging Provider — the basic methods for adding, deleting, and getting log entries.
LogDetailInfo	Holds a single key/value pair of information from a log entry.
LoggingProvider	Provides the bridge to the implementation of the Logging Provider.
LogInfo	Container for the information that goes into a log entry.

Class	Description
LogInfoArray	Holds an array of LogInfo objects.
LogProperties	Holds an array of LogDetailInfo objects.
LogTypeConfigInfo	Container for the configuration data relating to how logs of a specific log type are to be handled.
LogTypeInfo	Container for the log type information.
PurgeLogBuffer	Scheduler task that can be executed regularly if Log Buffering is enabled.
SendLogNotifications	Scheduler task that can be executed regularly if any log type is configured to send e-mail notifications.

The Controller Classes

The controller classes, EventLogController and ExceptionLogController, are the two that bring the most functionality to custom modules. Many of the other classes are used in concert with the controllers.

EventLogController

The EventLogController provides the methods necessary to log significant system events. This class is located in the DotNetNuke.Library in the Components/Providers/Logging/EventLogging/EventLogController.vb file. The class also defines the EventLogType enumeration that lists each log type that is handled by the EventLogController. The enumerations are shown in Listing 8-1.

Listing 8-1: EventLogController.EventLogType Enumeration

```
    Public Enum EventLogType
            USER_CREATED
            USER_DELETED
            LOGIN_SUPERUSER
            LOGIN_SUCCESS
            LOGIN_FAILURE
            CACHE_REFRESHED
            PASSWORD_SENT_SUCCESS
            PASSWORD_SENT_FAILURE
            LOG_NOTIFICATION_FAILURE
            PORTAL_CREATED
            PORTAL_DELETED
            TAB_CREATED
            TAB_UPDATED
            TAB_DELETED
            TAB_SENT_TO_RECYCLE_BIN
            TAB_RESTORED
            USER_ROLE_CREATED
            USER_ROLE_DELETED
            ROLE_CREATED
            ROLE_UPDATED
```

(continued)

Listing 8-1: *(continued)*

```
              ROLE_DELETED
              MODULE_CREATED
              MODULE_UPDATED
              MODULE_DELETED
              MODULE_SENT_TO_RECYCLE_BIN
              MODULE_RESTORED
              SCHEDULER_EVENT_STARTED
              SCHEDULER_EVENT_PROGRESSING
              SCHEDULER_EVENT_COMPLETED
              APPLICATION_START
              APPLICATION_END
              APPLICATION_SHUTTING_DOWN
              SCHEDULER_STARTED
              SCHEDULER_SHUTTING_DOWN
              SCHEDULER_STOPPED
              ADMIN_ALERT
              HOST_ALERT
        End Enum
```

The `EventLogController.AddLog()` method has several method overloads that enable a developer to log just about any values derived from an object or its properties. Following are descriptions of these overloaded methods, along with brief explanations of their parameters:

❑ The primary `AddLog` method is ultimately used by all of the other `AddLog` overloads and accepts a single LogInfo object. This method provides easy access to the base logging method in inherited LogController class:

```
Public Overloads Sub AddLog(ByVal objEventLogInfo As LogInfo)
```

❑ To log the property names and values of a Custom Business Object, use the following method:

```
Public Overloads Sub AddLog(ByVal objCBO As Object, ByVal _PortalSettings As _
PortalSettings, ByVal UserID As Integer, ByVal UserName As String, ByVal _
objLogType As Services.Log.EventLog.EventLogController.EventLogType)
```

Parameter	Type	Description
objCBO	Object	Custom Business Object.
_PortalSettings	PortalSettings	Current PortalSettings object.
UserID	Integer	UserID of the authenticated user of the request.
UserName	String	UserName of the authenticated user of the request.
objLogType	EventLogType	Event log type.

❑ To add a log entry that has no custom properties, use the following method:

```
Public Overloads Sub AddLog(ByVal _PortalSettings As PortalSettings, ByVal UserID _
As Integer, ByVal objLogType As _
Services.Log.EventLog.EventLogController.EventLogType)
```

This is useful if you simply need to log that an event has occurred, but you have no requirement to log any further details about the event.

Parameter	Type	Description
_PortalSettings	PortalSettings	Current PortalSettings object.
UserID	Integer	UserID of the authenticated user of the request.
objLogType	EventLogType	Event log type.

❏ To add a log entry that has a single property name and value, use the following method:

```
Public Overloads Sub AddLog(ByVal PropertyName As String, ByVal PropertyValue As _
String, ByVal _PortalSettings As PortalSettings, ByVal UserID As Integer, ByVal _
objLogType As Services.Log.EventLog.EventLogController.EventLogType)
```

Parameter	Type	Description
PropertyName	String	Name of the property to log.
PropertyValue	String	Value of the property to log.
_PortalSettings	PortalSettings	Current PortalSettings object.
UserID	Integer	UserID of the authenticated user of the request.
objLogType	EventLogType	Event log type.

❏ To add a log entry that has a single property name and value and the LogType is not defined in a core enumeration, use the following method:

```
Public Overloads Sub AddLog(ByVal PropertyName As String, ByVal PropertyValue As _
String, ByVal _PortalSettings As PortalSettings, ByVal UserID As Integer, ByVal _
LogType As String)
```

This is useful for custom modules that define their own log types.

Parameter	Type	Description
PropertyName	String	Name of the property to log.
PropertyValue	String	Value of the property to log.
_PortalSettings	PortalSettings	Current PortalSettings object.
UserID	Integer	UserID of the authenticated user of the request.
LogType	String	Event log type string.

❏ To add a log entry that has multiple property names and values, use the following method. To use this method, you must send into it a LogProperties object that is comprised of a collection of LogDetailInfo objects:

```
Public Overloads Sub AddLog(ByVal objProperties As LogProperties, ByVal _
_PortalSettings As PortalSettings, ByVal UserID As Integer, ByVal LogTypeKey As _
String, ByVal BypassBuffering As Boolean)
```

Parameter	Type	Description
objProperties	LogProperties	A collection of LogDetailInfo objects.
_PortalSettings	PortalSettings	Current PortalSettings object.
UserID	Integer	UserID of the authenticated user of the request.
LogTypeKey	String	Event log type.
BypassBuffering	Boolean	Specifies whether to write directly to the log (true) or to use log buffering (false) if log buffering is enabled.

Listings 8-2 through 8-6 show how to use the two most common overloaded methods for
`EventLogController.AddLog()`. To exemplify the flexibility of this method, Listing 8-2 illustrates how
you can send in a Custom Business Object and automatically log its property values.

Listing 8-2: EventLogController.AddLog Example

```
Private Sub TestUserInfoLog()
    Dim objUserInfo As New UserInfo
    objUserInfo.FirstName = "John"
    objUserInfo.LastName = "Doe"
    objUserInfo.UserID = 6
    objUserInfo.Username = "jdoe"
    Dim objEventLog As New Services.Log.EventLog.EventLogController
    objEventLog.AddLog(objUserInfo, PortalSettings, UserID, UserInfo.Username, _
        Services.Log.EventLog.EventLogController.EventLogType.USER_CREATED)
End Sub
```

The resulting log entry written by the XML Logging Provider for this example includes each property
name and value in the objUserInfo object as shown in the `<properties/>` XML element in Listing 8-3.

Listing 8-3: EventLogController.AddLog Log Entry for the XML Logging Provider

```
<logs>
      <log LogGUID="92ca39e4-a135-475a-8c0c-7e4949c359b7" LogFileID="b86359bb-
e984-4483-891b-26a2b95bf9bd"
          LogTypeKey="USER_CREATED" LogUserID="-1" LogUserName="" LogPortalID="0"
LogPortalName="DotNetNuke"
          LogCreateDate="2005-02-04T14:33:46.9318672-05:00"
LogCreateDateNum="20050204143346931"
          LogServerName="DNNTEST">
          <properties>
              <property>
                  <name>UserID</name>
                  <value>6</value>
```

```
                        </property>
                        <property>
                                <name>FirstName</name>
                                <value>John</value>
                        </property>
                        <property>
                                <name>LastName</name>
                                <value>Doe</value>
                        </property>
                        <property>
                                <name>UserName</name>
                                <value>jdoe</value>
                        </property>
                </properties>
        </log>
</logs>
```

If you are using the default DB LoggingProvider, this same information is stored in the EventLog table. The properties element is saved in the LogProperties column as an XML fragment as shown in Listing 8-4. This format is similar to the properties node for the corresponding XML log version.

Listing 8-4: EventLogController.AddLog LogProperties for the DB Logging Provider

```
<ArrayOfAnyType
        xmlns:xsd="http://www.w3.org/2001/XMLSchema"
        xmlns:xsi="http://www.w3.org/2001/XMLSchema-instance">
        <anyType xsi:type="LogDetailInfo">
                <name>UserID</name>
                <value>4</value>
        </anyType>
        <anyType xsi:type="LogDetailInfo">
                <name>FirstName</name>
                <value>Joe</value>
        </anyType>
        <anyType xsi:type="LogDetailInfo">
                <name>LastName</name>
                <value>Brinkman</value>
        </anyType>
        <anyType xsi:type="LogDetailInfo">
                <name>UserName</name>
                <value>tuser2</value>
        </anyType>
        <anyType xsi:type="LogDetailInfo">
                <name>Email</name>
                <value>joe.brinkman@tag-software.net</value>
        </anyType>
</ArrayOfAnyType>
```

> Because the XML log format is a little easier to read, the XML Logging Provider is used for all additional examples in this chapter and will note any substantial differences with the DB Logging Provider.

This example logs each of the properties of a Custom Business Object. There are other overloaded `EventLogController.AddLog()` methods available if you need to log less information or information that isn't stored in a Custom Business Object. The example in Listing 8-5 shows how you can use `EventLogController.AddLog()` to add a single key/value pair to the log.

Listing 8-5: EventLogController.AddLog Example

```
Private Sub TestCreateRole()

    Dim objRoleController As New RoleController
    Dim objRoleInfo As New RoleInfo

    'create and add the new role
    objRoleInfo.RoleName = "Newsletter Subscribers"
    objRoleInfo.PortalID = 5
    objRoleController.AddRole(objRoleInfo)

    'log the event
    Dim objEventLog As New Services.Log.EventLog.EventLogController
    objEventLog.AddLog("Role", objRoleInfo.RoleName, PortalSettings, _
    UserId, objEventLog.EventLogType.USER_ROLE_CREATED)

End Sub
```

In this case, the key `Role` and the value `Newsletter Subscribers` will be logged. The resulting log entry written by the default XML Logging Provider for this example is shown in the `<properties/>` XML element in Listing 8-6.

Listing 8-6: EventLogController.AddLog Log Entry

```
<logs>
     <log LogGUID="2145856a-1e4a-4974-86f6-da1f0ae5dcca" LogFileID="b86359bb-
e984-4483-891b-26a2b95bf9bd"
          LogTypeKey="ROLE_CREATED" LogUserID="1" LogUserName="host"
LogPortalID="0" LogPortalName="DotNetNuke"
          LogCreateDate="2005-02-04T22:00:22.0413424-05:00"
LogCreateDateNum="20050204220022041"
          LogServerName="DNNTEST">
          <properties>
               <property>
                    <name>RoleName</name>
                    <value>Newsletter Subscribers</value>
               </property>
          </properties>
     </log>
</logs>
```

ExceptionLogController

The ExceptionLogController exposes the methods necessary for adding information about exceptions to the log. This controller class also defines four exception types in the ExceptionLogType enumeration: `GENERAL_EXCEPTION`, `MODULE_LOAD_EXCEPTION`, `PAGE_LOAD_EXCEPTION`, and `SCHEDULER_EXCEPTION`. By defining different log types for exceptions, the configuration of the Logging Provider can treat each exception log type differently regarding how and if the exceptions get logged.

The next section covers exceptions in more detail. For now, the focus is on how to log the exceptions. The `ExceptionLogController.AddLog()` method has three overloaded methods that enable you to pass in various types of exceptions. The first method enables you to send in a System.Exception or any exception that inherits System.Exception, as shown in Listing 8-7.

Listing 8-7: ExceptionLogController.AddLog Example

```
Public Sub test()
    Try
        If 1 = 1 Then
            Throw New Exception("Oh no, an exception!")
        End If
    Catch exc As Exception
        Dim objExceptionLog As New Services.Log.EventLog.ExceptionLogController
        objExceptionLog.AddLog(exc)
        'a shortcut to this is simply "LogException(exc)"
    End Try
End Sub
```

In this case, the properties of the System.Exception will be logged along with a collection of properties that are specific to the request. For instance, it will log the filename, line, and column number the exception occurred in if it is available. The resulting log entry written by the default XML Logging Provider for this example is shown in Listing 8-8.

Listing 8-8: ExceptionLogController.AddLog Log Entry

```
<logs>
      <log LogGUID="39c72059-bcd1-42ca-8886-002363d1c9dc" LogFileID="6b780a60-
cf46-4588-8a76-75ae9c577277"
          LogTypeKey="GENERAL_EXCEPTION" LogUserID="-1" LogUserName=""
LogPortalID="-1" LogPortalName=""
          LogCreateDate="2005-02-04T23:25:44.6873456-05:00"
LogCreateDateNum="20050204232544687"
          LogServerName="DNNTEST">
          <properties>
              <property>
                  <name>AssemblyVersion</name>
                  <value>03.00.10</value>
              </property>
              <property>
                  <name>Method</name>
                  <value>DotNetNuke.Framework.CDefault.test</value>
              </property>
              <property>
                  <name>FileName</name>
                  <value>c:\public\dotnetnuke\Default.aspx.vb</value>
              </property>
              <property>
                  <name>FileLineNumber</name>
                  <value>481</value>
              </property>
              <property>
                  <name>FileColumnNumber</name>
                  <value>21</value>
```

(continued)

Listing 8-8: *(continued)*

```xml
                </property>
                <property>
                        <name>PortalID</name>
                        <value>0</value>
                </property>
                <property>
                        <name>PortalName</name>
                        <value>DotNetNuke</value>
                </property>
                <property>
                        <name>UserID</name>
                        <value>-1</value>
                </property>
                <property>
                        <name>UserName</name>
                        <value />
                </property>
                <property>
                        <name>ActiveTabID</name>
                        <value>36</value>
                </property>
                <property>
                        <name>ActiveTabName</name>
                        <value>Home</value>
                </property>
                <property>
                        <name>AbsoluteURL</name>
                        <value>/DotNetNuke/Default.aspx</value>
                </property>
                <property>
                        <name>AbsoluteURLReferrer</name>
                        <value />
                </property>
                <property>
                        <name>ExceptionGUID</name>
                        <value>128455d6-064a-4222-993f-b54fd302e21e</value>
                </property>
                <property>
                        <name>DefaultDataProvider</name>
                        <value>DotNetNuke.Data.SqlDataProvider,
DotNetNuke.SqlDataProvider</value>
                </property>
                <property>
                        <name>InnerException</name>
                        <value>Oh no, an exception!</value>
                </property>
                <property>
                        <name>Message</name>
                        <value>Oh no, an exception!</value>
                </property>
                <property>
                        <name>StackTrace</name>
                        <value>   at DotNetNuke.Framework.CDefault.test() in
c:\public\dotnetnuke\Default.aspx.vb:line 481</value>
```

```
            </property>
            <property>
                <name>Source</name>
                <value>DotNetNuke</value>
            </property>
        </properties>
    </log>
</logs>
```

Notice that Listing 8-8 does not tell you the portal module that the exception was thrown from. This is because a general exception was thrown (System.Exception). If a ModuleLoadException is thrown, more details about the portal module that throws the exception will be logged.

Exception Handling

The exception handling API in DotNetNuke provides a framework for handling exceptions uniformly and elegantly. Exception handling primarily uses four methods, most of which have several overloaded methods. Through these methods, developers can gracefully handle exceptions, log the exception trace and context, and display a user-friendly message to the end user.

The Exception Handling API

The exception handling API lives under the DotNetNuke.Services.Exceptions namespace. Table 8-2 lists the classes that comprise the Exception Handling API.

Table 8-2: Exception Handling Classes

Class	Description
BasePortalException	Inherits from System.Exception and contains many other properties specific to the portal application.
ErrorContainer	Generates formatting for the error message that will be displayed in the web browser.
ExceptionInfo	Stores information from the stack trace.
Exceptions	Contains most of the methods that are used in custom modules. It contains the methods necessary to process each type of portal exception.
ModuleLoadException	An exception type for exceptions thrown within portal modules. It inherits from BasePortalException.
PageLoadException	An exception type for exceptions thrown within pages.
SchedulerException	An exception type for exceptions thrown within the Scheduling Provider. It also inherits from BasePortalException.

The Exceptions Class

Although there are many classes in the exception handling namespace, the primary class that module developers deal with regularly is the Exceptions class. This class contains all of the methods necessary to gracefully handle exceptions in DotNetNuke. The most widely used method for exception handling is `DotNetNuke.Services.Exceptions.ProcessModuleLoadException()`.

ProcessModuleLoadException Method

The `ProcessModuleLoadException` method serves two primary functions: to log the exceptions that are thrown from within a module to the Logging Provider, and to display a friendly error message in place of the module that threw the exception. The friendly error message is displayed only if the host option Use Custom Error Messages is enabled on the Host Settings page (see Chapter 5).

`ProcessModuleLoadException` has seven overloaded methods:

❑   To process an exception that occurs in a portal module, use the following method. If the Custom Error Messages option has been enabled in Host Settings, this method will also handle displaying a user-friendly error message to the client browser:

```
Public Sub ProcessModuleLoadException(ByVal ctrlModule As _
Entities.Modules.PortalModuleBase, ByVal exc As Exception)
```

Parameter	Type	Description
ctrlModule	PortalModuleBase	Portal module object.
exc	Exception	Exception that was thrown.

❑   This method is the same as the previous one, although it provides the capability to suppress the error message from being displayed on the client browser:

```
Public Sub ProcessModuleLoadException(ByVal ctrlModule As _
Entities.Modules.PortalModuleBase, ByVal exc As Exception, ByVal _
DisplayErrorMessage As Boolean)
```

Parameter	Type	Description
ctrlModule	PortalModuleBase	Portal module object.
exc	Exception	Exception that was thrown.
DisplayErrorMessage	Boolean	Indicates whether the portal should render an error message to the client browser.

❑   This is the same as the previous method; however, it adds the capability to provide a custom friendly message to the client browser:

```
Public Sub ProcessModuleLoadException(ByVal FriendlyMessage As String, ByVal _
ctrlModule As Entities.Modules.PortalModuleBase, ByVal exc As Exception, _
ByVal DisplayErrorMessage As Boolean)
```

Parameter	Type	Description
FriendlyMessage	String	Friendly message to display to the client browser.
ctrlModule	PortalModuleBase	Portal module object.
exc	Exception	Exception that was thrown.
DisplayErrorMessage	Boolean	Indicates whether the portal should render an error message to the client browser.

❑   Use the following overloaded method if you are handling exceptions in a control that isn't directly in a portal module. For instance, if your portal module uses a server control, you can use this method to handle exceptions within that server control. It displays a friendly error message if custom error messages are enabled:

```
Public Sub ProcessModuleLoadException(ByVal FriendlyMessage As String, _
ByVal UserCtrl As Control, ByVal exc As Exception)
```

Parameter	Type	Description
FriendlyMessage	String	Friendly message to display to the client browser.
UserCtrl	Control	The control. It can be anything that inherits from System.Web.UI.Control.
exc	Exception	Exception that was thrown.

❑   This is the same as the previous method; however, it adds the capability to specify whether to display an error message to the client browser (the Host Settings option to Use Custom Error Messages takes precedence over this value):

```
Public Sub ProcessModuleLoadException(ByVal FriendlyMessage As String, _
ByVal ctrlModule As Control, ByVal exc As Exception, _
ByVal DisplayErrorMessage As Boolean)
```

Parameter	Type	Description
FriendlyMessage	String	Friendly message to display to the client browser.
ctrlModule	Control	The control. It can be anything that inherits from System.Web.UI.Control.
exc	Exception	Exception that was thrown.
DisplayErrorMessage	Boolean	Indicates whether the portal should render an error message to the client browser.

❑ This is a simple method that has only two parameters. It displays a generic error message to the client browser if custom error messages are enabled:

```
Public Sub ProcessModuleLoadException(ByVal UserCtrl As Control, _
ByVal exc As Exception)
```

Parameter	Type	Description
UserCtrl	Control	The control. It can be anything that inherits from System.Web.UI.Control.
exc	Exception	Exception that was thrown.

❑ This is the same as the previous method except it provides the capability to suppress the error message that is displayed in the client browser (the Host Settings option to Use Custom Error Messages takes precedence over this value):

```
Public Sub ProcessModuleLoadException(ByVal UserCtrl As Control, _
ByVal exc As Exception, ByVal DisplayErrorMessage As Boolean)
```

Parameter	Type	Description
UserCtrl	Control	The control. It can be anything that inherits from System.Web.UI.Control.
exc	Exception	Exception that was thrown.
DisplayErrorMessage	Boolean	Indicates whether the portal should render an error message to the client browser.

ProcessPageLoadException Method

Similar to the ProcessModuleLoadException method, the ProcessPageLoadException method serves two primary functions: to log the exceptions thrown from outside of a module to the Logging Provider, and to display a friendly error message on the page. The friendly error message will only be displayed if the host option Use Custom Error Messages is enabled on the Host Settings page (see Chapter 5).

ProcessPageLoadException has two overloaded methods:

❑ To process an exception that occurs in an ASPX file or in logic outside of a portal module, use the following overloaded method. If the Use Custom Error Messages option has been enabled in Host Settings, this method also handles displaying a user-friendly error message to the client browser:

```
Public Sub ProcessPageLoadException(ByVal exc As Exception)
```

Parameter	Type	Description
exc	Exception	Exception that was thrown.

❑ This is the same as the previous method; however, you must send in the URL parameter to redirect the request after logging the exception:

```
Public Sub ProcessPageLoadException(ByVal exc As Exception, _
ByVal URL As String)
```

Parameter	Type	Description
exc	Exception	Exception that was thrown.
URL	String	URL to redirect the request to.

LogException Method

The LogException method is used for adding exceptions to the log. It does not handle displaying any type of friendly message to the user. Instead, it simply logs the error without notifying the client browser of a problem. LogException has four overloaded methods:

❑ To log an exception thrown from a module, use the following overloaded method:

```
Public Sub LogException(ByVal exc As ModuleLoadException)
```

Parameter	Type	Description
exc	ModuleLoadException	Exception that was thrown.

❑ To log an exception thrown from a page or other logic outside of a module, use the following overloaded method:

```
Public Sub LogException(ByVal exc As PageLoadException)
```

Parameter	Type	Description
exc	PageLoadException	Exception that was thrown.

❑ To log an exception thrown from within a Scheduling Provider Task, use the following overloaded method:

```
Public Sub LogException(ByVal exc As SchedulerException)
```

Parameter	Type	Description
Exc	SchedulerException	Exception that was thrown.

❑ If you need to log an exception of another type, use the following overloaded method:

```
Public Sub LogException(ByVal exc As Exception)
```

Parameter	Type	Description
exc	Exception	Exception that was thrown.

ProcessSchedulerException Method

The `ProcessSchedulerException` method is used to log exceptions thrown from within a scheduled task. It simply logs the error.

To log an exception thrown from a scheduled task, use the following overloaded method:

```
Public Sub LogException(ByVal exc As ModuleLoadException)
```

Parameter	Type	Description
exc	ModuleLoadException	Exception that was thrown.

The exception handling API abstracts developers from the complexity of logging exceptions and presenting error messages gracefully. It provides several powerful methods that handle all of the logic involved in working with the Logging Provider and the presentation layer. The next section covers the various interfaces that module developers can take advantage of to bring more core features to life in their modules.

Scheduler

The Scheduler in DotNetNuke is a mechanism that enables developers to schedule tasks to run at defined intervals. It is implemented using the Provider pattern; therefore, it can easily be replaced without modifying core code. Creating a scheduled task is a fairly simple process. First, though, it's important to understand which types of tasks are suitable for the Scheduler.

Because the Scheduler is run under the context of the web application, it is prone to the same types of application recycles as a web application. In a web-hosting environment, it is a common practice to conserve resources by recycling the worker process for a site periodically. When this happens, the Scheduler stops running. Therefore, the tasks run by the Scheduler do not run 24 hours a day, 7 days a week. They are executed according to a defined schedule, but they can only be triggered when the worker process is alive. For this reason, you cannot specify that a task should run every night at midnight. It is not possible in the web environment to meet this type of use case. Instead, you can specify how often a task is run by defining the execution frequency for each task. The execution frequency is defined as every x minutes/hours/days.

To create a scheduled task, you must create a class that inherits from DotNetNuke.Services.Scheduling .SchedulerClient. This class must provide a constructor and a `DoWork` method. An example of a scheduled task is shown in Listing 8-9. This sample scheduled task will move all event log files to a folder named with the current date. By configuring this scheduled task to run once per day, the log files will be automatically archived daily, which keeps the log file sizes manageable.

Listing 8-9: Scheduled Task Example

```
Public Class ArchiveEventLog
    Inherits DotNetNuke.Services.Scheduling.SchedulerClient
    Public Sub New(ByVal objScheduleHistoryItem As _
        DotNetNuke.Services.Scheduling.ScheduleHistoryItem)
        MyBase.new()
        Me.ScheduleHistoryItem = objScheduleHistoryItem    'REQUIRED
    End Sub
    Public Overrides Sub DoWork()
        Try
            'notification that the event is progressing
            'this is optional
            Me.Progressing()    'OPTIONAL
            'get the directory that logs are written to
            Dim LogDirectory As String
            LogDirectory = Common.Globals.HostMapPath + "Logs\"

            'create a folder with today's date
            Dim FolderName As String
            FolderName = LogDirectory + Now.Month.ToString + "-" + _
                Now.Day.ToString + "-" + Now.Year.ToString + "\"
            If Not IO.Directory.Exists(FolderName) Then
                IO.Directory.CreateDirectory(FolderName)
            End If

            'get the files in the log directory
            Dim s As String()
            s = IO.Directory.GetFiles(LogDirectory)
            'loop through the files
            Dim i As Integer
            For i = 0 To s.Length - 1
                Dim OldFileInfo As New IO.FileInfo(s(i))
                'move all files to the new folder except the file
                'used to store pending log notifications
                If OldFileInfo.Name <> _
                    "PendingLogNotifications.xml.resources" Then
                    Dim NewFileName As String
                    NewFileName = FolderName + OldFileInfo.Name
                    'check to see if the new file already exists
                    If IO.File.Exists(NewFileName) Then
                        Dim errMessage As String
                        errMessage = "An error occurred archiving " + _
                            "log file to " + _
                            NewFileName + ".  The file already exists."
                        LogException(New _
                            BasePortalException(errMessage))
                    Else
                        IO.File.Move(OldFileInfo.FullName, NewFileName)
                        Me.ScheduleHistoryItem.AddLogNote("Moved " + _
                            OldFileInfo.FullName + _
                                " to " + FolderName + _
                                OldFileInfo.Name + ".")    'OPTIONAL
                    End If
```

(continued)

259

Listing 8-9: *(continued)*

```
            End If
        Next

        Me.ScheduleHistoryItem.Succeeded = True     'REQUIRED

    Catch exc As Exception     'REQUIRED

        Me.ScheduleHistoryItem.Succeeded = False    'REQUIRED

        Me.ScheduleHistoryItem.AddLogNote(String.Format( _
            "Archiving log files failed.", _
            exc.ToString))    'OPTIONAL

        'notification that we have errored
        Me.Errored(exc)     'REQUIRED

        'log the exception
        LogException(exc)     'OPTIONAL
    End Try
    End Sub
End Class
```

After the class has been compiled into the bin directory, the task can be scheduled from the Scheduling module under the Host page (see Chapter 6 for details). It is important to include each of the lines of code in Listing 8-9 that is labeled REQUIRED. These collectively ensure both the exception handling and schedule management are handled uniformly throughout all scheduled tasks.

HTTP Modules

ASP.NET provides a number of options for extending the path that data takes between client and server (known as the HTTP Pipeline). A popular method to extend the pipeline is through the use of custom components known as *HTTP modules*. An HTTP module enables you to add pre- and post-processing to each HTTP request coming into your application.

DotNetNuke implements a number of HTTP modules to extend the pipeline. They include features such as URL Rewriting, Exception Management, Users Online, Profile, Anonymous Identification, Role Management, DotNetNuke Membership, and Personalization.

Originally, a lot of the HTTP modules were implemented inside the core application (global.asax.vb). There were a number of reasons why the functionally was moved to HTTP modules:

❏ Administrators can optionally enable or disable an HTTP module.

❏ Developers can replace or modify HTTP modules without altering the core application.

❏ Provides templates for extending the HTTP Pipeline.

HTTP Modules 101

This section further examines the concepts of HTTP modules so you'll know when and where to implement them. To comprehend how HTTP modules work, it's necessary to understand the HTTP Pipeline and how ASP.NET processes incoming requests. Figure 8-1 shows the HTTP Pipeline.

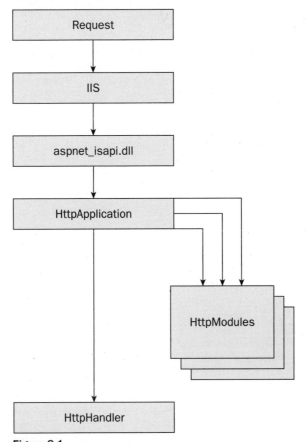

Figure 8-1

When a request is first made, it passes through a number of stages before it is actually handled by your application. The first participant in the pipeline is Microsoft Internet Information Server (IIS); its job is to route ASP.NET requests to the ASP.NET runtime. When an ASPX file is requested (or any other ASP.NET file), IIS forwards the request to the ASP.NET runtime (via an ISAPI extension).

Now that the request has been received by ASP.NET, it must pass through an instance of HttpApplication. The HttpApplication object handles application-wide methods, data, and events. It is also responsible for pushing the request through one or more HTTP module objects. The ASP.NET runtime determines which modules to load by examining the configuration files located at either machine level (machine.config) or application level (web.config). Listing 8-10 shows the HTTP modules configuration section of DotNetNuke.

Listing 8-10: HTTP Modules Configuration Section

```
<httpModules>
 <add name="UrlRewrite" type="DotNetNuke.HttpModules.UrlRewriteModule,
                              DotNetNuke.HttpModules.UrlRewrite" />

 <add name="Exception" type="DotNetNuke.HttpModules.ExceptionModule,
                             DotNetNuke.HttpModules.Exception" />

 <add name="UsersOnline" type="DotNetNuke.HttpModules.UsersOnlineModule,
                               DotNetNuke.HttpModules.UsersOnline" />

 <add name="Profile" type="Microsoft.ScalableHosting.Profile.ProfileModule,
                           MemberRole,
                           Version=1.0.0.0,
                           Culture=neutral,
                           PublicKeyToken=b7c773fb104e7562" />

 <add name="AnonymousIdentification"
       type="Microsoft.ScalableHosting.Security.AnonymousIdentificationModule,
             MemberRole,
             Version=1.0.0.0,
             Culture=neutral,
             PublicKeyToken=b7c773fb104e7562" />

 <add name="RoleManager"
       type="Microsoft.ScalableHosting.Security.RoleManagerModule,
             MemberRole,
             Version=1.0.0.0,
             Culture=neutral,
             PublicKeyToken=b7c773fb104e7562" />

 <add name="DNNMembership" type="DotNetNuke.HttpModules.DNNMembershipModule,
                                 DotNetNuke.HttpModules.DNNMembership" />

 <add name="Personalization" type="DotNetNuke.HttpModules.PersonalizationModule,
                                   DotNetNuke.HttpModules.Personalization" />

</httpModules>
```

To invoke each HTTP module, the `Init` method of each module is invoked. At the end of each request, the `Dispose` method is invoked to enable each HTTP module to clean up its resources. In fact, those two methods form the interface (IHttpModule) each module must implement. Listing 8-11 shows the IHttpModule interface.

Listing 8-11: The IHttpModule Interface Implemented by Each HTTP Module

```
Public Interface IHttpModule
    Sub Init(ByVal context As HttpApplication)
    Sub Dispose()
End Interface
```

During the Init event, each module may subscribe to a number of events raised by the HttpApplication object. Table 8-3 shows the events that are raised before the application executes. The events are listed in the order in which they occur.

Table 8-3: HTTP Module Events (Before the Application Executes)

Event	Description
BeginRequest	Signals a new request; guaranteed to be raised on each request.
AuthenticateRequest	Signals that the request is ready to be authenticated; used by the Security module.
AuthorizeRequest	Signals that the request is ready to be authorized; used by the Security module.
ResolveRequestCache	Used by the Output Cache module to short-circuit the processing of requests that have been cached.
AcquireRequestState	Signals that the per-request state should be obtained.
PreRequestHandlerExecute	Signals that the request handler is about to execute. This is the last event you can participate in before the HTTP handler for this request is called.

Table 8-4 shows the events that are raised after an application has returned. The events are listed in the order in which they occur.

Table 8-4: HTTP Module Events (After the Application Has Returned)

Event	Description
PostRequestHandlerExecute	Signals that the HTTP handler has completed processing the request.
ReleaseRequestState	Signals that the request state should be stored because the application is finished with the request.
UpdateRequestCache	Signals that code processing is complete and the file is ready to be added to the ASP.NET cache.
EndRequest	Signals that all processing has finished for the request. This is the last event called when the application ends.

In addition, there are three per-request events that can be raised in a nondeterministic order. They are described in Table 8-5.

Table 8-5: HTTP Module Events (Nondeterministic)

Event	Description
PreSendRequestHeaders	Signals that HTTP headers are about to be sent to the client. This provides an opportunity to add, remove, or modify the headers before they are sent.
PreSendRequestContent	Signals that content is about to be sent to the client. This provides an opportunity to modify the content before it is sent.
Error	Signals an unhandled exception.

After the request has been pushed through the HTTP modules configured for your application, the HTTP handler responsible for the requested file's extension (.ASPX) handles the processing of that file. If you are familiar with ASP.NET development, you'll be familiar with the handler for an ASPX page — System.Web.UI.Page. The HTTP handler then handles the life cycle of the page-level request raising events such as Page_Init, Page_Load, and so on.

DotNetNuke HTTP Modules

As stated earlier, DotNetNuke (like ASP.NET) comes with a number of HTTP modules. These modules enable developers to customize the HTTP Pipeline to provide additional functionality on each request. In this section, you explore several DotNetNuke HTTP modules, and examine their purpose and possibilities for extension.

URL Rewriter

The URL rewriter is an HTTP module that provides a mechanism for mapping virtual resource names to physical resource names at runtime — in other words, it provides a URL that is friendly. The term "friendly" has two aspects. One is to make the URL search-engine friendly, which is solved with the default implementation.

Most search engines ignore URL parameters, and because DotNetNuke relies on URL parameters to navigate to portal pages, the older application is not search-engine friendly. To effectively index your site, you need a parameterless mechanism for constructing URLs that search engines will process.

If you browse to a DotNetNuke site that is version 3.0 or greater, you may notice different URLs from earlier versions. Traditionally, a DotNetNuke URL looks something like the following:

```
http://www.dotnetnuke.com/default.aspx?tabid=622
```

With friendly URLs enabled, the preceding URL might look like this:

```
http://www.dotnetnuke.com/RoadMap/Friendly URLs/tabid/622/default.aspx
```

URL rewriter is invoked during the HTTP Pipeline's processing of a request and can optionally subscribe to application-wide events. The particular event of interest for this module is BeginRequest. This event enables you to modify the URL before the Page HTTP handler is invoked and make it believe the URL requested was that of the old non-friendly format.

The transformation process occurs through the use of regular expressions defined in SiteUrls.config in the root of your DotNetNuke installation. This file contains a number of expressions to LookFor and with corresponding URLs to SendTo. Listing 8-12 shows the default SiteUrls.config.

Listing 8-12: SiteUrls.config

```
<?xml version="1.0" encoding="utf-8" ?>
<RewriterConfig>
<Rules>
    <RewriterRule>
        <LookFor>.*/TabId/(\d+)(.*)/Logoff.aspx</LookFor>
        <SendTo>~/Admin/Security/Logoff.aspx?tabid=$1</SendTo>
    </RewriterRule>
    <RewriterRule>
        <LookFor>.*/TabId/(\d+)(.*)/rss.aspx</LookFor>
        <SendTo>~/rss.aspx?TabId=$1</SendTo>
    </RewriterRule>
    <RewriterRule>
        <LookFor>[^?]*/TabId/(\d+)(.*)</LookFor>
        <SendTo>~/Default.aspx?TabId=$1</SendTo>
    </RewriterRule>
</Rules>
</RewriterConfig>
```

The rules defined in this configuration file cover the default login and logoff page. You could potentially add any number of additional rules, and even hardcode some extra rules in there. For example, if you wanted to hardcode a link such as http://www.dotnetnuke.com/FriendlyUrl.aspx and have it map to another URL elsewhere, your entry might look like Listing 8-13.

Listing 8-13: SiteUrls.config with a Modified Rule

```
<?xml version="1.0" encoding="utf-8" ?>
<RewriterConfig>
<Rules>
    <RewriterRule>
        <LookFor>.*/FriendlyUrl.aspx</LookFor>
        <SendTo>~/default.aspx?tabid=622</SendTo>
    </RewriterRule>
    <RewriterRule>
        <LookFor>.*/TabId/(\d+)(.*)/Logoff.aspx</LookFor>
        <SendTo>~/Admin/Security/Logoff.aspx?tabid=$1</SendTo>
    </RewriterRule>
    <RewriterRule>
        <LookFor>.*/TabId/(\d+)(.*)/rss.aspx</LookFor>
        <SendTo>~/rss.aspx?TabId=$1</SendTo>
    </RewriterRule>
    <RewriterRule>
        <LookFor>[^?]*/TabId/(\d+)(.*)</LookFor>
        <SendTo>~/Default.aspx?TabId=$1</SendTo>
    </RewriterRule>
</Rules>
</RewriterConfig>
```

The preceding URL scheme is an excellent implementation for your own applications as well, particularly those with fixed pages. Unfortunately DotNetNuke has potentially any number of pages, so the team added some functionality that would transform any number of query string parameters.

Take a look at the default scheme for URL rewriting. You can see from the friendly URL shown earlier (`http://www.dotnetnuke.com/RoadMap/Friendly URLs/tabid/622/default.aspx`) that the requirement is met — that is, the URL would have no parameters. URLs generally adhere to the following pattern:

- ❑ `http://www.dotnetnuke.com/`: The site Host URL.
- ❑ `RoadMap/Friendly URLs/`: The breadcrumb path back to the home page.
- ❑ `tabid/622/`: The query string from the original URL transformed (`?tabid=622`).
- ❑ `default.aspx`: The standard web page for DotNetNuke.

The advantage of this scheme is that it requires no database lookups for the transformation, just raw regular expression processing that is typically quite fast.

For some situations, the breadcrumb path may not be desired. In those cases, simply modify the web.config `friendlyUrl` provider setting to turn off the feature. To turn it off, change the `includePageName` value shown in Listing 8-14 from `"true"` to `"false"`:

Listing 8-14: Modifying SiteUrls.config

```
<friendlyUrl defaultProvider="DNNFriendlyUrl">
    <providers>
        <clear />
        <add name="DNNFriendlyUrl"
        type="DotNetNuke.Services.Url.FriendlyUrl.DNNFriendlyUrlProvider,
        DotNetNuke.HttpModules.UrlRewrite" includePageName="true"
        regexMatch="[^a-zA-Z0-9 _-]" />
    </providers>
</friendlyUrl>
```

Earlier in this chapter, it was mentioned that there are two aspects of friendly URLs; so far, only one (search-engine friendly) has been discussed. The second aspect, known as human-friendly URLs, can sometimes impact performance.

A URL that is human friendly is easily remembered or able to be worked out by a human. For example, if you had a login to `dotnetnuke.com` and you wanted to visit your profile page without navigating to it, you might expect the URL to be `http://www.dotnetnuke.com/profile/smcculloch.aspx`.

That URL could easily be remembered, but would require additional processing on the request for two reasons:

- ❑ The URL contains no TabID. That would have to be looked up.
- ❑ The URL contains no UserID. A lookup on `smcculloch` is needed to find the corresponding UserID.

For these reasons, this approach was not chosen. Human-friendly URLs can be implemented by hardcoding the tabid and any other necessary parameters in the rewriter rules. You can see this in action on the Industrial Press web site at www.industrialpress.com/en — the left column contains links like http://www.industrialpress.com/en/AutoCAD/default.aspx. Listing 8-15 shows the rewriter rule for implementing this link.

Listing 8-15: Human Readable URL Example

```
<RewriterRule>
    <LookFor>[^?]*/AutoCad/(.*)</LookFor>
    <SendTo>~/Default.aspx?TabId=108</SendTo>
</RewriterRule>
```

So far, how incoming requests are interpreted has been explained, but how outgoing links are transformed into the friendly URL scheme have not. A number of options have been explored on how to transform the outgoing links, but the best option was to implement a provider-based component that would transform a given link into the chosen scheme. Figure 8-2 shows the URL rewriter architecture.

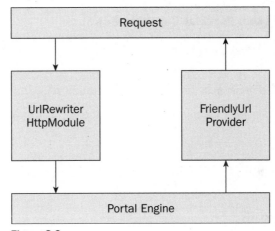

Figure 8-2

Luckily, DotNetNuke already had used two shortcut methods for building links within the application (NavigateUrl and EditUrl). It was relatively simple to place a call to the provider from each of these methods, effectively upgrading the site to the new URL format instantly.

This approach also tightly coupled the HTTP module with the provider, which is why you can find them in the same assembly (DotNetNuke.HttpModules.UrlRewrite.dll).

You can see from the architecture that it is quite plausible for you to write your own URL rewriting scheme. If it was more important for your site to have human-friendly URLs, you could write a scheme by creating a new provider to format outgoing URLs, and a new HTTP module to interpret the incoming requests.

Writing a new provider involves supplying new implementations of the methods in the FriendlyUrlProvider base class. Listing 8-16 shows these methods.

Listing 8-16: Friendly URL Provider Methods

```
Public MustOverride Function FriendlyUrl(ByVal objtab as TabInfo, _
    ByVal path As String) As String
Public MustOverride Function FriendlyUrl(ByVal objtab as TabInfo, _
    ByVal path As String, ByVal pageName As String) As String
Public MustOverride Function FriendlyUrl(ByVal objtab as TabInfo, _
    ByVal path As String, ByVal pageName As String, _
    ByVal settings As PortalSettings) As String
Public MustOverride Function FriendlyUrl(ByVal objtab as TabInfo, _
    ByVal path As String, ByVal pageName As String, ByVal portalAlias As String) _
    As String
```

As you can see, there are only four methods to implement so that you can write your URLs in your desired format. The most important part is to come up with a scheme and to find an efficient, reliable way of interpretation by your HTTP module. After you have written your provider, you can make an additional entry in the providers section of web.config as shown in Listing 8-17. Make sure to set the defaultProvider attribute.

Listing 8-17: Friendly URL Provider Configuration

```
<friendlyUrl defaultProvider="CustomFriendlyUrl">
  <providers>
    <clear />
    <add name="DNNFriendlyUrl"
      type="DotNetNuke.Services.Url.FriendlyUrl.DNNFriendlyUrlProvider,
      DotNetNuke.HttpModules.UrlRewrite" includePageName="true"
      regexMatch="[^a-zA-Z0-9 _-]"/>
    <add name="CustomFriendlyUrl"
        type="CompanyName.FriendlyUrlProvider, CompanyName.FriendlyUrlProvider" />
  </providers>
</friendlyUrl>
```

Exception Management

The exception management HTTP module subscribes to the error event raised by the HttpApplication object. Any time an error occurs within DotNetNuke, the error event is called. During the processing of this event, the last error to have occurred is captured and sent to the exception logging class, which calls the Logging Provider that handles the writing of that exception to a data store (the default is the DB Logging Provider).

Users Online

Users Online was implemented during version 2 of DotNetNuke. It allows other modules to interrogate the applications' data store for information regarding who is online, expressed as registered users and anonymous users. Previously it had been a custom add-on and was session-based. Before the addition of the functionality to the core (like many add-ons incorporated into the core), research was undertaken to investigate the best way to handle not only registered users, but also anonymous users.

The module subscribes to the AuthorizeRequest event. This event is the first chance an HTTP module has to examine details about the user performing the request. The HTTP module examines the request, determines whether the user is anonymous or authenticated, and stores the request in cache. Anonymous users are also given a temporary cookie so they are not counted twice in the future. A scheduled job from the Scheduler executes every minute on a background thread, pulling the relevant details out of cache and updating them in the database. It also clears up any old records. The records are stored within two tables: AnonymousUsers and UsersOnline.

The HTTP module is a good module to disable (comment out of web.config) if you do not need this information within your portal. Alternatively, you can just disable it in Host Settings.

DNNMembership

The DNNMembership HTTP module performs tasks around the security of a user. It stores role information about a user in an HTTP cookie so the same information does not have to be requested again and performs security checks for users switching portals.

There is no real need to extend this module because it is critical to DotNetNuke's operation.

Personalization

The Personalization HTTP module is very similar to the Microsoft-provided Profile HTTP module, and in fact, was based on the same concept, just integrated much earlier. It loads a user's personalized information into a serialized XML object at the beginning of the request, and saves it at the end of the request.

If you are interested in storing personalized information about a user, see the personalization classes (described in Table 8-6) under /Components/Personalization/.

Table 8-6: Personalization Classes

Class	Purpose
Personalization	The primary API for using the personalization system. It encapsulates the few DotNetNuke business rules for using the personalization system.
PersonalizationController	Represents a low-level API that converts personalization database references into business objects.
PersonalizationInfo	The data transfer object that represents the data in a programming friendly object.

Module Interfaces

Modules represent a discrete set of functionality that can extend the portal framework. In past versions of DotNetNuke, module interactions with the portal were primarily limited to making method calls into the core portal APIs. Though this one-way interaction provides some capability to use portal services and methods within the module, it limits the capability of the portal to provide more advanced services.

To provide two-way interactions with modules, the portal needs to have a mechanism to make method calls into the module. There are several distinct mechanisms for allowing a program to call methods on an arbitrary set of code, where the module code is unknown at the time the portal is being developed. Three of these "calling" mechanisms are used within DotNetNuke:

- ❑ Inheritance
- ❑ Delegates
- ❑ Interfaces

As discussed previously, every module inherits from the PortalModuleBase class (located in the components/module directory). This base class provides a common set of methods and properties that can be used by the module as well as the portal to control the behavior of each module instance. Because the module must inherit from this class, the portal has a set of known methods that it can use to control the module. The portal could extend the base class to add methods to handle new services. One downside to this approach is that there is not an easy mechanism for determining whether a subclass implements custom logic for a specific method or property. Because of this restriction, inheritance is generally limited to providing services that are needed or required for every subclass.

A second method for interacting with the modules involves the use of delegates. A delegate is essentially a pointer to a method that has a specific set of parameters and return type. Delegates are useful when a service can be implemented with a single method call and are the underlying mechanism behind VB.NET's event handling. DotNetNuke uses delegates to implement callback methods for the Module Action menu action event. Although delegates are very useful in some situations, they are more difficult to implement and understand than alternative methods.

The third calling mechanism used by DotNetNuke is the use of interfaces. An interface defines a set of methods, events, and properties without providing any implementation details for these elements. Any class that implements an interface is responsible for providing the specific logic for each method, event, and property defined in the interface. Interfaces are especially useful for defining optional services that a module may implement. The portal can detect if a class implements a specific interface and can then call any of the methods, events, or properties defined in the interface.

Starting in version 3.0, DotNetNuke significantly extended its use of module interfaces. Six main interfaces are intended for use by modules:

- ❑ IActionable
- ❑ IPortable
- ❑ IUpgradeable
- ❑ IModuleCommunicator
- ❑ IModuleListener
- ❑ ISearchable

IActionable

Every module has a menu that contains several possible action items for activities like editing module settings, module movement, and viewing help. These menu items are called Module Actions. The module menu can be extended with your own custom actions. When your module inherits from the PortalModuleBase class, it receives a default set of actions, which are defined by the portal to handle common editing functions. Your module can extend these actions by implementing the IActionable interface.

Interface

As shown in Listing 8-18, the IActionable interface consists of a single method that returns a collection of Module Actions. The `ModuleActions` property is used when DotNetNuke renders the module.

Listing 8-18: IActionable Interface Definition

```
Namespace DotNetNuke.Entities.Modules
   Public Interface IActionable
      ReadOnly Property ModuleActions() As Actions.ModuleActionCollection
   End Interface
End Namespace
```

Listing 8-19 shows an example usage as implemented in the Announcements module. The first two lines tell the compiler that this method implements the `ModuleAction` method of the IActionable interface. It is a read-only method, so you only need to provide a `Get` function. The first step is to create a new collection to hold the custom actions. Then you use the collection's `Add` method to create a new action item in the collection. Finally, you return the new collection.

Listing 8-19: IActionable.ModuleActions Example

```
Public ReadOnly Property ModuleActions() As ModuleActionCollection _
   Implements IActionable.ModuleActions
   Get
      Dim Actions As New ModuleActionCollection

      Actions.Add(GetNextActionID, _
               Localization.GetString(ModuleActionType.AddContent, _
                                    LocalResourceFile), _
               ModuleActionType.AddContent, _
               "", _
               "", _
               EditUrl(), _
               False, _
               Security.SecurityAccessLevel.Edit, _
               True, _
               False)

      Return Actions
   End Get
End Property
```

This is a simple example that demonstrates the basic steps to follow for your own custom module menus. DotNetNuke provides extensive control over each Module Action.

ModuleAction API

To take full advantage of the power provided by Module Actions and the IActionable interface, you need to examine the classes, properties, and methods that make up the Module Action API.

Table 8-7 lists the classes that comprise the Module Action API.

Table 8-7: Module Action Classes

Class	Description
ModuleAction	Defines a specific function for a given module. Each module can define one or more actions that the portal will present to the user. Each module container can define the skin object used to render the Module Actions.
ModuleActionType	Defines a set of constants used for distinguishing common action types.
ModuleActionCollection	A collection of Module Actions.
ModuleActionEventListener	Holds callback information when a module registers for Action events.
ActionEventArgs	Passes data during the click event that is fired when a Module Action is selected by the user.
ActionEventHandler	A delegate that defines the method signature required for responding to the Action event.
ActionBase	Creates ModuleAction skin objects. The core framework includes three different implementations: SolPartActions.ascx, DropDownActions.ascx, and LinkActions.ascx.

The ModuleAction class is the heart of the API. Tables 8-8 and 8-9 show the properties and methods available in the ModuleAction class. Each item in the Module Action menu is represented by a single ModuleAction instance.

Table 8-8: ModuleAction Properties

Property	Type	Description
Actions	ModuleActionCollection	Contains the collection of Module Action items that can be used to form hierarchical menu structures. Every skin object that inherits from ActionBase may choose how to render the menu based on the capability to support hierarchical items. For example, the default SolpartActions skin object supports submenus, while the DropDownActions skin object only supports a flat menu structure.
Id	Integer	Every Module Action for a given module instance must contain a unique Id. The PortalModuleBase class defines the GetNextActionId method, which can be used to generate unique Module Action IDs.

Property	Type	Description
CommandName	String	Distinguishes which Module Action triggered an action event. DotNetNuke includes 19 standard ModuleActionTypes that provide access to standard functionality. Custom Module Actions can use their own string to identify commands recognized by the module.
CommandArgument	String	Provides additional information during action event processing. For example, the DotNetNuke core uses CommandArgument to pass the Module ID for common commands like DeleteModule .Action.
Title	String	Sets the text that is displayed in the Module Action menu.
Icon	String	Name of the Icon file to use for the Module Action item.
Url	String	When set, this property allows a menu item to redirect the user to another web page.
ClientScript	String	JavaScript to run during the menuClick event in the browser. If the ClientScript property is present, it is called prior to the postback occurring. If the ClientScript returns false, the postback is canceled.
UseActionEvent	Boolean	Causes the portal to raise an Action Event on the server and notify any registered event listeners. If UseActionEvent is false, the portal handles the event, but does not raise the event back to any event listeners. The following CommandNames prevent the Action Event from firing: ModuleHelp, OnlineHelp, ModuleSettings, DeleteModule, PrintModule, ClearCache, MovePane, MoveTop, MoveUp, MoveDown, and MoveBottom.
Secure	SecurityAccessLevel	Determines the required security level of the user. If the current user does not have the necessary permissions, the Module Action is not displayed.
Visible	Boolean	If set to false, the Module Action will not be displayed. This property enables you to control the visibility of a Module Action based on custom business logic.
NewWindow	Boolean	Forces an action to open the associated URL in a new window. This property is not used if UseActionEvent is true or if the following CommandNames are used: ModuleHelp, Online Help, ModuleSettings, or PrintModule.

Table 8-9: ModuleAction Method

Method	Return Type	Description
HasChildren	Boolean	Returns true if the ModuleAction .Actions property has any items (Actions.Count > 0).

DotNetNuke includes several standard Module Actions that are provided by the PortalModuleBase class or that are used by several of the core modules. These ModuleActionTypes are shown in Listing 8-20. ModuleActionTypes can also be used to access localized strings for the ModuleAction.Title property. This helps promote a consistent user interface for both core and third-party modules.

Listing 8-20: ModuleActionTypes

```
Public Class ModuleActionType
  Public Const AddContent As String = "AddContent.Action"
  Public Const EditContent As String = "EditContent.Action"
  Public Const ContentOptions As String = "ContentOptions.Action"
  Public Const SyndicateModule As String = "SyndicateModule.Action"
  Public Const ImportModule As String = "ImportModule.Action"
  Public Const ExportModule As String = "ExportModule.Action"
  Public Const OnlineHelp As String = "OnlineHelp.Action"
  Public Const ModuleHelp As String = "ModuleHelp.Action"
  Public Const PrintModule As String = "PrintModule.Action"
  Public Const ModuleSettings As String = "ModuleSettings.Action"
  Public Const DeleteModule As String = "DeleteModule.Action"
  Public Const ClearCache As String = "ClearCache.Action"
  Public Const MoveTop As String = "MoveTop.Action"
  Public Const MoveUp As String = "MoveUp.Action"
  Public Const MoveDown As String = "MoveDown.Action"
  Public Const MoveBottom As String = "MoveBottom.Action"
  Public Const MovePane As String = "MovePane.Action"
  Public Const MoveRoot As String = "MoveRoot.Action"
End Class
```

DotNetNuke provides standard behavior for the following ModuleActionTypes: ModuleHelp, OnlineHelp, ModuleSettings, DeleteModule, PrintModule, ClearCache, MovePane, MoveTop, MoveUp, MoveDown, and MoveBottom. All ModuleActionTypes in this subset will ignore the UseActionEvent and NewWindow properties. The ModuleActionTypes can be further subdivided into three groups:

❑ **Basic redirection**: The ModuleActionTypes that perform simple redirection and cause the user to navigate to the URL identified in the URL property: ModuleHelp, OnlineHelp, ModuleSettings, and PrintModule.

❑ **Module movement**: The ModuleActionTypes that change the order or location of modules on the current page: MovePane, MoveTop, MoveUp, MoveDown, and MoveBottom.

❑ **Custom logic**: The ModuleActionTypes with custom business logic that use core portal APIs to perform standard module-related actions: `DeleteModule` and `ClearCache`.

DotNetNuke uses a custom collection class for working with Module Actions. The ModuleActionCollection inherits from .Net System.Collections.CollectionBase class and provides a strongly typed collection class. That minimizes the possibility of typecasting errors that can occur when using generic collection classes such as ArrayList.

Most module developers only need to worry about creating the ModuleActionCollection to implement the IActionable interface. Listing 8-21 shows the two primary methods for adding ModuleActions to the collection. These methods wrap the ModuleAction constructor method calls.

Listing 8-21: Key ModuleActionCollection Methods

```
Public Function Add(ByVal ID As Integer, _
    ByVal Title As String, _
    ByVal CmdName As String, _
    Optional ByVal CmdArg As String = "", _
    Optional ByVal Icon As String = "", _
    Optional ByVal Url As String = "", _
    Optional ByVal UseActionEvent As Boolean = False, _
    Optional ByVal Secure As SecurityAccessLevel = SecurityAccessLevel.Anonymous, _
    Optional ByVal Visible As Boolean = True, _
    Optional ByVal NewWindow As Boolean = False) _
    As ModuleAction

Public Function Add(ByVal ID As Integer, _
    ByVal Title As String, _
    ByVal CmdName As String, _
    ByVal CmdArg As String, _
    ByVal Icon As String, _
    ByVal Url As String, _
    ByVal ClientScript As String, _
    ByVal UseActionEvent As Boolean, _
    ByVal Secure As SecurityAccessLevel, _
    ByVal Visible As Boolean, _
    ByVal NewWindow As Boolean) _
    As ModuleAction
```

The first method in Listing 8-21 uses optional parameters that are not supported by C#. This method is likely to be deprecated in future versions to simplify support for C# modules and its use is not recommended.

The ModuleAction framework makes it easy to handle simple URL redirection from a Module Action. Just like the `Delete` and `ClearCache` actions provided by the DotNetNuke framework, your module may require the use of custom logic to determine the appropriate action to take when the menu item is clicked. To implement custom logic, the module developer must create a response to a menu click event.

In the DotNetNuke architecture, the ModuleAction menu is a child of the module container. The module is also a child of the container. This architecture allows the framework to easily change out the menu implementation; however, it complicates communication between the menu and module. The menu never has a direct reference to the module and the module does not have a direct reference to the menu. This is a classic example of the Mediator design pattern. This pattern is designed to allow two classes without direct references to communicate. Figure 8-3 shows the steps involved to implement this pattern.

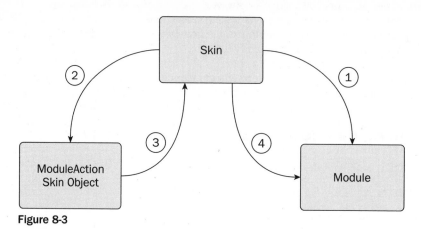

Figure 8-3

The following sections examine those steps and explore ways you can extend the framework.

Step 1: Register the Event Handler

The first step to implementing the Mediator pattern is to provide a mechanism for the module to register with the portal. The portal will use this information later when it needs to notify the module that a menu item was selected. Handling the click event is strictly optional. Your module may choose to use standard MenuActions, in which case you can skip this step. Because the module does not contain a direct reference to the page on which it is instantiated, you need to provide a registration mechanism.

The Skin class, which acts as the mediator, contains the `RegisterModuleActionEvent` method, which allows a module to notify the framework of the event handler for the action event (see Listing 8-22). Registration should occur in the module's `Page_Load` event to ensure that it happens before the event can be fired in the Skin class. The code in Listing 8-22 is from the HTML module and provides a working example of module-based event registration for the `ModuleAction` event. Although you could use another interface to define a known method to handle the event, the registration mechanism turns out to be a much more flexible design when implementing a single method.

Listing 8-22: Registering an Event Handler

```
'----------------------------------------------------------------------------
'-                      Menu Action Handler Registration                    -
'----------------------------------------------------------------------------
'This finds a reference to the containing skin
Dim ParentSkin As UI.Skins.Skin = UI.Skins.Skin.GetParentSkin(Me)

'We should always have a ParentSkin, but need to make sure
If Not ParentSkin Is Nothing Then

    'Register our EventHandler as a listener on the ParentSkin so that it may
```

```
      'tell us when a menu has been clicked.
      ParentSkin.RegisterModuleActionEvent(Me.ModuleId, AddressOf ModuleAction_Click)
   End If
   '-----------------------------------------------------------------------------
```

Listing 8-23 shows the `ModuleAction_Click` event handler code from the HTML module.

Listing 8-23: Handling the Event

```
Public Sub ModuleAction_Click(ByVal sender As Object, _
                              ByVal e As Entities.Modules.Actions.ActionEventArgs)

   'We could get much fancier here by declaring each ModuleAction with a
   'Command and then using a Select Case statement to handle the various
   'commands.
   If e.Action.Url.Length > 0 Then
     Response.Redirect(e.Action.Url, True)
   End If

End Sub
```

The DotNetNuke framework uses a delegate (see Listing 8-24) to define the method signature for the event handler. The `RegisterModuleActionEvent` requires the address of a method with the same signature as the `ActionEventHandler` delegate.

Listing 8-24: ActionEventHandler Delegate

```
Public Delegate Sub ActionEventHandler(ByVal sender As Object, _
                                       ByVal e As ActionEventArgs)
```

Step 2: Display the Menu

Now that the skin (the Mediator class) can communicate with the module, you need a mechanism to allow the menu to communicate with the skin as well. This portion of the communication chain is much easier to code. Handling the actual click event and passing it to the skinning class is the responsibility of the ModuleAction rendering code.

Like much of DotNetNuke, the ModuleAction framework supports the use of custom extensions. In this case, skin objects handle rendering the Module Actions. Each ModuleAction skin object inherits from the DotNetNuke.UI.Containers.ActionBase class. The Skin class retrieves the Module Action collection from the module by calling the `IActionable.ModuleActions` property and passes the collection to the ModuleAction skin object for rendering. The ActionBase class includes the code necessary to merge the standard Module Actions with the collection provided by the Skin class.

Each skin object includes code in the pre-render event to convert the collection of Module Actions into an appropriate format for display using an associated server control. In the case of SolPartActions.ascx, the server control is a menu control that is capable of fully supporting all of the features of ModuleActions including submenus and icons. Other skin objects like the DropDownActions.ascx may only support a subset of the Module Action features (see Table 8-10).

Table 8-10: ModuleAction Skin Objects

Action Skin Object	Menu Separator	Icons	Submenus	Client-Side JavaScript
Actions or SolPartActions	Yes	Yes	Yes	Yes
DropDownActions	Yes	No	No	Yes
LinkActions	No	No	No	No

Step 3: Notify the Portal of a Menu Item Selection

Each skin object handles the click event of the associated server control. This event, shown in Listing 8-25, calls the `ProcessAction` method, which is inherited from the ActionBase class. `ProcessAction` is then responsible for handling the event as indicated by the ModuleAction properties. If you create your own ModuleAction skin object, follow this pattern.

Listing 8-25: Click Event Handler

```
Private Sub ctlActions_MenuClick(ByVal ID As String) Handles ctlActions.MenuClick
   Try
      ProcessAction(ID)
   Catch exc As Exception    'Module failed to load
      ProcessModuleLoadException(Me, exc)
   End Try
End Sub
```

Step 4: Notify the Module That a Custom ModuleAction Was Clicked

If the `UseActionEvent` is set to `True`, the `ProcessAction` method (see Listing 8-26) calls the `OnAction` method to handle actually raising the event (see Listing 8-27). This might seem like an extra method call when `ProcessAction` could just raise the event on its own. The purpose of `OnAction`, though, is to provide an opportunity for subclasses to override the default event handling behavior. Although this is not strictly necessary, it is a standard pattern in .NET and is a good example to follow when developing your own event handling code.

Listing 8-26: ProcessAction Method

```
Public Sub ProcessAction(ByVal ActionID As String)
   If IsNumeric(ActionID) Then
      Dim action As ModuleAction = GetAction(Convert.ToInt32(ActionID))
      Select Case action.CommandName
         Case ModuleActionType.ModuleHelp
            DoAction(action)
         Case ModuleActionType.OnlineHelp
            DoAction(action)
         Case ModuleActionType.ModuleSettings
            DoAction(action)
         Case ModuleActionType.DeleteModule
            Delete(action)
         Case ModuleActionType.PrintModule
```

```
            DoAction(action)
          Case ModuleActionType.ClearCache
            ClearCache(action)
          Case ModuleActionType.MovePane
            MoveToPane(action)
          Case ModuleActionType.MoveTop, _
              ModuleActionType.MoveUp, _
              ModuleActionType.MoveDown, _
              ModuleActionType.MoveBottom
            MoveUpDown(action)
          Case Else
            ' custom action
            If action.Url.Length > 0 And action.UseActionEvent = False Then
              DoAction(action)
            Else
              ModuleConfiguration))
            End If
        End Select
    End If
End Sub
```

Listing 8-27: OnAction Method

```
Protected Overridable Sub OnAction(ByVal e As ActionEventArgs)
    RaiseEvent Action(Me, e)
End Sub
```

Because the skin maintains a reference to the ModuleAction skin object, the Skin class can handle the Action event raised by the skin object. As shown in Listing 8-28, the Skin class iterates through ActionEventListeners to find the associated module event delegate. When a listener is found, the code invokes the event, which notifies the module that the event has occurred.

Listing 8-28: Skin Class Handles the ActionEvent

```
Public Sub ModuleAction_Click(ByVal sender As Object, ByVal e As ActionEventArgs)
    'Search through the listeners
    Dim Listener As ModuleActionEventListener
    For Each Listener In ActionEventListeners

        'If the associated module has registered a listener
        If e.ModuleConfiguration.ModuleID = Listener.ModuleID Then

            'Invoke the listener to handle the ModuleAction_Click event
            Listener.ActionEvent.Invoke(sender, e)
        End If
    Next
End Sub
```

You are now ready to take full advantage of the entire ModuleAction API to create custom menu items for your own modules, handle the associated Action event when the menu item is clicked, and create your own custom ModuleAction skin objects.

IPortable

DotNetNuke provides the capability to import and export modules within the portal. Like many features in DotNetNuke, it is implemented using a combination of core code and module-specific logic. The IPortable interface defines the methods required to implement this feature on a module-by-module basis (see Listing 8-29).

Listing 8-29: IPortable Interface Definition

```
Public Interface IPortable
   Function ExportModule(ByVal ModuleID As Integer) As String

   Sub ImportModule(ByVal ModuleID As Integer, _
                    ByVal Content As String, _
                    ByVal Version As String, _
                    ByVal UserID As Integer)
End Interface
```

This interface provides a much-needed feature to DotNetNuke and is a pretty straightforward interface to implement. To fully support importing and exporting content, implement the interface within your module's business controller class.

As modules are being loaded by the portal for rendering a specific page, they are checked to determine whether they implement the IPortable interface. To simplify checking whether a module implements the interface, a shortcut property has been added to the ModuleInfo class. The ModuleInfo class provides a consolidated view of properties related to a module. When a module is first installed in the portal, a quick check is made to determine if the module implements the IPortable interface, and if so, the IsPortable flag is set on the base ModuleDefinition record. This property allows the portal to perform the interface check without unnecessarily loading the business controller class. Adding the check at the point of installation removes a requirement by previous DotNetNuke versions for a module control to implement unused stub methods. If the control implements the IPortable interface, DotNetNuke automatically adds the Import Content and Export Content menu items to your Module Action menu (see Figure 8-4).

Figure 8-4

Each module should include a controller class that is identified in the BusinessControllerClass property of the portal's ModuleInfo class. This class is identified in the module manifest file discussed later in the book. The controller class is where you implement many of the interfaces available to modules.

Adding the IPortable interface to your module requires implementing logic for the ExportModule and ImportModule methods shown in Listing 8-30 and Listing 8-31, respectively.

Listing 8-30: ExportModule Stub

```
Public Function ExportModule(ByVal ModuleID As Integer) As String _
   Implements Entities.Modules.IPortable.ExportModule

   Dim strXML As String = ""

   Dim objHtmlText As HtmlTextInfo = GetHtmlText(ModuleID)
   If Not objHtmlText Is Nothing Then
      strXML += "<htmltext>"
      strXML += "<desktophtml>{0}</desktophtml>"
      strXML += "<desktopsummary>{1}</desktopsummary>"
      strXML += "</htmltext>"

      String.Format(strXML, _
                    XMLEncode(objHtmlText.DeskTopHTML), _
                    XMLEncode(objHtmlText.DesktopSummary))
   End If

   Return strXML

End Function
```

Listing 8-31: ImportModule Stub

```
Public Sub ImportModule(ByVal ModuleID As Integer, _
                        ByVal Content As String, _
                        ByVal Version As String, _
                        ByVal UserId As Integer) _
   Implements Entities.Modules.IPortable.ImportModule

   Dim xmlHtmlText As XmlNode = GetContent(Content, "htmltext")

   Dim objText As HtmlTextInfo = New HtmlTextInfo

   objText.ModuleId = ModuleID
   objText.DeskTopHTML = xmlHtmlText.SelectSingleNode("desktophtml").InnerText
   objText.DesktopSummary = xmlHtmlText.SelectSingleNode("desktopsummary").InnerText
   objText.CreatedByUser = UserId
   AddHtmlText(objText)

End Sub
```

The complexity of the data model for your module determines the difficulty of implementing these methods. Take a look at a simple case as implemented by the HTMLText module.

In Listing 8-30, the ExportModule method is used to serialize the content of the module to an XML string. DotNetNuke saves the serialized string along with the module's FriendlyName and Version. The XML file is saved into the portal directory.

The ImportModule method in Listing 8-31 reverses the process by deserializing the XML string created by the ExportModule method and replacing the content of the specified module. The portal passes the version information stored during the export process along with the serialized XML string.

The IPortable interface is straightforward to implement and provides much needed functionality to the DotNetNuke framework. It is at the heart of DotNetNuke's templating capability and therefore is definitely an interface that all modules should implement.

IUpgradeable

One of DotNetNuke's greatest features is the capability to easily upgrade from one version to the next. The heart of that is the creation of script files that can be run sequentially to modify the database schema and move any existing data to the new version's schema. In later versions, DotNetNuke added a mechanism for running custom logic during the upgrade process. Unfortunately, this mechanism was not provided for modules. Therefore, third-party modules were forced to create their own mechanism for handling custom upgrade logic.

This was fixed in DotNetNuke 3.0 and updated again in 4.1. The IUpgradeable interface (see Listing 8-32) provides a standard upgrade capability for modules, and uses the same logic as used in the core framework. The interface includes a single method, UpgradeModule, which enables the module to execute custom business logic depending on the current version of the module being installed.

Listing 8-32: IUpgradeable Interface

```
Public Interface IUpgradeable
   Function UpgradeModule(ByVal Version As String) As String
End Interface
```

UpgradeModule is called once for each script version included with the module. It is called only for script versions that are later than the version of the currently installed module.

> Due to the behavior of ASP.NET when a new assembly is added to the \bin directory, the IUpgradeable interface could fail during installation. This behavior has been corrected in the 3.3 and 4.1 releases. If your module needs this interface for proper installation, have your users upgrade to the latest version of DotNetNuke.

Inter-Module Communication

DotNetNuke includes the capability for modules to communicate with each other through the Inter-Module Communication (IMC) framework. The IMC framework enables modules to pass objects rather than simple strings. Additionally, other properties enable a module to identify the Sender, the Target, and the Type of message. Take a look at the two main interfaces that provide this functionality to your module: IModuleCommunicator and IModuleListener.

IModuleCommunicator

The IModuleCommunicator interface defines a single event, ModuleCommunication, for your module to implement (see Listing 8-33).

Listing 8-33: IModuleCommunicator Interface

```
Public Interface IModuleCommunicator
  Event ModuleCommunication As ModuleCommunicationEventHandler
End Interface
```

To communicate with another module, first implement the IModuleCommunicator interface in your module. You should have an event declaration in your module as shown in Listing 8-34.

Listing 8-34: ModuleCommunication Event Implementation

```
Public Event ModuleCommunication(ByVal sender As Object, _
                    ByVal e As ModuleCommunicationEventArgs) _
                    Implements IModuleCommunicator.ModuleCommunication
```

IModuleListener

Whereas the IModuleCommunicator is used for sending messages, the IModuleListener interface (see Listing 8-35) is used for receiving messages.

Listing 8-35: IModuleListener Interface

```
Public Interface IModuleListener
  Sub OnModuleCommunication(ByVal s As Object, _
                    ByVal e As ModuleCommunicationEventArgs)
End Interface
```

This interface defines a single method, OnModuleCommunication, which is called when an IModuleCommunicator on the same page raises the ModuleCommunication event. What you do in response to this event notification is totally up to you.

> *DotNetNuke does not filter event messages. Any module that implements the IModuleListener interface is notified when the event is raised. It is the responsibility of the module to determine whether it should take any action.*

ISearchable

DotNetNuke provides a robust search API for indexing and searching content in your portal. The API is divided into three distinct parts:

❑   Core search engine

❑   Search data store

❑   Search indexer

Like the ModuleAction framework, the search framework also implements a Mediator pattern. When combined with the Provider pattern, this framework provides lots of flexibility. In Figure 8-5, you can see the relationship between these patterns and the three parts of the search API.

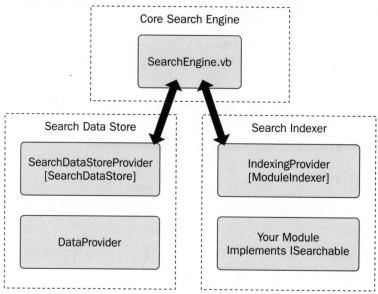

Figure 8-5

The core search engine provides a simple API for calling the IndexProvider and then storing the results using a SearchDataStoreProvider. This API is intended for use by the core framework. Future versions of the API will be extended to allow modules greater control over the indexing process.

DotNetNuke includes a default implementation of the SearchDataStoreProvider, which is meant to provide basic storage functionality, but could be replaced with a more robust search engine. As for other providers, third-party developers are implementing providers for many of the current search engines on the market. You can find links to these providers and more at www.dotnetnuke.com and in the DotNetNuke Marketplace at http://marketplace.dotnetnuke.com.

The IndexingProvider provides an interface between the core search engine and each module. DotNetNuke includes a default provider that indexes module content. This provider can be replaced to provide document indexing, web indexing, or even indexing legacy application content stored in another database. If you decide to replace it, keep in mind that DotNetNuke only allows for the use of a single provider of a given type. This means that if you want to index content from multiple sources, you must implement this as a single provider. Future versions of the framework may be enhanced to overcome this limitation.

When using the ModuleIndexer, you can incorporate a module's content into the search engine data store by implementing the ISearchable interface shown in Listing 8-36.

Listing 8-36: ISearchable Interface

```
Public Interface ISearchable
   Function GetSearchItems(ByVal ModInfo As ModuleInfo) As SearchItemInfoCollection
End Interface
```

This interface is designed to allow almost any content to be indexed. By passing in a reference to the module and returning a collection of SearchItems, the modules are free to map their content to each SearchItem as they see fit. Listing 8-37 shows a sample implementation from the Announcements module included with DotNetNuke.

Listing 8-37: Implementing the Interface

```
Public Function GetSearchItems(ByVal ModInfo As Entities.Modules.ModuleInfo) _
   As Services.Search.SearchItemInfoCollection _
   Implements Services.Search.ISearchable.GetSearchItems
     Dim SearchItemCollection As New SearchItemInfoCollection

     Dim Announcements As ArrayList = GetAnnouncements(ModInfo.ModuleID)

     Dim objAnnouncement As Object
     For Each objAnnouncement In Announcements
       Dim SearchItem As SearchItemInfo
       With CType(objAnnouncement, AnnouncementInfo)

         Dim UserId As Integer
         If IsNumeric(.CreatedByUser) Then
           UserId = Integer.Parse(.CreatedByUser)
         Else
           UserId = 2
         End If
         SearchItem = New SearchItemInfo(ModInfo.ModuleTitle & " - " & .Title, _
                       ApplicationURL(ModInfo.TabID), _
                       .Description, _
                       UserId, _
                       .CreatedDate, _
                       ModInfo.ModuleID, _
                       "Anncmnt" & ModInfo.ModuleID.ToString & "-" & .ItemId, _
                       .Description)
         SearchItemCollection.Add(SearchItem)
       End With
     Next

     Return SearchItemCollection
End Function
```

In this code, you make a call to your module's Info class, just as you would when you bind to a control within your ASCX file, but in this case the results are going to populate the SearchItemInfo, which will populate the DNN index with data from the module.

The key to implementing the interface is figuring out how to map your content to a collection of SearchItem Info objects. Table 8-11 lists the properties of the SearchItemInfo class.

Table 8-11: SearchItemInfo Properties

Property	Description
SearchItemId	An ID assigned by the search engine. It's used when deleting items from the data store.
Title	A string that is used when displaying search results.
Description	Summary of the content and is used when displaying search results.
Author	Content author.
PubDate	Date that allows the search engine to determine the age of the content.
ModuleId	ID of the module whose content is being indexed.
SearchKey	Unique key that can be used to identify each specific search item for this module.
Content	The specific content that will be searched. The default search data store does not search on any words that are not in the content property.
GUID	Another unique identifier that is used when syndicating content in the portal.
ImageFileId	Optional property used to identify image files that accompany a search item.
HitCount	Maintained by the search engine and used to identify the number of times that a search item is returned in a search.

Now that the index is populated with data, users of your portal can search your module's information from a unified interface within DNN.

Summary

This chapter examined many of the core APIs that provide the true power behind DotNetNuke. By leveraging common APIs, you can extend the portal in almost any direction. You can replace core functions or just add a custom module — the core APIs are what make it all possible. Now that you know how to use most of the core functions, the next several chapters examine how to create your own custom modules to really take advantage of this power.

9

Member Role

In December 2004, Microsoft made available its ASP.NET v1.1 Membership Management Component Prototype. This was distributed as an SDK which, when used by a developer in a project, was referenced as an assembly named MemberRole.dll. Microsoft defines it as "a collection of classes and sample scripts that allows a developer to more easily authenticate users, authorize users, and store per-user property data in a user profile." MemberRole.dll was simply a backport of a series of classes, from the then ASP.NET 2.0 Beta 2 framework, compiled under the 1.1 framework. This backported version conforms to the same API as is found in ASP.NET 2.0.

Just before releasing the SDK, Microsoft informed the DotNetNuke Core Team of its intentions with this backport. The Core Team discussed the pros and cons of taking advantage of the backport and, after much debate, decided to implement it at that time, using the backport, rather than waiting eleven months to prepare for a future upgrade of DotNetNuke to the ASP.NET 2.0 framework. When it was time to upgrade to the ASP.NET 2.0 framework with DotNetNuke's 4.0 release, the upgrade task was less complicated because of this decision. The majority of the changes required replacing the DLL reference with a reference to the new classes within the 2.0 framework.

Other factors that weighed in this decision included what MemberRole.dll offered in addition to the easier migration path. In adapting MemberRole.dll, DotNetNuke was also preparing itself for exposure to the hosting market through Microsoft's Shared Hosting Initiative. This initiative not only placed DotNetNuke in front of a new audience, but also helped DotNetNuke form a solid relationship with Microsoft. That relationship allows DotNetNuke to work closely with Microsoft and reap additional benefits, such as the special license for MemberRole.dll usage that extends the length this DLL can remain in production use. For example, the typical MemberRole.dll license was only permitted for production usage for a period of 90 days after the release of the ASP.NET 2.0 framework. The MemberRole.dll included in framework version 1.1 DotNetNuke releases does not contain this restriction.

For developers, it's important to understand that the MemberRole.dll referenced in the DotNetNuke 3.x versions, which use the ASP.NET 1.1 framework, is now part of the ASP.NET 2.0 framework. In DotNetNuke 4.x versions, which use the ASP.NET 2.0 framework, it is referenced from the System .Web.Security namespace.

Before discussing the details of how DotNetNuke uses Member Role, it is first essential that you understand how security works in ASP.NET 2.0.

Security in ASP.NET 2.0

In ASP.NET 1.x, the native authentication and authorization services relied on external data stores or configuration in the web.config file. For example, in ASP.NET 1.1 an application can provide forms-based authentication. This requires the developer to create a login form and associated controls to acquire, validate, and manage user credentials. After authentication, authorization is provided through XML configurations in the web.config file.

In ASP.NET 2.0, several new security enhancements expand on these services in three distinct ways:

❑ **Login and user controls:** A new suite of login and user-management controls reduce the need to rewrite standard user code for each application. You can, for example, create a set of pages for registering a new user, allowing an existing user to log in, and sending a forgotten password to a user simply by placing the appropriate controls on the page and setting a few properties.

❑ **User management:** Each ASP.NET 2.0 application can be accessed through a special set of administrative pages, which enable an authorized user to create new users, assign users to roles, and store user information. If you want to write your own management tools, you can access all of the same features programmatically. Note that the ASP.NET Web Configuration can only be run in a development, non-production environment, meaning the developer has to create his own solution for the production environment.

❑ **Membership/Roles Provider:** The membership feature creates a link between the front-end features (login controls and user-management site) and the persistence mechanism. A Membership provider encapsulates all the data access code that is required to store and retrieve users and roles. Thanks to the Provider Model, this component can easily be replaced with a provider that supports your particular data source.

Together these three components reduce the amount of code that is required to provide authentication and authorization services and persist the data to a data store. In designing these classes, Microsoft understood that it could not account for all possible use cases. Realizing this, Microsoft implemented them by using a Provider Model design pattern — the same one DotNetNuke uses in its own architecture throughout the application, as discussed in Chapter 7.

In the Member Role backported version, only the Membership/Roles Provider described earlier was actually backported to the 1.1 framework. This was not an issue for DotNetNuke because it already had its own login and user controls as well as its own user-management interface. Because the controls existed, all that was left to do was to modify the controls to use the API exposed by the Membership Provider.

The Membership/Roles Provider can actually be divided into the three distinct services outlined in Table 9-1. As a group, they are referred to as Membership Provider Services. Notice that all these default concrete providers use Microsoft SQL Server or SQL Server Express as their data store.

Table 9-1: ASP.NET 2.0 Membership Services Default Providers

Service	Default Concrete Provider Namespace
Membership	System.Web.Security.SqlMembershipProvider
Role Management	System.Web.Security.SqlRoleProvider
Profile	System.Web.Profile.SqlProfileProvider

The Profile service hasn't been mentioned until now because it is not part of the System.Web.Security namespace. Despite this, it was part of the Member Role backported version and was utilized in the DotNetNuke implementation. Keep in mind that it is possible to implement your own concrete providers using a different data store if you so desire.

With the basics of ASP.NET 2.0 security and Membership Provider Service in mind, the following section moves on to how DotNetNuke implements these service providers.

DotNetNuke Membership Overview

Before DotNetNuke began using Member Role, it had its own data schema and services to handle membership. Because of this, when it came time to implement Member Role, there were some challenges ahead.

Portals and Applications

Among the challenges was that DotNetNuke supports running many portals from a single DotNetNuke installation. Each portal has its own users and roles that are not shared with any other portals. A portal is identified by a unique key, the PortalID. Because the default Membership/Roles Provider implementation is a generic solution, it does not natively support the concept of having multiple portals, each with their own users and roles. The default Membership/Roles Provider implementation was designed in a way that only supports a single portal site in a DotNetNuke installation. The Membership/Roles Provider refers to the DotNetNuke installation as an "application," and without customization, that application can only support a single set of users and roles (a single portal instance).

> Microsoft abstracted the Membership/Roles Provider to enable a common source for validating users/roles across multiple applications. The design just didn't anticipate the kind of virtual segmentation within an application that DotNetNuke provides through portals, each with its own users and roles.

To overcome this limitation, a wrapper was needed for the Membership/Roles Providers' SQL data providers. This customization enables DotNetNuke to support application virtualization. The end result is that the Membership/Roles Providers, as implemented in DotNetNuke, can support multiple applications (multiple portal instances in a single DotNetNuke installation). PortalID in DotNetNuke was mapped to the ApplicationName in the Membership/Roles Provider. When a call was made to the Membership/Roles Provider, the ApplicationName was switched on-the-fly to match the PortalID of the portal instance using a concatenation of the object qualifier and the PortalID. Listing 9-1 shows the way this is set.

Listing 9-1: Setting ApplicationName

```
Public Function GetApplicationName(ByVal PortalID As Integer) As String

    Dim appName As String

    'Get the Data Provider Configuration
    Dim _providerConfiguration As ProviderConfiguration = ⤵
ProviderConfiguration.GetProviderConfiguration("data")

    ' Read the configuration specific information for the current Provider
    Dim objProvider As Provider = CType(_providerConfiguration.Providers⤵
(_providerConfiguration.DefaultProvider), Provider)

    'Get the Object Qualifier frm the Provider Configuration
    Dim _objectQualifier As String = objProvider.Attributes("objectQualifier")
    If _objectQualifier <> "" And _objectQualifier.EndsWith("_") = False Then
            _objectQualifier += "_"
    End If

    appName = _objectQualifier + Convert.ToString(PortalID)

    Return appName
End Function
```

Data Model for Users and Roles

To gain the full benefit from the Membership/Roles Provider, it's important to recognize that User and Role information can be externalized from the DotNetNuke and kept in a data store independent of the main data store. For instance, DotNetNuke may use Microsoft SQL Server as its database to store content and system settings, but the Membership/Roles Provider may use Windows authentication, LDAP, or another mechanism to handle authentication and authorization. Because security can be externalized using the Provider Model, it was essential to ensure that the implementation of the Membership/Roles Provider didn't customize any code or database tables used by the provider. The data tables used by the provider had to be independent of the other core DotNetNuke tables. Referential integrity could not be enforced between DotNetNuke data and the Membership/Roles Provider data, nor could cascade deletes or other data-level synchronization methods be used. In a nutshell, all of the magic had to happen in the business logic layer.

One of the challenges faced in implementing the Membership/Roles Provider was dealing with the fields supported by DotNetNuke but not by the provider. Ideally, a solution would have been achieved by completely replacing the DotNetNuke authentication/authorization-related tables with the tables used by the Membership/Roles Provider. This could not be accomplished because the authentication/authorization tables in DotNetNuke were already tied to so many existing and necessary features of the application. For instance, the DotNetNuke Users table has a column named UserID, which holds a unique identifier for each user. The UserID is used in nearly all core and third-party modules as well as the core itself. The most significant problem with UserID was that it didn't exist in the Membership/Roles Provider. Instead, the Membership/Roles Provider uses the username as the unique key for a user within an application. The challenge was that DotNetNuke needed a way to maintain the

UserID to preserve the DotNetNuke functionality that depended on it. This is just one example of an attribute that cannot be handled by the default Membership/Roles Provider provided by Microsoft.

Ultimately, it was decided that DotNetNuke would need to maintain satellite tables to support the DotNetNuke attributes that could not be managed by the Membership/Roles Provider. The goal was to maintain enough information in the DotNetNuke tables so that functionality was not lost, and offload whatever data we can to the Membership/Roles Provider tables. The end result is a data model that mirrors the Membership/Roles Provider tables, as shown in Figure 9-1.

Figure 9-1

Note that none of the tables on top have database relationships to any of the tables on the bottom. The lines connecting them simply show their relationship in theory, not an actual relationship in the database.

Because the data for portals, profiles, users, and roles is stored in multiple unrelated tables, the business layer is responsible for aggregating the data. For instance, you cannot get a complete representation of a user without collecting data from both the aspnet_Users table (from the Membership/Roles Provider) and the Users table (native DotNetNuke table).

Membership, Roles, and Profile Providers

Understanding the limitations DotNetNuke had to conquer and how all three of the providers were affected is important to comprehending why the current solution works the way it does. After the original implementation of Member Role in the first official DotNetNuke 3.x release, the DotNetNuke Core Team found its implementation of Member Role to be less extensible than it could be. To overcome the restrictions that DotNetNuke imposed on itself, the Membership, Roles, and Profile providers have been abstracted out even further. In doing this, a new set of three concrete AspNet Providers was created. They are the revised versions of the original Member Role implementation and can be found in $AppRoot\Library\Providers\MembershipProviders\CoreProvider\DataProviders\AspNetMembershipProvider.

In all abstract/concrete provider implementations, the concrete public methods override the methods exposed by the abstract provider. In the concrete providers, a set of private methods and properties are used to extend and customize the concrete provider along with custom logic in the business layer. In DotNetNuke, additional logic is responsible for combining data from the data store in this layer.

Because Member Role is the current default provider set, the schema shown in Figure 9-1 is still relevant today. When creating this new set of concrete providers, extreme caution was taken to make sure the new implementation would not alter the previous one, therefore minimizing upgrade implications.

As with the previous Member Role implementation, the new AspNet set of providers, which are still technically a Member Role implementation, follows the Provider Model design pattern discussed in Chapter 7. Keep in mind that it is possible to create a custom concrete profile provider of your own and still use the AspNet membership and AspNet roles concrete providers. This is important because it can greatly reduce the amount of effort for your next DotNetNuke project if only one of these concrete providers does not meet your requirements.

A word of caution: Because users and roles are so heavily tied together, if you are creating a custom concrete provider of your own for either of these, you probably need to create a custom concrete provider for the other.

Membership Provider

The function of a membership provider is to interface with a data store that contains data regarding a site's registered users and to provide methods for creating and deleting users, verifying login credentials, changing passwords, and more. Within the ASP.NET 2.0 framework System.Web.Security namespace is a MembershipUser class that defines the basic attributes of a membership user. Table 9-2 shows the methods and properties required by DotNetNuke to implement a custom membership provider. If you compare this table to the Member Role table on Microsoft's site, you'll notice they are very similar.

Table 9-2: DotNetNuke Abstract Provider Membership Methods/Properties

Method/Property	Description
MinPasswordLength	Minimum length each password must be.
MinNonAlphanumericCharacters	Number of non-alphanumeric characters required in a user's password.
PasswordFormat	How the passwords are stored in the data store. The options are Clear, Hashed, or Encrypted.
PasswordStrengthRegularExpression	A regular expression each password is passed through to verify it meets additional criteria.
RequiresQuestionAndAnswer	Determines if users are required to have a question and answer for accessing their password.
ChangePassword	Changes a user's password.
ChangePasswordQuestionAndAnswer	Changes a user's password question and answer.
CreateUser	Creates a single user.
DeleteUser	Deletes a single user.
GetPassword	Returns the password of a user.
GetUser	Returns a single user.
GetUserByUserName	Returns a single user by their username.
GetUserMembership	Returns all the membership-specific information for a single user.
GetUsers	Returns a list of users.
GetUsersByEmail	Returns a list of users by e-mail address.
GetUsersByUserName	Returns a list of users by username.
GetUsersByProfileProperty	Returns a list of users who meet criteria by various profile properties.
ResetPassword	Resets a user's password.
UnLockUser	Unlocks a user account so they can login to the portal.
UpdateUser	Updates a single user.
UserLogin	Authenticates a single user.

All methods listed in the table that return more than a single row of records are set up to use record paging. All the properties listed in Table 9-2 are retrieved from the web.config file. Listing 9-2 shows the set of properties for the default AspNet membership provider. This is contained in the memberrolesprototype section of the web.config file. Although this listing is specific to the default AspNet concrete provider, having a value set for each of these for any concrete membership provider is required by the abstract provider within DotNetNuke.

Listing 9-2: Membership Provider Set in web.config

```
<membership userIsOnlineTimeWindow="15">
  <providers>
    <add name="DNNSQLMembershipProvider" type="DotNetNuke.Security.
    Membership.AspNetSqlMembershipProvider, DotNetNuke.
    Provider.AspNetProvider" connectionStringName="SiteSqlServer"
    enablePasswordRetrieval="true" enablePasswordReset="true"
    requiresQuestionAndAnswer="false" minRequiredPasswordLength="4"
    minRequiredNonalphanumericCharacters="0" requiresUniqueEmail="false"
    passwordFormat="Encrypted" applicationName="/" description="Stores
    and retrieves membership data from the local Microsoft SQL Server
    database" />
  </providers>
</membership>
```

One of the properties in this listing is `passwordFormat`. By default, its value is set to `Encrypted`. The value uses the `machinekey` property, which is also set and stored in the web.config file as shown in Listing 9-3. This node is located within the system.web node in that file.

Listing 9-3: MachineKey Values Set in web.config

```
<add key="MachineValidationKey" value=
   "C505D402B1EC5185E5447F2F5DFD16263715D6D3" />
<add key="MachineDecryptionKey" value=
   " 28F7B5984BAF6B7706B6E63FAB0481B713818EAA0F12E033" />
<add key="MachineValidationMode" value="SHA1" />
```

At installation, the validationKey and the decryptionKey are regenerated and replaced with a custom value unique to your install. Because this is what encrypts your passwords, you must be very careful to safeguard the values assigned during DotNetNuke installation. If these values are altered by someone or the entire file is overwritten, no passwords will match for any of the users who registered while the application used the old key. If none of the passwords match, nobody can log in to your install. This could become an even bigger problem if the values are changed and additional users are registered using the newest keys. You would have the previous registered users having passwords encrypted using the old key and the new users' passwords encrypted using the new key. The key set you decide to use results in one set of your users not being able to log in.

> To avoid possible future catastrophe, it is critical to back up these keys after they are set by the DotNetnuke installation. It's also recommended that you keep a backup copy of the web.config file in a safe place just in case it is accidentally overwritten.

Listing 9-4 shows the `CreateUser` method from the AspNet concrete provider code located in the AspNetMembershipProvider.vb file.

Listing 9-4: CreateUser Method in the Concrete AspNet Membership Provider

```
Public Overrides Function CreateUser(ByRef user As UserInfo) As
UserCreateStatus
```

```
Dim createStatus As UserCreateStatus

Try
    ' check if username exists in database for any portal
    Dim objVerifyUser As UserInfo = GetUserByUserName(Null. ⤸
    NullInteger, user.Membership.Username, False, False)
    If Not objVerifyUser Is Nothing Then
        If objVerifyUser.IsSuperUser Then
            ' the username belongs to an existing super user
            createStatus = UserCreateStatus.UserAlreadyRegistered
        Else
            ' the username exists so we should now verify the password
            If ValidateUser(objVerifyUser.PortalID, user. ⤸
            Membership.Username, user.Membership.Password) Then

                ' check if user exists for the portal specified
                objVerifyUser = GetUserByUserName(user.PortalID, ⤸
                user.Membership.Username, False, False)
                If Not objVerifyUser Is Nothing Then
                    ' the user is already registered for this portal
                    createStatus = ⤸
                    UserCreateStatus.UserAlreadyRegistered
                Else
                    ' the user does not exist in this portal - add them
                    createStatus = UserCreateStatus.AddUser
                End If
            Else
                ' not the same person - prevent registration
                createStatus = UserCreateStatus.UsernameAlreadyExists
            End If
        End If
    Else
        ' the user does not exist
        createStatus = UserRegistrationStatus.AddUser
    End If

    If createStatus = UserRegistrationStatus.AddUser Then
        createStatus = CreateMemberhipUser(user)

        If createStatus = UserCreateStatus.Success Then
            'Create the DNN User Record
            createStatus = CreateDNNUser(user)

            If createStatus = UserCreateStatus.Success Then
                'Persist the Profile to the Data Store
                ProfileController.UpdateUserProfile(user)
            End If
        End If
    End If

Catch exc As Exception       ' an unexpected error occurred
    'LogException(exc)
    createStatus = UserCreateStatus.UnexpectedError
```

(continued)

Listing 9-4: *(continued)*

```
        End Try

        Return createStatus

    End Function
```

The method first calls the `GetUserByUserName` function, necessary in any custom concrete provider, to see if the username is used and return the user object if it is. If no result is returned, the `CreateStatus` variable is set to `AddUser`. If a result is returned, however, a series of steps is required to see how this should be handled:

1. A check is done to see if the username is a SuperUser's:

   ❑ If so, the `CreateStatus` variable is set to `AlreadyRegistered`.

   ❑ If not, the PortalID, username, and password are passed to the private `ValidateUser` function.

2. `ValidateUser` looks to the data store to determine if a matching username/password combination is found for this application and returns the result:

   ❑ If the result of the function is false, the `CreateStatus` variable is set to `UsernameAlreadyExists`.

   ❑ If the result is true, a check is done to see if the user exists for the specific portal by calling the function `GetUserByUserName`.

   ❑ Where no result is returned from `ValidateUser`, the `CreateStatus` variable is set to `AddUser` because the user does not exist for this specific portal. When a result is returned from `ValidateUser`, `CreateStatus` is set to `UserAlreadyRegistered`.

With the `CreateStatus` variable set, the required information is populated and the create user process can proceed. Finally, the `CreateStatus` variable is compared to the available `CreateStatus` options exposed by the `UserCreateStatus` enumerator and the proper action is taken. The `UserCreateStatus` enumerator is defined within the core in the file UserCreateStatus.vb. You can find this file and the others required to construct the abstract provider in $AppRoot\Library\Components\Users\Membership\.

Now you know how the abstract membership provider uses web.config to determine what concrete provider is needed for an install of DotNetNuke to run, and how additional properties needed by the provider to function properly can be retrieved from web.config. This adds flexibility for developers and those who implement DotNetNuke because they can easily change how they want their install to function without requiring them to write a single line of code.

Roles Provider

A Roles Provider interfaces with a data store that contains information mapping users to roles, and provides methods for creating and deleting roles, adding users to roles, and more. The role manager relies on the Roles Provider, given a username, to determine what role or roles the user belongs to. Table 9-3 shows the methods required by DotNetNuke to implement a custom Roles Provider.

Table 9-3: DotNetNuke Abstract Roles Provider Methods

Method	Description
CreateRole	Creates a single role.
DeleteRole	Deletes a single role.
GetRole	Returns a single role. There are two methods: one uses Role-Name and the other uses RoleID.
GetRoleNames	Returns all the role names a single user belongs to.
GetRoles	Returns a list of all roles used in a single portal.
UpdateRole	Updates a single role.
AddUserToRole	Adds a single user to a role.
GetUserRole	Returns a user/role object.
GetUserRoles	Returns a list of roles a single user belongs to. There are two methods: one uses UserID and the other uses RoleName and UserName.
GetUsersByRoleName	Returns a list of users who belong to a role, retrieved using RoleName (as User objects).
GetUserRolesByRoleName	Returns a list of users who belong to a role, retrieved using RoleName (as UserRole objects).
RemoveUserFromRole	Removes a user from a role.
UpdateUserRole	Updates a user/role object.

Listing 9-5 shows the default AspNet Roles Provider property set used in a standard DotNetNuke install. It is contained in the web.config file's memberrolesprototype section. Unlike the Membership Provider, it is not necessary to gather properties from here. You could, however, have properties here for use in your own custom Roles Provider, but doing so would require you to gather the value for these properties from within the Business Logic Layer of your custom provider code.

Listing 9-5: AspNet Roles Provider Set in web.config

```
<roleManager cacheRolesInCookie="true" cookieName=".ASPXROLES"
cookieTimeout="30" cookiePath="/" cookieRequireSSL="false"
cookieSlidingExpiration="true" createPersistentCookie="false"
cookieProtection="All">
  <providers>
    <add name="DNNSQLRoleProvider" type=
    "DotNetNuke.Security.Membership.AspNetSqlRoleProvider,
    DotNetNuke.Provider.AspNetProvider" connectionStringName=
    "SiteSqlServer" applicationName="/" description="Stores and retrieves
    roles data from the local Microsoft SQL Server database" />
  </providers>
</roleManager>
```

Again, as mentioned in the Membership Provider section, if you are creating your own concrete roles provider, you may need to create your own concrete membership provider. Of course, this depends on your implementation. Listing 9-6 shows the `AddUserToRole` method from the AspNet concrete provider code located in the AspNetRoleProvider.vb file.

Listing 9-6: AddUserToRole Method in the Concrete AspNet Roles Provider

```
Public Overrides Function AddUserToRole(ByVal portalId As Integer, ⊃
ByVal user As UserInfo, ByVal userRole As UserRoleInfo) As Boolean
    Dim createStatus As Boolean = True

    'Set Application Name
    SetApplicationName(portalId)

    Try
        'Add UserRole to DNN
        userRole = AddDNNUserRole(userRole)

        'Add UserRole to AspNet
        AspNetSecurity.Roles.AddUserToRole(user.Membership.Username, ⊃
        userRole.RoleName)
    Catch ex As Exception
        'Clear User (duplicate User information)
        userRole = Nothing
        createStatus = False
    End Try

    Return createStatus
End Function
```

In this listing, the method first makes a call to the `SetApplicationName` method, which is located within the same file. This is required by this concrete provider and may not be necessary in your own implementation. Next, another private method is called that adds the user to DotNetNuke's UserRoles table, which is necessary because that's how DotNetNuke relates users and roles to one another throughout the entire application and is required for any custom concrete provider implementation. Finally, the custom logic specific to this concrete provider is called, which adds the user to the provider's data store. This last step may not be necessary in your own custom roles provider if you plan to use your data store only for DotNetNuke and have no plans to extend the Roles Provider further from what is provided by DotNetNuke's abstract provider.

Profile Provider

A profile provider writes profile property values supplied by an ASP.NET application to a persistent profile data store and reads the property values back from the data store when requested by the application. Profile providers also implement methods that enable users and administrators to manage profile data stores using specific parameters. Table 9-4 shows the methods required by DotNetNuke to implement a custom profile provider.

Table 9-4: DotNetNuke Abstract Profile Provider Methods

Method	Description
GetUserProfile	Returns a user's profile.
UpdateUserProfile	Updates a user's profile.

Listing 9-7 sets properties for the default AspNet profile provider. It's contained in the web.config's memberrolesprototype section. The items listed as properties are what will be exposed to each user at time of registration by default.

Listing 9-7: Profile Provider Set in Web.Config

```
<profile enabled="true">
  <providers>
    <add name="AspNetSqlProvider" type=
    "DotNetNuke.Security.Membership.AspNetSqlProfileProvider,
    DotNetNuke.Provider.AspNetProvider" connectionStringName=
    "SiteSqlServer" applicationName="/" description="Stores and retrieves
    profile data from the local Microsoft SQL Server database" />
  </providers>
  <properties>
    <add name="FirstName" type="string" allowAnonymous="true" />
    <add name="LastName" type="string" allowAnonymous="true" />
    <add name="Unit" type="string" allowAnonymous="true" />
    <add name="Street" type="string" allowAnonymous="true" />
    <add name="City" type="string" allowAnonymous="true" />
    <add name="Region" type="string" allowAnonymous="true" />
    <add name="PostalCode" type="string" allowAnonymous="true" />
    <add name="Country" type="string" allowAnonymous="true" />
    <add name="Telephone" type="string" allowAnonymous="true" />
    <add name="Fax" type="string" allowAnonymous="true" />
    <add name="Cell" type="string" allowAnonymous="true" />
    <add name="Website" type="string" allowAnonymous="true" />
    <add name="IM" type="string" allowAnonymous="true" />
    <add name="TimeZone" type="integer" allowAnonymous="true" />
    <add name="PreferredLocale" type="string" allowAnonymous="true" />
  </properties>
</profile>
```

A Profile Provider needs to be more flexible than the other Membership Service Providers. In the Membership Service Providers already discussed, the data items are consistent one way or another. For example, the Membership Provider has a series of consistent methods that are required in your data schema in the majority of any web-facing sites. You will always need a UserName and Password set of columns using a defined data type that works for all cases. In a Roles Provider, you always need a RoleId and RoleName set of columns that are also using a defined data type that works for all its cases. Things aren't as straightforward in the Profile Provider. One install can require a list of 10 properties collected at time of registration, whereas another install may require 20 properties. Because you cannot account for how many properties an install will require, the flexibility needs to be there to allow changes without requiring changes to the actual provider that result in schema changes or changes in the code that would need a recompile.

A Profile Provider also must supply you with the capability to add profile items from other aspects of your application. For example, you may want to add a profile item such as an avatar image for a user in a web site's membership base. If you want the avatar image to persist with the user and be accessible anytime, it needs to be part of the user's profile object regardless of when it is collected from the user. This permits the avatar image in this example to be exposed to all modules used in a DotNetNuke portal and allows the module developers to know ahead of time where to access this image.

If you want to create your own concrete profile provider, you need to add some additional properties that are exposed throughout the DotNetNuke application and can be consumed by items plugged into the framework, such as modules. Table 9-5 shows these properties, each of which has a constant assigned to it in case the concrete provider does not include these properties. (If the property is not used in the concrete provider, the value will be assigned to that of the constant.)

Table 9-5: DotNetNuke Concrete Profile Provider Properties

Property	Description
Cell	User's cell/mobile phone
City	User's city
Country	User's country
Fax	User's Fax number
FirstName	User's first name
FullName	User's first and last names
IM	User's instant messenger name
IsDirty	Determines if a property in the Hash table has changed.
LastName	User's last name
ObjectHydrated	If the object is hydrated or not
PostalCode	User's postal code
PreferredLocale	User's preferred locale
ProfileProperties	Hash table of profile properties of a user
Region	User's region or state
Street	User's street address
Telephone	User's telephone number
Unit	User's address unit
TimeZone	User's time zone
Website	User's web site address

These properties look familiar because most of them are the same ones exposed in the web.config used by the default AspNet Profile Provider. The files containing the logic to construct the abstract profile provider can be found within a single folder at $AppRoot\Library\Components\Users\Profile\.

In the default AspNet concrete provider, a user's profile is stored as what has been referred to as a "blob" of data. This means that instead of having multiple columns, each with a clearly defined data type and column name, the entire set of properties is stored within a single column. This provides the flexibility to add properties to or remove properties from a profile without requiring major changes in the architecture. Listing 9-8 shows how a user's profile is created or updated.

Listing 9-8: UpdateUserProfile Method in the Concrete AspNet Profile Provider

```
Public Overrides Sub UpdateUserProfile(ByVal user As UserInfo)
    Dim objProfile As AspNetProfile.ProfileBase
    Dim objSecurity As New PortalSecurity
    Dim propHash As Hashtable = user.Profile.ProfileProperties

    'Set Application Name
    If user.IsSuperUser Then
        SetApplicationName(Common.Globals.glbSuperUserAppName)
    Else
        SetApplicationName(user.PortalID)
    End If

    objProfile = AspNetProfile.ProfileBase.Create⊃
    (user.Membership.Username, True)

    'Looping through each key in profile hashtable.
    'Each key is profile property name.
    Dim profProperty As ProfileProperty
    For Each key As Object In propHash.Keys
        profProperty = propHash(key)

        'checking if property's datatype is string.
        'if it is string then we do input filter on value.
        If AspNetProfile.ProfileBase.Properties⊃
        (key.ToString()).PropertyType Is GetType(String) Then
            'Checking if value is set or not? if value is set ⊃
             then do input filter
            'otherwise assign Nullstring.
            If Not profProperty Is Nothing Then
                objProfile(key.ToString()) = objSecurity.InputFilter⊃
                (profProperty.PropertyValue.ToString(), ⊃
                PortalSecurity.FilterFlag.NoScripting Or ⊃
                PortalSecurity.FilterFlag.NoMarkup)
            Else
                objProfile(key.ToString()) = Null.NullString
            End If
        Else
            objProfile(key.ToString()) = ⊃
            Null.SetNull(profProperty.PropertyValue, ⊃
```

```
                    AspNetProfile.ProfileBase.Properties(key.ToString()).⊃
                    PropertyType)
            End If
        Next
        objProfile.Save()

    End Sub
```

As with the other concrete provider examples, this method first sets the application name using a private function. However, the next step is different because essentially several rows of data are being passed in so they can be combined into a single row that will ultimately be a single column in the data store. The logic loops through each row of the hash table that was passed in as a parameter and verifies that the data is not nothing. If it is nothing, a default Null string value is assigned. After all of this is complete for each row of the hash table, the object is passed to the save method of the concrete provider. The save method is what actually sends the profile data to the data store.

Summary

This chapter described the Member Role. Simply put, it is a set of classes to be used by an ASP.NET application to handle its sites membership base and communicate with the data store. You looked at some limitations uncovered in the Member Role implementation due to DotNetNuke's multiple portals within the same application and how DotNetNuke overcame these limitations. You learned how DotNetNuke extended its abstract membership, roles, and profile providers so the concrete providers could be more flexible, and saw how a developer could create his own custom concrete providers. Now that you have an understanding of how the membership base is handled, you can move on to the next chapter where you explore some of the latest trends in web site development using DotNetNuke's ClientAPI.

10

Client API

One of the main goals in developing a web site is to provide the best possible experience for the site's users. To achieve that goal, the site developer must do many things, including but not limited to creating a pleasant look and feel for the site, making the site intuitive for the end users, and finally, keeping the time it takes to communicate between the client and server as limited as possible. That last item has been a challenge for web site developers for years.

When a user goes to a web site, the remote web server performs a series of events. It receives the request, processes events required by the web application, and then sends the rendered HTML to the client browser. The events are processed on the server side, and what this means is the server must use valuable resources to parse each page and then send it to the client browser as HTML, which is often seen as a disadvantage. One of the major advantages of using server side is that it is browserindependent, so you don't have to worry about variations between browsers. Everything done by the ASP.NET framework is done on the server side.

When events are rendered on the user's machine instead of on the remote server, they are rendered on the client side. The major advantage of using client side is that each web browser uses its own resources to execute the code found on the web page, thus taking the workload away from the remote web server. The main disadvantages are that a developer cannot use client-side code to access local files, directories, or databases. In addition, various browsers may not be able to support all methods received from the server. Probably the best general example of something being done on the client side is JavaScript.

Over the years, developers have found that a combination of both client-side and server-side scripting is often best to achieve the desired results. One of the disadvantages of this combination is that it requires the developer to understand how to write code for both the server side and the client side. For example, a DotNetNuke developer would be required to understand one of the .NET languages, probably VB.NET, and JavaScript in addition to HTML. This can be difficult for a developer because a solid understanding of all three programming languages in this example would be required to achieve the best possible result.

Postbacks and View State

With the introduction of ASP.NET 1.0, an ASP.NET web page had the option of posting back to itself. How postbacks work is that each time an ASP.NET web page is requested, a series of events that follow an ASP.NET page's life cycle fire off in a well-defined order. Figure 10-1 outlines the life cycle of a typical ASP.NET page.

The great thing about postbacks is that they allow the developer to use view state to maintain data collected from the user on each postback to the same page. Developers can also use this data during the page's postback process as long as they do so when it is accessible, which is defined by the page life cycle. A simple example of this is when a user fills out a feedback form. When he's finished, he clicks the Submit button. The data collected from the user is then sent to the server, which may do validation on the data. If the data does not meet requirements set by the developer, a flag can be set to postback the page with the error message presented to the end user. This, with the combination of view state, allows the page to be re-rendered and the values previously collected from the user can be bound to the controls where the user already entered the data. This makes for a better end-user experience because it keeps the user from having to input all of the data a second time.

> View state is encrypted on the server side before being passed to the client and is then decrypted on the server side as well when needed again.

The downside of postbacks is that each time a postback is required, the entire page life cycle must be iterated through and the page reproduced. This not only increases the workload on the remote web server, but it also increases the time end users must spend for this to be processed and returned to them with the error message. In addition, it increases traffic across the network because after the users are presented the page for a second time and they make their corrections, the page must be processed on the server side a second time, plus each control exposing itself to the view state must pass the collected data to and from the server on each postback. Although this is a simple example that can be completely avoided using one of ASP.NET's built in client-side validation controls, not all situations are quite this simple.

When Microsoft introduced ASP.NET 2.0, one of the embellishments was the capability to postback to other pages and not just the same page. This allows data to be passed from one page to another without sending the data to the data store before moving to the next page, or requiring the developer to use query string parameters containing the values gathered on the first page but needed on the new page. This is accomplished using the view state embedded in a hidden input field named __POSTBACK, which is passed from the first page to the new page. This field is embedded only when there is an IButtonControl on the page and its PostBackUrl property is set to a non-null value. To access the view state of the first page, the developer can use the PreviousPage property on the new page.

A detailed explanation of the page life cycle and view state are far beyond the scope of this chapter. If you require more information on either of these topics, refer to the MSDN web site or Visual Studio's MSDN Library. The basics covered in this section are here to give you a briefing on these items so you can understand other sections of this chapter.

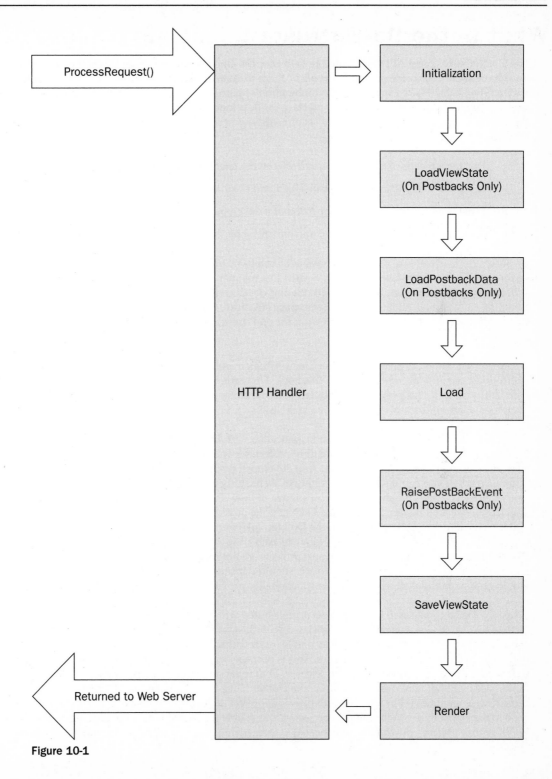

Figure 10-1

What Is the DotNetNuke Client API?

The DotNetNuke Client API was created to help ease the amount of knowledge DotNetNuke developers must have about client-side scripting, yet allow them to take full advantage of all the benefits associated with it. The DotNetNuke Client API is a combination of both server-side and client-side code that work together to enable a simple and reliable interface for developers to provide a rich client-side experience. Prior to development of the Client API, a set of goals was established that the finished project should achieve:

❑ Provide a means of communication between the client-side script and the server code

❑ Allow for the functionality to be disabled and postbacks to be used as a last resort

❑ Provide a uniform cross-browser API that a developer can program against to provide a rich UI

❑ Allow for the API to be extended and enhanced by the Core Team and third-party developers

Because most DotNetNuke developers have at least a basic understanding of one of the ASP.NET languages, the DotNetNuke Client API was written in a manner that the majority of ASP.NET developers should be comfortable working with. Methods and objects within the Client API are accessible using a naming convention similar to .NET's namespace structure. For example, if you wanted to use the Client API to determine what browser version the end user is browsing your site with, you would call `dnn.dom.browser.version`.

Before you get into more details about the Client API, first look at some of the things that make this different from the majority of code covered in this book. For starters, the Client API is part of the DotNetNuke Web Utility project. This project is distributed with the DotNetNuke source versions and is found at $Approot\Library\Controls\DotNetNuke.WebUtility.

One thing quite different than most projects associated with DotNetNuke is that the DotNetNuke project itself depends on the DotNetNuke Web Utility project. Most DotNetNuke development requires your custom project to reference DotNetNuke. As a developer, the most important thing to know about this difference is that you could use the DotNetNuke Web Utility in other ASP.NET projects that are not DotNetNuke-related. This should give you an idea of how abstracted this project is, unlike most DotNetNuke-related projects, because the DotNetNuke project depends on the Web Utility project instead of the Web Utility project depending on the DotNetNuke project. The fact that most DotNetNuke-related projects are not as abstracted as the DotNetNuke Web Utility project should not turn you away from DotNetNuke development. The reason most projects are not this abstracted is because DotNetNuke is a web application framework that other projects should depend on and, at best, removing that dependency would require minimal effort to duplicate functionality provided by DotNetNuke.

While the DotNetNuke Web Utility project is distributed with the core, there is another project — the DotNetNuke Web Controls project — associated with the Client API. This project's source code is not distributed with the DotNetNuke releases available for download from the official web site. It is distributed only in its binary form with those releases. This is because the project is an official DotNetNuke project independently developed from the core releases. That separation allows the project to develop at a more rapid pace by utilizing resources outside of the DotNetNuke Core Team and not having to adhere to the same release timelines set by the DotNetNuke Core project. If you are interested in obtaining the source code to the DotNetNuke Web Controls project, it is available for download on the official DotNetNuke Web Controls project's download page located at www.dotnetnuke.com/Default.aspx?tabid=873.

The DotNetNuke Web Controls project exposes a set of web controls used throughout the DotNetNuke Core project. These controls are also available for use in other DotNetNuke functionality such as modules. The Web Controls project actually references the DotNetNuke Web Utility project. This project is also architected in a manner that enables you to use it in ASP.NET applications outside of DotNetNuke.

Using the DotNetNuke Client API

When using the Client API code in your application, you first want to check your .NET code to see if the client browser supports that functionality. If it does, you need to register the namespace scripts on the client as shown in Listing 10-1.

Listing 10-1: Verifying that a Client Browser Supports DHTML and Registering the Namespace

```
If ClientAPI.BrowserSupportsFunctionality(ClientAPI.⊃
ClientFunctionality.DHTML) Then
    ClientAPI.RegisterClientReference(objPage, ClientAPI. ⊃
ClientNamespaceReferences.dnn)
End If
```

The first line of Listing 10-1, within the If statement, calls this function located within the ClientAPI class and passes it a value for the ClientFunctionality enumerator. This enumerator consists of the various client-side browser checks the class currently supports, shown in Listing 10-2. This enumerator is also located in the ClientAPI class.

Listing 10-2: Client-Side Browser Functionality Tests Supported

```
Public Enum ClientFunctionality As Integer
    DHTML = CInt(2 ^ 0)
    XML = CInt(2 ^ 1)
    XSLT = CInt(2 ^ 2)
    Positioning = CInt(2 ^ 3)    'what we would call adequate positioning support
    XMLJS = CInt(2 ^ 4)
    XMLHTTP = CInt(2 ^ 5)
    XMLHTTPJS = CInt(2 ^ 6)
    SingleCharDelimiters = CInt(2 ^ 7)
End Enum
```

The BrowserSupportsFunctionality function retrieves the client browser's major and minor build values. The value passed into the function is then compared against a list of supported browsers that are grouped by the enumerator names. The file containing this grouped list is named ClientAPICaps.config and it follows the basic XML version 1.0 structure, as shown in Listing 10-3. By default, ClientAPICaps .config is stored in the $Approot\Website\js\ folder. Isolating this file outside of the code was done for a good reason. There is always the possibility that a new browser or new version of an existing browser may be released to the public, and that it will support functionality contained within the current ClientAPICaps.config file. If it's a new type of browser, it won't be listed in the ClientAPICaps.config file. When a new browser or new version of a browser is released, there should be no need to require a recompile of the DotNetNuke or Web Utili projects. The only alternative to a recompile would be for developers and users to wait for the next release of DotNetNuke to add support for client-side functionality, which the framework is already capable of providing. Keeping functionality tests in a separate configuration file that can be edited with a text editor allows changes that can be made by almost anyone instead of waiting for another release or having to edit the code and recompile. This configuration file also offers DotNetNuke developers an easy way to extend and add functionality tests of their own.

Listing 10-3: ClientAPICaps.config File

```xml
<?xml version="1.0" encoding="utf-8" ?>
<capabilities>
    <functionality nm="DHTML" desc="Dynamic HTML">
        <supports>
            <browser nm="IE" minversion="4" />
            <browser nm="Netscape" minversion="5" />
            <browser nm="Gecko" minversion="1" />
            <browser nm="Opera" minversion="7" />
            <browser contains="Konqueror" />
            <browser contains="Safari" />
            <browser contains="FireFox" />
        </supports>
        <excludes>
        </excludes>
    </functionality>
    <functionality nm="XML" desc="Client Side XML Parsing">
        <supports>
            <browser nm="IE" minversion="4" />
            <browser nm="Netscape" minversion="5" />
            <browser nm="Opera" minversion="7" />
            <browser contains="Konqueror" />
            <browser contains="Safari" />
            <browser nm="Gecko" minversion="1" />
            <browser contains="FireFox" />
        </supports>
        <excludes>
            <browser contains="Mac_PowerPC)" />
        </excludes>
    </functionality>
    <functionality nm="XMLJS" desc="Requires JavaScript Client Side XML Parsing">
        <supports>
            <browser contains="Opera" />
            <browser contains="Konqueror" />
            <browser contains="Safari" />
        </supports>
    </functionality>
    <functionality nm="XMLHTTP" desc="Client Side HTTP Requests">
        <supports>
            <browser nm="IE" minversion="4" />
            <browser nm="Netscape" minversion="5" />
            <browser nm="Opera" minversion="7" />
            <browser contains="Konqueror" />
            <browser contains="Safari" />
            <browser nm="Gecko" minversion="1" />
            <browser contains="FireFox" />
        </supports>
```

```
            <excludes>
                <browser contains="Mac_PowerPC)" />
            </excludes>
        </functionality>
        <functionality nm="XMLHTTPJS" desc="Requires JavaScript HTTP Requests">
            <supports>
                <browser contains="Opera" />
                <browser contains="Konqueror" />
                <browser contains="Safari" />
            </supports>
        </functionality>
        <functionality nm="XSLT" desc="Client Side XSLT Processing">
            <supports>
                <browser nm="IE" minversion="4" />
            </supports>
            <excludes>
                <browser nm="Netscape" minversion="6" />
                <browser contains="Konqueror" minversion="5" />
                <browser nm="Opera" minversion="7" />
                <browser contains="Safari" />
                <browser contains="Mac_PowerPC)" />
                <browser nm="Gecko" minversion="1" />
                <browser contains="FireFox" />
            </excludes>
        </functionality>
        <functionality nm="Positioning" desc="Dynamic Positioning of Elements">
            <supports>
                <browser nm="IE" minversion="4" />
                <browser nm="Netscape" minversion="5" />
                <browser nm="Opera" minversion="7" />
                <browser nm="Gecko" minversion="1" />
                <browser contains="Konqueror" />
                <browser contains="Safari" />
                <browser contains="FireFox" />
            </supports>
            <excludes>
            </excludes>
        </functionality>
        <functionality nm="SingleCharDelimiters" desc="Supports single character ⤶
delimiters (i.e. Char(18))">
            <supports>
                <browser nm="*" />
            </supports>
            <excludes>
                <browser contains="Mac_PowerPC)" />
            </excludes>
        </functionality>
    </capabilities>
```

As you can see, each functionality group enables you to clearly define which browsers are supported and excluded for each separate test. In the test shown in Listing 10-1, the functionality being tested for is whether the client browser supports DHTML. Based on the ClientAPICaps.config file, you can see that if the user is browsing a web site using Client API with Internet Explorer version 4 or above, the user's browser is supported, and a value of true is returned.

After a functionality test is done, the next step is to register something on the client's browser. This can be a namespace for use on the client side as shown in Listing 10-1, or a variable or script block. When calling the `RegisterClientReference` function, you have to send it the Page object along with the `ClientNamespaceReferences` enumerator telling the function what namespace you are attempting to register. Each namespace is stored in a separate JavaScript file stored within the same folder as the ClientAPICaps.config file. When the `RegisterClientReference` function runs, it adds the corresponding file to the page so it can be downloaded by the client browser.

Client-Side Script Caching

Any time you are developing a web site, you want to keep the amount of data being passed from the server to the client machine minimal. That keeps the load time low for the web page so the end result improves the end-user experience. To use a large amount of client-side functionality, however, you need a large collection of JavaScript functions on the client machine. The dilemma is determining exactly how to divide up the JavaScript functions so you are only sending what you need when you need it.

There are some other factors to consider when dividing this up. When the JavaScript files are sent to the client browser, they are locally cached by the browser based on the current URL. Each time a page is sent from the server side to the client side, the browser has to send a request to the server for each separate JavaScript file to see if the client-side file's date is the same or older than that of the corresponding file on the server side. If the file on the server side is newer, or the client-side file does not exist yet, the server-side sends the JavaScript file to the client web browser.

Another factor that should be taken into consideration is the payload of the initial page. The more functions in a single JavaScript file, the bigger the file will be. If all client-side code were sent in a single file, that file would be rather large. The larger the file, the longer it takes to send to the client side. You never want the first page hit to your site to take so long that users have no desire to see the rest of your site. Despite the ever-increasing speed, availability, and usage of broadband connections, this is still a factor that merits your attention.

How this is handled in the DotNetNuke Client API, like many other decisions, is a compromise. The JavaScript files are grouped by functional area. These functional area groupings are similar, as is the naming of the entire Client API, to working with namespaces in ASP.NET. The JavaScript files are also structured so that all common functions are broken out into separate files. Those files make use of the functions by referring to the other JavaScript files containing that logical grouping, which is similar to working with ASP.NET namespaces.

To avoid too many requests needed on every page hit to determine if a new JavaScript file should be downloaded, the number of JavaScript files has been limited, and few will be added over time. A subsequent page hit is going to happen much more often than the initial page hit because the end user is more likely to view that page hundreds or even thousands of times again. Weighing all of this, the Core Team determined that it would be more beneficial for the end-user experience to not require a high number of requests for each page hit rather than focusing too much on the initial page hit payload.

Thus far you have touched only on how to get files and data from the server side to the client side and how to deliver them. The next section looks at how to start communicating between the client-side code (now that you know how to check what the client-side browser supports) and the server-side code.

Client and Server Communication

There is no point to doing all these client-side tests if you are not going to do anything based on their results. Earlier, this chapter pointed out that the view state is encrypted prior to going to the client browser. Because it is encrypted, it isn't really helpful to handle things on the client side. To you, as a developer, this means you need to find a way to get items onto the client side that you can use, and then pass those back to the server side where you can also make use of them.

Starting on the Server Side

The "Using the DotNetNuke Client API" section touched on how to register a variable, namespace, or script block. This was primer to show you how to get something over to the client side that you can communicate with. Normally this is done in one of two ways:

❑   Setting the value of a hidden form field on the server side and then reading its value on the client side using the Document Object Model (DOM)

❑   Setting the JavaScript variable directly on the server side by writing out a string the client side can read

With the Client API, you need to use the method `RegisterClientVariable` in your .NET code to register a variable on the server side for use on the client side. You will need to pass this method the Page object, a variable name/value pair, and a Boolean value to determine if the variable should be appended or overwritten. As shown in Listing 10-4, the first thing `RegisterClientVariable` does is create the client variable control. This is an HTML input control that is hidden — the input will always have a name and id of `_dnnVariable`. The method then builds a name/value set so it can then be added as the value for the hidden HTML input control.

Listing 10-4: Registering a Variable on the Client Side

```
Public Shared Sub RegisterClientVariable(ByVal objPage As Page, ByVal strVar ⤸
As String, ByVal strValue As String, ByVal blnOverwrite As Boolean)
    'only add once
    Dim ctlVar As HtmlInputHidden = ClientVariableControl(objPage)
    Dim strPair As String = GetClientVariableNameValuePair(objPage, strVar)
    If strPair.Length > 0 Then
        strPair = strPair.Replace("""", ClientAPI.QUOTE_REPLACEMENT)
'because we are searching for existing string we need it in its posted format
(without quotes)
        If blnOverwrite Then
            ctlVar.Value = ctlVar.Value.Replace(ROW_DELIMITER & strPair, ⤸
ROW_DELIMITER & strVar & COLUMN_DELIMITER & strValue)
        Else
            'appending value
            Dim strOrig As String = GetClientVariable(objPage, strVar)
            ctlVar.Value = ctlVar.Value.Replace(ROW_DELIMITER & strPair, ⤸
ROW_DELIMITER & strVar & COLUMN_DELIMITER & strOrig & strValue)
        End If
    Else
        ctlVar.Value &= ROW_DELIMITER & strVar & COLUMN_DELIMITER & strValue
    End If
```

(continued)

Listing 10-4: *(continued)*

```
    ctlVar.Value = ctlVar.Value.Replace("""", ClientAPI.QUOTE_REPLACEMENT)
'reduce payload of &quot;

    System.Diagnostics.Debug.WriteLine(GetClientVariableNameValuePair(objPage, ↵
strVar))
    System.Diagnostics.Debug.WriteLine(GetClientVariable(objPage, strVar))
        End Sub
```

The method starts to build the name/value set by first calling the GetClientVariableNameValuePair function. This function parses the hidden HTML input control's current value and returns the delimited name/value pair. If there is a matching variable name/value pair returned, based on the passed-in strVar value, it uses the Boolean value passed in to determine if it should append or overwrite the value of the current name/value pair. After all of this is finished, the set of name/value pairs is finally written to the page being sent to the client as the value of the hidden HTML input control.

A good example of registering a variable for client-side use is in the DotNetNuke Tree control. If you look inside the DotNetNuke.WebControls\DNNTree.vb file, you will see the DnnTree_PreRender method. In Listing 10-5, the part of the DnnTree_PreRender method is shown where it calls the RegisterClientVariable method. This steps through the method as explained earlier and builds the name/value set using dnn_controlid_xml as the name part, and XML data will be written out as its value part. The name/value set will be the value for the __dnnVariable. To avoid confusion, please note that the dnn_controlid represents the ClientID variable that is generated by ASP.NET at runtime.

Listing 10-5: Example of RegisterClientVariable in DNNTree

```
DotNetNuke.UI.Utilities.ClientAPI.RegisterClientVariable(Me.Page, Me.ClientID ↵
& "_xml", Me.TreeNodes.ToXml, True)
```

Continuing with the example, the HTML input control named __dnnVariable has a value assigned to it. Although not outlined previously, this example registers the proper JavaScript files to be sent to the client before assigning any values to the input control. Listing 10-6 includes the RegisterClientScript method, which determines the files to send to the client side. Pay attention to the part toward the bottom where it calls RegisterStartUpScript. This is part of the System.Web.UI namespace that allows ASP.NET server controls to add client-side script blocks to the page. Looking into this further, you can see the script block being passed in calls the dnn.controls.initTree client-side function. It also adds the parameter of the control id before sending the script block.

Listing 10-6: Registering a Startup Script

```
Public Sub RegisterClientScript()
    If IsDownLevel = False Then
        DotNetNuke.UI.Utilities.ClientAPI.RegisterClientReference(Me.Page, ↵
DotNetNuke.UI.Utilities.ClientAPI.ClientNamespaceReferences.dnn_dom)
        DotNetNuke.UI.Utilities.ClientAPI.RegisterClientReference(Me.Page, ↵
DotNetNuke.UI.Utilities.ClientAPI.ClientNamespaceReferences.dnn_xml)
        If Me.PopulateNodesFromClient Then DotNetNuke.UI.Utilities.ClientAPI. ↵
BrowserSupportsFunctionality(Utilities.ClientAPI.ClientFunctionality.XMLHTTP) ↵
Then DotNetNuke.UI.Utilities.ClientAPI.RegisterClientReference(Me.Page, ↵
DotNetNuke.UI.Utilities.ClientAPI.ClientNamespaceReferences.dnn_xmlhttp)
        End If
        If Not ClientAPI.IsClientScriptBlockRegistered(Me.Page, ↵
```

```
"dnn.controls.dnntree.js") Then ClientAPI.RegisterClientScriptBlock(Me.Page, ⤸
"dnn.controls.dnntree.js", "<script src="""" & TreeScriptPath & ⤸
"dnn.controls.dnntree.js""></script>")
        End If
        ClientAPI.RegisterStartUpScript(Page, Me.ClientID & "_startup", ⤸
"<script>dnn.controls.initTree(dnn.dom.getById('" & Me.ClientID & "')); ⤸
</script>")  'wrong place
    End If
End Sub
```

On the Client Side

All of the code discussed so far has been rendered on the server side. If you are an ASP.NET developer, everything should have seemed fairly familiar to you because it was all .NET code. Now you are about to enter client-side territory, which may be completely new to you. Because the DotNetNuke Client API took the namespace approach with its client-side script, it should help level the learning curve for those .NET developers who are working with client-side script for the first time.

In the "Starting on the Server Side" section, the DotNetNuke Tree control was used as an example. Before any values were set, the proper client-side namespaces were registered. Registering the client-side namespace sends the necessary JavaScript files and script blocks to the client. This is an important step because after the page is sent to the client, the dnn.controls.initTree function (see Listing 10-7) is called by the client side. dnn.controls.initTree creates a new instance of the DNNTree on the client side by creating a new XML document on the client side. The XML document retrieves its data from the controlid_xml variable created on the server side by calling the dnn.getVar client-side function. This getVar function basically does the opposite of RegisterClientVariable and selects the matching variable on the client side, and then populates the newly created XML document with data.

Listing 10-7: Beginning of the dnn.controls.dnntree.js File

```
dnn_control.prototype.initTree = function (oCtl)
{
    //oCtl.innerHTML = '';//temp
    dnn.controls.controls[oCtl.id] = new dnn.controls.DNNTree(oCtl);
    dnn.controls.controls[oCtl.id].generateTreeHTML();
    return dnn.controls.controls[oCtl.id];
}

//------- Constructor -------//
dnn_control.prototype.DNNTree = function (o)
{
    this.ns = o.id;                  //stores namespace for tree
    this.container = o;                    //stores container

    //--- Data Properties ---//
    //this.xml = dnn.getVar(o.id + '_xml');
    this.DOM = new dnn.xml.createDocument();
    this.DOM.loadXml(dnn.getVar(o.id + '_xml'));

    //--- Appearance Properties ---//
    this.css = __dt_getAttr(o, 'css', '');
    this.cssChild = __dt_getAttr(o, 'csschild', '');
```

(continued)

Listing 10-7: *(continued)*

```
        this.cssHover = __dt_getAttr(o, 'csshover', '');
        this.cssSel = __dt_getAttr(o, 'csssel', '');
        this.cssIcon = __dt_getAttr(o, 'cssicon', '');

        this.sysImgPath = __dt_getAttr(o, 'sysimgpath', '');
        this.imageList = __dt_getAttr(o, 'imagelist', '').split(',');
        this.expandImg = __dt_getAttr(o, 'expimg', '');
        this.workImg = __dt_getAttr(o, 'workimg', 'dnnanim.gif');
        this.collapseImg = __dt_getAttr(o, 'colimg', '');

        this.indentWidth = new Number(__dt_getAttr(o, 'indentw', '10'));
        if (this.indentWidth == 0)
            this.indentWidth = 10;
        this.checkBoxes = __dt_getAttr(o, 'checkboxes', '0') == '1';
        this.target = __dt_getAttr(o, 'target', '');
        this.defaultJS = __dt_getAttr(o, 'js', '');

        this.postBack = __dt_getAttr(o, 'postback', '');
        this.callBack = __dt_getAttr(o, 'callback', '');
        this.callBackStatFunc = __dt_getAttr(o, 'callbackSF', '');
        //if (this.callBackStatFunc != null)
        //    this.callBackStatFunc = eval(this.callBackStatFunc);

        //obtain width of expand image
        this.expImgWidth = new Number(__dt_getAttr(o, 'expcolimgw', '12'));

        this.hoverTreeNode = null;
        this.selTreeNode=null;
        this.rootNode = null;
        if (this.container.tabIndex <= 0)
        {
            this.container.tabIndex = 0;
            dnn.dom.addSafeHandler(this.container, 'onkeydown', this, 'keydownHandler');
            dnn.dom.addSafeHandler(this.container, 'onfocus', this, 'focusHandler');
        }
        else
        {
            var oTxt = document.createElement('input');
            oTxt.type = 'text';
            oTxt.style.width = 0;
            oTxt.style.height = 0;
            oTxt.style.background = 'transparent';
            oTxt.style.border = 0;
            oTxt.style.positioning = 'absolute';
            this.container.parentNode.appendChild(oTxt);
            dnn.dom.addSafeHandler(oTxt, 'onkeydown', this, 'keydownHandler');
            dnn.dom.addSafeHandler(oTxt, 'onfocus', this, 'focusHandler');
        }
    }
}
```

After the page is fully loaded and everything has been rendered on the client side, there is the possibility that a user may interact — selecting, expanding, collapsing, and so on — with the items enabled on the client side, like the DotNetNuke Tree. The entire time the user is interacting with the DotNetNuke Tree, the variable used in the example is being manipulated with each change on the client side. Assuming postbacks and callbacks are not enabled for these changes, the variable keeps getting altered until some type of state change is made. An example would be expanding a tree view until the end user sees the node he wants to select. The user then selects the node and clicks the Submit button, sending the manipulated code is sent back to the server side for processing.

Returning to the Server Side

So far, the variables have been created on the server side and sent to the client side. When they were on the client side, these variable values were manipulated based on the actions performed by the end user. After the manipulation, the variables are sent back to the server side for processing after some type of event is thrown or a callback is done. (The details of callbacks are discussed later in this chapter.) No matter how the variable was returned, it needs to be processed on the server side. Listing 10-8 shows the function called to retrieve the value of a client-side variable. This function retrieves the value of the variable and returns it so you can do something with the result.

Listing 10-8: Retrieving the Value of a Client-Side Variable

```
Public Shared Function GetClientVariable(ByVal objPage As Page, ByVal strVar ⟂
As String) As String
    Dim strPair As String = GetClientVariableNameValuePair(objPage, strVar)
    If strPair.IndexOf(COLUMN_DELIMITER) > -1 Then
        Return Split(strPair, COLUMN_DELIMITER)(1)
    Else
        Return ""
    End If
End Function
```

In the DotNetNuke Tree example, the client side manipulated the __dnnVariable item stored in the HTML input area that was hidden. The submit button click handler is processed and in there, assuming only single selection was permitted, you want to see what tree node the user selected. Similar to the earlier discussion regarding registering the client-side variable using the RegisterClientVariable function, the DotNetNuke Tree control handles the GetClientVariable function for you. It processes the variable, enabling you as a developer to focus on its results in your preferred ASP.NET programming language. At this point, you would write custom logic to handle the changes made on the client side with the DotNetNuke Tree and possibly send those changes to the data store.

That completes the round trip. What happens next depends on what you want your application to do. By now you should start to see that the Client API handles most of the work for you. This type of functionality has been used on the Internet for several years now but never has it been this easy to use in DotNetNuke, especially for those not familiar with client-side programming. Although not necessary in this example because it made use of the DotNetNuke Tree control, a solid understanding of the areas discussed is necessary if you want to create a custom control of your own that handles changes on the client side.

Client API's Callback

As you've seen, one of the best reasons for learning and making use of the Client API is to improve the end-user experience. Minimizing postbacks to the server was identified earlier as one of the goals that would help you achieve an improved end-user experience. Thus far this has been accomplished by sending client-side variables to the client that can be manipulated and returned to the server-side code, in a format it can read, when a postback occurs. This helps minimize postbacks because the client side handles the client-side events — such as expanding — raised in the DotNetNuke Tree example. The control changes, the changes are saved to a variable, and then the variable is processed when the client side finally communicates with the server side.

The question you are probably asking yourself now is, "What if I want to communicate with the server-side code more often without causing a postback?" Unless you are just beginning web development, you have probably heard some hype lately about Ajax and Atlas. Although the buzz about them is relatively new, the concept behind them has been around since the late '90s. Most of the reason for the hype now is probably because communication between the server-side and client-side code without requiring a postback — which Ajax and Atlas offer — is becoming easier to do and therefore more web sites are making use of it. However, to answer the question asked at the beginning of this paragraph, the answer is asynchronous callbacks. These callbacks enable communication between the client side and server side without the need for a postback.

Life Cycle of a Client Callback

When you're working with the Client API and Client Callback, it is just as important to understand the callback life cycle as it is to understand the page life cycle when dealing with view state. The remainder of this section is broken down into the steps within the Client Callback life cycle and describes what happens at each phase. Figure 10-2 illustrates the main areas of interest in the Client Callback lifecycle.

Setup and Registration

To get started using callbacks, the first thing you must do is implement IClientAPICallbackEventHandler in the page or your control. In the earlier example of the DotNetNuke Tree control, this was handled for you. After implementing the handler, you have to obtain JavaScript to invoke a callback. This is done by making a call to the `GetCallbackEventReference` method. The parameters required when calling the method are described in Table 10-1.

Table 10-1: GetCallBackEventReference Parameters

Argument	Description
ObjControl	The control that is responsible for handling the callback. It must implement IClientAPICallBackEventHandler.
StrArgument	The string is evaluated on the client side and is passed to the server-side callback handler.
strClientCallback	The pointer to the client-side function that is to be invoked when a callback is successful and complete.
strContext	The string is evaluated on the client side and passed to the client-side callback methods.
strErrorClientCallback	The pointer to the client-side function that is invoked when a callback errors out.

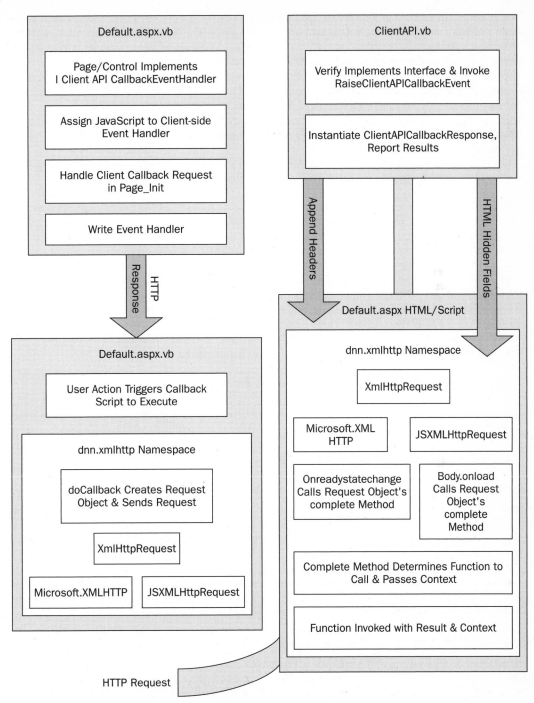

Figure 10-2

The result of this method will be JavaScript that needs to be assigned to the client-side event handler. After you have completed this, you would normally have to write logic to handle potential callbacks. This must be done early on in the page's life cycle, such as in the `Page_Init`, so that no response is written back other than the result of the callback. You handle potential callbacks by calling the `HandleClientAPICallbackEvent` method and passing it the Page object, as shown in Listing 10-9. When working on a DotNetNuke project making use of callbacks, it is not necessary to write this logic because it is already handled by the code in default.aspx.vb.

Listing 10-9: Handling Potential Callbacks in Page_Init

```
' ClientCallback Logic
DotNetNuke.UI.Utilities.ClientAPI.HandleClientAPICallbackEvent(Me)
```

It is assumed that prior to completing this phase in the callback life cycle, the proper namespaces and variables discussed in the "Using the DotNetNuke Client API" section have been registered. For callbacks, specifically, it requires the registering of the dnn.xmlhttp client-side namespace. Note that if you are making a call to the `GetCallbackEventReference` method, the registering of the dnn.xmlhttp client-side namespace will be handled for you. Now, after registering the client-side namespace and setting up the server side for handling any potential callbacks, you need to implement the IClientAPICallbackEventHandler interface. When implementing an interface in your page or control, you must also implement the methods contained within it. The IClientAPICallbackEventHandler interface contains only a single method, `RaiseClientAPICallbackEvent`. This function needs to be passed the `eventArgument` variable, which is some data returned from the client side, as a string. An example of implementing the `RaiseClientAPICallb kEvent` method is shown in Listing 10-10.

Listing 10-10: RaiseClientAPICallbackEvent Function

```
Public Function RaiseClientAPICallbackEvent(ByVal eventArgument As String) ⤶
As String Implements DotNetNuke.UI.Utilities.IClientAPICallbackEventHandler. ⤶
RaiseClientAPICallbackEvent
Return "Hello World! " & eventArgument
End Function
```

Essentially, this function is on the server side waiting for the client side to make a callback. When a callback is made, the function grabs the variable passed to it and returns a string as its result. What is done with the result after it's returned to the client side is up to the developer. In most situations, you will present users with some type of notification that their callback is complete and show them any necessary changes or errors that were a result of it.

If your only goal is to implement client callbacks, you need go no further. Everything required to get going has been covered. The remaining steps in the life cycle are handled via the Client API and should be reviewed for a better understanding of what is actually done by the Client API.

Client-Side Handling of the Callback

In the client-side handling of the callback, all variables are on the client side along with the necessary script files. One of the client-side namespaces that was required to be registered is the dnn.xmlhttp namespace. That's because the script contains the client-side function necessary to create a callback to the server side from the client side. The client-side code function, named `doCallBack`, is shown in Listing 10-11.

Listing 10-11: dnn.xmlhttp.doCallBack Client-Side Function

```
dnn_xmlhttp.prototype.doCallBack = function(sControlId, sArg, pSuccessFunc, ⊃
sContext, pFailureFunc, pStatusFunc, bAsync)
{
   var oReq = dnn.xmlhttp.createRequestObject();
   var sURL = document.location.href;
   oReq.successFunc = pSuccessFunc;
   oReq.failureFunc = pFailureFunc;
   oReq.statusFunc = pStatusFunc;
   oReq.context = sContext;
   if (bAsync == null)
      bAsync = true;

   if (sURL.indexOf('.aspx') == -1)    //fix this for url's that dont have page name
in them...  quickfix for now...
      sURL += 'default.aspx';

   if (sURL.indexOf('?') == -1)
      sURL += '?';
   else
      sURL += '&';

   //sURL += '__DNNCAPISCI=' + sControlId + '&__DNNCAPISCP=' + ⊃
encodeURIComponent(sArg);

   oReq.open('POST', sURL, bAsync);
   //oReq.send();

   if (encodeURIComponent)
      sArg = encodeURIComponent(sArg);
   else
      sArg = escape(sArg);
   oReq.send('__DNNCAPISCI=' + sControlId + '&__DNNCAPISCP=' + sArg);
}
```

As demonstrated in Listing 10-11, the first thing this client-side function does is create a new XmlhttpRequestObject by calling the `createRequestObject` function , which is located in the same client-side namespace. `createRequestObject` is responsible for determining the callback method supported by the user's browser. After XmlhttpRequestObject is created, this method assigns the pointers to the client-side function for success and the client-side function for failure. These function names, along with other important parameters passed in to the `doCallBack` client-side function, are described in Table 10-2.

> *If the current browser type does not support the XmlHttp request, it will use the JsHttp request that is referred to as the IFRAME request. Most browsers support XmlHttp requests, but this is worth mentioning.*

Table 10-2: Important doCallBack Parameters

Argument	Description
sControlId	The control that is responsible for handling the callback. It must implement IClientAPICallBackEventHandler.
pSuccessFunc	Stores a pointer to the function to be invoked upon a successful request.
pFailureFunc	Stores a pointer to the function to be invoked upon a failed request.
sContext	Stores the context of the request to be passed along to the success/failure function.

When the XmlHttp request object is created, the return URL for the request is set, the XmlHttp request object is opened, and communication with the server side begins using the XmlHttp request object's send function. At the end of this phase in the callback life cycle, focus is switched to the server side again.

Page_Init Handling of Callback Requests

Earlier in this chapter, you reviewed the life cycle of the page and were able to see how view state was involved at the various phases of the life cycle. This not only helps you understand the behavior of post-backs, but it also aids in clarifying things at this point in the callback life cycle.

The main reasons for handling callbacks in the Page_Init is that it is not possible to handle this any sooner in the life cycle of the page. Prior to this phase in the page life cycle, the controls on the page are not loaded yet. If the controls are not loaded yet, the page will not be able to use the FindControl method on them because prior to this phase there are no controls. On the other hand, you should not attempt to handle this later in the page life cycle than Page_Init because there is a chance some unwanted response text may be generated. As Listing 10-9 showed, the Startup and Registration phase of the callback life cycle is handled for you by DotNetNuke in its default.aspx.vb code.

Handle the Client API Callback Event

Part of handling the callback request is passing the request to the server-side callback event. The HandleClientAPICallbackEvent method, located within the ClientAPI.vb file, is now invoked and is responsible for creating a new ClientAPICallbackResponse object. With the new ClientAPICallbackResponse object created, the first order of business is to determine if certain criteria are met. The criteria are that the control must exist and be located on the server side, and the IClientAPICallbackEventHandler interface must be implemented. If those are met, the RaiseClientAPICallbackEvent method is called and a response and status code must be assigned.

ClientAPICallbackResponse ultimately reports back this status code and response from the server to the client side. The available status codes to return back to the client side are shown in Listing 10-12. Also handled in the ClientAPICallbackResponse, but not discussed, is how the response will be sent. This is either in the XmlHttp or JsHttp format, which is determined based on how the data was received from the client.

Listing 10-12: Callback Response Status Code Enumerator

```
Public Enum CallBackResponseStatusCode
OK = 200
        GenericFailure = 400
        ControlNotFound = 404
        InterfaceNotSupported = 501
End Enum
```

If the format is XmlHttp, which it normally is, the response appends the header of the page. If not, a `Response.Write` is added to the page.

Callback Response Handling

It is recommended, but not required, that callbacks be handled asynchronously. If they are not handled asynchronously, though, the browser won't be usable while it is checking for a callback. When that happens, it may appear to the end user that the browser is locked, which leads to confusion and lessens the end-user experience.

When a response is returned to the client side, it needs to be received by an event handler. This requires an event handler to be registered on the client side when the page is loaded. The responsibility of this client-side event handler is to determine if the callback was successful or if it failed. Listing 10-13 demonstrates how this is handled on the client side.

Listing 10-13: XmlHttpRequest's Client-Side Complete Function

```
dnn_xmlhttp.prototype.XmlHttpRequest.prototype.complete = function (sRes)
{
    var sStatusCode = this.getResponseHeader('__DNNCAPISCSI');
    this.completed=true;

    if (sStatusCode == '200')
       this.successFunc(sRes, this.context);
    else
    {
       var sStatusDesc = this.getResponseHeader('__DNNCAPISCSDI');
       if (this.failureFunc != null)
          this.failureFunc(sStatusCode + ' - ' + sStatusDesc, this.context);
       else
          alert(sStatusCode + ' - ' + sStatusDesc);
    }
}
```

Inside the complete method, the status code and status description are obtained by calling the `getResponseHeader` method. This method reads the response that was written on the server side to the header of the current page. If the JsXmlHttpRequest object was being used instead of the XmlHttpRequest object, its complete method would read the textbox's value from the IFRAME document that matches the header name.

Using either of the request object types works the same after reading the value from the server side. If the function is successful, it is passed to the success function that was assigned during the registration phase of the life cycle. If the function was anything other than successful, the client-side failure method — if one exists — is invoked.

The life cycle of a callback is now complete. You probably noticed that the majority of this is handled for you when using DotNetNuke. If you only want to use the current set of DotNetNuke Client API-enabled controls, which is discussed next, only a minimal understanding of this life cycle is required. However, if you want to extend the Client API or make web controls of your own, you'll need a solid understanding of the life cycle to efficiently achieve a proper end result.

Client API–Enabled DotNetNuke Controls

With DotNetNuke's focus on reusability and making the developer's experience as pleasant as possible, a series of Client API-enabled controls is included with the Core releases. In addition to the Tree control, which has been used in previous examples, all of the controls described in Table 10-3 are part of the DotNetNuke.WebControls project. These controls reside under the DotNetNuke.UI.WebControls namespace and are used in various areas of the Core framework. To make module development less of a task and also offer some nice client-side functionality, try to make use of these controls when appropriate.

Table 10-3: Client API–Enabled Controls

Control Name	Example Usage	Description
DNNLabelEdit	Module title of a container	Allows a label to be edited on the client side with no postback done. Uses callback to update the value in the data store.
DNNMenu	Core skins using solpart navigation	Allows a menu to be dynamically populated from the data store and built on the client side.
DNNTextSuggest	N/A	Allows a user to start typing in the textbox and results are immediately populated. Uses callback.
DNNTree	Core file manager	Enables you to display hierarchical data in a tree view format.

Each of these controls also has its own JavaScript file, located in the js folder, which is named dnn .controls.*controlname*.js where *controlname* corresponds to the specific control's name. When using these controls in your own development, they will register the namespaces, variables, and the script blocks that they need. This makes it easier for developers to use these controls with less code. It is possible to use the controls and not be required to prepare anything for the client side — simply using one of these controls in your module will handle all of it for you.

Of course, if you would like to get fancy, you could use callbacks as explained in the previous section. Keep in mind that all of this functionality is relatively new. As time goes on, you will see more examples in modules and throughout the core itself.

If you are looking for some examples to get started with but are not at the point of getting hands-on just yet, visit the webcontrols.dotnetnuke.com site. It is a live example of these controls being used in a simple ASP.NET application and not running within DotNetNuke. It enables you to view how rich the collections of controls are without requiring you to download source and install it locally. This site also displays a live version of the latest developer documentation generated at compile time. If you would like to download the example ASP.NET application utilizing these controls outside of the DotNetNuke environment, please visit the official DotNetNuke project's download page. You can also download any of the latest DotNetNuke source code discussed in this chapter as well as the project's unit tests.

In addition to these controls, there are two series of methods used often in the core that were not covered. The first is the EnableMaxMin series of methods that enable you to show and hide a module's content all from the client side. The capability to use callbacks, if supported, is part of this series as well. The other series is the module drag-and-drop functionality exposed to site or page administrators. This is what enables you to move a module from one content pane to another and save the change to the database using callback.

Writing Custom Web Controls Using the Client API

One of the original goals outlined when the Client API was created was to allow for the API to be extended and enhanced by developers within and outside of the Core Team. It is strongly recommended that anyone attempting to create their own custom web control utilizing the Client API have a solid understanding of both the Client API and ASP.NET Web Controls. Notice that this section is about creating custom web controls, not custom DotNetNuke controls. That's because more likely than not, a custom web control developed using the Client API will be reusable outside of DotNetNuke as long as the DotNetNuke Web Utility and, in projects making use of the pre-built web controls, the DotNetNuke Web Controls projects or binaries are available as well.

The following is a brief outline of steps that should help you start creating your own custom web controls that take advantage of the Client API:

1. Create a new Web Control Library in Visual Studio.
2. Add a reference to DotNetNuke.WebUtility.dll and, if you're using the pre-built web controls, DotNetNuke.WebControls.dll.
3. Create a class and set its inheritance:
   - ❑ Completely new web controls inherit from the .NET Framework's WebControl class.
   - ❑ Extending an existing control inherits from the control you are extending.
4. Define properties.
5. Create your events and event handlers in the class:
   - ❑ Use PreRender to register client-side scripts and postback handler.
   - ❑ Handle postback using RaisePostBackEvent.
   - ❑ Handle callbacks using RaiseClientAPICallbackEvent.
6. Create the web control's script:
   - ❑ Initialize the control using a constructor.
   - ❑ Declare and create methods.
   - ❑ Create event handlers.
   - ❑ Add mandatory script to handle random script order.

In addition, outline what you need to make your own design and functionality decisions, weighing the factors and determining what is best for your control. For example, an abundance of callbacks in a control ruins the end-user experience because each round trip between the client and server consumes valuable resources and Internet bandwidth. When creating a control that makes use of callbacks, you must decide what an appropriate interval is that still maintains the efficiency you want.

An important note about the JavaScript files is that ASP.NET 1.x cannot guarantee the order in which the client-side scripts are sent to the client. This can cause problems when a client-side method relies on another script that should already be present because the parent namespaces should have already been loaded by the browser. Because of this, there is a mandatory script block added to each JavaScript file included in the Client API. When DotNetNuke no longer supports framework 1.x, this script block will no longer be necessary and can be handled using the ClientScriptManager class readily available in the ASP.NET 2.0 framework. Until then, the mandatory script block addition is required in all custom scripts to ensure the proper loading order and the expected behavior from both versions of the ASP.NET framework.

Summary

This chapter introduced you to some of the common problems developers face when trying to produce a web site that offers the best possible experience for end users by utilizing a combination of server-side and client-side code. To offer this capability in a consistent manner, DotNetNuke provides the Client API for developers to limit the learning curve required for this type of functionality. When you're working with the Client API, however, there are a few major points to keep in mind:

- ❑ The Client API provides a means of communication between the client-side script and the server code yet allows the functionality to be disabled and postbacks to be used as a last resort.

- ❑ ClientAPICaps.config is a configuration file that allows browser functionality tests to be added and or extended without the need for a recompile.

- ❑ Client-side callbacks have a lifecycle of their own, which is important to understand with regard to the lifecycle of an ASP.NET page.

- ❑ DotNetNuke offers its own ASP.NET pre-built web controls that make use of the Client API, thus providing client-side functionality for use in custom modules.

- ❑ Developers with a minimal understanding of ASP.NET web control development can create custom web controls of their own that make use of the Client API.

The next chapter introduces you to localization. Localization is currently used in combination with the Client API to send localizable content via a JavaScript dialog box to the end user.

11

Localization

The World Wide Web is an international network that must accommodate users from hundreds of cultures, speaking many different languages. This poses a significant challenge for every web application that is targeted at a worldwide audience. To address this challenge, DotNetNuke provides a built-in localization framework that addresses many of the issues required to make DotNetNuke useable by a global audience. This framework is built to take advantage of the ASP.NET localization features while tackling some of its shortcomings.

This chapter examines DotNetNuke's core localization API, which can be used from within your own code to allow your modules to be usable by the widest audience. The declarative programming framework is also discussed. It simplifies the localization task for module developers, thereby removing a major barrier to acceptance and usage by module developers.

Overview

The localization API in DotNetNuke provides developers with an interface for performing multilingual translations in custom portal modules. As of this writing, DotNetNuke includes only static localization features. In other words, only text labels and other static strings are localized by the core.

Dynamic content localization is a feature that is closely related to content versioning. In traditional versioning systems, content changes along a single axis represented by time. By extending your view of versioning to include a second axis based on culture, you can overcome many of the challenges of dynamic content localization. This approach to dynamic localization will be addressed in a future DotNetNuke release.

Locales

A *locale* is the combination of a country code and a language code. For the sake of accurate translations, it is important to use both a country code and a language code to perform localization. Many languages are spoken in more than one country, and dialects may differ from country to country. For instance, French spoken in Canada is different from French spoken in France. A locale accounts for this differentiation. DotNetNuke supports four types of locales:

❑ **System locale:** The locale (en-US) that DotNetNuke is natively coded. It cannot be changed.

❑ **Default portal locale:** The portal's default locale, which is specified in the Site Settings screen (see Chapter 5). This locale will be automatically selected for any users who have not yet defined their default locale.

❑ **User-selected locale:** The locale that a user selects from the Registration or User Account page.

❑ **Custom locale:** A custom locale allows for customized translations to be defined for each portal. The localization framework manages this by appending the PortalID onto the locale. For instance, if Portal 2 has configured custom German translations, the custom locale for de-DE for Portal 2 is de-DE.Portal-2.

Resource Files

To align closely to the ASP.NET 2.0 localization implementation, DotNetNuke uses the Windows Resource Files (RESX) format to store translations. This file format uses XML tags to store key/value pairs of string values. Developers often use the Template.resx file in the root App_Resources directory as a starting place to create their resource files.

Here's an example of the Data Provider form field on the Host Settings page that shows the format of a resource file's data elements:

```
. . .
      <data name="plDataProvider.Text">
            <value>Data Provider:</value>
      </data>
      <data name="plDataProvider.Help">
            <value>The provider name which is identified as the default data
provider in the web.config file</value>
      </data>
. . .
```

Each name attribute is referred to as a resource key. Notice that the two resource keys in this example have extensions. DotNetNuke uses a number of extensions that help identify translations more easily:

❑ .Text: Used for the text properties of controls (default if not included in resource key).

❑ .Help: Used for help text.

❑ .Header: Used for the HeaderText properties of DataGrid columns.

❑ .EditText: Used for the EditText properties of DataGrids.

❑ .ErrorMessage: Used for the ErrorMessage property of Validator controls.

There are three types of static translations in DotNetNuke: Application Resources, Local Resources, and Global Resources. These static translations are defined in the following sections.

Application Resources

Application Resources translations are shared throughout many controls in DotNetNuke. Application Resources files are the storage area for generic translations. For example, to localize the words "True" and "False," you would store the translations in the Application Resources files. Other examples of Application Resources are Yes, No, Submit, and Continue.

Application Resources are stored in the App_GlobalResources directory, which is directly under the DotNetNuke root installation directory. The filename for the system locale (en-US) for Application Resources is SharedResources.resx. The file naming convention for other locales is SharedResources.[locale].resx. For example, the German Application Resource file would be named `SharedResources.de-DE.resx`.

Local Resources

Local Resources translations are unique to a user control. For example, to localize the Announcements module's user control, you would store the translations in a Local Resources file that lives in a child directory beneath the Announcements module's directory.

> If the Announcements module has static translations that are generic in nature (such as True and False), the translations should be gathered from Application Resources.

Local Resources files are stored in a directory named App_LocalResources. Each directory that contains localized user controls must have a directory named App_LocalResources. The filename for the System Locale follows this naming convention:

```
[control_directory]/App_LocalResources/[user_control_file_name].resx.
```

For example, for the en-US locale, the resource file for the Announcements module would be as follows:

```
Announcements/App_LocalResources/Announcements.ascx.resx.
```

The filename for other locales follows this naming convention:

```
[control_directory]/App_LocalResources/[control_files_name].[locale].resx.
```

Global Resources

Global Resources translations are for localizing strings from components that do not have Local Resource files, are not necessarily shared translations, and don't fit in the first two categories. Because all Local Resources are associated with a user control or a page, there is no place to store translations for components. For this reason, there's now this third category for resource files. An example of Global Resources usage is in the component admin/Containers/ActionBase.vb, which needs to localize the word Help in the module action lists.

Global Resources are stored in the same directory as Application Resources (/App_Resources). The filename for the system default locale is /App_Resources/GlobalResources.resx. For locales other than the system default, the naming convention is as follows:

```
/App_Resources/GlobalResources.[locale].resx
```

The API

The DotNetNuke.Services.Localization.Localization class provides the methods necessary for localizing strings. These methods are described in Table 11-1.

Table 11-1: Localization Methods

Method	Description
AddLocale	Used to add a locale to the list of supported locales in the App_GlobalResources/Locales.xml file.
GetResourceFile	Returns the path and filename of the resource file for a specified control.
GetString	Returns the localized string based on the resource key specified.
GetSupportedLocales	Returns the list locales from the App_GlobalResources/Locales .xml file.
GetSystemMessage	Localizes a string and replaces system tokens with personalized strings.
GetTimeZones	Returns a key/value pair collection of time zones.
LoadCultureDropDownList	Fills a DropDownList control with the supported cultures.
LoadTimeZoneDropDownList	Fills a DropDownList control with the list of time zones.
LocalizeDataGrid	Localizes the headers in a DataGrid control.
LocalizeRole	Localizes the three system roles.

The GetString Method

Of the methods in Table 11-1, the most widely used is GetString. It performs localization based on the resource key passed into it. GetString has five overloaded methods, detailed here:

❑ To localize a string value that has a translation in an Application Resource file, use the following method:

```
Public Shared Function GetString(ByVal name As String) As String
```

The resource file to be used will be selected based on the currently active locale. This automatically uses the active PortalSettings object to derive the portal's default locale.

Parameter	Type	Description
name	String	The string to be localized.

❑ The following is identical to the previous method, except you can send in a PortalSettings object to derive the portal's default locale:

```
Public Shared Function GetString(ByVal name As String, ByVal objPortalSettings _
As PortalSettings) As String
```

Parameter	Type	Description
name	String	The string to be translated.
objPortalSettings	PortalSettings	The PortalSettings object for the current context. It determines the default locale used for anonymous users.

❑ To localize a string value that has a translation in a Local Resource file, use the following method:

```
Public Shared Function GetString(ByVal name As String, ByVal ResourceFileRoot _
As String) As String
```

The following method accepts an incoming parameter (ResourceFileRoot) from which the resource file to use is derived. It automatically uses the active PortalSettings object to derive the portal's default locale.

Parameter	Type	Description
name	String	This is the string to be translated.
ResourceFileRoot	String	This is the value of a module's LocalResourceFile property. It is used to derive the resource file to be used for the translation.

❑ The following method enables you to specify the key name to translate, and both the resource file and portal settings to use for the translation:

```
Public Shared Function GetString(ByVal name As String, ByVal ResourceFileRoot _
As String, ByVal strLanguage As String) As String
```

Parameter	Type	Description
name	String	The string to be translated.
ResourceFileRoot	String	The value of a module's LocalResourceFile property. It is used to derive the resource file to be used for the translation.
strLanguage	String	The name of the language used to look up the string.

❑ The following method enables you to specify the key name to translate, and both the resource file and portal settings to use for the translation:

```
Public Shared Function GetString(ByVal name As String, ByVal ResourceFileRoot _
As String, ByVal objPortalSettings As PortalSettings, ByVal strLanguage _
As String) As String
```

Parameter	Type	Description
name	String	The string to be translated.
ResourceFileRoot	String	The value of a module's LocalResourceFile property. It is used to derive the resource file to be used for the translation.
objPortalSettings	PortalSettings	The PortalSettings object for the current context. If the localized string does not exist for the given language, then the default locale specified in objPortalSettings is used.
strLanguage	String	The name of the language used to look up the string.

The GetSystemMessage Method

The GetSystemMessage method is used throughout the core code to produce localized and personalized strings. For example, it is used frequently to send e-mail to registered users. The user registration page calls GetSystemMessage to localize the content of the e-mail that gets sent to the user. The e-mail contains personalized content, too, so rather than concatenating several dozen strings using the GetString method and wrapping them around personalized data, GetSystemMessage takes care of all of this with just one call.

GetSystemMessage has eight overloaded methods, described here:

❑ Use the following method if you need to localize and personalize a string when the personalization can be derived from the objPortal property. The translation must be stored in the Application Resources file.

```
Public Shared Function GetSystemMessage(ByVal objPortal As PortalSettings, _
ByVal MessageName As String) As String
```

Parameter	Type	Description
objPortal	PortalSettings	The PortalSettings object for the current context. It is used to derive any personalized content within the localized system message string.
MessageName	String	The resource key used to get the localized system message from the resource file. Because no user information is included in this overload, "User:" MessageName types are not supported.

❑ Use the following method if you need to localize and personalize a string when the personalization can be derived from either the objPortal or objUser properties. The translation must be stored in the Application Resource file.

```
Public Shared Function GetSystemMessage(ByVal objPortal As PortalSettings, _
ByVal MessageName As String, ByVal objUser As UserInfo) As String
```

Parameter	Type	Description
objPortal	PortalSettings	The PortalSettings object for the current context. It is used to derive any personalized content within the localized system message string.
MessageName	String	The resource key used to get the localized system message from the resource file.
objUser	UserInfo	The UserInfo object to derive any personalized content within the localized system message string.

❏ Use the following method if you need to localize and personalize a string when the personalization can be derived from the objPortal or objUser object's properties. You must specify the language to use for the translation, and the translation must be stored in the Application Resource file.

```
Public Shared Function GetSystemMessage(ByVal strLanguage As String , _
ByVal objPortal As PortalSettings, ByVal MessageName As String, _
ByVal objUser As UserInfo) As String
```

Parameter	Type	Description
strLanguage	String	The name of the language used to look up the string.
objPortal	PortalSettings	The PortalSettings object for the current context. It is used to derive any personalized content within the localized system message string.
MessageName	String	The resource key used to get the localized system message from the resource file.
objUser	UserInfo	The UserInfo object to derive any personalized content within the localized system message string.

❏ Use the following method if you need to localize and personalize a string when the personalization can be derived from the objPortal property values. You must specify the resource file to use for the translation.

```
Public Shared Function GetSystemMessage(ByVal objPortal As PortalSettings, _
ByVal MessageName As String, ByVal ResourceFile As String) As String
```

Parameter	Type	Description
objPortal	PortalSettings	The PortalSettings object for the current context. It is used to derive any personalized content within the localized system message string.
MessageName	String	The resource key used to get the localized system message from the resource file.
ResourceFile	String	The resource file that the localized system message is stored in.

331

❑ Use the following method if you need to localize and personalize a string when the personalization can be derived from either the objPortal or objUser properties. You must specify the resource file from which to retrieve the translation.

```
Public Shared Function GetSystemMessage(ByVal objPortal As PortalSettings, _
ByVal MessageName As String, ByVal objUser As UserInfo, ByVal ResourceFile _
As String) As String
```

Parameter	Type	Description
objPortal	PortalSettings	This is the PortalSettings object for the current context. It is used to derive any personalized content within the localized system message string.
MessageName	String	This is the resource key used to get the localized system message from the resource file.
objUser	UserInfo	This is the UserInfo object to derive any personalized content within the localized system message string.
ResourceFile	String	This is the resource file that the localized system message is stored in. It is usually the value of the module's LocalResourceFile property.

❑ Use the following method if you need to localize and personalize a string when the personalization can be derived from the objPortal object's properties and the Custom ArrayList collection items. You must specify the resource file to use for the translation.

```
Public Shared Function GetSystemMessage(ByVal objPortal As PortalSettings, _
ByVal MessageName As String, ByVal ResourceFile As String, ByVal Custom As _
ArrayList) As String
```

Parameter	Type	Description
objPortal	PortalSettings	The PortalSettings object for the current context. It is used to derive any personalized content within the localized system message string.
MessageName	String	The resource key used to get the localized system message from the resource file.
ResourceFile	String	The resource file that the localized system message is stored in.
Custom	ArrayList	A collection of strings that can be used for personalizing the system message.

❑ Use the following method if you need to localize and personalize a string when the personalization can be derived from objPortal, the objUser properties, and the Custom ArrayList collection items. You must specify the resource file from which to retrieve the translation.

```
Public Shared Function GetSystemMessage(ByVal objPortal As PortalSettings, _
ByVal MessageName As String, ByVal objUser As UserInfo, ByVal ResourceFile As _
String, ByVal Custom As ArrayList) As String
```

Parameter	Type	Description
objPortal	PortalSettings	The PortalSettings object for the current context. It is used to derive any personalized content within the localized system message string.
MessageName	String	The resource key used to get the localized system message from the resource file.
objUser	UserInfo	The UserInfo object to derive any personalized content within the localized system message string.
ResourceFile	String	The resource file that the localized system message is stored in. It is usually the value of the module's LocalResourceFile property.
Custom	ArrayList	A collection of strings that can be used for personalizing the system message.

❑   Use the following method if you need to localize and personalize a string when the personalization can be derived from the objPortal object's properties and the Custom ArrayList collection items. Also, you must specify the resource file and the language to use for the translation.

```
Public Shared Function GetSystemMessage(ByVal strLanguage As String, _
ByVal objPortal As PortalSettings, ByVal MessageName As String, _
ByVal objUser As UserInfo, ByVal ResourceFile As String, _
ByVal Custom As ArrayList) As String
```

Parameter	Type	Description
strLanguage	String	The name of the language used to look up the string.
objPortal	PortalSettings	The PortalSettings object for the current context. It is used to derive any personalized content within the localized system message string.
MessageName	String	The resource key used to get the localized system message from the resource file.
objUser	UserInfo	The UserInfo object to derive any personalized content within the localized system message string.
ResourceFile	String	The resource file that the localized system message is stored in. It is usually the value of the module's LocalResourceFile property.
Custom	ArrayList	A collection of strings that can be used for personalizing the system message.

When you use GetSystemMessage, you can specify several *system tokens* in the localized string. The tokens are used as keys to render property values from either the UserInfo or PortalSettings objects. Here's an example:

```
DotNetNuke.Services.Localization.Localization.GetSystemMessage(PortalSettings, _
"EMAIL_USER_REGISTRATION_PRIVATE_BODY", objNewUser, Me.LocalResourceFile)
```

This code calls the `GetSystemMessage` method to localize and personalize the body of an e-mail message that is sent to a newly registered user. The code is found in the Admin/Security/Register.ascx portal module. The `MessageName` parameter value is `EMAIL_USER_REGISTRATION_PRIVATE_BODY`. It is the resource key to look up the system message in the resource file. The resource key and associated translation from the resource file /Admin/Security/App_LocalResources/Register.ascx.resx is shown in Listing 11-1.

Listing 11-1: System Message Resource Example

```
<data name="EMAIL_USER_REGISTRATION_PRIVATE_BODY.Text">
    <value>
        Dear [User:FullName],

Thank you for registering at the [Portal:PortalName] portal website. Please read
the following information carefully and be sure to save this message in a safe
location for future reference.

Portal Website Address: [Portal:URL]
Username: [Membership:UserName]
Password: [Membership:Password]

Your account details will be reviewed by the portal Administrator and you will
receive a notification upon account activation.

Thank you, we appreciate your support...

[Portal:PortalName]

    </value>
 </data>
```

`GetSystemMessage` first localizes the string within the `<value>` XML node. Then it iterates through the system tokens (enclosed in brackets), replacing the tokens with the appropriate property values. For example, in Listing 11-1 you can see the token `[User:FullName]`. This will be replaced with the `FullName` property value of the User object. In this case, the User object is the objUser object passed into the `GetSystemMessage` method. Listing 11-2 shows that the system message has been personalized and localized with the en-US locale.

Listing 11-2: System Message Rendered Example

```
Dear John Doe,

Thank you for registering at the DotNetNuke portal website. Please read the
following information carefully and be sure to save this message in a safe location
for future reference.

Portal Website Address: http://test.dotnetnuke.com
```

```
Username: jdoe1234
Password: pwdjdoe1234

Your account details will be reviewed by the portal Administrator and you will
receive a notification upon account activation.

Thank you, we appreciate your support...

DotNetNuke
```

Localizing Modules

The current versions of DotNetNuke support localizing any static text within a module. Although full content localization is not yet supported, it is still important to localize your module so that the module can be used for non-English-speaking sites. Imagine the frustration of your users if all the content for their site is written in Spanish, yet all of the static text in your module is written in English.

Though the localization API is very powerful, it would add a lot of work for module developers if it was the only mechanism for localization. To simplify the job for developers, DotNetNuke includes a localization framework that applies localization using declarative markup in the ASCX or ASPX files. This approach provides a couple of benefits:

❏   It simplifies the programming model because the developer adds a single attribute/value pair to the server control markup, and the framework handles calling the appropriate localization APIs.

❏   It allows localization to be applied or changed without recompiling the application.

So look at what it takes to declaratively provide localization for your module.

After all static strings have been identified, you must determine the best approach for localizing each individual string. Each string should be categorized into one of four cases depending on how the string is used within a module:

❏   Text placed directly into the HTML in the ASCX files.

❏   Text declaratively set in a server control in the ASCX files.

❏   Text modified or set in the source code for the module.

❏   Text embedded in images.

The following sections show you how to use the localization framework and localization API to correct each of these potential problem areas.

Case 1: Handling Static Strings in the ASCX File

The key to resolving the problem of text placed directly into the HTML in the ASCX files is to understand that localization is handled programmatically. Whether it is your code or framework code, you need to have the string in a format that is easily accessed programmatically. This means that you must make sure that the code-behind file — and thus the DotNetNuke framework — is aware of the string's existence. This is actually quite easy to fix — just wrap the string in an HTML control. Essentially, this step transforms the problem into Case 2 and enables you to use a common approach for all strings in the ascx file. Table 11-2 shows an example of applying this step to a simple string located in a table cell.

Table 11-2: Wrapping a String with a Web Control

Before	After

```<TD class="SubHead">```
  ```Title:```
```</TD>```
	```<TD class="SubHead">```
	  ```<asp:Label id="lblTitle" runat="server">```
	    ```Title:```
	    ```</asp:Label>```
	  ```</TD>```

At this point, your strings are ready to be localized.

Case 2: Handling Static Text in Server Controls

After all of your static strings are encapsulated in server controls, it is easy to tell the localization framework how to localize your strings. To localize a control, add a `resourcekey` attribute with a value that tells the framework which string resource to use for this control. Table 11-3 takes the previous example and makes this additional change.

Table 11-3: Adding a resourcekey

Before	After

```<TD class="SubHead">```
  ```<asp:Label id="lblTitle"```
```runat="server"```
    ```Title:```
  ```</asp:Label>```
```</TD>```
	```<TD class="SubHead">```
	  ```<asp:Label id="lblTitle"```
	```runat="server">```
	    ```resourcekey="TestLabel">```
	    ```Title:```
	  ```</asp:Label>```
	  ```</TD>```

Now the framework has all the information it needs to find your string resources and localize this content.

As mentioned earlier in the chapter, your module should include the App_LocalResources directory with a resource file named after the user control that is being localized. When you first localize a module, it's best to leave the resource file empty. That will let you know if you have missed localizing strings. Figure 11-1 shows the sample, the `Title:` string, before it has been localized.

Figure 11-1

To verify that you have applied the localization settings correctly, ensure that the web.config file's AppSettings section includes the following line:

```
<add key="ShowMissingKeys" value="true" />
```

If you have applied the `resourcekey` and set `ShowMissingKeys` correctly, you should see the image in Figure 11-2, the localized string with a missing value.

Figure 11-2

Notice that the text shows you that it is looking for `TestLabel.Text`. This makes it easy to see where you have localized a control, and where you still need to create the localized version of the string. If you were to create the `TestLabel.Text` resource string with a `Localized Title;` value in your resource file, you'd get the localized content shown in Figure 11-3.

Figure 11-3

When you localize content, keep in mind that different cultures may use different punctuation. In this example, the colon (:) from the original string was changed to a semicolon (;) when it was localized.

A Label control shows how easy it can be to localize a web control. But each control is different and contains different attributes that might need to be localized. Table 11-4 shows which attribute will be localized using the default behavior.

Table 11-4: Default Localized Attributes

Control Type	Localized Attribute
System.Web.UI.WebControls	
Label	Text
Button	Text
LinkButton	Text
ImageButton	AlternateText
Hyperlink	Text
Image	AlternateText
CheckBox	Text
BaseValidator	ErrorMessage
RadioButtonList	Items(i).Text
DropDownList	Items(i).Text
System.Web.UI.HtmlControls	
HtmlImage	Alt

If the web control you are localizing is not listed in Table 11-4, you need to localize a different attribute, or if you need to localize multiple attributes for the same control, you must use the localization techniques shown in Case 3.

Case 3: Handling Static Text Programmatically

You will find several cases where text cannot be localized using a declarative approach. This will require programmatically setting the text using the localization API. The API section outlines the most frequently used methods of the API.

Continuing with the same example, take a look at how to handle localizing the `Tooltip` attribute for the label you created. Notice that this attribute is not the default attribute for the Label control listed in Table 11-4. To localize the attribute, add the following line of code to the code-behind:

```
lblTitle.Tooltip = Localization.GetString("TestLabel.ToolTip", _
                              Me.LocalResourceFile)
```

Because this is a new control, you are safe adding it to the `Page_Load` event. As you will see shortly, this is not always the appropriate spot for localizing strings. Now that you have the code, the only step left is to add the localized value to the resource file. This example uses `LocalResourceFile` because it is specific to the module. Also note that although the key is named `TestLabel.ToolTip`, you are free to use whatever key makes sense to you. Because you're using the API, you have much more control over how the keys are named.

If your key does not include a period (.), the framework will automatically add .text to your key and use that as the key for looking up the localized value. Keep this in mind when creating your keys. Assuming that you have named your key appropriately, you should see something like the localized tooltip shown in Figure 11-4 when you compile and navigate to a page with your module.

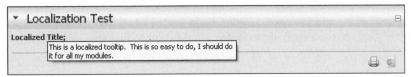

Figure 11-4

There are many instances where you might have embedded strings in your code that are changed depending on the application state. A good example of this is the Login skin object. This skin object changes between Login and Logout depending on the authentication state of the current user. To localize this control, just replace all the references to the static text with a call to one of the GetString methods described earlier.

The DotNetNuke localization API includes a few helper methods to simplify localizing complex controls like datagrids. Although you could use the standard programmatic techniques, a helper method makes it trivial to localize the HeaderText values. To localize column headers, include a key in the local resource file for each column in the datagrid. This key should be the same as the HeaderText value for the column with .Header appended. For example, say your grid looks something like this:

```
<asp:datagrid id="dgSample" runat="server" >
<Columns>
<asp:TemplateColumn HeaderText="Title">
...
</asp:TemplateColumn>
</asp:datagrid>
```

In this case, your resource key would be Title.Header. After you have the keys defined, just add the following method call to your code:

```
Localization.LocalizeDataGrid(dgSample, LocalResourceFile)
```

This method automatically iterates through the datagrid and localizes each of the column headers.

Case 4: Localizing Images

Images are a special case. It is recommended that you never include text in your images because it complicates localization and can usually be avoided through the use of background images and CSS. If your design requires you to embed text in an image, you need to make a few changes to make it easier to localize the image.

No module will ever include localized resources for every language supported by DotNetNuke — the effort to maintain the resource files would greatly exceed the cost for all other development. Most module developers will include resource files for their native language and maybe one or two other languages depending on the language skills of the module development staff. This means that many users will be forced to create the resource files for their own language. That's not usually a significant problem.

If an image file contains embedded text, though, the user is forced to re-create the image with a localized version of the text. To ease the burden for the user, include the base image without text, so that the user can easily create the text label in his language. Keep in mind that different languages have different space requirements. Just because a word or phrase is short in one language does not mean that it will be equally short in another language. That's one of the reasons for avoiding embedded text.

When your user has the image file with the localized text, he or she can use the standard `GetString` methods to set the `ImageUrl` attribute to the appropriate image filename, depending on the language they select.

Summary

In this chapter, you learned how resource strings are stored for the core framework and for each module. You looked at the main API methods for accessing the appropriate localized values and saw how to use the framework to localize your modules. You are now ready to localize your own modules and code so that they are usable by a wider audience. For more information about localization, check the documentation included with DotNetNuke.

12

Beginning Module Development

This chapter begins the tour of module development in DotNetNuke. As you have read, DotNetNuke provides a large amount of functionality right out of the box, but we also realize that each user is going to have separate business requirements that DotNetNuke may not meet. Fortunately, DotNetNuke provides developers and third-party independent software vendors (ISVs) the capability to extend the core framework by developing modules.

This chapter focuses on the architecture of one of those modules: the Events module. (Chapters 13 through 15 cover various other aspects of module development.) You'll begin by setting up DotNetNuke to interface with your module development in Visual Studio .NET 2005, exploring some configuration issues along the way.

Although Visual Studio 2005 is used in this book, you can still use Visual Studio 2003 to develop modules for DotNetNuke. The core team evaluated this situation extensively and made every effort to ensure the development process would be similar for developers employing either platform.

With the release of ASP.NET 2.0 and the new line of development tools, Microsoft has attempted to bring low-cost tools to the developer community. This suite of tools is known as the Express edition of Visual Studio. The Visual Web Developer is a free IDE that you can use to develop modules in DotNetNuke or for other ASP.NET projects. You can obtain the VWD download from `http://msdn.microsoft.com/vstudio/express/vwd/default.aspx`.

The Visual Web Developer interface is essentially the same as the Visual Studio 2005 interface that is illustrated in this chapter.

Planning Your Module Project

Of course, to succeed in any project, you should plan it out before you start writing even one line of code. Planning includes considering the answers to any number of questions as well as readying your resources.

Business Considerations

You're going to have to ask yourself or your project team a few questions before beginning your application development. For example:

Q   **Can the development effort justify the savings that your application will provide?**

A   Many factors can come into play: skills of in-house staff, costs associated with obtaining the skills, and many others that you will have to account for.

Q   **Can the module be purchased from a third party?**

A   DotNetNuke has grown in popularity over the past couple of years, and the outlook is for continued growth. More independent software vendors are developing modules, so more than likely there is no need to develop a module to accomplish a specific task — you can purchase it for very little cost. As of this writing, more than 250 modules are currently available for sale, and many more are available as free downloads. Some of these modules are written specifically for the 1.1 version of DotNetNuke, but there is an increasing number specifically targeting the ASP.NET 2.0 platform and DotNetNuke 4.0. If the module developer has written the module to conform to the same standards as the DotNetNuke core modules, the module will function in either the 3.2 version for ASP.NET 1.1 or the 4.0 version developed for ASP.NET 2.0.

Q   **Is training required for developers?**

A   Module development does require some additional skills. You develop modules in DotNetNuke using the standard tools you would use to do any ASP.NET development, but knowing how to take advantage of the available interfaces requires some understanding of the framework's inner workings. In addition to this book, many resources are available for learning about DotNetNuke if you want to investigate further. You may develop modules in any language supported by the .NET framework, including C#, J#, and VB.Net. This discussion sticks with VB.Net, the language in which DotNetNuke is written.

Q   **Should you hire an outside resource to do the development?**

A   Training becomes less of an issue when you have your development done by an outside resource. DotNetNuke's popularity has increased at such a phenomenal rate that many solution providers specialize in module development.

Q   **What infrastructure issues are there?**

A   How many developers are going to be working on the same code base? The more developers working on the same code, the more there is a need for source control. Scalability also may be something to consider. In addition, if you have to access resources over the Web, you need to read some of the application settings configured at a host level in DotNetNuke.

Q   Do you need to develop multiple data providers for the module?

A   What database are you going to use for the backend? DotNetNuke supports a Provider Model that enables developers to abstract out the physical database interaction, allowing the actual DotNetNuke core and module logic to be separate from the database logic. DotNetNuke supports SQL Server out-of-the-box, but a provider can be developed for basically any database backend. How many physical databases you need to support will determine how many providers you need to develop. Module development closely mirrors the DotNetNuke architecture, and you should create a provider for each platform you want to support. If you're going to distribute your module on various DotNetNuke installs with different databases like SQL Server, Oracle, or MySQL, you need to develop a provider to support those individual databases.

Q   Do you need to support different versions of DotNetNuke?

A   DotNetNuke is a mature product with several released versions. There have been many major architectural changes going from version 1.x to 2.x and to 3.x. DotNetNuke 4.x uses essentially the same provider model as DotNetNuke 3.x. At the time of this writing, the latest release was DotNetNuke 4.0.2. If you are developing on a later version, verify that there have not been any changes to the provider model for your version. If your module needs to be available on these various versions of DotNetNuke, you will need to manage the various code bases to accommodate all the required versions.

Modules developed for version 3.2 (on ASP.NET 1.1) will run on version 4.02 (on ASP.NET 2.0) unaltered because of their binary compatibility.

Q   What resources are needed for ongoing support of the module?

A   This may not be as much of an issue for modules purchased or developed by an outside party. You may be able to obtain adequate support from the vendor. If you develop in-house, you'll need to set aside resources to provide ongoing support of the module.

Of course, this list is not all-inclusive, but the example questions should be enough to help you determine the questions you need to ask regarding your own application.

Ready Your Resources

Now that you have decided to begin module development, you need to prepare your development environment. The source and project files are available in the DotNetNuke distribution file that you can download from www.dotnetnuke.com. Just as you installed DotNetNuke on the production server in Chapter 2, you need to configure a development machine with the source code — and the process is the same.

Ensure that your development environment is configured with Visual Studio .NET 2003/2005, SQL Server 2000/2005, or MSDE/SQL Server Express (or your specific data provider). In addition, if you are working with your source files in a location other than the DotNetNuke default (c:\dotnetnuke), you may need to change the solution file (dotnetnuke.sln) and the web information contained within the solution (dotnetnuke.webinfo) to point to the location of the virtual directory for your environment. That will ensure that you can open the solution correctly in Visual Studio .NET.

You may want to consider installing Visual Source Safe, or some other source control to ensure integrity of your project source code. Installing Source Safe is beyond the scope of this book, but it is recommended that you use some sort of source control to protect your development.

Another item to note is the publishing process from your development environment to your production environment. Because DotNetNuke is ASP.NET-compiled into several assemblies, the most it takes to publish to production is simply copying the development assemblies, user controls, associated ASPX, and resource files. Before you compile your module for production, ensure that the build configuration in Visual Studio.NET is set to Release, not Debug.

In many environments, an extra stage in the development process is added by placing a sandbox or testing server between development and production. The testing server should mirror your production environment as closely as possible — install your module to the testing server and test first. After the business units review the functionality and ensure it meets the requirements, publish the module to the production servers.

Starting Development

With your development decisions made, it's time to begin developing your module. In this example, you are going to work with the Events module that is included in the DotNetNuke distribution. This chapter and the next three chapters provide an in-depth study of this module.

At the time of this writing, the DotNetNuke 4.x source code download does not include the module source code for all the modules. This is because the module structure is essentially the same as the 3.2.x version. To obtain the source code for the Events module, download the source for 3.2.x.

Configuring Your Visual Studio .NET 2003 Project

DotNetNuke is broken down into several solutions. The primary solution, located in the root directory of the distribution file, contains all the projects that make up the entire core. This includes controls, web forms, class files, and any other files required for the core application. With the release of DNN 4, the solution organization is restructured into more manageable pieces for each specific section of DotNetNuke. The module code is not included in the source download for DotNetNuke 4.x, as mentioned earlier in this chapter. For module developers, there is the module solution located within the <approot>\Solutions\ DotNetNuke.DesktopModules directory of the 3.x source download.

Open the DotNetNuke.DesktopModules.sln file in Visual Studio .NET. You will see a solution containing approximately 30 projects, which are the individual modules that make up DotNetNuke. This part of the chapter shows you how to work with a module using Visual Studio 2003, which is essentially the same method you use if you are targeting your module for the ASP.NET 1.1 version of the framework. Later you'll see how to create a module using Visual Studio 2005 and the DotNetNuke starter project.

When you open the solution, you should see the project listings in the upper-right pane (Solution Explorer), as shown in Figure 12-1.

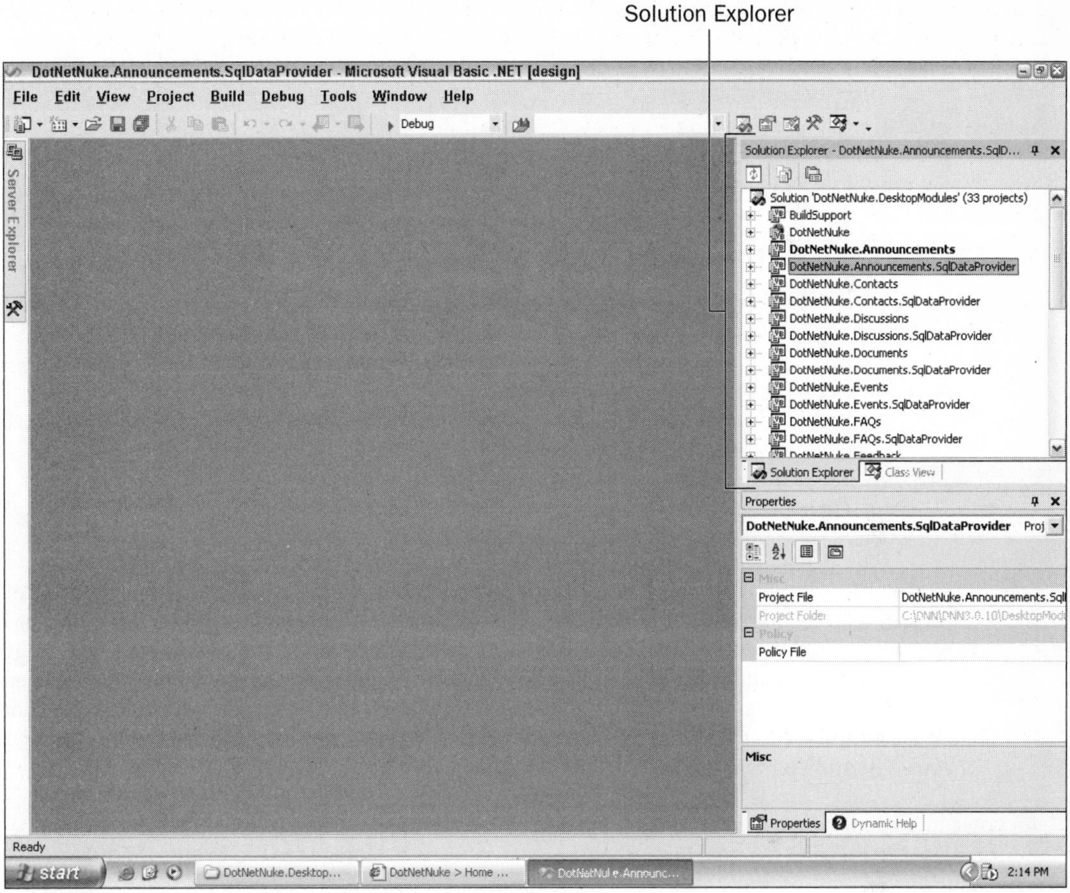

Solution Explorer

Figure 12-1

Create Your Project

To begin module development, first create a module project within the DesktopModules solution. Several projects are already included in the solution, and in this example you will be using the Events module. To create your own project, step through the following process:

1. With the Visual Studio .NET DotNetNuke.DesktopModules solution open, right-click the solution at the top of the Solution Explorer. Select Add ➪ New Project from the context menu. The Add New Project dialog opens.

2. Select Class Library from the Templates section, provide a name for your module in the Name text box, and click Browse to pick a location for the project files. For module development, select <approot>\DesktopModules\ for the project directory (see Figure 12-2). Your module should now be listed at the bottom of the Solution Explorer.

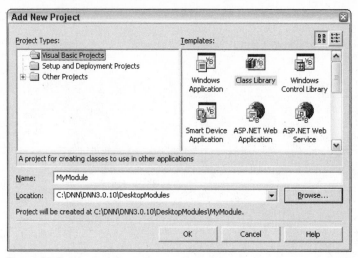

Figure 12-2

3.   Notice the BuildSupport project within the solution. This ensures that when you compile your project, your assemblies will be copied to the bin directory of the main DotNetNuke core project; then, any time you make a change in your development code and compile, those changes are displayed in your module when you view it within your portal in a web browser. This eliminates the need to manually copy the DLL file to the bin directory every time you make a change and recompile. To accomplish this, add a reference to your module project to the BuildSupport project as shown in Figure 12-3.

As you can see in the figure, a reference is created to each of the module projects in DNN. For the example used in this and the next three chapters, you can see a reference to the Events module — SQLDataProvider (more about this in the next chapter).

After your module project has been created, follow the same procedure to create your SQLDataProvider project. The only difference for the Data Provider project is the name, which will be ModuleName .SQLDataProvider (depending on your physical provider — if you were using Access, it would be AccessDataProvider). It is generally acceptable to place the Data Provider project in a subdirectory off of your module, so the full path would be <approot>\DesktopModules\ModuleName\Providers\ DataProviders\SQLDataProvider\. You then create a directory for each physical database you plan on supporting for your module.

Add Controls

Now that your project has been created, you need to add some controls for your users to interface with and some classes for data operations.

Add reference

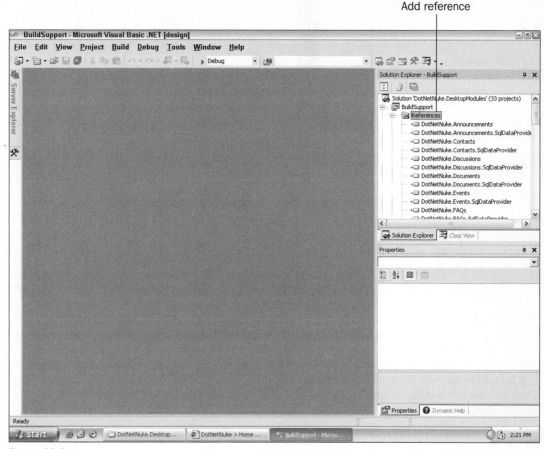

Figure 12-3

There is a limitation with Visual Studio .NET in adding user controls in class projects: you can't do it. In many cases, developers copy an existing ASCX control from another module project and paste it into their newly created project.

For most modules you need to create three controls:

❑ **View control** (Events.ascx): The default view users will see when they first access your module.

❑ **Edit control** (EditEvents.ascx): For updating the data contained in the module's tables within the database.

❑ **Settings control** (Settings.ascx): For specifying unique values for a particular instance of a module.

The Events module example has all three of these controls.

> *A member of the DNN Core Team created templates that you can use to install into your Visual Studio .NET application to ease the process of creating controls, as well as project files. They can be freely downloaded from* http://dnnjungle.vmasanas.net. *In addition, you can download Code Smith templates that will reduce the amount of code needed to create a data provider for your module. You also can download the AtGen SDK module development project at* http://projects.apptheory.com— *it will generate much of the code necessary for module development.*

Create Your Classes

You also need to create the supporting classes within the module. Generally, you'll have three classes contained in your main module project:

❑ **DataProvider class:** Contains methods that provide your abstraction layer with the database. These methods will be overridden by your data provider class in the Data Provider project (see Chapter 14).

❑ **Controller class:** Contains the methods for manipulating and obtaining data from the abstraction layer (see Chapter 14).

❑ **Info class:** Contains properties that define your objects (see Chapter 14).

The Data Provider project has one class, the DataProvider class, which holds the actual methods for obtaining and updating the data contained within a specific vendor's database (see Chapter 11).

In the Events module, the classes are DataProvider.vb, EventsController.vb, EventsInfo.vb, and SQLDataProvider.vb. We'll get into more detail on what these classes do in subsequent chapters, but for now we just want to cover what files need to be created to begin a module development project.

Configuring DotNetNuke to Interface with Your Module

Now that you have your Visual Studio .NET 2003 projects configured, you need to let DotNetNuke know about your module so you can test your development within your portal. DotNetNuke needs to know the location and type (view, edit, or settings) of your user controls to display them within the portal.

To manually configure your modules in DotNetNuke, log in as the host account. Then follow these steps:

1. Select Host ⇨ Module Definitions.

2. In the Module Definitions page, select Add New Module Definition from the menu options (see Figure 12-4).

3. Enter a Name and Description for your module. Select the check box for Premium if this module requires an additional payment for each portal admin to use the module.

4. Click the Update link button. Additional text boxes appear for you to enter a definition for the Desktop module (see Figure 12-5).

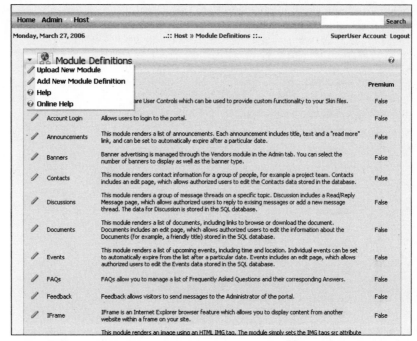

Figure 12-4

Figure 12-5

5. Provide a name for your module definition. The controls listing appears below the Definitions text box (see Figure 12-6).

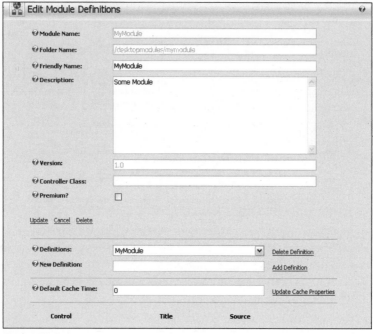

Figure 12-6

6. Define the location and type of control that you created in Visual Studio .NET 2003. Click the Add Control link button to bring up the Edit Module Control page (see Figure 12-7).

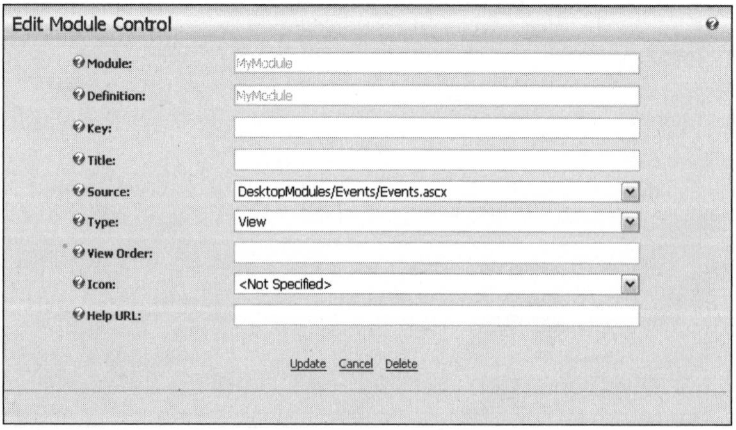

Figure 12-7

7. Define a key. For a default view control, leave the Key field empty; for an edit control, use Edit; and for a settings control, use Settings for your key. Keys they provide you with a mechanism to define which control to load at a point in your logic (discussed in more detail in Chapter 15). You can have as many controls as you want within your module — you just need to define a unique key to refer to each one in your code.

8. Provide a title for your control. It is displayed in the module container when viewing the control in DotNetNuke.

9. Select a source for the module — this is the actual filename and path to your ASCX control located in the DesktopModules directory. DotNetNuke will iterate through the directory structure and find all controls that are located in module projects under the DesktopModules directory. This is why you want to ensure you are creating your projects using the proper directory paths as described earlier in this chapter.

10. Select the type of control: Skin Object, Anonymous, View, Edit, Admin, or Host (more on this in Chapter 15).

11. You can enter in an optional View Order for the control. This is used to manage the order in which your controls are displayed on your module's action menu.

12. You can select an optional icon to be displayed next to your control. You must first upload the image file to your portal for it to be displayed in the drop-down menu.

13. Finally, there is an option for the Help URL, which enables you to provide online help for your module.

14. Click Update. Go through each control that makes up your module project and add a definition. Figure 12-8 shows an example of the definition for the Events module.

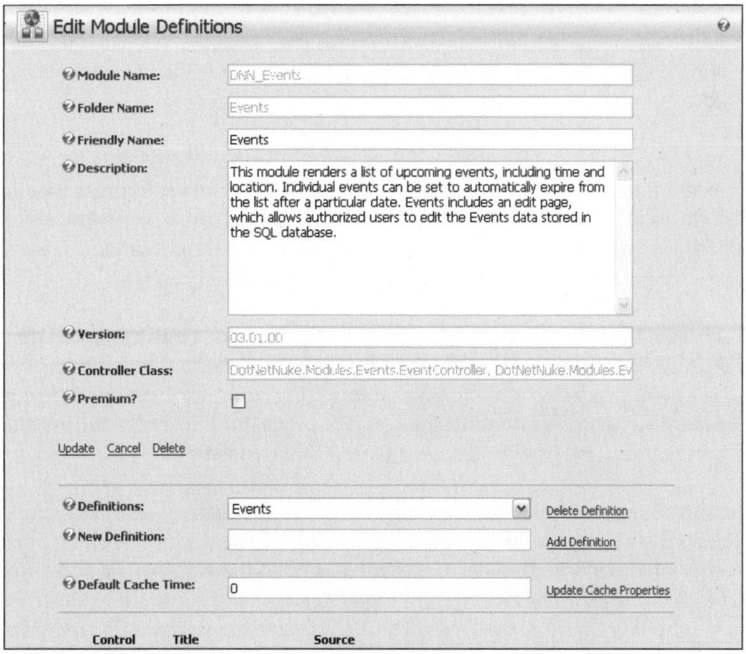

Figure 12-8

Another option on the Module Definitions screen is the capability to create a private assembly. A private assembly enables you to distribute your module to other portals using an automated setup. This is covered in more detail in Chapter 16.

After you define your module, place an instance within a page in your development DotNetNuke. You should see the initial view control after placing the module in the page, enabling you to view and debug your module within a live portal installation. Any changes that you make and then compile are instantly seen in this development page.

Developing Modules with Visual Studio .NET 2005

Now let's look at the methods for creating a module using Visual Studio .NET 2005. Note that developing a module with VS 2005 means that you cannot run the module on DotNetNuke 3.x and the ASP.NET 1.1 framework.

First take a look at some of the changes you will encounter as you start to utilize this platform for developing your modules.

In the VS 2005 line of products, Microsoft wanted to reduce the entry barriers that many developers have historically experienced with their integrated development environment products. The professional Microsoft's IDEs have usually been expensive, which prevented a lot of novice and hobby developers from utilizing the Microsoft platform. This could probably account for some of the rapid growth seen with the LAMP suite of technologies.

> LAMP is a free, open source web platform that utilizes Linux, Apache, and MySQL, and Perl, PHP, or Python scripting languages. The free software programs are used together to run dynamic Web sites or servers.

With the launch of ASP.NET 2.0, Microsoft is releasing a full suite of free development tools, which make up the Express line of development tools for .NET 2.0. The main Express tool you need to create DotNetNuke modules is the Visual Web Developer (VWD). You can also download and manage the SQL 2005 Express database engine and control it through VWD. You can download these products from `http://msdn.microsoft.com/vstudio/express/vwd/default.aspx`.

ASP.NET also comes with a file system web server, Cassini, which enables you to develop and test on your machine without having to set up IIS to accomplish these tasks. The web server is integrated with the Visual Studio line of products, which makes debugging your applications simpler. Integrating the simpler development structure along with the concept of Starter Kits helps reduce the learning curve associated with understanding how to develop DotNetNuke modules.

Starter kits were introduced with VS 2005. Microsoft has released several starter kits ranging from a Personal Site Starter kit to a PayPal- Enabled Ecommerce Start Kit. A starter kit essentially performs some of the remedial tasks associated with module development and what the AtGen SDK and VS templates mentioned earlier are used to accomplish. The DotNetNuke core team saw the benefit of these starter kits, especially for programmers who were new to the DotNetNuke framework, so the core created a DotNetNuke Starter kit, which you can download from `www.dotnetnuke.com/tabid/125/default.aspx`.

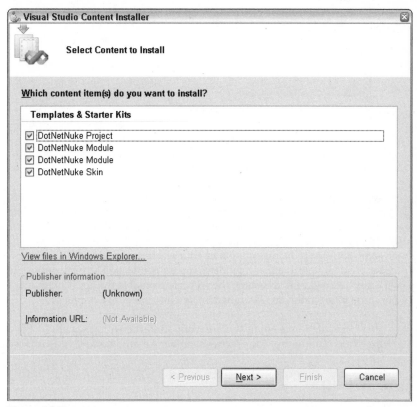

Installing the DotNetNuke Starter Kit

After you've downloaded the Starter Kit, execute DotNetNuke_4.0.2_StarterKit.vsi to install it on your computer. The Video Studio Content Installer dialog box (see Figure 12-9) opens, enabling you to select the kit components you want to install.

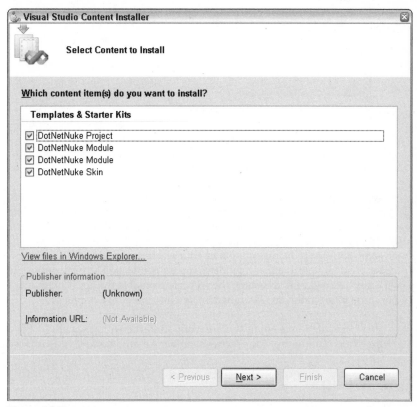

Figure 12-9

For now, leave all the items selected so the various options will be available for you to use in your projects. You may notice there is no publisher defined for this file, so you will receive a dialog telling you the file does not have a valid signature. The DotNetNuke core team will eventually start signing these files so you can be sure you're getting an official copy. This time, though, just click through the warning.

The next screen provides an overview of the projects you are installing. Click Finish and your templates will install.

Launch either Visual Web Developer or Visual Studio 2005 and choose New Web Site. (This example uses Visual Studio Team Suite, but the function is essentially the same if you are using VWD or one of the other versions of Visual Studio.) The New Web Site dialog's Templates page opens (see Figure 12-10).

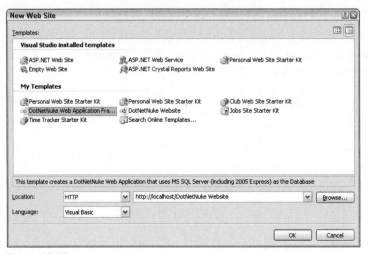

Figure 12-10

Select the DotNetNuke Web Application Framework project because you will be creating a fully functional instance of DotNetNuke to develop against. Change the default web site name to DotNetNuke402,
but accept the defaults for everything else and click OK. The application instance is created and you are
presented with some additional documentation in your web browser that will guide you through the
rest of the process: creating your database, modifying your connection string, configuring your web
server and NTFS permissions, and launching the web site to enable the application to install the needed
SQL scripts. For more information on installing DotNetNuke, refer to Chapter 2.

You now have a basic installation running and are ready to start creating a module. For this example,
you create a Hello World module, but the process is similar for any module you are developing.

Hello World Module

Open the DotNetnuke project you created earlier in the process using either Visual Web Developer or
Visual Studio 2005.In the Solutions Explorer, right-click the web site root — `http://localhost/`
`DotNetNuke402` — and select Add New Item. A dialog box like the one shown in Figure 12-11 opens.

Select the DotNetNuke Module template, rename your module **HelloWorld**, and click Add. The module is created with the structural work already done, so all you need to do is add your specific logic.
Figure 12-12 shows all files created for you with the DotNetNuke Module template.

A document loads into your web browser, detailing a couple of manual steps you need to perform.
Rename the Module Name folder to coincide with your module name, HelloWorld. This ensures that
you won't have naming conflicts as you develop additional module for your portal. You must change
this in two places:

❑   Rename \App_Code\ModuleName to **\App_Code\HelloWorld**.

❑   Rename \DesktopModules\ModuleName to **\DesktopModules\HelloWorld**.

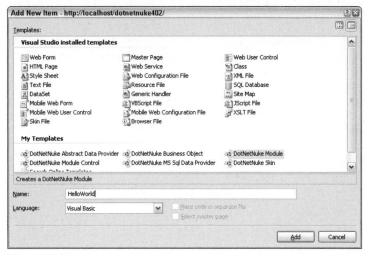

Figure 12-11

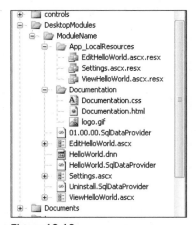

Figure 12-12

You can accomplish this in your development environment by right-clicking the folder name in the Solutions Explorer and selecting Rename from the menu.

Now you need to put in your application logic. Add a simple label control to ViewHelloWorld.ascx with the text **hello world**. You can enter any logic you want into these files and the process is essentially the same as discussed in the Event module earlier in this chapter. After you have dropped the label onto the form, you can rebuild the web site and register your module into the DotNetNuke web site as you did earlier in the chapter. Your Hello World Module is ready to use in your portal.

That was really simple and if you are not planning to distribute your module to other developers, this is really the easiest and most efficient method for extending the functionality of your DotNetNuke web site. You still need to create the logic for your DataProvider, but that process is essentially the same as if you where developing in VS2003 and will be covered in the next three chapters.

Summary

This chapter discussed some of the issues you will face as you begin any module development project, and showed you how to create your development environment.

The chapter also explored creating Visual Studio .NET projects and provided an overview of the DesktopModules solution file contained in the DotNetNuke distribution. You added some controls for your users as well as some classes for data operations in your development DotNetNuke portal, and examined methods for creating a module utilizing Visual Web Developer and the DotNetNuke starter kit.

The next three chapters cover each layer of module development — Database Layer, Business Logic Layer, and Presentation Layer — in detail.

13

Developing Modules: The Database Layer

Now that you understand the concept of modules and are getting ready to develop your own, this chapter guides you on how to begin development starting with the database layer. As in most application development, you want to build a database structure for your application. This chapter covers some basic database development and how to expose your data to a DotNetNuke module.

Chapter 7 introduced the concept of the Provider Model and how DotNetNuke uses it to abstract the business layer logic from the physical database. In this chapter, you develop your modules by modeling the three-tier architecture of DotNetNuke.

The sections on creating tables and stored procedures review some basic SQL Server development concepts. From there, you learn how to expose the stored procedures through a custom Data Provider that you will develop for your module. Extending on the DotNetNuke architecture, you develop an abstraction layer for the module to provide a separation from the physical database for your module.

Developing with SQL Server is beyond the scope of this book, but this chapter covers how you expose your database's structure to DotNetNuke. It covers table structure and stored procedures as a reference on how the structure relates to your module development.

> *Again, the Events module is used in the example for this chapter and the next two chapters on module development. The Events module project is located within the DotNetNuke.DesktopModules solution in the Solutions directory contained off of the root of the DotNetNuke distribution package.*

Database Design

This section reviews the tables and stored procedures that make up the backend database for the Events module.

The DotNetNuke (DNN) development team wanted a module that could track events, provide a time for the event, and expire the event so it would no longer be displayed after the expiration date was met. To accomplish this, the team needed to create a database structure to store event information, associate the information with DNN, and then create stored procedures to add, update, and delete event information. In the next sections, you learn the structure of the database tables for the module and the stored procedures for performing actions on the data.

For your database manipulation, you can use SQL Enterprise Manager, Query Analyzer, or Visual Studio .NET. The examples in this chapter use Visual Studio .NET 2003 for module development and database design. The idea behind this chapter and the next three chapters on module development is to give you a comprehensive review of the module structure contained within the DNN distribution.

As discussed in Chapter 12, keep in mind that you are not bound by the underlying physical database. You can use any other database as your backend for module development, and you can develop modules for whatever database your DotNetNuke install is using. SQL Server 2000 is used throughout the book because DotNetNuke natively supports SQL Server 2000 and SQL Server 2005 out of the box. The point of this exercise is to help you understand the physical database structure and how it applies to the database provider and abstraction layer you will create for your modules.

The next section covers the tables used to store the information. After a table is created, you can begin writing stored procedures to manipulate the data. One table is used for storing the event information: the Events table.

Events Table

The Events table stores your event information for the module. It is defined as shown in Figure 13-1.

The most important field contained within the structure as far as DNN integration goes is ModuleID. It contains an integer value that is assigned by DNN when you create an instance of your module. This value identifies the specific instance of the module with which you are working. It's important because multiple instances of a module can exist on a single page and a button click on one instance of the module must not operate on data from another instance of the module. Any values you store specific to this module instance will key off the value contained in this field. You will see this as you go create the stored procedures. The other fields within the database are specific to the module itself, and all depend on how you structure your application.

The ItemID field is for identifying the primary key of a specific item within your table. The main concept here, however, is to fully integrate and create a unique instance of your module with unique instance items. You need to specify a ModuleID value that relates to the key provided by DotNetNuke for every module instance.

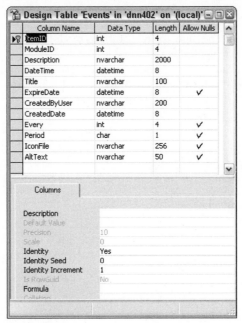

Figure 13-1

The following list describes each item in the Events table:

❑ **ItemID:** The primary key of the event information within the table.

❑ **ModuleID:** Because DNN can contain many instances of a module all with different information, this key consolidates all event information into the one module instance.

❑ **Description:** A text description of your event for display.

❑ **DateTime:** A date and time for when the event begins.

❑ **Title:** The title of the event presented to the user.

❑ **ExpireDate:** When the event will no longer be displayed in your portal.

❑ **CreatedByUser:** Tracks the ID of the portal user that created the event.

❑ **CreatedDate:** When the event was created.

❑ **Every:** If this is a recurring event, the period of time the event occurs. This is related to the Period field, which defines the amount of time between events.

❑ **Period:** Related to the Every field, this specifies the period between events, that is, days, weeks, months, years.

❑ **IconFile:** Displays an icon next to the event listing within the module.

❑ **AltText:** Alternate text to be displayed when you hover your mouse cursor over the icon. This also aids your portal in complying with the Americans with Disabilities Act (ADA) Section 508.

This covers how you're going to store the data that is entered into the module. Next, you create the stored procedures necessary for working with the data.

AddEvent Stored Procedure

The first stored procedure you're going to create for this module is AddEvent (see Listing 13-1). This procedure is used to add an event to the Events table.

Listing 13-1: The AddEvent Stored Procedure for the Events Module

```
create procedure dbo.AddEvent

    @ModuleID     int,
    @Description  nvarchar(2000),
    @DateTime     datetime,
    @Title        nvarchar(100),
    @ExpireDate   datetime = null,
    @UserName     nvarchar(200),
    @Every        int,
    @Period       char(1),
    @IconFile     nvarchar(256),
    @AltText      nvarchar(50)

as

insert into Events (
    ModuleID,
    Description,
    DateTime,
    Title,
    ExpireDate,
    CreatedByUser,
    CreatedDate,
    Every,
    Period,
    IconFile,
    AltText
)
values (
    @ModuleID,
    @Description,
    @DateTime,
    @Title,
    @ExpireDate,
    @UserName,
    getdate(),
    @Every,
    @Period,
    @IconFile,
    @AltText
)

select SCOPE_IDENTITY()


GO
```

There is nothing special about this stored procedure — it's a basic `insert` statement, and it accepts parameters from your database provider for populating the event information. One thing to keep in mind throughout all the stored procedures is that the `ModuleID` parameter is always passed when creating a new record that is associated with your module. In Chapter 14, you learn how to obtain the module ID from DotNetNuke and pass it to your stored procedure.

DeleteEvent Stored Procedure

The `DeleteEvent` stored procedure (see Listing 13-2) is for deleting an event previously added to DotNetNuke.

Listing 13-2: The DeleteEvent Stored Procedure for the Events Module

```
create procedure dbo.DeleteEvent

    @ItemId int

as

delete
from    Events
where   ItemId = @ItemId


GO
```

There is no need to pass a parameter value for `ModuleID` in this procedure. Because you're only concerned about performing a delete operation on the data, you only need to determine the primary key of the specific event record.

GetEvent Stored Procedure

You use the `GetEvent` stored procedure (see Listing 13-3) to get a single event's information.

Listing 13-3: The GetEvent Stored Procedure for the Events Module

```
CREATE procedure dbo.GetEvent

    @ItemId   int,
    @ModuleId int

as

select
    Events.ItemId,
    Events.ModuleId,
    Events.Description,
    Events.DateTime,
    Events.Title,
    Events.ExpireDate,
```

(continued)

Listing 13-3: *(continued)*

```
    'CreatedByUser' = Users.FirstName + ' ' + Users.LastName,
    Events.CreatedDate,
    Events.Every,
    Events.Period,
    'IconFile' = case when Files.FileName is null then Events.IconFile else
Files.Folder + Files.FileName end,
    Events.AltText
from    Events
left outer join Users on Events.CreatedByUser = Users.UserId
left outer join Files on Events.IconFile = 'fileid=' +
convert(varchar,Files.FileID)
where   ItemId = @ItemId
and     ModuleId = @ModuleId


GO
```

Here you are passing the `ModuleID` parameter along with the specific `ItemID` for the event. Use this stored procedure for obtaining a single event for modification or display.

GetEvents Stored Procedure

You use the `GetEvents` stored procedure (see Listing 13-4) for obtaining several events for a listing of a specific module instance.

Listing 13-4: The GetEvents Stored Procedure for the Events Module

```
CREATE procedure dbo.GetEvents

    @ModuleId int

as

select
    Events.ItemId,
    Events.ModuleId,
    Events.Description,
    Events.DateTime,
    Events.Title,
    Events.ExpireDate,
    Events.CreatedByUser,
    Events.CreatedDate,
    Events.Every,
    Events.Period,
    'IconFile' = case when Files.FileName is null then Events.IconFile else ⤸
Files.Folder + Files.FileName end,
    Events.AltText,
    'MaxWIdth' = (select max(WIdth) from Events left outer join Files on ⤸
Events.IconFile = 'fileid=' + convert(varchar,Files.FileID) where ⤸
```

```
     ModuleId =   @ModuleId and (ExpireDate > getdate() or ExpireDate is null))
     from    Events
     left outer join Files on Events.IconFile = 'fileid=' + ⊃
     convert(varchar,Files.FileID)
     where   ModuleId = @ModuleId
     and     (ExpireDate > getdate() or ExpireDate is null)
     order by DateTime


     GO
```

The only parameter passed to this stored procedure is the ModuleID value. This pulls all events for one module instance.

GetEventsByDate Stored Procedure

The GetEventsByDate stored procedure (see Listing 13-5) pulls all events within a specified date range for a specific module instance.

Listing 13-5: The GetEventsByDate Stored Procedure for the Events Module

```
CREATE procedure dbo.GetEventsByDate

   @ModuleId int,
   @StartDate datetime,
   @EndDate datetime

as

select
   Events.ItemId,
   Events.ModuleId,
   Events.Description,
   Events.DateTime,
   Events.Title,
   Events.ExpireDate,
   Events.CreatedByUser,
   Events.CreatedDate,
   Events.Every,
   Events.Period,
   'IconFile' = case when Files.FileName is null then Events.IconFile else ⊃
Files.Folder + Files.FileName end,
   Events.AltText
from    Events
left outer join Files on Events.IconFile = 'fileid=' + ⊃
convert(varchar,Files.FileID)
where   ModuleId = @ModuleId
and     ( (Period is null and (DateTime >= @StartDate and DateTime ⊃
<= @EndDate)) or Period is not null )
order by DateTime


GO
```

UpdateEvent Stored Procedure

The final stored procedure for the Events module is the `UpdateEvent` module (see Listing 13-6). This
enables you to update an existing event's information.

Listing 13-6: The UpdateEvent Stored Procedure for the Events Module

```
create procedure dbo.UpdateEvent

    @ItemId       int,
    @Description  nvarchar(2000),
    @DateTime     datetime,
    @Title        nvarchar(100),
    @ExpireDate   datetime = null,
    @UserName     nvarchar(200),
    @Every        int,
    @Period       char(1),
    @IconFile     nvarchar(256),
    @AltText      nvarchar(50)

as

update Events
set     Description = @Description,
        DateTime = @DateTime,
        Title = @Title,
        ExpireDate = @ExpireDate,
        CreatedByUser = @UserName,
        CreatedDate = getdate(),
        Every = @Every,
        Period = @Period,
        IconFile = @IconFile,
        AltText = @AltText
where   ItemId = @ItemId

GO
```

That's it for your database procedures. The next section covers how to wrap this up and create your own
physical database provider for DotNetNuke.

Database Providers

Module development closely mirrors DotNetNuke architecture. Each module should provide its own
abstraction to the underlying database. This enables you to change physical databases without having to
change or recompile the underlying code of DotNetNuke and your module. Remember, if you want to
support multiple databases with your module, you need to create a physical provider for each database
you want to support. So even if your DotNetNuke implementation is using a provider other than the
one included in SQL Support, such as Oracle, for example, you need to create a provider for your module to support Oracle as well.

The only direct interaction with the previous stored procedures contained in your database will be done in the provider project. In the modules solution of DotNetNuke, all modules have a corresponding project for a SQL Data Provider. For example, the main module project called DotNetNuke.Events is contained in the DesktopModules solution. In addition to this project, you have the DotNetNuke.Events .SQLDataProvider project. This project contains the class and methods necessary to interact with the stored procedures covered earlier in this chapter. The following sections cover this class and the methods it contains to create a provider for this module.

The SQLDataProvider class for the Events module and all modules within the DotNetNuke .DesktopModules solution closely mirrors the structure of the DotNetNuke core architecture. Therefore, you will see the same methods contained with this project as you would see in the main DotNetNuke .SQLDataProvider project included in the Solutions directory within the DotNetNuke distribution.

This section breaks down the structure of the database provider class for the Events module beginning with Listing 13-7.

Listing 13-7: Importing Namespaces for the Events Module Data Provider Class

```
Imports System
Imports System.Data
Imports System.Data.SqlClient
Imports Microsoft.ApplicationBlocks.Data
```

You import various namespaces into your class for dealing with the database. System.Data.SqlClient is used to connect to the SQL Server database. Because this assembly connects to the physical database, you need to use specific classes for connecting and manipulating the database. Microsoft.ApplicationBlocks .Data provides your assembly, which helps to reduce the code required for calling stored procedures and commands.

You can find more information on Microsoft Application Blocks in the "Patterns and Practices" section within the MSDN site at http://msdn.microsoft.com/library/en-us/dnanchor/html/ Anch_EntDevAppArchPatPrac.asp.

After importing the namespaces, the namespace DotNetNuke is added: Namespace DotNetNuke .Modules.Events. One thing to note here is that you're using a DotNetNuke core module as an example. If you develop your own modules for DotNetNuke, you should create your own unique namespace in the form of CompanyName.ModuleName and CompanyName.ModuleName.SQLDataProvider. This ensures that your namespace is unique and should not conflict with other third-party modules with a single DotNetNuke portal framework.

From here you have your standard class name, and because you're creating a physical data provider class, you'll also inherit the DataProvider class of DotNetNuke (see Listing 13-8). Each Data Access Layer must implement the methods contained in its DataProvider class, which are overridden for each physical database type (as you'll see later in this chapter).

Listing 13-8: Inheriting the DataProvider Class for the Module

```
Public Class SqlDataProvider
        Inherits DataProvider
```

Each of the following sections of code for the Data Access Layer is broken down by regions. Regions are used in DotNetNuke development to organize code and make the code more readable.

The first region in the class is the Private Members region (see Listing 13-9). In this region, you define the variables for your provider, which is defined within web.config.

Listing 13-9: The Private Members of the Data Access Layer

```
#Region "Private Members"

    Private Const ProviderType As String = "data"
    Private _providerConfiguration As Framework.Providers.⊃
ProviderConfiguration = Framework.Providers.ProviderConfiguration.⊃
GetProviderConfiguration(ProviderType)
    Private _connectionString As String
    Private _providerPath As String
    Private _objectQualifier As String
    Private _databaseOwner As String
#End Region
```

As in the overall DotNetNuke architecture, the code refers to the provider configuration within the data section of web.config (see Listing 13-10). In this section, you define the values for properties in the SqlDataProvider class.

Listing 13-10: Defining the Default Data Provider in the web.config

```
<data defaultProvider="SqlDataProvider">
     <providers>
       <clear />
       <add name="SqlDataProvider"
         type="DotNetNuke.Data.SqlDataProvider, DotNetNuke.SqlDataProvider"
         connectionStringName="SiteSqlServer"
         upgradeConnectionString=""
         providerPath="~\Providers\DataProviders\SqlDataProvider\"
         objectQualifier="" templateFile="DotNetNuke_template.mdf"
         databaseOwner="dbo" />
     </providers>
</data>
```

Next is the Constructors region, where you read web.config and then populate the values from the data section to your private members within your class (see Listing 13-11).

Listing 13-11: Constructors Regions in the SQLDataProvider Class of the Events Module

```
#Region "Constructors"

    Public Sub New()
        ' Read the configuration specific information for this provider
        Dim objProvider As Framework.Providers.Provider = _CType(_provider
Configuration.Providers(_providerConfiguration.DefaultProvider), _ Framework
.Providers.Provider)
        ' Read the attributes for this provider
        If objProvider.Attributes("connectionStringName") <> "" AndAlso _
```

```
System.Configuration.ConfigurationSettings.AppSettings(objProvider.Attributes ↩
("connectionStringName")) <> "" Then
        _connectionString = System.Configuration. ↩
ConfigurationSettings.AppSettings(objProvider.Attributes("connectionStringName"))
    Else
        _connectionString = objProvider.Attributes("connectionString")
    End If
    _providerPath = objProvider.Attributes("providerPath")

    _objectQualifier = objProvider.Attributes("objectQualifier")
    If _objectQualifier <> "" And _objectQualifier.EndsWith("_") = False Then
        _objectQualifier += "_"
    End If

    _databaseOwner = objProvider.Attributes("databaseOwner")
    If _databaseOwner <> "" And _databaseOwner.EndsWith(".") = False Then
        _databaseOwner += "."
    End If

End Sub

#End Region
```

After populating your private members with values from web.config, you then expose some public properties for your class (see Listing 13-12). These properties are read-only and contain the values from web.config.

Listing 13-12: Public Properties — Exposing the Database Connection Information in the SQLDataProvider Class

```
#Region "Properties"

    Public ReadOnly Property ConnectionString() As String
        Get
            Return _connectionString
        End Get
    End Property

    Public ReadOnly Property ProviderPath() As String
        Get
            Return _providerPath
        End Get
    End Property

    Public ReadOnly Property ObjectQualifier() As String
        Get
            Return _objectQualifier
        End Get
    End Property
    Public ReadOnly Property DatabaseOwner() As String
        Get
            Return _databaseOwner
        End Get
    End Property
#End Region
```

The database operations of your class are contained within the Public Methods region (see Listing 13-13). Remember the stored procedures discussed earlier? Now you're going to expose those procedures to your module so you can do your add, update, and delete operations, as well as obtain the data so it can be displayed in your module.

Listing 13-13: Public Methods within the SQLDataProvider Class

```
#Region "Public Methods"

    Private Function GetNull(ByVal Field As Object) As Object
        Return Common.Utilities.Null.GetNull(Field, DBNull.Value)
    End Function

    Public Overrides Function AddEvent(ByVal ModuleId As Integer, _
        ByVal Description As String, ByVal DateTime As Date, _
        ByVal Title As String, ByVal ExpireDate As Date, _
        ByVal UserName As String, ByVal Every As Integer, _
        ByVal Period As String, ByVal IconFile As String, _
        ByVal AltText As String) As Integer
        Return CType(SqlHelper.ExecuteScalar(ConnectionString, _
        DatabaseOwner & ObjectQualifier & "AddEvent", ModuleId, _
        Description, DateTime, Title, GetNull(ExpireDate), _
        UserName, GetNull(Every), GetNull(Period), _
        GetNull(IconFile), GetNull(AltText)), Integer)
    End Function

    Public Overrides Sub DeleteEvent(ByVal ItemId As Integer)
        SqlHelper.ExecuteNonQuery(ConnectionString, DatabaseOwner & _
ObjectQualifier & "DeleteEvent", ItemId)
    End Sub

    Public Overrides Function GetEvent(ByVal ItemId As Integer, _
ByVal ModuleId As Integer) As IDataReader
        Return CType(SqlHelper.ExecuteReader(ConnectionString, _
DatabaseOwner & ObjectQualifier & "GetEvent", ItemId, _
ModuleId), IDataReader)
    End Function

    Public Overrides Function GetEvents(ByVal ModuleId As Integer) As _
IDataReader
        Return CType(SqlHelper.ExecuteReader(ConnectionString, _
DatabaseOwner & ObjectQualifier & "GetEvents", ModuleId), _ IDataReader)
    End Function

    Public Overrides Function GetEventsByDate(ByVal ModuleId As Integer, _
        ByVal StartDate As Date, ByVal EndDate As Date) As IDataReader
        Return CType(SqlHelper.ExecuteReader(ConnectionString, _
DatabaseOwner & ObjectQualifier & "GetEventsByDate", _
```

```
    ModuleId, StartDate, EndDate), IDataReader)
        End Function

        Public Overrides Sub UpdateEvent(ByVal ItemId As Integer, _
            ByVal Description As String, ByVal DateTime As Date, _
            ByVal Title As String, ByVal ExpireDate As Date, _
            ByVal UserName As String, ByVal Every As Integer, _
            ByVal Period As String, ByVal IconFile As String, _
            ByVal AltText As String)
            SqlHelper.ExecuteNonQuery(ConnectionString, DatabaseOwner & _
                ObjectQualifier & "UpdateEvent", ItemId, Description, _
                DateTime, Title, GetNull(ExpireDate), UserName, _
                GetNull(Every), GetNull(Period), GetNull(IconFile), _
                GetNull(AltText))
        End Sub

#End Region
```

You can see that there is a one-to-one relationship within this class, so each method has a corresponding stored procedure within your SQL database. Here's a break down of the `GetEvents` method to explain what is happening.

Each event is a public method that overrides a corresponding method within the base class (DataProvider), which you inherited in the beginning of the class. So not only do you have a corresponding method in this class for each stored procedure, but you also have a corresponding method in the base DataProvider class, which is located in the main module project. The method within the base class is an abstracted method that your module implements, which enables you to separate the physical database interactions from your module assembly.

Next you'll notice that all parameters the stored procedure accepts are passed to your methods as well. In addition, you then execute the command and pass the database connection information such as the connection string, database owner account, object qualifier, name of the stored procedure, and the parameters it accepts.

The method then returns an `IDataReader` containing the result set from the database using the SQLHelper.ExecuteReader provided by the Microsoft Data Access Application Block you imported at the beginning of the class.

Finally, to handle null values returned from the database, DotNetNuke provides the `GetNull` method. When you create a method for your database, as was done in `AddEvent` and `UpdateEvent` in Listing 13-13, you should wrap the parameters with the `GetNull` method. This prevents errors from being raised in your Data Provider due to the null values.

That's it for the Data Access Layer. Remember this layer is compiled into its own assembly binary separate from the module's main assembly. By maintaining this separation, you can easily plug in providers for other databases. In addition, you don't need to recompile your base class when changing database operations or when replacing physical providers.

Data Abstraction

The next part of the module for data operations is the creation of the abstraction class. In the Data Access Layer, you created methods that overrode the base class. Now you need to cover that base class and gain some insight on how you provide an abstraction class for the Events module.

You need to switch over to the main module project (DotNetNuke.Events). In this project, you have a class file called DataProvider.vb. The class contains nothing but overridable methods, which you over-rode within your Data Access Layer class in the previous section.

The first thing you'll do within this class is import the necessary namespaces and define your class (see Listing 13-14). You use the `MustInherit` keyword within your class to specify that the class can be used only as a base class, as it is used in the SqlDataProvider class.

Listing 13-14: Creating the Abstraction Class for the Events Module

```
Imports System
Imports DotNetNuke

Namespace DotNetNuke.Modules.Events
   Public MustInherit Class DataProvider
```

Next is the Shared and Static region (see Listing 13-15) within the class. When the class is instantiated, you call the `CreateProvider` method.

Listing 13-15: Shared/Static Methods in the DataProvider Class of the Events Module

```
#Region "Shared/Static Methods"

        ' singleton reference to the instantiated object
        Private Shared objProvider As DataProvider = Nothing

        ' constructor
        Shared Sub New()
            CreateProvider()
        End Sub

        ' dynamically create provider
        Private Shared Sub CreateProvider()
                objProvider = CType(Framework.Reflection.CreateObject("data", _
                "DotNetNuke.Modules.Events", "DotNetNuke.Modules.Events"), _
                DataProvider)
        End Sub

        ' return the provider
        Public Shared Shadows Function Instance() As DataProvider
            Return objProvider
        End Function

#End Region
```

Finally, within the abstraction class you have what provides the abstraction: the abstraction methods (see Listing 13-16). Remember these methods from your `SqlDataProvider`? Each method contained in this base class has a corresponding method within your Data Access Layer's class. You'll notice each method uses the `MustOverride` keyword to specify that its method will be overridden by the class inheriting the abstraction class.

Listing 13-16: The Abstraction Methods in the DataProvider Class of the Events Module

```
#Region "Abstract methods"

        Public MustOverride Function AddEvent(ByVal ModuleId As Integer, _
            ByVal Description As String, ByVal DateTime As Date, _
            ByVal Title As String, ByVal ExpireDate As Date, _
            ByVal UserName As String, ByVal Every As Integer, _
            ByVal Period As String, ByVal IconFile As String, _
            ByVal AltText As String) As Integer
        Public MustOverride Sub DeleteEvent(ByVal ItemID As Integer)
        Public MustOverride Function GetEvent(ByVal ItemId As Integer, _
            ByVal ModuleId As Integer) As IDataReader
        Public MustOverride Function GetEvents(ByVal ModuleId As Integer) _
            As IDataReader
        Public MustOverride Function GetEventsByDate(ByVal ModuleId As Integer, _
            ByVal StartDate As Date, ByVal EndDate As Date) As IDataReader
        Public MustOverride Sub UpdateEvent(ByVal ItemId As Integer, _
            ByVal Description As String, ByVal DateTime As Date, _
            ByVal Title As String, ByVal ExpireDate As Date, _
            ByVal UserName As String, ByVal Every As Integer, _
            ByVal Period As String, ByVal IconFile As String, _
            ByVal AltText As String)

#End Region

    End Class

End Namespace
```

Now you should see the separation of the module from the physical database. Module development closely mirrors DotNetNuke architecture: all aspects of the application are totally separated from the underlying physical database.

Summary

This chapter covered the physical database creation all the way to the abstraction class contained in your module project. Here are points to remember when developing your database and data classes for your module:

❑   In addition to a primary key for module records, add a module ID field, because each module instance is assigned a unique module ID by the DotNetNuke framework.

❑   Each stored procedure will have a corresponding method contained within the Data Access Layer.

Chapter 13

❑   Each physical database provider will be created in its own assembly project in the same namespace as the module.

❑   Each abstraction base class will contain duplicate method names in the Data Access Layer that must be overridden.

That's it for the Database Layer. The next chapter covers the Business Logic Layer (BLL), in which you take the data from your database and create objects that you later bind to your user controls for display.

Developing Modules: The Business Logic Layer

Previous chapters covered how to create a physical database provider for your module, and how all the methods contained in the provider directly correlate to stored procedures within the database. After the provider was completed, you created an abstraction class that abstracts the methods contained in the provider to be used by the Business Logic Layer (BLL).

In this chapter, you will transform the record set returned by the provider into a collection of objects that is provided by the Business Logic Layer within your module. This chapter continues with concepts that were introduced in Chapter 7 on the DotNetNuke (DNN) architecture, because module architecture mirrors the architecture provided by DNN.

The idea here is to totally separate the physical database from the module or application logic that you create. Separating the two enables plug-and-play extensibility when you want to change a database provider. Because the provider is abstracted from the actual business logic, you can use the same code, but different data stores, and because they're compiled separately, there is no need to recompile the application to change database providers.

You will now extend this provider architecture to the business logic of the application. Here you create a collection of objects with specific properties that will be exposed to your user layer, which is covered in Chapter 15.

Developing the Business Logic Layer

Start by opening the Events module project located in the DotNetNuke.DesktopModules solution in the Solutions directory off of the root of the DotNetNuke distribution package. Open the solution in Visual Studio .NET 2005 to view the module projects; specifically, the DotNetNuke.Events module project you were working with in the previous chapter.

As you'll recall, the DataProvider.vb class within this project is the abstraction class, and it contains overridable methods for each method contained in the physical provider class. Now you will take these methods and wrap them with additional classes to populate an array of objects with specific properties.

Defining the Properties for the Info Class

This section covers the EventsInfo.vb class contained in the project folder. This class is what describes your objects for the Events module that will be returned from the database.

At the top of the class file, do your imports as in the following code:

```
Imports System
Imports System.Configuration
Imports System.Data
```

Following this you have your namespace. For this example, you'll stay within the DotNetNuke namespace, but if you were creating your own modules separate from DNN, you could use a custom namespace in the form of CompanyName.ModuleName:

```
Namespace DotNetNuke.Modules.Events
```

Listing 14-1 shows the Private Members region at the top of the class. Here you define private variables and their types. These variables will be used to store the values for each property for your class.

Listing 14-1: The Private Members Region of the EventInfo Class

```
Public Class EventInfo

#Region "Private Members"

    Private _ItemId As Integer
    Private _ModuleId As Integer
    Private _Description As String
    Private _DateTime As Date
    Private _Title As String
    Private _ExpireDate As Date
    Private _CreatedByUser As String
    Private _CreatedDate As Date
    Private _Every As Integer
    Private _Period As String
    Private _IconFile As String
    Private _AltText As String
    Private _MaxWidth As Integer


#End Region
```

Below the Private Members region is the Constructors region (see Listing 14-2). In object-oriented programming, the constructor is a special method for this class that must be present for the object to be instantiated. In the Events module with VB.NET, it is New. If you needed to write special initialization code for the EventInfo class, you would do so here to ensure the code is executed.

Listing 14-2: The Constructors for the EventInfo Class

```
#Region "Constructors"

    Public Sub New()
    End Sub

#End Region
```

Next are the public properties of the EventInfo class, which are used to define your object (see Listing 14-3). For example, an event has an ItemID, ModuleID, Description, and other properties. These correspond to the fields contained within the database for this module (see Chapter 13).

Listing 14-3: The Public Properties for the EventInfo Class

```
#Region "Properties"

    Public Property ItemId() As Integer
      Get
        Return _ItemId
      End Get
      Set(ByVal Value As Integer)
        _ItemId = Value
      End Set
    End Property

    Public Property ModuleId() As Integer
      Get
        Return _ModuleId
      End Get
      Set(ByVal Value As Integer)
        _ModuleId = Value
      End Set
    End Property

    Public Property Description() As String
      Get
        Return _Description
      End Get
      Set(ByVal Value As String)
        _Description = Value
      End Set
    End Property

    Public Property DateTime() As Date
      Get
        Return _DateTime
      End Get
```

(continued)

Listing 14-3: *(continued)*

```
       Set(ByVal Value As Date)
          _DateTime = Value
       End Set
    End Property

    Public Property Title() As String
       Get
          Return _Title
       End Get
       Set(ByVal Value As String)
          _Title = Value
       End Set
    End Property

    Public Property ExpireDate() As Date
       Get
          Return _ExpireDate
       End Get
       Set(ByVal Value As Date)
          _ExpireDate = Value
       End Set
    End Property

    Public Property CreatedByUser() As String
       Get
          Return _CreatedByUser
       End Get
       Set(ByVal Value As String)
          _CreatedByUser = Value
       End Set
    End Property

    Public Property CreatedDate() As Date
       Get
          Return _CreatedDate
       End Get
       Set(ByVal Value As Date)
          _CreatedDate = Value
       End Set
    End Property

    Public Property Every() As Integer
       Get
          Return _Every
       End Get
       Set(ByVal Value As Integer)
          _Every = Value
       End Set
    End Property

    Public Property Period() As String
```

```
        Get
           Return _Period
        End Get
        Set(ByVal Value As String)
          _Period = Value
        End Set
     End Property

     Public Property IconFile() As String
        Get
           Return _IconFile
        End Get
        Set(ByVal Value As String)
          _IconFile = Value
        End Set
     End Property

     Public Property AltText() As String
        Get
           Return _AltText
        End Get
        Set(ByVal Value As String)
          _AltText = Value
        End Set
     End Property

     Public Property MaxWidth() As Integer
        Get
           Return _MaxWidth
        End Get
        Set(ByVal Value As Integer)
          _MaxWidth = Value
        End Set
     End Property

  #End Region

  End Class


  End Namespace
```

Notice that each property you expose for your object corresponds to a field name in the Events table in DotNetNuke.

Creating Objects Using the Controller Class

Now that you have the properties defined for your objects, you need to populate the objects with values from your database. Object population begins with the Controller class. In this case, the controller is contained in the EventsController.vb class file in the module project. Open the file and review its contents.

Again, at the top of the file are the library imports:

```
Imports DotNetNuke.Services.Search
Imports System
Imports System.Configuration
Imports System.Data
Imports System.XML
```

Following this you again have to specify your namespace:

```
Namespace DotNetNuke.Modules.Events
```

Next, you implement a couple of interfaces after you define your class (see Listing 14-4). In this module, you implement the `Entities.Modules.ISearchable` and `Entities.Modules.IPortable` interfaces. These are two interfaces that provide your module with the capability to tie into the search mechanism and the capability to export data from your module and import it into another instance of your module on another page within the portal. These interfaces are covered in more detail later in this chapter.

Listing 14-4: Defining the Controller Class for the Events Module

```
Public Class EventController
    Implements Entities.Modules.ISearchable
    Implements Entities.Modules.IPortable
```

Listing 14-5 shows the public methods within the Controller class that are used to populate an ArrayList of objects from the record set received from your abstraction class.

Listing 14-5: Public Methods of the EventsController Class

```
#Region "Public Methods"

    Public Sub AddEvent(ByVal objEvent As EventInfo) _
        DataProvider.Instance().AddEvent(objEvent.ModuleId, _
        objEvent.Description, objEvent.DateTime, objEvent.Title, _
        objEvent.ExpireDate, objEvent.CreatedByUser, objEvent.Every, _
        objEvent.Period, objEvent.IconFile, objEvent.AltText)
    End Sub

    Public Sub DeleteEvent(ByVal ItemID As Integer)
        DataProvider.Instance().DeleteEvent(ItemID)
    End Sub

    Public Function GetEvent(ByVal ItemId As Integer, _
            ByVal ModuleId As Integer) As EventInfo
        Return CType(CBO.FillObject(DataProvider.Instance().GetEvent(ItemId, _
            ModuleId), GetType(EventInfo)), EventInfo)
    End Function

    Public Function GetEvents(ByVal ModuleId As Integer, _
            ByVal StartDate As Date, ByVal EndDate As Date) As ArrayList
        If (Not Common.Utilities.Null.IsNull(StartDate)) And _
            (Not Common.Utilities.Null.IsNull(EndDate)) Then
```

```
            Return _
            CBO.FillCollection(DataProvider.Instance().GetEventsByDate(ModuleId, _
                StartDate, EndDate), GetType(EventInfo))
        Else
            Return _
            CBO.FillCollection(DataProvider.Instance().GetEvents(ModuleId), _
                GetType(EventInfo))
        End If
    End Function

    Public Sub UpdateEvent(ByVal objEvent As EventInfo)
        DataProvider.Instance().UpdateEvent(objEvent.ItemId, _
            objEvent.Description, objEvent.DateTime, objEvent.Title, _
            objEvent.ExpireDate, objEvent.CreatedByUser, objEvent.Every, _
            objEvent.Period, objEvent.IconFile, objEvent.AltText)
    End Sub

#End Region
```

In Listing 14-5, notice that AddEvent, DeleteEvent, GetEvent, GetEvents, and UpdateEvent are all methods in the Data Abstraction class (DataProvider.vb) in the Events module project of the solution. Each method creates an instance of the DataProvider class, and calls its corresponding event. Recall from Chapter 13 that each method in the abstraction class (DataProvider.vb in the Events module project) also has a corresponding method in the physical provider (the SQLDataProvider project) as a wrapper to the stored procedures contained in the SQL Server database. Each method accepts a value that corresponds to values passed to parameters contained in the stored procedure. For example, the DeleteEvent stored procedure contains a parameter of ItemID for specifying the primary key of the event contained in the Events table. As such, Sub DeleteEvent in the Controller class accepts an ItemID of type Integer.

Custom Business Object Help Class

As an item of note here, DotNetNuke provides the Custom Business Object (CBO) helper class. The class file is located in the <webroot>\Components\Shared\CBO.vb class file.

This class provides several methods, but for this area of concern, you want to focus on two:

❑   FillObject: Creates an object with one item as in the case with the GetEvent method in Listing 14-5.

❑   FillCollection: Creates an ArrayList of objects from matching records returned from the database.

Optional Interfaces for the Events Module Controller Class

The last code region in the EventsController class is the Optional Interfaces region. Contained in this region are methods for interacting with the ISearchable and IPortable interfaces provided by DotNetNuke. You do not have to use these methods, but it is recommended to provide a fully functional module that is capable of exposing all the features of DotNetNuke.

ISearchable

Listing 14-6 defines properties of the individual events from your module to be placed in the search catalog of the DotNetNuke index.

Listing 14-6: Defining Search Items of the Module for DotNetNuke Search

```
Public Function GetSearchItems(ByVal ModInfo As Entities.Modules.ModuleInfo) As _
            Services.Search.SearchItemInfoCollection Implements _
            Entities.Modules.ISearchable.GetSearchItems
    Dim SearchItemCollection As New SearchItemInfoCollection
    Dim Events As ArrayList = GetEvents(ModInfo.ModuleID, _
            Convert.ToDateTime(Common.Utilities.Null.NullDate), _
            Convert.ToDateTime(Common.Utilities.Null.NullDate))

    Dim objEvents As Object
    For Each objEvents In Events
        Dim SearchItem As SearchItemInfo
        With CType(objEvents, EventInfo)
            Dim UserId As Integer = Null.NullInteger
            If IsNumeric(.CreatedByUser) Then
                UserId = Integer.Parse(.CreatedByUser)
            End If
            SearchItem = New SearchItemInfo(ModInfo.ModuleTitle & _
                " - " & .Title, .Description, UserId, .CreatedDate, _
                ModInfo.ModuleID, .ItemId.ToString, .Description, "ItemId=" & _
                .ItemId.ToString)
            SearchItemCollection.Add(SearchItem)
        End With
    Next
    Return SearchItemCollection

End Function
```

Listing 14-6 contains a function called `GetSearchItems`, which will return a type of `SearchItemInfoCollection` that contains the values from the Events module when you call the `GetEvents` method. You loop through the events returned from calling `GetEvents` and create a new object of `SearchItem`. You then define the properties of the `SearchItem` by using the `SearchItemInfo`. You'll pass the values for the object to the `SearchItem`, which will be populated into the DotNetNuke catalog for searching. If you do not want to make the items searchable in the portal, do not implement the interface and exclude the `GetSearchItems` function.

This should sound very familiar after getting to this point in the book. Module development closely mirrors the architecture of DotNetNuke. Not only does the core application support abstraction classes and the Provider Model extensively, but you should also duplicate this methodology in your own development. This ensures your development is consistent with other modules contained in DotNetNuke and also eases the process of upgrading for future versions of DotNetNuke.

Note that the SearchItemInfo class exposes properties for the `SearchItem` object, similar to the Events class. This structure is consistent throughout the DotNetNuke architecture and in module development as well.

IPortable

Another DotNetNuke interface that the Events module implements is `IPortable`. This interface provides the module with the capability to export the data contained for that module instance to another module instance.

Listing 14-7 looks at how you export data from the module instance.

Listing 14-7: The ExportModule Function for the EventsController Class

```
Public Function ExportModule(ByVal ModuleID As Integer) As _
        String Implements Entities.Modules.IPortable.ExportModule
    Dim strXML As String = ""
    Dim arrEvents As ArrayList = GetEvents(ModuleID, _
            Convert.ToDateTime(Common.Utilities.Null.NullDate), _
            Convert.ToDateTime(Common.Utilities.Null.NullDate))
    If arrEvents.Count <> 0 Then
        strXML += "<events>"
        Dim objEvent As EventInfo
        For Each objEvent In arrEvents
            strXML += "<event>"
            strXML += "<description>" & XMLEncode(objEvent.Description) & _
                    "</description>"
            strXML += "<datetime>" & XMLEncode(objEvent.DateTime.ToString) & _
                    "</datetime>"
            strXML += "<title>" & XMLEncode(objEvent.Title) & "</title>"
            strXML += "</event>"
        Next
        strXML += "</events>"
    End If
    Return strXML
End Function
```

Again as in the population of the search catalog, you call the `GetEvents` method to obtain all events for this particular instance of the module. You then loop through the results and generate an XML string, which will be returned by the function. In your user layer, you will implement the method that will then be called based on the user action.

Listing 14-8 looks at how you import the data from the previously generated XML string.

Listing 14-8: The ImportModule Function for the EventsController Class

```
Public Sub ImportModule(ByVal ModuleID As Integer, ByVal Content As String, _
        ByVal Version As String, ByVal UserId As Integer) _
        Implements Entities.Modules.IPortable.ImportModule
    Dim xmlEvent As XmlNode
    Dim xmlEvents As XmlNode = GetContent(Content, "events")
    For Each xmlEvent In xmlEvents.SelectNodes("event")
        Dim objEvent As New EventInfo
        objEvent.ModuleId = ModuleID
        objEvent.Description = xmlEvent.Item("description").InnerText
```

(continued)

Listing 14-8: *(continued)*

```
            objEvent.DateTime = Date.Parse(xmlEvent.Item("datetime").InnerText)
            objEvent.Title = xmlEvent.Item("title").InnerText
            objEvent.CreatedByUser = UserId.ToString
            AddEvent(objEvent)
        Next

    End Sub
```

As you can see in Listing 14-8, the XML generated by the ExportModule routine in Listing 14-7 is processed. This time, you call the AddEvent method of the EventController to populate an event for an element in the XML file.

Summary

This chapter completes the process of obtaining data from your database. In Chapter 13, you learned how to write a provider for a physical database. In this chapter, you learned the following:

❑ You converted the data to a collection of objects that will get bound to user controls in your modules.

❑ In building your Business Logic Layer for your modules, you can take advantage of two interfaces provided by the DotNetNuke core:

    ❑ IPortable — Provides your modules with the capability to export the data and settings of one module instance over to another module instance within your portal.

    ❑ ISearchable — Enables your modules to take advantage of the full-text indexing capabilities that are native to DotNetNuke to allow your module to be included in the portal search mechanism.

Chapter 15 covers the user interface of the module. You'll take the collections created by the Business Logic Layer and bind them to controls on your module.

Developing Modules: The Presentation Layer

Now you're at a point where you can start making your presentation layer for your desktop module. You have learned how to pull data from the database, provide abstraction, and then transform the data to a collection of objects from your Controller class. This chapter provides you with examples on how to display, modify, and work with the various controls that make up your desktop module in DotNetNuke (DNN).

The examples in this chapter first show you how to make a call to the business object to obtain the information, and then you'll create an Edit control to update the data and to specify settings that are specific to the module instance.

From there, the chapter moves on to the various user controls and interfaces that you can use to your advantage in your module development.

Module User Interfaces

Chapter 12 introduced you to module structure and how to manually create references to controls to define your module. Each module consists of a couple of user controls that enable the user to interface with your application logic. These controls provide a means to view and modify the data contained in the database supporting the module. DotNetNuke provides you with the ability to define these controls and interface them into your application using a module definition.

Table 15-1 lists the files that make up a module, their keys (see Chapter 12), and their function. This example continues with the Events module as in previous chapters.

Table 15-1: Module Definitions in Relation to the Events Module

Type	Filename (Events Module)	Key	Description
View	DesktopModules\Events\ Events.ascx		The control your users will see on the first request to the module. You can define multiple view controls for your module. The main thing to keep in mind is that the purpose of the view is to display your data.
Edit	DesktopModules\Events\ EditEvents.ascx DesktopModules\Events\ Settings.ascx	Edit Settings	Used to edit information contained in the database. A DesktopModule can consist of several edit controls based on the complexity of the module. Security for edit permissions is normally done at the module level contained within a specific page.
Admin	N/A	N/A	Not used in the Events module example, but this control will be displayed to administrators for a portal.
Anonymous	N/A	N/A	Provides an anonymous view of your data for your DesktopModule.
Host	N/A	N/A	For displaying a host-only control for your module.

As you can see from this table, several controls are available that you can make use of in your development. The defined types are specific to the user role within a portal. For module development, there may be data that you want to allow certain roles to access. For example, if the module manipulates the application settings or file system, you would want to restrict that functionality to the host who has control over the overall application instance. Your module may modify settings configured at a portal level, like the banner ad management system, in which case you could restrict the control to just administrators within a portal.

You can select many different configurations when doing module development. For now, the focus is to continue the Events module development covered in the previous two chapters.

The preceding table covered the controls specific to the Events module. The Events module consists of three primary user controls for displaying and manipulating data:

❑ **View** (DesktopModules\Events\Events.ascx): Displays the events either in a listing format sorted by event date or in a calendar format.

❑ **Settings** (DesktopModules\Events\Settings.ascx): Used to configure module-specific settings like the display.

❑ **Edit** (DesktopModules\Events\EditEvents.ascx): Used to add and update information for each specific event

The next few sections describe each control, and display data from the collection that was defined in the Business Logic Layer covered in Chapter 14.

View Control

In the Events module, the View control is located in the DesktopModules\Events directory and is called Events.ascx. Open the Events project and look at the user interface to see the controls it contains. There are two primary controls: DataList and Calendar. These two controls provide the module with two different views on the events data based on what is configured via the Edit control (discussed later in the chapter). Listing 15-1 reviews the DataList control from the Events.ascx file.

Listing 15-1: DataList Control in the Events.ascx Page

```
<asp:datalist id="lstEvents" runat="server" EnableViewState="false"
summary="Events Design Table">
    <itemtemplate>
        <table summary="Events Design Table">
            <tr>
                <td id="colIcon" runat="server" valign="top" align="center"
rowspan="3" width='<%# DataBinder.Eval(Container.DataItem,"MaxWidth") %>'>
                    <asp:Image ID="imgIcon" AlternateText='<%#
DataBinder.Eval(Container.DataItem,"AltText") %>' runat="server" ImageUrl=
'<%# FormatImage(DataBinder.Eval(Container.DataItem,"IconFile")) %>' Visible=
'<%# FormatImage(DataBinder.Eval(Container.DataItem,"IconFile")) <> ""
%>'></asp:Image>
                </td>
                <td>
                    <asp:HyperLink id="editLink" NavigateUrl='<%# EditURL
("ItemID",DataBinder.Eval(Container.DataItem,"ItemID")) %>' Visible="<%#
IsEditable %>" runat="server"><asp:Image id="editLinkImage" ImageUrl=
"~/images/edit.gif" Visible="<%# IsEditable %>" AlternateText="Edit"
runat="server" /></asp:HyperLink>
                    <asp:Label ID="lblTitle" Runat="server" Cssclass=
"SubHead" text='<%# DataBinder.Eval(Container.DataItem,"Title") %>'></asp:Label>
                </td>
            </tr>
            <tr>
                <td>
                    <asp:Label ID="lblDateTime" Runat="server" Cssclass=
"SubHead" text='<%# FormatDateTime(DataBinder.Eval(Container.DataItem,
"DateTime")) %>'></asp:Label>
                </td>
            </tr>
            <tr>
                <td>
                    <asp:Label ID="lblDescription" Runat="server" CssClass=
"Normal" text='<%# DataBinder.Eval(Container.DataItem,"Description") %>'>
</asp:Label>
                </td>
            </tr>
        </table>
    </ItemTemplate>
</asp:datalist>
```

You are going to bind the DataList to values from your database that are returned from a stored procedure and then up to the provider covered in Chapter 13. The field names are MaxWidth, AltText, IconFile, ItemID, Title, DateTime, and Description.

The Calendar control contained in the page provides an alternative view for the module (see Listing 15-2).

Listing 15-2: Calendar Control within the Events.ascx Provides Another View

```
<asp:calendar id="calEvents" runat="server" BorderWidth="1" CssClass="Normal" ⟲
SelectionMode="None" summary="Events Calendar Design Table">
    <dayheaderstyle backcolor="#EEEEEE" cssclass="NormalBold" borderwidth="1">⟲
</DayHeaderStyle>
    <daystyle cssclass="Normal" borderwidth="1" verticalalign="Top"></DayStyle>
    <othermonthdaystyle forecolor="#FFFFFF"></OtherMonthDayStyle>
    <titlestyle font-bold="True"></TitleStyle>
    <nextprevstyle cssclass="NormalBold"></NextPrevStyle>
</asp:calendar>
```

View Control Code-Behind Class

Now that you have some controls on the form, you need to bind some data to them for display. Recall from Chapter 13 that you can take data from an abstraction class, which DotNetNuke can then convert to a collection of objects via the Custom Business Object (CBO) helper class (see Chapter 7). Now you need to take the ArrayList of objects and bind them to your controls in the Events.ascx.vb code-behind file, located in the Events project.

At the top of your class, you first need to do your name imports, declare your namespace, and define your class:

```
Imports DotNetNuke
Imports System.Web.UI.WebControls

Namespace DotNetNuke.Modules.Events
Public MustInherit Class Events

        Inherits Entities.Modules.PortalModuleBase
```

PortalModuleBase Class

You inherit from the Entities.Modules.PortalModuleBase class. The PortalModuleBase class file is located in the main DotNetNuke project in the <webroot>\Components\Modules\PortalModuleBase.vb file. In addition to inheriting from the UserControl class of ASP.NET, this class is central to your module development efforts. It provides several important methods and properties for your module (see Table 15-2).

Table 15-2: Some PortalModuleBase Class Exposed Methods and Properties

Property	Type	Description

IsEditable	Boolean	Can be used as a reference to check and see if the current user has permissions to edit the module. This is defined in the properties for the DesktopModule in DotNetNuke. For example:
		`If IsEditable Then`
		`        txtEditField.Visible = True`
		`End If`

LocalResourceFile	String	Contains the path value of the resource file that is being used for the module. This enables you to support localization for your modules. This is covered in more detail in Chapter 8.
HelpFile	String	Contains a value to a local path for a text file containing help information.
HelpURL	String	Contains a value for a URL for an external help file for the specific module.
ModuleConfiguration	ModuleInfo	Provides information about a specific module.
PortalId	Integer	ID of the current portal that the request is for. This is an integer value that is generated by DotNetNuke when a host creates a new portal.
TabId	Integer	ID of the current page that the request is going to. This is generated by DotNetNuke when an admin creates a new page within the portal.
TabModuleId	Integer	Contains a value of module within a tab. Multiple tab modules can point to the same Module ID, allowing two instances of a module to point to the same date.
ModuleId	Integer	Returns the current ID of a specific module instance. This is an integer value that is generated by DotNetNuke when you add a new instance of a module into a page.
UserInfo	UserInfo	Contains information for the portal users.
UserId	Integer	Returns the ID of the current logged-on user.
PortalAlias	PortalAliasInfo	Contains various information pertaining to the current portal.

Table continued on following page

Property	Type	Description
PortalSettings	PortalSettings	Contains setting information specific to a portal, such as the admin e-mail.

Settings	HashTable	The Settings hash table is very important to module development, and is probably one of the most common tools you'll use. Consider it analogous to the registry in Windows. You can use the Settings hash to store and retrieve a key/value pair specific to your module instance. For example, to retrieve a value from the Settings hash:
		
		`Dim myVar As String =`
		`Settings("mykey").ToString`
		
		To set a value:
		
		`Dim objModules As New`
		
		`    Entities.Modules.ModuleController`
		`objModules.UpdateTabModuleSetting`
		`(TabModuleId, "mykey", myVar)`

ContainerControl	Control	Provides a container to wrap a module (see Chapter 6 to learn about what a container is).
HasModulePermission	Boolean	Checks permissions for a specific module instance, such as edit and view.

DotNetNuke Optional Interfaces

Right below your class declaration, you have the option to implement several interfaces:

```
Implements Entities.Modules.IActionable
Implements Entities.Modules.IPortable
Implements Entities.Modules.ISearchable
```

These interfaces provide you with the ability to tie into the Menu control for your module. As covered previously in this book, each module contains a menu with a list of action items. To add items to the menus you need to implement the IActionable interface. This is also true with the IPortable interface, which provides an export and import function for the module, and the ISearchable interface, which enables your module to take advantage of the integrated search engine within DotNetNuke. (See Chapter 8 and Chapter 14 for more information on these interfaces and how to use them in your modules.)

These interfaces are optional. At the bottom of the Events.ascx.vb class file, there is a code region with the name "Optional Interfaces." Within this region is the code showing you how to implement these interfaces (see Listing 15-3).

Listing 15-3: Optional Interfaces Region of the Events Module

```
#Region "Optional Interfaces"

        Public ReadOnly Property ModuleActions() As _
                Entities.Modules.Actions.ModuleActionCollection Implements _
                Entities.Modules.IActionable.ModuleActions
            Get
                Dim Actions As New _
                    Entities.Modules.Actions.ModuleActionCollection
                Actions.Add(GetNextActionID, _
    Localization.GetString(Entities.Modules.Actions.ModuleActionType.AddContent, _
    LocalResourceFile), Entities.Modules.Actions.ModuleActionType.AddContent, _
    "", "", EditUrl(), False, Security.SecurityAccessLevel.Edit, True, False)
                Return Actions
            End Get
        End Property

        Public Function ExportModule(ByVal ModuleID As Integer) As String _
            Implements Entities.Modules.IPortable.ExportModule
            ' included as a stub only so that the core knows this
            ' module Implements Entities.Modules.IPortable
        End Function

        Public Sub ImportModule(ByVal ModuleID As Integer, _
            ByVal Content As String, ByVal Version As String, ByVal UserId As _
            Integer) Implements Entities.Modules.IPortable.ImportModule
            ' included as a stub only so that the core knows
            ' this module Implements Entities.Modules.IPortable
        End Sub

        Public Function GetSearchItems(ByVal ModInfo As _
            Entities.Modules.ModuleInfo) As _
            Services.Search.SearchItemInfoCollection Implements _
            Entities.Modules.ISearchable.GetSearchItems
            ' included as a stub only so that the core knows this
            ' module Implements Entities.Modules.ISearchable
        End Function

#End Region
```

As you can see in Listing 15-3, the first method is ModuleActions. Here you implement the IActionable interface to add items into the menu for the module. You have a collection of menu items, with an accompanying action. In this example, you add a menu item using the Actions.Add method. You can see that instead of passing an absolute value for the menu listing, you're using a localized string using the Localization.GetString method. By using the localization interface provided by DotNetNuke (see Chapter 8), you can have menu items displayed in the language of the current user's profile. Because this action is going to be for editing the module, you will pass EditURL as the action property for this item. This will load your Edit control when the user selects this option from the menu. In addition to localization and the control to load properties, there are security parameters to pass as well. By specifying the security type for the item display, you can restrict the functionality to specific roles configured within your portal. In this example, you check for users with edit permissions for the module by passing the value Security.SecurityAccessLevel.Edit.

Below the menu action item method in Listing 15-3 are the methods covered in Chapter 14 for implementing search and import/export functionality for the module. Recall that these methods make a call to the GetEvents method within the Business Logic Layer (BLL) class. You then iterate through all the events for this module instance and either load them into the search or generate an XML feed for export. Now, you need to implement a stub for these methods for the core to know that the module implements the interfaces. DotNetNuke will then execute the corresponding methods contained in your BLL class.

Code-Behind Regions

You need to break your class into several regions. DotNetNuke makes use of named regions throughout the code to provide some organization to the code, and for better readability. Here's a breakdown of the code regions for this specific module. The first of these regions are the Controls and Private Members regions. As in any ASP.NET development, you need to declare your web controls to expose the actions, properties, and methods that they contain. In addition, for this specific example there are some private members — an array of events defined and an integer value for the current month (see Listing 15-4).

Listing 15-4: Controls and Private Members Regions of the Events Module

```
#Region "Controls"
            Protected WithEvents lstEvents As System.Web.UI.WebControls.DataList
            Protected WithEvents calEvents As System.Web.UI.WebControls.Calendar
#End Region

#Region "Private Members"
            Dim arrEvents(31) As String
            Dim intMonth As Integer
#End Region
```

Following these two regions, you begin to get into some code that is going to do something. This code is contained in the Private Methods region. Normally, your private methods are going to contain methods that will obtain your data and bind to your controls. In this example, there is one method called the GetCalendarEvents subroutine, which accepts a start date and an end date for obtaining information from your database (see Listing 15-5). Chapter 13 covered the various stored procedures for this module, and this method is what calls that process of obtaining a collection from the Business Logic Layer by calling the GetEvents method. With abstraction, the BLL then calls the abstraction layer, which contains a method that is overridden by the physical provider class that calls the SQL stored procedure GetEvents. The stored procedure then returns the fields matching the query to the physical provider, which finally is converted by DotNetNuke's Custom Business Object helper class to a collection of objects you define in the BLL. This collection, or ArrayList, is then bound to the controls that were placed on the page, in this case either a Calendar or DataList control.

Listing 15-5: GetCalendarEvents Method of the Events Module

```
#Region "Private Methods"
    Private Sub GetCalendarEvents(ByVal StartDate As String, ByVal _
        EndDate As String)
        Try
            Dim objEvents As New EventController
                Dim strDayText As String
                Dim datTargetDate As Date
                Dim datDate As Date
```

```
                    Dim blnDisplay As Boolean
                    Array.Clear(arrEvents, 0, 32)
                    Dim Arr As ArrayList = objEvents.GetEvents(ModuleId, _
                        Convert.ToDateTime(StartDate), _
                            Convert.ToDateTime(EndDate))
                    Dim i As Integer
                    For i = 0 To Arr.Count - 1
                        Dim objEvent As EventInfo = CType(Arr(i), EventInfo)
                        'While dr.Read()
                        If objEvent.Period.ToString = "" Then
                            strDayText = "<br>"
                        If Not objEvent.IconFile = "" Then
                            strDayText += "<img alt=""" & objEvent.AltText & """ _
                                src=""" & FormatImage(objEvent.IconFile) & """ _
                                border=""0""><br>"
                        End If
                        If IsEditable Then
                            strDayText += "<a href=""" & _
                                CType(Common.Globals.ApplicationPath, String) & _
                                "/" & glbDefaultPage & "?tabid=" & TabId & _
                                "&mid=" & ModuleId & "&ctl=Edit" & "&ItemID=" & _
                                objEvent.ItemId & "&VisibleDate=" & _
                                calEvents.VisibleDate.ToShortDateString & _
                                """><img alt=""Edit"" src=""" & _
                                CType(Common.Globals.ApplicationPath, String) & _
                                "/images/edit.gif"" border=""0""></a> "
                        End If
                        strDayText += "<span class=""ItemTitle"">" & _
                            objEvent.Title & "</span>"
                        If objEvent.DateTime.ToString("HH:mm") <> "00:00" Then
                            strDayText += "<br><span class=""Normal"">" & _
                                objEvent.DateTime.ToShortTimeString & "</span>"
                        End If
                        strDayText += "<br><span class=""Normal"">" & _
                            Server.HtmlDecode(objEvent.Description) & "</span>"
                        arrEvents(CDate(objEvent.DateTime).Day) += strDayText
                    Else                                    ' recurring event
                            datTargetDate = CType(objEvent.DateTime, Date)
                        datDate = Date.Parse(StartDate)

While datDate <= Date.Parse(EndDate)
    blnDisplay = False
    Select Case objEvent.Period
Case CType("D", Char)                           ' day
    If DateDiff(DateInterval.Day, datTargetDate.Date, _
            datDate) Mod objEvent.Every = 0 Then
blnDisplay = True
            End If
Case CType("W", Char)                           ' week
    If DateAdd(DateInterval.WeekOfYear, _
            DateDiff(DateInterval.WeekOfYear, _
            datTargetDate.Date, datDate), _
            datTargetDate.Date) = datDate Then
```

(continued)

Listing 15-5: *(continued)*

```
If DateDiff(DateInterval.WeekOfYear, _
        datTargetDate.Date, datDate) Mod _
        objEvent.Every = 0 Then
                                blnDisplay = True
                    End If
                End If
            Case CType("M", Char)        ' month
If DateAdd(DateInterval.Month, _
      DateDiff(DateInterval.Month, datTargetDate.Date, _
      datDate), datTargetDate.Date) = datDate Then
If DateDiff(DateInterval.Month, _
        datTargetDate.Date, datDate) Mod _
        objEvent.Every = 0 Then blnDisplay = True

                    End If
                End If
            Case CType("Y", Char)              ' year
                If DateAdd(DateInterval.Year, _
                  DateDiff(DateInterval.Year, datTargetDate.Date, _
                  datDate), datTargetDate.Date) = datDate Then
                    If DateDiff(DateInterval.Year, datTargetDate.Date, _
                      datDate) Mod objEvent.Every = 0 Then
                        blnDisplay = True
                    End If
                End If
        End Select
        If blnDisplay Then
          If datDate < datTargetDate.Date Then
            blnDisplay = False
          End If
        End If
        If blnDisplay Then
          If Not _
            Common.Utilities.Null.IsNull(objEvent.ExpireDate) Then
              If datDate > CType(objEvent.ExpireDate, Date) Then
                blnDisplay = False
              End If
          End If
        End If
        If blnDisplay Then
          strDayText = "<br>"
          If Not objEvent.IconFile = "" Then
            strDayText += "<img alt=""" & objEvent.AltText & """ _
               src=""" & FormatImage(objEvent.IconFile) & """ _
               border=""0""><br>"
          End If
          'check to see if the current user has edit permissions
          If IsEditable Then
            strDayText += "<a href=""" & _
               CType(Common.Globals.ApplicationPath, String) & _
               "/" & glbDefaultPage & "?tabid=" & TabId & _
               "&mid=" & ModuleId & "&ctl=Edit" & "&ItemID=" & _
```

```
                           objEvent.ItemId & "&VisibleDate=" & _
                           calEvents.VisibleDate.ToShortDateString & _
                           """><img alt=""Edit"" src=""" & _
                           CType(Common.Globals.ApplicationPath, String) & _
                           "/images/edit.gif"" border=""0""></a> "
                   End If
                   strDayText += "<span class=""ItemTitle"">" & _
                       objEvent.Title & "</span>"
                   If objEvent.DateTime.ToString("HH:mm") <> "00:00" Then
                       strDayText += "<br><span class=""Normal"">" & _
                           objEvent.DateTime.ToShortTimeString & "</span>"
                   End If
                   strDayText += "<br><span class=""Normal"">" & _
                       Server.HtmlDecode(objEvent.Description) & "</span>"
                   arrEvents(datDate.Day) += strDayText
                       End If
                   datDate = DateAdd(DateInterval.Day, 1, datDate)
               End While
           End If
       Next
     intMonth = CDate(StartDate).Month
     calEvents.DataBind()
     Catch exc As Exception                     'Module failed to load
     ProcessModuleLoadException(Me, exc)
     End Try
   End Sub

#End Region
```

The majority of the code in Listing 15-5 is specific to what you're doing for displaying the data. In a simple module, you'd bind the result set to a control, like so:

```
Dim objEvents As New EventsController
myDatalist.DataSource = objEvents.GetEvents(ModuleId, _
                        Convert.ToDateTime(StartDate), _
                        Convert.ToDateTime(EndDate))
myDataList.DataBind
```

However, because you have some criteria on how you want to display events, you load the result set into an ArrayList, which you then iterate through and format the data for display.

Other items to note in Listing 15-5 include the use of the IsEditable Boolean value to check to see if the user has permissions to edit content for the module. If the value is true, you display an edit icon to enable the user to edit events that are displayed.

Finally, in the exception catching, there's a call to ProcessModuleLoadException. The DotNetNuke framework provides this method for error trapping, which is discussed later in this chapter.

The next region in this example is the Public Methods region, where you expose any methods that you want to make available outside of this class. Here you're dealing primarily with formatting methods and calculating the day of the month (see Listing 15-6). Note that these methods should be declared public because your acsx class needs to access them at runtime.

Listing 15-6: Public Methods Contained in the Events Module

```
#Region "Public Methods"
    Public Function FormatDateTime(ByVal DateTime As Date) As String
Try
    FormatDateTime = DateTime.ToLongDateString
    If DatePart(DateInterval.Hour, DateTime) <> 0 Or _
        DatePart(DateInterval.Minute, DateTime) <> 0 Or _
        DatePart(DateInterval.Second, DateTime) <> 0 Then
FormatDateTime = FormatDateTime & " at " & _
        DateTime.ToShortTimeString
                End If
            Catch exc As Exception              'Module failed to load
                ProcessModuleLoadException(Me, exc)
            End Try
        End Function

        Public Function FormatImage(ByVal IconFile As String) As String
            Try
                If Not IconFile = "" Then
                FormatImage = PortalSettings.HomeDirectory & IconFile.ToString
                End If
            Catch exc As Exception              'Module failed to load
                ProcessModuleLoadException(Me, exc)
            End Try
        End Function

    Public Function GetFirstDayofMonth(ByVal datDate As Date) As String
            Try
                Dim datFirstDayofMonth As Date = DateSerial(datDate.Year, _
            datDate.Month, 1)
                Return GetMediumDate(datFirstDayofMonth.ToString)
            Catch exc As Exception              'Module failed to load
                ProcessModuleLoadException(Me, exc)
            End Try
        End Function

        Public Function GetLastDayofMonth(ByVal datDate As Date) As String
            Try
                Dim intDaysInMonth As Integer = Date.DaysInMonth(datDate.Year, _
            datDate.Month)
                Dim datLastDayofMonth As Date = DateSerial(datDate.Year, _
            datDate.Month, intDaysInMonth)
                Return GetMediumDate(datLastDayofMonth.ToString)
            Catch exc As Exception              'Module failed to load
                ProcessModuleLoadException(Me, exc)
            End Try
        End Function

#End Region
```

The next region in the code is the Event Handlers section. As you know from ASP.NET programming, event handlers are methods that respond to a certain action, be it an action performed by a user, such as a click event, or a system action such as the page loading. The page load event in your module is usually where you determine the initial state of your user control. For example, you may check to see if the request is a postback, which means the user clicked a link button or form button to call the module again. Listing 15-7 looks at the code in the Event Handlers section to see how the page load is handled in this module.

Listing 15-7: Event Handlers Region in the Events Module

```
#Region "Event Handlers"
        Private Sub Page_Load(ByVal sender As System.Object, ByVal e As _
        System.EventArgs) Handles MyBase.Load
            Try
                Dim EventView As String = CType(Settings("eventview"), _
                String)
                If EventView Is Nothing Then
                   EventView = "C"                         ' calendar
                End If

                Dim objEvents As New EventController
            Select Case EventView
                Case "L"                                 ' list
                     lstEvents.Visible = True
                     calEvents.Visible = False
                     lstEvents.DataSource = objEvents.GetEvents(ModuleId, _
                      Convert.ToDateTime(Common.Utilities.Null.NullDate), _
                      Convert.ToDateTime(Common.Utilities.Null.NullDate))
                     lstEvents.DataBind()
                Case "C"                                 ' calendar
                     lstEvents.Visible = False
                     calEvents.Visible = True
                If Not Page.IsPostBack Then
                        If Not Request.QueryString("VisibleDate") _
                        Is Nothing Then
                          calEvents.VisibleDate = _
                          CType(Request.QueryString("VisibleDate"), _
                          Date)
                    Else
                          calEvents.VisibleDate = Now
                    End If
                    If CType(Settings("eventcalendarcellwidth"), _
                    String) <> "" Then

    calEvents.Width = _
System.Web.UI.WebControls.Unit.Parse(CType(Settings("eventcalendarcellwidth"), _
                    String) & "px")

                End If
```

(continued)

Listing 15-7: *(continued)*

```
                    If CType(Settings("eventcalendarcellheight"), _
                       String) <> "" Then
                       calEvents.Height = _
   System.Web.UI.WebControls.Unit.Parse(CType(Settings("eventcalendarcellheight"), _
                       String) & "px")
                    End If
                 Else
                    If calEvents.VisibleDate = #12:00:00 AM# Then
                       calEvents.VisibleDate = Now
                    End If
                 End If

                 Dim StartDate As String = _
                 GetFirstDayofMonth(calEvents.VisibleDate) & " 00:00"
                 Dim EndDate As String = _
                 GetLastDayofMonth(calEvents.VisibleDate) & " 23:59"
                 GetCalendarEvents(StartDate, EndDate)
              End Select
           Catch exc As Exception                  'Module failed to load
              ProcessModuleLoadException(Me, exc)
           End Try
        End Sub

        Private Sub calEvents_DayRender(ByVal sender As Object, ByVal e As _
           System.Web.UI.WebControls.DayRenderEventArgs) Handles _
           calEvents.DayRender
           Try
              If e.Day.Date.Month = intMonth Then
                 Dim ctlLabel As Label = New Label
                 ctlLabel.Text = arrEvents(e.Day.Date.Day)
                 e.Cell.Controls.Add(ctlLabel)
              End If
           Catch exc As Exception                  'Module failed to load
              ProcessModuleLoadException(Me, exc)
           End Try
        End Sub

        Private Sub calEvents_VisibleMonthChanged(ByVal sender As Object, _
          ByVal e As System.Web.UI.WebControls.MonthChangedEventArgs) Handles _
          calEvents.VisibleMonthChanged
           Try
              Dim StartDate As String = GetFirstDayofMonth(e.NewDate.Date) & _
              " 00:00"
              Dim EndDate As String = GetLastDayofMonth(e.NewDate.Date) & _
              " 23:59"
              GetCalendarEvents(StartDate, EndDate)
          Catch exc As Exception                   'Module failed to load
              ProcessModuleLoadException(Me, exc)
           End Try
        End Sub
#End Region
```

In the `Page_Load` event, one of the first things you do is check the value contained within the Settings hash. Remember from Table 15-2 that the `Settings` hash is similar to the Windows registry where you can store key/value pairs. For example, you first check to see the view:

```
Dim EventView As String = CType(Settings("eventview"), String)
```

This is the purpose of the `Settings` hash — it enables you to have unique values for each module's instance. It provides maximum code reuse to similar functions. In the Events module example, you can specify different displays for events for each instance. That could be applied to any module to provide maximum flexibility for your application. You can see that throughout this method there are various keys checked for this module to obtain values.

Continuing through Listing 15-7, you can see that some of the private methods covered earlier in this chapter are called for displaying of date information. In addition, you also make a call to the EventsController to bind to your DataList. This is based on the value contained within your Settings (`"eventview"`) key. If you're in list view (L), you will bind to the controller and call the `GetEvents` method. Remember, you bring the data from the various layers starting with the physical database provider to the BLL:

```
Dim objEvents As New EventController
::
::
lstEvents.DataSource = objEvents.GetEvents(ModuleId, _
                    Convert.ToDateTime(Common.Utilities.Null.NullDate), _
                    Convert.ToDateTime(Common.Utilities.Null.NullDate))
lstEvents.DataBind()
```

The call to `Common.Utilities.Null.NullDate` provides you with a null object of the date type to pass to your method to return all events rather than just events within a specified range, as you did previously in this chapter.

This section explored the basic structure of a View control for a DesktopModule, but there are more items to deal with to complete the module. For instance, several times in the View control's code-behind class, you made calls to values contained within a Settings hash. These values are going to be configured within the Edit control, which is used for configuring the settings for this specific module instance. The Settings.ascx control was defined in the module definition in DotNetNuke for the Events module (see Chapter 12).

Settings Control

Now you need to create a control that enables you to customize your module. In the Events module, this will set the values contained in the Settings hash table. The keys you create are primarily for defining the display of the module. You set options for defining whether to display events in a list format or a calendar format.

Listing 15-8 reviews the user control for this module. This file is located in the Events project folder called Settings.ascx.

Listing 15-8: Settings User Control for the Events Module

```
<%@ Control language="vb" CodeBehind="Settings.ascx.vb" AutoEventWireup=
"false" Explicit="True" Inherits="DotNetNuke.Modules.Events.Settings" %>
<%@ Register TagPrefix="dnn" TagName="Label" Src="~/controls/LabelControl.ascx" %>
<table cellspacing="0" cellpadding="2" summary="Edit Events Design Table"
border="0">
  <tr>
    <td class="SubHead" width="175"><dnn:label id="plView" runat="server"
controlname="optView" suffix=":"></dnn:label></td>
    <td valign="bottom" width="125">
      <asp:radiobuttonlist id="optView" runat="server" repeatdirection=
"Horizontal" cssclass="NormalTextBox">
        <asp:listitem resourcekey="List" value="L">List</asp:listitem>
        <asp:listitem resourcekey="cmdCalendar" value="C">Calendar</asp:listitem>
      </asp:radiobuttonlist>
    </td>
  </tr>
  <tr valign="top">
    <td class="SubHead" width="175"><dnn:label id="plWidth" runat="server"
controlname="txtWidth" suffix=":"></dnn:label></td>
    <td valign="bottom" width="125"><asp:textbox id="txtWidth" runat=
"server" cssclass="NormalTextBox" columns="5"></asp:textbox></td>
  </tr>
  <tr valign="top">
    <td class="SubHead" width="175"><dnn:label id="plHeight" runat="server"
controlname="txtHeight" suffix=":"></dnn:label></td>
    <td valign="bottom" width="125"><asp:textbox id="txtHeight" runat=
"server" cssclass="NormalTextBox" columns="5"></asp:textbox></td>
  </tr>
</table>
```

You can see the various controls used here to display data — most are standard ASP.NET controls. One exception to this is the use of the DNN Label control. By using DotNetNuke intrinsic controls, you can take advantage of localization within your modules.

In addition to the DNN Label control, you can see how to specify the Settings hash table values for the view type. If you review Listing 15-7, you can see you checked the value of the Settings ("eventview") to determine in the View control how the events would be displayed. In the Settings.ascx control, you can see the optView form field, which has options for how to display the events in the module. You read these values in your code-behind page for the Settings.ascx control and then pass the values to the Settings hash, which you then use to check the view for the module.

Settings Control Code-Behind Class

If you look through the code-behind, you'll notice this file is much smaller than the code-behind for the View control because you're primarily concerned with specifying how you want the module to look. Listing 15-9 shows the class imports and the class definition in the Settings.ascx.vb file.

Listing 15-9: Defining the Settings Control for the Events Module

```
Imports DotNetNuke

Namespace DotNetNuke.Modules.Events
    Public MustInherit Class Settings
        Inherits Entities.Modules.ModuleSettingsBase
```

You can see here that you inherit the Entities.Modules.ModuleSettingsBase class. This class is provided by DotNetNuke and inherits PortalModuleBase as discussed earlier in the chapter, but it extends the PortalModuleBase to include some additional properties. The ModuleSettingsBase class provides methods and properties specific to configuring values for the module instance. Table 15-3 reviews what this class provides for your module development.

Table 15-3: ModuleSettingsBase Class

Name	Type	Description
ModuleId	Integer	ID of a specific single module instance.
TabModuleId	Integer	ID of the module container within a tab. For example, two module instances in two different tabs could point to the same Module ID, enabling them to mirror data.
ModuleSettings	Hashtable	Configuration options that affect all instances of a module.
TabModuleSettings	Hashtable	Affects only a specific instance of a module. This enables you to display the same information for a module, but in a different way.

One item to clarify here is the difference between the two module IDs (ModuleID and TabModuleID) and the two hash tables (ModuleSettings and TabModuleSettings). This is provided so you can use the same data in two different module instances. So, for example, if you want to update the event view for all instances of the same type of module, you would do so as follows:

```
Dim objModules As New Entities.Modules.ModuleController
        objModules.UpdateModuleSetting(ModuleId, "eventview", _
            optView.SelectedItem.Value)
```

In the next section, you update the specific instance using the UpdateTabModuleSettings method. This updates the view of all module containers pointing to the same data for a specific module, which is identified by its Module ID.

Code-Behind Regions

Next in the Settings class, the various code sections are broken down into code regions.

You'll notice that throughout DotNetNuke, certain standards are applied for coding conventions. As a module developer, you should strive to emulate the DotNetNuke coding style for easier readability and management.

The first and only section in the Settings.ascx.vb file is the Base Method Implementations region (see Listing 15-10). Here you have two methods: `LoadSettings` to load settings from your hash table, and `UpdateSettings` to update the settings values in the hash table.

Listing 15-10: Base Method Implementations of Events Module's Settings.ascx.vb

```
#Region "Base Method Implementations"
    Public Overrides Sub LoadSettings()
Try
    If (Page.IsPostBack = False) Then
                If CType(TabModuleSettings("eventview"), String) <> ""
Then optView.Items.FindByValue(CType(TabModuleSettings("eventview"), _
                String)).Selected = True
                Else
                  optView.SelectedIndex = 1        ' calendar
                End If
                txtWidth.Text = _
                 CType(TabModuleSettings("eventcalendarcellwidth"), String)
                txtHeight.Text = _
                 CType(TabModuleSettings("eventcalendarcellheight"), String)
            End If
        Catch exc As Exception                    'Module failed to load
            ProcessModuleLoadException(Me, exc)
        End Try
    End Sub

    Public Overrides Sub UpdateSettings()
        Try
            Dim objModules As New Entities.Modules.ModuleController
          objModules.UpdateTabModuleSetting(TabModuleId, "eventview", _
            optView.SelectedItem.Value)
            objModules.UpdateTabModuleSetting(TabModuleId, _
            "eventcalendarcellwidth", txtWidth.Text)
            objModules.UpdateTabModuleSetting(TabModuleId, _
            "eventcalendarcellheight", txtHeight.Text)
        Catch exc As Exception                    'Module failed to load
        ProcessModuleLoadException(Me, exc)
        End Try
      End Sub
#End Region
```

That's all it takes to configure the settings for your module. The next section covers the second Edit control for editing events for the module.

Edit Control

Because you're displaying events in your module, you need a way to add and update events in the database to display them. As in the View control, you're going to make a call to your BLL to pass an update or insert SQL command to your physical provider.

Open the EditEvents.ascx control contained in the Events module project to look at the user interface for adding your events data (see Listing 15-11).

Listing 15-11: Registering Controls for the EditEvents.ascx Control

```
<%@ Register TagPrefix="dnn" TagName="Label" Src="~/controls/LabelControl.ascx" %>
<%@ Register TagPrefix="Portal" TagName="URL" Src="~/controls/URLControl.ascx" %>
<%@ Register TagPrefix="Portal" TagName="Audit" Src=⊃
"~/controls/ModuleAuditControl.ascx" %>
<%@ Register TagPrefix="dnn" TagName="TextEditor" Src=⊃
"~/controls/TextEditor.ascx"%>
<%@ Control language="vb" CodeBehind="EditEvents.ascx.vb" AutoEventWireup=⊃
"false" Explicit="True" Inherits="DotNetNuke.Modules.Events.EditEvents" %>
```

You're registering several DotNetNuke intrinsic controls. You did this with the Label control in your Settings class, but you're implementing several more in this file. Table 15-4 lists the controls provided by DotNetNuke and explains their purpose.

Table 15-4: DotNetNuke Controls

Control	Location	Description
Label	\<approot\>\controls\ LabelControl.ascx	Provided by the DotNetNuke framework, supports features provided by DNN such as multiple languages based on user profile.
URL	\<approot\>\controls\ URLControl.ascx	Additional support for multi-language support of DotNetNuke based on profile.Portal structure, security, and other DNN intrinsic information.
Audit	\<approot\>\controls\ ModuleAuditControl.ascx	Provides information on who created the information and the creation date.
Text Editor	\<approot\>\controls\ TextEditor.ascx	Provides both a text-based and WYSIWYG environment for editing text and HTML for your module.
Address	\<approot\>\controls\ Address.ascx	Provides an address entry form used in the user registration within DotNetNuke.
Dual List	\<approot\>\controls\ DualListControl.ascx	Provides two lists for passing values from one list to the other. An example of this control is implemented in the security settings for a module or page.
Help	\<approot\>\controls\ Help.ascx	Provides inline help for your controls. Supports localization.
Section Head	\<approot\>\controls\ SectionHeadControl.ascx	Provides expandable areas for sections of your module. This is implemented throughout DotNetNuke.
Skin	\<approot\>\controls\ SkinControl.ascx	A drop-down list of skins installed for a portal. Primarily used in framework applications like under the Admin and Host menus.
Skin Thumbnail	\<approot\>\controls\ SkinThumbnailControl .ascx	Generates a thumbnail image of the skin. You can view the functionality in the DotNetNuke skins section under the Admin menu.
URL Tracking	\<approot\>\controls\ URLTrackingControl.ascx	Supports localization and click tracking.

As you can see from this table, DotNetNuke provides several controls, all of which you can use in your own development. Because DotNetNuke is open source, you can easily open any of the pages of code to find an implementation of these controls. This example covers controls specific to this module.

Now that the control has been registered in the page and your code-behind declared, you can continue on with the rest of the control and remove some of the formatting parameters for readability (see Listing 15-12).

Listing 15-12: EditEvents.ascx Control

```
<asp:panel id="pnlContent" runat="server">
      <TABLE width="600" summary="Edit Events Design Table">
      <TR vAlign="top">
            <TD>
                 <dnn:label id="plTitle" runat="server" controlname="txtTitle"
             suffix=":"></dnn:label></TD>
            <TD width="450">
                 <asp:textbox id="txtTitle" runat="server"></asp:textbox>
<asp:requiredfieldvalidator id="valTitle" runat="server" resourcekey=⤸
"valTitle.ErrorMessage" controltovalidate="txtTitle" errormessage="Title Is ⤸
Required" display="Dynamic"></asp:requiredfieldvalidator></TD>
            </TR>
            <TR vAlign="top">
             <TD>
                 <dnn:label id="plDescription" runat="server"
             controlname="txtDescription" suffix=":"></dnn:label></TD>
            <TD width="450">
                 <dnn:texteditor id="teDescription" runat="server"></dnn:texteditor>
                 <asp:requiredfieldvalidator id="valDescription" runat="server"
             resourcekey="valDescription.ErrorMessage"
             controltovalidate="teDescription" errormessage="Description Is
             Required" display="Dynamic"></asp:requiredfieldvalidator></TD>
            </TR>
            <TR vAlign="top">
             <TD>
                 <dnn:label id="plImage" runat="server" controlname="cboImage"
             suffix=":"></dnn:label></TD>
            <TD width="450">
                 <portal:url id="ctlImage" runat="server" showtabs="False"
             showurls="False" urltype="F" showtrack="False" showlog="False"
             required="False"></portal:url></TD>
            </TR>
            <TR>
             <TD>
                 <dnn:label id="plAlt" runat="server" controlname="txtAlt"
             suffix=":"></dnn:label></TD>
            <TD width="450">
                 <asp:textbox id="txtAlt" runat="server"></asp:textbox>
                 <asp:requiredfieldvalidator id="valAltText" runat="server"
             resourcekey="valAltText.ErrorMessage" controltovalidate="txtAlt"
             errormessage="<br>Alternate Text Is Required"
             display="Dynamic"></asp:requiredfieldvalidator></TD>
            </TR>
```

```
      <TR>
        <TD>
          <dnn:label id="plEvery" runat="server" controlname="txtEvery"
        suffix=":"></dnn:label></TD>
        <TD width="450">
          <asp:textbox id="txtEvery" runat="server"></asp:textbox> 
          <LABEL style="DISPLAY: none"
        for="<%=cboPeriod.ClientID%>">Period</LABEL>
          <asp:dropdownlist id="cboPeriod" runat="server">
            <asp:listitem value=""></asp:listitem>
            <asp:listitem resourcekey="Days" value="D">Day(s) ⟳
</asp:listitem>
            <asp:listitem resourcekey="Weeks" value="W">Week(s) ⟳
</asp:listitem>
            <asp:listitem resourcekey="Months"
          value="M">Month(s)</asp:listitem>
            <asp:listitem resourcekey="Years" value="Y">Year(s) ⟳
</asp:listitem>
          </asp:dropdownlist></TD>
      </TR>
      <TR>
        <TD class="SubHead" width="125">
          <dnn:label id="plStartDate" runat="server"
        controlname="txtStartDate" suffix=":"></dnn:label></TD>
        <TD width="450">
          <asp:textbox id="txtStartDate" runat="server"
        columns="20"></asp:textbox> 
          <asp:hyperlink id="cmdStartCalendar" runat="server"
        resourcekey="Calendar">Calendar</asp:hyperlink>
          <asp:requiredfieldvalidator id="valStartDate" runat="server"
        resourcekey="valStartDate.ErrorMessage"
          controltovalidate="txtStartDate" errormessage="<br>Start Date Is
        Required" display="Dynamic"></asp:requiredfieldvalidator>
          <asp:comparevalidator id="valStartDate2" runat="server"
        resourcekey="valStartDate2.ErrorMessage"
          controltovalidate="txtStartDate" errormessage="<br>Invalid start
        date!" display="Dynamic" type="Date"
          operator="DataTypeCheck"></asp:comparevalidator></TD>
      </TR>
      <TR>
        <TD class="SubHead" width="125">
          <dnn:label id="plTime" runat="server" controlname="txtTime"
          suffix=":"></dnn:label></TD>
        <TD width="450">
          <asp:textbox id="txtTime" runat="server"></asp:textbox></TD>
      </TR>
      <TR>
        <TD class="SubHead" width="125">
          <dnn:label id="plExpiryDate" runat="server" controlname=⟳
```

(continued)

Listing 15-12: *(continued)*

```
"txtExpiryDate"
              suffix=":"></dnn:label></TD>
          <TD width="450">
              <asp:textbox id="txtExpiryDate" runat="server"></asp:textbox> 
              <asp:hyperlink id="cmdExpiryCalendar" runat="server"
          resourcekey="Calendar">Calendar</asp:hyperlink>
              <asp:comparevalidator id="valExpiryDate" runat="server"
          resourcekey="valExpiryDate.ErrorMessage"
              controltovalidate="txtExpiryDate" errormessage="<br>Invalid expiry
          date!" display="Dynamic" type="Date"
              operator="DataTypeCheck"></asp:comparevalidator></TD>
          </TR>
      </TABLE>
      <P>
          <asp:linkbutton id="cmdUpdate" runat="server" resourcekey="cmdUpdate"
      text="Update"></asp:linkbutton> 
          <asp:linkbutton id="cmdCancel" runat="server" resourcekey="cmdCancel"
      text="Cancel" causesvalidation="False"></asp:linkbutton> 
          <asp:linkbutton id="cmdDelete" runat="server" resourcekey="cmdDelete"
      text="Delete" causesvalidation="False"></asp:linkbutton></P>
          <portal:audit id="ctlAudit" runat="server"></portal:audit>
  </asp:panel>
```

As you can see in Listing 15-12, the EditEvents form consists of several controls. Many are ASP.NET controls, such as the linkbutton, textbox, validators, and others. In addition to the ASP.NET controls, there are several of the DotNetNuke controls covered in Table 15-4. The first control you encounter is the DNN Label control:

```
<dnn:label id="plTitle" runat="server" controlname="txtTitle"
suffix=":"></dnn:label></TD>
```

Initially you registered the control, and now it is placed into the form. Since the label is a DNN control, it performs like any other label because it inherits from the ASP.NET control, but in addition you can associate information with the control, such as multiple languages from a resource file.

Further down the code is the TextEditor control:

```
<dnn:texteditor id="teDescription" runat="server"></dnn:texteditor>
```

By default, DotNetNuke uses FreeTextBox, which is a freely available open source control that you can use in your own applications. Because DotNetNuke uses a Provider Model for the TextEditor control, you can easily use any third-party control.

Next in line are controls that were registered using the "portal" prefix. These controls are for tracking activity within the portal. For example, when someone clicks on an event or any item in the portal, you can use these controls to track how many were clicked and who clicked on them. Of course to track who clicked on an item, users need to be logged on to the portal:

```
<portal:url id="ctlImage" runat="server" showtabs="False" showurls="False"
urltype="F" showtrack="False" showlog="False" required="False"></portal:url>
```

Some of the options enable you to show a log of clicks next to the item, tracking and other information for tracking activity, and display of the item. The control also integrates with DNN security, which enables you to display navigation of tab structure and still maintain the security so only those who have permissions for the resource see the information.

At the bottom of the page is an Audit control for tracking activity of the module. The Portal Audit control provides you with information on who created the information and the created date:

```
<portal:audit id="ctlAudit" runat="server"></portal:audit>
```

Now check out the code-behind to see how to work with the data and the controls. So far, you've dealt with displaying data from the BLL. Next you're going to be adding and updating information, so you'll need to pass parameters to your stored procedures in SQL. Refer to Chapters 13 and 14 to see how this all comes together.

Edit Events Code-Behind Class

Now that you've covered the front-end control that the user interacts with, take a look at the code-behind file and see how the class is structured. As before, you import the namespaces and define the class:

```
Imports DotNetNuke
Imports System.Web.UI.WebControls

Namespace DotNetNuke.Modules.Events
    Public MustInherit Class EditEvents
        Inherits Entities.Modules.PortalModuleBase
```

You'll notice again you inherit from the PortalModuleBase class as you did in the View control. Because this control is for adding data specific to your application, you'll inherit PortalModuleBase. Just to be clear on the difference between this control and the Settings control, which inherits from the ModuleSettingsBase class of DotNetNuke, the Settings control is specific to the operation of the module, not the item data that is entered in tables that you create. The Settings data is stored within internal tables native to DotNetNuke, so you need to inherit from the ModuleSettingsBase, which is focused on this task. An Edit control is specific to your application so it inherits from PortalModuleBase.

Edit Events Code Regions

Again, each section in the class is broken down into code regions for readability and organization. Here you review the regions specific to the EditEvents.ascx.vb file.

The first region is the Controls region, where you declare the controls you have created in your web form in the EditEvents.ascx control (see Listing 15-13).

Listing 15-13: Controls Region of the EditEvents.ascx.vb File

```
#Region "Controls"

    Protected WithEvents pnlContent As System.Web.UI.WebControls.Panel
    Protected plTitle As UI.UserControls.LabelControl
    Protected WithEvents txtTitle As System.Web.UI.WebControls.TextBox
    Protected WithEvents valTitle As _
        System.Web.UI.WebControls.RequiredFieldValidator
    Protected plDescription As UI.UserControls.LabelControl
    Protected WithEvents teDescription As UI.UserControls.TextEditor
    Protected WithEvents valDescription As _
        System.Web.UI.WebControls.RequiredFieldValidator
    Protected plImage As UI.UserControls.LabelControl
    Protected WithEvents ctlImage As UI.UserControls.UrlControl
    Protected plAlt As UI.UserControls.LabelControl
    Protected WithEvents txtAlt As System.Web.UI.WebControls.TextBox
    Protected WithEvents valAltText As _
        System.Web.UI.WebControls.RequiredFieldValidator
    Protected plEvery As UI.UserControls.LabelControl
    Protected WithEvents txtEvery As System.Web.UI.WebControls.TextBox
    Protected WithEvents cboPeriod As System.Web.UI.WebControls.DropDownList
    Protected plStartDate As UI.UserControls.LabelControl
    Protected WithEvents txtStartDate As System.Web.UI.WebControls.TextBox
    Protected WithEvents cmdStartCalendar As _
        System.Web.UI.WebControls.HyperLink
    Protected WithEvents valStartDate As _
        System.Web.UI.WebControls.RequiredFieldValidator
    Protected WithEvents valStartDate2 As _
        System.Web.UI.WebControls.CompareValidator
    Protected plTime As UI.UserControls.LabelControl
    Protected WithEvents txtTime As System.Web.UI.WebControls.TextBox
    Protected plExpiryDate As UI.UserControls.LabelControl
    Protected WithEvents txtExpiryDate As System.Web.UI.WebControls.TextBox
    Protected WithEvents cmdExpiryCalendar As _
        System.Web.UI.WebControls.HyperLink
    Protected WithEvents valExpiryDate As _
        System.Web.UI.WebControls.CompareValidator
    'tasks
    Protected WithEvents cmdUpdate As System.Web.UI.WebControls.LinkButton
    Protected WithEvents cmdCancel As System.Web.UI.WebControls.LinkButton
    Protected WithEvents cmdDelete As System.Web.UI.WebControls.LinkButton
    'footer
    Protected WithEvents ctlAudit As _
        DotNetNuke.UI.UserControls.ModuleAuditControl
#End Region
```

Most of the controls are ASP.NET controls as previously covered in Listing 15-12. You can see where you declare the DotNetNuke controls:

❑   Label controls:

```
Protected plTitle As UI.UserControls.LabelControl
Protected plDescription As UI.UserControls.LabelControl
Protected plImage As UI.UserControls.LabelControl
```

```
Protected plEvery As UI.UserControls.LabelControl
Protected plTime As UI.UserControls.LabelControl
Protected plExpiryDate As UI.UserControls.LabelControl
```

❑   URL control:

```
Protected WithEvents ctlImage As UI.UserControls.UrlControl
```

❑   Audit control:

```
Protected WithEvents ctlAudit As DotNetNuke.UI.UserControls.ModuleAuditControl
```

The next region is the Private Members region for storing an item ID value (see Listing 15-14). Because you're in the module's Edit control, you use this to add and update individual items. This variable is used to store the primary key of the individual event contained in the Events table.

Listing 15-14: Private Members Region of the Edit Control

```
#Region "Private Members"

        Private itemId As Integer = -1

#End Region
```

The next region is the Event Handlers region for dealing with click events and the Page_Load event for the control. Here you start with the Page_Load event and then see what is happening in each event for the Edit control of the Events module (see Listing 15-15).

Listing 15-15: Events Handlers Region of the Edit Control — Page Load Event

```
Private Sub Page_Load(ByVal sender As System.Object, ByVal e As _
    System.EventArgs) Handles MyBase.Load
    Try
            ' Determine ItemId of Events to Update
        If Not (Request.QueryString("ItemId") Is Nothing) Then
            itemId = Int32.Parse(Request.QueryString("ItemId"))
            End If
        'this needs to execute always to the
        'client script code is registered in InvokePopupCal
        cmdStartCalendar.NavigateUrl = _
          CType(Common.Utilities.Calendar.InvokePopupCal(txtStartDate), String)
        cmdExpiryCalendar.NavigateUrl = _
          CType(Common.Utilities.Calendar.InvokePopupCal(txtExpiryDate), String)
        ' If the page is being requested the first time, determine if an
        ' event itemId value is specified, and if so populate page
        ' contents with the event details
        If Page.IsPostBack = False Then
            cmdDelete.Attributes.Add("onClick", "javascript:return confirm('" & _
                Localization.GetString("DeleteItem") & "');")
            If Not Common.Utilities.Null.IsNull(itemId) Then
                ' Obtain a single row of event information
                Dim objEvents As New EventController
                Dim objEvent As EventInfo = objEvents.GetEvent(itemId, ModuleId)
                ' Read first row from database
```

(continued)

Listing 15-15: *(continued)*

```
                If Not objEvent Is Nothing Then
                    txtTitle.Text = objEvent.Title
                    teDescription.Text = objEvent.Description
                    ctlImage.FileFilter = glbImageFileTypes
                    ctlImage.Url = objEvent.IconFile
                    If Not objEvent.IconFile = "" Then
                        valAltText.Visible = False
                    Else
                        valAltText.Visible = True
                    End If
                    txtAlt.Text = objEvent.AltText
                    txtEvery.Text = objEvent.Every.ToString
                    If txtEvery.Text = "1" Then
                        txtEvery.Text = ""
                    End If
                    If objEvent.Period <> "" Then
                        cboPeriod.Items.FindByValue(objEvent.Period).Selected = _
                        True
                    Else
                        cboPeriod.Items(0).Selected = True
                    End If
                    txtStartDate.Text = objEvent.DateTime.ToShortDateString
                    txtTime.Text = objEvent.DateTime.ToShortTimeString
                    If objEvent.DateTime.ToString("HH:mm") = "00:00" Then
                        txtTime.Text = ""
                    End If
                    If Not Common.Utilities.Null.IsNull(objEvent.ExpireDate) Then
                        txtExpiryDate.Text = objEvent.ExpireDate.ToShortDateString
                    Else
                        txtExpiryDate.Text = ""
                    End If
                    ctlAudit.CreatedByUser = objEvent.CreatedByUser
                    ctlAudit.CreatedDate = objEvent.CreatedDate.ToString
                Else  ' security violation attempt to
                      ' access item not related to this Module
                    Response.Redirect(NavigateURL(), True)
                End If
            Else
                cmdDelete.Visible = False
                ctlAudit.Visible = False
                valAltText.Visible = False
            End If
        End If
    Catch exc As Exception    'Module failed to load
        ProcessModuleLoadException(Me, exc)
    End Try
End Sub
```

The first thing the Page_Load event does is to check the query string to determine whether you're working with a new or existing item in the Events table.

Further down you check for a null value by using the `Common.Utilities.Null.IsNull` method and passing it the itemID value. If the event ID is not null, you instantiate the EventsController class and execute the `GetEvent` method. Remember, this `GetEvent` method is contained in the Business Logic Layer, which then executes a call to the abstraction class, and eventually the physical provider that executes the corresponding stored procedure within the SQL database:

```
Dim objEvents As New EventController
Dim objEvent As EventInfo = objEvents.GetEvent(itemId, ModuleId)
```

You pass not only the itemID value to the stored procedure, but when you add a record you also add a value for ModuleID. The ModuleID is being provided by PortalModuleBase, which exposes the current module instance's ID to your class. The ID is a unique identifier provided by DotNetNuke that is generated each time a module is placed in the page. This ID provides the developer with a means to reuse modules, but have unique data for each instance.

Further down in the `Page_Load` event, you can see another DotNetNuke-specific item, and that is where you populate your Audit control with the information on the user creating the new event item:

```
ctlAudit.CreatedByUser = objEvent.CreatedByUser
ctlAudit.CreatedDate = objEvent.CreatedDate.ToString
```

This provides tracking internally so you can see who performed what action in your module. All these controls are optional for you to use in your module development.

Now you can move on to button action events. Listing 15-16 contains click events for cmdCancel, cmdDelete, and cmdUpdate link buttons.

Listing 15-16: Handling Linkbutton Events in the EditEvents Class

```
Private Sub cmdCancel_Click(ByVal sender As Object, ByVal e As EventArgs) _
    Handles cmdCancel.Click
    Try
        Response.Redirect(NavigateURL(), True)
    Catch exc As Exception     'Module failed to load
        ProcessModuleLoadException(Me, exc)
    End Try
End Sub

Private Sub cmdDelete_Click(ByVal sender As Object, ByVal e As EventArgs) _
    Handles cmdDelete.Click
    Try
        Dim objEvents As New EventController
        objEvents.DeleteEvent(itemId)
        objEvents = Nothing
        ' Redirect back to the portal home page
        Response.Redirect(NavigateURL(), True)
    Catch exc As Exception     'Module failed to load
            ProcessModuleLoadException(Me, exc)
```

(continued)

Listing 15-16: *(continued)*

```
        End Try
    End Sub

    Private Sub cmdUpdate_Click(ByVal sender As Object, ByVal e As EventArgs) _
        Handles cmdUpdate.Click
        Try
            Dim strDateTime As String
            ' Only Update if the Entered Data is Valid
            If Page.IsValid = True Then
                strDateTime = txtStartDate.Text
                If txtTime.Text <> "" Then
                    strDateTime += " " & txtTime.Text
                End If
                Dim objEvent As New EventInfo
                objEvent.ItemId = itemId
                objEvent.ModuleId = ModuleId
                objEvent.CreatedByUser = UserInfo.UserID.ToString
                objEvent.Description = teDescription.Text
                objEvent.DateTime = Convert.ToDateTime(strDateTime)
                objEvent.Title = txtTitle.Text
                If txtEvery.Text <> "" Then
                    objEvent.Every = Convert.ToInt32(txtEvery.Text)
                Else
                    objEvent.Every = 1
                End If
                objEvent.Period = cboPeriod.SelectedItem.Value
                objEvent.IconFile = ctlImage.Url
                objEvent.AltText = txtAlt.Text
                If txtExpiryDate.Text <> "" Then
                    objEvent.ExpireDate = Convert.ToDateTime(txtExpiryDate.Text)
                End If
                ' Create an instance of the Event DB component
                Dim objEvents As New EventController
                If Common.Utilities.Null.IsNull(itemId) Then
                    ' Add the event within the Events table
                    objEvents.AddEvent(objEvent)
                Else
                    ' Update the event within the Events table
                    objEvents.UpdateEvent(objEvent)
                End If
                objEvents = Nothing
                ' Redirect back to the portal home page
                Response.Redirect(NavigateURL(), True)
            End If
        Catch exc As Exception          'Module failed to load
            ProcessModuleLoadException(Me, exc)
        End Try
    End Sub
```

The first event you're handling in Listing 15-16 is `cmdCancel_Click`. Basically all you want to do is redirect the users back to where they started from, which is the default view of the module. In this case, it would be the View control talked about earlier in the chapter. One thing you'll notice is the use of `NavigateURL`, which is a function that returns a string for your module's view page. `NavigateURL` is provided by the DotNetNuke framework to provide navigation through your module logic to load the appropriate controls based on the module's key that you defined when you first configured DotNetNuke to interface with the module (see Chapter 12). Another key feature to the navigation methods provided by DotNetNuke is the support of friendly URLs (which you learn about later in this chapter), which eliminates query strings being passed in the URL and uses a directory structure for passing parameters.

The second event is `cmdDelete_Click`, which captures when the user deletes a specific event from the listing. You make another call to your EventsController, and pass the ID of the event you want deleted so eventually the stored procedure is called to delete the event. After the event is deleted, you redirect back to the initial View control of the module.

The final event is `cmdUpdate_Click`. This event handler contains a little more code than the previous methods. Initially you create an instance of the EventController class and populate the properties for an EventInfo object. These values are passed from the user controls contained in the web form on the web control. After the values are populated, you check to see if this is an existing event by looking at the item ID. If it's an existing event, you call the `UpdateEvent` method of the controller class. If you're adding an event, you call the `AddEvent` method of the EventController class. Finally, you use the `NavigateURL` function and redirect to the initial View control of the module.

That completes the architectural review of a DotNetNuke module.

DotNetNuke Helper Functions

In the previous code samples, you may have noticed several functions provided by the DotNetNuke core framework to ease your module development. These helper functions consist of error handling and URL navigation. This section provides some quick examples on what these functions do and how to use them in your own modules. More detail is provided in Chapter 8, but this section reviews common methods that were used in the examples in this chapter.

Error Handling

If you've been developing ASP.NET for any length of time, you've probably seen the yellow error dump on a web page when something goes wrong. This isn't a very nice sight for your users to see, and sometimes it displays a little more information about your application than you would like. Sometimes you don't even realize there is a problem. You could write your own error-handling routines, but with DotNetNuke you don't have to. The core framework provides module developers with the ability to check a logged-on user's security level, and display an appropriate error based on who is logged on. For example, an administrator can be presented with a little bit more detail about what specifically erred out, and average users can just be presented with a friendly error informing them that something is wrong. In addition, with the Logging Provider in DotNetNuke, you can view a log of the errors that occurred within a timeframe. This ensures you can see what has been happening with your portal and any errors your modules may have raised.

In this chapter, the code examples call the `ProcessModuleLoadException` method. For example:

```
Try
    'some logic
Catch exc As Exception
    ProcessModuleLoadException(Me, exc)
End Try
```

By using this method, you raise the error to DotNetNuke built-in error handling. To view any errors, logon as an admin or host-level account, and select Admin ⇨ Log Viewer. This brings up the Log Viewer screen. Errors are presented with a red entry by default. Just double-click the entry to view the error information.

Navigation URLs

Also covered in the sample code was the use of `NavigateURL` and `EditURL`. These provide two major functions: to load the appropriate control based on the key being passed to the function, and to support for friendly URLs in your module. Friendly URLs allow your module to eliminate the need to pass query strings in the URL. By using friendly URLs, you make it easier for spiders to spider your site, and it is an overall easier method to display and remember URLs to various pages in your site. For example, instead of using something like `http://www.dotnetnuke.com/default.aspx?tabid=233` to navigate to a page within a portal, friendly URLs would provide you with `http://www.dotnetnuke.com/tabid/233/default.aspx` as a path to the page. You can find more about the friendly URLs interface in Chapter 8.

`NavigateURL` provides you with the ability to load the appropriate control. This function is provided by DotNetNuke.Common.Globals.NavigateURL, located within the Globals.vb file in the <approot>\ components\shared\ directory in the DotNetNuke solution. This method accepts a `TabID`, which is the unique identifier of a page in your portal; `ControlKey`, which is the unique key you defined when you configured your module definition and identifies which user control to load for the module; and `AdditionalParameters`, which is for additional parameters. The additional parameters are a string array of the query string parameters you may need to pass in the URL. By using `AdditionalParameters`, you can easily implement friendly URLs for your module because DotNetNuke converts the string array to a directory structure to be displayed in the URLs.

For example, the following code snippet sets the `NavigateURL` property of a link button control using the `DotNetNuke.Common.Globals.NavigateURL` method:

```
hypRegister.NavigateUrl = NavigateURL(PortalSettings.ActiveTab.TabID, "Edit", _
    "mid=" & objModules.GetModuleByDefinition(PortalSettings.PortalId, _
    "User Accounts").ModuleID, "UserId=" & objUserInfo.UserID)
```

The ID of the currently active page is passed to the URL, and the control you want to load is the control with the Edit key. In addition, you pass several parameters for the control such as the Module ID and current User ID.

In addition to the features provided by the `NavigateURL` method, `EditURL` is another function for building navigation for your module. It is provided by PortalModuleBase. This method does not accept a Tab ID value because it assumes it is being used for the module instance currently in use. For example, if you list a record set and you want to edit a particular item, you would pass the key of ItemID and then the value. The `EditURL` function would pass the information to the Edit control:

```
<asp:HyperLink id="editLink" NavigateUrl='<%# EditURL("ItemID",
DataBinder.Eval(Container.DataItem,"ItemID")) %>' Visible="<%# IsEditable %>"
runat="server"><asp:Image id="editLinkImage" ImageUrl="~/images/edit.gif"
Visible="<%# IsEditable %>" AlternateText="Edit" runat="server" /></asp:HyperLink>
```

In this example, you're listing the events in a view user control and displaying an edit link to the user if he or she has edit permissions using the `IsEditable` Boolean value.

Summary

This chapter finishes the series on module development and architecture. In Chapter 13, you developed your physical provider class, which provides methods to expose your stored procedures in the database. From there, you moved on to creating an abstraction class, and finally exposing the result set of records as a collection of objects from your Business Logic Layer (see Chapter 14).

In this chapter, you did the following:

❑ You combined your work with those classes from the previous two chapters and then bound them to your module controls. Modules consist of several types of controls. The more common ones are as follows:

❑ The View control, for the first initial view of a module

❑ The Settings control, for configuring properties of a module instance

❑ The Edit control, for editing information specific to your business logic for the module application

❑ You learned the various helper functions that you can use in your own projects to reduce the amount of custom code.

This should provide you with enough information to begin developing your own module for DotNetNuke. In Chapter 17, you learn how to package these modules for distribution in other DotNetNuke portals. But first, in Chapter 16, you explore skinning the DotNetNuke application and provide your own unique look for your installation.

16

Skinning DotNetNuke

The capability to skin DotNetNuke was introduced in version 2 of the application and was a much-anticipated addition. The term "skinning" refers to an application's ability to change the look of the design by a setting in the application. This allows for the separation of the application logic from the user interface or object abstraction. As you learned in previous chapters, DotNetNuke uses a three-tier object-oriented design approach, with the user interface segmented as its own tier. This is what enables skinning to work and what enables the framework to present a unique feel depending on the parameters passed to the page. This chapter looks at the finer points of skinning and provides you with the tools to start building your own skins for DotNetNuke.

An Introduction to DotNetNuke Skinning

DotNetNuke uses templates to accomplish skinning because they provide for the separation of the presentation and layout attributes from the application logic required to display content to the user. We studied various approaches to enable this functionality and have created a solution that will give both developers and designers independence when implementing DotNetNuke sites. This results in faster deployment times and, more importantly, reduced expense with getting your portal functional and performing its intended purpose.

The abstraction of the user interface elements from a page can be accomplished using different methodologies. The method chosen includes some degree of parsing to merge the presentation with the business logic. Therefore, defining where, when, and how this parsing will take place becomes critical to the success of the entire solution.

The use of tokens or identifiers in the user interface files to represent dynamic functionality is a popular technique employed in many skinning solutions. DotNetNuke uses this approach in its skinning engine solution: as the page is processed, the token is replaced to the proper skin object or control for the function the token identifies. Some of these tokens serve as what are referred to as *Content Panes*. Content Panes, simply put, are areas of HTML where dynamic content will be populated at runtime. The dynamic content is populated by the use of modules. Details of how this is accomplished will be discussed later.

DotNetNuke enables you to create skins using your favorite editor, which gives you as a skin developer a good amount of flexibility — you only need to follow the rules for creating a skin; the tool you use to create it is up to you. You can create either an .ascx or .html skin. The type you create depends on your choice of editor and the set of rules you choose to follow. Offering designers the ability to create the skins in HTML or ASP.NET was a conscious choice made to allow for the most flexibility with creating these skins and to help bridge the gap between designers and developers. The Core Team realizes there are still many more HTML developers in the world than ASP.NET developers, so allowing skins to be created in HTML enables many more individuals to use this functionality of the application without having to learn new skills other than how to place the tokens within your skin design. Now that you have a little history of why the engine was architected, the following section looks at why it is still being used despite the introduction of Master Pages.

ASP.NET 2.0 Master Pages versus Skinning

The goal behind this section is to offer a minimal understanding of ASP.NET 2.0 Master Pages so there is a basis for comparison between them and the DotNetNuke skinning engine. This section is not a definitive guide on how to get started using Master Pages.

A Brief Introduction to Master Pages

With ASP.NET 2.0 a new concept of Master Pages was introduced. For those who have done HTML design work in the past with Dreamweaver, this concept is similar to Dreamweaver HTML templates that have a file extension of .dwt. The idea behind Master Pages is a pretty simple one: create a page template that allows for a consistent look and feel throughout an ASP.NET application while also allowing for various content areas to be replaced at runtime. Each Master Page template uses the .master file extension and can be created and used when you're working within Microsoft's Visual Web Developer.

One of the things that makes Master Pages different from normal HTML design templates is that they use a ContentPlaceHolder that allows for content to be merged from Content Pages at runtime. These content placeholders are represented by `<asp:contentplaceholder>` controls in the HTML code view of the Master Page template. As a developer or designer, you have the ability to use more than one ContentPlaceHolder within a single Master Page as long as you give each one its own unique ID within that page. Each ContentPlaceHolder on a Master Page is replaced with a Content Page at runtime. This means that for each ContentPlaceHolder you want to have replaced at runtime, you must create a Content Page for it. If you do not have a Content Page for every ContentPlaceHolder, default content will be loaded into the ContentPlaceHolders with no corresponding Content Pages. These Content Pages are linked to the Master Page using the @ Page directive at the top of the page and the actual content area is enclosed within the `<asp:content>` tag and its corresponding closing tag. Because the Content Page is linked to the Master Page, and will get injected into that Master Page at runtime, the normal HTML, BODY, HEAD, and FORM markup tags are not necessary. In fact, using one of these HTML markup tags outside of the Content control throws the following error at time of compilation: "Only Content controls are allowed directly in a Content Page that contains Content control."

Master Pages are definitely a step in the right direction for Microsoft and the .NET platform. They allow for the separation of content from the page and provide an easier way to get a consistent look and feel throughout the entire application

Why DotNetNuke Still Uses Its Skinning Engine

Considering all the advancements that were made for developers and designers with the introduction of Master Pages, you are probably asking yourself, "Why is DotNetNuke still using its proprietary skinning engine rather than taking advantage of Master Pages?" Even with the flexibility introduced with Master Pages, they are not without restrictions of their own.

One restriction of Master Pages is the lack of complete separation between the developer and the designer. It's great that with Master Pages a developer can isolate the content area and then ask the designer to work on that specific area. Although this isolates the designer to a specific area, many designers are not comfortable working within the Visual Studio environment despite the IDE used in Visual Studio, which shows the Master Page with the Content Page loaded into it at design time. For designers to be as productive as possible, they must be able to use the tools they feel most comfortable with. One thing that should not be overlooked is that many designers use an Apple operating system, which will not run Visual Studio, therefore making the concept of Master Pages useless to these designers unless they work in a text editor. Why should HTML design be limited to a designer using a Microsoft Windows operating system?

> This is one of the great benefits of the DotNetNuke skinning engine. It removes these restrictions placed on the designers. They are free to design on whatever operating system using whatever tools they choose, thus allowing them to be more productive.

Another restriction of Master Pages is that even though the designer is limited to a specific content area, there is still .NET code throughout that area. If designers open a Content Page in Visual Studio or their favorite HTML editor, they will see the @ Page directive and server control tags. If the designer has little or no experience working with ASP.NET applications, he could easily, and possibly unknowingly, alter one of these lines of code. If this happens, it means the developer has to spend time tracking down the problem. Because DotNetNuke completely isolates the design from the code by using the skins in combination with modules and skin objects, this situation is less likely to occur. Not only do the chances of a designer altering a developer's work decrease exponentially, it also allows them to work completely independent of one another. The developers can now spend their time developing modules, and the designers can spend their time creating skins and containers. With this complete separation between the two, both designers and developers can be working on the same site simultaneously instead of one waiting for the other.

As you can see, there are several good reasons why DotNetNuke still uses its own proprietary skinning engine instead of implementing Master Pages. One thing that was not addressed is the amount of development effort it would have taken to implement the Master Pages model. Just because a new feature was introduced to the ASP.NET framework, it is not necessarily better than one that was architected to fill a void left by the previous version of the ASP.NET framework. Using the DotNetNuke skinning engine, designers can work more efficiently and produce a better design without having to be concerned with altering the developer's code. The decision to still use the DotNetNuke skinning engine instead of Master Pages was not one that held DotNetNuke back, but one that kept it a step ahead.

File Organization

A skin package must meet certain conditions before it will install into the application. After the requirements are met, you can upload a compressed zip file containing your skin using the built-in File Manager, and the application will convert your files for use as a portal skin. The After the portal skins are successfully installed, they may be applied at several levels within the application — you can define a skin to be Host-, portal-, or page-level, depending on your needs.

Though skins can be applied at three separate levels, they can be stored in basically only two separate places on the file system. Where these files actually reside depends on where they are installed from and what portal you installed them on, if applicable.

When the skin is installed from the Host's Skins menu item — something that is only possible if you are logged in as a SuperUser — it is placed in the Portals/_default/Skins directory. During the skin install process, a folder is created in this directory matching the name of your zip file minus the .zip extension. This folder will contain the contents of your installed zip file, retaining the directory structure it had within this zip file. Please note that you can have a zip file of one name that contains a skins.zip file, which during the install process is stored in a folder with the same name as the zip file you uploaded. A skin package often has a master zip file such as skinpackage.zip that contains a skin.zip, so that the skin package can also contain a containers.zip, which includes all containers designed for the skin package. This installs the containers.zip following the same rules with the exception that it places the files in the Portals/_default/Containers folder instead.

If a skin is installed from the Admin's Skins menu item, the resulting folder will be placed in the Portals/*PortalId*/Skins directory. *PortalId* varies, depending on which portal you installed this on. If you are running only one portal on a DotNetNuke install, for example, this normally is named 0. Depending on your Host Settings, it may only be possible for a SuperUser to install skins at the portal level. Anywhere in the remainder of this chapter that you see Portals/PortalId/Skins, assume that you could also substitute _default for PortalId and accomplish the same thing, except the skin will be available at the Host level.

No matter which Skins menu item you used to install your skin package, the resulting directories are mapped to their corresponding skin ID, which uniquely identifies the skin in the application. These settings are stored in the Skins table in the database and enable the application to correctly determine the skin to load at runtime.

Processing Pages and Loading Skins

The application primarily uses a single page to process the functionality of displaying information to the user, Default.aspx. This page is the container for all the controls and skin elements the application needs to effectively serve its purpose of displaying the content to the portal user. You could refer to Default.apsx as a placeholder for the other information because its content is basic. If you view the source of the page from your IDE, it includes a placeholder for the content to be loaded and some error handling for the application. As you can see in Listing 16-1, there is a lot more that will be injected in the page than it would appear from looking at the code for the page.

Listing 16-1: Default.aspx Source Code

```
<%@ Page Language="vb" AutoEventWireup="false" Explicit="True"
Inherits="DotNetNuke.Framework.DefaultPage" CodeFile="Default.aspx.vb" %>
<%@ Register TagPrefix="dnn" Namespace="DotNetNuke.Common.Controls"
Assembly="DotNetNuke" %>
<!DOCTYPE HTML PUBLIC "-//W3C//DTD HTML 4.0 Transitional//EN">
<html>
<head id="Head" runat="server">
    <title><%= Title %></title>
    <%= Comment %>
    <meta name="DESCRIPTION" content=<%= Description %>>
    <meta name="KEYWORDS" content=<%= KeyWords %>>
    <meta name="COPYRIGHT" content=<%= Copyright %>>
    <meta name="GENERATOR" content=<%= Generator %>>
    <meta name="AUTHOR" content=<%= Author %>>
    <meta name="RESOURCE-TYPE" content="DOCUMENT">
    <meta name="DISTRIBUTION" content="GLOBAL">
    <meta name="ROBOTS" content="INDEX, FOLLOW">
    <meta name="REVISIT-AFTER" content="1 DAYS">
    <meta name="RATING" content="GENERAL">
    <meta http-equiv="PAGE-ENTER" content="RevealTrans(Duration=0,Transition=1)">
    <style id="StylePlaceholder" runat="server"></style>
    <asp:placeholder id="CSS" runat="server"></asp:placeholder>
    <asp:placeholder id="FAVICON" runat="server"></asp:placeholder>

    <script src="<%= Page.ResolveUrl("js/dnncore.js") %>"></script>

    <asp:placeholder id="phDNNHead" runat="server"></asp:placeholder>
</head>
<body id="Body" runat="server" onscroll="__dnn_bodyscroll()"
bottommargin="0" leftmargin="0"
    topmargin="0" rightmargin="0" marginwidth="0" marginheight="0">
    <noscript></noscript>
    <dnn:Form id="Form" runat="server" ENCTYPE="multipart/form-data"
style=""height: 100%;">
        <asp:Label ID="SkinError" runat="server" CssClass="NormalRed"
Visible="False"></asp:Label>
        <asp:PlaceHolder ID="SkinPlaceHolder" runat="server" />
        <input id="ScrollTop" runat="server" name="ScrollTop" type="hidden">
        <input id="__dnnVariable" runat="server" name="__dnnVariable" type="hidden">
    </dnn:Form>
</body>
</html>
```

So how does all this work? When a URL is requested and the user enters the application, the request is inspected and the proper skin is determined from the database tables. As you can see in Listing 16-2, the Page_Init goes through a series of logical steps until it finally has a skin value to load. The first step is to determine if the skin to be loaded is an applied preview. You can see an applied preview from several areas where skin selection is possible, such as Page Settings, by clicking the preview link next to the skin selection drop-down list. Doing this opens a new browser window that loads a portal page with the selected skin applied. This is done by adding the SkinSrc query string parameter to the URL. When a page is loaded containing the SkinSrc parameter, its corresponding value, which is the skin name converted for use in the URL, is applied to the page. If this parameter does not exist, the next step is to check the user's cookie for this site to see if it has a skin value set in it.

Listing 16-2: Default.aspx.vb Init_Page Directives

```
        Private Sub Page_Init(ByVal sender As System.Object, ByVal e As ⊃
System.EventArgs) Handles MyBase.Init

            ' set global page settings
            InitializePage()

            ' load skin control
            Dim ctlSkin As UserControl = Nothing

            ' skin preview
            If (Not Request.QueryString("SkinSrc") Is Nothing) Then
                PortalSettings.ActiveTab.SkinSrc = SkinController.FormatSkinSrc ⊃
(QueryStringDecode(Request.QueryString("SkinSrc")) & ".ascx", PortalSettings)
                ctlSkin = LoadSkin(PortalSettings.ActiveTab.SkinSrc)
            End If

            ' load user skin ( based on cookie )
            If ctlSkin Is Nothing Then
                If Not Request.Cookies("_SkinSrc" & PortalSettings.PortalId. ⊃
ToString) Is Nothing Then
                    If Request.Cookies("_SkinSrc" & ⊃
PortalSettings.PortalId.ToString).Value <> "" Then
                        PortalSettings.ActiveTab.SkinSrc = ⊃
SkinController.FormatSkinSrc(Request.Cookies("_SkinSrc" & ⊃
PortalSettings.PortalId.ToString).Value & ".ascx", PortalSettings)
                        ctlSkin = LoadSkin(PortalSettings.ActiveTab.SkinSrc)
                    End If
                End If
            End If

            ' load assigned skin
            If ctlSkin Is Nothing Then
                If IsAdminSkin(PortalSettings.ActiveTab.IsAdminTab) Then
                    Dim objSkin As UI.Skins.SkinInfo
                    objSkin = SkinController.GetSkin(SkinInfo.RootSkin,
PortalSettings.PortalId, SkinType.Admin)
                    If Not objSkin Is Nothing Then
                        PortalSettings.ActiveTab.SkinSrc = objSkin.SkinSrc
                    Else
                        PortalSettings.ActiveTab.SkinSrc = ""
                    End If
                End If

                If PortalSettings.ActiveTab.SkinSrc <> "" Then
                    PortalSettings.ActiveTab.SkinSrc = ⊃
SkinController.FormatSkinSrc(PortalSettings.ActiveTab.SkinSrc, PortalSettings)
                    ctlSkin = LoadSkin(PortalSettings.ActiveTab.SkinSrc)
```

```
                End If
            End If

            ' error loading skin - load default
            If ctlSkin Is Nothing Then
                ' could not load skin control - load default skin
                If IsAdminSkin(PortalSettings.ActiveTab.IsAdminTab) Then
                    PortalSettings.ActiveTab.SkinSrc = Common.Globals.HostPath & ⤶
SkinInfo.RootSkin & glbDefaultSkinFolder & glbDefaultAdminSkin
                Else
                    PortalSettings.ActiveTab.SkinSrc = Common.Globals.HostPath & ⤶
SkinInfo.RootSkin & glbDefaultSkinFolder & glbDefaultSkin
                End If
                ctlSkin = LoadSkin(PortalSettings.ActiveTab.SkinSrc)
            End If

            ' set skin path
            PortalSettings.ActiveTab.SkinPath = ⤶
SkinController.FormatSkinPath(PortalSettings.ActiveTab.SkinSrc)

            ' set skin id to an explicit short name to reduce page payload ⤶
and make it standards compliant
            ctlSkin.ID = "dnn"

            ' add CSS links
            ManageStyleSheets(False)

            ' add Favicon
            ManageFavicon()

            ' add skin to page
            SkinPlaceHolder.Controls.Add(ctlSkin)

            ' add CSS links
            ManageStyleSheets(True)

            ' ClientCallback Logic
            DotNetNuke.UI.Utilities.ClientAPI.HandleClientAPICallbackEvent(Me)

    End Sub
```

If the application still does not have a value for the skin to load, and the majority of the time it won't, the application will try to assign a value based on a set of substeps. First, it will look to see if the current page loading is an Admin page. If it is, it will look to the database to get the assigned skin based on the admin skin set in the Site Settings. If no skin was set in the Site Settings, it will then check for a value for the Host Settings admin skin.

In the case where the loading page is not an Admin page, the skin will then be assigned based on the active page's settings. This will check to see if a value exists for this particular page in the database. If it does not, it will then go through a process similar to the Admin page process just discussed. The difference is that instead of checking for the assigned admin skin, it will now check for the assigned portal skin. Also similar to the Admin page skin assignment process, the application will first check for an assignment at the site level, and if no results are found, it will then check for an assignment at the Host level.

Finally, if a skin value has still not been assigned, the application will load the default skin included with every DotNetNuke distribution as the default. It's also important to note that if a skin is found but it has an error that prohibits the framework from rendering it, the default skin with an error message at the top of the rendered page will be loaded.

Once the application is at this point, the `ctlSkin` variable will have a value. With the `ctlSkin` variable now populated, the application can move on to creating links in the rendered page for the skin's Cascading Style Sheets. The function responsible for handling this is the `ManageStyleSheets` function, shown in Listing 16-3. This function is actually called twice from within Page_Init:

❑ The first time it creates a link for the default.css file, located in the Portals/_default/ folder. It then attempts to load a link to the skin.css file if it exists for the current skin package. Finally, the application attempts to load a link to the CSS filename corresponding to the name of the current ASCX skin file being loaded if one exists.

❑ The second time this function is called it simply loads the portal.css file located in the Portals/PortalId folder. By default, unless the portal.css in the Portals/_default folder was changed prior to the portal being created, the portal.css file is a skeleton file with only the names of the styles commonly used throughout the DotNetNuke user interface.

If you would like an introduction to the default CSS styles used throughout the framework, please review `default.css` *, which contains all the styles with the default values that are applied at runtime. Those default values can also be seen in Table 16-2 later in this chapter.*

Listing 16-3: Default.aspx.vb ManageStyleSheets Function

```vb
Private Sub ManageStyleSheets(ByVal PortalCSS As Boolean)

    ' initialize reference paths to load the cascading style sheets
    Dim objCSS As Control = Me.FindControl("CSS")
    Dim objLink As HtmlGenericControl
    Dim ID As String

    Dim objCSSCache As Hashtable = CType(DataCache.GetCache("CSS"), Hashtable)
    If objCSSCache Is Nothing Then
        objCSSCache = New Hashtable
    End If

    If Not objCSS Is Nothing Then
        If PortalCSS = False Then
            ' default style sheet ( required )
            ID = CreateValidID(Common.Globals.HostPath)
            objLink = New HtmlGenericControl("LINK")
            objLink.ID = ID
            objLink.Attributes("rel") = "stylesheet"
            objLink.Attributes("type") = "text/css"
            objLink.Attributes("href") = Common.Globals.HostPath & "default.css"
            objCSS.Controls.Add(objLink)

            ' skin package style sheet
            ID = CreateValidID(PortalSettings.ActiveTab.SkinPath)
            If objCSSCache.ContainsKey(ID) = False Then
                If File.Exists(Server.MapPath(PortalSettings.ActiveTab.
SkinPath) & "skin.css") Then
                    objCSSCache(ID) = PortalSettings.ActiveTab.SkinPath &
```

```
"skin.css"
                    Else
                        objCSSCache(ID) = ""
                    End If
                    If Not Common.Globals.PerformanceSetting = ⏎
Common.Globals.PerformanceSettings.NoCaching Then
                        DataCache.SetCache("CSS", objCSSCache)
                    End If
                End If
                If objCSSCache(ID).ToString <> "" Then
                    objLink = New HtmlGenericControl("LINK")
                    objLink.ID = ID
                    objLink.Attributes("rel") = "stylesheet"
                    objLink.Attributes("type") = "text/css"
                    objLink.Attributes("href") = objCSSCache(ID).ToString
                    objCSS.Controls.Add(objLink)
                End If

                ' skin file style sheet
                ID = CreateValidID(Replace(PortalSettings.ActiveTab.SkinSrc, ⏎
".ascx", ".css"))
                If objCSSCache.ContainsKey(ID) = False Then
                    If File.Exists(Server.MapPath(Replace ⏎
(PortalSettings.ActiveTab.SkinSrc, ".ascx", ".css"))) Then
                        objCSSCache(ID) = Replace ⏎
(PortalSettings.ActiveTab.SkinSrc, ".ascx", ".css")
                    Else
                        objCSSCache(ID) = ""
                    End If
                    If Not Common.Globals.PerformanceSetting = ⏎
Common.Globals.PerformanceSettings.NoCaching Then
                        DataCache.SetCache("CSS", objCSSCache)
                    End If
                End If
                If objCSSCache(ID).ToString <> "" Then
                    objLink = New HtmlGenericControl("LINK")
                    objLink.ID = ID
                    objLink.Attributes("rel") = "stylesheet"
                    objLink.Attributes("type") = "text/css"
                    objLink.Attributes("href") = objCSSCache(ID).ToString
                    objCSS.Controls.Add(objLink)
                End If
            Else
                ' portal style sheet
                ID = CreateValidID(PortalSettings.HomeDirectory)
                objLink = New HtmlGenericControl("LINK")
                objLink.ID = ID
                objLink.Attributes("rel") = "stylesheet"
                objLink.Attributes("type") = "text/css"
                objLink.Attributes("href") = PortalSettings.HomeDirectory & ⏎
"portal.css"
                objCSS.Controls.Add(objLink)
            End If

        End If

    End Sub
```

One final note about the loading of skins is that there is a performance hit with these DB calls and enabling the portal to use this dynamic skinning solution, as there is with any application that can change its appearance on-the-fly. Even though there is a performance hit, this is one of the killer features DotNetNuke contains and is worth the additional overhead the process requires.

Packaging Skins and Containers

Now that you understand the process of getting a skin bound to the proper page, this section looks at the different parts of a skin package. The package is a compilation of the files and definitions you will use to tell DotNetNuke how and what to process for your skin when you install it into your application instance. A skin or container package can contain the following file types:

❑   ***.htm,*.html:** These files can contain the layout representing how you want the various skin objects to be located in your design. These files will be converted to *.ascx files upon installation to the application.

❑   ***.ascx:** These are skin-definition user controls that are precompiled in the format the skinning engine requires.

❑   ***.css:** These files contain the style sheet definitions you will use to define the files in your skin or container.

❑   ***.gif, *.jpeg, *.jpg, *.png:** These file extensions are used in support of the graphics files included in your skin.

❑   ***.xml:** These file extensions are used to inform the parsing engine how to handle specific skin objects and are also referred to as the manifest file.

❑   ***.* Others:** You can use any other resource files in your package, but these must be of an allowed file type in the Host-allowed file settings on the Host Settings page.

A package can contain multiple skins and/or containers. This enables you to create complementing skins for a site in one package. Because the layout will allow for various panes that contain the module content at runtime, this is a powerful feature because you may not want the same layout for all pages in a site, but you will probably want common graphics and defined styles throughout the same site. This ability to package multiple skins and containers enables you to install all of the skins for a portal in one installation.

A skin package should make use of a manifest file to identify the various files and elements to be included in the skin. Including this file enables you to combine all the files into one package and give the application the needed instructions for processing the skin to your specifications. Although the manifest file adds some overhead to the skin creation process, it greatly enhances the abilities of the installation process and allows greater control in a single step.

The manifest file as outlined is used only during the skin parsing process. What this XML file actually does is extend, or override, the attributes set in the generated ASCX file at the time of parsing. This enables the designer to assign attributes, such as CSS class names, to a skin object. The finer points of creating manifest files and how they work together with skin objects are discussed later in this chapter because this is an important mechanism for controlling the installation of your skins.

Creating Your Skin

You have two methods for creating your skin. The method you choose depends on your comfort level with the technology and your personal preference. You can create skins using HTML, or if you prefer, you can create *.ascx skins with VS.NET. This enables you to develop your skin in a comfortable environment and provides flexibility while creating skins. If you are more of a designer who has developed traditional web sites in the past, you may prefer creating your skins in HTML using your favorite editor, but if you are more of a programmer, you may prefer using ASP.NET code and developing your skin with Visual Studio. Both of these methods are basically the same except you use tokens when developing in HTML and you use the user controls when creating your skin. Of course, the file extension will change depending on your choice of methods.

At a minimum, you want to develop two skins for each package: one to display to your users and another to display the administrative modules discussed in Chapters 4 and 5. The reason for this is that the user content areas probably need multiple panes to properly lay out the content as your business needs require, but the administrative areas are likely to display only a single module per page, so these two layouts will need to be architected differently to adequately serve the purpose of the area.

There are several steps to creating a skin. The order in which you perform these steps is not important, but the following is a valid method to get everything accomplished and your skin into production.

Designing Your Skin

To simplify the development of skin files as well as expedite the packaging process later, it is recommended that you use the following organizational folder structure:

```
\Skins
    \SkinName (this is the package you are developing)
    ... (this is where you create the skin package zip files for
deployment)
    \containers (this is a static name to identify the container files
for the skin package)
    ... (this will contain all resource files related to your
containers)
    \skins (this is a static name to identify the skin files for the
skin package)
    ... (this will contain all resource files related to your skins)
```

This provides an easy structure to develop your skins—a structure that also simplifies preparing your package for deployment and installation into your portal. The free-form nature of skinning provides you a level of creative freedom within designing your skins. Designers may want to create the initial site designs as full graphical images and then slice the images to meet their needs after the concept is mature. One thing to be aware of when creating skins is that you need to include all user interface elements in your design—static elements such as graphics and text, active elements such as Login links, a navigation/menu system, and the other skin objects required for DotNetNuke to adequately display your content to your users.

This is where you need to be aware of the technical issues that will arise in terms of how to most effectively divide the graphical elements into the HTML representation you need. HTML layout is different from free-flow graphics, and the translation from a graphical image to an HTML representation determines the layout of the final design. Decisions such as what resolution you want to target for your site need to be made at this stage. If you want the site to remain fixed regardless of resolution of the user's browser or if the design should adapt to the resolution, you should make adjustments to your design accordingly. The download includes several example skins that display the differences between fixed-width skins and full-width skins, so you can see the differences between the two approaches.

Building the Skin

Now that you have your design completed, you will need to actually build the skin. As mentioned earlier, you can use any HTML editor, Visual Studio, or if you prefer, even your favorite text editor to build the skin for your design. The one thing to remember is the HTML in your skin must be well formed or the process will fail. This means you must ensure you close any HTML tags you open, including image tags. Image tags do not normally have closing tags so you should include the trailing / after the image content and before you end the tag. Most modern HTML editors will handle the process of ensuring tags are closed for you, but you should still double-check your work to make sure a bug is not introduced into your skin with a missing tag.

Normally you want to include your images and support files within the same folder as the rest of your skin elements, but that isn't a requirement. You can place them in any folder you want, but care must be taken to ensure the paths will remain valid after the skin upload process. As part of the upload process the skinning engine adds `<%= SkinPath %>` to the beginning of your image paths for you. This allows your skin to be portable across installs and also to display properly when using the friendly URL feature of the framework. This variable will be populated at runtime with a relative value similar to /Portals/PortalId/Skins/YourSkinName/.

Before this inline variable was added to all the image paths during the skin upload, if someone was developing a site on his local machine in a virtual directory of `http://localhost/VirtualDirectory` and then decided to move it to production at a location of `http://www.YourDomain.com`, the skin would not render images properly. This left you with two options: you could install the skin again, effectively overwriting the original skin, or you could choose to directly edit the skin file and correct the image paths manually. Although the rendering of this variable does add overhead to the HTML output processing, it provides portability across installs.

If you would like to sacrifice portability in favor of performance, you can manually trigger the parsing process. To do this, select either Admin ⇨ Skins or Host ⇨ Skins. This opens the skin administration section where you will see a drop-down list with all the skins available to you based on your permissions. Choose the skin you want to alter from this drop-down list. If you have any skin preview images available (discussed later in the chapter), they are shown here. To complete the process, select the Localized option instead of Portable from the Parse Options radio button list and click the Parse Skin Package button. This parses your skin package the same as it does during the skin uploading process with the exception of how the image paths are altered.

Figure 16-1 shows the parsing options available to the administrator after a skin is installed.

The Skins page also has an About link, with its name based on the skin package name. The link displays an HTML file that provides details about the company and skin package for the administrator. This file, created by the skin designer, must be named About.htm or About.html and should be contained within the skins.zip file. Although the file is not necessary to create a functional skin, it is a nice addition to a skin package.

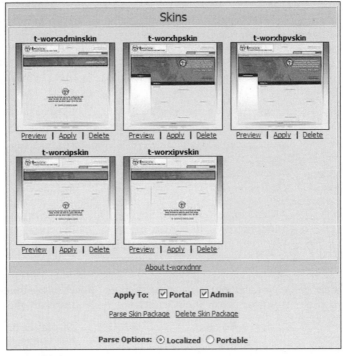

Figure 16-1

Skin Objects

Now that you have your design and a good idea of how your skin will be architected, you need to add the skin objects to the proper location in your skin file. This is so DotNetNuke will know where to insert the various content panes, portal elements, and navigation objects. This process will change to meet the method you choose to create your skin. If you are using ASCX skins, you need to specify the @Register and the actual user control tag in your skin. For example, `<dnn:Login runat="server" id="dnnlogin">` inserts the Login user control in the section of your skin where you specify the control. If you are using HTML skins, you simply need to include the token for the accompanying skin element. So for HTML skins, you just add `[Login]` in the location you want the Login control to appear, and the engine will replace it with the actual control when the skin is parsed during upload. Each of the skin objects has its own unique functions, and you must understand the use of each to build a functional skin. Table 16-1 lists each of these DotNetNuke core skin objects by token and control examples, and describes their purpose.

Table 16-1: DotNetNuke Core Skin Objects

Token	Control	Description
[SOLPARTMENU]	`< dnn:SolPartMenu runat= "server" id="dnnSolPartMenu">`	Displays the hierarchical navigation menu (formerly [MENU]).[SOLPARTMENU] skin object

Token	Control	Description
[LOGIN]	`< dnn:Login runat="server" id="dnnLogin">`	Dual state control — displays "Login" for anonymous users and "Logout" for authenticated users.
[BANNER]	`< dnn:Banner runat="server" id="dnnBanner">`	Displays a random banner ad.
[BREADCRUMB]	`< dnn:Breadcrumb runat= "server" id="dnnBreadcrumb">`	Displays the path to the currently selected tab in the form of Page-Name1 > PageName2 > Page-Name3.
[COPYRIGHT]	`< dnn:Copyright runat= "server" id="dnnCopyright">`	Displays the copyright notice for the portal.
[CURRENTDATE]	`< dnn:CurrentDate runat= "server" id="dnnCurrentDate">`	Displays the current date.
[DOTNETNUKE]	`< dnn:DotNetNuke runat= "server" id="dnnDotnetNuke">`	Displays the copyright notice for DotNetNuke (not required).
[HELP]	`< dnn:Help runat="server" id="dnnHelp">`	Displays a link for help, which will launch the user's e-mail client and send mail to the portal administrator.
[HOSTNAME]	`< dnn:HostName runat="server" id="dnnHostName">`	Displays the host title linked to the host URL.
[LINKS]	`< dnn:Links runat="server" id="dnnLinks">`	Displays a flat menu of links related to the current tab level and parent node. This is useful for search engine spiders and robots.
[LOGO]	`< dnn:Logo runat="server" id="dnnLogo">`	Displays the portal logo.
[PRIVACY]	`< dnn:Privacy runat="server" id="dnnPrivacy">`	Displays a link to the privacy information for the portal.
[SIGNIN]	`< dnn:Signin runat="server" id="dnnSignin">`	Displays the sign-in control for providing your username and password.
[TERMS]	`< dnn:Terms runat="server" id="dnnTerms">`	Displays a link to the terms and conditions for the portal.
[USER]	`< dnn:User runat="server" id="dnnUser">`	Dual state control — displays a "Register" link for anonymous users or the user's name for authenticated users.

Token	Control	Description
[CONTENTPANE]	`<div runat="server" id="ContentPane">`	Injects a placeholder for module content.
[LANGUAGE]	`<dnn:LANGUAGE runat="server" id="dnnLANGUAGE" />`	Displays a language selector drop-down list if the DotNetNuke install has more than one available option.
[SEARCH]	`< dnn:Search runat="server" id="dnnSearch">`	Displays the search input box
[TREEVIEWMENU]	`< dnn:TreeViewMenu runat="server" id="dnnTreeViewMenu">`	Displays a navigation menu using the DNN treeview control to provide a Windows Explorer-like menu.

These are the skin objects available for use in your skin creation, and some additional objects are available for use in the creation of containers. You can place these objects anywhere in your skin and control the placement of the portal elements. Not all these elements are required, but you should choose the elements you need to accomplish your purpose.

> Each skin must have at least one content pane, and it must be identified as the Content Pane or the modules will not display correctly.

If you are able to log in to a DotNetNuke installation as a SuperUser, you can view these and any additional skin objects available to you. To view them, navigate to the Host's Module Definitions menu item. Usually, the first item listed is the [Skin Objects] module name. Click the edit pencil next to it, and a page opens with all the skin objects installed on that DotNetNuke install.

Using Skin Object Attributes

Quite a few attributes are also available for use in the skin creation process. The attributes are defined in skin.xml, the manifest file, mentioned earlier in the chapter. This file is where you tell DotNetNuke how you want to use the various skin objects. For example, if you want your navigation menu to display horizontally in your skin, set that in the skin.xml file so the engine will know how to properly insert the menu into the skin. Table 16-2 lists the attributes available for use in the manifest file for the skin objects.

Table 16-2: DotNetNuke Core Skin Attributes

Token	Attribute	Default	Description
[SOLPARTMENU]	separatecss	True	Determines whether the CSS defined in a style sheet is used (values: `true`, `false`).
	backcolor	#333333	Background color.

Table continued on following page

Token	Attribute	Default	Description
	forecolor	white	Forecolor of menu item when selected.
	highlightcolor	white	Color of top and left border to give a highlight effect.
	iconbackground color	#333333	Background color in area where icon is displayed.
	selectedborder color		Color of border surrounding selected menu item.
	selectedcolor	#CCCCCC	Background color of menu item when selected.
	selectedfore color	white	Forecolor of menu item when selected.
	display	horizontal	Determines how the menu is displayed (values: vertical, horizontal).
	menubarheight	16	Menu bar height in pixels.
	menuborderwidth	1	Menu border width in pixels.
	menuitemheight	21	Menu item height in pixels.
	forcedownlevel	false	Flag to force the downlevel menu to display (values: true, false).
	moveable	false	Flag to determine if menu can be moved (values: true, false).
	iconwidth	0	Width of icon column in pixels.
	menueffects shadowcolor	dimgray	Color of the shadow.
	menueffects mouseouthide delay	500	Number of milliseconds to wait until menu is hidden on mouse out (0 = disable).
	menueffects mouseover display	Highlight	Adjusts the effect when mouse moves over a menu bar item (values: Outset, Highlight, None)
	menueffects mouseover expand	true	Makes the menu expand on mouse-over, unlike any menu found within the Windows environment (values: true, false).

Token	Attribute	Default	Description
	menueffects style	filter: progid:DX Image Transform .Microsoft .Shadow(color= 'DimGray', Direction=135, Strength=3) ;	IE-only property for submenu styles and transitions.
	fontnames	Arial	Name of the font used by the menu.
	fontsize	12	Size of the font used by the menu.
	fontbold	false	Determines whether the font used by the menu is bold (values: true, false).
	menueffects shadowstrength	3	Determines how many pixels the shadow extends.
	menueffects menutransition	None	Determines which direction the shadow will fall (values: None, AlphaFade, AlphaFadeBottom-Right, Barn, Blinds, Checker-board, ConstantWave, Fade, GradientWipe, Inset, Iris, RadialWipe, Random, Random-Bars, Slide, Spiral, Stretch, Strips, Wave, Wheel, Zigzag).
	menueffects menutransition length	0.3	Number of seconds the transition will take.
	menueffects shadowdirection	Lower Right	Determines which direction the shadow will fall (values: None, Top, Upper Right, Right, Lower Right, Bottom, Lower Left, Left, Upper Left).
	menucontainer cssclass	MainMenu_ MenuContainer	Menu container CSS class.
	menubarcssclass	MainMenu_ MenuBar	Menu bar CSS class.
	menuitemcssclass	MainMenu_ MenuItem	Menu item CSS class.
	menuiconcssclass	MainMenu_ MenuIcon	Menu icon CSS class.

Table continued on following page

Token	Attribute	Default	Description
	menuitemselcss class	MainMenu_ MenuItemSel	Menu item CSS class for mouse-over.
	menubreakcss class	MainMenu_ MenuBreak	Menu break CSS Class.
	submenucssclass	MainMenu_ SubMenu	Submenu CSS class.
	menuarrowcss class	MainMenu_ MenuArrow	Menu arrow CSS class.
	menuroot arrowcssclass	MainMenu_ MenuRootArrow	Menu root arrow CSS class.
	forcefull menulist	false	Displays the full menu as an indented list of normal hyperlinks, much like a sitemap (values: true, false).
	useskinpath arrowimages	false	Determines whether arrow images located in the skin are used and not those in the /images folder (values: true, false).
	userootbread crumbarrow	true	Determines whether a bread crumb arrow is used to identify the root tab that is listed in the breadcrumb ArrayList (values: true, false).
	usesubmenu breadcrumbarrow	false	Determines whether a bread crumb arrow is used to identify the submenu tabs that are listed in the breadcrumb ArrayList (values: true, false).
	rootbreadcrumb arrow		Image used for root-level menu breadcrumb arrows; for example, file.gif.
	submenubread crumbarrow		Image used for submenu menu breadcrumb arrows; for example, file.gif.
	usearrows		Uses arrows to indicate child sub-menus.
	downarrow	menu_down .gif	Arrow image used for downward-facing arrows indicating child sub-menus.
	rightarrow	breadcrumb .gif	Arrow image used for right-facing arrows indicating child submenus.

Token	Attribute	Default	Description
	level	Root	Root level of the menu in relationship to the current active tab (values: Root, Same, Child).
	rootonly	false	Indicator to turn off submenus (values: true, false).
	rootmenuitem breadcrumbcss class		CSS class used for root menu items when they are found in the breadcrumb ArrayList.
	submenuitem breadcrumbcss class		CSS class used for submenu items when they are found in the bread crumb ArrayList.
	rootmenuitemcss class		CSS class used for root menu items.
	rootmenuitem activecssclass		CSS class used for root menu items when they are the active tab.
	submenuitem activecssclass		CSS class used for submenu items when they are the active tab.
	rootmenuitem selectedcss class		CSS class used for root menu items when they are moused over.
	submenuitem selectedcss class		CSS class used for submenu items when they are moused over.
	separator		The separator between root-level menu items. This can include custom skin images, text, and HTML (for example, <![CDATA[<img src="file.gif">]]>).
	separatorcss class		CSS class used for the root-level menu item separator.
	rootmenuitem lefthtml		HTML text added to the beginning of the root menu items.
	rootmenuitem righthtml		HTML text added to the end of the root menu items.
	submenuitem lefthtml		HTML text added to the beginning of the submenu items.
	submenuitem righthtml		HTML text added to the end of the submenu items.

Table continued on following page

Token	Attribute	Default	Description
	tooltip		Tooltips added to the menu items. These come from the tab object properties, which are filled from the tabs table (values: Name, Title, Description).
	leftseparator		The separator used just before a root-level menu item, such as a left edge of a tab image.
	rightseparator		The separator used just after a root-level menu item, such as a right edge of a tab image.
	leftseparator active		The separator used just before an active root-level menu item.
	rightseparator active		The separator used just after an active root-level menu item.
	leftseparator breadcrumb		The separator used just before a root-level menu item found in the breadcrumb ArrayList.
	rightseparator breadcrumb		The separator used just after a root-level menu item found in the breadcrumb ArrayList.
	leftseparator cssclass		CSS class used for the left separator.
	rightseparator cssclass		CSS class used for the right separator.
	leftseparator activecssclass		CSS class used for the left separator active
	rightseparator activecssclass		CSS class used for the right separator active.
	leftseparator breadcrumbcss class		CSS class used for the left separator breadcrumb.
	rightseparator breadcrumbcss class		CSS class used for the right separator breadcrumb.
	menualignment	Left	Alignment of the menu within the menu bar (values: Left, Center, Right, Justify).

Token	Attribute	Default	Description
	cleardefaults	false	If true, this value clears (empties) the default color settings of the menu so that they can be left empty and not just overridden with another value
	delaysubmenuload	false	If true, this setting delays the loading of the menu until the rest of the page has rendered.
[LOGIN]	Text	Login	Text of the login link.
	CssClass	OtherTabs	Style of the login link.
	LogoffText	Logoff	Text for the logoff link.
[BANNER]	BorderWidth	0	Border width around the banner.
[BREADCRUMB]	Separator	breadcrumb .gif	The separator between bread crumb links. This can include custom skin images, text, and HTML (for example, <![CDATA[<img src="file.gif" >]]>).
	CssClass	SelectedTab	Style name of the breadcrumb links.
	RootLevel	1	The root level of the breadcrumb links. Valid values include:
			-1 (shows word "Root" and then all breadcrumb tabs)
			0 (shows all breadcrumb tabs)
			n, where n is an integer greater than 0 (skips n breadcrumb tabs before displaying).
[COPYRIGHT]	CssClass	SelectedTab	Style name of portal copyright link.
[CURRENTDATE]	CssClass	SelectedTab	Style name of date text.
	DateFormat	MMMM dd, yyyy	Format of the date text.
[DOTNETNUKE]	CssClass	Normal	Style name of DotNetNuke portal engine copyright text.
[HELP]	CssClass	OtherTabs	Style name of help link.
[HOSTNAME]	CssClass	OtherTabs	Style name of Host link (powered by xxxxxxxxx).

Table continued on following page

Token	Attribute	Default	Description
	Separator		The separator between links. This can include custom skin images, text, and HTML (for example, `<![CDATA[ <img src="file.gif"> ]]>`).
	Alignment	Horizontal	Links menu style (values: `Horizontal`, `Vertical`).
	Level	Same	Determines the menu level to display (values: `Same`, `Child`, `Parent`, `Root`).
[LOGO]	BorderWidth	0	Border width around the logo.
[PRIVACY]	Text	Privacy Statement	Text of the privacy link.
	CssClass	OtherTabs	Style name of privacy link.
[SIGNIN]			The entire login control (not just a link to a page that contains the login control) will be placed within the skin where this token is used. This is legacy and not recommended for use.
[TERMS]	Text	Terms of User	Text of the terms link.
	CssClass	OtherTabs	Style name of terms link.
[USER]	Text	Register	Text of the register/user link.
	CssClass	OtherTabs	Style name of register/user link.
[CONTENTPANE]	ID	ContentPane	Content pane key identifier to be displayed in the user interface and stored in the database.
[LANGUAGE]	CssClass		Style name of the drop-down list.
[SEARCH]	Submit	Submit	HTML to activate the search lookup (for example, `"Search"` or `"Go"` or `<img src="mybutton.gif">`).
	CssClass		CSS class for the search control.
[TREEVIEWMENU]	BodyCssClass		CSS class for the body of the tree-view menu.
	CssClass		CSS class for the treeview control.
	HeaderCssClass		CSS class for the header.

Token	Attribute	Default	Description
	HeaderTextCss Class	Head	CSS class for the header text.
	HeaderText		Text for the header of the tree menu.
	IncludeHeader	True	
	Level		Indicates the root level of the tree menu (blank = root).
	NodeChildCss Class	Normal	CSS class for a child node.
	NodeClosedImage	folderclosed .gif	Image for a closed (not in current breadcrumbs but has children) node.
	NodeCollapse Image	min.gif	Image to show that will activate a collapse of the menu node.
	NodeCssClass	Normal	CSS class for the nodes.
	NodeExpandImage	max.gif	Image to show that will activate an expansion of the menu node.
	NodeLeafImage	file.gif	Image used for a "leaf" node (no children).
	NodeOpenImage	folderopen .gif	Image for an opened (in current breadcrumbs and has children) node.
	NodeOverCssClass	Normal	CSS class for a node on mouse over.
	NodeSelected CssClass	Normal	CSS class for the selected node.
	NoWrap	false	Replaces spaces in the text of the node with nonbreaking spaces.
	ResourceKey		Resource key to localize the Title text. If blank, Text property will be used.
	RootOnly	false	Show only the root menu (no children).
	TreeCssClass		CSS class for the tree.
	TreeGoUpImage	folderup.gif	Image to go up a level on the tree.
	TreeIndentWidth	10	Additional width to indent each tree level.
	Width	100%	Width of the tree control.

As you can see, there are quite a few attributes for each skin object. This complicates the process of creating skins a bit, but it is important that you learn to use the attribute functions of each skin object to adequately realize the true power and flexibility of the DotNetNuke skinning engine. You may notice that the menu control monopolizes the majority of the available attributes—this shows the flexibility of the menu system DotNetNuke uses. One thing to note here is that the menu control is a fluid development control, which means it is constantly receiving revision and this list of attributes may not be complete by the time you are reading this book. Take a look at the menu documents available for download to ensure you are aware of all the options available to you with this powerful control.

Creating Multiple Instances of a Skin Object

The skinning engine will support multiple instances of the skin objects where you can define multiple menus for your skin or any other instance. You must of course give each instance an unique name, so you could have a menu skin object defined as [MENU] and a second menu defined as [MENU:1]. The value of 1 was used as the example name here but any descriptive name can be used here such as [MENU:Top]. These are also important for your content areas because it is likely you will want more than one content area for your skin. You must have at least one pane named [ContentPane], but you will likely want other areas to organize your content in so you can use the named instances like with the menu, only use the content skin object instead of the menu.

You can also set the attributes for each of your skin objects according to the ones previously listed in Table 16-2. Each skin object will support the attributes and you can specify them when you define the skin object. For example, in the earlier example of defining your Login control, you could have specified the text for your control such as <dnn:Login runat="server" id="dnnLogin" Text="Signin" />. This example works only if you are creating ASCX skins. If you are working with HTML skins, you must include the attribute setting in the manifest file.

A skin package may contain global attributes specified in a file named skin.xml (or container.xml for containers) that will apply to your skin files. You can also override the global skin attribute specification with a skin-specific attribute specification by providing a YourSkinFile.xml file. The Skin Uploader will merge the skin attributes with the HTML presentation file to create an ASCX skin file. Listing 16-4 shows a section of the manifest file where these attributes are set.

Listing 16-4: Skin Attribute Example

```
<Objects>
    <Object>
        <Token>[LOGIN]</Token>
        <Settings>
            <Setting>
                <Name>Text</Name>
                <Value>Signin</Value>
            </Setting>
        </Settings>
    </Object>
</Objects>
```

As you can see, the code in Listing 16-4 accomplishes the same thing as in the ASCX example, but you are able to keep the additional attributes separate from the presentation. This allows for cleaner and easier-to-understand HTML as you create HTML skins because the attributes do not congest the code with additional overhead.

There is a one-to-one relationship of skin object definitions in the skin file (that is, [MENU]) with the attribute specification in the skin.xml file. This is also true for all named instances. For example, if you want to include a vertical and horizontal menu in your skin, you can specify [MENU:1] and [MENU:2] named instances in your skin file and then create definitions for each with different attributes in the skin.xml file.

When creating HTML skins and specifying multiple ContentPanes, you need to stipulate the ID attribute in the attributes file. That enables DotNetNuke to identify the proper pane to insert your modules into while you are administering the portal. It also gives you the ability to add some friendly descriptive names to the various panes you may require. For example, Listing 16-5 shows how the ID of the pane is defined in the manifest file. You can define as many nodes of these various pane IDs as required to accomplish your design.

Listing 16-5: Content Pane Attributes

```
<Objects>
    <Object>
        <Token>[CONTENTPANE:1]</Token>
        <Settings>
            <Setting>
                <Name>ID</Name>
                <Value>RightPane</Value>
            </Setting>

        </Settings>

    </Object>
</Objects>
```

The code creates a pane named RightPane that you can use to display content to the user. You could also define a LeftPane or NavigationPane — basically whatever your business rules require you to include in the skin. This shows some of the flexibility the solution provides because you are able to use the number of panes necessary to accomplish your design. The solution enables you to create a layout to use the application as necessary. By using a combination of the code within your skin and the attributes file, you can create almost any iteration of a skin design you can imagine.

The reason one content pane must be named ContentPane is for consistency across all installed skins. During the page rendering, modules are loaded into content panes based on the name of the pane the module is assigned to. Having this required pane name enables you to change from one skin to another, which may have content panes of completely different names or a layout with fewer content panes, and not cause an error to occur. This is because if the pane the module was assigned to is not found, it will simply be loaded in the commonly named ContentPane, which must exist in all installed skins.

Creating Style Sheets for Your Skin

Now that you understand the way skins are designed, you can look at building a Cascading Style Sheet (CSS) for your skin. The CSS file will need to be defined and saved in your skin directory along with your other resource files. DotNetNuke uses an external style sheet specification, which enables you to define your styles separate from your skin files, and there are several levels of these files. This means it is not essential for you to create a CSS file for your skin because one of the other files will define the styles for you. But to keep a unique look to your skin design, you will want to build a style sheet specific for your skin design. The multiple style sheets in the application are structured in a hierarchal nature, so one style sheet's definitions may override another. There is a distinct priority of the order in which overriding of styles can occur. The cascading order of the style sheets is summarized in the following list with the previous item overriding the next:

1. **Modules**: The modules style sheet determines the styles that can be used in the individual module.

2. **Default**: This is the default style sheet for the host-level styles and the styles are defined in default.css.

3. **Skin**: These are the skin styles you will create and apply to your skin.

4. **Container**: Each container can contain styles unique to its design.

5. **Portal**: These are custom styles defined by the Portal Administrator and named portal.css.

You can define your skin's style sheet in one of two ways. You can create a style sheet named skin.css and place it in your skin directory. That file will apply to all skins that may reside in the skin package. You can also name your style sheet with the format of skinname.css, and it will apply to the skin file with the same name as the one you define here. You can add any style definitions you need, but at the minimum, you should override the default styles with those that complement the design of your skin.

Creating a Skin Preview Image

After you have the skin created, you need to create an image so you will be able to display the skin in the preview gallery. In order to do this, you need to create a high-quality image file with a .jpg extension that must be named the same as your skin file. For example, if your skin is named mySkin.ascx, then your image file must be named mySkin.jpg. At the time of upload, a thumbnail image will be generated for each properly named .jpg. This same concept is also true of container files you have created as part of your skin design. The skin preview images are displayed on the same page as the About.htm link discussed previously in this chapter and shown in Figure 16-1.

Deploying Your Skin

The last step in skin creation is to package the skin for deployment. The compressed file must be a *.zip file. You can use any number of third-party compression utilities, such as WinZip or Windows XP's built-in utility. One thing to watch out for when zipping your package is to ensure there are no buried folders between your skin files and the first-level compressed folder. This is a common mistake that causes the upload process to fail.

In many cases, you will want to package a complementary set of skin files and container files (which will be discussed shortly) in one distribution file. To do this, package your container files in a compressed *.zip file named containers.zip. Similarly, package your skin files in a compressed *.zip file named skins.zip, which was mentioned at the beginning of this chapter. Then, package these two files into a single *.zip file that is named after your skin. This allows people to install the full skin package (skins and containers) by uploading a single file through the Skin Uploader.

Creating Containers

This section looks at the procedures associated with creating a container for your skin. Containers are basically skin definitions applied at the container level. The process for creating a container is similar to the process for creating a skin, with the only real difference being the attributes and skin objects available for a container.

One requirement of creating a container is that you must include an Actions control so you will be able to administer the module's functions. The Actions control is a mechanism that allows binding of the module functionality to the portal framework. It is essentially the user control the module requires to do its intended work. Each module can define its own additional actions, but generally you will have standard functions to add and edit the module's content as well as the portal-level functions to move the module between panes and pages and edit the module settings including permissions, title, and so on. These are the minimum actions required, but the module developer can also create additional actions to perform unique functions of the module in question. The default actions menu uses the `SolPartActions` control, which functions as a pop-up menu when you hover over the edit icon located in the module container. This menu works best on the latest browsers and performs most reliably when using Internet Explorer 6+. There is a downlevel version of the control that will automatically be rendered to produce a drop-down box when you connect with one of the older browsers that doesn't support the advanced browser capabilities.

As mentioned throughout this chapter, you will want your skins and containers to complement each other and produce a consistent look throughout your design. So it's best (and probably a little easier) to design the skin and containers in conjunction with one another, even though they are really separate entities. Now that you have the basics, you can look at an example for a container manifest file. You will recall the manifest is where you define the attributes you want for the associated skin objects. To simplify this operation and provide a higher degree of granularity, a concept known as Pane Level skinning is also available. Pane Level skinning can be configured only at design time when the skin designer constructs the skin. It involves the use of some custom attributes, which can be included in the markup for the pane. The `ContainerType`, `ContainerName`, and `ContainerSrc` attributes can be used to identify a specific container to be used with all modules injected into the pane. For this to work correctly, the container must exist in the location specified; otherwise, the default container is displayed. Listing 16-6 demonstrates a basic example of this concept.

Listing 16-6: Pane Level Skinning

```
<Objects>
    <Object>
        <Token>[CONTENTPANE:1]</Token>
        <Settings>
            <Setting>
                <Name>ID</Name>
                <Value>LeftPane</Value>
            </Setting>
            <Setting>
                <Name>ContainerType</Name>
                <Value>G</Value>
            </Setting>
            <Setting>
                <Name>ContainerName</Name>
```

(continued)

Listing 16-6: *(continued)*

```
                <Value>DNN</Value>
            </Setting>
            <Setting>
                <Name>ContainrSrc</Name>
                <Value>standard.ascx</Value>
            </Setting>
        </Settings>
    </Object>
</Objects>
```

This example shows that it is possible to define standard containers for each section of the skin's design. You can also set the default container at the portal level, which will apply to any new modules created in the portal. The preceding example makes the process of adding content less time-intensive because you won't need to set the container after the module is added to the page.

As you can see, the container functionality in DotNetNuke is just as powerful as the skinning process, and the distinct look of your design can be accomplished using this technology. Table 16-3 showcases the skin objects available to you when you are developing your containers.

Table 16-3: DotNetNuke Core Container Skin Objects

Token	Control	Description
[ACTIONBUTTON]	`<dnn:ActionButton runat= "server" id="dnnAction Button">`	Generic button control used for various actions involving a module.
[SOLPARTACTIONS]	`< dnn:SolPartActions runat="server" id="dnn SolPartActions">`	Pop-up module actions menu (formerly [ACTIONS]).
[DROPDOWNACTIONS]	`< dnn:DropDownActions runat="server" id="dnn DropDownActions">`	Simple drop-down combo box for module actions.
[LINKACTIONS]	`< dnn:LinkActions runat= "server" id="dnnLink Actions">`	Links list of module actions.
[ICON]	`< dnn:Icon runat="server" id="dnnIcon">`	Displays the icon related to the module.
[TITLE]	`< dnn:Title runat="server" id="dnnTitle">`	Displays the title of the module.
[VISIBILITY]	`< dnn:Visibility run at="server" id="dnn Visibility">`	Displays an icon representing the minimized or maximized state of a module.
[CONTENTPANE]	`<div runat="server" id= "ContentPane">`	Injects a placeholder for module content.

Notice that you have some of the same functions available to your skinning functions, but you have also added a few objects that do not make sense from a page level but become important on a module level. These are powerful objects that can increase the use of your modules and containers, so you should take some time to experiment with the various uses of these skin objects. Table 16-4 covers the associated attributes you can use in conjunction with the skin objects for containers.

Table 16-4: DotNetNuke Core Container Skin Object Attributes

Token	Attribute	Default	Description
[ACTIONBUTTON]	CommandName		Maps to ModuleActionType in DotNetNuke.Entities.Modules.Actions:[AddContent | EditContent | ContentOptions | Syndicate-Module | ImportModule | Export-Module | OnlineHelp | Module-Help | HelpText | PrintModule | ModuleSettings | DeleteModule | ClearCache | MoveTop | MoveUp | MoveDown | MoveBottom | MovePane | MoveRoot].
	CssClass	CommandButton	CSS class for the button.
	DisplayLink	True	Displays the localized text for the command (value: True, False).
	DisplayIcon	False	Displays the icon for the command (value: True, False).
	IconFile		File to use for command icon if you're not using the built-in command icon (for example, myicon.gif).
[SOLPARTACTIONS]			The module action Solpart dynamic menu that is exposed to logged-in users who have permission to perform various module actions.
[DROPDOWNACTIONS]			The module action drop-down list that's exposed to logged-in users who have permission to perform various module actions.
[LINKACTIONS]			The module actions listed as links that are exposed to logged-in users who have permission to perform various module actions.
[ICON]	BorderWidth	0	Border width around the module icon (if applicable).

Table continued on following page

Token	Attribute	Default	Description
[TITLE]	CssClass	Head	Style name of title.
[VISIBILITY]	BorderWidth	0	Border width around the max/min icon.
	MinIcon	min.gif	Custom min icon file located in the skin file.
	MaxIcon	max.gif	Custom max icon file located in the skin file.
[CONTENTPANE]	ID	ContentPane	Content pane key identifier to be displayed in the user interface and stored in the database.

Now that the objects and attributes are defined, here's an example container for the DotNetNuke project. Listing 16-7 displays the DNN-Blue container from the default install. This container uses the attributes discussed previously.

Listing 16-7: Example Container

```
<TABLE class="containermaster_blue" cellSpacing="0" cellPadding="5"
align="center" border="0">
  <TR>
    <TD class="containerrow1_blue">
      <TABLE width="100%" border="0" cellpadding="0" cellspacing="0">
        <TR>
          <TD valign="middle" nowrap><dnn:ACTIONS runat="server"
id="dnnACTIONS" /></TD>
          <TD valign="middle" nowrap><dnn:ICON runat="server" id="dnnICON" /></TD>
          <TD valign="middle" width="100%" nowrap> <dnn:TITLE
runat="server" id="dnnTITLE" /></TD>
          <TD valign="middle" width="20" nowrap><dnn:VISIBILITY
runat="server" id="dnnVISIBILITY" /></TD>
        </TR>
      </TABLE>
    </TD>
  </TR>
  <TR>
    <TD id="ContentPane" runat="server" align="center"></TD>
  </TR>
  <TR>
    <TD>
      <HR class="containermaster_blue">
      <TABLE width="100%" border="0" cellpadding="0" cellspacing="0">
        <TR>
          <TD align="left" valign="middle" nowrap><dnn:ACTIONBUTTON1
runat="server" id="dnnACTIONBUTTON1" CommandName="AddContent.Action"
DisplayIcon="True" DisplayLink="True" /></TD>
          <TD align="right" valign="middle" nowrap><dnn:ACTIONBUTTON2
runat="server" id="dnnACTIONBUTTON2" CommandName="SyndicateModule.Action"
```

```
DisplayIcon="True" DisplayLink="False" /> <dnn:ACTIONBUTTON3 ⤸
runat="server" id="dnnACTIONBUTTON3" CommandName="PrintModule.Action" ⤸
DisplayIcon="True" DisplayLink="False" /> <dnn:ACTIONBUTTON4 ⤸
runat="server" id="dnnACTIONBUTTON4" CommandName="ModuleSettings.Action" ⤸
DisplayIcon="True" DisplayLink="False" /></TD>
            </TR>
        </TABLE>
    </TD>
  </TR>
</TABLE>
<BR>
```

The example in Listing 16-7 is a simple container that helps the display and feel of a portal with a blue-colored theme. You may notice that an ASCX container option is included here. If you were going to use this container, you'd need to add the Register directive for each of the controls added.

When creating a container, the designer should keep in mind that the container will hold the modules' content and also expose module actions through use of the module action menu. This is important to remember because the majority of DotNetNuke modules need this functionality, which is exposed only by the container. With regard to a container holding the content of a module, the designer should keep flexibility in mind because not all modules are going to expose content and functionality that can be confined within the same width and height constraints. Some designers may refer to this as an *elastic* layout.

Summary

DotNetNuke skinning has only a few basic requirements. If you can design and program in HTML and follow the few simple rules enforced by the skinning engine, you can build beautiful designs for your DotNetNuke site. A few things to keep in mind when working with a DotNetNuke Skin package are:

❑   Skins can be set at the site level and overridden at the page level, with the exception of Admin skins.

❑   Containers can be set at the site level, overridden at the page level, and then at the module level, with the exception of Admin containers.

❑   Each skin or container must have one Content Pane named ContentPane.

❑   Tokens are extended using XML files also referred to as manifest files.

❑   Skins and containers are installed using the DotNetNuke web interface and sometimes the capability to install them is only available only to SuperUsers.

Many examples of both free and commercial skins are available for you to use as references when creating your skins and containers. There are quite a few examples on the www.dotnetnuke.com web site and in the solution, as well as a multitude of resource sites in the DotNetNuke directory. Download some of these examples and, coupled with the knowledge contained in this chapter, you will create high-quality skins of your own in no time. If you can imagine it, then you can build it with the DotNetNuke skinning engine.

17

Distribution

This chapter examines how DotNetNuke add-ons can be distributed and installed. As DotNetNuke has progressed, functionality has been added to enable developers to package and distribute extensions to the DotNetNuke framework. These add-ons enable the administrators and users to customize the portal to suit their particular needs. Add-ons can provide additional functionality or can alter the visual presentation style for the portal. DotNetNuke uses zip files to package and redistribute add-ons. Each add-on type defines the specific files that can be included in the package. The custom add-ons are divided into three major categories:

❑ **Code add-ons**

    ❑ Modules

    ❑ Skin objects

    ❑ Providers

❑ **Skinning add-ons**

    ❑ Skins

    ❑ Containers

❑ **Language add-ons**

    ❑ Language packs

There are many aspects to consider in the distribution of add-ons, and this chapter answers the following questions as you look at each of these add-on types:

❑ What is the format of the manifest or configuration files for the add-on?

❑ How do you package all of the elements that go into a single add-on?

❑ How do you install the add-on?

Code Add-Ons

DotNetNuke provides mechanisms to extend the core portal functionality through the use of code add-ons. These add-ons can be packaged for easy distribution and installation. DotNetNuke supports three types of redistributable code packages: modules, skin objects, and providers. Although these are not the only mechanisms available for extending portal functionality, they are the only officially supported ones for distributing code add-ons.

Modules

A module, also known as a DotNetNuke Private Assembly (PA), represents a discrete set of application code that is used to extend the functionality of the DotNetNuke portal. A module provides a user interface for managing and displaying custom content in the portal. Unlike the other DotNetNuke code add-ons — skin objects and providers — modules are designed to be easily added to a page by the administrator. Each module can comprise one or more ASP.NET user controls and compiled assemblies. Like the main portal application, the module can take advantage of the Data Provider model to package providers for multiple database management systems. In addition to user controls and assemblies, a module can use other resources, including images, XML files, SQL scripts, text files, cascading style sheets, and resource archives.

Module Manifest File

Included in the module package is the module manifest file, an XML file that delineates the various elements that comprise a module package. The manifest file is organized to allow the portal to easily identify the module files and to determine the appropriate database entries necessary for the proper functioning of the module. Listing 17-1 shows the basic manifest file format. DotNetNuke recognizes two versions of DotNetNuke manifest files: version 2.0 and version 3.0. Each manifest file format recognizes different nodes, which directly correlate with various DotNetNuke features.

Listing 17-1: Module Manifest File Format

```
<?xml version="1.0" encoding="utf-8" ?>
<dotnetnuke version="D.D" type="Module">
  <folders>                              -- Contains one or more folder nodes
    <folder>
      <name />
      <friendlyname />                   -- V3.0* only
      <foldername />                     -- V3.0* only
      <modulename />                     -- V3.0* only
      <description />
      <version />
      <businesscontrollerclass />        -- V3.0 only
      <resourcefile />
      <modules>                          -- Contains one or more module nodes
        <module>
          <friendlyname />
```

```
        <cachetime />                    -- V3.0* only
        <controls>                       -- Contains one or more control nodes
          <control>
            <key />
            <title />
            <src />
            <iconfile />
            <type />
            <vieworder />
            <helpurl />                  -- V3.0 only
            <helpfile />                 -- V2.0 only
          </control>
        </controls>
      </module>
    </modules>
    <files>                              -- Contains one or more file nodes
      <file>
        <path />
        <name />
      </file>
    </files>
  </folder>
 </folders>
</dotnetnuke>
```

Let's take a few minutes to explore the individual XML nodes.

The root element is the `dotnetnuke` node. It contains two attributes, `version` and `type`:

```
<dotnetnuke version="D.D" type="Module">
```

The `version` attribute takes a numeric value. DotNetNuke supports two manifest file versions — `"2.0"` and `"3.0"`. Version 1.0 modules are no longer supported.

The `type` attribute must be set to `"Module"` for both v2 and v3 formats but can contain additional values to distinguish between the different manifest file formats used by skin objects and providers. These two additional formats are discussed later in this chapter.

> The v3 format has undergone some nonbreaking changes since it was first released. The additional supported elements are highlighted with an asterisk on the version number.

The manifest provides a `<folders>` element for identifying a collection of individual module folders. A `folder` node represents a single DotNetNuke module. The `folder` node can contain 10 child elements as defined in Table 17-1.

Table 17-1: Folder Elements

Element	Description	Required	Versions Supported
Name	Defines the default name of the module as well as the name of the directory that DotNetNuke will create in the DesktopModules folder if `foldername` is not set.	Yes	2.0, 3.0
friendlyname	Used to identify the module in the module drop-down list located on the Admin Control Panel that appears when a user is logged in as a Portal or Host Administrator. The Host Administrator can change the `friendlyname` at any time. This enables the administrator to present module names in a language other than English to his or her administrative users.	No	3.0*
foldername	Defines the name of the folder where the module will be installed. This folder becomes the root from which all other module files are installed (.dll files are an exception to this rule because they must be installed to the application \bin directory).	No	3.0*
modulename	Defines the name of the module that uniquely identifies it in the system. After a module is installed, the `modulename` cannot be changed. This name is only used internally to identify each distinct module type.	No	3.0*
description	Used for creating the module description that is presented to the host when viewing modules on the Module Definitions page.	Yes	2.0, 3.0
version	The version of the module. This element must be in the format `XX.XX.XX` where `X` is a digit from 0 to 9. It is used to determine which dataprovider scripts to execute. During installation, any script that has a higher version number than the currently installed module version will be executed. If this is the first time the module has been installed, all script files will be executed. Scripts are executed in the order of their version numbers.	Yes	2.0, 3.0

Element	Description	Required	Versions Supported
businesscontrollerclass	Defines the qualified name of the primary business controller in the module. If the IPortable, ISearchable, or IUpgradeable interfaces are implemented by the module, they must be implemented in this class. This entry uses the format `[namespace].[class name], [assembly name]`. Here's an example entry: `< businesscontrollerclass > DotNetNuke.Modules.Survey .SurveyController, DotNetNuke .Modules.Survey</ businesscontrollerclass>`.	No	3.0
resourcefile	Identifies a zip file that is included in the module package. The resource file may contain any number of files, which will be installed using folder information defined in the resource file. Files placed in the resource file do not need to be delineated in the files collection of the manifest.	No	2.0, 3.0
modules	Defines a collection of modules that are installed in the current folder. These modules will be associated with the Desktop module defined by the current folder. See Table 17-2 for a description of each module element.	Yes	2.0, 3.0
files	Defines a collection of files that are installed in the current folder. See Table 17-4 for a description of each file element.	Yes	2.0, 3.0

Additionally, the folder node contains two collection child elements, Modules and Files, which are described in Tables 17-2 and 17-4, respectively.

Table 17-2: Module Elements

Element	Description	Required	Versions Supported
friendlyname	Defines the name of the current module. This element is used primarily for display purposes to distinguish between multiple modules in a single Desktop module.	Yes	2.0, 3.0

Table continued on following page

Table 17-2: *(continued)*

Element	Description	Required	Versions Supported
cachetime	Currently unused. When activated in future versions, it will define the default cachetime value for the module when it is added to a page.	No	3.0*
controls	Defines a collection of user controls that are installed as part of the current module. These controls may provide different user or administrative screens for this specific module. See Table 17-3 for a description of each control element.	Yes	2.0, 3.0

As shown in Listing 17-1, every module contains one or more controls that are described in the controls collection. Each control can contain the various elements described in Table 17-3.

Table 17-3: Control Elements

Element	Description	Required	Versions Supported
key	A unique identifier that distinguishes each control in a single module. The primary View control does not use the key element and must not be included in the control definition. The module can use these key values to determine the appropriate screen to display for the current module state. The portal will display this control on the Module Settings screen if the control key is set to Settings.	No	2.0, 3.0
title	Defines the text displayed in the module title bar for the module edit screen associated with the current control. The title is not used for the primary View control.	No	2.0, 3.0
src	The filename of the ASP.NET user control corresponding to the current control definition. The filename includes any path information relative to the current module folder.	Yes	2.0, 3.0

Element	Description	Required	Versions Supported
iconfile	Defines the icon file to display in the module title bar. The iconfile setting is ignored for the primary View control and a control with a key of Settings.	No	2.0, 3.0
type	Defines the security access level required to view the current control. This level is defined as a subset of the SecurityAccessLevel enumeration. Valid values include Anonymous, View, Edit, Admin, Host.	Yes	2.0, 3.0
vieworder	Orders the controls when they are injected into the admin UI when multiple controls are associated with the module using the same key.	No	2.0, 3.0
helpurl	Defines a URL for help information related to the current control.	No	3.0
helpfile	Defines a file for help information related to the current control. The file location is relative to the current module folder. This element was deprecated in 3.0 and has been replaced through the use of LocalResources.	No	2.0

Table 17-4: File Elements

Element	Description	Required	Versions Supported
path	Defines a relative path to the module folder. The file defined by this node will be installed in this folder.	No	2.0, 3.0
name	The name of the file in the module package. If the file does not exist in the module package, an error is logged.	Yes	2.0, 3.0

Listing 17-2 shows the manifest file for the Survey module. The Survey module is included with DotNetNuke as an example of how to build, package, and deploy modules. You can find the module package and source code in the /desktopmodules/survey directory of the standard DotNetNuke installation.

Listing 17-2: Sample Manifest for the Survey Module

```xml
<?xml version="1.0" encoding="utf-8" ?>
<dotnetnuke version="3.0" type="Module">
  <folders>
    <folder>
      <name>DNN_Survey</name>
      <friendlyname>Survey</friendlyname>
      <foldername>Survey</foldername>
      <modulename>DNN_Survey</modulename>
      <description>
        Survey allows you to create custom surveys to obtain public feedback
      </description>
      <version>03.01.00</version>
      <businesscontrollerclass>
        DotNetNuke.Modules.Survey.SurveyController, DotNetNuke.Modules.Survey
      </businesscontrollerclass>
      <resourcefile>SurveyResources.zip</resourcefile>
      <modules>
        <module>
          <friendlyname>DotNetNuke.Survey</friendlyname>
          <cachetime>0</cachetime>
          <controls>
            <control>
              <src>DesktopModules/Survey/Survey.ascx</src>
              <type>View</type>
              <helpurl>http://www.dotnetnuke.com/default.aspx?tabid=787</helpurl>
            </control>
            <control>
              <key>Edit</key>
              <title>Create Survey</title>
              <src>DesktopModules/Survey/EditSurvey.ascx</src>
              <iconfile>icon_survey_32px.gif</iconfile>
              <type>Edit</type>
              <helpurl>http://www.dotnetnuke.com/default.aspx?tabid=787</helpurl>
            </control>
            <control>
              <key>Settings</key>
              <title>Survey Settings</title>
              <src>DesktopModules/Survey/Settings.ascx</src>
              <iconfile>icon_survey_32px.gif</iconfile>
              <type>Edit</type>
              <helpurl>http://www.dotnetnuke.com/default.aspx?tabid=787</helpurl>
            </control>
          </controls>
        </module>
      </modules>
      <files>
        <file>
          <name>Survey.ascx</name>
        </file>
        <file>
          <name>EditSurvey.ascx</name>
        </file>
```

```
        <file>
          <name>Settings.ascx</name>
        </file>
        <file>
          <name>DotNetNuke.Modules.Survey.dll</name>
        </file>
        <file>
          <name>DotNetNuke.Modules.Survey.SqlDataProvider.dll</name>
        </file>
        <file>
          <name>03.01.00.SqlDataProvider</name>
        </file>
        <file>
          <name>Uninstall.SqlDataProvider</name>
        </file>
      </files>
    </folder>
  </folders>
</dotnetnuke>
```

Packaging Modules

DotNetNuke private assemblies are packaged as zip files. Files included in the package are placed in predetermined directories as defined by the file type and manifest file settings. Any directory information contained in the zip file is ignored. Only files that are specifically delineated in the manifest file are extracted and saved to the portal directories. Figure 17-1 shows the survey module package that is included with DotNetNuke.

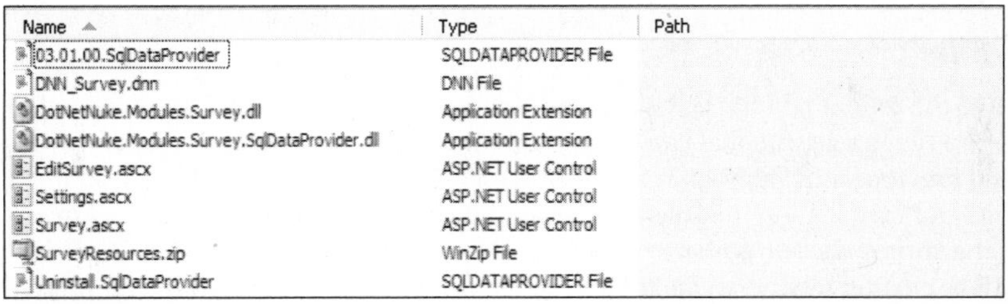

Name ▲	Type	Path
03.01.00.SqlDataProvider	SQLDATAPROVIDER File	
DNN_Survey.dnn	DNN File	
DotNetNuke.Modules.Survey.dll	Application Extension	
DotNetNuke.Modules.Survey.SqlDataProvider.dll	Application Extension	
EditSurvey.ascx	ASP.NET User Control	
Settings.ascx	ASP.NET User Control	
Survey.ascx	ASP.NET User Control	
SurveyResources.zip	WinZip File	
Uninstall.SqlDataProvider	SQLDATAPROVIDER File	

Figure 17-1

Special File Types

DotNetNuke recognizes four specific file types in the private assembly archive: DNN, DLL, ASCX, and dataprovider script. Although other file types may be included in the package, DotNetNuke treats these four types as special cases. The following list looks at each of these types and how they are handled during installation:

❑ **DNN:** The .dnn file is the manifest file for the Module package. Each package must include a single manifest file that follows the format previously discussed. The manifest file can use any name, but it must have the .dnn extension. The manifest fully describes each file included in the package and identifies information needed by the portal to create the proper module definition entries and install the module files to the appropriate directories required by DotNetNuke. The .dnn file is copied to the module folder defined in the manifest.

❑   **DLL:** .dll files are .NET assemblies. In DotNetNuke, these assemblies can represent the com-
    piled module code, a dataprovider assembly, or even an ASP.NET Server Control used in the
    module. All DLL files are installed to the application directory (/bin).

❑   **ASCX:** .ascx files are the visual portion of a user control in ASP.NET. An .ascx file defines the
    layout of the user interface for the specific module. It is copied to the module folder and a spe-
    cial entry is made in the DotNetNuke system tables as specified in the manifest file. The ASCX
    file can represent a single module control or can be a constituent control that is used on multiple
    screens within the module. All module controls are defined in the manifest, whereas constituent
    controls appear only in the manifest file list.

❑   **Dataprovider script:** Dataprovider files contain SQL scripts that define the database-specific code
    for the module. This file type uses an extension that follows a standard pattern: .[DataProvider
    Type]DataProvider, where [DataProviderType] corresponds to the provider type defined in the
    DotNetNuke web.config file (Access, Sql, Mysql, Oracle, Firebird and so on). For example, the
    default dataprovider supports SQL Server and is designated with the .sqldataprovider extension.
    New dataproviders may be written by third-party vendors, in which case new dataprovider
    script file types will be defined by the vendor. Dataprovider scripts are installed to a subdirec-
    tory of the Providers/DataProviders folder. The subdirectory is created with the same name as
    the dataprovider type (for example, SQLDataProvider files are installed in the providers/
    dataproviders/sqldataprovider directory).

> DotNetNuke 4.0 only includes a dataprovider for Microsoft SQL Server. Additional
> dataproviders will be provided as part of a separate DotNetNuke-sponsored project.
> Data providers for Oracle and MySQL are also available from third-party vendors.

Resource File

In addition to the predefined file types, the module package also allows for the inclusion of a resource
file. A resource file is a zip file that can contain any file that is not one of the special types defined earlier.
As indicated previously in Table 17-1, the resource file is designated with the <resourcefile> node of the
manifest file. Unlike the main module zip file, all directory information in the resource file is used to
determine the appropriate directory in which to place the individual resources. Any directory that is
defined will be created relative to the main module directory as defined in the manifest. Files that are
placed in the resource file should not be delineated in the manifest file; however, the resource file must
be specified in the manifest. Figure 17-2 shows the contents of the SurveyResources.zip file defined in
the survey module manifest previously presented in Listing 17-2.

Name	Type	Path
EditSurvey.ascx.de-DE.resx	.NET Managed Resources File	App_LocalResources\
EditSurvey.ascx.resx	.NET Managed Resources File	App_LocalResources\
icon_survey_32px.gif	GIF Image	
module.css	Cascading Style Sheet Document	
red.gif	GIF Image	
Settings.ascx.de-DE.resx	.NET Managed Resources File	App_LocalResources\
Settings.ascx.resx	.NET Managed Resources File	App_LocalResources\
Survey.ascx.de-DE.resx	.NET Managed Resources File	App_LocalResources\
Survey.ascx.resx	.NET Managed Resources File	App_LocalResources\

Figure 17-2

Notice that the *.resx files included in the resource file include path information. These files must be
installed in the [module folder]/App_LocalResources directory to function correctly. DotNetNuke will

place these files in the folder you designate (relative to the module folder), so you need to make sure to include the correct folder when building your resource file.

Installing Modules

After you have created a manifest file and properly packaged your module, it is ready for installation. The use of the zip file format and a well-defined manifest format greatly simplifies module installations. Because of the potential security risk, only the Portal Host has permissions to install modules. DotNetNuke supports two distinct methods for installing modules as well as other add-ons: web-based file upload and FTP-based file upload. These two methods differ primarily in the mechanism used for transferring the file to the server. After DotNetNuke receives the file, all processing is the same.

Web-Based File Upload

Follow these four simple steps to install a new module into your portal using the web-based installer.

1. Log in with the Host account and go to the Module Definitions page from the Host menu (see Figure 17-3). Only the Host account is authorized to install modules because modules have full access to the portal including file and database access.

> Modules can pose a security risk because they have unlimited access to the portal. Module code has the same security privileges as the core application. This means that modules could alter key portal tables, manipulate application files, or even gain access to other server resources. Modules should be fully tested in a "safe" environment prior to installation in a production system. In addition, the portal should run in a partial trust environment, which would limit the capability of any module to access restricted resources.

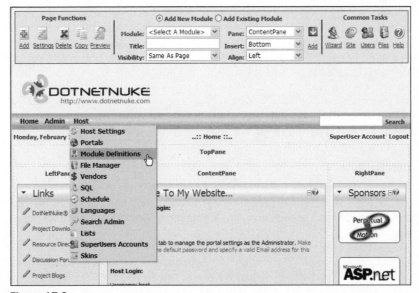

Figure 17-3

457

2. On the Module Definitions page, select the Upload New Module menu item from the module action menu (see Figure 17-4).

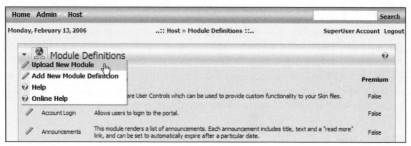

Figure 17-4

3. The File Upload screen provides a simple interface for uploading one or more modules (see Figure 17-5), and different add-on types. Browse to the desired module package, click OK on the Browse dialog, and click the Add link on the File Upload page. Use the Upload New File link button to finish installing the module.

Figure 17-5

4. After installing a new module, review the upload logs (see Figure 17-6). Errors will be highlighted in red. If no errors are shown, the module is ready for use in your portal.

FTP-Based Installation

DotNetNuke includes support for file-based installation of all defined add-on types. The framework includes a scheduled task that runs every minute to check installation folders for new add-ons to install. If you do not need this service, you can disable the scheduled task from the Schedule page in the Host menu.

To install a new module using FTP or any file manager, copy the module into the Install/Module directory of your DotNetNuke installation. When the ResourceInstaller task runs, it will install the module using the standard module installation code. If an error occurs, it will be noted in the task history, which you can access by selecting the History link for the ResourceInstaller task on the Schedule page (see Figure 17-7).

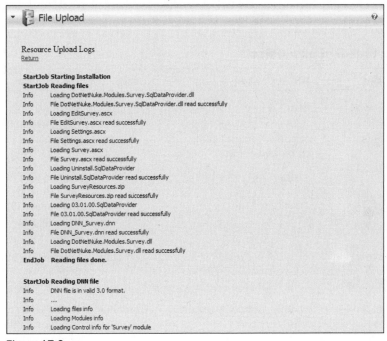

Figure 17-6

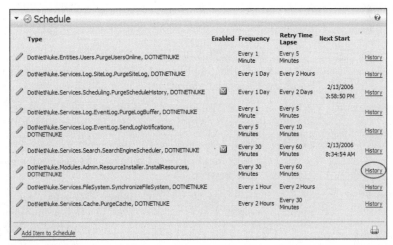

Figure 17-7

Skin Objects

Skins objects, like modules, are active elements designed to programmatically extend the functionality of DotNetNuke. Skin objects are used in skins and containers to produce a dynamic user interface. A number of default skin objects are included with DotNetNuke for common portal functions such as login, status, and navigation, as described in Table 17-5.

Table 17-5: Standard Skin Objects

HTML Token	ASCX Control	Usage	Description
[ACTIONBUTTON]	< dnn: ActionButton runat=>"server" id= "dnnActionButton" command name.	Container	Displays a list of link buttons that correspond to action menu items with a specified
[ICON]	< dnn:Icon runat= "server" id=> "dnnIcon"	Container	Displays an icon for the module. If the icon module was not set on the Module Settings page, no icon is displayed.
[PRINTMODULE]	< dnn: PrintModule runat="server" id= "dnnPrintModule">	Container	Displays an image button for printing module contents.
[ACTIONS]	< dnn: Actions runat= "server"id= "dnnActions">	Container	Displays the module action menu using the Solpart Menu control.
[SOLPARTACTIONS]	< dnn:SolpartActions runat="server" id= "dnnSolpartActions">	Container	Displays the module action menu using the Solpart Menu control. This is the same as the [ACTIONS] skin object.
[DROPDOWNACTIONS]	< dnn: DropDownActions runat="server" id= "dnnDropDownActions">	Container	Displays the module action menu items using a drop-down list.
[LINKACTIONS]	< dnn: LinkActions runat=>"server" id= "dnnLinkActions"	Container	Displays the module action menu items using a series of link buttons.
[TITLE]	< dnn:Title runat= "server" id="dnnTitle">	Container	Displays the module title.
[VISIBILITY]	< dnn:Visibility runat=>"server" id= "dnnVisibility"	Container	Displays the expand/collapse button for hiding or displaying module contents.
[SIGNIN]	< dnn:Signin runat= "server" id= "dnnSignin">	Skin	Displays the sign-in control for providing your username and password.

HTML Token	ASCX Control	Usage	Description
[BANNER]	< dnn:Banner runat= "server" id= "dnnBanner">	Skin	Displays a random banner ad.
[BREADCRUMB]	< dnn:Breadcrumb runat="server" id= "dnnBreadcrumb">	Skin	Displays the path to the currently selected page in the form of PageName1 > PageName2 > PageName3.
[CONTENTPANE]	<div runat="server" id="ContentPane" >	Skin	A placeholder for content modules.
[COPYRIGHT]	< dnn:Copyright runat= "server" id= "dnnCopyright">	Skin	Displays the copyright notice for the portal.
[CURRENTDATE]	< dnn:CurrentDate runat="server" id= "dnnCurrentDate">	Skin	Displays the current date.
[DOTNETNUKE]	< dnn:DotNetNuke runat="server" id= "dnnDotNetNuke">	Skin	Displays the copyright notice for DotNetNuke.
[HELP]	< dnn:Help runat= "server" id="dnnHelp">	Skin	Displays a link for Help that will launch the user's e-mail client and send mail to the portal administrator.
[HOSTNAME]	< dnn:HostName runat= "server" id= "dnnHostName">	Skin	Displays the Host Title linked to the Host URL.
[LANGUAGE]	< dnn:Links runat= "server" id= "dnnLanguage">	Skin	Displays a language selector drop-down list that allows the user to select the localized version of the site to display. This overrides the user's default language setting. This skin object is displayed only if a second language is installed for the portal.
[LINKS]	< dnn:Links runat= "server" id="dnnLinks">	Skin	Displays a flat menu of links related to the current tab level and parent node. This is useful for search engine spiders and robots.

Table continued on following page

Table 17-5: *(continued)*

[LOGIN]	< dnn:Login runat= "server" id="dnnLogin">	Skin	Dual-state control. Displays "Login" for anonymous users and "Logout" for authenticated users.
[LOGO]	< dnn:Logo runat= "server" id="dnnLogo">	Skin	Displays the portal logo.
[PRIVACY]	< dnn:Privacy runat=" server" id= "dnnPrivacy">	Skin	Displays a link to the privacy information for the portal.
[SEARCH]	< dnn:Search runat= "server" id= "dnnSearch">	Skin	Displays a search input box and link button.
[MENU]	< dnn:Menu runat= "server" id=>"dnnMenu"	Skin	Displays the hierarchical navigation menu.
[SOLPARTMENU]	< dnn:SolpartMenu runat="server" id= "dnnSolpartMenu">	Skin	Displays the hierarchical navigation menu. This is the same as the [MENU] skin object.
[TERMS]	< dnn:Terms runat= "server" id="dnnTerms">	Skin	Displays a link to the terms and conditions for the portal.
[TREEVIEW]	< dnn:TreeView runat=> "server" id= "dnnTreeView"	Skin	Displays a tree-based menu of links for the portal pages. The menu can be set to limit the tree to various menu levels.
[USER]	< dnn:User runat= "server" id=>"dnnUser"	Skin	Dual-state control. Displays a "Register" link for anonymous users or the user's name for authenticated users.

Custom skin objects are packaged and installed using the same processes as custom modules. All of the necessary skin object resource files are combined with a DotNetNuke manifest file (*.dnn) and packaged into a compressed zip file. Follow the installation steps outlined in the "Installing Modules" section earlier in the chapter. The primary difference between modules and skin objects is the manifest file format.

The skin object manifest file format (see Listing 17-3) is derived from version 2 of the module manifest format (shown previously in Listing 17-1). Changes are highlighted.

Listing 17-3: Skin Object Manifest File Format

```
<?xml version="1.0" encoding="utf-8" ?>
<dotnetnuke version="D.D" type="SkinObject">  -- Changed type value
  <folders>
    <folder>
      <name />
```

```
        <description />                    -- Not used
        <version />                        -- Not used
        <resourcefile />
        <modules>
          <module>
            <friendlyname />               -- Not used
            <controls>
              <control>
                <key />
                <title />
                <src />
                <iconfile />
                <type />                   -- Changed valid values
                <vieworder />
              </control>
            </controls>
          </module>
        </modules>
        <files>
          <file>
            <path />
            <name />
          </file>
        </files>
      </folder>
    </folders>
  </dotnetnuke>
```

The type attribute of the root `dotnetnuke` node must be set to `"SkinObject"`. Unlike modules, skin objects ignore the version value. The version must still be a decimal number in the format D.D where D is a single digit.

> Although there is no restriction on the actual number, it should be set to `2.0` to prevent conflicts with future versions of the skin object format.

The `description`, `version`, and `friendlyname` elements are no longer used but are still allowed in the manifest file without causing a validation error. The `type` element must be set to `"SkinObject"`. The name element will be used to set the `friendlyname`, `foldername`, and `modulename` attributes for the skin object in the database.

Providers

Providers are a third mechanism for extending the functionality of the DotNetNuke portal framework. The primary difference between modules, skin objects, and providers is in the usage pattern. Modules provide a mechanism for extending system functionality. No two modules are guaranteed to provide the same functionality or implementation. Skin objects follow this behavior, with each skin object being free to implement whatever functionality is desired. Providers are unique in that each provider of a given type must implement the same functionality. The implementation details may change but the basic functionality (that is, the programming interface) is defined by the portal.

Because providers are a programmatic extension to the portal framework, they use the packaging and installation mechanism defined for modules. Like skin objects, providers have their own manifest file format (see Listing 17-4), which is derived from the module manifest format.

Listing 17-4: Provider Manifest File Format

```
<?xml version="1.0" encoding="utf-8" ?>
<dotnetnuke version="D.D" type="Provider">  -- Changed type value
  <folder>
    <name />
    <type />
    <files>
      <file>
        <path />
        <name />
      </file>
    </files>
  </folder>
</dotnetnuke>
```

The `type` attribute of the root `dotnetnuke` node must be set to `"Provider"`. Providers follow the same rules as skin objects for the version attribute. Tables 17-6 and 17-7 describe the manifest folder and file elements.

Table 17-6: Provider Manifest Folder Elements

Element	Description	Required
Name	Defines the name of the provider. This name is used to create the folder in the appropriate provider directory.	Yes
Type	The provider type. It can be either `DataProviders` or `LoggingProviders`. Additional provider types will be supported in future releases.	Yes
Files	Defines a collection of files that are installed in the current folder. See Table 17-7 for a description of each file element.	Yes

Table 17-7: Provider Manifest File Elements

Element	Description	Required
Path	Defines a relative path to the provider folder.	No
Name	The name of the file in the provider package. If the file does not exist in the provider package, an error will be logged.	Yes

Files in the provider package are installed as follows:

```
[DotNetNuke Root Folder]/Providers/[ProviderType]/[FolderName]/[FilePath]/[FileName]
```

Skinning Add-Ons

Whereas code add-ons are designed to extend the functionality of the portal, skinning add-ons are aimed at giving the portal administrator complete control over the visual appearance of the portal. To simplify development and maintenance of these skinning packages, no manifest files are required. Instead, skinning packages rely on zip files to package and group the files to be installed in support of a skin. Although they do not utilize manifest files, skinning packages include support for XML-based configuration files. Configuration files enable the designer to set properties on individual skin elements that are identified inside the skinning source files. These skin elements include all skin objects as well as content panes defined within the skin definition file.

DotNetNuke uses two mechanisms for grouping content in the portal: pages and modules. Skins provide a method for changing the appearance of individual pages, whereas containers provide this function for each module instance placed on a page. First take a look at how skins are packaged and deployed.

Skins

As discussed in Chapter 16, skins provide the primary method for controlling the appearance of individual portal pages. One of the primary goals for the DotNetNuke skinning solution was to create a simple the process for developing and packaging skins. This process should allow web designers as well as developers to create skins using a variety of tools, from simple HTML editors to complex IDEs like Visual Studio .NET. This separation of form and function is one of the strengths of the DotNetNuke skinning solution.

Packaging Skins

A skin package comprises multiple files that constitute a complete skin:

- ❑   **.htm, .html files:** Abstract skin definition files that will be processed by the Skin Uploader to create an .ascx file.

- ❑   **.ascx files:** Skin-definition user controls that are written in the format required by the skin engine.

- ❑   **.css files:** Styles sheets that are related to skins.

- ❑   **.gif, .jpg, .jpeg, .png files:** Support graphics files.

- ❑   **.xml files:** Abstract skin properties files that will be combined with the abstract skin definition files during the upload processing.

- ❑   **.zip files:** Skin and container packages that are named according to the parent package.

> You can include any additional files needed by the skin, but they must be one of the allowable file types defined in the Host File Upload Extensions setting.

A skin package can contain multiple skin files. This enables you to create skins that leverage the same graphics but vary slightly based on layout. Obviously, the more skin files you have in a package, the more maintenance is required when you want to make a general change to the presentation in the future.

When you're packaging files for the skin, zip the files using relative file paths to the skin definition files. When unpacked, all file paths in the definition file will be corrected to point at the new file locations in the portal. Files are unzipped using the file path information contained in the skin package.

> **Make sure that relative file path information in the zip file matches the relative path information in the skin definition files.**

The following example shows two different graphic images from an abstract skin definition file:

```
<IMG src="top_left.gif" height="10" width="10" border="0">
<IMG src="images/top_right.gif" height="10" width="10" border="0">
```

The files should be included in the package as shown in Figure 17-8.

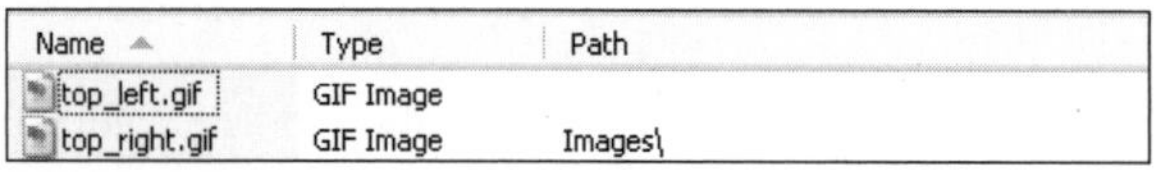

Name ▲	Type	Path
top_left.gif	GIF Image	
top_right.gif	GIF Image	Images\

Figure 17-8

If the preceding code snippet was contained in a package called MySkin.zip, the resulting image tags after installation would look this:

```
<IMG src="/Portals/_default/Skins/MySkin/top_left.gif" height="10" width="10"
border="0">
<IMG src="/Portals/_default/Skins/MySkin/images/top_right.gif" height="10"
width="10" border="0">
```

Skin packages can contain files that are applied to all skin definition files in the package or that are specific to an individual skin definition as outlined in Table 17-8. Any properties or styles set in the global file (if present) are overwritten with the value from the corresponding file that is specific to an individual skin. Graphics and any additional files stored in the skin package are global in scope and may be referenced by any skin definition file included in the package.

Table 17-8: Skin Filenames

File Type	Global Name	Individual Skin Name
Configuration file	Skin.xml	[skin filename].xml
Style sheet	Skin.css	[skin filename].css

In many cases, you will want to package a complementary set of skin files and container files in one distribution file. To do so, you need to package your container files in a zip file named containers.zip. Similarly, you must package your skin files in a zip file named skins.zip. Then you need to package these two files into a single zip file that is named after your skin. This enables people to install the full skin package (skins and containers) by uploading a single file through the Skin Uploader.

DotNetNuke contains a Skin Gallery for previewing skins installed in the portal. For the skin to be viewable in the Skin Gallery, you need to create a high-quality screenshot of your skin. For each skin or container definition file (both HTML- and ASCX-based definitions) you should also have a corresponding screenshot stored with a .jpg file extension (that is, if your skin file is named myskin.html, your screenshot needs to be named myskin.jpg).

If the skin package contains an about.htm file, the Skin Gallery will include an About <skin name> button below the gallery images. Clicking that button opens the designer-supplied about.htm file.

Skin Configuration Files

When creating abstract skin definition files (HTM or HTML files), the designer places tokens in the skin to designate locations for skin objects or content panes. To control the behavior and appearance of the skin objects and panes, the author may optionally choose to include one or more configuration files in the skin package. Any public property or field of a skin object or content pane can be set using the configuration file. As noted earlier, the global Skin.xml file property settings are applied to all skins. If present, these property settings may be overridden by a skin-specific configuration file as well.

The skin configuration file uses a simple format, as shown in Listing 17-5.

Listing 17-5: Skin Configuration File Format

```
<Objects>
  <Object>
    <Token />
    <Settings>
      <Setting>
        <Name />
        <Value />
      </Setting>
    </Settings>
  </Object>
</Objects>
```

Table 17-9 describes the relevant elements from the skin configuration file.

Table 17-9: Configuration File Elements

Element	Description
Objects	Contains one or more Object nodes that provide property settings for the individual skin element.
Token	Defines the skin element to update with the associated settings. This value must match a token that exists in the associated skin definition files.
Settings	Contains one or more Setting nodes that provide the individual name/value pairs for a single skin element property.
Name	The name of the skin object property or attribute. If the skin object does not support this attribute, an error may be thrown when the skin is used in the portal.
Value	The value to assign to the skin object attribute. If this is an invalid value, an error may be thrown when the skin is used.

The skin configuration file format enables the author to easily set one or more attributes for each token included in the skin. As you know, each skin object has its own set of supported attributes. The Skin Uploader merges the skin attributes with the HTML presentation file to create an ASCX skin file.

> If you are creating ASCX skins, you need to specify the attribute directly in your skin file (that is, `<dnn:Login runat="server" id="dnnLogin" Text="Signin" />`), and no configuration file is necessary.

Please note there is a one-to-one correspondence of skin object declarations in your skin file with the attribute specification in the XML file. This is also true for named instances. For example, if you want to include a vertical and horizontal set of navigation links in your skin, you can specify `[LINKS:Vertical]` and `[LINKS:Horizontal]` named instances in your skin file and then create definitions for each with different attributes in your XML file.

Listing 17-6 shows a sample configuration file that is used in the PHPDupe skin.

Listing 17-6: Skins Configuration File Format

```
<Objects>
  <Object>
    <Token>[LINKS:Horizontal]</Token>
    <Settings>
      <Setting>
        <Name>Separator</Name>
        <Value><![CDATA[  |  ]]></Value>
      </Setting>
      <Setting>
        <Name>Level</Name>
        <Value>Root</Value>
      </Setting>
    </Settings>
  </Object>
  <Object>
    <Token>[LINKS:Vertical]</Token>
    <Settings>
      <Setting>
        <Name>Level</Name>
        <Value>Child</Value>
      </Setting>
      <Setting>
        <Name>Alignment</Name>
        <Value>Vertical</Value>
      </Setting>
      <Setting>
        <Name>Separator</Name>
        <Value><![CDATA[<b><big> &middot;  </big></b>]]></Value>
      </Setting>
    </Settings>
  </Object>
  <Object>
    <Token>[DOTNETNUKE]</Token>
    <Settings>
```

```
      <Setting>
        <Name>CssClass</Name>
        <Value>Copyright</Value>
      </Setting>
    </Settings>
  </Object>
</Objects>
```

When settings are applied to the abstract skin file, they are injected in the control tag as attributes and take the form Name="Value". So based on the skin objects previously defined in Table 17-5, when the preceding configuration file is used, the [DOTNETNUKE] token will be replaced with the following control reference:

```
< dnn:DotNetNuke runat="server" id="dnnDotNetNuke" CssClass="Copyright">
```

Installing Skins

Unlike code add-ons, skins can be installed by portal administrators as well as by hosts. Skins also support web-based file upload or FTP based-file upload.

Web-Based File Upload

Use the following four steps to install a new skin into your portal using the web-based installer. Where the skin files are saved and which portals in a multi-portal site will have access to the skin depend on whether you install the skin from the Admin or the Host menu.

1. Log in with an Admin or Host account. If you are installing a skin for the current portal, go to the Admin/Site Settings menu (see Figure 17-9). Skin files will be stored in the individual portal directory. If multiple portals upload the same skin, duplicate files will exist in the portal directories.

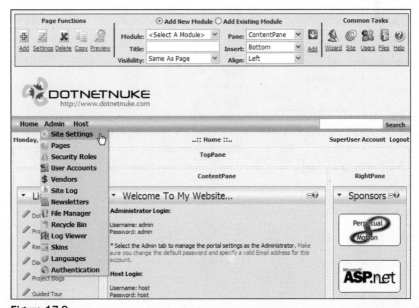

Figure 17-9

469

If you want all of the portals in a multi-portal installation to have access to the skin, log in with the Host account and select the Host/Host Settings menu (see Figure 17-10).

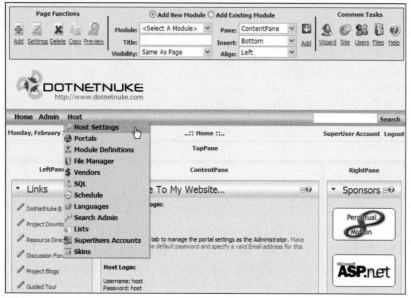

Figure 17-10

2. Figures 17-11 and 17-12 show the key portions of the Portal Settings and Host Settings screens. Select the Upload Skin link to go the File Upload screen.

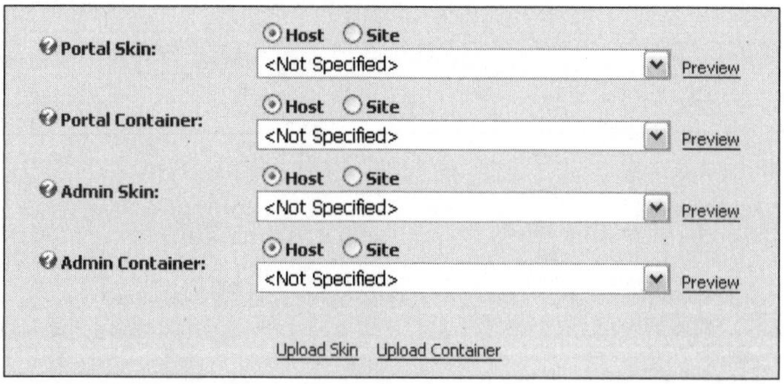

Figure 17-11

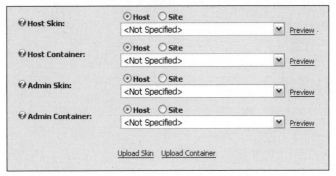

Figure 17-12

3.   The File Upload screen provides a simple interface for uploading one or more skins (see Figure 17-13). Browse to the desired skin package, click OK on the Browse dialog, and click the Add link on the File Upload page. Use the Upload New File link button to finish installing the module.

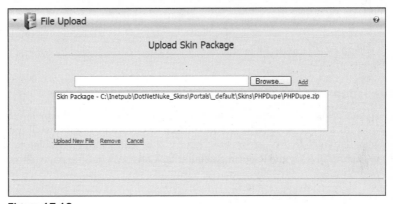

Figure 17-13

4.   After installing a new skin package, review the upload logs (see Figure 17-14). Errors are high-lighted in red. If no errors are shown, the skin is ready for use in your portal. The location of the installation directory is displayed at the top of the logs. Note that the directory matches the name of the skin package and will only vary based on whether the skin is installed from the Admin menu or the Host menu.

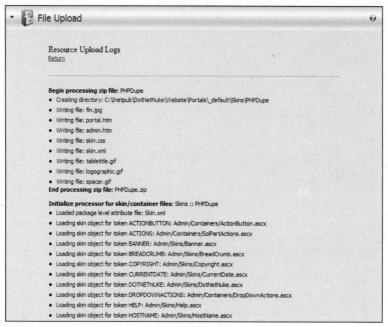

Figure 17-14

FTP-Based Installation

To install a new skin using FTP or any file manager, copy the module into the Install/Skin directory of your DotNetNuke installation. When the ResourceInstaller task runs, it will install the skin using the standard skin installation code. Any errors that occur will be noted in the task history, which is available by selecting the History link for the ResourceInstaller task on the Schedule page (shown previously in Figure 17-7).

Containers

Containers, like skins, provide the ability to control the appearance of portal. Whereas skins work at the "page" level, containers are designed for wrapping individual modules that appear on the page. Each module on a given page can use any one of the installed containers. Containers follow many of the same packaging and installation processes as skins and differ primarily in the allowable content inside the HTML or ASCX definition files. The following sections provide a look at these differences.

Packaging Containers

Containers follow the same packaging rules as skins. Container packages can contain files that are applied to all container definition files in the package or that are specific to an individual container definition as outlined in Table 17-10. The behavior and purpose of these files is the same as for skins; only the names of the files are different.

Table 17-10: Container Filenames

File Type	Global Name	Individual Container Name
Configuration file	Container.xml	[container filename].xml
Style sheet	Container.css	[container filename].css

Installing Containers

Containers follow the same procedures for web- and FTP-based installations. For web-based installations, in step 2, select the Upload Container link instead of the skin link (shown previously in Figures 17-11 and 17-12). Containers will be installed in the Portal or Host containers directory. To install containers using FTP, place the container package in the Install/Container directory.

Language Add-Ons

Support for multiple languages was added in DotNetNuke 3.0. The DotNetNuke implementation loosely follows the localization architecture and naming conventions of the ASP.NET 2.0 framework. DotNetNuke 4.0 recognizes language add-ons for the core framework, modules, providers, and a full language pack, including resources for both the core framework and all installed modules and providers. The only difference between the various language pack types are the specific string resource files included.

The multi-language architecture poses a unique challenge for creating and installing Language Packs due to the number of directories and files involved. Like code add-ons, Language Packs utilize a manifest file to manage the meta-data necessary to get all of the files installed to the correct directory.

Language Pack Manifest File

The Language Pack manifest file follows a very simple format, as shown in Listing 17-7.

Listing 17-7: Language Pack Manifest File Format

```
<?xml version="1.0"?>
<LanguagePack xmlns:xsd="http://www.w3.org/2001/XMLSchema"
xmlns:xsi="http://www.w3.org/2001/XMLSchema-instance" Version="3.0">
  <Culture Code="" DisplayName="" />
  <Files>
    <File FileName="" FileType="" ModuleName="" FilePath=""/>
  </Files>
</LanguagePack>
```

This file relies on the use of attributes, which is a more compact format than using simple elements. Table 17-11 lists the file's key elements.

Table 17-11: Manifest File Elements

Element	Description
LanguagePack	The root element for the manifest file. It must be created exactly as shown in Listing 17-7. The installation code will validate the file against the listed schemas.
Culture	Defines the culture information associated with the current Language Pack. The Culture contains two attributes: Code and DisplayName. The Code attribute takes a value corresponding to a valid culture name as defined by the .NET Framework System.Globalization.CultureInfo class. DisplayName defines the name to display when languages are selected in the portal framework.
Files	Contains one or more File nodes that provide the information necessary to properly install the individual resource file identified by the File node. See Table 17-10 for more information about the individual attributes of the File element.

Each language resource included in the Language Pack must be identified by a corresponding file element in the manifest (see Table 17-12). The files will be saved based on predefined rules depending on the file type.

Table 17-12: Manifest File Elements

Attribute	Description	Required
FileName	Defines the name of the physical file. It should not include any path information.	Yes
FileType	Defines the type of file identified by this node and is used by the portal to determine the root directory where the file will be installed. The FileType must be one of four values: GlobalResource, AdminResource, ControlResource, or LocalResource. See Table 17-11 for more information on these i file types.	Yes
ModuleName	Required for files marked AdminResource or LocalResource. This value identifies the name of the Admin or Desktop module that is associated with this file. ModuleName is the same as the name of the directory name in which the module is installed.	No
FilePath	Defines a path relative to the default resource path. The file path where the file will be saved is: [RootPath]\[ModuleName]\[FilePath]\[ResourceDirectory]. The RootPath and ResourceDirectory values are determined by the file type and are i defined in Table 17-11.	No

The FileType attribute is used to determine the appropriate RootPath and Resource directory (see Table 17-13). The RootPath value corresponds to specific directories defined by DotNetNuke. Admin modules, controls, and Desktop modules are the only DotNetNuke elements that are permitted to have local language resources. All other elements should use the Global resources. The Resource directory is defined to correspond to ASP.NET 2.0.

Table 17-13: FileType Values

FileType	Description	RootPath	Resource Directory
GlobalResource	Shared resources	\	App_GlobalResources
AdminResource	Admin module resources	\admin	App_LocalResources
ControlResource	Control resources	\controls	App_LocalResources
LocalResource	Desktop module resources	\Desktopmodules	App_LocalResources

To simplify the creation of the manifest file, DotNetNuke includes the capability to generate the Language Pack to include the manifest file. Although the manifest file may be hard to maintain by hand, it is a format that lends itself well to automatic generation and is easily read during the installation process. Listing 17-8 shows a partial listing of the generated Deutsch (German) manifest file.

Listing 17-8: German Language Pack Manifest

```xml
<?xml version="1.0"?>
<LanguagePack xmlns:xsd="http://www.w3.org/2001/XMLSchema"
xmlns:xsi="http://www.w3.org/2001/XMLSchema-instance" Version="3.0">
  <Culture Code="de-DE" DisplayName="Deutsch" />
  <Files>
    <File FileName="GlobalResources.de-DE.resx" FileType="GlobalResource" />
    <File FileName="SharedResources.de-DE.resx" FileType="GlobalResource" />
    <File FileName="TimeZones.de-DE.xml" FileType="GlobalResource" />
    <File FileName="Announcements.ascx.de-DE.resx" FileType="LocalResource"
ModuleName="Announcements" />
    <File FileName="EditAnnouncements.ascx.de-DE.resx" FileType="LocalResource"
ModuleName="Announcements" />
...
...
...
...
...
...

    <File FileName="Address.ascx.de-DE.resx" FileType="ControlResource" />
    <File FileName="DualListControl.ascx.de-DE.resx" FileType="ControlResource" />
    ...
    ...
    <File FileName="Classic.ascx.de-DE.resx" FileType="AdminResource"
ModuleName="ControlPanel" />
    <File FileName="IconBar.ascx.de-DE.resx" FileType="AdminResource"
ModuleName="ControlPanel" />
    ...
    ...
  </Files>
</LanguagePack>
```

Packaging Language Packs

A Language Pack includes three different types of files:

- **Language resource:** A language resource file is a standard .NET resource file that includes a key name and the localized value. A call to the DotNetNuke method `GetString(key)` returns the value that corresponds to the key.

- **Time zones:** The TimeZones.[locale].xml file includes a list of time zones that are recognized by the DotNetNuke portal.

- **Manifest:** The manifest file identifies the resource files included in the Language Pack.

DotNetNuke includes the capability to generate Language Packs for any of the languages and cultures that are currently installed on your portal. Given the number of files and directories involved in putting together a complete Language Pack, the generator is the recommended method for creating it. Not only does the generator simplify the creation process, but it also ensures that all necessary files are included and that the manifest file is properly formatted. Follow these simple steps to create a Language Pack.

1. Log in with the Host account and go to the Languages page on the Host menu (see Figure 17-15). Although the Admin account has some capability to edit language resources, it does not have the necessary permissions to generate or import Language Packs.

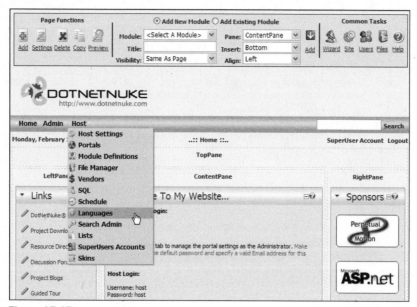

Figure 17-15

2. The Languages screen provides a number of options for adding new locales and languages to your portal. If you want to generate a Language Pack for a language that does not appear in the Supported Locales list, you must first add the language to your portal. (See Chapter 5 for more information about adding languages.) Select Create Language Pack from the Action menu or from the links at the bottom of the screen as shown in Figure 17-16.

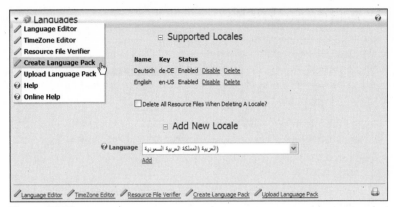

Figure 17-16

3. The latest versions of DotNetNuke enable you to create language packs for different subsets of the installed localized resources. (Earlier versions required you to create a Language Pack that included all localized strings. This behavior would include module strings that could cause problems for users who do not have the same modules in their installation.) As shown in Figures 17-17 through 17-20, each resource pack type provides specific options to customize the resource pack name and to select the resources that will be included in the package. For this example, select Full as the Resource Pack Type and then select the locale for which you want to create a Language Pack. Click the Create link (see Figure 17-20) to generate the Language Pack after you've made your selections.

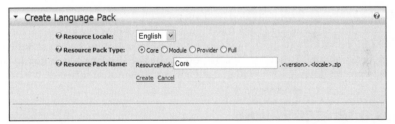

Figure 17-17

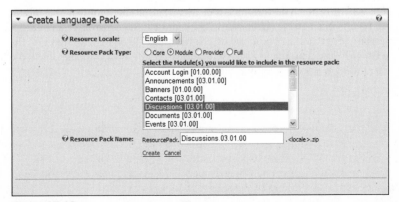

Figure 17-18

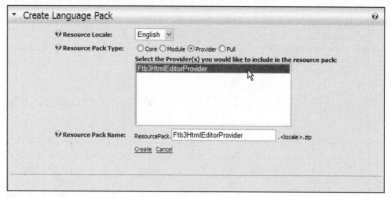

Figure 17-19

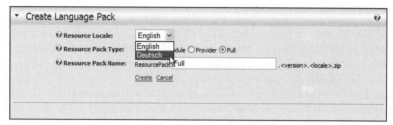

Figure 17-20

4. After the Language Pack is created, you are presented with a complete log showing all of the files added to the Language Pack (see Figure 17-21). Review the logs for errors, which are highlighted in red. Additionally, the log shows you important information about the directory in which the generated Language Pack is stored. The log also provides a link to the File Manager so that you can download the Language Pack from the portal server.

Installing Language Packs

Just like code and skinning add-ons, Language Packs also support two installation methods: web-based and FTP-based. Language Packs can include hundreds of files, which must be properly referenced in the manifest file. Any mismatch between the files identified in the manifest and files included in the Language Pack results in an error. Additionally, the manifest file controls where each resource will be installed. An error in the manifest could result in a resource file being installed into the wrong directory. If you use the DotNetNuke Language Pack Generator to create the Language Pack, the likelihood of errors during installation is significantly reduced.

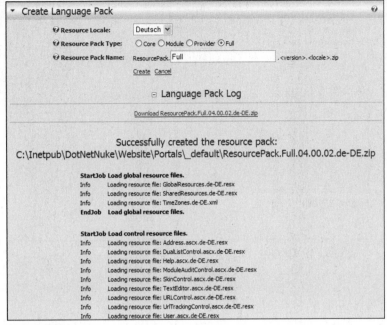

Figure 17-21

Web-Based File Upload

Follow these four steps to install a new language into your portal using the web-based installer:

1. Log in with the Host account and go to the Languages page on the Host menu (shown previously in Figure 17-15). Although the Admin account has some capability to edit language resources, it does not have the necessary permissions to generate or import Language Packs.

2. The Languages screen provides a number of options for new locales and languages. If you want to generate a Language Pack for a language that does not appear in the Supported Locales list, you must first add the language to your portal. (See Chapter 5 for more information about adding additional languages.) Select Upload Language Pack from the Action menu or from the links at the bottom of the screen (see Figure 17-22).

3. The File Upload screen appears (see Figure 17-23). Select the file you want to upload and click the Upload New File link.

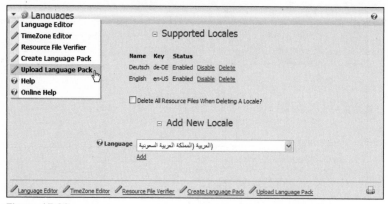

Figure 17-22

Figure 17-23

4. After the Language Pack is uploaded, you are presented with another File Upload screen. This screen displays the complete Resource Upload Logs showing all of the files that have been uploaded (see Figure 17-24). Review the logs for errors, which are highlighted in red. Additionally, the log shows you important information about the directory where the generated Language Pack is stored, and the log provides a link to the File Manager so that you can download the Language Pack from the portal server.

FTP-Based Installation

To install a new Language Pack using FTP or any file manager, copy the Language Pack into the Install/Language directory of your DotNetNuke installation. When the ResourceInstaller task runs, it will install the Language Pack using the standard skin installation code. If an error occurs, it's noted in the task history, which is available by selecting the History link for the ResourceInstaller task on the Schedule page (shown previously in Figure 17-7).

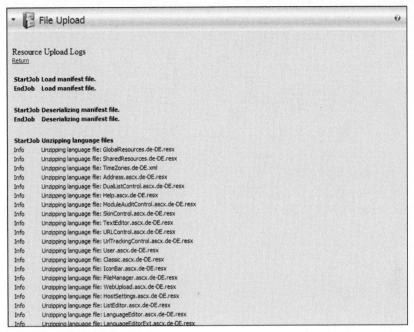

Figure 17-24

Summary

This chapter completes the discussion of DotNetNuke development. It has progressed from administering standard DotNetNuke installations to creating DotNetNuke modules and skins, and finished by documenting the steps needed to package, distribute, and install these add-ons. You are now ready to begin work on using DotNetNuke to build professional web sites that take full advantage of the power, flexibility, and extensibility provided by the portal.

Resources

There are numerous effective resources that bring value to the development or business aspects of using DotNetNuke. Table A-1 describes a number of great developer tools, many of which are used by the DotNetNuke community and Core Team members. Some of these developer tools are free and others have fees.

Table A-1: Developer Tools

Tool	Description
Beyond Compare by Scooter Software `www.scootersoftware.com`	Helpful for comparing files and folders to identify changes in code and to keep directories in synch.
Reflector for .NET by Lutz Roeder `www.aisto.com/roeder/dotnet`	A class browser for .NET assemblies. It includes call and called graphs, code viewers for IL, Visual Basic, Delphi, and C#, dependency trees, and more.
Nunit by James W. Newkirk, Michael C. Two, Alexei A. Vorontsov, Philip A. Craig, and Charlie Poole `www.nunit.org`	A powerful unit-testing framework for all .NET languages. It is a port of the Unit Java utility.
SQL Backup by Red-Gate `www.red-gate.com`	Creates compressed, encrypted and secured backups of SQL Server databases on user-defined schedules.
SQL Compare by Red-Gate `www.red-gate.com`	Compares the structures of Microsoft SQL Server databases and generates scripts to synchronize the databases objects.

Table continued on following page

Tool	Description
SQL Data Compare by Red-Gate `www.red-gate.com`	Compares the data in Microsoft SQL Server databases and generates scripts to synchronize the data.
ANTS Profiler by Red-Gate `www.red-gate.com`	A code and memory profiler for applications writing in any .NET language.
ANTS Load by Red-Gate `www.red-gate.com`	Load tests web sites and web services.

FileZilla
by Tim Kosse
`http://sourceforge.net/projects/`
`filezilla`
	A great open-source FTP client.

CodeSmith by Eric J. Smith `www.codesmithtools.com`	A commercial template-based code generator. It can generate code for any ASCII-based language, including .NET.
CodeSmith Templates for DotNetNuke 3.0 by Vicenç Masanas `http://dnnjungle.vmasanas.net`	A great collection of CodeSmith templates that help you create business controllers, business objects, stored procedures, data providers, and SQLData Provider code very quickly.
ATGen SDK for DotNetNuke by AppTheory `http://projects.apptheory.com`	This SDK, based on the commercial code generator MyGeneration, enables developers to quickly create modules and the associated data access layers. It generates the DAL, UI, Business Logic Layer, and installation items required for any module
FXCop by Microsoft `www.gotdotnet.com/team/fxcop`	Analyzes .NET-managed code assemblies to verify that they conform to the Microsoft .NET Framework Design Guidelines.
SnagIt by TechSmith `www.techsmith.com`	A terrific tool for taking screenshots. It can even take screen captures of scrolling windows (like long web pages).
Araxis Merge by Araxis LTD `www.araxis.com`	An advanced file comparison and merging tool with integrated folder comparison and synchronization. It allows for two-way or three-way comparisons.
SourceGear Vault by Araxis LTD `www.sourcegear.com`	Vault is the source control tool used by the Core Team. It is a fantastic source control tool for a distributed development team.
Draco.NET by Chive Software Limited `http://draconet.sourceforge.net`	A Windows service application that facilitates continuous integration. It monitors your source code repository, rebuilds your project, and e-mails the results automatically.

Tool	Description
Cruise Control .NET by ThoughtWorks `http://ccnet.thoughtworks.com`	A powerful open source Automated Continuous Integration server, implemented using the Microsoft .NET Framework.
Gemini by CounterSoft `www.countersoft.com`	Comprehensive issue, task, and defect management tracking for multiple projects. Generous support of open-source, non-profit, and academic use.
Camtasia Studio by TechSmith `www.techsmith.com`	A robust application for easily creating compelling training and presentations for Web and CD-ROM delivery.

Table A-2 describes several useful custom third-party modules. As of the date of the publication of this book, several of these modules are free. Because DotNetNuke 4 is a relatively new release, there aren't many DotNetNuke 4.0-only modules on the market yet, but the Core Team went to great lengths to ensure that modules developed for the DotNetNuke 3.x versions still function on the new 4.0 version.

Table A-2: Modules

Module	Description
Aggregator – Tabbed Modules by DNN Stuff `www.dnnstuff.com`	Acts as a tabbed container for one or more modules.
Enterprise Forms by ethuongmai `www.ethuongmai.com`	Designed to enable an average DNN user to create and manage forms and content without any knowledge of HTML or DNN custom-module development.
DNNPhoto Gallery by Dave Wilson `www.dnnphotogallery.com`	Highly configurable professional photo gallery that offers a "lite" version as well as a free trial download.
Active Forums by ActiveModules `www.activemodules.com`	Feature-packed forum module that provides built-in conversion utilities for Adverageous and the DNN Core forum.
Module Wrapper by ZLDNN `www.zldnn.com`	Enables you to combine multiple modules into a single container using a table format that permits row and column spanning.
SQLView by DNN Stuff `www.dnnstuff.com`	Displays the results from any SQL query in tabular format.
Multi Page Content by BonoSoft `www.dotnetnuke.dk`	Shows multiple pages of content within a single module. It is helpful for displaying long articles and tutorials in a condensed format.

Table continued on following page

Module	Description
DnnBB by Bonosoft and Nimo Software `www.dnnbb.net`	An open-source bulletin board/forum module that is easy to install and use.
Speerio File Manager Pro v3.0 by Speerio, Inc. `www.speerio.net`	Provides enhanced file-management capabilities for DotNetNuke portals, including multi-server file management, customizable meta data, WebDAV and photo/audio/video content, and metadata management.
Speerio Community Studio v1.0 by Speerio, Inc. `www.speerio.net`	Integrated solution for community-centric DotNetNuke portals, providing collaborative file and media sharing, blogging, calendar, forum, chat, and an advanced folksonomy engine that helps users quickly and easily locate information.
Private Messages by Scott McCulloch `www.ventrian.com`	A module that enables you to send private messages to other users of a portal.
Simple Gallery by Scott McCulloch `www.ventrian.com`	Allows photos to be uploaded, thumbnailed, and displayed. Advanced functionality includes approval of photos, albums, bulk upload, search integration, and syndication via RSS.
Swirl AJAX Chatroom by Swirlhost `www.swirlhost.com`	Simple but fast, customizable chatroom client based on AJAX technology.
InfoMap by Vicenç Masanas `http://dnnjungle.vmasanas.net`	Dynamically displays information on a picture. It can position user contact lists on a map. InfoMap presents a clickable map with "hot" areas where some information has been entered. When you click in any given area, the list of contacts for this area is displayed.
TemplatePrint, PagePrint by Vicenç Masanas `http://dnnjungle.vmasanas.net`	Skin objects to enhance the printing capabilities of DNN. You can define skins and containers for the printing.
Podcaster by Arrow Consulting & Design, Inc. `www.vbdotnetexpert.com`	Publish single or multiple episode podcasts optimized for iTunes. RSS 2.0 compliant.
Help Desk by DnnToolset `www.dnntoolset.com`	Powerful, easy-to-use system for the management and tracking of help system tickets.
Weather.com Feed by Oliver Hine `www.oliverhine.com`	Provides an instant weather forecast for any site using a feed from `weather.com` (requires free signup as a weather.com partner).

Module	Description
Email Management by Jason Koskimaki `www.yapclub.com/dnn`	Open source e-mail and newsletter management module that can perform scheduled mailing and logging.
MMLinks by Mauricio Maurquez `http://dnn.tiendaboliviana.com`	Template-based links module with extensive support for localization, role-based access, custom CSS, and JavaScript effects.
HrefExchanger by Anthony Glenright `www.inventua.com`	Automatically swaps outgoing DotNetNuke URLs for friendly URLs, and incoming friendly URLs for DotNetNuke URLs (requires IIS configuration).
XMod by Kelly Ford `www.dnndev.com`	Highly configurable and extensible form builder that can be leveraged to create applications without the use of traditional programming.
ListX by bi4ce `http://dnn.bi4ce.com`	Powerful presentation/reporting engine that builds fully functional, hierarchical views of data. ListX modules can interact with one another, each configured to perform complex display logic and runtime actions.

Projects are the newest addition to the DotNetNuke offerings and all the core modules have now been broken out into their own subprojects. This allows the module projects to release new versions of the modules as they are ready without needing to wait for a core framework release. You can read the latest news on the various module projects and download the latest releases from the DotNetNuke web site.

B

System Message Tokens

System tokens were introduced in Chapter 4 in the context of customizing portal e-mail templates (although they are also used for other purposes). The tables in this appendix identify and briefly describe the properties of each token. Recall that token properties may be referenced in e-mail templates using the pattern [Token:Property].

Table B-1 describes the HostSettings properties that are available for the token Host (such as [Host:ControlPanel]).

Table B-1: Standard HostSettings Properties

Property Name	Description
AutoAccountUnlock	Number of minutes after which an account that has been locked due to successive failed login attempts will reset.
ControlPanel	Determines whether the new 3.0+ Control Panel is displayed or version 2.0.
Copyright	Determines whether the copyright information is displayed in the Page Title. (Y/N)
DemoPeriod	Number of days that a demo portal will be active.
DemoSignup	Determines whether users are allowed to sign up for a demo portal. (Y/N)
DisableUsersOnline	Determines whether the the UsersOnline scheduler tasks are disabled. (Y/N)
EnableModuleOnlineHelp	Determines whether the online help option for modules is enabled. (Y/N)

Table continued on following page

Property Name	Description
EventLogBuffer	Determines whether buffering of event log entries is enabled. (Y/N)
FileExtensions	List of acceptable file extensions that can be uploaded to the site using any of the file upload mechanisms.
HelpURL	URL for online help.
HostCurrency	Default currency used when making payments for host services.
HostEmail	E-mail address of the portal host.
HostFee	The base fee for site hosting.
HostPortalId	ID of the default portal.
HostSpace	Amount of file space allowed for an account in megabytes.
HostTitle	Name of the hosting account. This name is used throughout the site for identifying the host.
HostURL	URL for the host web site.
ModuleCaching	Module caching method, either memory or disk (M/D).
PaymentProcessor	Payment processing gateway used for handling payments from client sites.
PerformanceSetting	Determines the optimization level (1–4) for site performance versus memory consumption.
ProxyPort	Port number of the proxy server.
ProxyServer	Server used for proxying web requests.
SchedulePollingRate	Defines the interval between scheduled task execution cycles.
SchedulerMode	Determines which method will execute scheduled tasks in the scheduling provider.
SiteLogBuffer	How many items to hold in the SiteLog before purging the log to disk.
SiteLogHistory	Number of days of activity to keep in the SiteLog.
SiteLogStorage	Identifies storage location for the SiteLog (File or Database).
SkinUpload	Determines whether skins can be uploaded by portal administrators.
SMTPAuthentication	SMTP authentication method: Anonymous, Basic, or NTLM.
SMTPServer	URL of the SMTP server used for sending e-mail messages.
SMTPUsername	Name of user account used for sending messages.
UseCustomErrorMessages	Determines whether the portal displays the standard DotNetNuke custom error messages or whether raw ASP.NET errors are shown.

Property Name	Description
UseFriendlyUrls	Enables or disables the URL rewriter used for implementing FriendlyURLs.
UsersOnlineTime	Length of the user's online buffer in minutes. If a user is inactive for this period of time, he or she will be marked as offline.

The PortalSettings properties are available for the token Portal (such as [Portal:PortalId]). Table B-2 describes them.

Table B-2: Standard PortalSettings Properties

Property Name	Description
PortalId	ID of the current portal.
PortalName	Name of the current portal. This name is used for branding the portal.
HomeDirectory	Folder name associated with the current portal. The name is a relative path to the portal root directory.
LogoFile	Graphic file used for displaying the portal logo.
FooterText	Information displayed in the copyright skin object.
ExpiryDate	Date that the hosting contract for the portal expires.
UserRegistration	Determines whether user registration is required and whether the registration is private (accounts created by the portal administrator), public (users can register for their own account and gain immediate access), or verified (users can register their own account but only get access after verification of e-mail address).
BannerAdvertising	Enables or disables use of default banner ads.
Currency	Default currency used for portal services.
AdministratorId	ID of the primary portal administrator.
Email	E-mail address for the portal administrator (this is generally set to a support e-mail address).
HostFee	Monthly charge the portal pays for hosting services.
HostSpace	Maximum amount of disk space allocated to this web site.
AdministratorRoleId	RoleId of the administrator's role for the portal.
AdministratorRoleName	RoleName of the administrator's role for the portal.
RegisteredRoleId	RoleId of the registered user's role for the portal.
RegisteredRoleName	RoleName of the registered user's role for the portal.

Table continued on following page

Property Name	Description
Description	Web site description. This information will be included in the meta tags used by search engines.
KeyWords	Specific meta tag keywords.
BackgroundFile	Graphic file used for the portal background.
SiteLogHistory	How many days to keep the SiteLog history for the portal.
AdminTabId	Page ID of the Admin page (PageId is the DotNetNuke 3 equivalent of TabID). This is the parent page for all portal administration pages.
SuperTabId	Page ID of the Host page. This is the parent page for all host administration pages.
SplashTabId	Page ID to use when no page is specified in the URL.
HomeTabId	Page ID to use as the portal home page. If no SplashTabId is designated, the HomeTabId is used.
LoginTabId	Page ID to use when the user selects the login link. This page should include the Login module.
UserTabId	Page ID to use when registering users or editing user profiles.
DefaultLanguage	Default locale of the web site. This will determine the language used when anonymous users visit the site.
TimeZoneOffset	Time zone where the web server is located.
Version	Build number for the current portal application.

Table B-3 describes the UserInfo properties available for the token User (such as [User:UserID]).

Table B-3: Standard UserInfo Properties

Property Name	Description
UserID	Unique identifier for a specific portal user.
Username	Logon name of the specific user.
FirstName	User's first name.
LastName	User's last name.
FullName	First name and last name with a single space between.
PortalID	PortalID to which this user belongs.
IsSuperUser	Does the user have Host permissions?
AffiliateID	Identifies the link used to navigate to the portal. When a user follows an affiliate link and registers on the portal, a unique AffiliateID is then associated with the user.

Table B-4 describes the `UserMembership` properties available for the token `Membership` (such as `[Membership:Password]`).

Table B-4: Standard UserMembership Properties

Property Name	Description
Password	User's password if available.
Email	E-mail address of the user.
Username	Login name of the user.
LastLoginDate	Last date/time the user logged in to the portal.
CreatedDate	Date/time when the user account was created.
Approved	If the user's account has been approved for access to the web site.
LockedOut	If the user's account has been locked due to potential security issues.

Table B-5 describes the `UserProfile` properties available for the `Profile` token (such as `[Profile:FirstName]`).

Table B-5: Standard UserProfile Properties

Property Name	Description
FirstName	User's first name.
LastName	User's last name.
Street	Street address.
City	City.
Region	State, province, or region for the user. Primarily used for U.S. and Canada.
PostalCode	Postal code for the user's mailing address.
Country	Country where the user lives.
Unit	Apartment, post office box, or suite for the user's address.
Telephone	Telephone number for the user.
Cell	Mobile phone number.
Fax	Fax number.
Website	Personal or corporate web site for the user.
IM	Instant messenger contact ID.
TimeZone	User's default time zone. This is used for translating times from the SiteLog.
PreferredLocale	User's preferred locale. This determines the language used for all static content on the portal.

Index

Index

A

ASP.NET 2.0, 44–45
DotNetNuke 3.0 and, 31
DotNetNuke and, 238
security, 237–238
security in, 288–289
ASPInsiders, 47
assigning privileges, 117
attributes
containers, 441
Content Pane, 439
skin objects, 429–438
Audit control, 401
authentication
modes, 133–134
portal configuration, 131–135
Windows, 132–133
authority, delegating, 117
AutoUpgrade function, installation and, 68
AutoUpgrade setting, web.config, 66

B

banner advertising, vendors, 138–140
Banner Advertising Site Setting, 112
Banner module, 199–201
Banners module, 91
Beadle, Phil, 46
benefactor program, 50–53
Birds of Feather, Tech Ed, 41
Birds of Feather session, PDC, 20
Body Background Site Setting, 107
branding, 38–40
[BREADCRUMB] skin object, 428
Brinkman, Joe, 20, 41
BSD (Berkely Software Distribution), 13
building skins, 426
objects, 427–429
attributes, 429–438
instances, 438–439
Burzi, Francisco (PHP-Nuke), 11
business conderations, module planning, 342–343

Business Logic Layer, 373
businesscontrollerclass element, folder node, 451

C

C#.NET, IBuySpy Portal and, 3
cachetime element, Module element (folder node), 452
caching, client-side script caching, 310
Calendar control, Events.ascx page, 386
callback requests, Page_Init handling, 320
callbacks
Client API, 315–321
life cycle, 316–321
registration, 316–318
setup, 316–318
response handling, 321–322
Campbell, Richard, 36
Caron, Dan, 20, 26, 41
CAS (Code Access Security) environment, 30
categories, add-ons, 447
CBO (Custom Business Object) helper class, 379
CBOs (Custom Business Objects), 226–231, 234
properties, 246
values, 246
CBO.FillCollection method, 229
CBO Hydrator, 228–231
Charitable Donations model, 52
child portals, 86, 165–166
classes
ActionBase, 272
ActionEventArgs, 272
ActionEventHandler, 272
CBO helper class, 379
controller
EventLogController, 245–250
ExceptionLogController, 250–253
Edit Events code behind class, 405
EditEvents, 409–410
EventLogController, 244
EventsController class, 378
EventsController.vb class, 377